T · R · E · N · T

Traditions of the Rabbis from the Era of the New Testament

VOLUME I

Prayer and Agriculture

T • R • E • N • T

Traditions of the Rabbis
from the Era of the
New Testament

1. Prayer and Agriculture

2. Feasts and Sabbaths

3. Women and Marriage

4. Crime and Punishment

5. Offerings and Temple

6. Pure and Impure

T·R·E·N·T

TRADITIONS OF THE RABBIS FROM THE ERA OF THE NEW TESTAMENT

VOLUME I

Prayer and Agriculture

David Instone-Brewer

WILLIAM B. EERDMANS PUBLISHING COMPANY

GRAND RAPIDS, MICHIGAN / CAMBRIDGE, U.K.

Wm. B. Eerdmans Publishing Co.
255 Jefferson Ave. S.E., Grand Rapids, Michigan 49503 /
P.O. Box 163, Cambridge CB3 9PU U.K.

Printed in the United States of America

09 08 07 06 05 04   7 6 5 4 3 2 1

ISBN 0-8028-4762-5

www.eerdmans.com

Contents

TRACTATE MAASER SHENI: SECOND TITHE

Foreword

The rabbinic material is fascinating but not easy to penetrate. One crux is the problem of dating; a perpetual headache for those who want to use rabbinic material in historical studies. That most of the material is older than the earliest written documents, in many cases even older than the first discernible redactions, used to be a universal conviction. But how early a dating is justified? Around 1960, scholars generally had greater confidence than we do today in the information the rabbis themselves have left us about who made a dictum or did what a rabbinic narrative relates.

Much has happened since, within both early rabbinic and New Testament research. The greatest contribution has been made by Dr. Jacob Neusner, in studies both detailed and broad. He has illuminated the rabbinic tradition with approaches both old and new, in a career of unprecedented productivity.

Jewish tradition is not simply a heritage to be preserved but is extraordinarily rich and living, variegated and variable, and freshly creative. Even the rabbis could rework their traditions, change formulations, cancel elements, and insert additions and new layers. I could mention this part of their activity only in passing in Memory & Manuscript, though in later works I have worked out more explicitly the hint I gave there concerning this complicated phenomenon.

Dr. Instone-Brewer is building on the foundations laid by myself and Dr. Jacob Neusner. He employs the discoveries about dating rabbinic traditions together with an analysis of their multilayered development. I commend his endeavor to bring the fruits of rabbinic studies to the world of New Testament scholars.

Birger Gerhardsson

Preface

The aim of this series is, for the first time, to provide ready access for New Testament scholars to the invaluable collection of those rabbinic traditions which can be shown to originate before 70 CE.

The dating of rabbinic material has been developed and tested during the last half century. Recent studies by Neusner and others, including my Cambridge doctoral work, *Techniques and Assumptions in Jewish Exegesis before 70 CE*, (*Texte und Studien zum Antiken Judentum* 30, Tübingen: J. C. B. Mohr, 1992), have now confirmed that it is possible to isolate early ideas and traditions which have been preserved within collections of rabbinic laws by their later editors. This approach is not peculiar to Jewish studies, because ancient Roman historians are now recovering early Roman legislation from the sixth-century CE Digest of Justinian.

Unlike Strack-Billerbeck's *Kommentar zum Neuen Testament aus Talmud und Midrasch*, which presented isolated quotations without sufficient regard to context or time periods, this work presents the ancient traditions in the context of related rabbinic thought and with careful consideration of dating.

The systematic application of new dating methods in this work has identified a fascinating corpus of traditions which originated during the time of the New Testament. These texts tell us more about the everyday social and religious world of early first-century Palestinian Judaism than those of Josephus, Graeco-Roman classics, Philo, or even Qumran. I have been amazed at the coherent picture of first-century Judaism which has gradually unfolded before me as I isolated this body of traditions. It has already produced many new insights which illuminate the New Testament and early Judaism,[1] but it will take rising generations of scholars to harvest this rich resource.

Each rabbinic tradition in this work is presented with comments on the meaning within its context, the methodology for dating it, with a 'level of confidence' for that date, and a literal English translation in parallel with the original text. The focus of this work is the primary texts, though references to important secondary literature are provided. The topics in these volumes follow the six orders of Mishnah, using the subject divisions which date back to the earliest origins of this material. Parallels to the New Testament and other ancient literature are noted throughout.

This methodology and sample results have been presented to a number of senior scholars to whom I am grateful for their responses concerning the project. In Lent

---

[1] For example, see my *Divorce and Remarriage in the Bible: The Social and Literary Context* (Grand Rapids: Eerdmans, 2002).

term 2003, I presented part of this work as the Tyndale Lectures at the Faculty of Divinity, Cambridge University, and I am gratful for the responses of the professors and postgraduate students. In the same year, the Society of New Testament Studies meeting in Bonn provided a further forum for the shaping of this project.

I am indebted to several readers of this work, including Dr Menahem Kister (Hebrew University, Jerusalem), Dr Jacob Neusner (Research Professor of Religion and Theology, Bard College, New York) and Dr Birger Gerhardsson (Lund, Sweden) who graciously provided the Foreword to this first volume. Several people helped me edit the work, especially Kate Gaze and Justin Hardin. I would also like to record my indebtedness to Professor Stefan Reif (Director of the Taylor-Schechter Genizah Research Unit, Cambridge University Library) who has worked as consultant on this volume and from whom I have gained many invaluable insights.

I would like to dedicate this volume to Professor William Horbury (Professor of Jewish and Early Christian Studies, University of Cambridge) who skilfully guided my first faltering steps into these deep waters during my doctoral research. I am grateful for the support of the Institute for Early Christianity in the Graeco-Roman World, Tyndale House, Cambridge and particularly Dr Bruce Winter who was the inspiration behind this project.

David Instone-Brewer, Tyndale House, Cambridge

Abbreviations

Major Modern Editions and Reference Works

Albeck   *Eiführung in die Mischna* (Berlin & New York, 1971)
Blackman   *Mishnayoth* (New York, 1963-64)
CRINT   *Compendia Rerum Iudaicarum ad Novum Testamentum* (Assen: 1974-76)
Danby   *The Mishnah* (London, 1933).
DJD   *Discoveries in the Judean Desert* (Oxford 1955-)
Enc.J.   *Encyclopaedia Judaica* (Jerusalem, 1972)
Jastrow   *A dictionary of the Targumim, the Talmud Babli and Yerushalmi, and the Midrashic literature* (New York, 1950)
JE   *Jewish Encyclopedia* (New York : 1901-1906)
Lieberman   *The Tosefta according to the Codex Vienna* (New York, 1955-1973)
Loeb   *Loeb Classical Library* (Cambridge MA & London)
Neusner's Jerusalem Talmud   *The Talmud of the land of Israel* (Chicago, 1982)
Neusner's Mishnah   *The Mishnah* (New Haven, 1988).
Neusner's Tosefta   *The Tosefta* (New York, 1977-1986)
Soncino Talmud   *Hebrew-English edition of the Babylonian Talmud* (London 1967)
Strack-Stemberger   *Introduction to Talmud and Midrash* (Minneapolis, 1996)
TDNT   *Theological Dictionary of the New Testament* (Grand Rapids, 1964)
Z or Zuckermandel   *Tosephta: based on the Erfurt and Vienna Codices* (Jerusalem, 1937)

Bible

Gen.	1Kgs.	Eccl.	Obad.	Mt.	Phil.	1Pet.
Exod.	2Kgs.	Song	Jon.	Mk.	Col.	2Pet.
Lev.	1Chr.	Isa.	Mic.	Lk.	1Thes.	1Jn.
Num.	2Chr.	Jer.	Nah.	Jn.	2Thes.	2Jn.
Deut.	Ezra	Lam.	Hab.	Acts	1Tim.	3Jn.
Josh.	Neh.	Ezek.	Zeph.	Rom.	2Tim.	Jude
Judg.	Est.	Dan.	Hag.	1Cor.	Tit.	Rev
Ruth	Job	Hos.	Zech.	2Cor.	Phlm.	
1Sam.	Ps.	Joel	Mal.	Gal.	Heb.	
2Sam.	Prov.	Amos		Eph.	Jas.	

Apocrypha

1Esd.	1 Esdras	Song Three	Song of the Three
2Esd.	2 Esdras		Children [Dan.3.24-90]
	[chs. 3–14 = *4 Ezra*]	Sus.	History of Susanna
Tob.	Tobit	Pr.Azar.	Prayer of Azariah
Jdt.	Judith		[Dan.3.26-45]
Gk.Est.	Greek adds. to Esther	Bel	Bel and the Dragon
Wis.	Wisdom of Solomon	Pr.Man.	Prayer of Manasseh
Sir.	Ben Sira, Ecclesiasticus	1Macc.	1 Maccabees
Bar.	Baruch	2Macc.	2 Maccabees
Ep.Jer.	Letter of Jeremiah		
	[Baruch 6]		

Early Pseudepigrapha & Christian Works

Ap.Const.	Apostolic Constitutions	T.Ash.	Testament of Asher
Aris.Ex.	Aristeas the Exegete	T.Benj.	Testament of Benjamin
Aristob.	Aristobulus	T.Dan	Testament of Dan
1En.	1 Enoch (Ethiopic)	T.Gad	Testament of Gad
2En.	2 Enoch (Slavonic)	T.Iss.	Testament of Issachar
3En.	3 Enoch (Hebrew)	T.Jos.	Testament of Joseph
4Ezra	4 Ezra	T.Jud.	Testament of Judah
Did.	Didache	T.Levi	Testament of Levi
Hel.Syn.Pr.	Hellenistic Synagogal	T.Naph.	Testament of Naphtali
	Prayers	T.Reu.	Testament of Reuben
Jan.Jam.	Jannes and Jambres	T.Sim.	Testament of Simeon
Jos.Asen.	Joseph and Aseneth	T.Zeb.	Testament of Zebulun
Jub.	Jubilees	T.Ab.	Testament of Abraham
Mart.Ascen.Isa.	Martyrdom and	T.Isaac	Testament of Isaac
	Ascension of Isaiah	T.Jac.	Testament of Jacob
Odes Sol.	Odes of Solomon	T.Adam	Testament of Adam
Ps-Philo	Liber antiquitatum	T.Job	Testament of Job
	biblicarum	T.Mos.	Testament of Moses
Ps-Phoc.	Pseudo-Phocylides	T.Sol.	Testament of Solomon
Pss.Sol.	Psalms of Solomon	Theod.	Theodotus, On the Jews
Sib.Or.	Sibylline Oracles		

Major works from Qumran and related texts

(specific manuscripts are referred to by number)

CD	Damascus Document (from Cairo Genizah)	4QHalakhah	Halakhah
CTLevi	Testament of Levi (from Cairo Genizah)	4QMish	Priestly Courses, Mishmarot
1Q20	1QapGen ar Genesis Apocryphon	4QMMT	Halakahic Letter, Miqsiat Ma'ase ha-Torah
1QapGen	Genesis Apocryphon	4QMSM	Midrash Sepher Mosheh
1QDM	Dibre Mosheh / Words of Moses	4QNJ	New Jerusalem[a]
1QH	Hodayot, Hymns	4QPEnosh	Prayer of Enosh
1QLitPr	Festival Prayers	4QpHos	Hosea Pesher
1QM	Milhiamah, War Scroll	4QpIsa	Isaiah Pesher
1QMyst	Mysteries	4QpNah	Nahum Pesher
1QNoah	Noah	4QpPs	Psalms Pesher
1QpHab	Pesher Habakkuk	4QPrFêtes	Festival Prayers
1QpMic	Micah Pesher	4QPrNab	Prayer of Nabonidus
1QpPs	Psalms Pesher	4QpsEzek	Pseudo-Ezekiel
1QpZeph	Zephaniah Pesher	4QPsJos	Psalms of Joshua
1QS	Serek Hayahiad, Community Rule / Manual of Discipline	4QpsMoses	Pseudo-Moses
		4QpZeph	Zephaniah Pesher
		4QShirShabb	Songs of the Sabbath Sacrifice
1QTLevi	Testament of Levi		
4QapocrJer	Jeremiah Apocryphon	4QSM	Sefer ha-Mihiamah
4QapocrJoseph	Apocryphon of Joseph	4QTanh	Tanhumin
4QapocrJoshua	Apocryphon of Joshua	4QTest	Testimonia
4QapocrMoses	Apocryphon of Moses	4QtgJob	Targum of Job
4QapPs	Non-Canonical Psalms	4QtgLev	Targum of Leviticus
4QBer	The Chariots of Glory, Blessings	4QTNaph	Testament of Naphtali
		4QTohiorot	Purificaltion Rules A
4QCalendrical	Calendrical Document	11QBer	Benedictions
4QDibHam	Words of the Luminaries	11QMelch	Melchizedek
		11QT	Temple Scroll
4QFlor	Florilegium	11QtgJob	Targum of Job

Josephus

Ant.	Antiquities of the Jews	Life	Life of Josephus
Apion	Against Apion	War	The Jewish War

Philo

Abr.	De Abrahamo, Abraham
Aet.	De aeternitate mundi, Eternity of the World
Agr.	De agricultura, Agriculture
Anim.	De animalibus, Animals (whether they have reason)
Cher.	De cherubim, Cherubim
Conf.	De confusione linguarum, Confusion of Tongues
Congr.	De congressu eruditionis gratia, Preliminary Studies
Contempl.	De vita contemplativa, Contemplative Life
Decal.	De decalogo, Decalogue
Deo	De Deo, God
Det.	Quod deterius potiori insidiari soleat, Worse Attacks the Better
Deus	Quod Deus sit immutabilis, God is Unchangeable
Ebr.	De ebrietate, Drunkenness
Exsecr.	De exsecrationibus, Curses (and Rewards)
Flacc.	Contra Flaccum, Against Flaccus
Fug.	De fuga et inventione, Flight and Finding
Gig.	De gigantibus, Giants
Her.	Quis rerum divinarum heres sit, Who is the Heir?
Hypoth.	Hypothetica, Hypothetica
Ios.	De Josepho, Joseph
Leg. 1-3	Legum allegoriae, Allegorical Interpretation
Legat	Legatio ad Gaium, Embassy to Gaius
Migr.	De migratione Abrahami, Migration of Abraham
Mos. 1-2	De vita Mosis, Life of Moses
Mut.	De mutatione nominum, Change of Names
Opif.	De opificio mundi, Creation of the World
Plant.	De plantatione, Planting
Post.	De posteritate Caini, Prosterity of Cain
Praem.	De praemiis et poenis, Rewards and Punishments
Prob.	Quod omnis probus liber sit, Every Good Person is Free
Prov.	De providentia, Providence
QE 1-2	Quaestiones in Exodum, Questions in Exodus
QG 1-4	Quaestiones in Genesin, Questions in Genesis
Sacr.	De sacrificiis Abelis et Caini, Sacrifices of Abel and Cain
Sobr.	De sobrietate, Sobriety
Somn. 1-2	De somniis, Dreams
Spec. 1-4	De specialibus legibus, Special Laws
Virt.	De virtutibus, Virtues

Tractates of Mishnah, Tosefta, and Talmuds

(Tosefta variations in brackets)

Ab.	(Pirqé) Abot	Naz.	Nazir (Nezirut)
Arak.	Arakhin	Ned.	Nedarim
AZ	Abodah Zarah	Neg.	Negaim
BB	Baba Batra	Nid.	Niddah
Bek.	Bekhorot	Ohol.	Oholot
Ber.	Berakhot	Orl.	Orlah
Betz.	Bétzah (Yom Tob)	Par.	Parah
Bik.	Bikkurim	Pea.	Peah
BM	Baba Metzia	Pes.	Pesachim (Pisachim)
BQ	Baba Qamma	Qid.	Qiddushin
Dem.	Demay	Qin.	Qinnim
Ed.	Eduyyot	RH	Rosh ha-Shanah
Er.	Érubin	San.	Sanhedrin
Git.	Gittin	Shab.	Shabbat
Hag.	Ḥagigah (Rayyaih)	Shebi.	Shebiit
Hal.	Ḥallah	Shebu.	Shebuot
Hor.	Horayot	Sheq.	Sheqalim
Hul.	Ḥullin	Sot.	Sotah
Kel.	Kelim	Suk.	Sukkah
(t.KBQ, t.KBB & t.KBM)		Taan.	Taanit
Ker.	Keritot	Tam.	Tamid
Ket.	Ketubbot	Tem.	Temurah
Kil.	Kilayim	Ter.	Terumot
Maas.	Maaserot	Toh.	Tohorot
	(Maaser Rishon)	TY	Tebul Yom
Makh.	Makhshirin	Uq.	Uqtzin
Makk.	Makkot	Yad.	Yadayim
Meg.	Megillah	Yeb.	Yebamot
Meil.	Meilah	Yom.	Yoma
Men.	Menachot		(Yom ha-Kippurim)
Mid.	Middot	Zab.	Zabim
Miq.	Miqvaot	Zeb.	Zebachim
MQ	Moed Qatan		
MS	Maaser Sheni		

Supplementary Talmud Tractates:

Abad.	Abadim	Mez.	Mezuzah
ARN.A / B	Abot deRabbi Natan	PS	Pereq ha-Shalom
	A & B	Sem.	Abel Rabbati or
DER	Derek Eretz Rabba		Semachot
DEZ	Derek Eretz Zuta	Sis.	Tzitzit
Ger.	Gerim	Soph.	Sopherim
Kall.	Kallah	ST	Sepher Torah
Kuth.	Kutim	Teph.	Tephillin

Other Rabbinic Works

Gen.R.	Genesis (Bereshit) Rabbah	Pes.R.	Pesiqta Rabbati
		Sif.Lev.	Siphra
Exod.R.	Exodus (Shemot) Rabbah	Sif.Num.	Siphré Numbers
etc.		Sif.Deut.	Siphré Deuteronomy
Agg.Ber.	Aggadat Bereshit	Sif.Zuta	Siphré Zuta
Frag.Tg.	Fragmentary Targum	Tanh.Yel.	Tanhuma Yelammedenu
Mekh.	Mekhilta (de R. Ishmael)	Tg.Jon.	Targum Jonathan (the
Mekh.Sim.	Mekhilta de R. Shimeon b. Yohai		Prophets)
		Tg.Neof.	Targum Neofiti
MHG	Midrash ha-Gadol		(Pentateuch)
Mid.Prov.	Midrash Mishlé	Tg.Onk.	Targum Onkelos
Mid.Pss.	Midrash Tehillim or Shoher Tob		(Pentateuch)
		Tg.Ps.Jon.	Targum Pseudo-Jonathan
Mid.R.	Midrash Rabbah		(Pentateuch)
Mid.Tann.	Midrash Tannaim	Yalq.	Yalqut (Shimeon)
MLT	Midrash Leqah Tob	Yalq.M.	Yalqut ha-Makhiri
Pes.K.	Pesiqta de Rab Kahana		

Introduction to Rabbinic Traditions

The aim of this work is to collect rabbinic traditions which originated in the New Testament era, which is defined as the first century before 70 CE. This collection is the best insight we have into the mindset of the Jews to whom both Jesus and Paul addressed most of their teaching. The sources are presented with the Hebrew text and a literal translation in parallel, with commentaries for the nonspecialist reader on their meaning, their dating, and their relevance to the New Testament.

Text which can be dated before 70 CE is printed in a bold font, and later or undateable text (which is sometimes included to provide the context) is in an unbold font. Square brackets contain explanatory words which do not occur in the original text. The Hebrew text is taken from standard sources, and variant readings are given only where these might change the meaning of the text. Textual criticism of rabbinic texts is still in its infancy, and no attempt is made in these volumes to estimate the relative importance of variants.

The cutoff point of 70 CE is significant for both Jewish and Christian sources. Most, and perhaps all, of the New Testament was completed by 70 CE,[1] and the whole of Judaism was transformed by the destruction of Jerusalem and the Temple in 70 CE. The Hillelites position came to dominate Judaism as a result of the destruction of the Essene community, the virtual disappearance of the Sadducees, and the victory of the Hillelite viewpoint over that of the Shammaites whose numbers declined to almost nothing soon after 70 CE.

The structure of this work is based on the Mishnah which is arranged according to subject matter. The Mishnah, which is the earliest collection of rabbinic traditions, inherited its structure from previous collections that are very ancient. This structure has the dual benefit of keeping material roughly in the same order that tradition has preserved it in, and at the same time of providing a convenient collection of material according to subject matter, using categories which are based in ancient Jewish thought. I have occasionally moved material within this structure, when a tradition has been preserved in one tractate but relates to a different subject.

The traditions collected here are, on the whole, a faithful reflection of the ideas and practices of rabbinic Judaism before 70 CE. However, they do not represent the actual words spoken or written before 70 CE, because they have been edited into later collections and then abbreviated and rewritten for easy memorization. The editors

---

[1] Parts of the Gospels, the Pastoral Epistles, and Revelation may originate from after 70 CE, but the fact that they do not overtly refer to the destruction of Jerusalem and its Temple is a good indication that they originated earlier.

worked with much care, with great attention to detail, and they were especially careful to preserve opinions which disagreed with their own. Although they can be trusted to transmit these traditions faithfully, one should always be aware of possible errors and innovations, and the wording should not be regarded as quotations from the early rabbis themselves.

The undateable and later traditions of the Mishnah have not been abandoned in this work because each tractate is summarized, section by section, in order to provide an overview of the subject. These summaries help to put the early traditions within a context, indicate the direction of later developments. Square brackets are used in the summaries to add necessary details which are not stated in Mishnah.

The style of the translation is deliberately literal, in order to accentuate the forms and structure which are necessary for understanding the meaning of the text.[2] This type of translation also helps to tie the English to the Hebrew, which is especially useful for the non-Hebrew reader. Danby's Mishnah remains the superlative translation based on the interpretation of Maimonides, while the Mishnah in Epstein's Talmud leans more on Rashi. In my translations I have attempted to be blind to later interpretations while considering what it meant in the first and second centuries.

Technical terms are explained when they first occur at the start of each tractate, and are collected in a glossary at the end of each volume. Transliterations are simplified, as in most Jewish works, without complex attempts to convey the exact Hebrew spelling. They are always accompanied by the Hebrew lettering when they are defined at the start of tractates and in the glossary. Technical terms which might be mistaken for normal vocabulary are identified by initial upper case (e.g., Afternoon Prayer) or by italics (e.g., *consecrated* food; *forgotten* crop), and great care is taken to translated these words consistently. Some words which rabbinic scholars tend to leave untranslated are translated in these works (e.g., '*demay*' as '*doubtfully tithed food*'; '*érub*' as '*community marker*'; '*hullin*' as '*deconsecrated*') and some words whose traditional translation is confusing have been translated more literally (e.g., '*impure*' instead of 'unclean'; '*elevation offering*' instead of 'heave offering';[3] '*holyday*' instead of 'special festival day'[4]).

---

[2] See J. Neusner "Redaction, Formulation, and Form: the Case of Mishnah" (*Jewish Quarterly Review* 70 [1980]: 131-47). Alan Avery-Peck agrees, though he points out that this is not so important in the case of the Talmuds which are not characterized by such a high degree of formulaic language and set linguistic forms (*The Talmud of the Land of Israel: A Preliminary Translation and Explanation*, 35 vols., Chicago *Studies in the History of Judaism* [Chicago: University of Chicago Press, 1982-94], vol. 6, p. 40).

[3] This helps to identify it with the verb 'to elevate' which is often the only indication that an *elevation offering* is being discussed.

[4] 'Festival Day' is confusing because this term only applies to special days within the festival and not to the other days which are known as Intermediate Festival Days.

The Authors of Rabbinic Literature

In this work, the collective term 'rabbis' (not 'Rabbis') is used to refer to the followers and guardians of the teaching which is contained in what we now called 'rabbinic literature,' both before and after 70 CE. In many ways this term is inappropriate, but it is the best one available.

Most individuals who are named in this literature have the title 'Rabbi' (meaning 'my teacher/master'), though some have the title 'Rabban' ('our teacher'), Mar ('master') or Abba ('father'), or a few other variations. Most individuals before 70 CE have no title at all, and although it would be an oversimplification to say that the title 'Rabbi' was not used until 70 CE, it is likely that it was adopted in some kind of official way after this time. Of the forty-two named individuals of the second Tannaitic generation (the first generation after 70 CE), all have the title 'Rabbi,' except for a few who were given other honorific titles and four who have no title,[5] while before 70 CE only six individuals are called 'Rabbi.'[6] It is possible that this title was given to these six in retrospect, but this is unlikely because it is not given to those who commanded the greatest respect by later generations, such as Hillel or Gamaliel. It may be significant that the title 'Rabbi' before 70 CE is always used for priests,[7] so it may originally have been an honorary title for priests who were either of very high rank or were respected among the later rabbis.

The later rabbis had various collective names for themselves:

➤ 'Sages' (*Ḥakhamim*, חֲכָמִים) was used for any 'anonymous' (i.e., unnamed) teachers

➤ 'Associates' (*Ḥaberim*, חֲבֵרִים) was used for observant Jews (who, in earlier times, may not necessarily have been teachers)

---

[5] Other titles are 'Rabban,' 'Abba,' or simply 'Ben.' Gamaliel is often called 'the Elder' which may merely distinguish him from Gamaliel II, though this title is also used of Hillel and Shammai, and of leaders in general (cf. m.Taan.3.6). The four individuals without any title are Boethus b. Zonin (a lay man who asked the Sages a question in b.Pes.37a, cf. b.BB.13b), Onkelos (a proselyte who is attributed with editing the Targum), Simeon brother of Azariah, and Nahum of Gimzu. Of these, Simeon and Nahum made halakhic rulings, so one would expect them to have the title 'Rabbi.' Later commentators were surprised at Simeon's lack of a title, and suggested that Azariah was given the credit because he supported Simeon financially (Lev.R.25.2). Nahum is only known for one ruling which he 'whispered' to Akiba (b.Ber.22a).
[6] R. Eleazar b. Harsom, R. Hanina, Chief of the priests, R. Ishmael b. Phabi, R. Johanan (Nehunia) b. Gudgada, R. Simeon of Mizpah, and R. Measha.
[7] Five of these six are specifically named as priests. The sixth, R. Measha, is only known from m.Pea.2.6, which does not tell us if he was a priest or not. Gamaliel I is frequently called "Rabban," but this may have been influenced by the title of Gamaliel II.

➤ 'Pietists' (*Ḥasidim*, חֲסִידִים) was used for those who were especially observant or spiritual

➤ 'Tannaim' (*Tannaim*, תַּנָּאִים) was used for teachers and their disciples before the Mishnah was finished at about 200 CE

➤ 'Elders' (*Zeqenim*, זְקֵנִים) was used for leaders or judges among the scholars.

There is no evidence that any of these terms were specifically used for referring to the predecessors of the rabbis before 70 CE, though 'Sages' was used for seekers of wisdom in general and 'Elders' was used for leaders in general. Outside rabbinic literature, in the NT and Josephus, they are called 'Pharisees' (*Perushim*, פְּרוּשִׁים, 'separatists'), though later rabbis tended to regard this as a disparaging title, and the NT suggests that they used the title 'Rabbi' (Mt.23.7-8), which was honorific enough also to be used of Jesus.[8] Therefore, in this work, 'rabbinic' and 'rabbis' will refer to all those who contributed to rabbinic texts, whether they lived before or after 70 CE.

The only Jewish group which survived the destruction of 70 CE with any strength was the Hillelites. A tradition tells the story that Johanan ben Zakkai went to pay homage to Vespasian after the fall of Jerusalem, prophesying that he would become emperor, and he was rewarded with a safe home for his followers at Yavneh (or Jamnia). This became the center of rabbinic Judaism where these Hillelites and a few others set up the new Sanhedrin. All the collections of rabbinic traditions which have survived are therefore edited by the successors of these Hillelites. Fortunately the debates between the schools of Hillel and Shammai appear to have been edited shortly before this destruction, and have been passed on relatively intact, as seen from the fact that the Shammaites win some of the debates. However, it is likely that many of these debates have been lost, and that many have been tampered with. A few Sadducee-Pharisee debates have also survived, though these are clearly biased against the Sadducees.

Most scholars believe that the rabbis at Yavneh excluded rival groups and contributed to their demise, and a few think that these rival groups survived but were ignored by rabbinic Judaism.[9] However, a good case can be made that all the rival groups simply lost their distinctiveness and impetus with the destruction of the Temple. The Sadducees lost their locus of activity, the Essenes lost the reason for their rebellion, and the Pharisees' attempt to replicate Temple activities in the home, synagogue, and schoolhouse became the only way to express Jewish rites. The

---

[8] Mt.26.25, 49; Mk.9.5; 11.21; 14.45; Jn.1.38, 49; 3.2, 26; 4.31; 6.25; 9.2; 11.8 — though in Matthew, which contains Jesus' teaching, "do not be called Rabbi" (Mt.23.7f), he is only addressed as Rabbi by Judas.

[9] This is well argued by Martin Goodman, "Sadducees and Essenes after 70 CE" in *Crossing the Boundaries: Essays in Biblical Interpretation in Honour of Michael D. Goulder,* ed. Stanley E. Porter et al., Biblical Interpretation 8 (Leiden: Brill, 1994), pp. 347-56.

defining characteristic of Yavneh became inclusiveness rather than sectarian exclusiveness, which explains why those who continued after 70 CE to call themselves 'Pharisee' ('*Perushim*' in rabbinic literature) were regarded as sectarians. This inclusivity is seen in the Mishnah, which was the first Jewish document to express rival views with equal authority, and which appears to 'agree to disagree' except when a clear decision was made by the voting of a majority.[10]

The editors of the legal material did not preserve all points of view, since a consensus was usually reached, but they aimed to preserve the different opinions that formed the route toward this consensus. Therefore the earliest strata of debate were preserved mainly when they served to explain the basis of later decisions, or where early rulings had continued unchanged, but they discarded rulings which had been superseded by later debate or case law.

The editors of Scripture commentaries, by contrast, had the dual motives of explaining the Scripture text and illustrating it interestingly. This meant that, like the legal editors, they often preserved early sources when recording the development of a debate about the meaning of a text. Other early sources were preserved simply because they were interesting, especially if they contained a story or something that could be applied in a sermon. Of course neither set of editors were as single minded as this, and all rabbinic literature contains a rich mix of material from legal discussions, stories and Scripture exposition, woven together in convoluted and ingenious ways.

The aim of this present work is to find the earliest traditions, which is in some ways contrary to the aims of the early editors of rabbinic material, who wished to preserve the *conclusions* of scholarly debate, rather than their *origins*. They recorded the early stages of discussions merely in order to understand later developments. The assumption of this present work is that these editors attempted to faithfully transmit early material, because the veracity of later conclusions was partially dependent on the accuracy of the earlier stages. However, caution is always needed, because although the whole ethos of scholarship in rabbinic circles involved accurate memorizing and transmitting of earlier teaching, mistakes and innovations are nevertheless found throughout these traditions.

---

[10] See Shaye J. D. Cohen, "The Significance of Yavneh: Pharisees, Rabbis, and the End of Jewish Sectarianism," *Hebrew Union College Annual* 55 (1984): 27-53.

Collections of Rabbinic Traditions

Rabbinic literature has traditionally been divided into *halakhic* (legal) material and *aggadic* (nonlegal) material. The *halakhic* collections are Mishnah, Tosefta, and the commentaries on Mishnah in the Babylonian Talmud and Jerusalem Talmud. The *aggadic* collections include Midrash Rabbah, Mekhilta, Sifra, Sifré, and other Midrashim. This distinction is useful mainly for those who use rabbinic rulings to determine answers to questions of Jewish law. There is little evidence that such a sharp distinction was made before 70 CE.

Another classification is between Talmudic literature and Midrashic, which is easier to justify, but still creates overlaps. Talmudic literature consists of the Babylonian Talmud and the Jerusalem or Palestinian Talmud, which contain the discussions that took place in the academies in the Eastern Diaspora and in Palestine, respectively. The Midrashim (plural of Midrash) are commentary-style discussions of Scripture. They include discussions of law (which overlap with Talmudic material) as well as the stories and other literature in Scripture. They can be regarded as the result of discussions in the synagogue schoolhouse which were reflected in sermons.

The Mishnah and Tosefta preserve the earliest rabbinic material. They consist of early traditions which have been sorted according to subject matter and then sorted according to the development of debates up to about 200 CE. Both Talmuds are structured around the Mishnah, which they quote and then comment on, a section at a time. The Babylonian and Jerusalem Talmud debates cover the periods up to about 430 CE and 500 CE, respectively. The Tosefta is also quoted in the Jerusalem Talmud, but the Babylonian Talmud appears to be ignorant of it.

Early Halakhic works:			(up to about 500 CE)
m.	Mishnah	מִשְׁנָה	Collection, edited about 200 CE
t.	Tosefta	תּוֹסֶפְתָּא	Collection, edited about 400 CE
b.	Talmud Babli or Babylonian Talmud	תַּלְמוּד בַּבְלִי	Commentary on Mishnah, edited about 400 CE
y.	Talmud Yerushalmi or Jerusalem Talmud	תַּלְמוּד יְרוּשַׁלְמִי	Commentary on Mishnah, edited about 500 CE
Meg. Taan.	Megillat Taanit with Scholion	מְגִלַּת תַּעֲנִית	Pre-70 list of Fast Days, with a post-Talmudic commentary

The origins of the Mishnah and Tosefta are subjects of tradition and speculation. According to tradition, Mishnah (meaning 'recitation') was compiled by Judah ha Nasi ('the Patriarch,' end of second century), based on earlier versions by Akiba (early second century) and Meir (mid second century). Earlier editions are referred to within Mishnah when it says "at first they said . . . ,"[11] or occasionally when a ruling in Mishnah appears to be a phrase by phrase commentary on a previous ruling.[12]

Prior to the written editions of Mishnah, the 'oral law' was deliberately not written down, in order to distinguish it from the written Mosaic law. It is known that sometimes oral law *was* written, though this may have been solely for private reference. Scholars would have specialized in memorizing different sections of oral law, and would be consulted like living books.

The school disputes, which enshrine the rulings made by the rival schools of Hillel and Shammai, were edited in order to be memorizable, though they are sometimes expanded and added to in their written form. For example, the two pairs of rulings at m.Shebi:4.2 would originally have had the form:

A field which was improved: (*nittaybah*, נְטַיְבָה)
The School of Shammai says: They do not eat.
The School of Hillel says: They do eat.
The School of Shammai says: They do not eat by favor (*betobah*, בְּטוֹבָה).
The School of Hillel says: They do eat by favor.

The first line is the subject of the debate and then the conclusion of each school is given. The second pair of rulings is linked to the subject by a similar sounding word which acts as a memory aid, and the schools are always named in the same order, so the memorized version probably would not include the words "The School of x say". The highly abbreviated form often makes these traditions difficult to interpret, but easy to memorize.

Written sources may have been used as well as oral transmission, but these were always regarded as inferior to oral sources. R. Johanan [PA2] appears to warn against using such sources: "Those who write *halakhot* are as one who burns Torah and he who learns from them receives no reward" (b.Tem.14b). Also there is a story of Rab [BA1] who found a secret scroll in the house of Hiyya [T6], containing *halakhic* sentences of Issi b. Judah [T5] (b.Shab.6b; 96b; b.BM.92a). Occasionally, when someone was unsure of a ruling, "he went out, examined, and found . . ." (b.Ber.19a; b.Pes.19a; b.Hag.19a; b.Ket.81b; b.BM.18b; 20b; b.AZ.68a), which suggests (but does not prove) that there may have been written sources. It is likely that these existed as crib notes for students, but most did not regard them as authoritative and some considered them to be immoral.[13]

---

[11] E.g., m.Shebi.4.1; m.Ned.9.6; m.Git.6.5; m.Nid.10.6.
[12] E.g., m.Ter.5.1.
[13] For further discussion see Hermann L. Strack, *Einleitung in Talmud und Midrasch* (München 1887); ET *Introduction to the Talmud and Midrash* was revised (or more properly, rewritten) by Günter Stemberger (Oscar Beck: München, 1982) ET by Markus N. A. Bockmuehl (London: T. & T. Clark, 1991; Minneapolis: Augsburg Fortress, 1992, 1996), pp. 31-44 (page numbers follow the 1996 ed.).

It is still uncertain whether the Tosefta developed earlier or later or generally contemporaneously with the Mishnah.[14] Probably they developed independently from some point in the second century. However, the Tosefta we have now is certainly dependent upon Mishnah, and was completed about 400 CE. The early traditions are virtually identical when they appear in both, but a great deal of material appears in only one of them. The Tosefta can be regarded as a repository of material which was left out of Mishnah because it did not fit the overall plan and conclusions of Mishnah, or as the first commentary on Mishnah. For the purposes of this present work, the Tosefta is relatively unimportant because the earliest material is either missing from it or is virtually identical to that which is preserved in Mishnah.[15]

Mishnah and Tosefta both share the same general outline, with the same subject headings for the tractates and the same style for recording the debates. Their overall structure is six *orders* which are named after the main subject they deal with: Agriculture, Festivals, Women, Punishments, Offerings, and Purity. Each of these is further divided into tractates which are also named after the subject covered by them. Within each tractate the material has chapter divisions which appear to predate the final redaction of the Mishnah.[16] The tractates are organized like a series of histories of individual debates, in which named individuals express their opinions and the voice of the majority is expressed anonymously.

It is likely that the overall structure was relatively old and represented different courses or the specialities of different teachers in the academies. The individual tractates are fairly self-contained and the vast majority fit naturally into one of the *orders* (except for a few obvious exceptions like *Berakhot*, 'Benedictions'). It seems that the traditions on the same subject were gradually associated with each other, perhaps as a result of organized teaching based on the structure of these *orders* and tractates. This suggests that the traditions grew in complexity when the overall structure of the *orders* had already been largely decided.

In spite of this elaborate and highly organized structure, a large number of traditions and debates are in the 'wrong' place. The internal structure of each tractate can be organised both by subject and by linguistic links. Digressions frequently occur, where one ruling is followed by other rulings which share related principles or common phrases. The traditions in these digressions are sometimes also found in the

---

[14] Most scholars, such as Lieberman, Goldberg, and Neusner, regard the Tosefta as the earliest commentary on an early form of the Mishnah. However there is a strong argument for regarding it as an earlier collection than Mishnah—see Judith Hauptman, "Mishnah as a Response to Tosefta," in *The Synoptic Problem in Rabbinic Literature*, ed. Shaye J. D. Cohen, Brown Judaic Studies 326, pp. 13-34.

[15] For further discussion see Strack and Stemberger, *Introduction,* pp. 149-58.

[16] The frequent variation in the order of chapters and the clear subdivisions of material suggest that they already represented independent units at the time of final editing.

'correct' tractate, but often they are not. In this present work they are moved to the tractate corresponding to the subject matter.

The large number of 'wrongly' placed traditions suggests that traditions were memorized and passed on in two forms. Sometimes sayings were collected according to a similar theme or the development of a single subject matter. Others were collected according to a similar phrase or a similar type of argument. For example, tractate *Gittin* (divorce) has a large digression which consists of all the rulings which were justified by the phrase "for the sake of peace" and other similar phrases. The digression starts at m.Git.4.2 which is dealing with the subject of divorce, and which ends with this phrase, and this is followed by a long list of traditions which contain the same or similar phrase, stretching all the way to m.Git.5.9. None of these other rulings which were "for the sake of peace" relates directly to divorce, which suggests that once a group of traditions became associated with each other, later editors were reluctant to break them up, even for the sake of the overall structure of Mishnah.

The principle purpose of the Mishnah appears to have been to organize legal material so that a reader could discover the majority opinion on any matter that had been debated, along with the principle stages in the history of the debate. The majority opinion is presented anonymously or as the opinion of the 'Sages.' The history of the debates is presented as a series of traditions attributed to named scholars or schools, interspersed with editorial headings and the anonymous majority rulings. One of the main differences between the Tosefta and Mishnah is the differences in the majority views as represented by the anonymous rulings. This suggests that they may have been rival publications.

The Mishnah and its Babylonian Talmud gained predominance because of the decline of the Palestinian academies. It retained its predominance because the Jerusalem Talmud is much shorter and the material it contains covers much the same ground as the Babylonian Talmud. The Babylonian and Jerusalem Talmuds are much more different from each other than the Mishnah and Tosefta. They represent the debates by the academies of the Eastern Diaspora and of Palestine, respectively. Neither of them are highly edited and the Jerusalem Talmud has a large number of repeated sections so it appears to be simply a collected record of teaching without any final redaction. The Babylonian Talmud does show signs of editing, but it also has a vast number of nonlegal sayings and stories among the legal debates which seem curiously out of place. Both Talmuds contain *beraytot*—traditions which claim to date from Mishnaic times but which are not preserved in Mishnah.

Only about half of the tractates of Mishnah and Tosefta are discussed in the Talmuds. It is possible that debates about the missing tractates occurred but were not preserved. The traditional answer is that the missing debates, such as almost all of the *order* on Agriculture, were no longer relevant outside the land of Palestine or after the destruction of the Temple, though debates on the *order* on Offerings are present because it was studied in lieu of Temple worship.

The Midrashim were all edited much later than Mishnah and Tosefta, and most are later than both Talmuds. They sometimes contain traditions which are attributed to early rabbis, but these are much less reliable than *halakhic* traditions, because there was less emphasis on accuracy in *aggadic* collections.

Halakhic Midrashim:			(traditions from second-third centuries though edited much later)	
Mekh.	Mekhilta (de R. Ishmael)	מְכִילְתָּא	Commentary on Exodus	I
Mekh. Sim.	Mekhilta de R. Shimeon b. Yohai	מְכִילְתָּא דְּרַבִּי שִׁמְעוֹן בֶּן יוֹחַאי	Commentary on Exodus (reconstructed from fragments)	A
Sif.Lev.	Siphra	סִפְרָא	Commentary on Leviticus	A
Sif.Num. Sif.Deut.	Siphré	סִפְרֵי	Commentary on Numbers and Commentary on Deuteronomy	I A
Sif.Zuta	Siphré Zuta	סִפְרֵי זוּטָא	Commentary on Numbers	A
Mid.Tann.	Midrash Tannaim	מִדְרַשׁ תַּנָּאִים	=Mek.Deut compiled from MHG	I

(it is widely thought that I = from the School of Ishmael, and A = from the School of Akiba)

Some Aggadic Midrashim:			(all edited after about 450 CE, but preserve some early traditions)
Gen.R.	Bereshit Rabbah	בְּרֵאשִׁית רַבָּה	Sermonic comments on Genesis
Lam.R.	Eykah Rabbah	אֵיכָה רַבָּה	Sermonic comments on Lamentations
Lev.R.	VaYiqra Rabbah	וַיִּקְרָא רַבָּה	Sermonic comments on Leviticus
Mid.R.	Midrash Rabbah	מִדְרַשׁ רַבָּה	The above three plus later books covering the rest of the OT.
Pes.K.	Pesiqta de Rab Kahana	פְּסִיקְתָּא דְּרַב כָּהֲנָא	Sermons for Holydays
Pes.R.	Pesiqta Rabbati	פְּסִיקְתָּא רַבָּתִי	Sermons for Holydays
Tanh.Yel.	Tanhuma Yelammedenu	תַּנְחוּמָא יְלַמְּדֵנוּ	Sermons on the Pentateuch
Agg.Ber.	Aggadat Bereshit	אַגָּדַת בְּרֵאשִׁית	Sermons on Genesis
Mid.Pss.	Midrash Tehillim or Shoher Tob	מִדְרַשׁ תְּהִלִּים	Sermons on Psalms
Mid.Prov.	Midrash Mishlé	מִדְרַשׁ מִשְׁלֵי	Sermonic comments on Proverbs

Some Collections of Aggadic Midrashim:		(all edited after about 1100 CE, but preserve some early traditions)
MHG	Midrash ha-Gadol מִדְרַשׁ הַגָּדוֹל	Large collection of older Midrashim covering the Pentateuch & 5 Scrolls (Song, Ruth, Lam., Eccl., Esther)
MLT	Midrash Leqaḥ Tob מִדְרַשׁ לֶקַח טוֹב	Covering the Pentateuch and 5 Scrolls
Yalq.M.	Yalqut ha-Makhiri יַלְקוּט הַמָּכִירִי	Covers much of Prophets and Writings
Yalq.	Yalqut (Shimeon) יַלְקוּט	Collection of comments on whole OT

The Structure of Rabbinic Law

All Talmudic literature follows the same structure of six *order*s, which each divide into tractates on different subjects. Some tractates occur only in Mishnah and Tosefta, though most are commented on in the two Talmuds. A few later tractates are found only in the Babylonian Talmud. In the following tables, the initials m, t, b and y in the right-hand column indicate the presence of the tractates in Mishnah, Tosefta and the two Talmuds. A few tractates have a different name in Tosefta, as indicated in brackets, but in this present work the Mishnaic name is used for Tosefta references— i.e., t.Bes. is used instead of t.YT, except for *Kelim* which is divided into three tractates in Tosefta.

Abbreviations in these volumes have minimal dots, spaces, italics and special symbols, e.g.:

m.Ab.1.1; t.Pes.1.1; b.AZ.2a; y.Maas.1.1

A wide variety of other abbreviation systems exist, which include more spaces, transliterations of the Hebrew letters, expanded abbreviations, different names for Tosefta tractates, folio pages for Jerusalem Talmud, 'p' or 'j' for Palestinian/Jerusalem Talmud, 'B.T' and 'P.T' for the Talmuds, or no prefixes for Mishnah and Babylonian Talmud. The above abbreviations may therefore occur in the following variety of ways:

'Abot. 1:1; T. Pis. 1.1; *B.T. 'Abod. Zar.* 2 a; j.Maȧś. 2a, 1.1

Tractates are arranged in six *order*s:

Agriculture (*Zeraim*) concerns mainly tithing, though it opens with a tractate on prayer, which was probably put there as a suitable opening for the whole Mishnah.

Festivals (*Moed*) concerns the various festivals including Sabbath, and the regulations limiting work and movement during them.

Women (*Nashim*) concerns matters relating to marriage and vows (which a man may remit for his wife or daughter).

Damages (*Neziqin*) concerns compensation for persons and property, criminal trials, punishments, and crimes such as false oaths and idolatry, which carry severe penalties. Summaries of some early rulings and early sayings are added.

Holy Things (*Qodashim*) concerns the Temple and its offerings, including their redemption and their misuse.

Purities (*Toharot*), concerns various sources of impurity (discharges, menstruation, corpses, leprosy), how they are spread, and how to purify them.

The Supplementary Tractates are relatively late and concern a variety of subjects including matters of non-Temple worship (Scripture scrolls, *tefillin*, *tassels*, *mezuzot*), family mores (funerals, manners, chastity, peace), and relations with *non-Jews* and slaves.

I	Zeraim	זְרָעִים	Seeds, i.e., agriculture	In:
Ber.	Berakhot	בְּרָכוֹת	'Blessings'—Prayers	mtby
Pea.	Peah	פֵּאָה	'Corner' of the field and other poor tax	mty
Dem.	Demay	דְּמַאי	'Doubtful' tithe, and how to tithe	mty
Kil.	Kilayim	כִּלְאַיִם	'Mixtures' which are unlawful	mty
Shebi.	Shebiit	שְׁבִיעִית	'Sabbath Year' rest for farmland	mty
Ter.	Terumot	תְּרוּמוֹת	'Elevation Offerings' for priests to eat	mty
Maas.	Maaserot	מַעֲשְׂרוֹת	'Tithes'	mty
	(Maaser Rishon)	[מַעֲשֵׂר רִאשׁוֹן]	('First Tithe'—in Tosefta)	
MS	Maaser Sheni	מַעֲשֵׂר שֵׁנִי	'Second Tithe' for spending in Jerusalem	mty
Hal.	Hallah	חַלָּה	'Cake' of dough offering	mty
Orl.	Orlah	עָרְלָה	Forefruit (lit. 'foreskin') of young trees	mty
Bik.	Bikkurim	בִּכּוּרִים	'Firstfruits'	mty

II	Moed	מוֹעֵד	Festivals	
Shab.	Shabbat	שַׁבָּת	'Sabbath' Day rest from work	mtby
Er.	Érubin	עֵירוּבִין	'Communities' for Sabbath movement	mtby
Pes.	Pesachim	פְּסָחִים	'Passover'	mtby
	(Pisachim)	[פִּסְחִים]	(different vowels in Tosefta)	
Sheq.	Sheqalim	שְׁקָלִים	Half 'Shekels' for temple tax	mty
Yom.	Yoma	יוֹמָא	'The Day' of Atonement	mtby
(Yom ha-Kippurim)		[יוֹם הַכִּפּוּרִים]	('The Day of Atonement'—in Tosefta)	
Suk.	Sukkah	סֻכָּה	'Booths' (i.e., Festival of Tabernacles)	mtby
Betz.	Bétzah	בֵּיצָה	'Egg' and other Holyday regulations	mtby
	(Yom Tob)	[יוֹם טוֹב]	('Holyday'—in Tosefta)	
RH	Rosh ha-Shanah	רֹאשׁ הַשָּׁנָה	'New Year'	mtby
Taan.	Taanit	תַּעֲנִית	'Fasting'	mtby
Meg.	Megillah	מְגִילָה	'Scroll' of Esther at Purim	mtby
MQ	Moed Qatan	מוֹעֵד קָטָן	'Lesser Festivals'	mtby
Hag.	Hagigah	חֲגִיגָה	'Festival Offering'	mtby
	(Rayyaih)	[רְאִייָה]	('Appearance'—in Tosefta)	

III	Nashim	נָשִׁים	Women	In:
Yeb.	Yebamot	יְבָמוֹת	'Sisters-in-Law' in Levirate marriage	mtby
Ket.	Ketubbot	כְּתוּבּוֹת	'Marriage Contracts'	mtby
Ned.	Nedarim	נְדָרִים	'Vows'	mtby
Naz.	Nazir	נָזִיר	'Nazirite' vow	mtby
	(Nezirut)	[נְזִירוּת]	('Abstinence'—in Tosefta)	
Sot.	Sotah	סוֹטָה	'Suspected Adulteress'	mtby
Git.	Gittin	גִּיטִּין	'Divorce Certificates'	mtby
Qid.	Qiddushin	קִדּוּשִׁין	'Betrothal'	mtby

IV	Neziqin	נְזִיקִין	Damages, i.e., litigation	
BQ	Baba Qamma	בָּבָא קַמָּא	'First Gate'—Damages and compensation	mtby
BM	Baba Metzia	בָּבָא מְצִיעָא	'Middle Gate'—Profits and wages	mtby
BB	Baba Batra	בָּבָא בַתְרָא	'Last Gate'—Property and inheritance	mtby
San.	Sanhedrin	סַנְהֶדְרִין	'Sanhedrin' court	mtby
Makk.	Makkot	מַכּוֹת	'Stripes' and other punishment	mtby
Shebu.	Shebuot	שְׁבוּעוֹת	'Oaths'	mtby
Ed.	Eduyyot	עֵדְיוֹת	'Testimonies' about early teaching	mt
AZ	Abodah Zarah	עֲבוֹדָה זָרָה	'Idolatry'	mtby
Ab.	[Pirqé] Abot	[פִּרְקֵי] אָבוֹת	'[Sayings of] the Fathers'	m
Hor.	Horayot	הוֹרָיוֹת	Erroneous 'Decisions'	mtby

V	Qodashim	קָדָשִׁים	Holy Things, i.e., Offerings	
Zeb.	Zebachim	זְבָחִים	'Sacrificial Victims'	mtb
Men.	Menachot	מְנָחוֹת	'Meal Offerings'	mtb
Hul.	Ḥullin	חוּלִּין	'Profane Things'	mtb
Bek.	Bekhorot	בְּכוֹרוֹת	'Firstborn'	mtb
Arak.	Arakhin	עֲרָכִין	'Assessments' of value for vows	mtb
Tem.	Temurah	תְּמוּרָה	'Exchange' for offerings	mtb
Ker.	Keritot	כְּרִיתוֹת	'Extirpations' from Israel	mtb
Meil.	Meilah	מְעִילָה	'Misuse' of consecrated things	mtb
Tam.	Tamid	תָּמִיד	'Daily Burnt Offering'	mb
Mid.	Middot	מִדּוֹת	'Measures' of Temple and furnishings	m
Qin.	Qinnim	קִנִּים	'Birds Nests' bird offerings	m

VI	Toharot	טָהֳרוֹת	Purities	In:
Kel.	Kelim	כֵּלִים	'Utensils'	mt
	(Divided into three tractates in Tosefta, like the start of Neziqin: t.KBQ, t.KBB and t.KBM)			
Ohol.	Oholot	אָהֳלוֹת	Under 'Roofs' with a corpse	mt
Neg.	Negaim	נְגָעִים	'Plagues' of leprosy	mt
Par.	Parah	פָּרָה	Red 'Heifer'	mt
Toh.	Tohorot	טָהֳרוֹת	Im-'Purities'	mt
Miq.	Miqvaot	מִקְוָאוֹת	'Immersion Pools'	mt
Nid.	Niddah	נִדָּה	menstrual 'Isolation'	mtby
Makh.	Makhshirin	מַכְשִׁירִין	'Predisposition' to defilement	mt
Zab.	Zabim	זָבִים	Impure 'Discharges'	mt
TY	Tebul Yom	טְבוּל יוֹם	'Bathed Same Day' for purifying	mt
Yad.	Yadayim	יָדַיִם	Washing of 'Hands'	mt
Uq.	Uqtzin	עוּקְצִין	Impurity from plant 'Stalks'	mt

Supplementary Tractates:		(Later tractates, only in the Babylonian Talmud)		
ARN.A	Abot deRabbi	אָבוֹת דְּרַבִּי נָתָן	'The Fathers by R. Nathan'	b
ARN.B	Natan A and B		(a commentary on Abot)	
Soph.	Sopherim	סוֹפְרִים	'Scribes'	b
Sem.	Abel Rabbati	אֵבֶל רַבָּתִי	'Mourning'	b
	(or Semachot)	[שְׂמָחוֹת]	or (euphemistically) 'Joy'	
Kall.	Kallah	כַּלָּה	'Bride' and chastity	b
DER	Derek Eretz Rabba	דֶּרֶךְ אֶרֶץ רַבָּא	'Conduct–Major' treatise	b
DEZ	Derek Eretz Zuta	דֶּרֶךְ אֶרֶץ זוּטָא	'Conduct–Minor' treatise	b
PS	Pereq ha-Shalom	פֶּרֶק הַשָּׁלוֹם	'Chapter on Peace'	b
Ger.	Gerim	גֵּרִים	'Non-Jews'	b
Kuth.	Kuthim	כּוּתִים	'Kuthim,' i.e., Samaritans	b
Abad.	Abadim	עֲבָדִים	'Slaves'	b
ST	Sepher Torah	סֵפֶר תּוֹרָה	'Section on Torah'	b
Tef.	Tefillin	תְּפִילִין	'Phylacteries' or 'Tefillin'	b
Sis.	Tzitzit	צִיצִית	'Tassels'	b
Mez.	Mezuzah	מְזוּזָה	'Doorposts'	b

Editions and Translations

Very few ancient manuscripts of Mishnah, Tosefta, and Talmud have survived. The Münich manuscript of 1334 is the only one with a complete text of the Babylonian Talmud and Mishnah, though individual tractates have survived in a few earlier manuscripts and in fragments from the Cairo Genizah. The only complete manuscript of the Jerusalem Talmud is MS Leyden of 1289. The only complete manuscript of the Tosefta is MS Vienna of the early fourteenth century, though the earlier MS Erfurt of 1260 covers the first four *orders*. The most important editions, on which virtually all future editions are based, are those of Daniel Bomberg who published the first complete copies of the Babylonian Talmud with Mishnah, Jerusalem Talmud, and Tosefta as well as 200 other Hebrew books. He published them in Venice in the 1520s, and was, like many other early printers of Hebraica, a Christian. There are many other manuscripts and many known variants, but full critical editions are still being completed.

The Babylonian Talmud is traditionally laid out, as in the Bomberg edition, with commentaries by medieval rabbis such as Rashi in the margins at the top, bottom, and sides. This layout is reproduced in most Hebrew editions of the Talmud, with the same text in the same positions. As a result, Talmudic references relate to page numbers. A typical reference is b.San.43a where "b" refers to the Babylonian Talmud, "San" is an abbreviation for the tractate (in this case "Sanhedrin") and "43a" is the page number. Each number refers to a folio sheet where the front (recto) is the "a" side and the back (verso) is the "b" side. The Talmud has chapter divisions, but these are not normally referred to in references.

The Palestinian or Jerusalem Talmud was given a similar reference system but with the prefix "p," "j," or "y" (for Yerushalmi). The Jerusalem Talmud has two possible types of reference—chapters and verses (known as *halakhot*), or page numbers and columns. The chapter and *halakhah* divisions correspond approximately to the Mishnah reference. Page numbers refer to both sides of a sheet, with two columns on each side which are referred to as a and b (on the first side) and c and d (on the reverse). A full reference such as y.San.12.4, 43a combines both the chapter/verse and the page/column reference. In this work, only the chapter/verse references are given, though the additional subdivisions of Neusner's translation (in Roman numbers) are given when the section is a long one.

References to Mishnah and Tosefta are normally in the style of chapters and verses. The chapters are roughly the same as chapter numbers in the Talmuds, and each verse is called a 'mishnah.' These sections are often much longer in the Tosefta, which contains about four times as much material as the Mishnah. The chapters in

Mishnah and Tosefta usually correspond to each other, and the order of material within the chapters is the same, but the *mishnah* (verse) divisions do not keep step with each other. Neither of them have traditional page layouts like the Talmuds, so they are not cited by page number, though Mishnah is sometimes cited by the page number where it occurs in the Babylonian Talmud. In this work, Tosefta is normally cited according to Lieberman's edition, which Neusner's translation follows, rather than Zuckermandel's edition, which has greater traditional acceptance but is often flawed. When numbering differs, Zuckermandel's reference is given in brackets after Lieberman's.

English translations are now available for most of the important rabbinic literature. Mishnah is translated into flowing English by Danby while a more literal translation is supplied by Neusner. Blackman's Mishnah is perhaps the most useful, because it has a pointed Hebrew text and numerous explanatory footnotes. Tosefta and Jerusalem Talmud are translated in full only by Neusner but Guggenheimer's new translation is progressing well. The Babylonian Talmud and Midrash Rabbah are also translated by Neusner, though the old Soncino translations are still very useful, especially for the footnotes. The German translation of the Babylonian Talmud by Goldschmidt is useful for easy access to the variants in MS München. The Soncino translations with their Hebrew texts are available on a searchable CD from Davka.com who also produce searchable Hebrew texts of most other rabbinic works. Hebrew texts of the main rabbinic works are also available on the Web at http://www1.snunit.k12.il/kodesh/.

Rabbinic Generations

The rabbis who contributed to the Mishnah and Tosefta are called Tannaim, and the rabbis who contributed to the Talmuds are called Amoraim. Both groups are traditionally classified in generations called T1, T2, etc. for the first and second generation of Tannaim etc., and in this study T0 will be used for the pre-Tannaitic scholars. The Amoraim are divided into Babylonian and Palestinian generations (PA1, BA1, PA2, BA2, etc.), according to their main center of authority. Although this classification appears to be crude, it is a fairly reliable way of identifying the general date of these individuals.

Approx. Dates	Generations	Period / Center	Titles and Works
200 BCE–10 CE	T0	Second Temple Period	The Great Assembly
10–80 CE	T1	**Temple Destroyed**	
80–120 CE	T2		Tannaim:
120–140 CE	T3	Yavnean Period	
140–165 CE	T4	**Bar Kokhba Revolt**	Mishnah
165–200 CE	T5	Ushan Period	Tosefta
200–220 CE	T6		Halakhic Midrashim
220–250 CE	BA1 and PA1	Palestine:	
250–290 CE	BA2 and PA2	Sepphoris	Amoraim:
290–320 CE	BA3 and PA3	Tiberias, Caesarea	Palestinian Talmud,
320–350 CE	BA4 and PA4	Babylon:	Babylonian Talmud,
350–375 CE	BA5 and PA5	Nehardea	Aggadic Midrashim
375–425 CE	BA6	Pumbeditha, Sura	

T0 covers several generations, from about 200 BCE to 10 CE
    i.e., "before New Testament times" or "before the first century"
T1 covers from about 10 ce to after the destruction of the Temple in 70 CE
    i.e., "in the first Century," or "in NT times," or "before 70 CE"
T2 covers the restoration of study from about 80 to 120 CE
    i.e., "soon after 70 CE," or "end of the first century"
    or "early Yavnean period" (Yavneh became the center of authority)
T3 covers the period of expansion of study from about 120 to 140 CE
    i.e., "early second century" or "later Yavnean period"
    or "before Bar Kokhba's revolt" (132–135 ce)

T4 covers the time of the last great Mishnaic debates in about 140 to 165 CE
  i.e., "mid second century" or "after Bar Kokhba's revolt"
  or "early Ushan period" (when Usha became the center of authority)
T5 covers the time of consolidation of Mishnah in about 165 to 200 CE
  i.e., "late second century" or "middle Ushan period"

The following tables are an exhaustive list of scholars in the Tannaitic generations, and scholars who occur more than 100 times in the Amoraic generations. Contracted names are given as they normally occur in rabbinic literature, with fuller names in brackets. Abbreviations are 'R.' for 'Rabbi' ('my teacher'), 'Rn' for 'Rabban' ('our teacher') and 'b.' for 'ben' or 'bar' ('son of' in Hebrew and Aramaic, respectively).

The individuals named in rabbinic works are usually easy to identify because they are referred to in standard ways, though this standard is not always the same in Mishnah as in Talmud. The following tables show which generations the scholars belong to, based on who speaks with who, who quotes who, and who is quoted by who. This is based on traditional rabbinic scholarship and largely verified by modern critical scholarship. The more often a rabbi is named, the more certain we can be about when he taught, so the tables indicate the relative importance of each scholar—bold type for very frequent occurrence, normal type for less frequent.

Italics are used in two different ways in these tables. For Tannaim italics indicate that they only occur once in Mishnah or, in a few cases indicated by curly brackets, they only occur in Talmud. For the Amoraim in the Babylonian Talmud, italics indicate occasional differences in the way the Jerusalem Talmud refers to them, and vice versa for Amoraim in the table for the Jerusalem Talmud. The English spellings of the names follow the Soncino translations for Babylonian Talmud, and Neusner's translations for Mishnah and Jerusalem Talmud. They have deliberately not been unified because these are the editions which an English reader are most likely to use.

There is still much uncertainty about some scholars. Sometimes the same scholar may have more than one name and sometimes two scholars may share the same name. However, rabbinic tradition was fairly careful to distinguish between such scholars, and so confusion is relatively rare. Many oft-cited individuals were known only by their first name (e.g., Judah) or their patronym (e.g., Ben Bathyra) or a title (e.g., Rabbi or Abba). Some of the more confusing short forms are listed at the end of the tables. The rabbinic traditions are normally careful to use the same form of name for the same individual, though occasional mistakes have occurred. There are also many individuals with the same name (such as Rn. Gamaliel) who can only be distinguished from each other by the names of the people with whom they are mentioned. They are normally distinguished in modern studies as I or II (e.g., Rn. Gamaliel I) and sometimes rabbinic literature will call the first one 'the Elder' or 'the Great,' though usually the ambiguity is left unresolved. Therefore one should always check that the individuals who are named in a debate come from the same or adjacent generations.

Authorities named in Mishnah

Bold indicates 10 or more occurrences in Mishnah; italics indicates less than two occurrences. Curley brackets indicates that the person is only named in Talmud. Spelling as in Soncino eds.

T0 - Pre-Tannaitic, before c. 10 CE

3rd C BCE: Simeon the Pious
 = Simeon I — Jos.Ant.12.43;
 or = Simeon II — Jos.Ant.12.224
2nd C BCE: *Antigonus of Soko*
2nd C BCE: Johanan the High Priest
 = John Hyrcanus
2nd C BCE: **Jose b. Joezer**
2nd C BCE: Jose b. Johanan
2nd C BCE: Joshua b. Perahiah
2nd C BCE: Nittai (Mittai) of Arbela
2nd C BCE: Jose b. Johanan
1st C BCE: Abtalion [1st C BCE]
1st C BCE? Akabia b. Mahalalel
1st C BCE: *Baba b. Buta*

1st C BCE: *Ben Hé Hé*
1st C BCE: {*Bené Bathyra*}
1st C BCE: **Hillel** (the Elder)
1st C BCE: *Honi the Circle Maker*
1st C BCE? Joshua b. Gamala
1st C BCE: Judah b. Tabbai
1st C BCE: *R. Measha*
1st C BCE: *Menahem*
1st C BCE: **Shammai** (the Elder)
1st C BCE: Shemaiah
1st C BCE: Simeon b. Shetah
1st C CE: Eliehoenai b. Hakof
1st C CE: *Hanamel (Hanan) the Egyptian*

T1 - Tannaim c. 10-80 CE

Abba Jose Cholikofri
Admon
Ben Bukri
Dosethai of Kefar Yathmah
{*R. Eleazar b. Harsom*}
Rn. Gamaliel (I, the Elder)
Hanan b. Abishalom
Hananiah b. Hezekiah b. G.
R. Hanina, Deputy of the priests
R. Ishmael b. Phabi (or *Fabi*)
Joezer of the Birah
R. Johanan (Nehunia) b. Gudgada

Johanan b. ha-Horanith
Rn./R. Johanan b. Zakkai
{*Jonathan b. Uzziel* }
{*Judah b. Durtai*}
Menahem b. Signai
Nahum the Mede
Nahum the Scribe
Rn. Simeon b. Gamaliel (I)
{*Simeon b. Hillel* }
R. Simeon of Mizpah
R. Zechariah b. Kubetal

T2 - Tannaim c. 80-120 CE

Abba Jose b. Hanan
Abba Saul b. Batnith
(Johanan) *Ben Bag Bag*
Ben Bathyra (R. Simeon)
{*Ben Patura* }
Boethus b. Zonin
R. Dosa b. Harkinas
R. Eleazar b. Arak
R. Eleazar b. Azariah
{*R. Eleazar b. R. Jose*}
R. Eliezer (b. Hyrcanus)
R. Eliezer b. Diglai
R. Eliezer b. Jacob (I)
R. Eliezer / Eleazar b. Zadok
Rn. Gamaliel (II)

R. Halafta
R. Hanina b. Dosa
R. Hanina b. Gamaliel (II)
R. Huzpith
R. Hyrcanus in Kefar Etam
R. Jose b. (R.) Honi
R. Jose the Priest
R. Joshua (b. Hananiah)
R. Joshua b. Bathyra
R. Joshua b. Hyrcanus
R. Judah b. Bathyra
{*R. Judah b. Lakish* }
R. Levitas of Yavneh
{*Nahum of Gimzu* }
R. Nehunia b. Elinathan

R. Nehunia b. ha-Kanah
{*Onkelos (Aquilas?)* }
R. Pappias
Samuel the Lesser
{*Simeon ha-Pakuli* }
R. Simeon b. Nethaneel
Simeon brother of Azariah
R. Simeon son of the Deputy
R. Yakim of Hadar
R. Yeshebab
R. Zadok
{*R. Zechariah b. Abkulas* }
R. Zechariah b. ha-Kazzab

Authorities named in Mishnah

Bold indicates 10 or more occurrences in Mishnah; italics indicates less than two occurrences.
Curley brackets indicates that the person is only named in Talmud. Spelling as in Soncino eds.

T3 - Tannaim c. 120-140 CE

Abtolemus	R. Hananiah b. Hakinai	**R. Jose the Galilean**
R. Akiba (b. Joseph)	R. Hananiah b. Teradion	*R. Jose b. Kisma*
(R. Simeon) **Ben Azzai**	**R. Hanina b. Antigonus**	*R. Joshua b. Mathia*
(Simeon) Ben Nanos	*R. Ilai or Ila*	R. Judah b. Baba
(Simeon) Ben Zoma	**R. Ishmael** (b. Elisha)	*R. Judah the Priest*
R. Eleazar (b.) Hisma	R. Johanan b. Beroka	R. Mathia(h) b. Heresh
R. Eleazar b. Judah of Bartotha	*R. Johanan b. Joshua*	Nehemiah of Bet Deli
R. Eleazar b. Perata (I)	*R. Johanan b. Mathia*	*R. Simeon b. Akashiah*
R. Eleazar of Modiim	**R. Johanan b. Nuri**	Simeon of Teman
Elisha b. Abuyah	*R. Jose son of the Damascene*	**R. Tarfon**

T4 - Tannaim c. 140–165 CE

Abba Eleazar b. Dulai	*R. Hanina of Ono*	**R. Judah** (b. Illai)
Abba Saul	R. Ishmael b. R. Johanan b. Beroka	**R. Meir**
R. Eleazar b. Mathia	R. Jacob (b. Korshai)	*R. Menahem (b. R. Jose*
R. Eleazar (b. Shammua in M)	R. Johanan the sandal-maker	*b. Halafta)*
R. Eliezer b. Jacob (II)	*R. Jonathan (b. Joseph)*	**R. Nehemiah**
R. Eliezer b. R. Jose the Galilean	R. Joshua b. Karha	{*R. Simai* }
R. Eliezer b. Pilai	**R. Jose** (b. Halafta)	**Rn. Simeon b. Gamaliel** (II)
R. Hananiah b. Akabia	*R. Jose b. ha-Hotef the Ephrathi*	R. Simeon of Shezuri
R. Hananiah b. Akashiah	{*R. Josiah (the Great)* }	**R. Simeon** (b. Yohai)

T5 - Tannaim c. 165–200 CE

Abba Gorion of Sidon	{*R. Isaac* }	R. Nathan
R. Dosa	*R. Ishmael b. R. Jose (b. Halafta)*	R. Nehorai
R. Dosethai b. Jannai	*Jaddua the Babylonian*	*R. Phinehas b. Jair*
R. Eleazar b. R. Simeon (b. Yohai)	**R. Jose b. R. Judah** (b. Illai)	**Rabbi** (Judah, ha-Nasi)
(= Eliezer b. Simeon in Babli)	*R. Jose Ketanta* [?= Jose	R. Simeon b. Eleazar
R. Eliezer (Eleazar) ha-Kappar	(Issi) b. Akabia - y.BQ 3.7, 3d]	*R. Simeon b. Halafta*
R. Eliezer (Eleazar) **b. Zadok** (II)	[?=Issi b. Judah - b.Pes.113b]	R. Simeon b. Menasia
R. Halafta (b. Dosa) of	R. Jose b. Meshullam	Symmachus (b. Joseph)
Kefar Hananiah	R. Judah b. Tema	

T6 - Tannaim c. 200–220 CE

{*Rn. Gamaliel (b. Rabbi)* (III)}	R. Simeon b. Judah (ha-Nasi)	{*R. Zakkai* }
{Hiyya (bar Abba, the Great) }	(= R. Simeon b. Rabbi)	
{Bar Kappara }	{*R. Shila* }	

PA1 – Palestinian Amoraim named in Mishnah c. 220–250 CE

R. Jannai	*R. Joshua b. Levi*

Babylonian & Palestinian Amoraim in Babylonian Talmud

Bold indicates 500 or more occurrences in Talmud; less than 100 occurrences are not included. Italics indicate the name in Jerusalem Talmud. Spelling as in Soncino eds.

BA1 - Babylonian Amoraim c. 220–250 CE	PA1 - Palestinian Amoraim c. 220–250 CE
Assi (I) (Mar) **Samuel** **Rab** (Abba b. Aibu or Abba Arikha 'the tall')	R. Hanina (bar Hama) R. Hoshaia (Hoshaia Rabba, *Oshaia*) **R. Jannai (Sabba, the Elder)** **R. Joshua b. Levi**
BA2 - Babylonian Amoraim c. 250–290 CE	PA2 - Palestinian Amoraim c. 250–290 CE
Rab Adda bar Ahabah (Ada . . .) **Rab Huna** (bar Hiyya) (I) Rab Jeremiah bar Abba (. . . *bar Wa*) **Rab Judah** (bar Ezekiel) Rabbah bar Abbuha	R. Hiyya bar Joseph R. Hiyya bar Ashi **R. Johanan** (bar Nappaha) R. Jose ben Hanina (Rab) Kahana (I) **Resh Lakish** (R. Simeon b. Lakish)
BA3 - Babylonian Amoraim c. 290–320 CE	PA3 - Palestinian Amoraim c. 290–320 CE
Abba (Ba) [BA3 => PA3] Rab Hamnuna (I) **Rab Hisda** **Rab Joseph** (bar Hiyya) **Rab Nahum** (bar Jacob) Rab Safra **Rab Shesheth** Rabbah bar bar Hanah (*Abba* . . .) [son of Abba bar Hana, hence 'bar bar'] **Rabbah, Raba** (bar Rab Nahmani) Rabbah bar Rab Huna Ulla (bar Ishmael)	R. Abbahu (of Caesarea) R. Assi (*Yose, Assa, Issi*) (II) R. Ammi (ben Nathan, *Immi*) **R. Eleazar** (ben Pedat, *Leazar*) Hanina (Hasid of the Rabbis) R. Hiyya bar Abba, *b. Ba* (II) R. Isaac (Nappaha, 'the blacksmith') (II) R. Levi (bar Sisi) (R. Samuel) Bar Nahmani **R. Zera** (I)
BA4 - Babylonian Amoraim c. 320–350 CE	PA4 - Palestinian Amoraim c. 320–350 CE
Abaye R. Aha bar Jacob R. Rami bar Hama **Rab Nahum b. Isaac** **Raba** (bar Joseph bar Hama)	R. Jeremiah Rabin (*R. Abin, R. Abun, R. Bun*)
BA5 - Babylonian Amoraim c. 350–375 CE	PA5 - Babylonian Amoraim c. 350–375 CE
Dimi (of Nehardea) Rab Huna bar Rab Joshua **Rab Papa** (bar Hanan) Rab Zebid (of Nehardea)	(None are named more than 100 times)
BA6 - Babylonian Amoraim c. 375–425 CE	
Rab Aha bar Raba [BA6] Amemar [BA6] **Rab Ashi** [BA6]	Rab Kahana [BA6] Mar Zutra [BA6] **Rabina** [I BA6]
BA7 - Babylonian Amoraim c. 425–460 CE	None are named more than 100 times
BA8 - Babylonian Amoraim c. 460–500 CE	None are named more than 100 times

Babylonian & Palestinian Amoraim in Jerusalem Talmud

Bold indicates 500 or more occurrences in Talmud; less than 100 occurrences are not included. Italics indicate the name in Babylonian Talmud. Spelling as in Neusner's translation.

BA1 - Babylonian Amoraim c. 220–250 CE	PA1 - Palestinian Amoraim c. 220–250 CE
Rab (Abba b. Aibu) (Mar) **Samuel**	R. Haninah (bar Hama) **(H)Oshaya** (bar Hama, Rabba) **R. Joshua b. Levi** R. Yannai **R. Yose bar Haninah**
BA2 - Babylonian Amoraim c. 250–290 CE	**PA2 - Palestinian Amoraim c. 250–290 CE**
R. Huna or Hunya	Hiyya bar Ashi (Rab) Kahana **R. Simeon b. Lakish** (or Resh Lakish) **R. Yohanan**
BA3 - Babylonian Amoraim c. 290–320 CE	**PA3 - Palestinian Amoraim c. 290–320 CE**
R. Hisda [BA3]	R. Abahu (of Caesarea) R. Assa, Assi, or Issi (II) R. Ammi or Immi (ben Nathan),
R. Jacob bar Idi R. Joshua R. Levi (bar Sisi) [T6] or R. Samuel b. Isaac R. Samuel bar Nahmani R. Simeon b. Ba or b. Abba R. Simeon b. Pazzi **R. Yose** (b. Zab(i)da) **R. Zeira** (I)	**Ba**, Abba Bar bar Mamel (*Abba . . .*) Bun bar Kahana (*Abba . . .*) **R. Eleazar** or **R. Leazar** R. Hinena (b. Pappai) R. Hiyya b. Abba, b. Ba (II) R. Ila (also Hela or Ela) R. Isaac (Nappaha) (II) **R. Jacob bar Aha**
PA4 - Palestinian Amoraim c. 320–350 CE	
R. Abin, Abun, Bun or *Rabin* (I) **R. Aha** (of Lydda) R. Haggai Huna, Hunya or Nehonya (b. Abin)	**R. Jeremiah** **R. Judah** (b. Pazzi or b. Simon) or Judah [IV PA5] R. Yudan
PA5 - Babylonian Amoraim c. 350–375 CE	
R. Abin, Abun, Bun or *Rabin* (II) R. Hananiah or Hanina(h) (II) **R. Hezekiah** **R. Jonah** **R. Mana** or Mani (b. Yonah) (II)	R. Pinhas (bar Hama) R. Tanhum(a) (bar Abba) **R. Yose b. Bun** (or bar Abin, bar Abun)

Alphabetic List

Ab(b)ahu (of Caesarea) [PA3]
Abaye [BA4]
Abba [BA3 => PA3]
Abba Arikha ('the tall') [BA1]
Abba b. Aibu [BA1]
Abba Bar bar Mamel [PA3]
Abba Bun bar Kahana [PA3]
Abba Eleazar b. Dula'i [T4]
Abba Gorion of Sidon [T5]
Abba Jose b. Hanan [T2]
Abba Jose Cholikofri [T1]
Abba Saul [T4]
Abba Saul b. Batnith [T2]
Abbah bar bar Hanah [BA3]
Ab(b)ahu (of Caesarea) [PA3]
Abin [PA4] or [PA3]
Abtalion [1st C BCE]
Abtolemus [T3]
Abun [I PA4] or [II PA5]
Adda or Ada b. Ahabah [BA2]
Admon [T1]
Aha (of Lydda) [PA4]
Aha b. Jacob [BA4]
Aha b. Raba [BA6]
Akabia b. Mahalalel [1st C BCE?]
Akiba (b. Joseph) [T3]
Amemar [BA6]
Ammi (b. Nathan) [PA3]
Antigonus of Soko [2nd C BCE]
Aquilas [T3]
Ashi [BA6]
Assa in Y = [II PA3]
Assi in B = [I BA1] or [II PA3]
Assi in Y = [II PA3]
Ba [BA3 => PA3]
Baba b. Buta [1st C BCE]
Bar bar Mamel [PA3]
Bar Kappara or Qappara [T6]
Bar Nahmani [PA3]
Ben Azzai (Simeon) [T3]
Ben Bag Bag [T2]
Ben Bathyra (Simeon) [T2]
Ben Bukri [T1]
Ben Hé Hé [1st C BCE]
Ben Nanos (Simeon) [T3]
Ben Patura [T2]
Ben Zoma [T3]
Bené Bathyra [1st C BCE]
Boethus b. Zonin [T2]
Bun b. Kahana [PA3]
Dimi (of Nehardea) [BA5]

Dosa in M = b. Harkinas [T2]
Dosa in B = [T5]
Dosa b. Harkinas [T2]
Dosethai b. Jannai [T5]
Dosethai of Kefar Yathmah [T1]
Ela [PA3]
Eleazar in M = (b. Shammua) [T4]
Eleazar in B and Y = (b. Pedat) [PA3]
Eleazar b. Arak [T2]
Eleazar b. Azariah [T2]
Eleazar b. Harsom [T1?]
Eleazar (b.) Hisma [T3]
Eleazar b. Judah of Bartotha [T3]
Eleazar b. Mathia [T4]
Eleazar b. Perata [I T3]
Eleazar b. Simeon (b.Yohai) [T5]
Eleazar ha-Kappar [T5]
Eleazar of Modiim [T3]
Eliehoenai b. Hakof [1st C CE]
Eliezer (b. Hyrcanus) [T2]
Eliezer b. Diglai [T2]
Eliezer b. Jacob [I T2] or [II T4]
Eliezer b. Jose the Galilean [T4]
Eliezer b. Pilai [T4]
Eliezer b. Simeon [T5]
Eliezer or Eleazar b. Zadok [I T2] or [II T5]
Eliezer ha-Kappar [T5]
Elisha b. Abuyah [T3]
Gamaliel (b. Rabbi) [III, T6]
Gamaliel (the Elder) [I T1]
Gamaliel [II T2]
Haggai [PA4]
Halafta [T2]
Halafta (b. Dosa) of Kefar Hananiah [T5]
Hamnuna [I BA2] or [II BA3]
Hananiah or Hanina(h) [II PA5]
Hanamel the Egyptian [1st C CE]
Hanan b. Abishalom [T1]
Hanan the Egyptian [1st C CE]
Hananiah b. Akabia [T4]
Hananiah b. Akashiah [T4]
Hananiah b. Hakinai [T3]
Hananiah b. Hezekiah b. Gurion [T1]
Hananiah b. Teradion [T3]
Hanina, Deputy of the priests [T1]
Hanina (Hasid of the Rabbis) [PA3]
   or (b. Hama) [PA1]
Hanina b. Antigonus [T3]
Hanina b. Dosa [T2]
Hanina b. Gamaliel [II T2]
Hanina of Ono [T4]

Hela [PA3]
Hezekiah [PA5]
Hillel (the Elder) [1st C BCE]
Hinena (b. Pappai) [PA3]
Hisda [BA3]
Hiyya (b. Abba) the Great [T6]
Hiyya b. Abba, b. Ba [II PA3]
Hiyya b. Ashi [PA2]
Hiyya b. Joseph [PA2]
Honi the Circle Maker [1st C BCE]
Hoshaya (b. Hama, Rabba) [I PA1]
Huna (b. Abin) [PA4] or (b. Hiyya) [I BA2]
Huna b. Rab Joshua [BA5]
Huzpith [T2]
Hyrcanus in Kefar Etam [T2]
Ila(i) (the Elder) [T3] or [PA3]
Immi (b. Nathan) [PA3]
Isaac [T5]
Isaac (Nappaha, 'the blacksmith') [II PA3]
Ishmael (b. Elisha) [T3]
Ishmael b. Johanan b. Beroka [T4]
Ishmael b. Jose (b. Halafta) [T5]
Ishmael b. Phabi (or Fabi) [T1]
Issi [II PA3]
Issi b. Judah [T5?]
J--- if a name is not here, try Y---
Jacob (b. Korshai) [T4]
Jacob b. Aha [PA3]
Jacob b. Idi [PA3]
Jaddua the Babylonian [T5]
Jannai (Sabba, the Elder) [PA1]
Jeremiah [PA4]
Jeremiah b. Abba (or b. Wa) [BA2]
Joezer of the Birah [T1]
Johanan Ben Bag Bag [T2]
Johanan (b. Nappaha) [PA2]
Johanan (Nehunia) b. Gudgada [T1]
Johanan b. Beroka [T3]
Johanan b. ha-Horanith [T1]
Johanan b. Joshua [T3]
Johanan b. Mathia [T3]
Johanan b. Nuri [T3]
Johanan b. Zakkai [T1]
Johanan the High Priest [2nd C BCE]
Johanan the sandal-maker [T4]
Jonah [PA5]
Jonathan (b. Joseph) [T4]
Jonathan b. Uzziel [T1]
Jose in B, M or T = (b. Halafta) [T4]
Jose in Y = (b. Zab(i)da) [PA3]
Jose (Issi) b. Akabia [T5?]
Jose b. Bun (or b. Abin, b. Abun) [PA5]
Jose b. ha-Hotef the Ephrathi [T4]

Jose b. Hanina [PA2]
Jose b. Honi [T2]
Jose b. Joezer [2nd C BCE]
Jose b. Johanan [2nd C BCE]
Jose b. Judah (b. Illai) [T5]
Jose b. Kisma [T3]
Jose b. Meshullam [T5]
Jose Ketanta [T5?]
Jose son of the Damascene [T3]
Jose the Galilean [T3]
Jose the Priest [T2]
Joseph (b. Hiyya) [BA3]
Joshua (b. Hananiah) [T2]
Joshua b. Bathyra [T2]
Joshua b. Gamala [1st C BCE?]
Joshua b. Hyrcanus [T2]
Joshua b. Karha [T4]
Joshua b. Levi [PA1]
Joshua b. Mathia [T3]
Joshua b. Perahiah [2nd C BCE]
Josiah (the Great) [T4]
Judah in M and B = (b. Illai) [T4]
Judah in Y = (b. Pazzi or b. Simon) [PA4] or
    Judah [IV PA5]
Rab Judah (b. Ezekiel) [BA2]
Judah b. Baba [T3]
Judah b. Bathyra [T2]
Judah b. Durtai [T1?]
R. Judah b. Lakish [T2]
Judah b. Tabbai [1st C BCE]
Judah b. Tema [T5]
Judah ha-Nasi or . . . Nesi'ah in Y = [T5]
Judah ha-Nasi or . . . Nesi'ah in B = [II PA2]
    or [III PA3]
Judah the Priest [T3]
Kahana [I PA2] or [II BA6] or [BA1]
    or [BA3]
Kappara, Bar [T6]
Leazar — see Eleazar
Levi (b. Sisi) [T6] or [PA3]
Levitas of Yavneh [T2]
Mana or Mani (b. Yonah) [II PA5]
Mar Samuel [BA1]
Mar Zutra [BA6]
Mattia(h) b. Heresh [T3]
Measha [1st C BCE]
Meir [T4]
Menahem [1st C BCE]
Menahem (b. Jose b. Halafta) [T4]
Menahem b. Signai [T1]
Mittai of Arbela [2nd C BCE]
Nahmani (Samuel b. Nahmani) [PA3]
Nahum (b. Jacob) [BA3]

Nahum b. Isaac [BA4]
Nahum of Gimzu [T2]
Nahum the Mede [T1]
Nahum the Scribe [T1]
Nathan [T5]
Nehemiah [T4]
Nehemiah of Bet Deli [T3]
Nehonya (b. Abin) [PA4]
Nehorai [T5]
Nehunia b. Elinathan [T2]
Nehunia b. ha-Kanah [T2]
Nittai of Arbela [2nd C BCE]
Onkelos [T3]
Oshaya or Oshaia (b. Hama, Rabba) [I PA1]
Papa (b. Hanan) [BA5]
Pappias [T2]
Phinehas b. Jair [T5]
Pinhas (b. Hama) [PA5]
Qappara, Bar [T6]
Rab (Abba b. Aibu) [BA1]
Rab Judah (b. Ezekiel) [BA2]
Raba (b. Joseph b. Hama) [BA4]
Rabbah (b. Rab Nahmani) [BA3]
Rabbah b. b. Hanah [BA3]
Rabbah b. Abbuha [BA2]
Rabbah b. Rab Huna [BA3]
Rabbi (Judah, ha Nasi) [T5]
Rabin [PA4] or [PA3]
Rabina [I BA6]
Rami b. Hama [BA4]
Resh Lakish (Simeon b. Lakish) [PA2]
Safra [BA3]
Samuel [BA1]
Samuel b. Isaac [PA3]
Samuel b. Nahmani [PA3]
Samuel the Lesser [T2]
Shammai (the Elder) [1st C BCE]
Shemaiah [1st C BCE]
Shesheth [BA3]
Shila [T6]
Simai [T4]
Simeon b. Akashiah [T3]
(Simeon) Ben Azzai [T3]
Simeon b. Azzai [T3]

Simeon b. Ba or b. Abba [PA3]
(Simeon) Ben Bathyra [T2]
Simeon b. Eleazar [T5]
Simeon b. Gamaliel [II T4] or [I T1]
Simeon b. Halafta [T5]
Simeon b. Hillel [T1]
Simeon b. Judah (ha-Nasi) [T6]
(Simeon b. Lakish) Resh Lakish [PA2]
Simeon b. Lakish [PA2]
Simeon b. Menasia [T5]
(Simeon) Ben Nanos [T3]
Simeon b. Nethaneel [T2]
Simeon b. Rabbi [T6]
Simeon b. Shetah [1st C BCE]
Simeon (b. Yohai) [T4]
Simeon b. Zoma [T3]
Simeon b. Pazzi [PA3]
Simeon brother of Azariah [T2]
Simeon ha-Pakuli [T2]
Simeon of Mizpah [T1]
Simeon of Shezuri [T4]
Simeon of Teman [T3]
Simeon son of the Deputy [T2]
Simeon the Pious [3rd C BCE]
Simon=Simeon
Symmachus (b. Joseph) [T5]
Tanhum(a) (b. Abba) [PA5]
Tarfon [T3]
Ulla (b. Ishmael) [BA3]
Y--- if a name is not here, try J---
Yakim of Hadar [T2]
Yannai — see Jannai
Yeshebab [T2]
Yohanan — see Johanan
Yose — see Jose
Yudan [PA4]
Zadok [T2]
Zakkai [T6]
Zebid (of Nehardea) [BA5]
Zechariah b. Abkulas [T2]
Zechariah b. ha-Kazzab [T2]
Zechariah b. Kubetal [T1]
Zera, or Zeira [I PA3]

Short forms that sometimes cause confusion

Abba or **Ba** in B or Y = Abba [BA3=>PA3] — studied in B, taught in P
Ben Bathyra = Simeon b. Bathyra. His brother is R. Judah b. Bathyra
Dosa in B is usually T5 and in M is usually T2
Eleazar in M or Leazar in T = b. Shammua [T4]; but in B or Y = b. Pedat [PA3]
Huna in B = b. Hiyya [I BA2]; but in Y = b. Abin [PA4]
Jose or **Yose** in B, M, T = b. Halafta [T4]; but in Y = b. Zab(i)da [PA3]
Mar ('the Master') refers to a rabbi previously named in the text
Rab = Abba b. Aibu [BA1]
Raba = Raba b. Joseph b. Hama [BA4]
Rabbah = Rabbah bar Rab Nahmani [BA3]
Rabbi in B or Y = Judah HaNasi [I T5]
Rab Nahmani in B = Samuel bar Nahmani [PA3]
Rab Judah = b. Ezekiel [BA2]
R. Judah in M or T or B = Judah b. Illai [T4]
R. Judah in Y = Judah b. Pazzi or b. Simon [PA4] or Judah [IV PA5]
R. Judah ha-Nasi ('the Prince' or 'the Patriarch') = Judah [I T5], often just 'Rabbi'
R. Judah Nesiah (Aramaic 'the Prince') = Judah [II PA2], or Judah [III PA3]

Note on Huna:
Stemberger points to Bacher *Tann* 2.389-90 which says that Dosa is T5 also in Mishnah, because he appears to debate with R. Jose [T4] at m.Toh.8.8. But this is attributed to Dosa b. Harkinas at m.Ed.3.2 and it is an independent ruling which may not originally have been part of the same debate. Other places in Mishnah where "R. Dosa" appears without a patronym are m.Hul.1.7; m.Shab.20.4; m.Bek.7.2 (where his opinion is stated before that of Hanina b. Antigonus [T3]); m.Ed.3.2, 3, 6 (in the midst of a long list of traditions of Dosa b. Harkinas in m.Ed.3.1–3.10). According to a later biographical story in b.Yeb.16a Dosa b. Harkinas was sometimes called Dosa. In the Babylonian Talmud he appears without the patronym at several places with Judah [b. Illai, T4]: b.Yom.12b, 23b, 24a, 60a and b.Zeb.46a (re clothes of the High Priest); b.Betz.9b (re moving a ladder during a festival); b.Ket.36b and b.Git.81a (re defilement of a priest's daughter, but cf. m.Ed.3.6); b.BK.69a (re gleaning); b.BM.76b-77b (re payment for uncompleted work); b.San.63a (re a last meal before punishment); b.Zeb.88b (re bells of the High Priest). Dosa also cites Abba Saul [T4] at b.Betz.37b and makes a ruling about Sukkah at Usha [i.e., T4 or T5] (b.Suk.20a, 20b) as well as occurring elsewhere in contexts which contain no clues about dating: b.Pes.26a; b.Suk.52a; b.San.99a; b.Men.50b; b.Hul.59b; b.Hul.117b; b.Ker.6a; b.Meil.7b. A few Dosa traditions may appear to refer to b. Harkinas: in b.Nid.4b, 5a, 9b he appears to debate with Eliezer, but the Amoraim assume he is referring to an older *baraytah*; in b.BM.47b Johanan says he "taught the same thing as Ishmael" which he similarly says of Dosa b. Harkinas at b.Hul.124b, though concerning a different matter.

Dating Rabbinic Traditions

The problems involved

No written rabbinic material has survived in its original form from before the third century. The rabbinic collections contain material which originated before this, but one must always be aware that this material was edited and re-ordered to fit in with the motives and organization of the Jewish world of later centuries. Having said this, there are good reasons to believe that much of the content of the early material has been faithfully preserved.

The whole ethos of rabbinic literature suggests that it was praiseworthy to record past rabbis accurately, even when they disagreed with the view of the consensus or the view of the person who recorded the saying.[1] Eliezer ben Hyrcanus was praised as "a plastered cistern which loses not a drop,"[2] because he faithfully passed on traditions of former teachers, whether he agreed with them or not. This praise for him is attributed to Johanan ben Zakkai, who was the foremost scholar when rabbinic Judaism was reestablished following the destruction of Jerusalem. He said, "If all the Sages of Israel were in the one scale of the balance and Eliezer b. Hyrcanus in the other, he would outweigh them all." For Johanan b. Zakkai, the faithful transmission of former teaching was the heart of scholarship, and it became the backbone of learning in post-70 Judaism.

The early traditions which have been preserved are not the actual words of the early rabbis. Editors abbreviated them and made them conform in vocabulary and style in order to make them more memorizable. However, all this was done with the motive of preservation, and traditions were not normally changed in order to fit in with later orthodoxy. Indeed, the sayings which have been preserved are generally those which do *not* agree with the standard position, in contrast to the majority view, which was recorded anonymously or attributed to 'the Sages.' When changes or additions were made, they were frequently tacked on to the end of an older tradition so that the older portion did not need to be changed, even if this resulted in somewhat clumsy prose.[3]

---

[1] E.g. m.Er.6.1-3a where R. Judah transmits a tradition which is opposed both to the majority *halakhah* and his own teaching, even though the majority version of that tradition is compatible with both.

[2] m.Avot.2.9.

[3] E.g., the list in m.Dem.1.1a, or the addition of Eliezer to the ruling in m.Qid.1.9.

The use of rabbinic material for historical research has been transformed by Jacob Neusner who acknowledged his indebtedness to his mentor Morton Smith, despite their later differences. Although he was by no means the first scholar to apply historico-critical methods to rabbinic texts, he highlighted the need to analyze them in the same way as any other historical text or religious-historical text. This approach has not been easy for many scholars to accept, because it appears to nullify huge sectors of previous research, including much of Neusner's early works. He demonstrated this by totally rewriting his *Life of Yohanan ben Zakkai* as *Development of a Legend*, and partly rewriting his *History of Jews in Babylonia* as *The Rabbinic Traditions about the Pharisees before 70*.[4]

This present work owes a great debt to Neusner's work. It is based on a synthesis of his historico-critical approach with the detailed studies of more traditional scholars. My aim is to apply the results of work by Neusner and his fellow scholars in a way which is sensitive to historico-critical methods, while also being sympathetic to the aims of the original editors of the early rabbinic corpus. I regard editors such as Rabbi Judah ha-Nasi as careful scholars who aimed to preserve the results of past scholarship in an accurate way. This does not mean that they always succeeded in passing on traditions accurately, or that the traditions they received were always accurate representations of what the attributed scholar actually said, but their aim was to preserve, and not to mislead.

The aim of this work is to identify all the sources which can arguably be dated before 70 CE. During the last few decades there has been some reluctance to find *any* evidence of the world before 70 CE in rabbinic literature, and the dating of rabbinic material is sometimes regarded as an impossible task. This conclusion is usually a reaction against the simplistic way in which rabbinic material has been used by previous generations of scholars.

Neusner's seminal article in 1978 on "The Use of the Later Rabbinic Evidence for the Study of First-Century Pharisaism"[5] warned about the dangers of using rabbinic literature for studying the New Testament without a very careful consideration of dating, and pointed out that current dating methods were uncritical and unreliable. This warning was taken so seriously that New Testament scholarship has tended to steer clear of Jewish sources. David Aus has complained:

> Many NT scholars today employ the genuine problem of dating rabbinic sources . . . as a cheap pretext for not even considering them. . . . I would be the first to concede that much of what is Amoraic and even some of what is ostensibly Tannaitic is late and of

---

[4] See Neusner's foreword to the 1998 edition of Birger Gerhardsson, *Memory and Manuscript, Acta Seminarii Neotestamentici Upsaliensis 22* (Uppsala, 1961), republished (Grand Rapids: Eerdmans, 1998).
[5] In William Scott Green, ed., *Approaches to Ancient Judaism: Theory and Practice*, Brown Judaic Studies 1 (Missoula, Mont.: Scholars Press for Brown University, 1978), pp. 215-25.

doubtful relevance to NT narratives. Yet a number of Jewish traditions from before 70 CE have been retained in the (patently later) rabbinic writings. Each individual tradition must be analyzed and evaluated on its own merits, which I try to do.[6]

Dating methods have been developed and tested critically during the last three decades by many scholars, especially by Neusner and his students. Huge advances have been made, and there is now a general consensus about some methods and a cautious acceptance of others. Rabbinic scholars have been able to identify the early rabbinic material and reconstruct a plausible picture of the proto-rabbinic world before 70 CE. Ed Sanders and Ze'ev Falk have both succeeded in constructing a coherent account of early Judaism using principles of dating which are similar to those used in this study.[7] They have come to their tasks from two disparate backgrounds—Sanders using all the historico-critical tools of the modern historian, and Falk depending on a more traditional, though not uncritical, approach. They have both succeeded in showing that this early material fits well with what we know of first-century Jewish belief and practice from other sources such as Josephus, Philo, Qumran, and epigraphy. The ongoing project which is being published as the *Compendia Rerum Iudaicarum ad Novum Testamentum* gives equal weight to early traditions with rabbinic literature and other material which can certainly be dated to the first century (Qumran, Josephus, Philo, etc.), and it too is building up a comprehensive and consistent picture of Second Temple Judaism.

Günter Stemberger, who produced what has become the standard *Introduction to Talmud and Midrash*[8] and who is usually cautious about such things, regards the two following dating methods as well established.

Dating sayings attributed to named individuals

The most important evidence for dating is the attributions, which have been found to be generally accurate. As Stemberger says:

> The study of extensive text units (e.g. by J. Neusner) has shown that at least in Tannaitic collections these attributions are largely reliable. Even if the accuracy of the

---

[6] Roger David Aus, *"Caught in the Act," Walking on the Sea, and the Release of Barabbas Revisited,* South Florida Studies in the History of Judaism 157 (Atlanta: Scholars, 1997), p. x.
[7] E. P. Sanders, *Judaism: Practice & Belief, 63 BCE–66 CE* (London; Philadelphia: SCM; Trinity Press International, 1992). On p. 6 he states the principles he used for selecting early rabbinic sources: "I use only passages that are attributed to a pre-70 Pharisee or to the Schools of Hillel and Shammai. Exceptions to this rule will be justified case by case." Ze'ev W. Falk, *Introduction to Jewish Law of the Second Commonwealth,* 2 vols. (Brill: Leiden, 1972; 1978). Falk does not appear to question the dating of traditions from named authorities—see, e.g., vol. 1, p. 3.
[8] Strack-Stemberger, *Introduction.* The issues of dating are dealt with mainly on pp. 57-62.

tradent's name cannot be positively proven, the historical period connected with that name generally can.[9]

Even though the attribution of given sayings to individual masters will freqently be in doubt, nevertheless they can quite safely be assigned to specific *generations* of scholars.[10]

Neusner has shown in massively detailed studies that attributions can generally be relied on in early *halakhic* sources, though these should always be treated with care and individual attention must be given in every instance.

The temporal order of attributions is generally sound. . . . In every instance [in the tractate *Kelim*], except that just cited [*m.Kel.* 17.5], in which we are able to establish the expectation that the substance of a given law is prior to that of another closely related rule, the earlier rule also will be assigned to an earlier authority, the later rule to a later authority.[11]

The attribution of a saying to a named rabbi cannot be assumed to be correct, but extensive historico-critical work has suggested that such attributions are generally correct. Even when the attribution is suspect, the saying can usually be assumed to date from the same time period as the person to whom it has been attributed.

The use of attributions has been validated in two completely different ways. The first is by studying all the sayings attributed to a single individual, in order to see if these form a coherent body of material. Neusner and others have studied Johanan ben Zakkai, Akiba, Eliezer ben Hyrcanus, and others, and found that the sayings attributed to these individuals form distinct and coherent bodies of material, as one would expect from a single individual or a school. They also found two main exceptions to this principle. Biographical details about individuals have to be treated with much greater care, because they mostly originate long after the death of the individual, as seen by the fact that they are largely absent from early collections. Also, attributions to very early authorities have to be treated with great care, because sometimes a ruling which had no scriptural support was given added authority by being attributed to a great man of the past.

The second way the attributions have been validated is by studying the style of the sayings. It is impossible to do form-critical studies on rabbinic collections because the form of the sayings was changed to aid memorization and to conform with later stages of a debate. However one can study the types of arguments which are used. My own work in this area[12] examined the exegetical techniques used in material attributed

---

[9] Strack-Stemberger, *Introduction*, p. 57.

[10] Strack-Stemberger, *Introduction*, p. 133.

[11] Jacob Neusner, *A History of the Mishnaic Law of Purities*, Studies in Judaism in Late Antiquity, vol. 3 (Leiden: Brill, 1974-97), p. 239.

[12] D. Instone-Brewer, *Techniques and Assumptions in Jewish Exegesis before 70 CE*, Texte und Studien zum antiken Judentum 30 (Tübingen: J. C. B. Mohr, 1992).

to pre-70 individuals and schools. I included the traditions of the Hillelite-Shammaite disputes and Pharisee-Sadducee disputes because the Sadducees and Shammaites declined to insignificance after the destruction of Jerusalem. I found that these exegetes never used allegory, never altered the text to fit the exegesis, always interpreted the text in its context, and always looked for a single plain meaning. In all these respects they were very different from exegetes after 70 CE when these types of exegesis became popular.

Traditions which are attributed to individuals or schools before 70 CE cannot simply be regarded as quotes which date from that time. None of the material in rabbinic sources comes to us unedited. Every saying has been preserved as part of an argument or as part of a larger tradition, mixed in with later material. It has almost certainly been abbreviated, and the vocabulary may have been changed to conform with the surrounding material. Although much care was taken to preserve the teachings of others faithfully, traditions are occasionally attributed to more than one person[13] and there are frequent discussions about attribution or about what the teacher actually said.[14] The fact that these discussions occur shows that attribution and accuracy were important issues, but it also shows that mistakes can happen.

Biographical and exegetical materials have to be treated with extra caution. One of the earliest results of Neusner's work was the demonstration that stories about the early rabbis are almost all recorded in later collections such as the Talmud and *aggadic* Midrashim which were edited two or more centuries after the events. This suggests that they originated long after the events or, at the very least, that there was not much interest by earlier rabbis in preserving such traditions. Exegetical traditions are also largely absent from the earlier collections, and tend to accumulate with time. It appears that later rabbis proposed scriptural foundations for established rulings, which may or may not have been the original basis for those rulings.

The lack of biographical and exegetical material in the earliest collections (i.e., Mishnah and Tosefta) may merely be due to the fact that early works are highly abbreviated and are interested mainly in matters of law. It might be argued that the details found in later collections are just as old as the rulings found in Mishnah, but they happen to not be recorded till later. Nevertheless, special caution must always be applied to exegetical traditions, and biographical details should be treated with extreme caution.

---

[13] These can usually be traced to errors in transmission—see Strack-Stemberger, *Introduction*, pp. 58-59.

[14] An interesting example is seen at b.Er.75b: "R. Joseph stated: 'Rabbi taught: If they were three they are forbidden.' Said R. Bebai to them: 'Do not listen to him. It was I who first reported it, and I did so in the name of R. Adda b. Ahabah, giving the following as a reason: Since I might describe them as many (*rabbim*) residents in the outer courtyard.' 'Lord of Abraham,' exclaimed R. Joseph, 'I must have mistaken *rabbim* for Rabbi.'"

Logical precedence in anonymous sayings

The second most important method for dating rabbinic traditions is logical precedence—i.e., identifying an anonymous tradition which is commented on or assumed in a datable tradition. As Stemberger says:

> Occasionally the context allows such cases to be identified as the presupposition or else the concluding decision of a datable discussion . . . [but] An anonymous statement is not automatically old, not in the Mishnah and much less in the Talmud.[15]

This second method has also been used effectively by Neusner who concluded in an early part of his work on *Purities* that it could be used to date a large number of anonymous sayings.

> Unattributed sayings are not a great problem. In mKel they account for 1/10 of the rulings, and most can be assigned to a time period. Of the 49 in mKel, 26 can be located to the Yavnean or Ushan period, and often to a particular circle of Rabbis within that period. They can be dated if they are 'closely tied to an attributed law, or are diametrically opposed to a tradition assigned to a specific person and so may with confidence be located in the same division as the contrary law.'[16]

Neusner was perhaps overenthusiastic here, and he certainly appears to be more cautious in later works. However, this principle that the development in the law codes can be used to date anonymous rulings has proved useful when used carefully. Unfortunately the majority of anonymous rulings remain impossible to date.

Anonymous rulings usually indicate the conclusions of the editor(s) concerning the view of the majority, which is sometimes made explicit by attributing the ruling to 'the Sages.' In another work by a second editor, this same ruling which is anonymous in one collection may attributed to a named individual. When the anonymity is removed in this way, there is almost always a contrary ruling to counter it, which suggests that the second editor has removed the anonymity in order to question it, because he did not regard this ruling as an undisputed view of the majority at the time. This indicates that the reason for making a ruling anonymous is to set it above dispute, as the conclusion of the majority, and that the only way to question such rulings was to name the person who first proposed it.[17]

The anonymous opinion of the majority may represent the oldest stage which forms the foundation for the ensuing debate, or it may represent the conclusion. In Talmudic literature, anonymous sayings which are not quotations from Mishnah or

---

[15] Strack-Stemberger, *Introduction*, p. 59.
[16] Neusner, *Purities*, vol. 4, p. 244.
[17] See David Weiss Halivni, "The Reception Accorded to Rabbi Judah's Mishnah" in E. P. Sanders et al., *Jewish and Christian Self-Definition,* 2 vols. (Philadelphia: Fortress, 1981), vol. 2: pp. 204-12, especially p. 209. Cf. b.BK.69b; b.San.34b; b.Shab.140a.

Tosefta usually date from late Amoraic times, when they felt that their names were not important enough to be preserved, or the issues were considered more important than the contributors, but in Mishnah and Tosefta they are more often the starting point of a debate. According to tradition, the anonymous sayings of Mishnah should all be attributed to Meir (mid second century—see b.San. 86a). Although several do indeed reflect teaching attributed elsewhere to Meir, this is not a useful guide because many others can be shown to predate or postdate Meir. The most reliable way to date anonymous traditions is that of logical precedence, as used by Neusner and referred to by Stemberger above.

Logical progression in the development of legal rulings is a relatively safe way to date anonymous traditions, but it should be used with caution. Datable traditions are often dependent on anonymous traditions, which presumably preceded them. Sometimes this is merely a logical dependence (i.e., the dateable ruling makes no sense unless the other anonymous ruling has already been established), and sometimes it is confirmed by a verbal dependence (i.e., the dateable ruling cites or refers to the anonymous ruling). However, a logically earlier anonymous ruling does not necessarily represent the view of an earlier generation, because it may represent the view of the majority at the time of the debate.

The anonymous sayings which are dated early by this method cannot be regarded as early traditions, because they are likely to be a construct of the editor, who has summarized the position of the majority or the starting point of the debate. However, they *are* likely to be an accurate reflection of the ideas and sometimes the vocabulary of the majority viewpoint which is being summarized. It was in the interest of the editor to accurately summarize the initial stages in the debate, because often the whole character of the debate was colored by this opening position. Therefore it is often possible to discover the viewpoints of earlier scholars, though their words are usually lost.

Other ways of dating anonymous sayings

Apart from these two important methods for dating, on which there has been a great deal of corroborative work, there are also three other methods which are less useful by themselves but which may provide supporting evidence.

First, the use of parallel sources may be able to show that a particular ruling or a social situation was recognized outside the rabbinic community. In particular, Josephus, Philo, Qumran, NT, and epigraphic sources are useful guides to both the pre-70 rabbinic movement and wider Judaism. These sources should be used with care because although Egyptian and sectarian Judaism had a great influence on rabbinic Judaism after the destruction of Jerusalem, their influence was much smaller before 70 CE. My work on rabbinic exegesis showed that popular Midrashic techniques such as allegory and *al tiqré* were not used in rabbinic Judaism before 70 CE, though they were common in Philo and Qumran. This means that there may be many parallels between Philo and later rabbis which do not represent the opinion of rabbinic Judaism before 70 CE. Having said that, Philo, Josephus, and Qumran often give useful corroborative evidence for dating traditions.[18]

Second, references to Temple practices can also sometimes be an indication of pre-70 sources in anonymous material. There are, of course, extensive discussions about Temple practices after 70 CE,[19] because meditation on the scriptural laws of the Temple were considered to be especially rewarding and some regarded it as equivalent to Temple practices.[20] These discussions are usually characterized by an interest in theoretical issues rather than practical outworking of the ritual,[21] but this type of distinction is not sufficient to decide whether a tradition is early or not. Nevertheless, some rituals are more likely to be debated after the destruction of the Temple than others. The following distinctions are useful when weighing the likelihood that a tradition originated before 70 CE.

Many rituals which were not linked to the Temple still continued after its destruction so references to them give little or no indication of an early date. These include:

> the priests' gift from unconsecrated animals,[22]
> *elevation offerings*,[23]

---

[18] Palestinian Judaism and Egyptian Judaism influenced each other in many ways, though the direction of the influence is often difficult to decide. Sandmel considered this problem for a long time and eventually gave up trying to decide, concluding that "independent, parallel developments seem the better explanation than that of major dependency in either direction" (Samuel Sandmel, *Philo of Alexandria: An Introduction* [Oxford: Oxford University Press, 1979], p. 134). However, his earlier, more detailed, work showed that Philo had more similarities with later Palestinian rabbis than with his contemporaries (*Philo's Place in Judaism: A Study of Conceptions of Abraham in Jewish Literature* [New York: Ktav, 1971]).

[19] For example, R. Meir and the Sages rule that someone who desecrates a sinner's meal offering or a *suspected adultery meal offering* should be *extirpated*, even though both of these offerings ended with or just before the Temple was destroyed (m.Men.2.5, cf. m.Sot.9.9), and m.Shebu opens with a long debate by rabbis of T4 and T6 about goat offerings.

[20] E.g., b.Taan.27b; b.San.51b; b.Men.110a.

[21] For example, the debate in y.Ter.1.3.II concerning the commands which a minor may and may not fulfill. He may fulfill any optional commands such as making a *dedication* to the Temple or bringing a peace offering, but he may not fulfill any of the compulsory commands such as bringing a Paschal sacrifice or a sin offering when it is required. However, as Alan Avery-Peck notes in his translation: "the central concern of the pericope is the delineation of a theory that governs the rights of a minor. The concern is not the final adjudication of specific cases" (*Talmud of the Land of Israel,* vol. 6, p. 78). Similarly, the debate concerning the validity of sacrifices offered by a priest who was later found to have been the son of a divorcee (y.Ter.8.2.I-II).

[22] m.Hul.10.1: "[The requirement to give to the priests] the shoulder, the two cheeks, and the maw [Deut.18.3] applies in the Land and outside of the Land, in the time of the Temple and not in the time of the Temple."

➤ *second tithe* money,[24]
➤ *dough offerings*,[25]
➤ tithes of grain and cattle,[26]
➤ giving the *firstborn* (or its monetary value) to a priest,[27]
➤ the first fleece,[28] and
➤ tithe of grain and cattle.[29]

A few rituals which required the Temple were practiced in a limited way for a limited period even after its destruction, especially:

➤ *second tithe* which was redeemed and the money put aside for the future, though no *firstfruit* food was put aside,[30]
➤ *firstfruits* which were put aside by some, against the advise of some rabbis,[31] and
➤ Temple *dedications* which could be redeemed for money and put aside.[32]

---

[23] They continued to give *elevation offerings*: "Once Tarfon was late in coming to the *bet midrash*. Rabban Gamaliel said to him, What is the reason for your delay? He replied: I was performing the [Temple] service. He then said to him: How come? Is there any service nowadays? He answered: It says in the Bible: 'I give you the priesthood as a service of gift' [Num.18.7], making the eating of *elevation offering* within the borders of Erez Israel equivalent to the service in the Temple" (Sif.Num.116 // b.Pes.72b-73a; cf. m.Bik.2.3; t.Hag.3.33.). There was a debate after the Temple destruction whether to give them to Levites or Priests, and gradually they were given to priests or Levites who were also scholars, and even perhaps to scholars who were neither. Eventually *elevation offering* were no longer given, but burned, presumably when the water of the Red Heifer ashes ran out so that priests could no longer be purified.

[24] After the Temple was destroyed, they turned the *second tithe* into money and put it aside for a future Temple (Sif.Deut.106; b.Makk.19a; b.Zeb.60a), and did this at least until the end of the Tannaitic period (m.MS.2.7; t.MS.3.18; 4.5), though not in the Amoraic period. See S. Safrai and M. Stern, eds., *The Jewish People in the First Century: Historical Geography, Political History, Social, Cultural and Religious Life and Institutions, Compendia rerum Iudaicarum ad Novum Testamentum*, section 1, v. II (Assen: Van Gorcum, 1974-76) (hereafter *CRINT* 1.II), p. 823.

[25] See the question put to Tarfon at m.Betz.3.5 and the ruling of Meir at m.Ter.7.5-6.

[26] m.Sheq.8.8; m.Bek.9.1.

[27] m.Bek.1.6; 6.6. But after 70 CE the priests had to keep the animal until a blemish developed (which made it ineligible for sacrifice), and then eat it—see b.Tem.8a and m.Bek.4.1, which distinguish between practices 'now' and in 'Temple times.'

[28] m.Hul.11.1.

[29] m.Sheq.8.8.

[30] E.g. m.MS.1.5, "If the Temple does not exist, let [*second tithe* food] rot."

[31] These were still discussed after 70 CE (e.g., R. Judah b Illai [T5] in m.Hal.4.9; Simeon b. Yohai [T4] in m.MS.5.6) though m.Bik.2.4 says they cannot be given because they require a sacrifice and waving before the altar. The implication of m.Sheq.8.8 is that some people still put aside *firstfruits,* though Simeon b. Yohai said that they should not be regarded as holy.

[32] The term *"dedication"* (*heqdesh*, הֶקְדֵּשׁ) refers to the specific practice of donating items to the Temple (cf. re m.Pea.1.6; m.Ter.6.4, and t.Ter.7.8a), and when it was something which is unsuitable as a sacrifice it was sold to pay for the Temple upkeep (see m.Sheq.4.6-8). Animals which had been incorrectly offered to the Temple, such as a female animal for a guilt offering,

Most rituals which required the Temple stopped immediate it was destroyed, and although they are discussed, there is no suggestion that anyone practiced them. These include:

- ➤ all sacrifices,
- ➤ the priests' portion from *consecrated* animals,[33]
- ➤ the *half shekel*,[34]
- ➤ *meal offerings*,[35]
- ➤ special priestly garments,[36]
- ➤ priests eating the *holy things*,[37]
- ➤ waving the *first sheaf* (though the date of this ceremony still continued to mark the first day when the new crop could be consumed),[38]
- ➤ Naziriteships,[39] and
- ➤ *suspected adultery*.[40]

---

could also be used in this way (m.Tem.3.3; m.Ker.6.1). *dedications* were occasionally discussed after 70 CE (e.g., m.Tem.7.3) but new *halakhot* concerning them were rare. In Mishnah there is only m.Ket.5.4 (which has the nature of a newly invented loophole using an antiquated law) and m.Pea.7.8 (which is so impractical that it was probably a purely theoretical ruling). It does not seem, from these traditions, that anyone *dedicated* actual produce to the Temple after 70 CE. In b.AZ.13a-b *dedications* are specifically prohibited, and if anyone did inadvertently do so, the animal had to be left to die or the plants left to rot, so that no one would accidentally commit *meilah* by gaining benefit from them. However, this does not mean that every occurence of the term "*dedication*" (*heqdesh*, הֶקְדֵּשׁ) indicates an early tradition, especially when it is listed along with other types of consecrated produce. One phrase in particular, "*second tithe* or *dedication* which is (not) redeemed" occurs frequently in Mishnah (e.g., m.Ber.7.1; m.Ter.1.5; 6.5; 8.2; m.Shab.18.1; m.Er.3.2; m.Pes.2.5; m.San.8.2; m.Makk.3.2), so these references to a *dedication* may simply be an archaic componant of a common phrase.

[33] In contrast to unconsecrated animals, which continued after 70, the breast and thighs of peace offerings (Lev.7.31) were not given after 70 according to m.Hul.10.1.

[34] m.Sheq.8.8; cf. m.MQ.3.6.

[35] R. Judah says meal offerings, sweet-smelling sacrifices (i.e., oil with meal offerings) and priestly garments, were restricted to the Temple or Tabernacle, and were not even part of worship in the legitimate High Places (m.Tem.14.10). Therefore one may assume that they could not continue after the Temple was destroyed.

[36] See previous note.

[37] The "*holy things*" are the priestly portions of offerings which were sacrificed in the Temple.

[38] The sacrifice of the lamb and meal offering, which was part of this ceremony, certainly stopped, but did they still cut a *first sheaf*? There was still some debate shortly after 70 CE (Ishmael [T3] in m.Men.10.1) about the process of cutting the *first sheaf*, but this appears to be a historical debate. However, the law that the new crop could not be eaten until after the *first sheaf* was waved (Lev.23.14) did continue. This did not mean that they still had to wave the *first sheaf*, but it meant that no one could sell the new crop until after the date when it would have been waved. Therefore Johannan b. Zakkai [T1] specifically says that this ruling was continued "after the Temple was destroyed" (m.Men.10.5). Eliezer [T2] said that this also applied outside Israel (m.Qid.1.9).

[39] cf. m.Naz.5.4, which refers to a former destruction of the Temple, but applies also later.

[40] m.Sot.9.9.

When considering whether or not a reference to a Temple ritual originated from Temple times, it is worth distinguishing between different types of discussions. Legal rulings about Temple practices or incidental references to Temple practices are more likely to have an early origin. Simple descriptions of what happened are sometimes early but they may also be a later synthesis based on what they knew. Details which are based on Scripture or which could be easily inferred from Scripture or from previous rulings are particularly suspect, and discussions which attempt to find an ethical principle behind Temple practices are almost certainly post-70. Archaic language has been used by some scholars as an indication of dating (especially Epstein and Ginzberg[41]), but I have avoided it, because this language may merely reflect an editor's wish to make a tradition *appear* old.[42] It can only be used as a method of dating if a later dateable tradition is clearly confused about the meaning of the archaic terms, and confusion about the practices themselves is also a good indication that they are discussing an older tradition.

The third additional indication of dating is the structure within the tractate. Most tractates have a clear structure that has been maintained by later editors by adding material to the end of sections or to the ends of individual paragraphs rather than inserting material in the middle of them. This is particularly clear with the comments of R. Judah and R. Meir which are normally appended onto the end of a mishnah (i.e., a paragraph). Other editing is often seen when a section starts again with the same subject but at a later time: for example, m.*Terumot* where m.Ter:1.1-3 and 1.4-5 answer 'Who?' and 'From what?' and then 1.6 and 1.7–3.2 answer these same questions again but with later material. Editing can also often be seen in a list, where subsequent additions are made without changing the original wording so that the list becomes untidy and sometimes almost ungrammatical (e.g., m.Dem.1.1a; 1.3). Finally one can see the work of editors in the miscellany of rulings which are frequently added to the end of a tractate, as if they have been put there because they cannot be slotted into the structure or in a desire to end the tractate with some moral teaching (e.g., m.Ber.9.5; m.Pea.8.9; m.Shebi.10.8). These types of structure may one day provide the basis for further methods of dating rabbinic material, especially if they are combined with philological studies of archaic language, but without a great deal more groundwork they provide very uncertain tools.

---

[41] e.g. Jacob N. Epstein, *Introduction to Tannaitic Literature: Mishnah, Tosephta, and Halakic Midrash* [Hebrew] (Jerusalem: Magnes Press, 1957). Louis Ginzberg, "Tamid, The Oldest Treatise of the Mishnah," *Journal of Jewish Lore and Philosophy*, later *Hebrew Union College Annual* 1 (1919): 33-44, 197-209, 265-95).

[42] For example, Epstein argues for an early origin of m.Qid.1.1 on the basis of the archaic Aramaic form *mamzere* instead of *mamzerim*, but Baruch A. Levine calls this "archaistic" language which is "evoking the atmosphere of Ezra's day" (see "Later Sources on the Netinim," in *Orient and Occident,* ed. Harry A. Hoffner [Neukirchen-Vluyn: Neukirchener Verlag, 1973], p. 108, n. 8).

Levels of confidence in dating

Some traditions can be dated more confidently than others. In this work, all the traditions which are dated as pre-70 are assigned a level of confidence to indicate how certain or uncertain the dating is. A level of confidence of 1 is used for those whose dating is fairly certain, and 2-8 indicate decreasing levels down to traditions whose dating is not very certain. Lower levels of confidence are 9 (doubtful, but interesting), 10-12 (very uncertain) and 13 (almost certainly a later fabrication).

The levels of confidence are assigned as follows:
(1) A legal tradition attributed to someone before 70 CE (T0-T1), including the school disputes between the Hillelites and Shammaites when there is no reason to doubt that they are genuine.
(2) A legal tradition not attributed to anyone but assumed or disputed as though it were already well established in a saying which is attributed to someone from T2 or earlier. The tradition must be cited by this person or recorded elsewhere; otherwise it is level 5.
(3) A tradition attributed to someone from T2 or T3 that refers to an event before 70 CE to establish a legal point. This must concern a specific event, and not just a general practice—which is level 7.
(4) A nonlegal tradition attributed to someone before 70 CE (T0-T1) that is transmitted by someone from T3 or earlier and preserved in Mishnah or Tosefta. Traditions outside these limits are level 10.
(5) A legal tradition not attributed to anyone that is assumed or disputed as though it was already well established in a saying that is attributed to someone from T2 or earlier. (This is an unrecorded tradition; if the tradition is recorded elsewhere, it is level 2.)
(6) A legal tradition not attributed to anyone but attested externally in a pre-70 source (Josephus, Philo, Qumran, NT, etc.). Note: parallels are not necessarily attestations.
(7) A legal tradition attributed to someone from T2 that refers to a practice from before 70 CE (mainly Temple-based activities). (Later traditions are level 8 and 9.)
(8) A legal tradition not attributed to anyone of T2 or earlier that refers to a practice from before 70 CE (mainly Temple-based activities) *with some confirmation* that it has a pre-70 origin.
(9) A legal tradition not attributed to anyone of T2 or earlier that refers to a practice from before 70 CE (mainly Temple-based activities) *without any confirmation* that has a either a pre-70 or post-70 origin.
(10) A nonlegal tradition attributed to someone before 70 CE (T0-T1) that is transmitted by someone from T4 or later or outside Mishnah and Tosefta. Earlier transmissions are level 4.
(11) A nonlegal tradition that refers to a practice from before 70 CE (mainly Temple-based activities) *without any confirmation* that has a either a pre-70 or post-70 origin.
(12) A biographical tradition attributed to someone from T3 or earlier about someone before 70 CE (T0-T1).

(13) A biographical tradition not attributed to anyone of T3 or earlier about someone before 70 CE (T0-T1).

These numbers should not give a false sense of accuracy to the process of dating rabbinic traditions, which is still somewhat an art rather than a science. But they do help the reader to make a quick appraisal of the relative value of a text.

These volumes contain all the traditions which can be dated with a confidence level between 1 and 8, and a few which have a level of 9 or 10 if they are of particular interest for other early traditions or the New Testament. Many traditions which 'feel' early have therefore been omitted because there is not enough evidence to safely say that they originated before 70 CE. Therefore these volumes do not contain *all* the pre-70 rabbinic traditions, but they contain all the traditions *for which there is sufficient evidence* to conclude that they originate before 70 CE.

In the future it is hoped that different forms of evidence may become useful and other traditions will become datable. In the meantime, this work helps to establish a corpus of texts which can be safely used for studying the Jewish world of the early and middle first century, when the New Testament was written.

Tractate *Berakhot*: Blessings (Prayer)

Definitions and Outline

The English terms 'blessing' and 'benediction' are both translations of the Hebrew root 'to bless' (*barak*, בָּרַךְ). Blessing comes from God to humanity in almost all biblical and extrabiblical sources, though later it was also used for blessing God in prayer. This development is already seen in Scripture which uses this formula twice.[1] The normal way of starting a communal Jewish prayer of thanks was "Blessed (*baruk*, בָּרוּךְ) are you LORD . . . ," and any prayer which starts with "Blessed . . ." is called a '*benediction.*'

Prayers consist mainly of the *Shema*, the Eighteen Benedictions, meal time benedictions and Grace after Meals, as well as various other blessings. The texts of these prayers are not recorded in Mishnah, or in other early rabbinic literature. However, one of the versions of the Eighteen that was preserved in the Cairo Genizah contains wording which is regarded by some scholars to originate before 70 CE, so this is included as an appendix.

m.Ber.1–3: The *Shema*

The *Shema* is a recital of a series of Scripture verses (Deut.6.4-9; 11.13-21; Num.15.37-41) that starts "Hear . . ." (*shema,* שְׁמַע). It is recited in the morning and evening and is preceded and concluded with specific prayers. The rabbis required the wearing of a prayer shawl (*tallit*, טַלִּית) and phylacteries or *tefillin* (תְּפִלִּין) during these prayers. The readings have been found on tiny scrolls at Qumran, which confirms that the practice of wearing *tefillin* and saying such prayers was widespread throughout Judaism before 70 CE.

m.Ber.4–5: The Eighteen Benedictions

The Eighteen Benedictions are usually called 'The Eighteen' (*Shemoneh Esreh*, שְׁמוֹנֶה עֶשְׂרֵה) or simply 'The Prayer' (*Tefillah*, תְּפִלָּה), and they were later called the '*Amidah*' (עֲמִידָה, 'standing'). They are prayed every morning and evening after the *Shema*, and every afternoon. A subset of them are prayed at the Additional

---

[1] Ps.119.12; 1Chron.29.10. The concept of blessing God is found at Gen.14.20; 24.27; Exod.18.10 etc. See the discussion in Joseph Heinemann, *Prayer in the Talmud: Forms and Patterns* (Berlin and New York: de Gruyter, 1977), translation of *ha-Tefilah bi-tequfat ha-Tana'im veha-'Amora'im* (Yerushalayim: Magnes Press, 1964), pp. 82, 88-89.

Service on a Sabbath. When time is short or when one is in danger, one may pray a shorter *abstract* (*meén*, מֵעֵין). In early times the Eighteen was a list of short blessings related to specific themes and prayer leaders varied the wording.

m.Ber.6–8: Blessings and Grace after Meals

The school disputes show that there was a great deal of interest in cultic etiquette at mealtimes. Most of this involved the *benedictions* by which one gave thanks for all the different constituents of the meal, and the way one conducted the invitation to say a communal Grace after Meals (*zimmun*, זִימוּן, 'invitation'). The last meal of the Sabbath was also followed by the *Habdalah* (הַבְדָלָה, 'separation'), which celebrated the uniqueness and end of the Sabbath.

m.Ber.9: Other blessings

Blessings which are used in the Temple and other blessings. The general principle that one should thank God for all things produced a wide array of blessings for all kinds of events. Most of these blessings originated after 70 CE.

Related text: The Eighteen Benedictions

The oldest of the surviving texts of the Eighteen contains references to "God's dwelling" in Jerusalem and other features from before 70 CE. The traditional story that the curse of the Minim originated after 70 CE has serious problems.

m.Ber.1.1-2: When to recite the Shema

Summary of Mishnah: You may recite the evening *Shema* from the close of the Temple services until midnight or perhaps dawn (1.1) and the morning *Shema* from the beginning to the end of sunrise (1.2).

The following traditions have elements (marked in bold) for which there is evidence of an origin before 70 CE:

m.Ber.1.1a: From when should you recite the evening Shema?

From when should one recite	מאימתי קורין
the Shema in the evening?	את שמע בערבית.
From the time the priests come in [home]	משעה שהכהנים נכנסים
to eat of their *elevation offerings*.	לאכול בתרומתן

Comments: The *Shema* was recited morning and evening because Deut.6.7 mentions "when you lie down and when you rise up." The evening *Shema* was therefore associated with bedtime (as in *Jos.Ant.*4.212 and *Sib.Or.*3.591-93), but the Sages wished to define the earliest time when it could be recited and decided that the end of the Temple service marked this time. They recorded this as the time when the priests returned home to eat their *elevation offering* (often known as the 'heave offering')— the small tithe (about one-fiftieth) of food products which were put aside by Jews for consumption by priests and their families. Perhaps this marked the earliest time when the priests could say the *Shema*, and they were known to be the enthusiasts who wanted to say it first, or perhaps more people would see the returning priests than the closing of the Temple gates. Later rabbis defined the earliest time for *Shema* as 'the time of the appearance of the stars,' which was more useful outside Jerusalem and after the destruction of the Temple. Qumran sectarians, who rejected the Temple, used sunset to define the time (1QS.9.26–10.1, 10).

This is not just a suggestion, but a precept. The participle, which represents the present tense in Mishnaic Hebrew, often also has a jussive force, especially when it has an impersonal plural subject ('they do,' i.e., 'one does'), as here. See the introduction to Mishnaic Hebrew in the appendix.

Dating (2): The saying in m.Ber.1.1a implies an origin in Temple times, when the priests would finish their duties and all return home at the same time. The *elevation offering* continued after the destruction at 70 CE (see, e.g., b.Ber.2a and m.Git.1.6), but the return of the priests all at the same time implies that they were all working in the same place—i.e., the Temple. This would give the early date a confidence level of 7 (see Introduction re Dating), but we can give it a much higher confidence level of 2 because the saying is commented on by R. Eliezer [T2] (i.e., a second generation Tanna, active about 80–120 CE (see Introduction re Dating for these abbreviations). R. Eliezer and his contemporaries debate about the latest time at which one may recite the evening *Shema* (in the rest of m.Ber.1.1).

m.Ber.1.2: From when should you recite the morning *Shema*?

From when should one recite the *Shema* in the morning?	מאימתי קורין את שמע בשחרית.
From when one can distinguish between blue and white.	משיכיר בין תכלת ללבן
R. Eliezer [b. Hyrcanus, T2] says "Between blue and green."	רבי אליעזר אומר בין תכלת לכרתי
and concludes it by sunrise.	וגומרה עד הנץ

Comments: The morning *Shema* is related to getting up, but the earliest time it can be recited is determined by the amount of natural light needed to recognise blue from white. R. Eliezer proposed blue and green because one could distinguish blue and white even by moonlight. He also proposed the latest time when one could say it (sunrise), though later rabbis allowed recital up to three hours after sunrise, when a king's children might rise (i.e., the last people to get up) and said that a later recital did not fulfill this obligation and was nothing more than a Torah reading (ibid).

Dating (2): Here, as in subsequent traditions, the portions which are likely to originate before 70 CE are marked in bold. The fact that Eliezer had a different viewpoint to this anonymous tradition indicates either that the ruling was made in his day (so the anonymous tradition is the viewpoint of the majority), or that it was already established by his day (so the anonymous tradition is the status quo). The latter is more likely in this case because Eliezer adds an additional comment about the final time when it can be recited, which is not addressed by the anonymous tradition. This suggests that Eliezer is not taking part in a debate but interacting with an established tradition. This is confirmed when his additional point is debated (later in this mishnah) by R. Joshua [T2], a contemporary of Eliezer, and not by an anonymous majority.

"Blue and white" probably refers to the colors of the *tassels* of the prayer shawl, which suggests that it was already worn at this time. The discoveries of numerous scrolls of *tefillin* and *mezuzahs* for doorposts show that they too were used before 70 CE, as confirmed by Josephus:

> They shall inscribe also on their doors the greatest of the benefits (τὰ μέγιστα—i.e., the Law, cf. *Ant.* 3.223) which they have received from God and each shall display them on his arms. (Jos.*Ant.* 4.212-13, 8.13)

m.Ber.1.3–2.4: How to recite the *Shema*

Summary of Mishnah: Do you literally lie down and stand up to recite (1.3)? The correct blessings must accompany the recital (1.4-5) and you must concentrate on the words (2.1). You should not interrupt the *Shema* to greet a friend, except at natural breaks [which are listed] though you may greet a dangerous person [such as a Roman soldier] at any time (2.1-2). You can recite the *Shema* anywhere, even up a tree (2.4), but you must recite it clearly (2.3).

The following traditions have elements (marked in bold) for which there is evidence of an origin before 70 CE:

m.Ber.1.3: Should you stand and recline for the Shema?

The School of Shammai says:	בית שמאי אומרים,
In the evening everyone must recline	בערב, כל אדם יטו
and must recite [the *Shema*]	ויקראו,
and in the morning they must stand, as it says:	ובבוקר יעמודו, שנאמר
"And at your lying down and at your rising."	ובשכבך ובקומך.
But the School of Hillel says:	ובית הלל אומרים,

Everyone should recite
according to the way he [is positioned]
as it says: "And at your walking in the way."

כל אדם קורא
כדרכו
שנאמר ובלכתך בדרך.

Comments: The Shammaites typically followed a more strictly literal understanding of the text, though this is not always what a modern reader would regard as the 'plain' meaning of the text. In this text they understood "reclining" and "rising" in a very literal sense, and taught that the evening *Shema* should be recited lying down and the morning *Shema* should be recited standing up. In contrast, the Hillelites argued from the double meaning of *derek*, 'way,' that you should remain in the 'way' you were when the time arrived for reciting. A later rabbi, Tarfon [T3], followed the Shammaite interpretation when he was on a journey, and got mugged. His fellow rabbis said that he deserved this because he followed the Shammaite teaching (ibid).

Dating (1): The school debates were collected together before 70 CE, though a few may have been added later (see Introduction—Dating). This is a typical school debate which is corroborated by the relatively early biographical event concerning R. Tarfon [T3].

m.Ber.1.4: Long and short blessings with the *Shema*

In the morning one says two *benedictions*
before [the *Shema*]
and one [*benediction*] after it,
and in the evening, two before it
and two after it.
One [of these last two *benedictions*] is long
and one is short.
When they said it is to be long,
one is not permitted to shorten (it)
[and when they said it is to be] short,
one is not permitted to lengthen (it).
[And when they said to] seal [the blessing]
one is not permitted not to seal it.
And where [they said] not to seal
one is not permitted to seal [the blessing].

בשחר מברך שתים
לפניה
ואחת לאחריה,
ובערב שתים לפניה
ושתים לאחריה
אחת ארוכה
ואחת קצרה
מקום שאמרו להאריך,
אינו רשאי לקצר.
לקצר,
אינו רשאי להאריך.
לחתום,
אינו רשאי שלא לחתום.
ושלא לחתום,
אינו רשאי לחתום.

Comments: The prayers before and after the Scripture readings of the *Shema* were:

Morning:	"Blessed art thou . . . who forms light and creates darkness. . ."
	"With abounding love you have loved us. . ."
	"Hear O Israel . . ." (Deut.6.4-9; 11.13-21; Num.15.37-41)
	"True and firm . . . is this thy word . . ."
Evening:	"Blessed art thou. . . who brings forth the evening twilight . . ."
	"With everlasting love you have loved the House of Israel . . ."

"Hear O Israel . . ." (Deut.6.4-9; 11.13-21; Num.15.37-41)
"True and trustworthy is all this . . . "
"Cause us, O LORD our God, to lie down in peace . . ."

The actual prayers used may not have been fixed before 70 CE and the wording of these prayers was almost certainly not fixed (see below, 4.4). The relative length of the original prayers is impossible to know, and although the final prayer in the evening is shortest, it is not much shorter than "With abounding love . . ." or "With everlasting love. . . ." When these prayers became fixed, the morning prayers were different from the evening prayers (as listed above) but the two sets follow the same themes. These themes probably represent a common set of guidelines which later were crystallized into two sets of slightly different prayers.

The search for the 'original' versions of such prayers, which were assumed to exist by scholars such as Elbogen,[2] has largely been abandoned. Heinemann[3] has shown convincingly that the huge variety of similar prayers in surviving Jewish prayers is probably due to local variations that have been amalgamated into the prayer books. He disputed the idea that these variants descended from a single original form; and argued that variations were encouraged before 70 CE and that some of these became popular enough to be preserved.[4]

Although these prayers are called '*benedictions*' (from *barak*, 'to bless') in this ruling, only the first prayers actually start with "Blessed. . . ." The 'seal' marks the end of a prayer with a short sentence of the form "Blessed art thou, O LORD,

---

[2] Ismar Elbogen, *Jewish Liturgy: a Comprehensive History,* translated by Raymond P. Scheindlin from the German edition of 1931 and the Hebrew edition 1972, which included supplements by other authors (Philadelphia: Jewish Publication Society, 1993).

[3] Heinemann showed, for example, that the prayer for the building of Jerusalem (the *Bonah Yerushalayim*) appears in various versions in different contexts: in the weekday *Amidah*, in Grace after Meals, in the benediction after reading from the Prophets (*Haftarah*), and in the benediction of the marriage ceremony. Some of these versions can be traced back to different communities, such as the version in the Grace after Meals, which is essentially identical with an Egyptian version which is preserved in the Geniza. He concluded from this that the later prayer books attempted to preserve as many different forms of prayers as possible by putting the different versions into different services. This means that the prayer books themselves are not evolving into new versions but are collecting a variety of older versions (see Heinemann, *Prayer,* pp. 49-59).

[4] Ezra Fleischer has argued against this, saying that there was no obligatory prayer in the Temple or in the synagogue during the time of the Temple, and that only the Qumran sectarians had fixed prayers before 70 CE ("On the Beginnings of Obligatory Jewish Prayer," *Tarbiz* 59 [1990]: 397-441). However, Carl Ostmeyer has shown that Qumran specifically avoided the use of the term *tephillah* and substituted *tehillah* whenever possible, because they wanted to avoid any connection with the Temple cult, with which *tephillah* is almost always connected in the OT ("Distinctive Features of Prayer-Terminology in Qumran," forthcoming). This suggests that the *Tephillah* was already intimately associated with Temple worship. See also the reply to Fleischer in Stefan C. Reif, "On the Earliest Development of Jewish Prayer," *Tarbiz* 60 (1991): 677-81.

who. . . ." A seal is found at the end of all these prayers, so they may be called '*benedictions*'.

Dating (5): The first part of the text (up to ". . . one is long and one is short") is commented on by the second half ("When they said: Long . . ."). The two halves do not form a debate by contemporary scholars, because they do not disagree or interact, but instead the second half has the form of a commentary on the first half. This suggests that the second half is at least a generation later than the first half, which had already gained the status of a fixed ruling. The reference to 'lengthening' and 'shortening' prayers assumes that the prayers are not yet fixed. The phrase "one is not permitted to shorten . . . or lengthen" either means 'You may not use another prayer which is shorter or longer' or 'You may not abbreviate or expand the standard prayer.'[5] Either way, this dates the second half to the time when prayers were becoming fixed, which was about the time of Eliezer, as seen in 4.4, and so the first half must be pre-70.

New Testament: There is nothing in the New Testament to indicate that Jewish prayers were fixed. There are no quotations from traditional Jewish liturgy in the New Testament, though there are several passages which probably have Jewish origins (the Lord's Prayer, the Magnificat, the Benedictus, and perhaps the 'songs' in Col.1.15-20 and Phil.2.6-11).[6] In contrast, early Christian liturgy has several allusions or even quotations from Jewish prayers (*Kyrie eleison, Audis nos Domine = anenu adonay* 'Answer us, O Lord'; *liberas nos Domine = Hoshienu adonay* 'Save us, O Lord'[7]; *Sanctus = Qedushah*, both based on Isa.6.3 and Ezek.3.12[8]).

m.Ber.1.5: The 'Exodus' in the *Shema*

One should commemorate	מזכירין
the "Exodus from Egypt"	יציאת מצרים
in the night [recital of *Shema*, as in the morning].	בלילות.

Comments: The "Exodus from Egypt" is the reading of Num.15.37-41, which contains the words "brought (הוצאתי) you out of Egypt." The reason you might not recite this passage at night is that it refers to the blue and white threads of the *tassels* that you should "look upon and remember all the commands" (v. 39). This is impossible at night and is only possible in the morning when there is enough light to distinguish between blue and white (see 1.2). This ruling argues that Num.15.37-41

---

[5] The terms 'long' and 'short' did not only refer to length but came to refer to other features of the prayer.
[6] For a sceptical viewpoint see Phillip Sigal, "Early Christian and Rabbinic Liturgical Affinities: Exploring Liturgical Acculturation," *New Testament Studies* 30 (1984): 63-90.
[7] Heinemann, *Prayer in the Talmud*, p. 147.
[8] Heinemann, *Prayer in the Talmud*, p. 230.

should be included at night because of the reference to the Exodus, which took place at night.

Dating (2): Toward the end of the generation of T2 (80–120 CE) the rabbis in Mishnah debated a scriptural proof for this ruling (ibid). Ben Zoma [T3] suggested to Eleazar b. Azariah [T2] that the words "So that you may remember the day on which you left Egypt all the days of your life" (Deut.16.3) could have said simply 'the days of your life,' and the apparently superfluous word 'all' implied 'the whole day,' including the night. This was contrary to the traditional interpretation of this word that it implied 'your whole life, even the afterlife.' This traditional interpretation was presumably anti-Sadducean, like other similar interpretations in support of the afterlife (see m.San.10.3). Both Ben Zoma [T3] and Eleazar b. Azariah [T2] take for granted that the Exodus passage was part of the *Shema*, which implies that it was already established at least a a generation previously. This is confirmed by Josephus who appears to allude to this reading:

> "Twice each day, at the dawn thereof and when the hour comes for returning to repose, let all acknowledge before God the bounties which He has bestowed on them through their deliverance from the land of Egypt: thanksgiving is a natural duty, and is rendered alike in gratitude for past mercies and to incline the giver to others yet to come." (Jos.*Ant.* 4.212-13, 8.13)

All this implies that the ruling in m.Ber.1.5 originated before 70 CE.

m.Ber.2.5–3.6: Who recites the *Shema*?

Summary of Mishnah: You do not recite the *Shema* on your wedding night, though you may, like Gamaliel (who also differed from general practice in other ways) (2.5-8). You do not recite at a wake or a funeral, unless you are unnecessary for the ceremony, and not within eyesight of the chief mourner (3.1-2). Women, slaves, and children are exempt from saying the *Shema*, though they must say the Eighteen (3.3). An *impure* person cannot recite until he has immersed himself (3.4-6).

The following traditions have elements (marked in bold) for which there is evidence of an origin before 70 CE:

m.Ber.2.5: *Shema* is not performed on the wedding night

A bridegroom is exempt from reciting Shema	חתן פטור מקריאת שמע
on the first night [of his marriage]	בלילה הראשון
until the end of the [following] Sabbath	עד מוצאי שבת,
if he has not 'done the deed' [i.e., consummation].	אם לא עשה מעשה.

Comments: The reason for this is not likely to be the time involved, because the *Shema* took only a few minutes, and the exemption did not extend to the Eighteen Benedictions. Other possible reasons are that women were not expected to recite the *Shema* (though they prayed the Eighteen—see m.Ber.3.3), so this activity would have separated the couple, or because concentration might have been difficult. Weddings normally took place on a Wednesday (m.Ket.1.1), and so this ruling lasted three nights on average.

Dating (2): This ruling dates from at least a generation before Rabban Gamaliel II [T2], who was gently reproved by his students for saying the *Shema* on his wedding night.

The last phrase looks as if it has been tacked on by a later generation, who looked at the matter from a more legalistic viewpoint. They regarded the command "go forth and multiply" (Gen.1.28) as taking precedence over the command to recite the *Shema*, but once the marriage was consummated the *Shema* must be recited. This effectively negated the ruling, because traditional marriages included a period of seclusion for the couple immediately after the ceremony, when consummation took place, in theory at least. This last phrase probably dates from a generation following Gamaliel [II, T2] who chose to recite the *Shema* even on his wedding night. The amended ruling was either intended to excuse Gamaliel (on the assumption that he had already consummated the marriage) or commend his example by giving a reason for it.

A later generation cited a saying by Simeon b. Gamaliel [II, T4] to show that you did not need to refrain from reciting the *Shema*, even if a marriage was unconsummated (m.Ber.2.8), which probably represented a gradually more stringent use of fixed liturgy.

New Testament: Paul's permission for couples to abstain from conjugal activity in order to make time for prayer (1Cor.7.3-5) suggests that he shared the same assumption that conjugal activity can interfere with prayer. However, there is a contrast in attitude, in that the rabbis are concerned that conjugal love should not interrupt prayer for too long, while Paul is concerned that prayer should not be used to interrupt conjugal love for too long.

y.Ber.2.8.I 21a: Noncompulsory observances are not prohibited

It was taught: In all rulings which restrict:	תני כל דבר שהוא של צער
All who wish to do them	כל הרוצה לעשות
to acquire devotion may do them.	עצמו יחיד עושה.
A disciple of the Sages	תלמיד חכם
may do them and gain themselves a blessing.	עושה ותבוא לו ברכה.

Comments: This principle is used here to excuse Rabban Gamaliel II [T2] for saying the *Shema* on his wedding night (see 2.5 above). It implies that the Sages did not like the performance of additional deeds over and above the law, because this caused individuals to 'stand out.' This was probably a pragmatic ruling to prevent excesses of piety or showing off, either of which could lead to extremes of asceticism. This ruling allows, perhaps grudgingly, for people to ignore the various exceptions from fasts and other duties, because these did not involve actions which were additional to the Law. This ruling may have been brought about by the ascetic movement.

Dating (2): This type of principle, which summarizes or generalizes many rulings, has the appearance of being late. However, the application of this saying was discussed by Rabban Gamaliel II and R. Joshua [T2] (ibid), which dates it to at least to the previous generation.

New Testament: This is similar to the injunction by Jesus that you should not do excessive acts of piety in public in order to be seen (Mt.6.1; 23.5)

m.Ber.3.1: *Shema* is not performed by the bereaved

He whose dead [relative] lies before him	מִי שֶׁמֵּתוֹ מוּטָל לְפָנָיו,
is exempt from reciting *Shema*	פָּטוּר מִקְּרִיאַת שְׁמַע
and from the Prayer [Eighteen Benedictions]*	וּמִן הַתְּפִלָּה
and from [wearing] the *tefillin*.	וּמִן הַתְּפִלִּין.

*Not all MSS have this line.

Comments: The obligations of purity, which are associated with wearing the *tefillin* and prayer, as well as the need to concentrate during prayer time, can be ignored for the sake of burial. This is not just during the burial service (which is unlikely to take place at dawn or dusk when the *Shema* is recited) but also during the time of the wake before burial. Eliezer [T2] and Joshua [T2] debated how long this continued after the burial. Mishnah (ibid) continues with a list of mourners who are similarly exempt, or even forbidden from reciting the Prayer (for fear of offending or distracting the chief mourner). Later discussions say that the bereaved are not able to concentrate sufficiently, so they should not be allowed to say the Prayer (b.Ber.31a) but this early version implies that the ruling was a concession rather than a command.

Dating (2): The original saying perhaps referred only to the *Shema* and *tefillin* , and the Prayer (the *Tefillah*) was added by inference—because if Torah law is exempt *(Shema* and *tefillin)* then certainly rabbinic law is exempt *(Tefillah)*. Or, possibly, *Tefillah* was missed by a scribe due to the similarity of the two lines. The version in the Babylonian Talmud adds the line "and from all precepts laid down in Torah." This line makes the foregoing superfluous, and was probably added after the other lines were well established. The reference to *tefillin* is amplified by Eliezer [T2] in y.Ber.3.1, which suggests that the ruling predates 70 CE.

New Testament: The importance of burial of near relatives is seen to overrule even the most pressing of religious commitments. This makes Jesus' demand "Follow me, and let the dead bury their dead" (Mt.8.21-22) sound very startling. He was effectively telling a prospective disciple that following him was the most supreme religious commitment imaginable.

m.Ber.3.3: *Shema* is not performed by women, slaves, or children

Women, slaves, and children	נשים ועבדים וקטנים,
are exempt from reciting *Shema*	פטורין מקריאת שמע
and from [wearing] the *tefillin*	ומן התפלין,
but they are obligated to [say] the Prayer	וחייבין בתפלה
and to [follow the law of the] *mezuzah*	ובמזוזה
and to [pray] the blessings of the meal.	ובברכת המזון.

Comments: This ruling is not an example of the lower status of women but an application of the general rule that women were excused every positive commandment which was limited by time (m.Qid.1.7). This was necessary to enable them to care for the household effectively. The Prayer is not time-limited by Law (except within a very wide range of time), and the Law did not state at which time the blessings of the meal should occur because there was no set time for meals. Or, this ruling may merely state that women were obligated "to prayer" in general, so that they did not have to say the Prayer (i.e., the Eighteen Benedictions).

The 'blessings of the meal' is the Grace after Meals (see m.Ber.6.1-8 below). This ruling does not make it clear whether or not women may lead the Grace. If they may not, then their obligation is limited to meals with two or fewer people where no men are present. The ambiguity may reflect a time when women were allowed to lead the Grace—this is discussed below at m.Ber.7.1-2.

Tefillin and *mezuzot* are the containers for biblical texts of the *Shema* which are attached to the head, hands, and houses, as prescribed in Deut.6.8-9.

Dating (5): This ruling only makes sense if it is related to the ruling that women are excused every positive command which is restricted to a set time (m.Qid.1.7). If this ruling in m.Ber.3.3 postdated the general rule about women and positive commands, the whole of this ruling would be superfluous (as implied in b.Ber.20b). Therefore this ruling must predate the general rule in m.Qid.1.7, which can be dated before 70 CE.[9]

---

[9] It is part of a collection of sayings in m.Qid.1.7-9a which is commented on by Eliezer [T2] in m.Qid.1.9b.

This ruling also fits well with what is known about slaves before 70 CE, contrary to the situation after 70 CE. Urbach has pointed out that even gentile slaves could be assumed to be converted and circumcised, though after 70 CE very few chose to convert. Gentile slaves had the same cultic rights and responsibilities as women, and a manumitted slave was expected to marry a Jew.[10] The schools assumed that slaves had the same responsibility as Israelites to procreate (m.Ed.1.13) and Rn. Gamaliel I entrusted his slave with roasting the Passover lamb (m.Pes.7.2—though this slave was exceptional—see m.Ber.2.7).

Tefillin and *mezuzot* have been found at Qumran, so their use is certainly pre-70, and they are attested as early as second century BCE (Aristeas 158-59), as well as in the NT era by Josephus *(Ant.* 4:213).

New Testament: There has been a huge debate about the role of women in the New Testament, especially with regard to the teaching on submission of women, children, and slaves to the *paterfamilias* in Ephesians 5.22–6.9; Colossians 3.18–4.1; 1 Peter 2.18–3.7; and 1 Timothy 2.9-15; 6.1-2. These are presumably related to similar codes involving this threefold submission, codes which were produced by Greek, Jewish, and Egyptian moralists.[11] It is likely that this moral movement was inspired by the perceived link between the freedom and licentiousness of the 'new Roman woman' in the first century CE.[12]

m.Ber.4.1-4: When to pray the Eighteen Benedictions

Summary of Mishnah: There are prayer services three times a day and one extra on Sabbaths (4.1). When can you pray an *abstract* of the Eighteen instead (4.3)? Should prayers be fixed (4.4)?

The following traditions have elements (marked in bold) for which there is evidence of an origin before 70 CE:

---

[10] Jewish and gentile slaves existed in Palestine before 70 CE. See E. E. Urbach, "The Laws Regarding Slavery As a Source for Social History of the Period of the Second Temple, the Mishnah and Talmud" in *Papers of the Institute of Jewish Studies London*, vol. 1, ed. J. G. Weiss (Jerusalem: Magnes Press, 1964), pp. 1-94. See especially pp. 42-55 for the differences between pre-70 and post-70 CE conditions.

[11] See summary and references in Craig S. Keener, *Paul, Women & Wives: Marriage and Women's Ministry in the Letters of Paul* (Peabody, Mass.: Hendrickson Publishers, 1992), pp. 145-46. For Jewish sources, see W. D. Davies, *Paul and Rabbinic Judaism: Some Rabbinic Elements in Pauline Theology*, 2nd ed. (London: SPCK, 1955), 130-33.

[12] B. Winter, "The 'New' Roman Wife and 1 Timothy 2.9-15: The Search for a Sitz im Leben," *Tyndale Bulletin* 51 (2000): 283-92.

m.Ber.4.1: Times for praying the Eighteen

The Morning Prayer [can be said] until midday
The Afternoon Prayer until evening.
The Evening Prayer has no fixed [time].
And the Additional [Sabbath Prayer]
[can be said during] the whole day.

תפלת השחר, עד חצות.
תפלת המנחה, עד הערב.
תפלת הערב, אין לה קבע.
ושל מוספין,
כל היום.

Comments: The timing of the times of Prayer appears to be based on the Temple sacrifices. The Afternoon Prayer, the *Minhah*, was even named the same as the *afternoon meal offering* (*Minhah*, מִנְחָה). The morning and afternoon sacrifices had no fixed time (other than morning and afternoon), and the additional Sabbath sacrifice was not time limited. There was no evening sacrifice, and the Evening Prayer may have been added later so that the Prayer would accompany the *Shema* in both morning and evening. The timing of the *Shema* was originally based on the start and end of bedtime, and it was natural that the morning and evening Prayer of Eighteen should follow immediately after the *Shema*, rather than create separate prayer times, but this ruling shows that it was not necessary to link the two, and they may originally have been separate.

Dating (5): It is difficult to know how early the Eighteen came into common use, but it is certain that they originated in some form before 70 CE—see the excursus on Early Prayer. It is also difficult to know when the Evening Prayer came into common use. The phrase 'not fixed' was understood as 'not compulsory' by R. Joshua [T2], though this interpretation was opposed by Rn. Gamaliel [II, T2] (y.Ber.4.1; b.Ber.27b-28a), and this controversy was still continuing in the days of Abaya [BA4] and Raba [BA4]. R. Joshua b. Levi [PA1] tried to relate the evening sacrifice to the continued burning of the afternoon sacrifice during the night (b.Ber.26b with Rashi *ad loc.*). A more likely explanation is found in a tradition that R. Jose the Galilean [T3], who lived in Temple times, used to recite the evening Prayer when the Temple gates were closed (t.Ber.3.2), which is the same as the beginning of the time allowed for the *Shema* (see 1.1 above), and suggests that the evening Prayer was associated with the evening *Shema* rather than with any sacrifice. Later anonymous discussions relate the three times of Prayer to the prayers of Daniel (Dan.6.11).

The comment about the Additional Service may have been added later, though this Service was already established by 70 CE (see m.Ber.4.7).

New Testament: Luke and Acts suggests that there were specific times for prayer in the Temple, during the afternoon and the morning (Lk.1.10; Acts 3.1; 10.9, 30), perhaps associated with the *incense offering* (cf. Lk.1.10; Acts 10.4; Rev.8.4). The Temple was also regarded as a place for prayer in general (Lk.18.10; Acts 22.17), and all three Synoptics call the Temple a "House of Prayer" (Mt.21.13; Mk.11.17; Lk.19.46). This time of public prayer may have occurred immediately after or during the prayer service held by the priests, which immediately preceded the *incense offering* (m.Tam.5.1). Peter's prayer "at about the sixth hour" could have been the morning prayer which had been delayed by his journey (Acts 10.9).

m.Ber.4.3: The Eighteen Benedictions and abstracts of them

Rabban Gamaliel [II, T2] says:	רבן גמליאל אומר,
Every day, a man prays	בכל יום מתפלל אדם
the Eighteen [Benedictions].	שמונה עשרה.
R. Joshua [(b. Hananiah, T2] says:	רבי יהושע אומר,
An *abstract* of the Eighteen.	מעין שמונה עשרה.
R. Akiba [T3] said:	רבי עקיבה אומר,
If his prayer is fluent in his mouth,	אם שגורה תפלתו בפיו,
he must pray the [full] Eighteen;	יתפלל שמונה עשרה.
and if not, an *abstract* of the Eighteen.	ואם לאו, מעין שמונה עשרה.

Comments: Although this debate occurred soon after 70 CE, it tells us that there was already a consensus that there were Eighteen Benedictions, and it was not yet decided whether these needed to be prayed in their full form. In later times, it was ruled that the full form had to be used except in times of danger or debilitating illness (cf. m.Ber.4.4), but this was still not the case in the mid second century when Akiba said that it depended on how the person felt at the time. Akiba was a charismatic,[13] so he probably meant whether or not a person felt inspired.

The number Eighteen is already being used as a title for this prayer, which suggests that the number of *benedictions* was already very firmly fixed. It is significant that Rn. Gamaliel II used this title, because according to later tradition he was responsible for fixing the number, though, as discussed below, it is likely that this ruling had already been made in the days of Gamaliel I.

There was a considerable dispute about the form of the *abstract*. Some regarded it as an outline of the Eighteen, and some as a prayer which encompassed the most important elements of the Eighteen. Rab [BA1] and Samuel [BA1] assumed it was an outline, but disagreed about whether it consisted of the first sentence of each or the last (y.Ber.4.3, VI.A; cf. b.Ber.29a). Later debates appear to assume that the *abstract* was a short prayer which encompassed the general sentiments of the Eighteen, or at least the first three and last three benedictions. This same ambiguity is seen in the word '*abstract*' (מעין) which can mean 'spring, fountain, womb,' which would suggest it was an outline, acting as a source or seed of the Eighteen, or it can mean 'essence' or 'reflection' (from עין, 'eye'), which would suggest that was a substitution for the Eighteen. In 6.8 it is used for one *benediction* which 'embodies' three others, which suggests the latter meaning is being used there.

---

[13] Cf. b.Ber.31a; b.Hag.14b.

Dating (5): All the participants in this debate (which took place in the generation immediately after 70 CE) assume that *abstract*s of the Eighteen exist and are legitimate in at least some circumstances, so some kind of *abstract*(s) already existed before 70 CE, and they may have been the first form of the Eighteen.

Various *abstract*s have been recorded,[14] the earliest of which is Eliezer's (see the Early Prayers below). The version which became the official one was "Give us discernment . . . ," which was attributed to Mar Samuel [BA1] (b.Ber.29a). This was generally accepted by the mid fourth century, as seen by the way that Abaye [BA4] could refer to 'Give us discernment' instead of to 'the *abstract*.' An anonymous discussion later made a distinction between 'Give us discernment' and other *abstract*s, saying that 'Give us discernment,' together with the first three and last three *benedictions*, is a substitute for the Eighteen, but other short versions were simply a stopgap until one was out of danger and could say the full Eighteen (b.Ber.30a). This development is an example of the gradual formalization and fixing of prayer in general.

New Testament: The Lord's Prayer appears to be an *abstract* of the Eighteen. It is very similar to the earliest *abstract* preserved in rabbinic literature, though with important differences.[15] It was used in the early church in the same way as the Eighteen—i.e., they prayed it three times, standing, and used it as an outline for a longer prayer.[16]

The Lord's Prayer is similar to many Jewish prayers, especially its reference to God's name and kingdom (which occurred in almost all Jewish prayers), God's holiness (as in the various versions of the Qiddush), prayer for God's will (as in Eliezer's *abstract*, below), food (as in Benediction #9), and forgiveness (as in Benediction #6). What is unusual is the call for ease from trouble and the prayer that

---

[14] R. Joshua at m.Ber.4.4. R. Eliezer b. Hyrcanus [T2] at t.Ber.3.7; b.Ber.29b. R. Nahum at y.Ber.4.3 and an anonymous source at y.Ber.4.4. Mar Samuel, R. Eleazar b. R. Zadok and an anonymous source at b.Ber.29b. Perhaps the Papyrus Egerton 5 is also an Abstract—see A. Marmorstein, "The Oldest Form of the Eighteen Benedictions," *Jewish Quarterly Review* NS 34 (1943/4): 137-59, based on the work of Joseph Wahrhaftig, "A Jewish Prayer in a Greek Papyrus" (*Journal of Theological Studies* 40 [1939]: 386-91). See also Pieter W. van der Horst, "Neglected Greek Evidence for Early Jewish Liturgical Prayer," *Journal for the Study of Judaism in the Persian, Hellenistic and Roman Period* 29 (1998): 278-96.

[15] Heinemann, *Prayer*, pp. 191-92; David Bivin, "Prayers for Emergencies," *Jerusalem Perspective* 5 (1992): 16-17. Contra: Israel Abrahams, *Studies in Pharisaism and the Gospels*, 2nd series (London: Cambridge University Press, 1924); cf. Charles Taylor, *Sayings of the Jewish Fathers, Comprising Pirqe Aboth in Hebrew and English: with Notes and Excursuses*, 2nd ed. (Cambridge: Cambridge University Press, 1897), esp. pp. 124-30.

[16] Gordon J. Bahr, "Use of the Lord's Prayer in the primitive church" (*Journal of Biblical Literature* 84 [1965], 153-59); Phillip Sigal, "Early Christian and rabbinic liturgical affinities: exploring liturgical acculturation [appendix: Hebrew text of alenu, tr]" (*New Testament Studies* 30 [1984]: 63-90).

God should 'forgive us as we forgive.' Eliezer's *abstract* is the clearest parallel to the call for protection, as well as containing a striking parallel to Jesus' prayer, "your will be done on earth as in heaven" (Mk.14.36 // Mt.26.42 // Lk.22.42):

t.Ber.3.7 (Z 3.11; cf. b.Ber.29b): Eliezer's abstract

R. Eliezer*1 [b. Hyrcanus, T2] says:	רבי אלעזר אומר
May your will be done in the heavens above*2	יעשה רצונך בשמים ממעל
and grant the ease of spirit to those who fear you*3	ותן נחת ריח ליראיך
and do what is good in your eyes.	והטוב בעיניך עשה
Blessed [is he] who listens to prayer.*4	ברוך שומע תפלה

The text follows Lieberman's edition of Tosefta here and elsewhere, when available.
*1 Z has אלעזר, "Eleazar," i.e., R. Eleazar b. Shammua [T4], but b.Ber.29b agrees with L. agrees with L. agrees with L. agrees with L. agrees with L. agrees with L. agrees with L. agrees with L. agrees with L. agrees with L.
*2 Z has the imperfect עשה and omits ממעל, "above."
*3 Z adds בארץ, "on earth," while b.Ber.29b adds מתחת, "below."
*4 b.Ber.29b says "Blessed are you Lord who . . . ," as was standard in later benedictions.

The most basic form of the prayer is:

> Your will be done in heaven
> Grant ease to those who fear you
> And do what is good in your eyes.

This prayer starts and finishes with the same word (עשה) which helps to make it memorable. Someone heightened the parallels between the first two lines by adding "on the earth" to the second line, then someone linked these two lines more memorably by changing "on the earth" to "below" and adding "above" to the first line. Someone also made a contrast between what happens on earth now and what will happen in heaven, by using the future perfect "may your will be done." And someone added the interpretative word "spirit" to explain the type of "ease" we should expect. Then a customary benediction was added which the Talmud unabbreviated, so we have:

> May your will be done in the heavens above
> And grant ease of spirit to those who fear you on earth below
> And do what is good in your eyes.
> Blessed are you O Lord who listens to prayer.

These expansions which add interpretation and balance to the prayer are similar to variations which we see between Matthew and Luke's versions of the Lord's Prayer (Mt.6.9-13 // Lk.11.2-4). Matthew's Lord's Prayer has various expansions which add theological content: "Father" is expanded to "Our Father who is in heaven," "your Kingdom come" is interpreted as "your will be done on earth as it is in heaven" (very similar to Eliezer's prayer), and "do not lead us into trials" gains the interpretative comment that trials come when we are "delivered" into the hand of "the evil one" (which is in line with first-century Jewish theology[17]). Similarly, Matthew interprets the first beatitude (Mt.5.3f // Lk.6.20f) by changing "poor" into "poor in spirit" (a similar change to that in Eliezer's prayer).

It is likely that the Lord's Prayer was an *abstract* which was used as a skeleton to help the disciple remember various components which should be included in his prayer. Therefore, like Eliezer's, it could exist in various forms which were shorter or longer.

m.Ber.4.4: R. Eliezer: Prayers should not be fixed

R. Eliezer [b. Hyrcanus, T2] says:	רבי אליעזר אומר,
He who makes his prayer fixed,	העושה תפלתו קבע,
his prayer is not [successful] supplications.	אין תפלתו תחנונים.

Comments: The context suggests that this refers to the wording of the Eighteen, and the curious mixture of singular 'prayer' and plural 'supplications' suggests that this may have been the original context, because the Eighteen were known as '*the* Prayer,' though it contained many supplications.

The word 'fixed' may mean a fixed time (as at 4.1) or fixed words (which makes more sense here). After the wording of prayers became fixed, this ruling came to mean 'who makes his prayers perfunctory.'[18] The wording of the Eighteen did not become fixed for several centuries, though the Sanhedrin at Yavneh started to rule about the wording of some of them. As seen in 4.3, people were allowed to pray an *abstract* instead of the full Eighteen, and so they were still allowed to shorten or lengthen it.

The following *baraytah* illustrates the way in which prayers varied. Its historical value is uncertain, partly because biographical stories are often later inventions, and also because some sources name the teacher as Eleazar, not Eliezer.

b.Ber.34a: Shortened and lengthened prayer

Our Rabbis taught:	תנו רבנן,
Once a certain disciple	מעשה בתלמיד אחד
went down before the Ark [to lead the prayers]	שירד לפני התיבה
in the presence of R. Eliezer,	בפני רבי אליעזר

---

[17] First-century Judaism regarded Satan as the origin of all trials (as in Jas.1.13), so that even the trial of Abraham sacrificing Isaac was regarded as a trial from Satan—see Jub.17.15f; cf. b.San.89b.

[18] קבע can mean either 'established, fastened' (i.e., fixed wording) or 'regular, appointed time' (i.e., fixed time). Jastrow suggests that it means 'perfunctory' on the basis of this passage and other passages which have derived from it.

and he used to extend the prayer to an inordinate length.	והיה מאריך יותר מדאי.
His disciples said to him:	אמרו לו תלמידיו,
Master, how longwinded this fellow is!	רבינו, כמה ארכן הוא זה!
He replied to them:	אמר להם,
Is he drawing it out any more than	כלום מאריך יותר
our Master Moses,	ממשה רבינו,
of whom it is written: (Deut.9.25)	דכתיב ביה,
"[he prayed] the forty days	את ארבעים היום
and the forty nights"?	ואת ארבעים הלילה וגו'.
Another time it happened that a certain disciple	שוב מעשה בתלמיד אחד
went down before the Ark	שירד לפני התיבה
in the presence of R. Eliezer,	בפני רבי אליעזר,
and he used to cut the prayer inordinately short.	והיה מקצר יותר מדאי.
His disciples said to him:	אמרו לו תלמידיו,
How concise this fellow is!	כמה קצרן הוא זה!
He replied to them:	אמר להם,
Is he any more concise than	כלום מקצר יותר
our Master Moses,	ממשה רבינו,
as it is written: (Num.12.13)	דכתיב,
"Heal her now, O God, I beseech Thee"?	אל נא רפא נא לה.

Even third generation Amoraim in the early fourth century continued to understand Eliezer's saying to mean 'insert something fresh into it.'[19] Flourishes and additional phrases continued to be added to the Eighteen for many centuries, which can be seen by comparing the various versions of this prayer in many manuscripts and prayer books which have survived.

Before the wording became fixed, these additions consisted of each individual's petitions, and even after the words became fixed and were said by the prayer leader, there was still an opportunity to add private petitions. Before they became fixed, there was a rule to tell people where to add them:

> One does not utter words [of private petition and supplication] after "True and firm" [the prayer immediately before the Eighteen] but he may utter words [of petition] after the Prayer, even if [the petition is] as [long as] the order of the confession on the Day of Atonement. (t.Ber.3.6)

However, this probably represents the later fixing of the Eighteen because another tradition which discusses this story about Eliezer said that one could insert private intercession at Benediction #P15, 'who hears prayers' (b.AZ.8a). Although this tradition is transmitted in the early third century, it may reflect very old behavior because the *abstract* of Eliezer has the form of three intercessions which end with this benediction (see t.Ber.3.7 above).

---

[19] Rabbah and R. Joseph at b.Ber.29b.

Dating (5): The above story (which is set just after 70 CE) assumes that they could summarize or lengthen the prayers as they wished. This implies that the wording of prayers was still unfixed at 70 CE, though Eliezer's opposition to fixed prayers (cf. m.Ber.4.4) suggests that fixed wording was starting to be introduced. Eliezer was a conservative authority in a changing world. His saying is a nostalgic complaint that prayers should be spontaneous in order to be sincere. A similar saying is attributed to Simeon b. Nathanael, who can probably be dated to the same time (m.Ab.2.13). The reluctance of rabbinic Judaism to write down prayers was perhaps related to this principle that prayers should not be fixed.

At Qumran prayers were apparently fixed because they were written down in great detail. Their prayers mirror, in many ways, the synagogue service of which we only have later evidence. They prayed in the morning and evening (4Q503, cf. Jos.*War*:2.128) when they said the *Shema* with the *Decalogue*, various blessings, confessions, and supplications (equivalent to the Eighteen), and sang songs of praise (the *Hodayot* and others).[20]

The fact that this is a story about Eliezer rather than a *halakhic* ruling makes us less confident about its early origin because non-*halakhic* sayings were generally transmitted with less accuracy and were often invented by later generations. However, as we have seen, it fits in well with what we know from elsewhere about this time period and about Eliezer.

New Testament: In the Gospels long public prayers are regarded as a mark of hypocrisy (Mk.12.40; Mt.23.14; Lk.20.47), and repetition as a feature of gentile prayer (Mt.6.7). The Lord's Prayer may be regarded as either an outline that could be expanded, so it had no fixed form, or an *abstract* that could be used when there was little time. The short version in Luke (Lk.11.2-4) and the larger version in Matthew (Mt.6.9-13), where several petitions have been expanded, suggests that early Christians regarded it as an outline as well as an *abstract*.

t.Ber.3.11: Sabbath Benedictions on an *ordinary festival day*

A Sabbath which fell	שבת שחלה להיות
on the New Moon	בראש חודש
or on an *ordinary festival day*:	ובחולו של מועד
In the morning and afternoon	בשחרית ובמנחה
pray seven [benedictions]	מתפלל שבע
and say the [benediction about] the holiness of the Day	ואומר קדושת היום
in the [benediction about the Temple] Service.	בעבודה
R. Eliezer says: [Say the *benediction* about the holiness of the Day]	רבי אליעזר אומר

---

[20] See Daniel K. Falk, "Qumran Prayer Texts and the Temple," in D. K. Falk et al., eds., *Sapiential, Liturgical and Poetical Texts from Qumran* (Leiden: Brill, 2000), pp. 106-26.

in the Thanksgiving [*benediction*]. בהודייה

None of this is in Zuckermandel's edition. Lieberman finds it in MS Erfurt.

Comments: The Eighteen are reduced to seven on a Sabbath, with only the first three and last three *benedictions* being said, and an extra *benediction* concerning the Sabbath. The question arose as to how many *benedictions* to recite on a day when the Sabbath fell on a day that had its own additional *benedictions*, such as a New Moon festival. This decision says that the total number of *benedictions* remains seven, and that the extra *benediction* is inserted into the *benediction* which concerns the Temple Service (the third nearest the end). Eliezer later suggested that it should be inserted into the following *benediction* which concerned Thanksgiving (the second to last one), probably because the additional *benediction* was a thanksgiving for the special day.

It is not clear from here whether the Eighteen originally consisted of these six *benedictions* and later expanded, or whether these six were part of a Temple service and the others were said by the people or outside the Temple only, or whether the Eighteen were abbreviated to six on Sabbaths because of the extra sacrifices or the extra afternoon service. It is unlikely that these six were the first *benedictions* without the existence of the others, because the others include all the matters of petition without which prayer is meaningless (petitions for forgiveness, protection, food, salvation, etc.). It seems likely that the six were either said by the priests while the people said the petitionary *benedictions*, or that the priests normally said all Eighteen but abbreviated them on Sabbaths because of the extra sacrifices. Either way, it is possible that these six were the ones which were said by the priests in the Temple.

Dating (2): It is possible that this was a debate which occurred in the time of Eliezer, after 70 CE, but it is recorded as though it was a decision from a previous generation which was commented on by Eliezer. The latter is more likely as it explains the difference of opinion, which was probably due to changes after the destruction of the Temple. In the time of the Temple, the most significant aspect of the festivals, including the intermediate days, was the huge increase in sacrifices brought by pilgrims. It was therefore natural that the *benediction* for the special day should be inserted into the *benediction* concerning Temple Service. After its destruction, the festival days became days for contemplation and thanksgiving for former blessings, so it would be more natural to move the special *benediction* to the *benediction* for Thanksgiving.

At Qumran there were no petitionary prayers on the Sabbath,[21] which agrees with the principle of omitting all the petitionary benedictions on the Sabbath.

---

[21] See Lutz Doering "New Aspects of Qumran Sabbath Law from Cave 4 Fragments" in *Legal Texts and Legal Issues: Proceedings of the Second Meeting of the International Organization*

New Testament: Luke and Acts records people going to the Temple at specific times to pray (Lk.1.10; Acts 3.1), which suggests that people prayed in the Temple in an organized manner. Perhaps these prayer times coincided with the *incense offering* (see 4.1 above) and perhaps these prayers were led by the priests, but we know almost nothing about prayer in the Temple.

t.Ber.3.13 (Z 3.15): Sabbath Benedictions on a *holyday*

A *holyday* of the *Rosh ha-Shanah* (New Year)	יום טוב של ראש השנה
which fell on the Sabbath:	שחל להיות בשבת
The School of Shammai says:	בית שמיי אומרים
He prays ten [*benedictions*]*	מתפלל עשר
But the School of Hillel says:	ובית הלל אומרים
He prays nine [*benedictions*].	מתפלל תשע
A *holyday* which fell on the Sabbath:	יום טוב שחל להיות בשבת
The School of Shammai says:	בית שמיי אומרים
He prays eight [*benedictions*] -	מתפלל שמנה
he says the Sabbath one by itself	ואומר של שבת בפני עצמה
and the *holyday* one by itself	ושל יום טוב בפני עצמו
and begins with the Sabbath one.	ומתחיל בשל שבת
And the School of Hillel says:	ובית הלל אומרים
He prays seven [*benedictions*]—	מתפלל שבע
he begins with the Sabbath one	ומתחיל בשל שבת
and closes with the Sabbath one,	ומסיים בשל שבת
and says the [*benediction* about the] Holiness of the Day	ואומר קדושת היום
in the middle [of the Sabbath one].	באמצע

---

* A few MSS read שמנה עשרה, "eighteen" and the parallel in t.RH.2.17 reads שמנה, "eight".
Tosefta parallel: t.RH.2.17

Comments: This appears to be two related traditions, the latter of which has been expanded with an explanation. They continue the problem dealt with in 3.11 by asking what happens if even more important days coincide with the Sabbath. In 3.11 New Moons are dealt with, with the *Rosh ha-Shanah* (New Year) festival being the most important New Moon festival. *Ordinary festival days* were also dealt with—the days between the first and last day of a festival, on which you could perform work if it was urgent; while the festival *holydays* (the first and last days of the festival) were governed by the restrictions of the Sabbath.

---

for Qumran Studies, Cambridge, 1995: Published in Honour of Joseph M. Baumgarten, ed. Moshe Bernstein, Florentino García Martínez, John Kampen (Leiden: E J Brill, 1997), pp. 251-74, esp. p. 255.

The debate apparently presupposes that there is an extra *benediction* for each *holyday*, and that there is also an extra *benediction* for the first New Moon, so that there are two extra *benedictions* on the New Year. The Hillelites inserted the *holyday benediction* into another one so that there was still only the normal total of seven *benedictions* on that Sabbath, but the Shammaites said it separately, making a total of eight. Both schools agreed that the two extra *benedictions* of the New Year should be said separately, making a total of nine *benedictions* for the Hillelites and ten for the Shammaites.

The simplicity of this explanation is unfortunately spoiled by variations in the transmitted text itself, because some editions have the Shammaites saying "eighteen" and others "eight". The reading "eight" is probably an attempt at a correction of "eighteen". The parallel at t.RH.2.17 and the logic behind this the passage suggests that the correct reading is "ten", which became "eighteen" by the influence of the phrase 'The Eighteen Benedictions'.

The explanation given to the second ruling says that the Hillelites inserted the extra *benediction* into the Sabbath *benediction*, while the Shammaites said it separately just after the Sabbath *benediction*.

This debate indicates that there was already a perception that the number of *benedictions* was important. The debate does not concern the words of the *benedictions*, and the fact that these extra *benedictions* should be said was assumed by both sides. The only issue was whether or not to increase the total number of discrete *benedictions*.

One possible reason that this had any great importance is that there was some kind of response at the end of each *benediction*. Perhaps each *benediction* was followed by the blowing of a *shophar* trumpet or prostrations (cf. Sir.50.16-21), or perhaps there was a communal 'Amen' at the end of each *benediction*, as was common later. Or perhaps there was a different response at the time of the Temple (see on m.Ber.9.5c below).

Dating (1): There is nothing to suggest that this school debate was a later invention, especially since someone felt it necessary to add an explanation. This explanation was almost certainly added later, because it is added only to one tradition, which should logically be the first of the pair. It appears that the pair were associated with each other in this order first, and then the explanation was added. The order was probably determined by the order of 'New Moon' and then '*ordinary festival day*' in 3.11. The explanation may not, therefore, be a true representation of what the schools taught.

New Testament: The blowing of the seven trumpets in Revelation in a vision seen "on the Lord's Day" (Rev.8.2, cf. 1.10) makes heaven look like the Temple and suggests that the Christian 'Lord's Day' is the heavenly Sabbath. Although Revelation is full of the number seven, it is significant that the seven trumpets are sounded at the time of *incense offering*, which is seen as representing the prayers of the saints (Rev.8.3-4).

m.Ber.4.5–5.2: How you should pray the Eighteen

Summary of Mishnah: You should dismount for the Eighteen, turn toward the Temple, and concentrate on the prayer (4.5-6). The Additional Service does not occur everywhere (4.7). You may not interrupt prayer even to greet the king (5.1). Rules about what prayers occur in which *benedictions* (5.2).

The following traditions have elements (marked in bold) for which there is evidence of an origin before 70 CE:

m.Ber.4.5-6: Stand, and turn to the Temple to pray

One who is riding on an ass	היה רוכב על החמור,
must dismount [to pray the Eighteen],	ירד.
and if he is not able to dismount,	ואם אינו יכול לירד,
he must turn his face.	יחזיר את פניו.
And if he is not able	ואם אינו יכול
to turn his face,	להחזיר את פניו,
he must direct his heart in the direction	יכון את לבו כנגד
of the House, the Holy of Holies,	בית קודש הקדשים.
6) One who was sitting on a ship*	היה יושב בספינה
or in a wagon or on a raft,	או בקרון או באסדה,
he must direct his heart in the direction	יכון את לבו כנגד
of the House, the Holy of Holies.	בית קודש הקדשים.

*Some editions read 'travelling' (מהלך) instead of 'sitting.'

Comments: This ruling depends on the assumption that you should stand when praying the Eighteen, and that you should pray it within a set time, whether it is convenient or not. It was a general rule of honor to get up and stand if you were approached by a superior, such as a gentile ruler (y.Ber.5.1, 9a) or an elder (t.Meg.3.24). Therefore it was considered necessary to stand when praying to God.[22] The main message of these rulings is that the inability to stand or to turn toward the Temple should not prevent you from praying.

The verb 'to direct' (כון) is particularly apt because it can also mean 'to stand, be firm.' To 'direct your heart' meant to 'concentrate with your mind.' This is particularly apt on a boat or a wagon, where it may be impossible to stand, and it may

---

[22] Uri Ehrlich, "'When You Pray Know Before Whom You Are Standing' (b.Ber 28b)," *Journal of Jewish Studies* 49 (1998): 38-50.

be impossible to know the direction of Jerusalem, so you have to 'direct your heart' instead.

Later rabbis thought that you dismounted so that you did not have an elevated position when praying (t.Ber.3.17). This may have been inspired by (or may have inspired) the phrase 'go down to pray' which is used constantly in the Babylonian Talmud, because the Ark, where the prayer leader stood, was in a lower part of the synagogue.

Dating (8): The use of 'the House' (i.e., the Temple) and the 'Holy of Holies' instead of 'Jerusalem' or 'Zion' probably indicates that the Temple was standing when this ruling was formulated. R. Simeon b. Halafta [T5] at the beginning of the third century clearly assumed that the ruling referred to the real Temple, while others had started to say that it referred to the heavenly Temple (Song.R.4.12).[23]

New Testament: Standing was the normal attitude of formal prayer in the Gospels. The humble publican stood to pray (Lk.18.13) and Mark 11.25 assumed that Christians, too, will stand to pray ("when you stand praying"). Therefore, when Jesus criticizes the Pharisees who "love to stand and pray in the synagogues" (Mt.6.5), he presumably means that they stood in a prominent place, and loved to be seen. Similarly he criticizes those who deliberately stood in the street and prayed (Mt.6.5). Although the above mishnah suggests that it was normal to stop and pray wherever you happened to be at the time of prayer, Jesus implies that they deliberately contrived to be in a public and prominent position at this time.

This did not mean that all prayer was to be conducted standing, because Jesus himself in Gethsemane "fell to the ground" (Mk.14.35; Mt.26.39) and "kneeled" (Lk.22.41), but the Lord's Prayer was probably prayed standing, as it was in the early church, because it was the equivalent to the *Amidah* (the 'Standing' prayer).[24]

---

[23] "It has been taught: 'A man should concentrate his mind on the Holy of Holies.' . . . R. Hiyya the Great [T6] says: It means, the celestial Holy of Holies. R. Simeon b. Halafta [T5] says: It means, the Holy of Holies here below. Phinehas [T5] said: I will harmonize your two statements; it means, the celestial Holy of Holies which is directly opposite the Holy of Holies here below." At a much later date the phrase could be used in a spiritual sense without any problem, e.g., Zohar III 8b: "a man should in his prayer fix his mind on the Holy of Holies, which is the Holy Name, and then say his prayer." There is also a discussion in y.Ber:4.6 which starts: "This [rule that one must pray facing the Temple] applies at a time when the Temple was standing. How do we know [it applies] when the Temple is destroyed [i.e., that all must still face the Temple mount when praying]?" This is discussed by R. Abun [A4].

[24] *Ap.Const.*7.44, discussed in Sigal, "Early Christian and Rabbinic Liturgical Affinities," p. 73; Gordon J. Bahr, "Use of the Lord's Prayer in the Primitive Church," *Journal of Biblical Literature* 84 (1965): 153-59.

m.Ber.4.7: The Additional Prayer

R. Eleazar b. Azariah [T2] says:
There is no **Additional Prayer**
except in a congregation of a city.
And the Sages say: [It is said by those who are]
in a congregation in a city
and [by those] who are not in a congregation in a city.

רבי אלעזר בן עזריה אומר,
אין תפלת המוספין
אלא בחבר עיר.
וחכמים אומרים,
בחבר עיר
ושלא בחבר עיר.

Comments: On a Sabbath there was an Additional Service for the saying of the Eighteen, but it appears from this dispute that it was not originally considered compulsory for all Jews. Eleazar argued that it was only compulsory if there was a substantial number of Jews in the community (i.e., in a city but not in a village), while the majority ('the Sages') ruled that it was compulsory for everyone.

The reason for an Additional Service was presumably to parallel the Sabbath sacrifice, which was in addition to the morning and afternoon sacrifice (Num.28.9). Perhaps the Additional Service was common in the larger synagogues, but it was not yet adopted by individuals. We may surmise that originally the Additional Service was only carried out in Jerusalem, perhaps in the Temple itself, and that after 70 CE the Sages wanted it to be adopted everywhere.

This is an interesting insight into the way that prayer changed from being a private activity before 70 CE and a communal activity after 70 CE. Before 70 CE, prayer was normally a private matter, even when it was performed in a synagogue.[25] People went to the synagogue, but they each prayed by themselves, starting at different times according to when they arrived. Josephus mentions someone greeting him in the synagogue while reciting morning prayers (*Life.* 294-95), which implies that the person who was greeting him had either finished his prayers or had not yet started them.

After 70 CE, prayer was increasingly a communal activity, conducted by a prayer leader in the synagogue, especially on a Sabbath when work did not prevent people attending. With this development came the assumption that someone who did not attend synagogue was not performing his prayers. The Additional Service may have become a point of conflict because many people were not used to performing this additional prayer in private, and so they did not turn up at the synagogue. Perhaps synagogues in smaller villages did not hold this Additional Service, because they knew that no one would turn up. The Sages wanted to make sure that every synagogue fell into line.

---

[25] The nature and even existence of synagogues in the first century has been a matter of much dispute, especially for synagogues in Palestine. The tide of scholarly opionion has turned in favor of early synagogues, thanks mainly to recent archeological work.

It is significant that both Eleazar and the Sages assumed that where the synagogue opened for this Additional Service, the local Jewish people should attend. Eleazar did not argue that people had the right to remain at home if they wished. This means that the concept of worship at synagogue was already established. Although you *could* pray the Eighteen in any place, it was assumed that you would go to the synagogue if possible.

Dating (5): Both sides in this dispute (which took place soon after 70 CE) assume the existence of the Additional Service, which must therefore already have been well established by 70 CE. It is likely that Eleazar is arguing for the old status quo, while the others want to enforce uniformity now that the Temple rite has gone. He is standing up for the right of smaller synagogues to omit this service, if they wish.

New Testament: This tradition suggests that daily prayers had not always been said in synagogues, but the synagogue or the Temple is already the normal place for prayer in the New Testament. Even the publican, who did not want to attract attention, went to the synagogue to pray (Lk:18.13), and when Paul was in a new city he went to find a Jewish congregation on a Sabbath, even if they did not meet in a building (Acts 16.13). This concurs with the assumption in Hebrews that Christians should meet together (Heb.10.25). However, Jesus assumed that Christians would pray more than just at prayer services, and that they would do this in secret (Mt.6.6).

m.Ber.5.2: Inserting *Rain* and *Separation* in the Eighteen

One should mention the power of the rains	מזכירין גבורות גשמים
in [Benediction #2] Reviving the Dead;	בתחיית המתים,
and one should ask for the rains	ושואלין הגשמים
in [Benediction #9] Blessing of the Years;	בברכת השנים,
and [one should insert] the *Habdalah*	והבדלה
in [Benediction #4] Endow Understanding.	בחונן הדעת.
R. Akiba [T3] says:	רבי עקיבה אומר,
One says it as the fourth blessing	אומרה ברכה רביעית
separately.	בפני עצמה.
R. Eliezer (b. Hyrcanus) [T2] says:	רבי אליעזר אומר,
[One says it] within [Benediction #P17] Thanksgiving.	בהודאה.

Comments: The first part of this ruling determines where to insert a prayer for rain. This was a very important issue in a country which depended on the annual heavy autumn rains. It distinguishes between thanksgiving for rain (which was inserted into Benediction #2 concerning God's power) and prayer for providing rain (which was inserted into Benediction #9 concerning crops). The prayer for rain was only inserted at particular times of the year (see m.Taan.1.1).

The *Habdalah* ('separation') gives thanks for the separation between holy and profane, and thereby gives thanks to God for the Sabbath and *holydays*. It is said in the evening prayers "at the end of the Sabbath, and at the end of festivals, and at the end of the Day of Atonement" (t.Ber.5.30). This debate concerns whether to increase the number of *benedictions* by saying the *Habdalah* as a separate *benediction*, or whether to insert the *Habdalah* into an existing *benediction*. We do not have any early text of the *Habdalah* prayer.

Dating (2): Eliezer and Akiba both assume that the *Habdalah* is said, but they disagree about whether to say it as a separate *benediction*. This indicates that the number eighteen is already seen as important it itself, so that one should try not to change the number of *benedictions*. Their opinions are attached to a previously assembled collection of rulings, which must therefore predate Eliezer [T2]. The *Habdalah* can confidently be dated to pre-70 in the school dispute of m.Ber.8.5; and Dosa [b. Harkinas, T2] debates the significance of the *Habdalah* in m.Hul.1.7.

New Testament: The separation of sacred and secular is one of the aspects of Judaism that Jesus disagrees with in the Gospels. In the *Habdalah* prayer which we now have, this concept of separation is applied also to 'Israel and other nations.'[26] This wording may have been present in some form in the first century, which would have exacerbated the friction between Jewish and gentile Christians.

m.Ber.5.3-5: Errors when you pray the Eighteen

Summary of Mishnah: A prayer leader stands before the Ark [of Scripture scrolls]. If he makes an error (common ones are listed), the others stop him and his replacement starts at the beginning of the faulty blessing (5.3). The leader should not do anything which might distract him unnecessarily (5.4). An error when leading prayers is a bad sign, but fluency in prayer is a good sign (5.5).

The following traditions have elements (marked in bold) for which there is evidence of an origin before 70 CE:

m.Ber.5.3: Unallowed phrases in public prayer

He who says [while leading prayer]:	האומר
"May your Mercy extend to a bird's nest"	על קן צפור יגיעו רחמיך,
or "May your Name be remembered for good"	ועל טוב יזכר שמך,

---

[26] Saadya's tenth-century text of the *Habdalah* reads: "Blessed art Thou, O Lord, our God, King of the Universe! Who hast made a separation between what is holy and what is profane; between light and darkness; between Israel and other nations; between the seventh day and the six days of creation. Blessed art Thou who hast separated the holy from the profane."

[or] "We give thanks, We give thanks":	מוֹדִים מוֹדִים,
One should silence him.	מְשַׁתְּקִין אוֹתוֹ.
He who goes before the ark [to lead prayers]	הָעוֹבֵר לִפְנֵי הַתֵּיבָה
and errs [in the wording of a prayer]:	וְטָעָה,
Another must serve instead	יַעֲבוֹר אַחֵר תַּחְתָּיו,
and he should not decline at that time.	וְלֹא יְהֵא סַרְבָן בְּאוֹתָהּ שָׁעָה.
From where does he begin?	מִנַּיִן הוּא מַתְחִיל,
[from] the beginning of the *benediction*	מִתְּחִלַּת הַבְּרָכָה
in which [the former leader] erred.	שֶׁטָּעָה בָּהּ.

Mishnaic parallel: m.Meg.4.9

Comments: If the person who is leading prayer uses some inappropriate phrases of which the rabbis disapproved, he should be silenced, and if he stumbles or makes a mistake he should be replaced. Normally you could decline to lead prayers, but if you were asked at this point you should not decline, presumably because the whole congregation is waiting. You should restart the *benediction* in which the mistake occurred.

The meanings of the three forbidden prayer phrases is not recorded, though later rabbis made some reasonable suggestions:

"May thy mercy reach the nest of a bird": This presumably refers to Deut.22.6-7 which forbids killing both the mother and her young if you discover a nest. The Babylonian Talmud has two possible interpretations: R. Jose b. Abin [PA5] said that it introduced insidious distinctions between animals (so they might become jealous); and R. Jose b. Zebida [PA3] said that it implied that God acts according to compassion rather than according to law (b.Ber.33b; b.Meg.25a). The Jerusalem Talmud records two similar opinions: R. Jose (i.e., b. Zebida) [PA3], in the name of R. Samuel, said that it implied that God's mercy went no further than a bird's nest; and R. Jose b. R. Bun (i.e., Abin) [PA5] said that it implied that God's actions are motivated solely by mercy (y.Ber.5.3 I; y.Meg.4.10 I). The two pairs of rabbis are actually the same with slightly different names in the two Talmuds,[27] and the two pairs of opinions are similar to each other, though the attributions appear to be reversed.

The two latter explanations in both Talmuds are especially similar, and, more significantly, they fit in with an example prayer which was said in the presence of Rabbah [BA3]: "You have shown mercy to the bird's nest, so show pity and mercy to us" (b.Ber.33b; cf. y.Meg.4.10 I). This implies that the phrase was used as a form of argument to persuade God to answer prayer. This type of persuasion in prayer was criticized by Simeon b. Shetah when Honi refused to leave his circle until God

---

[27] R. Jose b. Abin in Babylonian Talmud is the same as R. Jose b. R. Bun in Jerusalem Talmud, and R. Jose b. Zebida is simply called R. Jose in Jerusalem Talmud.

answered favorably (m.Taan.3.8). Heinemann points to many other rabbinic passages which criticize prayers of importunity.[28]

"For good may your name be mentioned": Only the Babylonian Talmud discusses the meaning of this, suggesting, anonymously, that it implies that you bless God only for good things, whereas you should bless God for *all* things (b.Ber.33b; b.Meg.25a). Mishnah states in an undateable saying that "One is obligated to say a *benediction* over evil just as he says a blessing over good" (m.Ber.9.5).

"We give thanks, we give thanks" (i.e., a repetition of the opening word of P17 in the Eighteen): The Babylonian Talmud gives the anonymous opinion that this was forbidden because it implies acknowledgement of two powers instead of one God (b.Ber.33b; b.Meg.25a).[29] However, the Jerusalem Talmud records the opinion of R. Samuel b. R. Isaac [PA3], who said that repetition like this is a trait of liars (y.Ber.5.3 II; y.Meg.4.10 II). Presumably he meant that one mistrusts someone who affirms their loyalty too often or who affirms the truth of what they are saying with too much emphasis. R. Samuel's explanation may have represented the older opinion since the editors of the Jerusalem Talmud had problems with it. They added the comment that "This applies only to public [prayer], because for an individual this is [normal in] supplication."

Dating (5): The system of replacing the prayer leader was already in place when Samuel the Lesser composed the curse of the Minim and later forgot the wording (b.Ber.28b.f). It will be shown below, in the section concerning the Dating of the Eighteen Benedictions, that this incident took place before or immediately after 70 CE.

The ruling about the "bird's nest" cannot be confidently dated alongside the ruling about replacing the prayer leader because they are not sufficiently linked. The former ruling says the person should be silenced and the latter says they should be replaced. Nevertheless, even if the ruling is later, the use of these phrases fits best into a pre-70 context when the wording of prayers was less fixed.

New Testament: The ruling against the "bird's nest" prayer assumes that God does indeed care for his smallest creatures. The ruling says, in effect, that one should not take advantage of God's love for his creatures to try to force him to answer prayer, in the way that a child might pray: "If you love me, you will give it to me," or "You love these little creatures more than me." The other explanations of this ruling are later and less plausible. This explanation also fits very closely to the teaching of Jesus who used the same argument (Mt.10.29: "not one sparrow will fall to the ground without your Father knowing"; Mt.6.26 "your heavenly Father feeds them") to

---

[28] Heinemann, *Prayer,* pp. 200-201.
[29] In y.Meg.4.10 this is confused with an explanation of the former saying.

encourage people that God cares for them (Mt.10.30: "you are of more value than many sparrows"; cf. Mt.6.26-32). Jesus did not tell people to use it to bend God's ear to their prayers but he did encourage importunate prayers (parable of the importunate widow, Lk.18.1-8; friend at midnight, Lk.11.5-8; 'knock and ask,' Mt.7.7 // Lk.11.9).

The ruling against repetition in prayer sounds like Jesus' teaching against meaningless babbling (Mt.6.7).

m.Ber.5.5b: Fluent prayers of Hanina b. Dosa

They said concerning	אמרו עליו על
R. Hanina b. Dosa [T2]	רבי חנינא בן דוסא,
that he used to pray for the sick	שהיה מתפלל על החולים
and said: This one will live.	ואומר, זה חי
or: This one will die.	וזה מת.
and they said to him:	אמרו לו,
From where do you know [this]?	מנין אתה יודע.
He said to them:	אמר להם,
If my prayer is fluent in my mouth,	אם שגורה תפלתי בפי,
I know that he is heard,	יודע אני שהוא מקובל.
and if not,	ואם לאו,
I know that he is rejected.*	יודע אני שהוא מטורף.

Comments: This is an example to illustrate the principle that errors or even stumbling in prayer are a bad sign. In the Talmud, two miracles are added to illustrate this—the healing of the sons of Gamaliel I and of Johanan b. Zakkai.

Our Rabbis taught: Once the son of R. Gamaliel fell ill. He sent two scholars to R. Hanina b. Dosa to ask him to pray for him. When he saw them he went up to an upper chamber and prayed for him. When he came down he said to them: Go, the fever has left him; They said to him: Are you a prophet? He replied: I am neither a prophet nor the son of a prophet, but I learnt this from experience. If my prayer is fluent in my mouth, I know that he is accepted: but if not, I know that he is rejected. They sat down and made a note of the exact moment. When they came to R. Gamaliel, he said to them: By the temple service! You have not been a moment too soon or too late, but so it happened: at that very moment the fever left him and he asked for water to drink. On another occasion it happened that R. Hanina b. Dosa went to study Torah with R. Johanan ben Zakkai. The son of R. Johanan ben Zakkai fell ill. He said to him: Hanina my son, pray for him that he may live. He put his head between his knees and prayed for him and he lived. Said R. Johanan ben Zakkai: If Ben Zakkai had stuck his head between his knees for the whole day, no notice would have been taken of him. Said his wife to him: Is Hanina greater than you are? He replied to her: No; but he is like a servant before the king, and I am like a nobleman before a king. (b.Ber.34b)

Although these miracles are folklore, it is certain that Hanina was known for healing miracles.

Dating (10): According to later traditions, Hanina b. Dosa was active both before and after 70 CE and the stories are consistent with his residence at Arav in Galilee before 70 CE, at which time Johanan b. Zakkai also lived at Arav (m.Shab.16.7; 22.3) before he lived at Jerusalem. Hence the Talmud says that Gamaliel sent two scholars to fetch him from Galilee to Jerusalem, so that Gamaliel could attend the lectures of Johanan b. Zakkai. These details do not help to confirm the historicity of these stories, but *if* they happened, it places them before 70 CE. Many other stories grew up about the miracles of Hanina.

This saying in Mishnah is much more likely to originate with Hanina than the stories, because it assumes that many of his prayers resulted in failure. This is not the type of saying which would be invented about a mythical miracle worker.

New Testament: The healing of Gamaliel's son, as recorded in the later traditions of the Talmud, is strikingly similar to Jesus' healing of the centurion's servant (Mt.8.5-13 // Lk.7.1-10 // Jn.4.46-53) and the Syro-Phoenician's daughter (Mt.15.21-28 // Mk.7.24-30), particularly in the way that the messengers affirmed the exact time of healing. Only Matthew has both of these healings and only he and John add that the healing took place 'that very hour.'

It is possible that Matthew and John both know about these miracle stories of Hanina and have crafted their accounts in reaction to them—Matthew making the miracles contrast with those of Hanina, while John was accentuating the similarities. Matthew emphasized the gentile identity of both the people healed, and pointed out that one is a servant and one a girl. This is in complete contrast to the two people healed by Hanina, who were sons of greatest rabbis of the day. John, by contrast, appears to make the story of the Centurion's servant fit more closely to the stories of Hanina. He obscures his gentile identity by calling him a 'nobleman,' and calls the servant his 'child' (παιδίον) and 'son' (υἱός). He also greatly emphasizes that this took place in Galilee (vv. 43, 45, 46, 47, 54), puts huge emphasis on the point of the exact time (vv. 52-53), and then says that this is one of the 'signs' by which the Jews should be convinced.[30]

m.Ber.6.1-8: Blessings and Grace after Meals

Summary of Mishnah: You say a different blessing [i.e., a *benediction* of thanks] for every new type of food as it arrives (6.1-4), unless a previous blessing already included that type of food (6.5, 7). After a meal you say the Grace [a final collection

---

[30] See further in Geza Vermes, *Jesus the Jew: A Historian's Reading of the Gospels* (London: Collins, 1973).

of *benedictions*]. When you do not recline [i.e., at informal meals] each person says these blessings for themselves (6.6). Do you say a blessing for fruit (6.8)?

The following traditions have elements (marked in bold) for which there is evidence of an origin before 70 CE:

t.Ber.4.1: A blessing must be said before food is eaten

A man must not taste anything	לא יטעום אדם כלום
until he has blessed it.	עד שיברך,
As it is said: (Ps.24.1)	שנאמר
"The earth is the Lord's, and all its fullness."	לה׳ הארץ ומלואה.
He who enjoys [anything] from the world	הנהנה מן העולם
which is without blessing, commits *misuse*,	הוה בלא ברכה מעל,
until he has [said the blessing and thereby] completed	עד שיתירו
all the commands [due] to him.	לו כל המצות

Comments: Although this saying is not recorded in the Mishnah, the second half is found as a *baraytah* in b.Ber.35a, and it is a prerequisite basis of all the rulings about *benedictions* over food. Scripture only mentions giving thanks *after* a meal (Deut.8.10), and so it was necessary to find support for this innovation.

The term '*misuse*' (*maal*, מעל, 'fraud') normally refers to using Temple property as if it were nonsacred. This exegesis implies that everything was considered the property of God, which either he gave as a gift (in which case we thank him for it) or it is stolen from him.

Dating (5): This is the general principle which lies behind all the rabbinic rules about thanks before food, and so it is certain that the principle predates them, even if it was not expressed in these terms. The principle of giving thanks before eating is already well established before 70 CE, as the following texts will show.

Scriptural proof texts are rarely recorded alongside rulings, though they were often added by later rabbis, perhaps based on traditional exegeses which had been the original basis of the ruling. The Babylonian Talmud attributes this exegesis to Samuel [BA1], transmitted by Rab Judah [BA2], and although it is possible that Samuel was citing a traditional exegesis, this attribution does make an early origin unlikely.

However, the argumentation of this exegesis may suggest that it has an early origin, because it uses an assumption which was later abandoned. This assumption is that when poetic parallelism appears in Scripture, both halves of the parallel are saying something different, even when they appear to say the same thing. After 70 CE rabbinic exegetes generally recognized that Scripture could contain redundant phrases in poetry just like secular literature did, and that Scripture poetry often contained pairs of phrases which balanced each other by saying virtually the same thing. But pre-70 rabbinic exegesis always tried to find a separate meaning for both halves of a parallelism, including parallelism in the Writings.[31] They knew about the normal function of parallelism (as seen by the many instances of parallelism in the Eighteen Benedictions and other poetry and prayers) but they did not think that God, the author of Scripture, would repeat himself like a human.

When a modern exegete reads the first verse of Psalm 24 in its context, it is an example of exact parallelism:

The earth is the Lord's and its fullness
The world and all those who live in it.

Standing in isolation, the first line might be regarded as different from the second in that it could be referring to the things in the earth whereas the second line refers to the people. However, the whole of verses 1-6 describes the people ("Who shall go up? ... He who is righteous. ... This is the generation ..."), which makes it likely that the "fullness" refers to the people who fill the earth. Also the words "earth . . . and its fullness" appears to be an allusion back to the vocabulary of Genesis 1.28 where Adam is told to "fill the earth" (i.e., with people). Therefore both halves of this parallelism are speaking about the people who live on the earth, and not about the 'things.'

The rabbis before 70 CE reasoned that God would never write a superfluous phrase in Scripture. Therefore, although they recognized parallelism as a rhetorical device, they always tried to find two meanings in the two lines of parallelism in Scripture. The second line clearly means 'all the people in the earth,' so the first line must mean 'all the things in the earth.' This kind of exegesis is characteristic of pre-70 Palestinian Judaism, and although it was not unknown after, the later rabbis tended to accept parallelism as a rhetorical device, even in Scripture.[32] It is, of course, possible that the meaning of "The earth is the LORD's and its fullness" had already become fixed before 70 CE (in the same way that it has also become fixed in most of Christendom), and that it was not applied to the matter of blessing food until later.

A further indication that this exegesis dates back to before 70 CE is the reliance on it by Paul (see below).

The explanation "He who enjoys . . ." may have been added later, and is undateable.

---

[31] For parallelism in pre-70 rabbinic teaching, see my *Techniques and Assumptions in Jewish Exegesis before 70 CE,* Texte und Studien zum antiken Judentum 30 (Tübingen: J. C. B. Mohr, 1992), pp. 166-67, 150-52, and my "The Two Asses of Zechariah 9:9 in Matthew 21" (forthcoming). See also the exegesis of Eccl.1.15 in m.Hag.1.6.

[32] R. Ishmael [T3] was attributed with the saying that "Scripture speaks with the language of men" (b.Ber.31b; b.Ned.3a) and with a new set of rules for interpretation. It is likely that some of these rules originated with Akiba [T3], whose exegeses illustrate this revolution far better than those of Ishmael. Both men thrived in the early second century.

New Testament: Psalm 24.1 is cited in 1 Corinthians 10.26 in the context of eating food. The passage is arguing that one may eat whatever is presented by a host, even if one is not sure whether the meat was bought from a gentile source (i.e., it might have been offered to an idol). Paul's argument could simply be based on the meaning of the text (i.e., the whole earth belongs to God, not to an idol), but it has much more force if the reader has already accepted that this was the proof text for giving thanks to God for every course in a meal.

m.Ber.6.5: Which blessings include other types of food?

[If one said the] blessing over the wine	בֵּרֵךְ עַל הַיַּיִן
which is before the meal,	שֶׁלִּפְנֵי הַמָּזוֹן,
one is exempt from the [blessing for]	פָּטַר
the wine which is after the meal.	אֶת הַיַּיִן שֶׁלְּאַחַר הַמָּזוֹן.
[If one said the] blessing over the dainties	בֵּרֵךְ עַל הַפַּרְפֶּרֶת
before the meal,	שֶׁלִּפְנֵי הַמָּזוֹן,
one is exempt from the [blessing for]	פָּטַר
the dainties after the meal.	אֶת הַפַּרְפֶּרֶת שֶׁלְּאַחַר הַמָּזוֹן.
[If one said the] blessing over the bread,	בֵּרֵךְ עַל הַפַּת,
one is exempt from the [blessing for] the dainties.	פָּטַר אֶת הַפַּרְפֶּרֶת.
[If one said the] blessing over the dainties,	עַל הַפַּרְפֶּרֶת,
one is not exempt from [the blessing for] the bread.	לֹא פָּטַר אֶת הַפַּת.
The School of Shammai say:	בֵּית שַׁמַּאי אוֹמְרִים,
Not even that made in a pot.	אַף לֹא מַעֲשֵׂה קְדֵרָה.

Comments: The principle is that a separate blessing must be said once during a meal for each course or related group of foods or, as later rabbis saw it, for each new intention to eat.

The 'dainties' is an attempt to translate the word *parperet*, 'small dish' (from a word meaning 'to grind' or 'small'), which was used for both appetizer and desert dishes. The rule says that a blessing for the bread includes these dainties, but a blessing for the dainties does not include the bread. The comment of the School of Shammai, that the blessing for the dainties does not include the food cooked in the pot (meat or vegetables, or both in a stew), implies that the blessing for the bread *did* include the cooked dishes. All this follows a natural logic if the bread is considered as 'the main dish,' which was eaten alongside all other foods, while the dainties are a 'minor dish' so thanks for them cannot include anything more major.

Dating (2): The comment by the School of Shammai indicates that these rulings were already established before 70 CE. They were probably already connected in this form, since the Shammaite comment appears to interact with the last two.[33] The first ruling implies that there was a separate blessing for wine after the meal (i.e., the Grace after Meals) which is also seen at 7.5; 8.1, 8.

In later times, there were many different blessings for all the elements of the meal. This early ruling appears to imply that thanks for all the food can be encompassed in the blessing for the bread and that this, with the blessing for the wine, was all that was necessary. However, people were already starting to say blessings for individual components of the meal, and they are warned that if they say a blessing for the dainties, they also have to say other separate blessings.

New Testament: The Gospels mention that Jesus said a blessing over the bread at the feeding of the thousands (Mt.14.19; Mk.6.41; 8.6; Lk.9.16), and with the two at Emmaus (Lk.24.30), and his prayers over the bread and wine at the Last Supper were perhaps modified blessings for bread and wine. Paul described the prayer over the wine as a 'blessing' (1Cor.10.16). The story of the thousands does not say that he blessed the bread, but it is implied because the breaking of the 'loaves' is linked with the blessing.

The story of Emmaus suggests that Jesus had a characteristic way of blessing bread, and all the Synoptics note that Jesus looked up to heaven as he blessed the bread for the thousands, so perhaps he did this in a particularly singular way. Later rabbis started making rules about when to bow and when to raise the head (cf. b.Ber.12a re Rab, mid third century); until now there are four set times when one bows the head during the Eighteen.

The principle behind the separate blessings for bread and wine is that every new thing which one comes across should be the subject of thanks to God. An undateable tradition in Mishnah emphasizes that one should give thanks to God even for seemingly bad things like earthquakes and storms (m.Ber.9.2), which concurs with Paul's teaching that we should give thanks to God in all circumstances (e.g., 1Thes.5.18; Eph.5.20; Phil.4.10-11). Paul refers to 'giving thanks' because, as seen in the Hodayot of the Dead Sea Sect, the formula with which individual prayers began was "I thank you LORD ... ," whereas communal prayers began with "Blessed are you LORD... ."

m.Ber.6.8a: Three Benedictions of the Grace after Meals

[If] he ate figs, or grapes or pomegranates,	אכל האנים ענבים ורמונים,
he blesses after them [with]	מברך אחריהן
the Three Benedictions [of Grace after Meals]	שלש ברכות,
—the words of Rn. Gamaliel [II T2].	דברי רבן גמליאל.

---

[33] b.Ber.42b debates whether they interact with the third or fourth ruling, and leave it undecided. I have suggested that they were interacting mainly with the third.

But the Sages say:
One *benediction* (an *abstract* of the Three).

וַחֲכָמִים אוֹמְרִים,
בְּרָכָה אַחַת ‹מֵעֵין שָׁלֹשׁ›.

Comments: The Grace after Meals later became an important ritual at the end of any meal which involved three or more males eligible to say the Grace (see the next section). This passage shows that this was already practiced by the generation immediately after 70 CE, but there was still much debate about it. The point of this ruling is to determine whether the full Grace after Meals is required after a minor meal. Gamaliel says that the full Grace ("the Three Benedictions") should be said even after a meal consisting of only fruit, but the Sages say that one may say a single *benediction* which is an *abstract* of the Three.

Something akin to the Three Benedictions was prayed by Isaac in Jubilees 22.6-9:

> Blessed be God Most High who created heaven and earth and who made all the fat of the earth and gave it to the sons of man so that they might eat and drink and bless their Creator.
>
> I thank you, my God, because you have let me see this day. Behold, I am one hundred and seventy-five years old, and fulfilled in days. And all of my days were peaceful for me. The sword of the enemy did not triumph over me in anything which you gave to me or my sons all the days of my life until this day.
>
> O my God, may your mercy and your peace be upon your servant and upon the seed of his sons so that they might become an elect people for you and an inheritance from all of the nations of the earth from henceforth and for all the days of the generations of the earth forever.[34]

Like all rabbinic prayers, we have no witness to their wording until several centuries later, and this wording in Jubilees is very different from the rabbinic versions when their wording became fixed. However, the subject matter is very similar. In the *Seder R. Amram Gaon*,[35] the first prayer blesses God who created all things and feeds his people. The second thanks God for ample land and food and prays for rescue from persecution and death. The third asks God to have mercy on Jerusalem and looks forward to the kingdom of the Messiah. A concluding blessing ("Who is good and bestows good") was added during the second century.

---

[34] Based on Charlesworth's translation with some minor changes. This passage has not been preserved at Qumran. James H. Charlesworth, *The Old Testament Pseudepigrapha*, vol. 1: *Apocalyptic Literature and Testaments;* vol. 2: *Expansions of the "Old Testament" and Legends, Wisdom and Philosophical Literature, Prayers, Psalms, and Odes, Fragments of Lost Judeo-Hellenistic* (London: Darton, Longman and Todd, 1983-85).

[35] The earliest full text of Jewish prayers is from the tenth century. There is considerable variation in the three main MSS of Seder Amram for these benedictions. The three most important MSS with their translations are found in David Hedegård's *Seder R. Amram Gaon* (Lund: Lindstedts Universitets-Bokhandel, 1951).

Dating (5): The only part of this tradition which can be dated before 70 CE is the phrase "the Three Benedictions," which was being used as a name for the Grace. This phrase appears to be used in an incidental way by Gamaliel, as if everyone would understand what he meant, because the main point of the ruling concerns whether or not an abbreviated Grace was sufficient.

The Three Benedictions are almost certainly from before 70 CE, as the passage in Jubilees shows. If the benedictions had been based on a passage in Scripture, we could assume that later rabbis adapted their prayer from it, but it is unlikely that they would decide to adapt a passage from Jubilees, which they considered uncanonical. It is therefore more likely that the passage in Jubilees is based on prayers which were already in common use. The additional concluding *benediction* is traditionally dated to the destruction of Bethar at the end of Bar Kokhba's revolt (135 CE). The other *three* are generally assumed to be older, and are traditionally ascribed to Moses, Joshua, and David (b.Ber.48b). Although these attributions are fanciful, the benedictions are certainly very old. As well as the citation in Jubilees, the third *benediction* is alluded to by Ben Sira (Sir.36.12-14, 17-19) and the thanksgiving prayer in Didache 10 is almost certainly dependent on them. The three were already known to Eliezer b. Hyrcanus [T2] who comments on changes made to the third blessing on the Sabbath (b.Ber.48b), and so the subject matter, if not the wording, of the first three must already have been settled before 70 CE.

m.Ber.7.1-5: Saying Grace after Meals for a group

Summary of Mishnah: If there are at least three who are eligible to say Grace after Meals, one of them should lead. Gentiles, women, slaves and children are not eligible together with the males; nor are any who have eaten *untithed* food or eaten less than an olive-sized portion (7.1-2). There are different calls for Grace for three eligible people, and for ten, and perhaps for larger numbers (7.3). No one may leave until Grace is said, though a subgroup of three or more may share Grace and leave (7.4-5). A final cup of wine has a blessing recited over it and is drunk with the Grace (7.5).

The following traditions have elements (marked in bold) for which there is evidence of an origin before 70 CE:

m.Ber.7.1-2: People excluded from saying the Grace after Meals

Three who ate together	שְׁלֹשָׁה שֶׁאָכְלוּ כְּאֶחָד,
are obligated to [recite] the Grace [together].	חַיָּבִין לְזַמֵּן.
One who ate *doubtfully tithed food,*	אֲבָל דְּמַאי,
or [one who ate] from *first tithe*	וּמַעֲשֵׂר רִאשׁוֹן
with the elevation *offering removed,*	שֶׁנִּטְּלָה תְרוּמָתוֹ,

or from the *second tithe*,	וּמַעֲשֵׂר שֵׁנִי
or from a *dedication* which was redeemed,	וְהַקְדֵּשׁ שֶׁנִּפְדּוּ,
or an attendant who ate an olive's [volume],	וְהַשַּׁמָּשׁ שֶׁאָכַל כְּזַיִת,
or a Samaritan,	וְהַכּוּתִי,
—they may say Grace with them.	מְזַמְּנִין עֲלֵיהֶם.
(But) one who ate *untithed* food,	<אֲבָל> אָכַל טֶבֶל,
or from *first tithe* from which	וּמַעֲשֵׂר רִאשׁוֹן
the *elevation offering* was not removed,	שֶׁלֹּא נִטְּלָה תְרוּמָתוֹ,
or from *second tithe*,	וּמַעֲשֵׂר שֵׁנִי
or from a *dedication* which was not redeemed	וְהַקְדֵּשׁ שֶׁלֹּא נִפְדּוּ,
or an attendant	וְהַשַּׁמָּשׁ
who ate less than an olive's [volume]	שֶׁאָכַל פָּחוֹת מִכְּזַיִת,
or a gentile*	וְהַנָּכְרִי,
—they may not say Grace with them.	אֵין מְזַמְּנִין עֲלֵיהֶם.
2) Women and slaves and minors	נָשִׁים וַעֲבָדִים וּקְטַנִּים,
may not say Grace on behalf of them.	אֵין מְזַמְּנִין עֲלֵיהֶם.

* Some MSS have עוֹבֵד כּוֹכָבִים, 'idolater' or literally 'a worshipper of the stars' which is a replacement by the censors.

Comments: This ruling defines who was eligible for leading Grace after Meals on behalf of others, and was therefore among those counted for the sake of deciding the form of the Grace. If there were fewer than three, no leader was needed, and if there were ten or more, a different formula was used (see 7.3 below). The first half lists people who might not be considered worthy, but who nevertheless could lead the Grace, and the second half lists those who could not.

The ruling about women, slaves, and minors has probably been added later. The whole of 7.1-2 is regarded as a single mishnah in the Babylonian Talmud, but these two rulings are separated elsewhere.[36] There is some confusion in rabbinic traditions about whether or not women are eligible for leading the Grace. We saw above that m.Ber.3.3 is ambiguous about whether or not women may lead the Grace. This mishnah (7.2) implies that they may not lead Grace, though an early *baraytah* states: "A woman may recite the *benediction* on behalf of her husband, a son may recite the *benediction* on behalf of his father, a slave may recite the *benediction* on behalf of his master" (t.Ber.5.17).[37] A solution was proposed by Joshua b. Levi [PA1] who said

---

[36] They are considered separately in the Jerusalem Talmud, and the Tosefta records 7.2 but not 7.1. They are divided in the editions of the Mishnah.

[37] In b.Ber.20b the same saying occurs (though the order of the units is 'a son,' 'a slave,' and 'a woman') with the addition: "But the Sages said: A curse light on the man whose wife or children have to say grace for him." In y.Ber.3.3 V the same saying (though in the order found in Tosefta) is found with the addition in the Babylonian Talmud (which is commented on later in the discussion). This is one of the instances where a lost source or sources must be inferred. Both Talmuds cite the addition of the Sages, but this is not present in either Tosefta nor

that women were not eligible to be one of the three, but they could be one of the ten (b.Ber.47b). It is likely that women, slaves, and minors were originally able to lead the Grace within the home, but this changed. The change may have been prompted by the fact that slaves were not regarded as religiously competent after 70 CE (see m.Ber.3.3). However, it is unlikely that a woman or minor was ever allowed to say the Grace at a public gathering.

Dating (9): The only reason for dating this before 70 CE is the reference to 'a *dedication*' (*heqdesh*, הֶקְדֵּשׁ). This refers, in Mishnah, to the specific practice of donating items to the Temple (see Dating in the Introduction). However, the phrase "*second tithe* or *dedication* which is (not) redeemed" occurs frequently in Mishnah, so this reference to a *dedication* may simply be present as an archaic component of a common phrase. The early date is strengthened by the next tradition (see below).

New Testament: The first three categories in the above ruling (gentiles, women, and slaves) are found in the well-known *benedictions* in the traditional Jewish prayer book just before the morning *Shema*, "Blessed are you Lord our God, King of the universe, who has not made me a gentile. Blessed . . . who has not made me a slave. Blessed . . . who has not made me a woman." This is very similar to a triple blessing attributed to Socrates: "He used to say there are three blessings for which he was grateful to Fortune: first that I was born a human being and not one of the brutes; next that I was born a man and not a woman; thirdly a Greek and not a barbarian."[38] This sentiment and this group of three was presumably behind Paul's affirmation that in Christ there is no inferiority for gentiles, women, or slaves (Gal.3.28). It is also significant that Paul says immediately after this that those in Christ are no longer children (Gal.4.1-7), which is the fourth category named in this mishnah as incapable of leading public worship. See also the comments re women at m.Ber.3.3.

m.Ber.7.3: Calling for the Grace before different numbers of eaters

How should one [invite] to say Grace?	כֵּיצַד מְזַמְּנִין.
When [there are] three, he says: Let us bless.	בִּשְׁלֹשָׁה, אוֹמֵר, נְבָרֵךְ.
When [there are] three in addition to himself	בִּשְׁלֹשָׁה וְהוּא,
he says: May you bless.	אוֹמֵר, בָּרְכוּ.
When ten, he says: Let us bless our God.	בַּעֲשָׂרָה, אוֹמֵר, נְבָרֵךְ לֵאלֹהֵינוּ.
When ten in addition to himself,	בַּעֲשָׂרָה וְהוּא,
he says: May you [bless God].	אוֹמֵר, בָּרְכוּ.
The same for ten or for ten thousand.	אֶחָד עֲשָׂרָה, וְאֶחָד עֲשָׂרָה רִבּוֹא.

Mishnah, and the Babylonian Talmud cannot be citing the Jerusalem Talmud because the order of units is different in both.

[38] *Diogenes Laertius* 184.1.33. This third century CE work cites Hermippus *Lives* from the third century BCE.

When a hundred, he says:	בְּמֵאָה, אוֹמֵר,
Let us bless the Lord, our God.	נְבָרֵךְ לה' אֱלֹהֵינוּ.
When a hundred in addition to himself	בְּמֵאָה וְהוּא,
he says: May you bless [the Lord, our God].	אוֹמֵר, בָּרְכוּ.
When a thousand, he says: Let us bless	בְּאֶלֶף, אוֹמֵר נְבָרֵךְ
the Lord our God, the God of Israel.	לה' אֱלֹהֵינוּ אֱלֹהֵי יִשְׂרָאֵל.
When a thousand in addition to himself	בְּאֶלֶף וְהוּא,
he says: "May you bless . . ."	אוֹמֵר, בָּרְכוּ.
When ten thousand, he says: Let us bless	בְּרִבּוֹא, אוֹמֵר, נְבָרֵךְ
the Lord God, God of Israel,	לה' אֱלֹהֵינוּ אֱלֹהֵי יִשְׂרָאֵל
God of Hosts,	אֱלֹהֵי הַצְּבָאוֹת
who sits [above] the Cherubim	יוֹשֵׁב הַכְּרוּבִים
for the meal which we have eaten.	עַל הַמָּזוֹן שֶׁאָכַלְנוּ.
When ten thousand in addition to himself	בְּרִבּוֹא וְהוּא,
he says: "May you bless . . ."	אוֹמֵר, בָּרְכוּ.
According to the formula with which he blessed,	כְּעִנְיָן שֶׁהוּא מְבָרֵךְ,
so is the formula with which they follow:	כָּךְ עוֹנִין אַחֲרָיו,
Blessed is the Lord God,	בָּרוּךְ ה' אֱלֹהֵינוּ
God of Israel, God of Hosts	אֱלֹהֵי יִשְׂרָאֵל אֱלֹהֵי הַצְּבָאוֹת
who sits [above] the Cherubim	יוֹשֵׁב הַכְּרוּבִים
for the meal which we have eaten.	עַל הַמָּזוֹן שֶׁאָכַלְנוּ.

Comments: When the time for Grace after Meals came, an eligible person would lead the others by saying the start of the first *benediction*, and the others would respond by starting the *benediction* in the form which the leader invited. The *benediction* was very simple for a gathering of three: The leader said "Let us bless" and they all responded "Blessed be [he] for the food we have eaten." If there were four eligible people, so that the leader was not necessary to make up the numbers, the leader would say "May *you* bless . . ." and (by implication) he might not respond with the others.

The opening formula grew progressively grander for larger groups, though in the middle of this long ruling a contrary opinion is expressed: "The same for ten or for ten thousand." It appears that not everyone agreed with the gradual additions to the formulae for 100, 1,000, or 10,000 eaters. It seems that the formulae for numbers above ten were a later addition which some rejected.

Heinemann suggested that the concept of congregations of ten may have originated with the Qumran sect, where members were arranged into units of 10, 50, 100 etc. (cf. 1QS 2.21-22; 6.3-7; *CD* 13.1-2).[39] However, it is equally likely that Qumran was influenced by practices which were already common in pre-70 rabbinic Judaism. These, and other complex rules for mealtimes, can probably be traced to the

---

[39] Heinemann, *Prayer*, p. 117.

Ḥaberim, who were probably the forerunners of rabbinic groups (cf. m.Dem.2.3 and below on m.Ber.8.1-8).

Dating (5): The internal controversy which is preserved within this ruling caused some consternation in later discussion, because a contrary opinion like this should normally be attributed to a named authority. R. Joseph [BA3] solved the problem by saying that the contrary opinion belonged to R. Akiba [T3], and the different blessings for numbers beyond 10 were proposed by R. Jose the Galilean [T3] (b.Ber.50a). This conclusion is based on a dispute between these two, on this topic, which follows immediately after. This solution is possible, but unlikely. It is more likely that the contrary opinion, which would normally have been omitted from the end of the tradition, was preserved because it was in the middle, and it was therefore difficult to remove from an already traditional form. Therefore, this anonymous contrary opinion is an indication that the tradition was already well established by the time of Akiba's debate.[40] The first part of the ruling (up to this contrary opinion) is therefore likely to be pre-70, but the rest is less likely to be so.

New Testament: The different blessings for different sizes of gatherings may explain the reason why the Gospels are particularly interested in the number of people who sat down to eat the miraculous loaves and fishes with Jesus (Mt.14.13-21; 15.32-38 and parallels). Mark 6.40 even says that they were sat down in groups of 50 and 100 and Luke 9.14 says that this was a specific instruction of Jesus, so it was presumably done to facilitate the counting. Part of the reason for giving the numbers was, no doubt, that 4,000 and 5,000 were impressive, but it would have been more impressive to give total numbers, and not just the number of men. Matthew specifically says on both occasions that the women and children were not counted (14.21; 15.38), which suggests that they were counting the number of eligible people for the saying of Grace, in order to decide on the form of the blessing.

It is not necessary to conclude that Jesus was especially concerned about the exact form of the Grace. It is likely that people at a public meal were already in the habit of sitting in groups of ten men or in larger numbered groups. Not only would this facilitate counting for the Grace, but it would mean that each group could decide for itself when it had finished the meal and say Grace together, if someone in that group had to leave before the whole gathering had finished.

It may be significant that the Synoptics say that "they all ate and were satisfied" (Mk.6.42 // Mt.14.20 // Lk.9.17), alluding to Deut.8.10, "you shall eat and be satisfied and bless the Lord your God," which was a proof text of Judah b. Illai [T4] for the practice of saying Grace after Meals (b.Ber.21a; 48b).

---

[40] Cf. the discussion in Heinemann, *Prayer,* p. 115.

m.Ber.7.5b: Blessing for the final cup of wine

One should not **bless the wine**
until one adds water into it
—the words of R. Eliezer [b. Hyrcanus, T2].
But the Sages say:
One should bless [before the water is added].

אֵין מְבָרְכִין עַל הַיַּין,
עַד שֶׁיִּתֵּן לְתוֹכוֹ מַיִם,
דִּבְרֵי רַבִּי אֱלִיעֶזֶר.
וַחֲכָמִים אוֹמְרִים,
מְבָרְכִין.

Comments: Eliezer's ruling applies to any blessing over wine, whether it is during a meal or at the Grace after Meals. However, the rest of this mishnah (m.Ber.7.5a) concerns the Grace after Meals, so the Talmudic discussion is concerned mainly with wine for this Grace. The Grace after Meals is said over a cup of wine which is called "the cup of blessing" (kos shel barukah, כוס של ברכה).[41] This cup became the central feature of the Grace. Many traditions have grown up around this cup, and they are summarized in a tradition which appears to date from some time before 200 CE and after 100 CE.[42]

> R. Zera [I PA3] said in the name of R. Abbahu [PA3]—according to others, it was taught in a baraytah: Ten things have been said in connection with the cup of blessing. It requires to be rinsed [inside] and washed [outside], it must be undiluted and full, it requires crowning and wrapping, it must be taken up with both hands and placed in the right hand, it must be raised a handbreadth from the ground, and he who says the blessing must fix his eyes on it. Some add that he must send it round to the members of his household. R. Johanan [PA2] said: We only know of four: rinsing, washing, undiluted and full. A Tanna taught: Rinsing refers to the inside, washing to the outside. (b.Ber.51a)

When Eliezer spoke about adding water, he probably referred to the final process in the production of wine, which was the diluting of the grape juice into a drinkable concentration. He was not talking about further diluting the drink in order to extend it.[43] The Babylonian Talmud has a slightly longer version of this mishnaic tradition, though it presents it as an anonymous baraytah to which was added 'so R. Eliezer':

> Our Rabbis taught: If wine has not yet been mixed with water, we do not say over it the blessing 'Who creates the fruit of the vine,' but 'Who creates the fruit of the tree,'

---

[41] Not in Mishnah, but it is cited in Talmud by Abaye [BA4] as if it is a timeless tradition to say: "bring a cup of blessing to say Grace" (b.Pes.107a), and by Joshua b. Levi [PA1] (b.Sot.38b).

[42] It is commented on by an anonymous Tanna. This suggests that it was already an accepted tradition by the time the Tannaim came to an end in about 220 CE. It appears to presuppose the ruling of m.Ber.7.5 that the blessing is said while the wine is undiluted, so it dates from the time of Eliezer or later.

[43] According to Raba (BA4, early fourth century) wine had to be diluted with three parts water, and wine production had probably changed little since the first century. This concentration was presumably to make the wine easier to transport.

and it can be used for washing the hands. Once water has been mixed with it, we say over it the blessing 'Who creates the fruit of the vine,' and it may not be used for washing the hands. (b.Ber.50b)

This indicates that before the water was added it should be regarded essentially as strong grape juice, which was not considered to be drinkable though it could be used like any other liquid for pouring over hands. After the process of making wine was complete, by the final addition of a suitable amount of water, the blessing for wine, rather than grape juice, could be said over it.

Dating (5): Eliezer's ruling assumes the blessing for a cup of wine already existed, and the context suggests that he was referring to the final cup of the meal, but this is not actually stated. The earliest datable reference to the phrase "cup of blessing" is in the NT (see below), and the earliest rabbinic reference is the *baraytah* cited above. There are several other references in Talmud, but all Amoraic.

New Testament: The "cup of blessing" which was prepared for the Grace after Meals was presumably in Paul's mind when he referred to "the cup of blessing which we bless" (1Cor.10.16), which he also called "the cup after supper" (1Cor.11.25). In Christian communities this universal Jewish ceremony had taken on a new meaning, ever since Jesus changed the course of a Passover meal on the last evening with his disciples. It appears that Christians celebrated the Lord's Supper at the end of communal meals (cf. Acts 2.42, 46; 1Cor.11.20-29). The Lord's Supper was celebrated with the 'cup of blessing'—i.e., a modification of the Grace after Meals which ended a normal Jewish communal meal.

This was natural for early Christians because they assumed that Jesus used this cup during the Passover meal. At a Passover meal there were four named cups, the third of which was accompanied by the Grace after Meals, so that this was the cup of blessing. The Gospel accounts are not clear about which one Jesus used for instituting the Lord's Supper, but there is a hint that it was not the final cup because he said: "I will not drink again from the fruit of the vine" (Mk.14.25 // Mt.26.29 // Lk.22.18). This saying is not explained and comes after the cup of the Lord's Supper in Mark and Matthew, though in Luke, which has the unusual sequence of cup-bread-cup (Lk.22.17-20), it comes after the first of his two cups for the Lord's Supper. It is likely that Jesus used the third of the four Passover cups, and then said that this would end the meal—hence the strong statement that he would not drink again.

The confusion in Luke's account may be due to confusion over which of the four cups is the 'cup of blessing'. Luke knew the tradition that Jesus used the third Passover cup but he also knew that the cup of blessing was the final cup at most meals, so he probably assumed that it was also the last cup of the Passover meal. Therefore he thought that Jesus used both the third cup and "also the cup after supper" (Lk.22.20).

m.Ber.8.1-8: School rulings concerning meals

Summary of Mishnah: A collection of school disputes about meals, not all of which concern blessings. Most of them concern the order in which blessings occur, and matters of *purity*.

The following traditions have elements (marked in bold) for which there is evidence of an origin before 70 CE:

m.Ber.8.1: Order of blessing for the day and for the wine

The School of Shammai says:	בית שמאי אומרים,
One should say the blessing over the day	מברך על היום
and after that say the blessing over the wine.	ואחר כך מברך על היין.
But the School of Hillel says:	ובית הלל אומרים,
One should say the blessing over the wine	מברך על היין
and after that say the blessing over the day.	ואחר כך מברך על היום.

Comments: When the meal took place on a Sabbath or a *holyday*, a special blessing for the day was said at the end of the meal. The Shammaites said this before the blessing for the wine and the Hillelites after.

This and the following disputes concerning blessings and other religious matters at mealtimes suggest that Hillelites and Shammaites often ate in groups, but rarely together. Nevertheless, their religious observances at these meals were remarkably similar, because these disputes concern very minor details, usually based on the order in which they did things. The agreement extends to the number and subject of the various blessings and cleansing activities, as well as their general order.

Perhaps the wording of some of these blessings was also established, although it is likely that the wording was not yet fixed. Extempore embellishments were encouraged for the Eighteen Benedictions at this time (see 4.4 above), and it is likely that no prayers were fully fixed at this time, which may explain why there are no disputes about precise wording of prayers.

Dating (1): There is no reason to believe that this dispute has been changed by later generations. The difference is stated simply, and no justification is given for the Hillelites, whose opinion prevailed. This dispute is the first of a series which spans m.Ber.8.1-8, and which starts and ends with a dispute about wine. Originally these disputes may have existed in two or more smaller groups which were then collected and put in the present order. Three of the disputes at the beginning and the last (8.1, 2, 4, 8) have the form 'they do this and after that they do the other.' The other disputes have been inserted in their chronological or logical order. The only ruling which is clearly out of order is the last. Although this last one was in a logical position when it was part of the smaller group (because they dealt with the order of events for blessing the wine, and this last one deals with differences caused by a small quantity of wine), it is out of order when the other disputes were inserted which involved rites which followed after the wine was blessed. This implies that they wanted to preserve the inclusio effect of leaving one of the original sayings at the end.

m.Ber.8.2-4: Hand washing and related matters during meals

The School of Shammai says:	בית שמאי אומרים,
One should wash the hands	נוטלין לידים,
and after that pour the cup.	ואחר כך מוזגין את הכוס.
But the School of Hillel says:	ובית הלל אומרים,
One should pour the cup	מוזגין את הכוס
and after that wash the hands.	ואחר כך נוטלין לידים.
3) The School of Shammai says:	בית שמאי אומרים,
He wipes his hands on a napkin	מקנח ידיו במפה
and rests it on the table.	ומניחה על השולחן.
But the School of Hillel says:	ובית הלל אומרים,
[He rests it] on the cushion.	על הכסת.
4) The School of Shammai says:	בית שמאי אומרים,
One should sweep the house	מכבדין את הבית
and after that wash the hands.	ואחר כך נוטלין לידים.
But the School of Hillel says:	ובית הלל אומרים,
One should wash the hands	נוטלין לידים
and after that sweep the house.	ואחר כך מכבדין את הבית.

Comments: Washing hands was a law of the rabbis, not of Torah,[44] but it appears to be deeply ingrained into the religious observance of all Jews in the first century. The disagreements concern very minor points and they show that both groups agreed on several matters: they expected the leader of Grace to wash his hands and dry them on a napkin,[45] and they wiped all the crumbs off the table at this time. The order for Shammaites was wipe, wash, wine, and for the Hillelites it was wine, wash, wipe.[46]

---

[44] See, e.g., b.Hul.106a: "R. Idi b. Abin said in the name of R. Isaac b. Ashian: The washing of the hands for common food was ordained only in order to acquire the habit with regard to *terumah*; moreover, it is a meritorious act. . . . [For it was taught:] It is written: And whomsoever he that hath the issue toucheth, without having rinsed his hands in water [Lev.15.11]. Herein, said R. Eleazar b. 'Arach, the Sages found a biblical support for the law of washing the hands. . . . For it is written: 'Without having rinsed his hands in water.' Can this mean that if he had rinsed his hands, [whatsoever he touched] would be clean? Surely he requires immersion, does he not? The meaning must be: And any other person that has not rinsed his hands is unclean." This does not mean that Lev.15.11 is a scriptural basis for handwashing, but only that it gives scriptural support.

[45] *Mapah*, מפה, which Jastrow relates to the Latin *mappa*, is of Punic origin.

[46] It is also possible to argue from this passage that there were two hand washings.

The Shammaites could place the napkin on the table because all the food had already been cleared away, so it would not be contaminated by a wet napkin. Hands were also washed by everyone before the meal, and it is unlikely that Shammaites put the napkin from this previous handwashing on the table.

The crumbs were important because they may have included the *elevation offerings* from *doubtfully tithed food,* which might not have been tithed properly. One hundredth of such food would be separated by eaters on their plate, and then crumpled so that no one would accidentally eat it. A pious householder would burn them to make sure that they were not accidentally eaten by a nonpriest. For details, see the tractate *Demay.*

The literal phrase 'mix the cup'[47] should probably be understood simply as 'pour' or 'prepare the cup.' There were continuing disputes about whether one adds the water before or after the blessing, and even whether this cup is undiluted.[48]

Dating (1): There is no reason to believe that this tradition has been altered by later authorities. In fact later authorities favored the Shammaite opinion in the third ruling, and yet there is no hint of this in the tradition as we have it.

It is likely that the order of these disputes was determined by a Hillelite. As pointed out above, the collection of 8.1-8 is a smaller collection (8.1, 2, 4, 8), with others inserted in a chronological or logical order. If a Shammaite had decided the order, he would have placed the ruling about the napkin (8.3) after the ruling about wiping the table (8.4), because this preceded handwashing.

New Testament: Jesus regarded hand washing as a non-Scriptural innovation (Mt.15.2-3; Mk.7.1-8; Lk.11.38). These passages suggest that his disagreement with the Pharisees on this matter concerned not so much the fact that they did something which was not commanded in Scripture, but that they criticized others for not following their rules.

m.Ber.8.5: Blessings for the lamp and for the spices

The School of Shammai says:	בית שמאי אומרים,
[The order of *bendictions* is:] *Lamp* and *Food*	נר ומזון
and *Spices* and *Habdalah*.	ובשמים והבדלה.
But the School of Hillel says:	ובית הלל אומרים,
[The order of *bendictions* is:] *Lamp* and *Spices*	נר ובשמים
and *Food* and *Habdalah*.	ומזון והבדלה.
The School of Shammai says:	בית שמאי אומרים,
"Who created the light of fire."	שברא מאור האש.
But the School of Hillel says:	ובית הלל אומרים,

---

[47] *mazag,* מזג, 'to mix.'
[48] See b.Ber.51a, cited at 7.5b above.

"Creator of the light of fire." בורא מאורי האש.

Comments: As well as the Grace after Meals giving thanks for the *Food*, there are three extra prayers at the end of a meal on a Sabbath: for the *Lamp*, for the *Spices*, and the *Habdalah*. The *Lamp* is thanksgiving for light, which is lit with the first making of fire after the Sabbath; *Spices* is thanksgiving for the expensive condiments, which are only on the table on a Sabbath;[49] and the *Habdalah* (or 'separation') was a thanksgiving for the difference of the Sabbath over normal days. Both schools agreed that these three extra *benedictions* were said, but disagreed about the order. According to this tradition, the Shammaites inserted Grace after Meals between *Lamp* and *Spices* whereas the Hillelites kept *Lamp* and *Spices* together. According to t.Ber.5.30 (Z 5.31) they both kept them together before Grace, but the Hillelites said *Spices, Lamp* and the Shammaites said *Lamp, Spices*.

The important thing which they all agreed about was that *Habdalah* should be separated and kept until the end. This is perhaps because it was celebrated with an extra cup of wine, which had to be separate from the cup of wine for the Grace (see m.Ber.8.8 below).

The disagreement about the wording for the *benediction* for the *Lamp* might suggest that the wording of the others was fixed and agreed. However, the blessing for the light was also said at the schoolhouse (see t.Ber.5.30 below), where both Hillelites and Shammaites would hear each other say their different blessings, and so the difference in this wording was important and obvious.

Dating (1): There is no reason to doubt that this dispute is recorded accurately. However, the following ruling in 8.6 looks like a later addition. It is not a school dispute, and it does not share the form of those disputes. It was added there because it concerned the blessing for the light. The ruling which immediately follows this (m.Ber.8.6: "They may not bless the light or spices of idolaters . . . of the dead . . . or of idols, nor bless the light until one can use it") was added at a later, indeterminable date.

m.Ber.8.7: If you forget to say Grace after Meals

He who ate and forgot and did not bless:	מי שאכל ושכח ולא ברך,
The School of Shammai says:	בית שמאי אומרים,
He must return to his place and he must bless.	יחזור למקומו ויברך.
But the School of Hillel says:	ובית הלל אומרים,
He must bless in the place where he remembered.	יברך במקום שנזכר.

Comments: If the Grace is forgotten after a meal, you may say it later, though the Shammaites said you had to return to the table.

---

[49] These came to be regarded as an amelioration for the sadness that the Sabbath will soon end.

Dating (1): There is no reason to believe that later authorities have changed this dispute. The ruling which immediately follows this ("How long may he delay blessing? Until the food in his stomach has been digested.") was added later, at an uncertain date.

m.Ber.8.8: The blessing for only one cup of wine

[If] Wine comes to them after the meal	בא להם יין לאחר המזון
and there is not [enough] there	ואין שם
except for the one cup:	אלא אותו הכוס,
The School of Shammai says:	בית שמאי אומרים,
[He says] blessings over the wine	מברך על היין
and after that, blessings over the meal.	ואחר כך מברך על המזון.
But the School of Hillel says:	ובית הלל אומרים,
[He says] blessings over the meal	מברך על המזון
and after that, blessings over the wine.	ואחר כך מברך על היין.
One should respond 'Amen' after	עונין אמן אחר
a Jew [says] the blessing,	ישראל המברך.
but one should not respond 'Amen' after	ואין עונין אמן אחר
a Samaritan [says] the blessing,	הכותי המברך,
until one hears the whole blessing.	עד שישמע כל הברכה.

Comments: What if there is not enough wine for the extra cup of wine after the meal? If one drinks the wine with the meal, both schools agree that one must give thanks for it, because there will not be a thanksgiving for wine after the meal (cf. m.Ber.6.5). The schools disagree only about whether the thanksgiving for the wine comes before or after the thanksgiving for the meal.

It is possible that the Hillelite ruling could mean that one saves the wine until after the meal, and then gives thanks for it, as suggested by a passage in Tosefta:

t.Ber.5.30b (Z 5.32): The blessing for only one cup of wine

And if he has only one cup	ואם אין לו אלא כוס אחד
he leaves it until after the meal	מניחו לאחר המזון
and links together all [the blessings]	ומשלשלן כולן
after [the meal].*	אחריו

*Z reads לאחריו ואומר, i.e., 'until after he has spoken.'

However, this passage concerns the *Habdalah* on a Sabbath, which would not be regarded as optional.

Dating (1): There is no reason to doubt that this was a genuine school dispute, and the most straightforward reading implies that the special cup of wine with the final blessing was optional. The version in t.Ber.5.30 ruling implies that a separate cup of wine was needed, at least for the *Habdalah*. Although the earliest reference to a separate and special cup of wine after the meal dates from the third century (y.Ber.5.2 IV), it is already spoken of as a very well established tradition. It is therefore likely that the special extra cup became compulsory either in the late first century or early second century.

The end of this section ("They respond 'Amen' . . .") was added later at an indeterminable time which was perhaps the same time as 8.6 and the end of 8.7. It is included here because of the NT parallels (see below).

New Testament: Paul warned the Corinthians that an outsider may not be sure about saying 'Amen' to a prayer of thanksgiving if it was spoken in tongues (1Cor.14.16). The ruling here, that one may not say 'Amen' to the prayer of a Samaritan without hearing the whole of it, suggests the same kind of caution. The 'outsider' (ἰδιώτου) would probably be a Jew, especially if Paul expected them to say 'Amen,' and he would be as suspicious of Christians as he would be of Samaritans. He would want to hear the whole prayer and understand it before he committed himself to agreeing with it, even if it was portrayed as a "prayer of thanksgiving." The "prayer of thanksgiving" may be the central prayer of the Grace after Meals, which is one of the few communal prayers which start "I thank you."[50] Although it is true that a 'prayer of thanksgiving' (εὐχαριστία) is used in the New Testament for general thanksgiving in worship (e.g., Phil.4.6; Col.4.2), it is also used specifically for the prayer of thanksgiving for food (1Tim.4.3-4), and much early Christian worship took place in the context of a meal.

t.Ber.5.29 (Z 5.30): Blessing for the final cup of wine and the oil

The School of Shammai says:	בית שמאי אומרים
He holds the cup of wine in his right hand*1	אוחז כוס יין בימינו
and the perfumed oil in his left hand.*1	ושמן ערב בשמאלו
He blesses over the wine*2	מברך על היין
and after that blesses over the oil.*2	ואחר כך מברך על השמן
But the School of Hillel says:	ובית הלל אומרים
He holds the perfumed oil in his right hand*2	אוחז שמן ערב בימינו
and the cup of wine in his left hand.*2 *3	וכוס יין בשמאלו
He blesses over the oil	מברך על השמן
and smears it on the head of the attendant.	וטחו בראש השמש
If the attendant was a disciple of the Sages	אם היה שמש תלמיד חכם
he wipes it on the wall	טחו בכותל

---

[50] In the Dead Sea *Hodayot* the communal prayers begin "Blessed . . ." and the private prayers begin "I thank you. . . ." But the central prayer of the Grace is a communal prayer which begins "I thank you . . . ," as seen in Jub.22.7 and continued right up to modern Jewish prayer books. See on m.Ber.6.8.

for it is not commendable	לְפִי שֶׁאֵין שֶׁבַח
for a disciple of the Sages	תַּלְמִיד חָכָם
to go about perfumed.	שֶׁיֵּצֵא מְבוּסָם

*1 Z swaps over 'right' and 'left' as also in Babli.
*2 Z swaps over 'wine' and 'oil' as also in Babli.
*3 Z adds "He blessed over the wine and turned and."

Comments: The oil referred to here may be the oil which was sent around after a meal for cleaning hands, or it may be the oil which was used for perfuming a room.[51]

The dispute underlying this tradition appears to be yet another dispute about the order of doing things, though this has become corrupted (see Dating, below). The original dispute presumably said that Shammaites blessed the oil and then the wine, and the Hillelites reversed this. This is the same order as the differences in m.Ber.8.5, so it is possible that there was originally just one blessing for oil and spices. Many spices were used for both flavorings and perfume.

The leader appears to put oil in his hand, although he does not want to anoint himself with it, and smears it on something when he has blessed it. He does not smear it on one of his guests, probably because they are all disciples, and yet he does not want to waste it so he smears it on a servant (unless he is also a disciple) or on the wall to perfume the room. This suggests that they are already applying the principle that one cannot bless something without using it (as seen in m.Ber.8.6, "They do not bless over the lamp until one makes use of the light").

In later times, when there were blessings for almost every occurrence of life (see on t.Ber.5.30c below), the blessing for spices or for perfumed oils was said whenever one smelled them for the first time during any one day (b.Ber.53a).

Dating (1): Lieberman's text (as given here) appears to be defective, because the order "wine and after that oil" is stated for the Shammaites, but the reverse is not given for the Hillelites. Zuckermandel's edition and the Babylonian Talmud fills this gap in an inexpert way, making both sides follow the same order, but instead of using the standard 'and after that' (וְאַחַר כָּךְ) they use 'and turned' (וְחָזַר). It might be theorized that the original text had the last words missing: ". . . he blesses over the oil and after [that he blessed over the wine]." Without the missing words in square brackets, this does not make sense, and so one tradition attempted to say what he did with the oil *after* blessing it (represented by the MSS behind Lieberman's text) and another attempted to supply the missing reference to *wine* (represented by the MSS behind Zuckermandel's text).[52] If this explanation is correct, then the Lieberman-type

---

[51] Both types of oil are referred to in the Babylonian Talmud, at b.Ber.43b and 43a, respectively.

[52] The actual MSS behind these readings are laid out clearly in Lieberman's edition, but not in Zuckermandel's edition. The number of MSS is extremely small and the large number of

text is older, because it has removed the word 'after,' which is necessary to prompt the expansion, but which is superfluous in the finished version. If the Zuckermandel-type text had been earlier, it would have retained the word 'after' and would probably have gotten the wine and oil of the Hillelites in the correct order, instead of making their order the same as the Shammaites.

All this confusion, due to a corrupt original text, suggests that the original dispute was already well established, and that the ending had been lost long before.

New Testament: This tradition shows that it was normal practice to perfume someone by putting perfumed oil on their head, though this practice was disdained by the rabbis. Luke records that Jesus contrasted the woman who anointed his feet with his Pharisaic host who "did not anoint my head" (Lk.7.46). It is possible that the Pharisee would have regarded this as something unworthy of a scholar, but Jesus reminded him that to offer it was part of natural hospitality, as was a kiss and foot washing.

m.Ber.9.1-5: Other blessings

Summary of Mishnah: You should give a blessing of thanks for all kinds of things, good and bad, whenever you come across them after a period of absence (9.1-2, 5). Some specific examples are given, as well as prayers when entering and leaving towns (9.3-4). Prayers to change things which have already happened are vain prayers (9.3). You should act respectfully on the Temple Mount, and not use it as a shortcut (9.4). Blessings in the Temple (9.4).

The following traditions have elements (marked in bold) for which there is evidence of an origin before 70 CE:

t.Ber.5.30c (Z 5.33): Blessings in the schoolhouse

In the School of *Midrash*	בבית המדרש
The School of Shammai says:	בית שמיי אומרים
One blesses for all.	אחד מברך לכולן
And the School of Hillel says:	ובית הלל אומרים
Each one blesses for himself.	כל אחד ואחד מברך לעצמו

Comments: Several blessings are listed in m.Ber.9.1-3 which are for new events or experiences, such as visiting a holy site, seeing a comet or the ocean, or completing a new house or hearing some news. You only bless once, not constantly, so you bless

---

missing MSS makes it impossible to construct families of MSS or infer dependencies between them.

God for rain when it starts after an interval, not every day. You bless God for bad news and bad events as well as good, because God is the true Judge. All of these blessings are undateable or post-70, but this text from Tosefta shows that the principle was already in place before 70 CE.

The Tosefta does not state what the blessing is for, which may mean that there was only one blessing to which it could apply, or it may be a general rule for all such blessings. Probably the former was true to start with, when the blessing for light from a lamp was the only such blessing, but in later times it was assumed to apply to all such blessings. In the Babylonian Talmud, a *baraytah* at b.Ber.53a has the same ruling (though in reverse) but after "In the School of Midrash" it adds "and light was brought before them" (והביאו אור לפניהם). This makes it clear that the ruling refers to the lighting of a lamp after the end of Sabbath. This lamp was different because, as it says in another *baraytah*, it was lit "after a rest"—i.e., after an interval when no light could be lit (b.Ber.52b).

The principle that you should thank God for the good and the bad probably stems from the use of Isaiah 45.7 ("I form light and create darkness") in the first blessing before the morning *Shema* (see b.Ber.11b). Although the first authority to which this can be attached is R. Oshaia [PA1], it may have been a very early tradition.

Dating (1): There is no reason to believe that this dispute is the product of later authorities. This is the only dateable example of a blessing for a new thing after an absence, apart from those which were parts of set prayers, such as the blessing for the lamp at the meal ending the Sabbath. These blessings grew in number until they were prescribed for almost every event and activity. In Amoraic times there were many more blessings, including blessings for entering and leaving a toilet which, according to Abaye [mid fourth century] blesses God who "has formed man in wisdom and created in him many orifices and many cavities."

The post-70 date of most of these blessings is probably indicated by their opening formula, "Blessed be. . . ." In the Dead Sea Scrolls, the *Hodayot* show that the general rule was to use "Blessed be . . ." for public thanks, and "I thank . . ." for private thanks. The blessing for the new light starts with "Blessed be . . . ," even though it is an early prayer, because it was originally a communal prayer.

New Testament: The Pauline injunction to 'give thanks in all circumstances' (e.g., 1Thes.5.18; Eph.5.20; Phil.4.10-11) is the same principle which underlies the blessing of God for every new thing, good or bad.

m.Ber.9.5b: Disrespectful behavior on the Temple Mount

A man must not act with levity[53]	לא יקל אדם את ראשו
opposite the East Gate	כנגד שער המזרח,
which is precisely opposite	שהוא מכוון כנגד
the Holy of Holies.	בית קדשי הקדשים.
One must not enter the Temple Mount	לא יכנס להר הבית,
with his walking stick or with his shoes	במקלו ובמנעלו
or with his money-bag	ובפונדתו
or with dust which is on his feet.	ובאבק שעל רגליו.
And one must not make a shortcut.	ולא יעשנו קפנדריא.
Or spit, from *major and minor*.	ורקיקה, מקל וחומר.

Comments: The East Gate entered straight into the Temple Mount—the large flat area which surrounded the Temple and occupied a large portion of West Jerusalem. If you were approaching Jerusalem from the west, the quickest route into the city was across the Temple Mount, which this ruling tries to discourage. It says, in effect, if you go onto the Temple Mount, you should be going there to worship. If you have a walking stick or shoes (as opposed to sandals[54]) and a money bag, this indicates that you are going on a journey. The walking stick of a disabled person was also excluded because the lame were not allowed in the Temple (Lev.21.18).

The ruling about 'dust on the feet' probably indicates that pious worshippers washed their feet before coming to worship. The ruling about a money bag would not prevent someone purchasing a sacrifice in the Temple, but would prevent someone carrying a traveling bag with a large amount of money into the Temple.

The argument from *major and minor* (*Qal vaHomer*) was a common exegetical technique before 70 CE and after. It argues from a major or accepted truth to a minor or derivative one. The argument in this case would be: If it is necessary to be respectful on the Temple Mount in all these different ways, then surely it is improper to spit. However, it is not obvious why someone would want to derive this ruling rather than any other act of disrespectful behavior. Perhaps it is based on an actual case which required a ruling.

Dating (9): The dating of this tradition is very uncertain. Although it speaks about matters which would be irrelevant after 70 CE, the rabbis continued to debate such things in order to be prepared for building a new Temple, or as an act of piety in place of carrying out the Temple rites. Some of the details discussed here might sit well in a pious discussion of the Temple, but it is not possible to say that they were invented with the synagogue in mind, because later rabbis found more differences than similarities with behavior in a synagogue (b.Ber.62b). In particular, the prohibition of

---

[53] Lit., 'A man should not lighten his head'. See the similar phrase in m.Ned.2.1.

[54] מנעול is *foot-covering*, or *shoe*, in contradistinction to *sole*. Neusner translates it *overshoes*.

walking sticks makes no sense in a synagogue, because there was no restriction about letting the lame into a synagogue. Therefore it is likely that at least the core of this tradition dates to before 70 CE. The last line, about spitting, has probably been added on, at an indeterminable date.

New Testament: The same sensibilities which inspired this ruling are found in a heightened degree in Jesus when he threw the traders out of the Temple (Mt.21.12-13; Mk.11.15-17; Lk.19.45; Jn.2.14-17). Sanders doubts that sheep and cattle were on sale there but agrees that birds probably were,[55] though the Gospels all place this event at Passover time, when Jerusalem was full of pilgrims wanting to purchase lambs, and so normal practices may not have applied at this time. Mark records that Jesus "would not allow any one to carry any vessel through the Temple," which may relate to the ruling about using the Temple Mount as a shortcut.

m.Ber.9.5c: Blessings in the Temple and God's name in greetings

[At] the end of all blessings	כל חותמי ברכות
which were in the Sanctuary,	שהיו במקדש,
they used to say, "From the age" [i.e., 'Forever'].	היו אומרים מן העולם.
The Heretics were ruining this and said:	משקלקלו המינין, ואמרו
"There is no age [i.e., world] but [this] one."	אין עולם אלא אחד,
They *decreed* that they say [from henceforth]	התקינו שיהו אומרים,
"From the age and to the age"	מן העולם ועד העולם.
[i.e., 'Forever and ever'].	
And they *decreed* that when a man	והתקינו שיהא אדם
greets his associate	שואל את שלום חברו
[he does so] in [God's] Name.	בשם

Comments: This explains why the phrase "forever" was changed to "forever and ever" in Temple prayers. It also mentions that normal greetings used to contain the name of God.

We do not know how 'forever' was used in the Temple. It is fairly certain that individual *benedictions* ended with 'Amen,' and perhaps the *benedictions* in the Temple ended with 'Forever, Amen,' or perhaps the priests said 'Forever' and the people responded 'Amen,' or perhaps this was only at the end of the final priestly blessing of Peace. According to a *baraytah*, 'forever' was part of the people's response instead of 'Amen':

> It was taught: They did not respond 'Amen' in the Temple. What did they respond? "Blessed be the name of his glorious kingdom forever." (y.Ber.9.5 VI)

---

[55] Sanders, *Judaism: Practice,* pp. 87-90. He cites Philo who spoke about the quiet Temple Mount, on which animals were not allowed *(Spec.*I.74-75).

The heretics *(minim)* are presumably the Sadducees who did not believe in an afterlife, so they interpreted 'from the age' to mean '*only* this age.' The Pharisees replaced this phrase which the Sadducees could not say without referring to the next age. It may be that the response ". . . for ever and ever" started as a vocal rebellion by the people during Temple prayers which were led by Sadducees.

The greeting 'in the name' refers to a greeting such as "YHWH bless you" in Ruth 2.4, according to a later comment which occurs immediately after this in Mishnah.

Both of these rulings are described as '*decreed*'—i.e., they were enacted as a *taqqanah*, a rabbinical *decree* for which there is no biblical prescription.

Dating (9): Although there is no corroboration of the dating of this tradition, and the origin is clearly post-70 (because it speaks about the Temple in the past), it is likely to represent the wording of prayers in the Temple, because it is reflected in the NT (see below). However, the real reason for the repetition of 'the age' may have been lost and this story was invented to supply it.

New Testament: The curious phrases "from the age" or "from the age and to the age" are reproduced almost precisely in Greek Jewish works (including the New Testament) as "to the ages" (εἰς τοὺς αἰῶνας) or "to the ages of the ages" (εἰς τοὺς αἰῶνας τῶν αἰώνων), both of which occur regularly with 'Amen' following (e.g., Rom.1.25; Gal.1.5 and Mt.6.13 in some editions).

The Eighteen Benedictions

Prayers were not written down during Talmudic times, apart from a few exerpts and short prayers from well after 70 CE. It was traditionally assumed that there was some kind of taboo or proscription preventing this, but the discovery of written prayers at Qumran shows that this was not true, at least for some Jews. Probably the feeling that prayers should not be fixed (see 4.4 above), or perhaps that prayers should be learned from your own teacher (cf. Lk.11.1), made people reluctant to commit them to writing.

Various prayers can be argued to originate before 70 CE,[56] but we do not have the words of any in rabbinic literature, except perhaps the prayer of the High Priest on the Day of Atonement (m.Yom.3.8; 4.2; 6.2). However, it may be possible that a surviving version of the Eighteen can be dated back to Temple times. The Cairo Genizah, which preserves documents from as early as the ninth century, contains one fragment of the Eighteen which has extremely early features, and it is possible that it preserves some wording from before 70 CE.

---

[56] Heinemann listed these, with extensive reasons, in *Prayer*, pp. 124-55.

The modern Jewish prayer books have developed mainly from the Babylonian traditions with some elements from the Palestinian traditions. The Sephadic rite (which is used by Jews from Spain and Portugal) is the closest to the Babylonian rite as described by Amram Gaon,[57] and the Ashkenazi rite (used in Germanic- and English-speaking countries) and old French rite (now disused) are slight developments of this. The Roman rite from Italy and Romanian rite from the Balkans are related to the Palestinian tradition as preserved best in the Genizah texts.[58] Although these prayer books undoubtedly contain early material, only minor elements can be dated before 70 CE.

Although we have no records of synagogue liturgy from the first century, this should not make us conclude that there was none. It is significant that the liturgy at Qumran has some similarities to that which is later known from synagogue liturgies, comprising the *Shema* and the Decalogue (in Qumran *tefillin*), prayers containing *benedictions* (4Q503, 4Q408), confessions, supplications (Words of the Luminaries), and songs of praise (*Hodayot*, songs of 4Q334, David song in 11QPsA).[59] This is similar to the synagogue service (Psalms, *Shema*, Eighteen Benedictions, and Supplications).

Early Christians were probably the cause of the most significant change to the recital of the *Shema* in the first century. Rabbinic sources tell us that the Decalogue used to precede the recitation of the *Shema*, and it is found alongside the biblical texts of the *Shema* at Qumran, but it was removed at some point. We do not know when this was, but Mishnah notes the inclusion of the Decalogue without any comment, and it is only in the Talmud that they feel the need to explain that this is not done any more,[60] so perhaps it happened sometime in the third century. Such a momentous change must have taken a long time to debate, decide, and implement, and so the cause would have started much earlier. Rab Judah (BA2, end third century) blamed "the insinuations of the heretics (*minim*)". We do not know what the heretics said, but we can guess. When Paul and other Jewish Christians recited their prayers, they had a problem when they came to the *Shema* verse of Numbers 15:40: "remember and do all my commandments", because this implied that all 613 commandments which were

---

[57] The earliest prayer book which we have is that of Amram Gaon from the mid tenth century, though different MSS have much variation, and it is often difficult to know what is the earliest reading. The three most important MSS with their translations are found in Hedegård's *Seder R. Amram Gaon.*

[58] See Elbogen, *Jewish Liturgy,* pp. 9-10. For an updated account see Stefan C. Reif, *Judaism and Hebrew Prayer: New Perspectives on Jewish Liturgical History* (Cambridge: Cambridge University Press, 1995).

[59] Daniel K. Falk, "Qumran Prayer Texts and the Temple," in D. K. Fralk et al., eds., *Sapiential, Liturgical and Poetical Texts from Qumran* (Leiden: Brill, 2000), pp. 106-26, esp. p. 120.

[60] See m.Tam.5.1; b.Ber.12a; y.Ber.1.8, 3c. The Nash Papyrus (second century BCE), which was probably a liturgical text, contains the Decalogue followed by the *Shema*.

found in the Old Testament had to be obeyed. However, the fact that the Ten Commandments preceded the *Shema* meant that Christians could give them a special status and relegate the ceremonial, food and purity laws to a secondary status, as having been fulfilled by Christ. Regular Jews wanted to emphasize that *all* the laws had to be obeyed equally, and they could not recite all 613, so they removed the 10 Commandments from the recitation.

The Eighteen Benedictions in the Palestinian (Genizah) version

A genizah is a repository of documents which are no longer needed, but which cannot be thrown away because they contain the name of God. Normally such repositories are emptied periodically, and the contents are buried, often in the context of a burial service. The Genizah of the Ben Ezra Synagogue in Cairo was larger than most, and documents accumulated for several hundred years until Solomon Schechter gained permission to take documents away for study. This collection, most of which is in Cambridge University Library, consisted of about 210,000 documents dating back to the tenth century.[61] Schechter soon discovered some texts which looked very similar to the modern prayer of the *Amidah* (the Eighteen Benedictions) but with very significant differences. It is now generally agreed that Genizah texts represent Palestinian prayer traditions, which were also followed in Egypt.

One text which Schechter published had extremely early features.[62] It is the most well known of the Genizah fragments of the Eighteen, and is generally known as *the* Genizah version of the Eighteen, though actually there are many other Genizah fragments which do not preserve these early features. It was translated by Heinemann,[63] but the English version accidentally omitted two very important lines about the Temple at Jerusalem, and so although it was generally acknowledged as old, the pre-70 date of this text was overlooked. In the following, words in bold are those which are shared with the Babylonian version, as represented by Amram, and reconstructed from various sources by Finkelstein.[64] *Benedictions* are numbered slightly differently in the Babylonian (B) and Palestinian (P) versions.

P1 = B1
Blessed are you Lord   ברוך אתה יי

---

[61] For the background and introduction to these texts see Stefan C. Reif, *A Jewish Archive from Old Cairo: A History of the Cambridge University's Genizah Collection* (Richmond: Curzon, 2000).

[62] T-S K27.33b in Cambridge University Library published in "Geniza Specimens," *Jewish Quarterly Review* OS 10 (1898): 654-59.

[63] Heinemann, *Prayer*, pp. 26-27.

[64] Louis Finkelstein, "Development of the Amidah," *Jewish Quarterly Review* 16 (1903): 1-43, 127-70.

our God and God of our fathers;
God of Abraham
God of Isaac and God of Jacob;
The great God, powerful and revered;
Exalted God, creator of heaven and earth;
Our shield, and shield of our fathers;
Our refuge in all generations.
Blessed are you, Lord, shield of Abraham.

אל הינו ואלהי אבותינו
אלהי אברהם
אלהי יצחק ואלהי יעקב
האל הגדול הגבור והנורא
אל עליון קונה שמים וארץ
מגנינו ומגן אבותינו
מבטחינו בכל דור ודור
ברוך אתה יי מגן אברהם

P2 = B2
You are powerful, humbling the proud;
Strong, and judging the violent;
Alive **forever**, raising **the dead**;
Making wind blow and dew fall;
sustaining the living, reviving the **dead.**
Like the fluttering of an eye,
make our **salvation** sprout.
Blessed are you Lord, reviving the dead.

אתה גבור משפיל גאים
חזק ומדין עריצים
חי עולמים מקים מתים
משיב הרוח ומוריד הטל
מכלכל חיים מחיה המתים
כהרף עין
ישועה לנו תצמיח
ברוך אתה יי מחיה המתים

P3 = B3
You are **holy**, and revered is your name,
and there is no God beside you.
Blessed are you Lord, the holy God.

קדוש אתה ונורא שמך
ואין אלוה מבלעדיך
ברוך אתה יי האל הקדוש

P4 = B4
Graciously give us, our Father,
understanding from you,
and discernment and insight from your Torah.
Blessed are you Lord,
gracious giver of understanding.

חנינו אבינו
דיעה מאתך
ובינה והשכל מתורתך
ברוך אתה יי
חונן הדעת

P5 = B5
Cause us to repent, Lord, to you,
and we will **repent.**
Renew our days as at the start.
Blessed are you Lord,[*1]
who desires repentance.

השיבנו יי אליך
ונשובה
חדש ימינו כקדם
ברוך אתה יי
הרוצה בתשובה

P6 = B6
Forgive us our Father,
for we have sinned against you.
Blot out and remove our **transgressions**
from before your eyes,
for your compassion is great.
Blessed are you Lord,
who abundantly forgives.

סלה לנו אבינו
כי חטאנו לך
מחה והעבר פשעינו
מנגד עיניך
כי רבים רחמיך
ברוך אתה יי
המרבה לסלוח

P7 = B7

Look on our affliction and plead our cause,
and redeem us for the sake of your name.
Blessed are you Lord, the redeemer of Israel.

ראה בעניינו וריבה ריבנו
וגאלנו למען שמך
ברוך אתה יי גואל ישראל

P8 = B8

Heal us, Lord our God,
from the pain of our heart and grief,
and remove sighing from us,
and bring healing for our **wounds.**
Blessed are you Lord, who heals*2
the sick of his people Israel.

רפאינו יי אלהינו
ממכאוב לבנו ויגון
ואנחה העבר ממנו
והעלה רפואה למכותינו
ברוך אתה יי רופא
חולי עמו ישראל

P9 = B9

Bless for us, Lord our God,
this year to our benefit,
with all kinds of produce,
and bring near quickly
the final year of our redemption.
Give dew and rain upon the ground,
and satisfy the world
from the storehouses of your **goodness,**
and give a blessing on the work of our hands.
Blessed are you Lord,
who blesses the years.

ברך עלינו יי אלהינו
את השנה הזאת לטובה
בכל מיני תבואתה
וקרב מהרה
שנת קץ גאולתינו
ותן טל ומטר על פני האדמה
ושבע עולם
מאוצרות טובך
ותן ברכה במעשה ידינו
ברוך אתה יי
מברך השנים

P10 = B10

Blow on the great *shophar*
for our freedom,
and lift up a **banner**
for the gathering of our redeemed [exiles].
Blessed are you Lord who gathers
the expelled of the people of Israel.

תקע בשופר גדול
לחירותינו
ושא נם
לקיבוץ גאליותינו
ברוך אתה יי מקבץ
נדחי עמו ישראל

P11 = B11

Restore our judges as in former times,
and our counsellors as in the beginning;
and reign over us—you alone.
Blessed are you Lord, lover of justice.

השיבה שופטנו כבראשונה
ויועצינו כבתחלה
ומלוך עלינו אתה לבדך
ברוך אתה יי אוהב המשפט

P12 = B12

For the apostates let there be no hope,
and may the kingdom of the arrogant
be quickly uprooted in our days;
and may the *natzarim* and *minim*
instantly perish;

למשומדים אל תהי תקוה
ומלכות זדון
מהרה תעקר בימינו
והנצרים והמינים
כרגע יאבדו

may they be blotted from the book of the living,
and may they not be written with the righteous.
Blessed are you Lord,
humbler of the arrogant.

ימחו מספר החיים
ועם צדיקים אל יכתבו
ברוך אתה יי
מכניע זדים

P13 = B13
To the righteous converts
may your compassion be aroused,
and give to us a good reward
with those who do your will.
Blessed are you Lord,
trust of the righteous.

על גירי הצדק
יהמו רחמיך
ותן לנו שכר טוב
עם עושי רצונך
ברוך אתה יי
מבטח לצדיקים

P14 = B14
Have **compassion,** Lord our God,
with your great compassion,
upon Israel your people,
and **upon Jerusalem your city,**
and upon Zion, the dwelling of your honor,
and upon your Temple,*3
and upon your Residence,*3
and upon the royal house of David,
your righteously anointed one.
Blessed are you Lord, God of David
builder of Jerusalem.

רחם יי אלהינו
ברחמיך הרבים
על ישראל עמך
ועל ירושלם עירך
ועל ציון משכן כבודך
ועל היכלך
ועל מעונך
ועל מלכות בית דויד
משיח צדקך
ברוך אתה יי אלהי דויד
בונה ירושלם

P15=B16
Hear, Lord our God,
the voice of our **prayers**
and have compassion upon us;
for you are God of grace and compassion.
Blessed are you Lord, hearer of prayer.

שמע יי אלהינו
בקול תפלתינו
ורחם עלינו
כי אל חנון ורחום אתה
ברוך אתה יי שומע תפלה

P16=B17
May it be your will, Lord our God,
to dwell in **Zion,**
and may your **servants** serve you
in Jerusalem,
Blessed are you Lord,
whom we shall serve in reverence.

רצה יי אלהינו
ושכון בציון
ויעבדוך עבדיך
בירושלם
ברוך אתה יי
שאותך ביראה נעבוד

P17=B18
We give thanks to you,
[for] **you are the Lord our God,**
and God of our fathers,
for all the goodness,

מודים אנחנו לך
אתה הוא יי אלהינו
ואלהי אבותינו
על כל הטובות

the loving-kindness and compassion	החסד והרחמים
which you bestowed on us,	שגמלתנו
and enacted for us	ושעשיתה עמנו
and for our fathers;	ועם אבותינו
and "if we say: our foot slipped" [Ps.94.18]	ואם אמרנו מטה רגלינו
from before you,	מלפנינו
"your loving-kindness, Lord, will hold us up" [Ps.94.18].	חסדך יי יסעדינו
Blessed are you Lord,	ברוך אתה יי
O Good One, thanks is [due] to you.	הטוב לך להודות

P18=B19

Place your peace	שים שלומך
upon Israel your people,	על ישראל עמך
and upon your city,	ועל עירך
and upon your inheritance.	ועל נחלתך
and bless us all as one.	וברכנו כולנו כאחד
Blessed are you Lord, maker of peace.*4	ברוך אתה יי עושה השלום

*1 Schechter omitted אתה which is clearly present in the Genizah MS.
*2 Schechter omitted יי which is clearly present in the Genizah MS.
*3 These crucial lines were omitted from Heinemann's translation, and others copied the mistake.
*4 Schechter accidentally repeated most of P18 in the middle of the last line.

Comments on the Eighteen Benedictions

These Eighteen are called '*benedictions*' because they end with "Blessed. . . ." The first three are doctrinal and could be said to form a statement of faith: God is the shield of the fathers (#1), he is the great resurrection life-giver (#2) and he is holy (#3). The last three are a final thanksgiving and commitment: His servants will do his will (#16) and give thanks (#17) and God gives them peace (#18). The middle ones are petitions: for understanding (#4), repentance (#5), forgiveness (#6), redemption (#7), healing (#8), prosperity (#9), the gathering of Israel (#10), Jewish rulers (#11), against apostates (#12), for converts (#13), and Jerusalem (#14), ending with "hear our prayers" (#15).

The theological emphasis of both the doctrinal statements and petitions are those of the Pharisees. The doctrinal issues concern the fathers of the covenant (#1 which refers to the covenant of Gen.15 with the phrase "shield of Abraham," cf. Gen.15.1), the resurrection of the dead (#2), and the need for purity (#3 which highlights the holiness of God). The petitions emphasize the supremacy of God's will rather than man's will, so that God himself is the source of understanding (#4) and repentance (#5). God's all-sufficiency is emphasized because he can provide forgiveness of sin (#6), protection from enemies (#7), healing of illnesses (#8), and food (#9). The eschatology dates from before the destruction of the Temple, being concerned with the continuing ingathering of Israel (#10), the restoration of Jewish self-rule (#11), and the speedy end to the "kingdom of the arrogant" (the Romans?) (#12). God's love is called on to protect his converts (#13), his city and Temple (#14), and "us" his people (#15).

The Babylonian version is very similar to the Palestinian, though sometimes there are many additional phrases. There are also some changes in emphasis, as well as indications that the Babylonian version dates from after 70 CE (see Dating below).

For example, in #2, the Palestinian version reads "Sustaining the living, reviving the dead," but the Babylonian version expands this to "Sustaining the living with loving-kindness, reviving the dead with great mercy."

Palestinian #2 (Genizah):	**Babylonian #2 (Amram):**
You are powerful,	**You are powerful,**
humbling the proud;	
Strong, and judging the violent;	
Alive **forever**, raising **the dead**;	**forever** Lord, reviving **the dead.**
Making wind blow and dew fall;	You are mighty to save
sustaining the living,	**sustaining the living**
	with loving-kindness,
reviving the **dead.**	**reviving** (the) **dead**
	with great mercy
	supporting the falling, healing the sick,
	and loosening the bound
	and keeping your faithfulness
	to those who sleep in the dust.
	Who is like you, Lord of great things
	and who resembles you, King
Like the fluttering of an eye,	who causes death and life
make our **salvation** sprout.	and makes **salvation** spring forth.
	You are faithful to make the dead live.
Blessed are you Lord,	**Blessed are you Lord,**
reviving the dead.	**reviving the dead.**

The text in bold, which indicates the same Hebrew in both (including text with the same vocabulary but different grammatical form), gives a good indication as to what the original wording of the *benediction* was, before it was developed by both Palestinian and Babylonian communities. Although it is always possible that one or other community removed words as well as adding them, the general trend was to add words. And although it is likely that different versions existed concurrently in both communities, before the wording became fixed, the words in bold nevertheless help to indicate which words were too traditional to be altered.

However, we must always be aware that the wording was flexible, and even the words in bold may not have represented traditions which were universally shared. For example, the Sadducees may not have been happy repeating this *benediction*, because they did not believe in resurrection. However, by just a small change of wording, this benediction could have been said by a Sadducee. Instead of praying *mihayeh ha-metim* (מחיה המתים "reviving the dead") they could pray *mihayeh mimmavet* (מחיה ממות "preserving from death"). Or, they might have said the same words with a different meaning, by interpreting the phrase as "preserving the [almost] dead," because the word for "reviving" can also mean to "preserve alive."

It is even possible that the original meaning of this word "revive" was a reference to preserving life and not to resurrection, because it is the normal use of this word in Scripture[65] including its only occurrence in the Pentateuch (which probably constituted the whole of Scripture for the Sadducees). The Pentateuchal text where 'revive' or 'preserve' is found in one of only two Pentateuchal passages which contains another important word in this benediction: 'sustain' (*kalkal*, כלכל).[66] Therefore it is possible that the original wording of the benediction was based on this passage, where Joseph says:

> God sent me before you to preserve [you] . . . and I will sustain you there, for there are still five years of famine. (Gen.45.5, 11)

This is clearly talking about the sustaining and preserving of the living who are close to death, and not to reviving from death. However, the wording was sufficiently ambiguous to become the basis of a benediction about resurrection from the dead. Therefore it is possible that the proposed Sadducean form was actually the original, and that the Pharisees changed it into the form which has survived.

The wording of #5 is significantly different in the Babylonian version where it gives much less emphasis to the sovereignty of God.

Palestinian #5 (Genizah):	Babylonian #5 (Amram):
Cause us to repent,	**Cause us to return**,
Lord, to you,	our Father, to your Law;
	draw us near, our King, to your service,
and we will **repent**.	and bring us back in perfect **repentance**
Renew our days as at the start.	to your presence.
Blessed are you Lord,	**Blessed are you Lord,**
who desires repentance.	**who desires repentance.**

In the above translation of the Babylonian version, the first occurrence of שוב is translated 'return' rather than 'repent,' as implied by the context of the prayer. The Palestinian version may suggest that God himself causes people to repent, whereas

---

[65] See Gen.45.5; 2Chr.14.13; Ezra 9.8-9; Neh.9.6, but contra Judg.6.5.
[66] Only at Gen.45.11 and 50.12.

the Babylonian version suggests that God draws near those who have chosen to repent (though this is not entirely unambiguous).

The emphasis of #12 appears to have changed even before the Genizah Palestinian version. The final blessing concerns the 'arrogant' or perhaps 'arrogantly sinful' (one who commits *zadon*, זדון, 'deliberate sin'), and the body of both versions relate this to a 'kingdom.' Both the Palestinian and Babylonian versions have inserted a curse on heretics. The Palestinian version refers to the *minim* ('heretics') and *nazarim* (which will be discussed below), and earlier versions may have referred to the *Perushim* (see Dating below) while the Babylonian has retained only the *minim*. The Palestinian version has inserted this curse after the "be quickly uprooted," and Babylonian has inserted it before these same words, which shows that the curse was added after the original *benediction* was already in a fairly fixed form.

Palestinian #12 (Genizah):	Babylonian #12 (Amram):
For the apostates let there be no hope,	**For the apostates let there be no hope, and may minim instantly perish** and all the enemies of your people be cut off
and may the kingdom of the arrogant be quickly uprooted in our days; **and may** *nazarim* and **minim instantly perish;** may they be blotted from the book of the living, and not be written with the righteous.	**and may the kingdom of the arrogant be quickly uprooted** and crushed and humbled **in our days.**
Blessed are you Lord, **humbler of the arrogant.**	**Blessed are you Lord,** breaker of enemies and **humbler of the arrogant.**

The reference to 'Nazarenes' is usually regarded as a reference to Christians, who were occasionally known as the "sect of the Nazarenes" (Acts 24.5), or to the early sect of Jewish Christians known as the Nazarenes. The early Church Fathers felt that it was directed at all Christians.[67]

The *minim* is a general term for 'heretic' in rabbinic literature, and they are not defined in this prayer, though many identities have been proposed.[68] The general consensus is that this referred generally to heretics, or perhaps to Christians because they are linked with the Nazarenes. However, it is possible that the *minim* was a reference to the Sadducees, and that this replaced the word *Perushim*, 'Pharisees,'

---

[67] Tertullian says specifically that 'the Jews call us *Nazareni*' *(Adversus Marcionem* 4.8.1), and Justin Martyr says repeatedly that the Jews curse Christians in the synagogue and speak disparagingly about them after their prayers (Justin Martyr, *Dialogue* 16, 93, 95, 96, 123, 133).
[68] These are summarized well in William Horbury, "The Benediction of the Minim and Early Jewish-Christian Controversy," *Journal of Theological Studies* NS 33 (1982): 19-61.

which was used when the Sadducees were in the ascendancy. Probably both versions continued to be used until 70 CE when the Sadducees virtually disappeared (see Dating below).

The "kingdom of the arrogant" sounds like the perception of the Roman occupation by Jews in the early first century. After this time the rabbis discouraged criticism of the Roman authorities (cf. m.Ab.3.2), and it is difficult to know what other 'kingdom' could be referred to. Later rabbis suggested that it was a reference to Christians. Hai Gaon (eleventh century) and Judah ha-Levi (twelfth century) derived 'apostates' *(meshumadim,* משומדים) from 'baptized' *(meshumad,* משועמד).[69] However, it is hardly likely that the new sect of Christians would have been regarded as a 'kingdom' before the fourth century, despite their claims about being a 'kingdom,' which must have sounded grandiose to most Jews in the early centuries.

The Babylonian version of #13 deemphasizes the importance of converts, and perhaps emphasizes 'trust' instead of 'works' for salvation. These changes took place long after 70 CE, but they are of significance to the debate about early Christian theology of grace and works.

Palestinian #13 (Genizah):	Babylonian #13 (Amram):
	To the righteous and to the pious and
	*toward the elders of the people of the
	*house of Israel and remnant of their scribes,
To the righteous converts	**to the righteous converts**
may your compassion be lavished,	**may your compassion be lavished,**
	Lord our God,
and give to us **a good reward**	**and give a good reward**
with those who do your will.	to all who faithfully trust in your name
	and set our portion with them
	forever, unashamed.
Blessed are you Lord,	**Blessed are you Lord,** support and
trust of the righteous.	**trust of the righteous.**

* Preserved in the rite of *Ez Hayyim* and a few other later rites.

The common wording which is shared by both versions may indicate that the original *benediction* concerned only converts. The Palestinian version adds after "a good reward" the words "and to us who do your will," while the Babylonian adds the "to all who faithfully trust in your name," and the Babylonian also precedes the whole *benediction* with "To the righteous and to the pious and. . . ." The effect of all this is to make God's blessing on converts apply to all Jews.

The two versions may also highlight differences between those who emphasized a reward based on 'doing God's will' and those who emphasized a reward based on

---

[69] Both Hai Gaon and Judah ha-Levi are cited in Horbury, "The Benediction," pp. 45-46.

'faithful trust.' The original *benediction* praised "the trust of the righteous," which is acceptable to both viewpoints. The Palestinian version added a reference to "those who do your will" (*oshé ratzonek*, עושי רצונך) while the Babylonian added, instead, "those who faithfully trust in your name" (*habotehim beamet*, הבוטחים באמת). The Babylonian version also added the word 'support' (*mishan*, משען) to the final *benediction* before "trust of the righteous," as if to explain what his phrase meant.

After #14, the Babylonian version adds a new *benediction* concerning David. The Palestinian version of #14 appears to be a *benediction* for Jerusalem with a *benediction* of David slotted in, while the Babylonian version has a separate *benediction* for David. The Palestinian version assumes that the Temple is still standing, while the Babylonian version assumes it is destroyed. The phrase "builder of Jerusalem" does not necessarily imply that Jerusalem requires rebuilding, as seen by its occurrence in the Hebrew text of Ben Sira 51.12.

Palestinian #14 (Genizah):

Have **compassion**, Lord our God,
with your great compassion,
upon Israel your people,
and **upon Jerusalem your city,**
and upon Zion,
the dwelling of your honor
and upon your Temple,
and upon your Residence,
and upon the royal house of David,
your righteously anointed one.
Blessed are you Lord, God of David
builder of Jerusalem.

Babylonian #14 (Amram):
Upon Jerusalem your city,
return in **compassion**
and build her soon in our days.

**Blessed are you Lord,
builder of Jerusalem.**

Babylonian #15 (Amram):
Cause the offshoot of David to flourish speedily.
Blessed are you Lord,
who causes the horn of salvation to flourish.

The two versions of #P15=B16 are almost identical and are addressed to the "hearer of prayer." Most of the *abstract*s of the Eighteen also end with "Hear our prayers" or something similar. At a later time private petitions could be added into #P15 (b.Ber.1a; b.AZ.8a), though originally, before the prayers were fixed, they could probably be added at any point in the section of petitionary prayers from #4 to #P15.

The last three *benedictions* (#P16–P18 = B17–B19) have very few words in common in the Palestinian and Babylonian versions. This may indicate that these were the most fluid and least fixed of the *benedictions*. The Babylonian versions do not even end with the same final one-line *benedictions*, which are identical or virtually identical in all the others, and the Babylonian version does not even have a final one-line *benediction*. This is probably where the verbose would show off and the hurried or faint-hearted would abbreviate (cf. 4.4 above).

Dating of the Eighteen Benedictions (5)

Traditionally these *benedictions* are said to originate with the "men of the Great Synagogue" (b.Ber.33a) or "120 elders, prophets among them" (b.Meg.17b). Finkelstein[70] attempted to trace the earliest development of the Eighteen using form criticism. Some, like Grant,[71] have embraced this enthusiastically, while others have criticized his simplistic approach and overconfident results.[72] Bickerman,[73] while critical of Finkelstein's methods, nevertheless found some value in his model of a gradually developing prayer which was originally based in the Temple. He argued that the first *benedictions* formed a 'civic prayer' in the model of Greek city-states, and even found a reference to it in 1 Maccabees 12.11 where High Priest Jonathan at about 150–145 BCE told the Spartans that the Jews unremittingly remembered them at festivals and "at other days . . . at the sacrifices which we offer and in prayers." The timing of the Eighteen appears to be linked to Temple sacrifices (see on 4.1 above), and it is possible that they were part of the private prayer service by the priests before starting their duties (m.Tam.5.1).

The origins and original wording of the Eighteen are probably now impossible to reconstruct, though their form goes back before the first century, because some similar ideas and even wording are found in various ancient sources, especially Ben Sira 36.1-17; 51.21-35 (Hebrew) and 2 Maccabees 1.24-29.[74] It is probable that there was no single official version of this prayer because prayers were not fixed, at least in the first century CE (cf. 1.4 and 4.4 above). However, it is also likely that the areas where variation was permitted were carefully limited. The differences between the Palestinian and Babylonian versions should not distract us from the very great similarities, and the identical wording in most of the final lines of each *benediction*. The Comments above suggest that the three doctrinal *benedictions* (#1–3) and many of the individual petitionary *benedictions* (#4–P15/B16) had a relatively fixed form,

---

[70] Finkelstein, "Development of the Amidah."

[71] Frederick C. Grant, "Modern Study of the Jewish Liturgy" [critique of L. Finkelstein, "Development of the Amidah," *Jewish Quarterly Review* 16 (1903): 1-43, 74-77], *Zeitschrift für die Alttestamentliche Wissenschaft* 65 (1953): 59-77.

[72] I. Elbogen, *Jewish Liturgy,* p. 393, Heinemann, *Prayer,* pp. 44-45.

[73] Elias J. Bickerman, "The Civic Prayer for Jerusalem [history of Tefillah]," *Harvard Theological Review* 55 (1962): 163-85.

[74] The parallels with 2Macc:1.24-29 are laid out usefully in Daniel K. Falk, *Daily, Sabbath, and Festival Prayers in the Dead Sea Scrolls* (Leiden: Brill, 1998), pp. 200-201. For other possible Qumran parallels, see 1QH.16.8-20; 1QS.9–11.

though their order and number may have been flexible and the final three were probably the least fixed.

The early Palestinian version, as represented by the Genizah fragments, may contain some wording which originated before 70 CE, while the earliest Babylonian version, as represented by Amram, has many differences, which suggest that it was changed for use by a post-70 community. This does not mean, of course, that the Genizah fragments represent the exact wording of a pre-70 community, but it does indicate that there was a great deal of conservatism in the transmission of this version.

The fixing of the order, number, and possibly the wording of the Eighteen was attributed to Gamaliel II at Yavneh:

b.Ber.28b.f (cf. b.Meg.17b): Composing the benediction for *minim*

Our Rabbis taught: Simeon ha-Pakuli [T2]	תנו רבנן, שמעון הפקולי
arranged the Eighteen Benedictions	הסדיר שמונה עשרה ברכות
before Rn Gamaliel [II, T2], in order,	לפני רבן גמליאל על הסדר
in Yavneh.	ביבנה.
Rn Gamaliel said to them,	אמר להם רבן גמליאל
to the Sages:	לחכמים,
Which man knows how to compose	כלום יש אדם שיודע לתקן
a *benediction* about the *minim*?	ברכת המינים
Samuel the Lesser [T2] arose and composed it.	עמד שמואל הקטן ותקנה,
The next year he forgot it,	לשנה אחרת שכחה.
and he considered it	והשקיף בה
for two or three hours	שתים ושלש שעות
and they did not remove him.	ולא העלווהו.

It is difficult to know when to date this tradition. It is a biographical tradition, which makes dating unsafe, and there are also indications that it has been edited. As it is written, the significance of this tradition is not so much the introduction of the *benediction* of the *minim*, but the fact that Samuel the Lesser was not dismissed from leading the prayers when he forgot the wording. A later tradition (y.Ber.5.4, 9c) says that a prayer leader is dismissed if he makes a mistake in one of the three *benedictions* which test the orthodoxy of the prayer leader. The three testing *benedictions* are #2 (because a Sadducee would have difficulty praying for resurrection), #14 (because a Samaritan would have difficulty blessing Jerusalem) and #12 concerning the *minim*. This tradition explains why Samuel the Lesser was not expelled—because he was the author of the *benediction*. Perhaps this tradition was invented by later rabbis to justify his non-dismissal, or perhaps he really *was* the author of the words of this *benediction*. It is therefore possible that the latter part of this tradition, from "The next year he forgot it . . ." was a later addition.

The words "in Yavneh" and "before the Sages" also appear to have been added later, because they are entirely superfluous to the text and out of place. If they had been in the original version, we would expect 'in Yavneh' immediately after 'Gamaliel'[75] and we would expect 'to the Sages' in place of 'to them.' It therefore is possible that these phrases have been added in order to link the tradition with Gamaliel II, who established the Sanhedrin at Yavneh when he succeeded Johanan b. Zakkai as *nasi* ('prince' or head of the rabbinic movement). Without these additional phrases, the tradition could refer to Gamaliel I who lived in the last generation of the Temple. To date the tradition, we have to look at the other datable elements within it. These are the two other individuals and the curse of the *minim*. Of the two individuals, Simeon ha-Pakuli is impossible to date because he occurs nowhere else, and Samuel the Lesser occurs very infrequently.

Samuel the Lesser is normally dated as T2 (80–120 CE), but the reason for this dating is the tradition which we are examining here. However, he is also attributed with sayings which fit into a pre-70 context, and he was supposed to be a disciple of Hillel (Song.R.8.13[76]); so, we would expect him to be of the T1 generation, the same as Gamaliel I. It is also significant that he and Simeon ha-Pakuli are not called 'Rabbi.' Very few named individuals lack this title after 70 CE, unless they lack rabbinic expertise,[77] and considering that these two have supposedly made

---

[75] This would also mean that 'in order' (על הסדר) would be at the end of the sentence unit, as is normal for this term (cf. m.Yom.5.7; b.RH.34b 2x; b.Yom.32a, 71a 2x, b.Meg.17b, 18a; b.San.49b)— his tradition is the only place in Babli where על הסדר is not at the end of a sentence unit.

[76] "On another occasion when the sages of Israel were taking a vote in the vineyard in Yavneh . . . a Bath Kol went forth and said to them, 'There is among you a man who is fitting to receive the holy spirit, but his generation is not worthy of the privilege,' and they all fixed their eyes on Samuel the Lesser. When he died, they mourned saying, 'Ah, modest, ah, pious soul, worthy disciple of Hillel the Elder!' He also said three things just before his death: Simeon and Ishmael will perish by the sword, and [the rest of] his colleagues will be put to death, and the rest of the people will be despoiled, and great tribulations will come upon the world! and he said this in Aramaic." The 'Simeon and Ishmael' are, according to Rashi on b.Sot.48b, Rabban Simeon the Patriarch and R. Ishmael the High Priest. This is a very uncertain and probably a completely unhistorical account, but it contains avoidable problems which would not be present if this was a complete fabrication. Samuel is supposedly in the Vineyard of Yavneh and yet he is also called a disciple of Hillel, who died in the first century BCE. Also he is attributed with sayings in Aramaic, when post-70 traditions are in Hebrew, and his sayings appear to be warnings of the destruction at 70 CE. His title as 'a worthy disciple of Hillel' may not indicate a direct discipleship, because in the tradition cited just immediately before this, Hillel is called a "worthy disciple of Ezra." However, this does not solve all the problems, which would be easily avoided if someone had constructed this tradition without any preexisting wording. It is likely that this tradition was based on older material, and that the location in the vineyard of Yavneh is a later addition, perhaps influenced by the tradition of the writing of the benediction of the *minim* which was 'in Yavneh' (b.Ber.28b).

[77] Of the forty-two individuals of the second Tannaitic generation which are named in rabbinic literature, all of them have the title 'Rabbi,' except for a few with an honorific title of

authoritative contributions before the Sanhedrin, we would expect them to have the title 'Rabbi.' Before 70 CE, however, Sages did not have this title unless they were also respected priests.[78] Therefore, although the few traditions which are associated with Samuel the Lesser are historically unreliable and contain obvious problems, they do, with this tradition, fit into an overall picture of someone who was active before 70 CE.

The wording of the curse of the *minim* also suggests a pre-70 date. The precise wording of the curse was clearly considered to be significant, because Samuel was almost dismissed for forgetting it. If the wording was not important, he could simply have cursed the *minim* with some other words, but it appears that this would not have been sufficient. The words "instantly perish" do not seem to be especially significant, until we look at the use of the Hebrew words in Scripture. The verb 'perish' (*abad*, אבד) occurs frequently in Scripture, but the word 'instantly' *(keraga,* כרגע) only occurs in two passages, and both of them alongside 'perish.' The context[79] of the first occurrence is the story of Korah and his followers, who wrongly offered incense in their censers before the Lord (Num.16.21, 45 [17.10]), and 'perished' (Num.16.33) as a result. Second, it occurs in Psalm 73 concerning the problem of sinners who are rich and at ease, whom the psalmist concludes will "become desolate instantly" (Ps.73.19) and will "perish" (Ps.73.27). It is probably significant that Samuel the Lesser, who is attributed with authoring this curse, is also attributed with an exegesis on Ecclesiastes 7.15 concerning the apparent prosperity of the wicked (Eccl.R.7.24), and an exegesis of Proverbs 24.17 on God's eventual judgment of the wicked (m.Ab.4.19).

---

familiarity ('Abba' or simply 'Ben'). The only exceptions are Boethus b. Zonin (a lay man who asked the Sages a question in b.Pes.37a; cf. b.BB.13b), Onkelos (a convert who is attributed with editing the Targum), Simeon brother of Azariah, and Nahum of Gimzu. Of these, only Simeon and Nahum made *halakhic* rulings, so that one would expect them to have the title 'Rabbi.' Later commentators were surprised at Simeon's lack of a title, and suggested that Azariah was given the credit because he supported Simeon financially (Lev.R.25.2). Nahum is known for only one ruling which he 'whispered' to Akiba (b.Ber.22a).

[78] Of the forty-six individuals of the first and pre-Tannaitic generations which are named in rabbinic literature, the only individuals which are given the title 'Rabbi' are R. Eleazar b. Harsom, R. Hanina, Chief of the priests, R. Ishmael b. Phabi, R. Johanan (Nehunia) b. Gudgada, R. Simeon of Mizpah, and R. Measha. All of these except one were priests who were either of very high rank or were respected among the Sages, and so it was probably a special title of respect for priests before 70 CE. The only exception, R. Measha, is only known from m.Pea.2.6; he may or may not have been a priest.

[79] The context of an allusion is extremely important in early rabbinic exegesis, as I have shown in my *Techniques*. The context of Scripture allusions in the Eighteen has also been shown to be significant by Reuven Kimelman in "The Daily Amidah and the Rhetoric of Redemption," *Jewish Quarterly Review* 79 (1988/9): 165-97.

Both of these passages would be regarded as damning the Sadducees. Rabbinic traditions and Josephus accused the Sadducees of luxuriating in their wealth,[80] and there must have been a great deal of debate about why God allowed the wicked Sadducees to prosper. The offering of incense by the High Priest was also a very important point of dispute between the Sadducees and Pharisees. The Pharisees said that on the Day of Atonement the incense should be lit only within the Holy of Holies, while the Sadducees said it should be lit before entering the Holy of Holies.[81] This was a huge problem to the Pharisees, because it threatened to invalidate the most important ceremony in the Temple. This suggests that the curse of the *minim*, "may they instantly perish," was a carefully crafted exegetical criticism of the Sadducees, which applied to them specifically when they were in charge of the High Priesthood.[82]

Therefore it seems likely that this tradition about the origin of the curse of the *minim* originally referred to Gamaliel I, before 70 CE. The individuals Simeon and Samuel are both named without the title 'Rabbi', and other traditions of Samuel the Lesser fit better before 70 CE. Also the wording of the curse of the *minim* may suggest a reference to the Sadducees of Temple times. The only reason for dating it later is the presence of the word 'in Yavneh' which, along with 'before the Sages,' appears to have been added later. The reason for attributing it to Gamaliel II instead of Gamaliel I was to give it the force of the Sanhedrin which was convened by Gamaliel II in "the vineyard of Yavneh"[83] with all of its authority, but without the dominance of Sadducees. This gave the new *benediction* greater force than if it was authorized by a single person, even if he was as great as Rn. Gamaliel I.

The reference to Gamaliel II may not be totally fictitious. He is attributed with other teaching on prayers and rites outside the Temple, and it seems that the establishment of liturgy after the destruction of the Temple was a special interest of his. It is therefore reasonable to assume that he was involved in the fixing of the

---

[80] ARNa.5=ARNb.10 "They used vessels all of silver and all of gold all their days, not because they were ostentatious but the Sadducees say: The Pharisees have a tradition that they subject themselves [to austerity] in this world, but in the world to come they will not have anything." Cf. Jos. *Ant.*13.297-98.

[81] t.Kipp.1.8 and parallels. See the discussion in my *Techniques,* pp. 101-4 and J. Z. Lauterbach, "A Significant Controversy between the Sadducees and the Pharisees," *Hebrew Union College Annual* 4 (1927): 173-205.

[82] Judah ha-Levi (twelfth century) said that the Sadducees and Boethusians are 'the *minim* for whose destruction we pray in the Prayer." It might be argued that his opinion was an attempt to avoid the charge that the benediction was anti-Christian. However, it is clear that this was not his motive, because he said that Christians are the 'apostates' (*meshumadim*, מֹשׁומדים) who are mentioned at the start of the benediction: "and as for Jesus and his companions, they are the 'baptized' *(meshumadim)* who joined themselves to the sect of those who perform immersions in the Jordan" (cited in Horbury, "The Benediction," pp. 45-46).

[83] See m.Ket.4.6; b.Ber.63b; b.Yeb.42b, 75a; b.BB131b.

Eighteen, and that he made final decisions on this, perhaps in the context of the Sanhedrin as this tradition implies. In this case, he would have decided on the acceptance of the rulings of Simeon and Samuel, though they would not have appeared before him. From the text as it now stands, it is impossible to know if Samuel did originally deliver his ruling 'before Gamaliel [I]' or whether this too was added to the tradition. Either way, it is most likely that his ruling, and that of Samuel, date from the generation before Gamaliel II who later considered them, as the head of the Sanhedrin at Yavneh, and ratified them as authoritative for all Israel.

The curse of the *minim* was not the only change made to *benediction* #12. As seen in the Comments above, the *benediction* into which this curse was inserted was originally directed against the "kingdom of the arrogant," which was probably a curse against the Romans from the early first century, because after this time the rabbis discouraged unnecessary criticism of Rome. However, it is likely that the original addition to this *benediction* concerned the *Perushim*, not the *minim*. This change, along with other changes about which there is greater confidence, is recorded in a tradition which has survived in two slightly different forms:

t.Ber.3.25: Inserting new benedictions into established ones

One inserts the [*benediction*] concerning *minim*	כולל של מינים
in the one concerning *Perushim* [*benediction* #12],	בשל פרושין
and the one concerning 'proselytes'	ושל גרים
in the one concerning 'elders' [#13],	בשל זקנים
and the one concerning 'David'	ושל דוד
in 'Jerusalem' [#14].	בירושלים
If he recited each of them separately	ואם אמר אלו לעצמן
he has [still] fulfilled his obligation.	ואלו לעצמן יצא.
(anonymous)	

y.Ber.4.3.I, 17a: Inserting new benedictions into established ones

One inserts the [benediction] concerning *minim*	כולל של מינים
in 'humbler of the arrogant' [benediction #12]	במכניע זידים,
and the one concerning 'proselytes'	ושל גרים
and the one concerning 'elders'	ושל זקנים
in 'the trust of the righteous' [#13],	במבטח לצדיקים,
and the one concerning 'David'	ושל דוד
in 'rebuilds Jerusalem' [#14]	בבונה ירושלים.
(cited by R. Eliezer b. R. Jose [T4])	

These traditions record rules about where to insert extra *benedictions*. The aim is probably to make sure that the total number of *benedictions* does not gradually increase. This suggests that the rules date from a time after the number has been fixed at Eighteen, but before the wording of the *benedictions* has been fixed.[84] In one version the *benedictions* are referred to by the main subject, and in the other they are referred to by the wording of the final line.

It is difficult to date either version, though the one in the Jerusalem Talmud is most likely to be earlier because its form is less symmetrical, and memorization tends to make traditions conform more closely to easily remembered structures. The unsymmetrical feature lies in the changes proposed for *benediction* #13, which has two proposed changes, while the *benedictions* #12 and #14 have only one. In Tosefta, each *benediction* has only one proposed change, so it is more symmetrical and easier to memorize. One of the insertions which the Jerusalem Talmud discusses for #13 (the 'elders') is actually the title of *benediction* #13 in the Tosefta version, which either means that this change had already taken place and the insertion had become the title of the *benediction*, or the actual title had disappeared from the tradition as part of the process of becoming more symmetrical and memorable.

The additional words in the Tosefta version ("If he recited each of them separately, he has [still] fulfilled his obligation") suggests that this version predates the fixing of the number at Eighteen, or perhaps it is a reaction against an attempt to fix the number. As a tentative conclusion, it would seem that the Jerusalem Talmud version is earliest, and that the Tosefta version predates the fixing of the number eighteen which (as we saw above) dates probably to the time of Gamaliel II. The same type of sentiment (that prayer should not be fixed) is expressed by R. Eliezer b. Hycanus [T2] at about this time (4.4 above), which tends to confirm this dating. It is not clear whether these additional words are part of the same tradition which forms the list of changes, or whether it was added as a comment to this list. The latter is possible, because this would explain why they are missing from the version in Jerusalem Talmud, but on the other hand, we would expect Eliezer b. R. Jose (who cited this tradition) to omit a ruling which had been supplanted when the number of the *benedictions* became fixed.

Therefore, we may conclude that the Tosefta version of the list of changes dates to the generation of Gamaliel II and Eliezer [T2]. By this time the list had already become simplified so that only one change was proposed for each *benediction*, and perhaps the additional words about reciting them separately had been added. So, the original list probably dated from at least a generation before, from the time of Gamaliel I [T1].

Most of these changes are known to us from various versions of the Eighteen Benedictions. The insertion of the *minim* is discussed above. The insertion of 'David' is discussed in the Comments above, where we saw that the Palestinian version

---

[84] One more benediction was eventually added in Babylon, but the name of the Eighteen was so firmly established that it was not changed when this happened.

inserts a blessing about David into #14, while the Babylonian version adds it as a separate *benediction* #15, which suggests that this ruling was enforced only in Palestine.

The changes proposed to #13 are puzzling, because only a few of the ancient versions contain a reference to the 'Elders,'[85] while the earliest versions of this *benediction* already appear to be already concerned with proselytes. The words of this *benediction* which are shared by both the Palestinian and Babylonian versions are: "To the righteous proselytes may your compassion be lavished, and give [them] a good reward. Blessed are you Lord, trust of the righteous." If this tradition about the insertions is correct, the word 'proselytes' is an addition, so the original *benediction* concerned the rewards of the righteous. This would agree with the fact that the final line (which is generally the most resistant to changes) does not mention 'proselytes.' Therefore it is likely that the word 'proselytes' was not part of the original *benediction*, and that it was probably added some time in the first century.

The other surprise in this tradition is the reference to פרושין which is either *paroshin,* '*separatists,*' or it is *Perushin,* 'Pharisees.'[86] In the Tosefta tradition this is the title of the *benediction* into which they inserted '*minim,*' which is identified as 'humbler of the arrogant' (i.e., #12) in the Jerusalem Talmud tradition. This is surprising because there is no surviving version of the Eighteen which retains the term פרושין, and yet it was important enough at one time to be known as the title of *benediction* #12.

The terms *paroshin* and *Perushin* are related and somewhat inseparable. It is likely that *Perushin* was originally a disparaging title given to the Pharisees by the Sadducees, who accused them of being separatists because of their holiness code which tended to make them avoid contact with people. This title came to be widely used, rather like the title 'Christians' which was originally assigned by outsiders (Acts 11.26). In rabbinic literature the title *Perushim* was used for referring to the early Pharisees, though in later rabbinic literature it was used for separatist or fanatical individuals.[87]

---

[85] Finkelstein, "Development of the Amidah," p. 132, n. 99, finds it, for example, in *Ez Hayyim,* the rite used by English congregations in preexpulsion times. He said that his text was a copy of Leipzig MS XVII which was in the library of the Jewish Theological Seminary of America (Cat. Adler, 4055-57). Elbogen failed to find "elders" in any early texts, though he found it in later rites of the Ashkenaz and Sepharad (*Jewish Liturgy,* pp. 46-47).

[86] Rivkin has analyzed all the occurrences of *Perushim* in rabbinic literature though Cohen and Bowker doubt whether they are the same as the predecessors of the Sages. See Shaye J. D. Cohen, "The Significance of Yavneh: Pharisees, Rabbis, and the End of Jewish Sectarianism," *Hebrew Union College Annual* 55 (1984): 27-53; John Bowker, *Jesus and the Pharisees* (Cambridge: Cambridge University Press, 1973); E. Rivkin, *A Hidden Revolution: The Pharisees' Search for the Kingdom Within* (Nashville: Abingdon, 1978).

[87] The fact that post-70 references to *Perushim* generally have the connotation of 'sectarians' suggests that only those who refused to join the Yavneh movement continued to be called by

The Tosefta tradition implies that the use of *Perushim* in #12 preceded the use of *minim*, which means that it was in use at least as early as the first century. This makes it likely that it referred to the Pharisees, and not to the small separatist groups which retained this title after 70 CE.

It therefore seems possible that the Sadducees originally inserted a reference to the *Perushim* into *benediction* #12 when they had control of the Temple, and that the Pharisees changed this to '*minim*' whenever they said the Eighteen. This explains why it was so important to gather the greatest possible authority behind an official change to '*minim*', in order to finally supplant a slur against the Pharisees in the traditional wording of the Eighteen. Although the original *benediction* against the *minim* was composed in the time of Gamaliel I, it was important to give it the authority of the Sanhedrin, so the tradition was changed to imply that it was done with the authority of Gamaliel II at Yavneh.

There is no mention of *Nazarim* in this record of insertions. This probably means that this insertion postdates this tradition. It is unlikely that the insertion of *Nazarim* predates this list of insertions because the list mentions elements which have already disappeared by the time of the Genizah version—i.e., '*Perushim*' and 'Elders.' I have argued above that this list dates back to at least the last generation of the Second Temple period. *Nazarim* are already named in the Genizah version, the wording of which suggests that it came from a pre-70 context. These factors, taken together, suggest that the curse of the *Nazarim* was added not long before 70 CE. However, this conclusion is based on many uncertainties. The list of changes may have come from a community which did not have a curse of *Nazarim*, and the curse may have been inserted into the Genizah version after 70 CE, despite the conservativeness shown in most of the wording of this version. If both of these were true, the curse of the *Nazirim* may date from after 70 CE, though it is much more likely that it comes from before 70 CE.

The Eighteen Benedictions and the New Testament

It is likely that Jesus himself said the Eighteen three times a day, though he may have said an *abstract*, such as the version which he taught to his disciples (see 4.3 above).

It is possible that Jesus referred to #2 (Resurrection) when he answers the Sadducees concerning resurrection. He said that they knew neither the Scriptures nor the "power of God" (Mt.22.29; Mk.12.27), which may be a reference to the title of this *benediction*, 'The Powers' (see m.RH.4.5) or to the opening words "You are

---

this title. The earliest such reference is by R. Joshua b. Hananiah (c. 80–120 CE) in m.Sot.3.4. See also a later reference to the *Perushim* 'after the Temple was destroyed' in t.Sot.15.11. Pharisees are criticized before 70 CE in the Gospels and in some Qumran texts (e.g., 4QpNah in 4Q169 2.8-10; 4QpPs in 4Q171 2.16-20).

powerful. . . ."[88] The description of the resurrection in #2 "like the fluttering of an eye" or "like the twinkling of an eye" (as in Heinemann's translation) is clearly parallel to Paul's phrase in the same context (1Cor.15.52).

The horticultural metaphor of 'offshoot' and 'flourishing'[89] with regard to salvation in B#15 may have been in Paul's mind when he spoke about Apollos planting and Paul watering, but God causing growth of salvation (1Cor.3.6)

If 'from death' was in the original, or in one of the original forms of this *benediction #2*, it may explain why the Babylonian version includes prayer for healing and rescue: "support the falling, heal the sick, and loose the bound." This is very similar to the list which Jesus presented to John the Baptist (Mt.11.5; Lk.7.22) and cited from Isaiah 61.1 and 58.6 in his sermon at Nazareth (Lk.4.18-19). Although the list is the same, the vocabulary of the *benediction* is not taken from Isaiah, but from the Psalms.[90] The only word from Isaiah which is in this *benediction* is 'bind,' which in Isaiah is 'bind the broken hearted' and in the *benediction* is 'release the bound,' and so the use is completely opposite. This suggests that the sermon at Nazareth has little to do with this *benediction*, but the list given to John may be a conscious reference to this form of the *benediction*. If that is the case, it explains the link of this list with resurrection, and for John, who is in prison, there is a very poignant omission of 'release the bound.' It may also have been an encouragement to John's disciples, to know that their master, who was to die soon, would share in the resurrection.

The dating of this version, and especially of the curse of the *minim*, suggests that there was an organized rejection of Christians within the synagogue which commenced before 70 CE.[91] This does not mean that such rejection was universal or even necessarily widespread. As McCready has pointed out, the early synagogues were not part of a cohesive or united movement which acted in concert.[92] The vast

---

[88] This was suggested by Loewe in *A Rabbinic Anthology* #979.

[89] Both from צמח which is used of growing plants.

[90] Ps.145.14; 103.3; 146.7—as analyzed in Reuven Kimelman, "The Daily Amidah and the Rhetoric of Redemption," *Jewish Quarterly Review* 79 (1988/9): 184.

[91] Steven T. Katz has argued very strongly against this conclusion in "Issues in the Separation of Judaism and Christianity after 70 CE: A Reconsideration," *Journal of Biblical Literature* 103 (1984): 43-76. However, much of his argument is based on silence, that the Mishnah contains no mention of any official ban and that there is no specific mention of the curse of the *Nazarim* by Christian apologists before Epiphanius and Jerome. However he does not take sufficient note of the complaints of Justin Martyr, does not mention *Nazareni* in Tertullian, and rules out New Testament evidence too glibly, saying that Paul's letters from Damascus are unhistorical, while John's Gospel exaggerated the synagogue's reaction and dates from after 70 CE.

[92] Wayne O. McCready, "Johannine Self-Understanding and the Synagogue Episode of John 9," in David J. Hawkin and Tom Robinson, eds., *Self-Definition and Self-Discovery in Early Christianity: A Study in Changing Horizons; Essays in Appreciation of Ben F. Meyer from Former Students*, Studies in the Bible and early Christianity, vol. 26 (Lewiston, N.Y., and Lampeter: E. Mellen Press, 1990), pp. 147-66, esp. 160-62.

majority of surviving manuscripts of the Eighteen lack any reference to the *Nazarim,* and although such references may have been removed, there is no evidence that this has occurred. The evidence of the New Testament and early Church Fathers is also patchy. Although anti-Christian letters from Jewish authorities in Damascus and Jerusalem are mentioned,[93] and Paul met Jewish persecution in some cities, he also managed to preach in many synagogues, and even when he arrived in Rome, the Jews did not appear to be prewarned about his heresy.[94] It would therefore appear that the curse of the *Nazarim* was introduced only in some places and perhaps at different times, unlike the curse of the *minim,* which was promulgated by the highest central authority.

Many scholars have dated John's Gospel at the end of the first century or even later, on the assumption that it reflects the anti-Christian feelings engendered by the curse of the *minim* or the *Nazarim* or both.[95] The Johannine community appeared to experience expulsion from the synagogue (John 9.22; 12.42; 16.2), which is not exactly what we would expect as a result of this curse. Katz has argued that there was no concept of excommunication from Judaism until the third century,[96] and he says that John may reflect the strong feeling that they weren't welcome as a result of this curse. If the 'expulsions' were related to this curse, then we may surmise that John was writing from one of the areas where the curse of the *Nazarim* was introduced, or where they chose to extend the definition of *minim* to Christians. Either of these could have occurred at any time during the latter half of the first century.

Summary and Conclusions

The *Shema* was already established as a recitation twice a day (m.Ber.1.1-3), accompanied by specific blessings (m.Ber.1.4) and readings (m.Ber.1.5). The *Shema* was exempted at a watch for the dead (m.Ber.3.1), and on the evenings of a new marriage (m.Ber.2.5), though this was not compulsory (y.Ber.2.8.I). Women,

---

[93] Letters from Damascus in the story of Paul (Acts 9.1-2; 22.5; 26.12). Justin Martyr says "you selected and sent out from Jerusalem chosen men through all the land to tell that the godless heresy of the Christians had sprung up, and to publish those things which all they who knew us not speak against us" *(Dialogue.*17.1).

[94] Acts 28.21 says the Jews of Rome "have had no communication from Judaea, nor has any countrymen of ours arrived with any report or gossip to your discredit." If there had been any anti-Christian sentiment, Katz points out that Luke would have been the first to note it, as he does throughout Acts.

[95] This was suggested by J. Louis Martyn, *History & Theology in the Fourth Gospel* (New York: Harper & Row, 1968), pp. 15-21 and developed by C. K. Barrett, *The Gospel of John and Judaism,* translated from the German *Johannesevangelium und das Judentum* by D. M. Smith (London: SPCK, 1975), pp. 47-48, 59-76, and is now very widely accepted. This is surveyed well in McCready, "Johannine Self-Understanding," esp. pp. 148-49, 152-57.

[96] "Separation," pp. 48-51.

children, and slaves were exempt from the *Shema* and *tefillin* but not the Eighteen and *mezuzot*.

The Prayer (Amidah) was already called the 'Eighteen' (m.Ber.4.3) which suggests that it already had this number of *benedictions*, though their wording was not fixed (m.Ber.4.4), unlike many of the prayers at Qumran. However, there were rules about where to insert various components (m.Ber.5.2). There were already extra *benedictions* on New Moons and *holydays* (t.Ber.3.13), and the eighteen were shortened to seven on Sabbaths (t.Ber.3.11). It is not clear if the eighteen grew from the seven or the eighteen were shortened to the seven.

Individuals were expected to say the Eighteen three times a day (m.Ber.4.1) or say an *abstract* of them (m.Ber.4.3). The earliest *abstract* (Eliezer's in t.Ber.3.7) is similar in some ways to the Lord's Prayer. In later times, an *abstract* was only permitted if you were in danger or ill. You had to stand to pray, and turn toward the Temple (m.Ber.4.5-6). There were rules about the way in which you should not pray (m.Ber.5.3), which included any language of coercion, such as used by Honi the Circler (m.Taan.3.8). Free-flowing prayer was considered best, as exemplified by Hanina b. Dosa (m.Ber.5.5b).

There are various traditions concerning the development of the Eighteen (especially b.Ber.28b.f; t.Ber.3.25; y.Ber.4.3.I, 17a). Although the wording of this prayer was not fixed before 70 CE, and did not become completely fixed for a few centuries, traditional forms already existed and the subjects and probably the final lines of each *benediction* were already fixed. Gamaliel II fixed the wording of the curse of the *minim* and perhaps fixed the order of the Eighteen, but it is unlikely that he invented a new *benediction*.

A comparison of the earliest **Genizah copy of the Eighteen** (which, it is argued here, contains wording from before 70 CE) with the earliest Babylonian version (which is certainly post-70) gives various insights into the development of the Prayer.

#2 probably referred originally to the power of God to revive the dying rather than raising the dead.

#5 may have had less emphasis on God's sovereignty.

#12 may have referred originally to the sinful Roman occupiers. Later the references to the *Perushim* (i.e., Pharisees) and *minim* (i.e., Sadducees) were added by the Sadducees and Pharisees respectively, both cursing each other. The reference to *Nazarim* (Christians) were added later still, but probably before 70 CE.

#13 probably referred originally to the Righteous, but the Sadducees added "Elders," and the Pharisees changed the emphasis to the "Converts." At a later stage, these converts were regarded in Palestine as "those who do your will" and in Babylon as "all who faithfully trust in your name."

#14 probably started as a prayer for Jerusalem and the Temple. Palestinians added a reference to David, though in Babylon this was a separate *benediction*. Later versions lost the reference to the Temple and prayed for Jerusalem to be rebuilt.

Thanksgiving should be offered for every type of food separately (t.Ber.4.1, citing Ps.24.1) and perhaps for every new thing. A multitude of blessings for non-food items are found in later traditions, but the principle probably dates back to before 70 CE. A blessing for one type of food may include a blessing for other items eaten with it (m.Ber.6.5), so a meal might have only two blessings, for bread (which is eaten with everything) and for wine.

The various events related to this blessing (clearing the table in preparation, hand washing, and the use of the right or left hand) were considered to be very important (m.Ber.8.2-4; t.Ber.5.29). There were also separate blessings for the light at the end of the Sabbath (m.Ber.8.5; t.Ber.5.30c), and for spices (m.Ber.8.5). On a Sabbath there was an additional prayer called the *Habdalah* (m.Ber.8.5) which celebrated the difference between the sacred and the profane, and perhaps another extra blessing (m.Ber.8.1).

Grace after Meals consisted of three blessings (m.Ber.6.8), the wording of which is already hinted at in Jubilees 22.6-9. If there were three or more males eligible to lead Grace, one would lead for the others (m.Ber.7.1-2), and the formula of invitation was different for different numbers of males (m.Ber.7.1-3). If you left without saying Grace, you had to do it when you remembered (m.Ber.8.7).

A few **miscellaneous sayings** at the end of the tractate rule that you may not use the Temple Mount as a shortcut (m.Ber.9.5b), that the phrase "forever and ever" which was used in the Temple was simply "forever" before the heresy of the Sadducees (m.Ber.9.5c), and that people used to say the name of God in normal greetings (m.Ber.9.5c).

Tractate *Peah*: Harvest Leftovers for the Poor

Definitions and Outline

Torah said (Lev.19.9-10; 23.22; Deut.26.12-13) that the poor should be allowed to take any crop which the farmer did not harvest, such as the difficult-to-reach *'corner'* crop of the field (*peah*, פֵּאָה, 'corner'), the *gleanings* which need to be picked up from the ground (*leqet*, לֶקֶט, 'glean' or 'gather') the individual *'separated'* fruit which has fallen off a bunch of grapes (*peret*, פֶּרֶט, 'separate'), *'defective'* bunches of grapes (*olelot*, עוֹלְלוֹת, 'bunches'), and any *'forgotten'* produce which the farmer left unharvested or uncollected (*shikhehah*, שִׁכְחָה, 'forgotten'). This tractate carefully defines these categories. The term *peah* is also used as an inclusive term for all these types of harvest *'leftovers'*[1], and it is sometimes difficult to decide if *peah* should be translated *'corner'* or *'leftovers'*.

The poor could also help themselves to crops which had been declared *ownerless* (*hephqer*, הֶפְקֵר), and to crops which grow wild in the Sabbath Year (*shebiit*, שְׁבִיעִית), and possibly to *fourth year [fruit]* (*rebai*, רְבָעִי) which may not be harvested by the owner.

This tractate also deals with the *'poor tithe'* (*maaser ani*, מַעֲשֵׂר עָנִי). Torah speaks about three tithes—the *first tithe* for the Levites (Lev.27.30), the *second tithe* which is eaten or spent in Jerusalem (Deut.14.22-26), and the *poor tithe* which was collected every third year (Deut.14.28-29; 26.12-13). A seven-year cycle had already been established by 70 CE[2] in which the *second tithe* is suspended during the third and sixth year when the *poor tithe* was given instead,[3] and all tithes are suspended in the seventh Sabbatical Year. The *poor tithe* is given to a poor person (who can also be a Levite). The Levites give a tithe of the *first tithe* to a priest (Num.18.26-28), but the poor do not give a tithe of the *poor tithe* or harvest *leftovers*, though they do tithe all other food.

m.Pea.1.1–4.9: *Corner* crop

Leviticus 19.9-10; 23.22 says that the *corners* of a crop should be left. It does not say what proportion should be left, which types of crop are included, or how one defines

---

[1] The term *'leftovers'* is not normally used in other works. The normal term is *peah*.
[2] Cf. m.Yad.4.3, which is dealt with at the end of this chapter.
[3] Though some sections of Judaism gave three tithes during the third and sixth years—cf. Jub.32.11; Jos. *Ant:*4.240-41; Tob.1.7-8; Tg.Ps.Jon.Deut.26.1-13.

the border of a plot (which determines where the corners are). The original law presumably meant that you should let the poor harvest whatever happened to be left, but the Sages wished to define exactly how much you should leave behind, and where.

m.Pea.4.10–5.6: *Gleanings*

Torah said that the poor could pick up what a farmer happened to drop during harvesting (Lev.19.9-10; 23.22). The Sages defined the time during which this applied. This is followed by a digression on the definition of a poor person.

m.Pea.5.7–7.2: *Forgotten* produce

Torah said that produce which the farmer forgot to harvest was available to the poor (Deut.24.19-21). The Sages defined the point at which the harvest was finished, which meant that any remainder was *forgotten*.

m.Pea.7.3–8.1: Grape harvest

The Torah said that *separated* grapes and *defective* bunches were for the poor (Lev.19.10; Deut.24.21). The Sages defined *separated* grapes as individual grapes, *defective* bunches as those which were not shaped like a bunch, and they added that grapes could be *forgotten* like other crops. A digression notes that those who are not poor may also collect harvest *leftovers*, but only after the poor have finished.

m.Pea.8.2-9: The *poor tithe*

The Sages defined who was 'poor' and how much they should be given. The *poor tithe* was supplemented by daily and weekly provisions for the hungry.

Related texts: m.Yad.4.3 re the *poor tithe* outside Israel

Jews in Ammon and Moab give *poor tithe* to support Israel during the Sabbath Year?

m.Pea.1.1-3: What proportion of a crop is *leftovers*?

Summary of Mishnah: There is no maximum for designating *leftovers*, just as there is no maximum for good deeds or Torah study, of which one enjoys the fruit in this life while storing the capital for the life to come (1.1). The minimum *leftovers* is one-sixtieth of the crop (1.2). Later rabbis [T4] pointed out that the theoretical maximum was the whole crop minus one stalk (1.3).

The following traditions have elements (marked in bold) for which there is evidence of an origin before 70 CE:

m.Pea.1.1: Things which have no measure, and bear fruit in this world

These are things which have no measure:	אֵלּוּ דְבָרִים שֶׁאֵין לָהֶם שִׁעוּר.
Peah [harvest *leftovers* for the poor],	הַפֵּאָה,
and *bikkurim* [*firstfruits*],	וְהַבִּכּוּרִים,
and *appearance* [*offerings*],	וְהָרֵאָיוֹן,
and deeds of charity,	וּגְמִילוּת חֲסָדִים,
and study of Torah.	וְתַלְמוּד תּוֹרָה.
These are things of which a man	אֵלּוּ דְבָרִים שֶׁאָדָם
eats the fruit in this life	אוֹכֵל פֵּרוֹתֵיהֶן בָּעוֹלָם הַזֶּה
and the capital [comes] to him	וְהַקֶּרֶן קַיֶּמֶת לוֹ
for the future life:	לָעוֹלָם הַבָּא.
Honoring a father and mother,	כִּבּוּד אָב וָאֵם,
and acts of loving-kindness	וּגְמִילוּת חֲסָדִים,
and bringing peace	וַהֲבָאַת שָׁלוֹם
between a man and his associate.	בֵּין אָדָם לַחֲבֵרוֹ.
And the study of Torah	וְתַלְמוּד תּוֹרָה
is equivalent to them all.	כְּנֶגֶד כֻּלָּם.

Comments: A 'measure' (*shiur*, שִׁעוּר) is a form of rabbinic fence which was constructed round many biblical commands which were silent about the quantities involved. By adding a measure, a pious person could be sure that they had fulfilled the law. This ruling suggests that *leftovers* originally had no measure associated with them, though, as m.Pea.1.2 indicates, a measure was later added.[4]

The Jerusalem Talmud debates why *elevation offerings* were not listed as something without measure (as stated at m.Ter.1.1). R. Jose concluded that 'measure' here means 'maximum measure,' because *elevation offerings* have a maximum, but others replied that *leftovers* also have a maximum, so this argument does not work (y.Pea.1.1 I). There may be an explanation to this (see Dating, below), but probably the list in this mishnah is not meant to be exhaustive.

The 'appearances' may refer to three times per year that they were required to 'appear' before the Lord (Exod.23.15; cf. m.Hag.1.1), but it is more likely to refer to the *appearance offerings* which they brought with them (Exod.23.15: 'Do not appear before me empty [handed]'—cf. discussion at b.Hag.7a). These offerings were treated like *peace offerings*, which were eaten with friends in Jerusalem. This fits very well with the other two, because this means that the list includes gifts to the poor (*leftovers*), gifts to the priests (*firstfruits*), and gifts which are shared with friends (*appearance offerings*).

Originally the first saying may have lacked its last line, because it is far more startling and effective without it:

---

[4] m.Pea.1.2: "One must not give for *leftovers* less than one-sixtieth, even though they said there is no measure to *leftovers*."

These are things which have no measure: *leftovers, firstfruits, appearance offerings*, and deeds of charity.

It says, in effect: Just as there is no limit to all kinds of legal requirements, so there should be no limit to our charitable giving. It seems likely that, at a later date when Torah study was greatly emphasized, the force of this was diluted by the addition of 'and study of Torah.' The removal of this final line also brings the saying into the normal structure of three plus a fourth (which was popular since the time of Proverbs 30 and Amos 1.11–2.6).

Later rabbis assumed that the 'measure' referred to here was a minimum, because they felt that it contradicted their ruling about a minimum for *leftovers* (defined as one-sixtieth of the crop in m.Pea.1.2). But if 'measure' meant 'minimum,' this would completely destroy the force of the saying. This would make it say, in effect: 'Just as there is no minimum set for various offerings, so also minuscule alms giving is sufficient.' The reason the later rabbis regarded 'measure' as meaning 'minimum' is that they were concerned about whether or not people had fulfilled the requirements of the law. In earlier days, some people kept the *halakhah* of the Sages, and some did not. Those who did so kept it out of piety, and there was no need to define lower limits—they had the opposite problem of defining upper limits to curb their enthusiasm. In later days, after 70 CE, when the Sages ruled Israel as the only religious authorities of any note, it is likely that more people attempted to keep the *halakhah* of the Sages and wanted to know the minimum requirements of the law, so the Sages had to make rulings on them.

The second saying has a similar final line, but it is much more likely that this was part of the original saying, because it is the fourth line after a set of three, and it is the startlingly different one which makes the listener take note. It is obvious that the first three result in heavenly rewards. The command to honor father and mother was associated with a promise of long life (Exod.20.12). Loving-kindness is specifically linked with a reward in Hosea, which also says that loving-kindness replaces sacrifices (Hos.10.12; 6.6) which was very important in the generation following 70 CE.[5] The rewards of peace might be regarded as commonplace, which needed no

---

[5] See the exegesis of Hos.6.6 in ARNa.4: "Once as Rn. Johannan b. Zakkai was coming forth from Jerusalem, R. Joshua followed after him and beheld the Temple in ruins. 'Woe unto us!' R. Joshua cried, 'That this, the place where the iniquities of Israel were atoned for, is laid waste!' Rn. Johanan b. Zakkai said to him, 'My son, be not grieved; we have another atonement as effective as this. And what is it? It is acts of loving-kindness, as it is said, *For I desire mercy, and not sacrifice* (Hos.6.6).'" The saying is attributed to R. Johanan b. Zakkai [T1] by R. Joshua [T2]. The attribution is probably for polemic reasons and is unlikely to be accurate, and so it should be dated to R. Joshua who wished to discourage the coming war by those who wanted to rebuild the Temple—see Jacob Neusner, *Development of a Legend: Studies on the Traditions concerning Yohanan Ben Zakkai*, Studia post-biblica, no. 16 (Leiden: E.J. Brill, 1970), pp. 113-14.

justification, though there may be a reference here to the rather antithetical text at Judges 4.17.[6]

The point of this saying is not that these things are rewarded in the future life, because all obedience of the commandments was assumed to do that. The point is that these commands result in 'fruit' in this life. The term 'fruit' can also mean 'interest' which is gained on capital, and so this is the interest on the capital being amassed in heaven. This list is not meant to be exhaustive, and later rabbis found other examples.[7] The force of the final line is in the final phrase 'equivalent to them all' which suggests that the reward for studying Torah is as great as all these added together.

Dating (8): The first saying can be dated to before 70 CE, except perhaps for the last line. The reference to '*appearance offerings*' suggests a context before 70 CE. This early date is confirmed by the contradiction with 1.2 which is acknowledged there ("though they said there is no measure to *leftovers*"). The casual acceptance of this contradiction suggests that this saying was already traditional and established.

At the earliest stages, neither *leftovers* nor *elevation offerings* had measures—both tractates open with this statement, and then go on to define a minimum (m.Pea.1.2; m.Ter.4.3). This change is acknowledged in *Peah* (at m.Pea.1.2) but it is ignored in *Terumot*. It is possible that the measure was added to the law of *Terumot* before it was added to *Peah*, and this saying originated from that time, so that *leftovers* is listed as unmeasured but *elevation offerings* are not.

The whole of the second saying is likely to originate after 70 CE, and it is included here mainly because the concept of 'capital in heaven' and 'fruit' in this life are found in the Gospels. The special nature of the commandment to love one's father and mother was already recognized in NT times (cf. Eph.6.2), but the teaching on loving-kindness and peace fits much better into the post-70 context, especially if they were derived from the texts suggested above.

The principle of 'treasure in heaven' is illustrated by a story in t.Pea.4.18 about Monobaz, king of Adiabene in the early first century, which says that he gave away all his riches during a famine. It quotes him as saying, "My ancestors stored up

---

[6] Judg.4.17: 'Sisera fled . . . to the tent of Jael . . . for there was peace between (שלום בין) Jabin the king of Hazor and between the house of Heber (חבר).' The reference to "peace between a man and his associate (חבר)" may be a play on words with Heber. This might be part of an exegesis which told those who wanted to revolt and rebuild the Temple that one can sometimes conquer by using peace. However, this is complete supposition, because we have no record of any exegesis like this.

[7] b.Shab.127a: 'R. Judah b. Shila said in R. Assi's name in R. Johanan's name [PA2]: There are six things, the fruit of which man eats in this world, while the principal remains for him for the world to come, viz.: Hospitality to wayfarers, visiting the sick, meditation in prayer, early attendance at the Beth Hamidrash, rearing one's sons to the study of the Torah, and judging one's neighbor in the scale of merit.'

treasures for this lower [world] but I have stored up treasures for [the world] above ... where [human] hand cannot reach." While the words of Monobaz cannot, of course, be regarded as genuine, this probably does relate to a historical incident concerning Helena, the wife of Monabaz. She was a convert to Judaism, and happened to be in Jerusalem during the famine in 47/48 CE. She and her son, who was now king and who was also a convert, spent considerable sums on famine relief.[8]

The principle of honoring father and mother is illustrated by a series of stories in the Jerusalem Talmud about Dama ben Natina, who is presumably pre-70 because the stories are attributed to Eliezer [b. Hyrcanus, T2]. The stories tell about the extreme honor he showed to his parents, by picking up a slipper for his mother after she had hit him with it, and by never sitting on the stone on which his father used to sit, and by refusing to wake his father even to make a sale worth 1,000 *dinars* (y.Pea.1.1.VIII). Although the stories are attributed to Eliezer, it is not safe to assume they originated with him. They are cited by Abbahu [BA3] in the name of Johanan [PA2], and so they are third hand, and their non-*halakhic* and ethical content means that they would be treated less rigorously than legal traditions. They are the type of story which is liable to be invented, or at least exaggerated, in the course of a sermon, without anyone being worried about their accuracy. Nevertheless, they are illustrative of the importance which was given to the commandment of honoring father and mother.

New Testament: Both sayings have clear parallels with the NT, but they also have points of contrast, because they use the same kind of ideas as the NT though in a completely different way.

The message of the first saying (without the final line) is that there should be no limit to deeds of loving-kindness. Loving-kindness is compared with a few commandments which are stated without measures in the Torah. The fact that these are highlighted makes the implied contrast with the fact that most commandments are known for being measured and proscriptive, whereas love should be free and should flow without measure. The NT makes a similar point about deeds of love and compassion, though it tends to say that these supplant the OT rites. Matthew has Jesus twice criticizing legalism by citing Hosea 6.6—"I desire mercy, not sacrifice" (Mt.9.13; 12.7)—and both Jesus and Paul say that love summarizes and perhaps replaces all the commandments (Mt.22.36-40 // Mk.12.28-31; Jn.13.34; Rom.13.9).

The second saying's concept of amassing treasure in heaven is at the heart of Jesus' teaching, and the sentiments attributed to Monobaz (see Dating) are very similar to Jesus' teaching about treasure in heaven which cannot be stolen (Mt.6.19-21 // Lk.12.33-34; Mt.19.21 // Mk.10.21 // Lk.18.22; cf. Tob.4.9).

---

[8] Jos.*Ant*.20.2.5, 309. See the analysis in Lester L. Grabbe, *Judaism from Cyrus to Hadrian* (Minneapolis: Fortress Press, 1992), vol. 2, p. 439.

However, Jesus' concept of 'fruit' is somewhat different from that in early rabbinic sources, where it is a reward during this life. In Jesus' teaching, the fruit is the repentance of a believer and perhaps a moral lifestyle by which he is judged (Mt.7.17-20 // Lk.6.43-44; cf. also the parables of the sower and the fruitless fig tree) which comes from the 'treasure in his heart' (Lk.6.45). John the Baptist has a similar emphasis (Mt.3.8 // Lk.3.9). In the epistles, 'fruit' is the moral improvement of a believer (Rom.6.22; Gal.5.22; Eph.5.9; Jas.3.18).

The concept of benefitting from the fruit of righteousness in this life is probably what Jesus criticizes in Mt.6.1-2: "Beware of doing your righteousness before men, in order to be seen by them . . . as the hypocrites do . . . that they may be praised by men. Amen, I tell you that they have received their reward."

The importance of the command to honor your father and mother is reemphasized by Jesus (Mt.15.4-6) though he also said that following him was more important than burying one's father (Mt.8.21f // Lk.9.59f).

m.Pea.1.4-6: Crops subject to *leftovers*, and to tithes

Summary of Mishnah: *Leftovers* are due from any crop harvested on private land which can be stored (1.4). This includes grain, legumes, and fruit from vines and trees (1.4-5). The farmer can designate part of his crop as *leftovers* after harvest. If he does so before he has measured the total crop, he does not have to pay tithes on it. Similarly, if he uses a portion of the crop for another purpose (such as animal feed) before measuring the total, he is not liable for tithes on that portion (1.6).

The following traditions have elements (marked in bold) for which there is evidence of an origin before 70 CE:

m.Pea.1.6: Designating *peah* before tithing

One may continue to give	לעולם הוא נותן
in the category of *leftovers*	משום פאה
and be exempt from tithes	ופטור מן המעשרות,
until it is smoothed [for measuring],	עד שימרח.
and give in the category of *ownerless property*	ונותן משום הפקר
and be exempt from tithes	ופטור מן המעשרות,
until it is smoothed [for measuring]	עד שימרח.
and feed [it] to cattle, beasts and birds	ומאכיל לבהמה ולחיה ולעופות
and be exempt from tithes	ופטור מן המעשרות,
until it is smoothed [for measuring],	עד שימרח.
and carry [it] from the granary and sow [it]	ונוטל מן הגורן וזורע
and be exempt from tithes	ופטור מן המעשרות,
until it is smoothed [for measuring],	עד שימרח,

—the words of R. Akiba.	דִּבְרֵי רִבִּי עֲקִיבָה.
A priest or Levite who bought the granary:	כֹּהֵן וְלֵוִי שֶׁלָּקְחוּ אֶת הַגֹּרֶן,
The tithes [belong] to them,	הַמַּעַשְׂרוֹת שֶׁלָּהֶם,
until it is smoothed [for measuring].	עַד שֶׁיְּמָרֵח.
He who *dedicates* [it to the Temple] and redeems [it]	הַמַּקְדִּישׁ וּפוֹדֶה,
is liable to tithes	חַיָּיב בְּמַעַשְׂרוֹת,
until it is smoothed by the [Temple] Treasurer.	עַד שֶׁיְּמָרֵחַ הַגִּזְבָּר.

Comments: Instead of leaving the *corners* of the field unharvested and letting the poor collect *gleanings* and *forgotten* produce, a farmer could designate a proportion of his crop as *leftovers*. [9] He could do this at any time, even after the harvest was all collected and measured, but if he waited until after 'smoothing over,' the *leftovers* became liable to tithes. The 'smoothing over' was the time when the harvest was measured by pouring into vessels and the top skimmed off so that it exactly filled the vessel. When it became liable for tithes, presumably the farmer paid them, because it was assumed that the poor received *leftovers* which were already tithed (see m.Pea.8.2).

After this general principle was stated in the first part of this mishnah, several other rulings were developed from it. If *leftovers* escaped tithing by being separated before 'smoothing over,' then the same applies to produce which is given away to the community (*ownerless property*) or which is used for animal feed or seed corn. If a priest or Levite buys it before it is measured, they should theoretically pay the tithe, but they are assumed to pay it to themselves, so they can ignore this requirement. But if it is sold to them after measuring, the farmer has to pay the tithes to another priest or Levite.

The final ruling concerns someone who *dedicates* all or part of the produce to the fund for the Temple upkeep. If he *dedicated* it and then decided to give a cash equivalent instead (i.e., 'redeem it'), he had to pay the tithe, because even if the crop was not measured when he made the *dedication*, it would be measured before he handed the money to the Temple.

The final part of this ruling ("until it is smoothed by the Treasurer") sounds impractical. It seems to suggest that someone might transport the crop to the Temple and hand it to the Temple Treasurer, and later decide to redeem it. In this case, the Temple would be liable for paying the tithes because they would own it when it was being measured—though the Temple does not pay tithes, so the produce would escape tithing. This is an absurd situation because no one would transport produce to

---

[9] This assumed that *peah* is being used here in its generic sense which includes all types of *leftovers*. If it were being used in the more restricted sense of *corner* crop, then the farmer would still have to let the poor come and collect *gleanings* and *forgotten* produce, but this would suggest that he had to invite them long before the final measuring, which takes place after threshing and winnowing.

the Temple and then decide to redeem it and transport it back again. This absurdity disappears if we assume that the farmer who redeems the crop is different from the farmer who presented it. In other words, this ruling says that someone who buys *dedicated* crop from the Temple escapes paying tithes on it because it belonged to the Temple when tithes became liable. Or perhaps there were local representatives of the Temple Treasurer who would take ownership of the crop and later accept redemption for the crop without the need to transport it. This latter solution would also make sense of the similar difficulty in m.Pea.4.8.

The first two and the last two rulings had no financial consequence for the farmer, because he had already decided to give away the produce, and the ruling only told him whether or not part of it should be given as tithes. These rulings are therefore a matter of piety rather than economics. The rulings about animal feed and seed corn include the financial benefit of avoiding tithes.

The 'Treasurer' was an official in the Temple. The highest officials in the Temple, in order of rank, were High Priest, Deputy High Priest, Commander, Treasurer, Chief of the Watch, and Chief of the Guard.[10] The Treasurer was responsible for testing the quality of the flour of the *first sheaf* (b.Men.85a), and other offerings such as wine (m.Men.8.7).

Dating (8): This collection of rulings presumably formed a unit before its insertion in this tractate, because only the opening ruling is related to the subject of *leftovers*.

The final ruling refers to *dedication* of produce to the Temple which suggests a pre-70 date for that ruling. The attribution to Akiba presumably refers to the three rulings about common property, animal feed, and seed corn, which all have a very similar form. Therefore it is likely that the first and last ruling formed the original group, to which the rulings of Akiba, and perhaps the ruling about priests and Levites, were added.

This is the first of a handful of references in Peah to *dedicating* produce to the Temple (the others are at m.Pea.2.8; 4.7-8; 7.8a). This practice almost certainly stopped with the destruction of the Temple, though an anonymous Talmudic tradition says what you should do if animals or crops are accidentally *dedicated* after the Temple was destroyed.[11] The function of these *dedications* was to pay for ongoing expenses in the Temple (m.Meil.3.5-6 "for Temple upkeep"), unless they were animals of sacrificial quality, in which case they were sacrificed (m.Sheq.4.7). If it

---

[10] According to b.Hor.13a, which also refers to a few other officials.

[11] One should lock it away until it dies or rots, to make sure that no one accidentally benefits from it. b.AZ.13a-b: "One should not declare anything as *dedicated* (מקדיש), or as devoted, or as set value upon at the present time; and if one did declare aught as *dedicated* or devoted or set value upon, then if it be cattle it should be disabled, if fruit clothes or utensils they should be allowed to rot, if money or metal vessels, he should carry them to the Salt Sea. What is meant by disabling? The door is locked in front of it, so that it dies of itself!"

had continued as a fund for rebuilding the Temple, we would expect a great deal of interest in the subject in Yavnean discussions. However, the only rulings in Mishnah relating to these *dedications* which can be dated after 70 CE appear to demonstrate a purely theoretical interest.[12]

m.Pea.2.1-4: What defines a single area for *leftovers*?

Summary of Mishnah: An individual portion of *leftovers* must be designated from every crop. A crop cannot be counted together with a different crop or with any crop from which it is separated by a natural boundary such as a river, road, or land which is cultivated in a different way (2.1). Later rabbis [T4] debated some definitions of natural boundaries (2.2-3). Trees can only be divided into separate crops by a fence, and some say that nothing can divide up trees (2.3-4).

The following traditions have elements (marked in bold) for which there is evidence of an origin before 70 CE:

m.Pea.2.1: Landmarks defining borders for *leftovers*

And these are separations re *leftovers*:	ואלו מפסיקין לפאה.
A stream and a pool [or rivulet]	הנחל, והשלולית,
a private road and public road*1	ודרך היחיד, ודרך הרבים,
a public footpath and a private footpath*2	ושביל הרבים, ושביל היחיד
[which is] permanent in [both] the hot season	הקבוע בימות החמה
and in the rainy season	ובימות הגשמים,
and uncultivated and ploughed [land]	והבור, והניר,
and [fields] with different seed.	וזרע אחר.
And [crop] reaped early [for fodder]*3	והקוצר לשחת
[makes] a separation	מפסיק,
—the words of R. Meir [T4].	דברי רבי מאיר.
But the Sages say:	וחכמים אומרים,
There is no separation	אינו מפסיק,
unless he ploughed [it].	אלא אם כן חרש.

*1, *2 Some editions reverse the order on one line so both have the same order.
*3 Some editions read והזורע לשחת והקוצר 'and seed for early reaping [for fodder].'

Comments: Each field required a separate designation of *leftovers,* and this ruling determined which types of boundaries divided a single field into more than one.

---

[12] m.Ket.5.4, which has the nature of a loophole used by someone with little interest in supporting the Temple, and m.Pea.7.8a, which looks logical but is impractical. See also the discussion at m.Ber.7.1-2.

The practical consequences of this became relatively minor when the ruling was introduced (probably after 70 CE) that you should designate one-sixtieth of the total crop (m.Pea.1.2) because this would be the same whether the field is subdivided or not. Before 70 CE, when there was no fixed proportion, the bulk of *leftovers* consisted of the *corner* crops, and if a field was divided into two, there were twice as many corners. Another practical consequence of dividing fields into smaller units was the increased likelihood that the farmer would leave *forgotten* sheaves behind. If he left three sheaves, these could not be considered to be *forgotten* (see m.Pea.6.5), but if the field was divided into two or more areas, it became much more likely that two sheaves would be left in a single area.

Dating (7): The concept of 'borders' for defining the area for *leftovers* is assumed in the rest of this section and the next (i.e., m.Pea.2.1–3.4), which includes some pre-70 material. This suggests that the *concept* of borders, if not the details listed here, dates from before 70 CE.

This list of border indicators appears to have grown with time. The beginning of the list has a pairing structure which makes it memorable, and probably indicates they were formed as a unit:

> stream and pool, private road and public road, public footpath and private footpath, permanent in the hot season and in the rainy season, uncultivated and ploughed.

The next item, concerning an area with different type of seed, may have been added as a result of the ruling in m.Pea.2.6, which is dated before 70 CE. The final item in the list was added by Meir (mid second century).

New Testament: Mark notes that the disciples who plucked corn on a Sabbath were on their 'way' or on a 'path' (Mk.2.23), which Casey suggests is an emphasis that they were not stealing, because a path marked a border, and crops on a 'border' could be eaten by the poor. He suggests that they understood *peat* (פאה) in Lev.19.9 as 'border' rather than 'corner.'[13] This means that the borders of every field were liable for designation as *leftovers*. After 70 CE this would make little difference, because they could harvest it all and designate one-sixtieth. Earlier, however, they would leave the borders unharvested. It may also have meant, in practice, that poor people might help themselves from the borders, even before harvest.

---

[13] Maurice Casey, *Aramaic Sources of Mark's Gospel,* Society for New Testament Studies Monograph Series 102 (Cambridge: Cambridge University Press, 1998), pp. 141-42. He points out that the Peshitta and LXX translations would fit this interpretation.

m.Pea.2.4: Trees form a single unit for *peah*

And concerning carob trees:	וּלֶחָרוּבִין,
All those visible from each other [are counted together].	כָּל הָרוֹאִין זֶה אֶת זֶה.
Rn. Gamaliel [I, T1] said:	אָמַר רַבָּן גַּמְלִיאֵל,
The practice which was in my father's house:	נוֹהֲגִין הָיוּ בֵּית אַבָּא,
One should give *leftovers* once for olive trees	נוֹתְנִין פֵּאָה אַחַת לַזֵּיתִים
which were in all directions.	שֶׁהָיוּ לָהֶם בְּכָל רוּחַ,
And for carob trees:	וּלֶחָרוּבִין
all those visible from each other.	כָּל הָרוֹאִין זֶה אֶת זֶה.
R. Eliezer b. Zadok [I, T2]	רַבִּי אֱלִיעֶזֶר בְּרַבִּי צָדוֹק
said in his name:	אוֹמֵר מִשְּׁמוֹ,
Even **for the carob trees**	אַף לֶחָרוּבִין
which were in all the town.	שֶׁהָיוּ לָהֶם בְּכָל הָעִיר.

Comments: With most crops, each separate field required a separate designation of *leftovers*, but with orchards there was some confusion about how to define the edges. If they were all planted together in an orchard, there was no problem, but trees were also planted in courtyards and in any other convenient spots.

This mishnah starts with a ruling that carob trees could be counted together if they could be seen from each other, but this is followed by a tradition from Gamaliel I about his father (start of first century) which gave a slightly different ruling for olive trees. However, R. Eliezer b. Zadok (start of second century) added that Gamaliel's tradition about olive trees applied also to carob trees, because he counted all his carob trees in town as one orchard, whether or not they could be seen from each other.

Dating (1): The fact that Eliezer's correction did not amend the other version of Gamaliel's ruling confirms that the tradition by Gamaliel was already established, and so it was not invented at a later date.

New Testament: This is a rare insight into the family of someone named in the New Testament. The fact that they owned several carob and olive trees, which were not all within sight of each other, suggests that they owned more than one property and perhaps several in the same town.

m.Pea.2.5–3.4: Borders of a *mixed* crop

Summary of Mishnah: Two types of wheat can be regarded as one crop if they are harvested together (2.5-6). Is grain sown between rows of trees regarded as separate crops (3.1)? If he harvests different portions as they become ripe, are these different crops (3.2-3)? If there are small plots of spices or onions, each are a separate crop (3.2, 4). If portions of a crop are processed in different ways, they are separate crops (3.3).

Digression in m.Pea.2.7-8: Circumstances when the owner of the field is not responsible for designating *leftovers*.

The following traditions have elements (marked in bold) for which there is evidence of an origin before 70 CE:

m.Pea.2.6: The ancient basis for 'two types of wheat'

It happened that:	מעשה
R. Simeon of Mizpah [T1] sowed	שזרע רבי שמעון איש המצפה
[and came]*1 before Rn. Gamaliel [I T1]	לפני רבן גמליאל,
and they went up to the Chamber	ועלו ללשכת
of Hewn-stone and inquired.	הגזית ושאלו.
Nahum the Scribe*2 said:	אמר נחום הלבלר,
I have received from R. Measha [BCE 1]	מקובל אני מרבי מיאשא,
who received from [his] father*3	שקבל מאבא,
who received from the Pairs	שקבל מן הזוגות,
who received from the Prophets	שקבלו מן הנביאים,
a *halakhah* of Moses from Sinai	הלכה למשה מסיני,
In sowing*4 the field	בזורע את שדהו
[with] two kinds of wheat:	שני מיני חטין,
If he made one grain-store	אם עשאן גורן אחת,
he gives one [set of] *leftovers*;	נותן פאה אחת.
[if he made] two grain-stores,	שתי גרנות,
he gives two [sets of] *leftovers*.	נותן שתי פאות.

*1 Some editions: ובא 'And came.'
*2 Some editions: הבבלי 'the Babylonian.'
*3 Some editions: הזורע 'He who sows.'
*4 Some editions: מאביו 'from his father.'

Comments: After deciding (in 2.5) that different crops in the same field all need a separate designations of *leftovers*, the question arose about two types of the same crop in one field. The decision was that if they were similar enough to store together (and therefore mix together for eating or selling), they can be regarded as one crop, but if they are stored separately, they need separate sets of *leftovers*. This ruling (which is stated in m.Pea.2.5) is justified here by a tradition about a court case which went before the Jerusalem Sanhedrin "in the Court of Hewn Stone." The traditional ruling was traced all the way back to oral law at Mt. Sinai.

It is difficult to imagine what practical consequences would cause this matter to be brought to the attention of the Sanhedrin. The crops were both in the same field, so this would not multiply the number of *corners*, and there is no reason why two types of crop would increase the amount of *gleanings* or *forgotten* crop. The farmer may have wished to avoid the poor trampling his fields when one crop had been harvested but the other was still standing, but he could have chosen to designate *leftovers* after harvest (as in 1.6). Perhaps the two crops meant that he had to leave four *corners* for each crop, or perhaps, like later generations, the Sanhedrin sometimes debated matters which were of legal interest but of little practical concern.

The reference to oral rulings which can be traced back to Mt. Sinai also occur elsewhere,[14] though this is the only early text where the chain of tradition is described so fully. The idea is that Moses was given both the Written Law (the Torah) and the Oral Law (the *Halakhah*) and that the latter developed and grew with time. These oral rulings make up the Oral Law which was accepted by the Pharisees but not the Sadducees.[15] Most Jewish scholars interpret the phrase "a *halakhah* of Moses from Sinai" to mean something like 'this law is timeless,'[16] though this text claims that at least some oral rulings were given at Mt. Sinai.

Dating (1): There is no reason to believe that this tradition was invented in order to give authority to the ruling. It is a relatively minor ruling, of little consequence, which stands relatively secure on a logical base of previous rulings. The tradition is added after the ruling has been stated, as though it is of historical interest rather than a necessary basis for the decision.

New Testament: Although Jesus appears to reject the Oral Law ('traditions of the elders,' Mt.15.1-9 // Mk.7.1-13), Paul does not regard this as a rejection of the system of passing on oral traditions, and he uses the same language of 'receiving' and 'passing on' traditions. He criticizes those who altered the traditions which he passed to his disciples (2Thes.3.6-9; Gal.1.9), and passes on the traditions which he received concerning the Lord's Supper (1Cor.11.23-26) and the resurrection (1Cor.15.3-7), though he also emphasizes that he received some teachings by revelation, not from other men (Gal.1.1–2.2).

m.Pea.2.7-8: Digression: When are you exempt from *leftovers*?

A field which was harvested by *non-Jews*,*1	שדה שקצרוה גוים,
harvested by thieves,	קצרוה לסטים,
withered by ants,*2	קרסמוה נמלים,
[or] broken down by the wind or cattle	שברתה הרוח או בהמה,
is exempt [from *leftovers*].	פטורה.
[If] he harvested half	קצר חציה
and [then] thieves harvested half,	וקצרו לסטים חציה,

---

[14] m.Ed.8.7; m.Yad.4.3 and various occasions in Tosefta, Sifra, and the Talmuds, though not in Mekhilta or Sifré.
[15] Jos.*Ant.*13.297: "The Pharisees had passed on to the people certain regulations handed down by former generations and not recorded in the Laws of Moses, for which reasons they are rejected by the Sadducean group."
[16] Safrai, *Literature of the Sages*, pt. I, pp. 181-83.

he is exempt, because the obligation	פטורה, שחובת
of *leftovers* concerns the standing corn.	הפאה בקמה.
8)*³ [If] thieves harvested half	קצרוה לסטים חציה
and [then] he harvested half,	וקצר הוא חציה,
he gives *leftovers* from that which he harvested.	נותן פאה ממה שקצר.
[If] he harvested half and sold half,	קצר חציה ומכר חציה,
the buyer gives *leftovers* for the whole.	הלוקח נותן פאה לכל.
[If] he harvested half	קצר חציה
and *dedicated* half [to the Temple],	והקדיש חציה,
he who redeems it from the Treasurer,	הפודה מיד הגזבר,
he gives *leftovers* for the whole.	הוא נותן פאה לכל.

*1 Some editions: כותים 'Samaritans.'
*2 Some editions add: אכלה חגב 'eaten by locusts.'
*3 In some editions this is a continuation of 7.

Comments: You are exempt from designating *leftovers* if you did not harvest the latter half of the crop because you are liable "when you harvest," and *leftovers* become liable when you "finish" (Lev.19.9). If you harvest the latter half by choice (e.g., you bought the crop), you designate *leftovers* for the whole, but if it is not by choice (e.g., thieves harvested the first half), you only designate *leftovers* from however much you harvested.

This also meant that someone who *dedicated* the second half to the Temple effectively passed on the responsibility for designating *leftovers* for the whole field to whoever redeemed that produce from the Temple.

This is a digression which fits in with the general topic, but it occurs in the middle of a discussion about the borders of a mixed crop (which continues at m.Pea.3.1). It is not clear why this digression is inserted here. Perhaps it was strongly linked to a preceding or later passage, so that rather than separate it, the editors decided to let it stay here. If this is so, it was most likely linked to m.Pea.3.1, which comes from roughly the same time period.

The Jerusalem Talmud editor(s) assumed that these rulings meant that you *cannot* designate *leftovers* after harvest has finished, and they therefore found a conflict with m.Pea.1.6 which says that you can designate *leftovers* after harvest has finished (y.Pea.2.7.III). They manage to resolve the problem by finding a special circumstance when you would have to designate *leftovers* from harvested produce. However, that circumstance is so contrived that it is almost certainly not what was envisioned in m.Pea.1.6, and Jerusalem Talmud concedes elsewhere that harvested produce is sometimes designated as *leftovers* in other circumstances (y.Pea.4.1.I). It is much more likely that m.Pea.2.7-8 rules what happened *if* the farmer is not actually the one who finishes harvesting the produce, which is the *normal* time for designating *leftovers*, so he does not have to designate it. This does not imply that he *cannot* designate *leftovers* from harvested produce.[17]

Dating (8): The date of this digression rests on the reference in the last ruling to '*dedication* [to the Temple]' (cf. 1.6; 4.7-8; 7.8a), which comes logically at the end of this set of rulings because it relies on all the previous rulings. It is therefore likely also to be the latest chronologically, so that the rest of the rulings can be dated before 70 CE.

However it should be noted that the ruling concerning *dedications* seems impractical, and may be a later comment. It was not practical because it assumes that purchasers of donated produce would have the information which was needed to calculate any *leftovers* which were due. This meant that each donation of produce would have to be kept separate, along with detailed notes about its provenance. The buyer would need to know the size of the complete harvest from which the donation had been made, and whether or not the donation included the last of the harvest. The ruling probably also implies that a purchaser would buy the complete donation. Although all of this is possible, it is unlikely that the Sadducean administrators of the Temple would bother to record all this information in case a pious Pharisee was the purchaser.

On the other hand, it is possible that this practice was a form of tax avoidance which was highlighted in order to encourage gifts to the Temple. The farmer could absolve himself of the burden of isolating and distributing *leftovers* by the simple procedure of *dedicating* the second half of the harvest. This was worth a saving of much more than one-sixtieth, because as soon as it was *dedicated*, the Temple was responsible for the cost of harvesting, processing, and transporting the produce (cf. m.Pea.4.8), as well as paying tithes on that half of the crop. In practice, the Temple would probably pay him to harvest and process the crop for them, so in a year of low grain prices, it might even be economically advantageous to *dedicate* the latter portion of the crop. The reference to "half" throughout these rulings may indicate the minimum *dedication* to which this could apply. The Temple would either offer to keep records of provenance, in order to encourage such donations, or these details might simply be noted as a theoretical obligation which was never enacted.

m.Pea.3.1: Trees as boundaries for *leftovers*

Plots of grain	מל בנות התבואה
which are between olive trees:	שבין הזיתים,
The School of Shammai says:	בית שמאי אומרים,
Leftovers [are due] from each one.	פאה מכל אחד

---

[17] *Yad Avraham*, ad loc., suggests that only someone who has forgotten to designate *peah* properly will do it after the harvest has finished.

And the School of Hillel says:	וְאֶחָד. בֵּית הַלֵּל אוֹמְרִים,
From one [set of *leftovers*] for all.	מֵאֶחָד עַל הַכֹּל.
And they agree that if the heads	וּמוֹדִים, שֶׁאִם הָיוּ רָאשֵׁי
of the rows intertwine,	שׁוּרוֹת מְעוֹרְבִין,
then one gives *leftovers*	שֶׁהוּא נוֹתֵן פֵּאָה
from one for all.	מֵאֶחָד עַל הַכֹּל.

Comments: The schools disagreed about whether olive trees which were planted in the same field as grain formed natural boundaries which divided the field into separate units, each of which was liable for *leftover*s separately. They both agree that if the crop in the small plots actually touch each other, they can be counted together. In many cases this would mean that the field could be counted as one.

This was an important concern to the farmer who might be faced with the complex task of designating *leftovers* from numerous small plots. The Hillelite ruling favored a small farmer.

This matter was even more serious if, as Casey suggests, the Sages regarded *peah* as meaning 'border' rather than 'corner' (see m.Pea.2.1). This would mean that pious individuals would have to leave not only the corners unharvested, but also the borders of every small plot. Tiny plots could become almost impossible to harvest in this situation, though they could choose to designate *leftovers* as a proportion of the crop, rather than leave portions unharvested.

Dating (1): There is no reason to doubt that this school debate is correctly reported. Although the Shammaite position would be clearly unpopular, there is no attempt to highlight this point. Indeed, the extra comment that both schools allowed subplots to be counted together if their crops touch each other ameliorates the Shammaite position. There is no reason to believe that this extra comment dates from after 70 CE because it would not be necessary to add this when the Hillelite position had become normative.

Although the Hillelite position almost certainly prevailed after 70 CE, it is likely that some individuals still applied the Shammaite ruling. This might be the reason why R. Tarfon (who is reported to have followed some Shammaite rulings, e.g., m.Ber.1.3) ruled that you should designate *leftovers* from even tiny plots of crop (m.Pea.3.6).

Jerusalem Talmud records that the School of Rabbi had a version of this ruling which referred to "trees" instead of "olive trees" (y.Pea.3.1.I). The reading "olive trees" is more likely to be original, because there would be a tendency to generalize rulings from specific cases and not vice versa.

m.Pea.3.5-8: Multiple ownership of a field

Summary of Mishnah: Joint owners of a field or tree can jointly designate *leftovers*, but individuals who own half a field or half a tree each designate *leftovers* themselves (3.5). What is the smallest part of a field from which you have to designate *leftovers* (3.6)?

Digression in m.Pea.3.7-8: Ownership of land can be passed to your sons or wife or slave before death. If you consigned it all on your deathbed, and recovered, it is not valid, unless you kept a little, indicating that you expected to recover. If the wife accepts any, you assume that this is in place of her *marriage settlement*. If you give a slave all your property, then he is free, but if you retain the smallest portion it is assumed that you also retain the slave.

The digression in 3.7-8 was probably part of the same tradition as 3.5, because both use the phrase "if the owner has retained." The mishnah in 3.6 has been inserted by a later editor so that it effectively finishes off the section about defining separate fields for *leftovers*. It is possible that 3.6 had already been inserted into the tradition of 3.5-8 before the whole became part of a Mishnah collection, but this is unlikely because there is no clear reason why this should be inserted here. There is no evidence that any of this section originated before 70 CE.

m.Pea.4.1-9: Restricting access of the poor to *leftovers*

Summary of Mishnah: The farmer should insist that he harvests *leftovers* on behalf of the poor if the produce is on a trellis or a palm tree, which may be damaged during harvesting, and he may also do so with other crops if the poor agree (4.1-2). A poor person cannot claim ownership of part of a crop which he has not yet collected, for example, by throwing his coat over it (4.3), and he cannot use sickles and spades to harvest *leftovers* (4.4). The poor can collect *leftovers* only three times a day (4.5), and the farmer cannot allocate *leftovers* to a specific person (4.9). No *leftovers* or tithes are due from a crop if it is *dedicated* to the Temple before it became liable and redeemed after it became liable (4.7-8).

The following traditions have elements (marked in bold) for which there is evidence of an origin before 70 CE:

m.Pea.4.5: When can the poor collect *peah*?

Three appearances per day,	שלש אבעיות ביום,
at morning, midday and afternoon.	בשחר ובחצות ובמנחה.
Rn. Gamaliel [II, T2] said:	רבן גמליאל אומר,
They said this only so that [the farmer]	לא אמרו אלא כדי

may not decrease [the number of appearances].	שלא יפחותו.
R. Akiba [T3] said:	רבי עקיבה אומר,
They said this only so that [the farmer]	לא אמרו אלא כדי
may not increase [the number of appearances].	שלא יוסיפו.
Those of the House of Namer used to	של בית נמר היו
gather [crops] by means of the rope,	מלקטין על החבל,
and give *leftovers* from all [the field]	ונותנים פאה מכל
furrow by furrow [one at a time].	אומן ואומן.

Comments: The poor could expect to go to the farmer and be available to collect *leftovers* three times a day. This ruling appears to be either a way to minimize the interference caused by the poor, or a way to make sure the farmer did not impose too many limits on access by the poor. Gamaliel and Akiba debated about which of these was correct—whether "three times" was the maximum or the minimum number of times the poor should come. Gamaliel thought that the farmer might not want his workers interrupted by beggars all day long, while Akiba thought that the farmer might want the poor to be constantly at work on the field. Akiba's view is less plausible, so it is given support by quoting the tradition of the House of Namer, that they used to like the field cleared row by row, at great inconvenience to the poor who had to be there all day, ready to work.

This debate suggests that the poor had to fit in with the working practice of the farm, by coming at times when the workers would have a break, or by working immediately behind the workers in roped off areas, according to the dictates of the farmer. Although the poor had legal rights to collect *leftovers*, they had to make sure that they fitted in with the working practices of the harvesters.

Dating (2): This debate, which occurred a few decades after 70 CE, suggests that the ruling which they were discussing was already very old, because the original reason for the ruling had been forgotten. It is also possible that the example from the House of Namer was pre-70, but this House (or place) is unknown, and there is no indication whether this was an example from ancient times or one which was roughly contemporaneous with the debate.

m.Pea.4.7-8: Dedicating and redeeming crops during harvest

He who *dedicates* standing corn [to the Temple]	הקדיש קמה
and redeems [it while it is still] standing corn	ופדה קמה,
is liable [to designate *leftovers*].	חייב.
[He who *dedicates*] sheaves [to the Temple]	עומרין
and redeems [it while it is still] sheaves	ופדה עומרין,
is liable [to designate *leftovers*].	חייב.
[He who *dedicates*] standing corn [to the Temple]	קמה
and redeems [it when it is] sheaves	ופדה עומרין,

is exempt [from designating *leftovers*]	פְּטוּרָה,
for at the time it became liable [to *leftovers*]	שֶׁבִּשְׁעַת חוֹבָתָהּ
it used to be exempt [because the Temple owned it].	הָיְתָה פְּטוּרָה.
8) Similarly he who *dedicated* [to the Temple]	כַּיּוֹצֵא בּוֹ, הַמַּקְדִּישׁ
his produce before the time came	פֵּרוֹתָיו עַד שֶׁלֹּא בָּאוּ לְעוֹנַת
that they were liable [to separating tithes]	הַמַּעַשְׂרוֹת,
and he redeemed them,	וּפְדָאָן,
they are liable[to separating tithes].	חַיָּבִין.
[He who *dedicated* them] before the time	מִשֶּׁבָּאוּ לְעוֹנַת
that they were liable [to separating tithes]	הַמַּעַשְׂרוֹת,
and he redeemed them	וּפְדָאָן,
they are liable [to separating tithes].	חַיָּבִין.
He who *dedicated* them before the time	הִקְדִּישָׁן עַד שֶׁלֹּא נִגְמְרוּ
and the [Temple] Treasurer processed them	וּגְמָרָן הַגִּזְבָּר,
and after that he redeemed them,	וְאַחַר כָּךְ פְּדָאָן,
they are exempt [from tithes]	פְּטוּרִים,
for at the time they became liable [to tithes]	שֶׁבִּשְׁעַת חוֹבָתָן
they were being exempt [because the Temple owned them].	הָיוּ פְּטוּרִים.

Mishnaic parallel for 4.8: m.Hal.3.4

Comments: After *dedicating* a crop to the Temple, you could redeem it (buy it back at its *full value* plus an *added fifth*), and if the crop belonged to the Temple at the time that *leftovers* or tithes became due, they did not have to be paid. *Leftovers* became due at the time when the last of the standing crop was harvested (see m.Pea.2.7), though you could designate them at any time during or after harvest (see m.Pea.1.6). Therefore the payment of *leftovers* depended on who owned the crop at the time the harvest ended. Similarly, tithes became due when the produce was 'smoothed' (see 1.6), so if the Temple owned it at this time, the farmer did not have to pay tithes.

This could have been used as a loophole by which the cost of tithes and *leftovers* could be avoided. The total cost of tithing was one-fiftieth (*elevation offering*) + two-tenths (*first & second tithes*) + one-sixtieth (*leftovers*), the total of which is 3.6% more than the cost of redeeming the crops (one-fifth). Although the financial advantage was small, this had the advantage of avoiding all the complexities of tithing, and the inconvenience of letting poor people onto your land. The Temple would benefit from this arrangement, because they would gain one-fifth of the value of the crop. The Temple would presumably add the cost of harvesting the crop, or perhaps subcontract the farmer to harvest his own crop. This type of procedure would only be practical if the Temple Treasurer had local representatives who would take ownership of crops (as suggested at 1.6).

Dating (8): The reference to '*dedication*' and 'Treasurer' link these rulings with the Temple, as also in m.Pea.1.6; 2.8; 7.8a. The explanations at the end of each mishnah looks like a later comment, especially with the use of "used to be" (היתה / היו) which is often used to indicate the past—e.g., m.Ber.9.5; m.Pea.2.4; 4.5). It is also possible that the whole of 4.8 was a later extrapolation from the rulings in 4.7.

m.Pea.4.10-11: Defining '*gleanings*'

Summary of Mishnah: 'Gleanings' must fall to the ground before the farmer touched it—i.e., *while* it was being harvested and not before (4.10-11).

There is no evidence that any of this section originated before 70 CE.

m.Pea.5.1-3: Poor portion which became mixed with the crop

Summary of Mishnah: If produce lies on top of *gleanings*, that which touches the ground belongs to the poor, but what if produce is spread too widely (5.1)? A single stalk which stands among harvested crop belongs to the poor if the harvest is finished. A stalk of *gleanings* which falls into the produce, is swapped for tithed produce (5.2). May you irrigate a field if it makes gleaning more difficult (5.3)?

The following traditions have elements (marked in bold) for which there is evidence of an origin before 70 CE:

m.Pea.5.1a: *Gleanings* mixed in with collected produce

A stack [of produce] from which nothing	גדיש שלא
was gleaned under it:	לוקט תחתיו,
All that touching the ground,	כל הנוגע בארץ,
behold, it is for the poor.	הרי הוא של עניים.

Comments: If harvested produce was heaped on the field, before the *gleanings* had been gathered by a poor person, there were probably *gleanings* underneath it which belonged to the poor. But how could you distinguish the *gleanings* from the collected produce? The only safe solution was to remove the pile and give to the poor anything which was touching the ground.

Dating (2): This ruling was already established before the dispute in m.Pea.5.2b which depends on it, and which is dated before or just after 70 CE (see below).

m.Pea.5.2b: A single stalk of *gleanings* mixed in with produce

An ear of *gleanings*	שבולת של לקט
which became mixed in a stack [of produce]:	שנתערבה בגדיש,

Tithe one ear and give [it] to [a poor man].
R. Eliezer [b. Hyrcanus, T2] said:
And how can this poor man
transfer ownership of something which has not
come into his possession.
But assign to the poor
[part] of the whole stack
and tithe one ear and give it to him.

מעשר שבולת אחת ונותן לו.
אמר רבי אליעזר,
וכי היאך העני הזה
מחליף דבר שלא
בא ברשותו,
אלא מזכה את העני
בכל הגדיש,
ומעשר שבולת אחת, ונותן לו.

Comments: When harvested produce was piled on the ground, it was likely to cover a few stalks of *gleanings* which could be gathered, even if the ground had already been gleaned by a poor person. A pious farmer needed a way of dealing with this situation. He could give a poor person an amount of grain according to the amount of *gleanings* which he estimated to be under the pile, but there was a problem of tithes. The poor were not expected to pay tithes on *leftovers*, and yet the *gleanings* under the pile had become liable for tithes, because they had become part of the harvest. Therefore he had to first pay the tithes on the *gleanings* which were covered, and then give the poor the equivalent amount of produce from the harvested produce.

R. Eliezer pointed out another problem—when the farmer gave the poor some produce from the harvest, he was, in effect, swapping some harvested produce for the *gleanings*, but how could there be a swap if the poor person never owned it? The only way that a poor person could own the *gleanings* was if the farmer moved his pile of produce so that the poor person could pick up the *gleanings*. Clearly, this would completely disrupt the process of harvesting. A poor person could, effectively, hold a pious farmer to ransom, by demanding that he be allowed to search under every pile of produce for even a single stalk of *gleanings* which might be buried.

Eliezer's solution is for the farmer to give the poor person a small part ownership of the pile of produce, which was equivalent to the estimated amount of *gleanings* which was buried under the pile, and then 'swap' some tithed produce for that part ownership.

It is interesting to speculate how this ruling originated. While it is possible that Eliezer was simply answering a theoretical question which arose while the Sages were debating, it is more likely that this was the response to an actual problem. Either a pious farmer wanted to know what to do about this problem, or a poor person wanted to know what his rights were. The terms of the answer suggest that the ruling was made in favor of the farmer because it speaks about a "single stalk" rather than the amount of *gleanings* estimated to be under a pile. This minimal amount suggests that a poor person had demanded his right to move piles of produce 'because there might be even a single stalk of *gleanings* lying under the pile.' The farmer took the dispute to a Courthouse, to defend himself from this economic blackmail. The court decided that the poor person was technically within his rights, but morally in the wrong, so they awarded him the minimal 'one stalk.'

Dating (2): This whole problem is based on the ruling in m.Pea.5.1a, which must have been well established before it could be used by the poor person as a basis for his action. It is also likely that the first part of the ruling here, about tithing the produce which is 'swapped' for the stalk of *gleanings*, also preceded Eliezer and this court case, so that this too would be pre-70, though it is possible that it was all part of the same court case.

   The situation behind Eliezer's ruling, as conjectured above, where a poor man threatened to disrupt the harvest by demanding his rights, fits the circumstances after 70 CE much better than before 70 CE. Before 70 CE, the wide variety of *halakhic* systems in Palestine (Hillelite, Shammaite, Essene, and probably many others) meant that it was difficult to define someone's rights, and an individual could always claim to have a different understanding of the law. After 70 CE, when there was an emphasis on consensus, as decided by the majority, and when there was a single source of *halakhic* authority, it was much more possible for people to demand their rights. We do not know enough about the society to determine whether the Yavnean authority was obeyed even by non-pious farmers, but it would be possible for a poor person to demand their rights from a farmer who was, or claimed to be, a pious person.

m.Pea.5.4-6: Who is a 'poor' person?

Summary of Mishnah: A poor person is someone who does not own the crop from which he wants to collect *leftovers*, and who does not own any farmland (5.5-6). [There is no other measure of wealth, such as ownership of houses or money.] Does this include a farmer who is away from home and therefore does not have access to his own crop (5.4)?

This digression which defines the 'poor' sits uneasily between a discussion of *gleanings* and *forgotten* produce. It would be better situated at the end of all the different types of harvest *leftovers*, at m.Pea.8.1, with the other general discussion about the poor who collect this food. It is presumably here because it was already linked to the preceding or the following passage. The link may have been with m.Pea.5.2, which introduces the subject of partial ownership (which, together with other issues of complicated ownership, is important in this section) and which has a tradition by Eliezer b. Hyrcanus (as also in the first of the traditions in this section). There is no evidence that any of this section originated before 70 CE.

m.Pea.5.7–6.6: When is a sheaf *forgotten*?

Summary of Mishnah: Produce is not *forgotten* if the farmer knew about it but had not gotten round to harvesting it, or if the poor deliberately hid it by putting a cloak over it (5.7). Produce can only be *forgotten* after the crop has been bundled and collected. and only remains *forgotten* up to the time of threshing (5.8). A harvester can only 'forget' produce which he has not noticed—i.e., not if it was in front of him (6.4), or if it was left in a prominent place (6.2). A pile of three (or four?) sheaves or other units of produce is clearly not *forgotten* (6.5-6). Produce can also be declared *ownerless* and harvested by anyone (or just by the poor?) (6.1).

The following traditions have elements (marked in bold) for which there is evidence of an origin before 70 CE:

m.Pea.6.1a: Is *ownerless property* only for the poor?

The School of Shammai says:	בית שמאי אומרים,
[If produce] is declared *ownerless**	הפקר
to the poor, it is [validly] declared *ownerless.**	לעניים, הפקר.
And the School of Hillel says:	ובית הלל אומרים,
It is not [validly] declared *ownerless*	אינו הפקר,
unless it is declared *ownerless* also to the rich	עד שיופקר אף לעשירים
like that which is *released* [in the Sabbatical Year].	כשמטה.

* Some editions have הבקר, which is הפקר in Jerusalem dialect.
Mishnaic parallel: m.Ed.4.3

Comments: If someone did not want to harvest their crop, perhaps because a glut made it uneconomical to harvest, they could declare it *ownerless*, so that anyone could come and harvest it for themselves, and it would not be liable for tithes (see m.Pea.1.6). This concept of *ownerless property* is not found in Scripture (though later rabbis found ways to infer it from apparently redundant phrases—y.Pea.6.1.I), so there was uncertainty about regulations concerning it.

The Shammaites said that only the poor should be allowed to harvest it, while the Hillelites said that anyone should be allowed. The reason given for the Hillelite position is an analogy with the Sabbath Year produce, which anyone can harvest (Lev.25.6), and which is also called '*ownerless* produce' (m.Shebi.9.4). The real reason may have been more pragmatic, because the Hillelite position would make it easy for a farmer to declare his field *ownerless* rather than leaving it to rot, whereas the Shammaite position would mean that the farmer would have to police it and make sure that only the poor came to harvest it.

This explanation follows the Tosefta, though the dispute was understood differently by the editor(s) of Jerusalem Talmud. Tosefta says that "the School of

Shammai and the School of Hillel agree that if produce is declared *ownerless* [lit., 'free'] for human but not beast, or for Jew but not gentile, it is [validly] declared *ownerless*." This assumes as above, that Shammaites say it is valid to declare a field *ownerless* "for the poor but not the rich," while Hillelites say it is invalid. Tosefta adds that both schools agreed that it was valid to say it is "for humans but not beasts or for Jews but not gentile." In contrast, the Jerusalem Talmud assumes that this dispute showed that Shammaites allowed *ownerless* fields to have the same benefits as *leftovers,* but Hillelites did not. This results in a problem because m.Pea.1.6 assumes that *ownerless* fields are exempt from tithes, and implies that this is the ruling of Akiba, who normally followed Hillelite rulings. They have to resort to saying that Akiba is simply reporting a Shammaite ruling without commending it.

Dating (1): There is no reason to doubt that this is an accurate representation of a Hillelite-Shammaite dispute. However, it is likely that the reason which is given in support of the Hillelite position has been added later. Without it, the Hillelites appear to be unsympathetic to the plight of the poor, so later editors would be tempted to bolster their position. The addition of this justification also makes the debate unbalanced, so it is likely that this was added later. This does not mean that this is necessarily wrong—it may have accurately represented how the Hillelites argued—but it is unlikely to have been part of the tradition as it was edited before 70 CE.

The tradition in Tosefta may or may not represent a pre-70 ruling. The Hillelite-Shammaite source available to the editor(s) of Mishnah appears to have consisted of disputes, and so the few agreements may have been added later.

m.Pea.6.1b-3: Distinctive crop cannot be *forgotten*

[If] all the sheaves of a field are each a *qab*	כל עומרי השדה של קב קב
and one of them is four *qabs*	ואחד של ארבעת קבין
and it is forgotten:	ושכחו,
The School of Shammai says:	בית שמאי אומרים,
It is not *forgotten* [produce].	אינו שכחה.
And the School of Hillel says:	ובית הלל אומרים,
[It is] *forgotten* [produce].	שכחה.
2) The sheaf which is close	העומר שהוא סמוך
to a stone wall or to a heap [of produce],*	לגפה ולגדיש,
to cattle or to tools, and it is forgotten:	לבקר ולכלים, ושכחו,
The School of Shammai says:	בית שמאי אומרים,
It is not *forgotten* [produce].	אינו שכחה.
And the School of Hillel says:	ובית הלל אומרים,
[It is] *forgotten* [produce].	שכחה.
3) At the start of rows:	ראשי שורות,
the sheaf in the opposite row proves it.	העומר שכנגדו מוכיח.
The sheaf which had been tied up by him	העומר שהחזיק בו

| to take to the town, and he forgot it: | לְהוֹלִיכוּ אֶל הָעִיר, וּשְׁכָחוֹ, |
| **they agree that it is not *forgotten*.** | מוֹדִים שֶׁאֵינוּ שְׁכָחָה. |

---

* Some editions have וְלַגָּדֵר, 'or to a fence.'
Mishnaic parallel for 6.1b-2: m.Ed.4.3b-4

Comments: A *forgotten* sheaf is one which has been unintentionally left in the field by the harvesters. The Shammaites argued that if it was a particularly significant sheaf or in a significant location, it would be unreasonable to assume that it had really been forgotten, and it is more reasonable to think that the farmer left it there on purpose, to collect it at the next stage of harvesting. The Hillelites said that no matter where it was left, you may regard it as *forgotten*.

The Hillelites appear to be on the side of the farmer who might' quite genuinely forget to bring in a sheaf. From the examples given here, it is unlikely that any sheaf could be regarded as *forgotten* unless it was clearly in the open in the middle of the field.

The first of these rulings is somewhat unsatisfactory, because one is left thinking 'What about a sheaf of two or three *qabs*?'[18] It will be suggested below that this question may have resulted in a more tightly defined version of the Shammaite ruling which said something like: "Three *qabs* is *forgotten*, but not four," which then inspired the Shammaite position at 6.5.

The two rulings in 6.3 appear to be related to 6.2 by the term 'they agree,' which presumably is meant to refer to the Schools in contrast to their disagreement in 6.2. The second ruling of 6.3 is debated alongside 6.2 in t.Pea.3.2 (see Dating), which makes this relationship more likely, at least for the first of these rulings.

The first ruling in 6.3 seems to refer to a sheaf which appears to be *forgotten* at the beginning of a row, but is actually there on purpose, probably as a marker for those harvesting 'the opposite row.' Or, as Tosefta explains it, if the sheaves at the ends of the rows down one side of the field are collected, and not those down the other side, it shows that the farmer has not yet finished clearing the field (t.Pea.3.4— anonymous undateable). However, Tosefta's explanation is unlikely because it would only apply if there were fewer than three sheaves down one side of the field (cf. m.Pea.6.5), which means the field has only one or two rows and yet the farmer was unable to clear it all at the same time.[19]

The second ruling in 6.3 says that a sheaf which has been left after being tied up securely enough to be carried to town cannot be *forgotten*, presumably because the farmer has already taken ownership of it before putting it down.

---

[18] Later Amoraim (PA2–PA5) puzzled over this—see y.Pea.6.1.IV.
[19] There has been a great deal of debate about the meaning. See the summary in *Yad Avraham* ad loc.

Dating (1): There is no reason to doubt that these are genuine Hillelite-Shammaite debates, though there was confusion in later generations about which school ruled what. According to Tosefta (t.Pea.3.2), R. Joshua b. Hananiah [T2] agreed with Mishnah, but R. Eliezer b. Hyrcanus [T2] said the reverse of Mishnah—i.e., the schools agreed re sheaves at fixed locations (cf. m.Pea.6.2), but disagreed re sheaves which were already picked up by the owner (cf. m.Pea.6.3). This confusion helps to confirm that these rulings are pre-70.[20]

The other version of the first ruling is totally conjectural, though if it did exist, it is likely to be a later version, because it does not balance with the Hillelite ruling. However, the later Amoraim who debated these problems did not know of this other version, and so it is likely that it never had any independent existence.

The last mishnah (6.3) is not specifically part of the Hillelite-Shammaite debates, but it continues this same subject with another two situations. Neither of the rulings in 6.3 have the typical debate format, which means they may have been added later, though the second one, on which 'they agree' (מודים, *modim*), is one of the school rulings that Eliezer and Joshua disagree about in t.Pea.3.2, so it is certainly earlier than 70 CE. The first one ('the row opposite') is undateable, though it is likely to be early, because the next mishnah (6.4) appears to be an attempt to expound it, and the fact that the second ruling of 6.3 has been left between the first ruling and its explanation suggests that these two were already a traditional unit which could not be separated.

m.Pea.6.5: How many sheaves can be *forgotten*?

Two sheaves are *forgotten*,	שני עומרים, שכחה.
but three are not *forgotten*.	ושלשה, אינן שכחה.
Two piles	שני צבורי
of olive or carob are *forgotten*	זיתים וחרובין, שכחה.
but three are not *forgotten*.	ושלשה, אינן שכחה.
Two flax stalks for linen are *forgotten*	שני הוצני פשתן, שכחה.
and three are not *forgotten*.	ושלשה, אינן שכחה.
Two grapes are *separated* [fruit]	שני גרגרים, פרט.
but three are not *separated*.	ושלשה, אינן פרט.
Two ears are *gleanings*	שני שבלים, לקט.
but three are not *gleanings*.	ושלשה, אינן לקט.
These according to the words of	אלו כדברי
the School of Hillel.	בית הלל.
And concerning all of these	ועל כולן

---

[20] Yerushalmi harmonizes the two by having Eliezer say that the schools disputed with regard to "a sheaf which the [farmer] picked up to take to the town, and placed near a wall or a heap, cattle or tools, and forgot" (y.Pea.6.2.III).

the School of Shammai says:	בית שמאי אומרים,
Three are for the poor,	שלשה לעניים,
and four for the householder.	וארבעה לבעל הבית.

Comments: The Hillelites said that if two sheaves or piles of other produce were left in a field, they could be regarded as *forgotten*, but the presence of three indicated that the farmer had not yet finished bringing in the harvest. The Shammaites said even three piles of produce could be regarded as *forgotten*, though not four. Similarly, three grapes in a small bunch cannot be regarded as single *separated* grapes, and three ears together cannot be counted as *gleanings*. The three grapes or ears are presumably together, because if it meant 'three in one field/vineyard,' there would be no point in collecting them.

These opinions have the reverse effect of their opinions in m.Pea.6.1b-2, where the Shammaite ruling aided the farmer while the Hillelite ruling aided the poor. Here, by contrast, the Shammaites allow the poor to take even three lots of produce left in the same field, though the Hillelites restrict them only to two lots or less. There is no exegetical basis which caused the Shammaites to think differently in this situation,[21] and no other reason is given for this difference, and so is it possible that there is an editorial mistake?

If we conjecture that the Shammaites originally said 'one but not two' instead of 'four but not three,' the result not only conforms to what we might expect, but it may also reveal the exegetical basis for this dispute. The Shammaites may have argued that the biblical passages always use the singular for *corner*, *gleanings,* and *forgotten*, so that one pile could be taken, but not two.[22] The Hillelites, taking the side of the poor, could use exegetical method of *gezerah shavah*[23] to link it with a verse like 'two or three witnesses' (Deut.17.6) or perhaps simply base it on pragmatic grounds.

It is possible that the Shammaite tradition was changed because it was influenced by 6.1b where Shammaites say that a sheaf of 4 *qabs* is not *forgotten*, which implies that a sheaf of 3 *could* be *forgotten*.

Dating (1?): The form of this Hillelite-Shammaite debate is not typical and must therefore be suspect. Also, as mentioned above, the Shammaite opinion is the reverse of what we might expect from the rulings on a similar subject in 6.1b-2. The solution proposed above suggests that the original form of the first ruling was something like:

---

[21] Later Amoraim tried to solve this by supplying an exegetical basis for these positions in y.Pea.6.4.VI.

[22] This is similar to the exegesis in m.Yeb.6.6 where both schools interpret 'children' as 'at least two children.'

[23] An exegetical method by which details in one text could be read into another if they were linked by subject or vocabulary. This method was employed commonly before 70 CE—see my *Techniques*.

The School of Shammai say: One sheaf is *forgotten* but two are not.

The School of Hillel say: Two sheaves are *forgotten* but three are not.

The Shammaite portion was lost for some reason, and it was replaced by something which was influenced by the Shammaite ruling of m.Pea.6.1b "a sheaf of four *qabs* is *forgotten* [but not three]." The rest of the rulings may have been derived from the first.

Unfortunately no evidence has survived of this original ruling, and it is not mentioned along with 6.1b and 6.2 at m.Ed.4.1–5.3, which lists all the rulings where the Shammaites are more lenient than the Hillelites (a reverse of the norm).[24] Therefore, the form of the School dispute as we have it is suspect, and there is no evidence for the proposed amendment.

In spite of these problems, the first ruling should still be dated before 70 CE because it is cited by Rabban Gamaliel [II, T2] in m.Pea.6.6.

New Testament: 'Householder,' literally 'Lord of the house,' is the normal term for a farmer in both Mishnah (בעל הבית, *baal ha-bét*) and in the New Testament (οἰκοδεσπότης). In the New Testament it is used even for an owner of a large estate (cf. the parables of vineyard owners, Mt.20.1; 21.33).

m.Pea.6.6: How large a sheaf can be *forgotten*?

The sheaf which contains [two] *seahs*,	הָעוֹמֶר שֶׁיֶּשׁ בּוֹ סָאתַיִם,
and it is forgotten: It is not *forgotten*.	וּשְׁכָחוֹ, אֵינוֹ שִׁכְחָה.
Two sheaves which contain [two] *seahs*,	שְׁנֵי עוֹמָרִים וּבָהֶם סָאתַיִם,
Rn. Gamaliel [II] said:	רַבָּן גַּמְלִיאֵל אוֹמֵר,
They [belong] to the householder.	לְבַעַל הַבָּיִת.
And the Sages said:	וַחֲכָמִים אוֹמְרִים,
[They belong] to the poor.	לָעֲנִיִּים.
Rn. Gamaliel said:	אָמַר רַבָּן גַּמְלִיאֵל,
Does an increase of sheaves	וְכִי מֵרוֹב הָעוֹמָרִים
strengthen the right of the householder	יֻפֶּה כֹחַ שֶׁל בַּעַל הַבַּיִת
or does it weaken his right [to keep the sheaves]?	אוֹ הוּרַע כֹּחַ.
They say to him: It strengthens his right.	אָמְרוּ לוֹ, יֻפֶּה כֹחוֹ.
He [Gamaliel] said to them [the Sages]:	אָמַר לָהֶם,
Now, if in the situation where it is	וּמָה אִם בִּזְמַן שֶׁהוּא
"one sheaf containing [two] *seahs*,	עוֹמֶר אֶחָד וּבוֹ סָאתַיִם וּשְׁכָחוֹ,
and it is forgotten: it is not *forgotten*,"	אֵינוֹ שִׁכְחָה.
[then] two sheaves containing [two] *seahs*	שְׁנֵי עוֹמָרִים וּבָהֶם סָאתַיִם,

---

[24] It is sometimes difficult to decide what is considered 'lenient' in the list in m.Ed.4–5, but one would expect to find this ruling in the list because it contains two other rulings where the Hillelites say that something is regarded as 'forgotten' while Shammaites say it is free of this designation (m.Ed.4.3-4).

it is not logical that they are not *forgotten*?	אֵינוּ דִין שֶׁלֹּא יְהֵא שִׁכְחָה.
They say to him: No.	אָמְרוּ לוֹ, לֹא.
If you say concerning one sheaf	אִם אָמַרְתָּ בָּעוֹמֶר אֶחָד
that it is [defined] as a pile [of produce],	שֶׁהוּא כְגָדִישׁ,
will you say [the same] concerning two sheaves,	תֹּאמַר בִּשְׁנֵי עוֹמָרִים
which are like bundles?	שֶׁהֵן כִּכְרִיכוֹת.

Comments: A ruling is stated, and it is then debated by Rn. Gamaliel II and the Sages (i.e., the majority). The ruling is that a large sheaf of more than two *seahs* cannot be said to be *forgotten*. The translation read "[two] *seahs*" because the rest of the discussion assumes that it is equivalent to two sheaves of one *seah* each. Strictly speaking, the rule concerns a sheaf of "more than one *seah*," and Rn. Gamaliel is testing the boundaries of this ruling by speaking about the smallest sheaf which would fit into this category.

This large sheaf is twelve times the size of a normal sheaf as described in the ruling of 6.1b,[25] and so without doubt this would be a memorable sheaf. The Shammaites would therefore argue that it cannot be forgotten, because it stands out. The Hillelites did not accept this type of argument (as seen in m.Pea.6.1b-2). So, how can the Sages defend the fact that this sheaf should not be counted as *forgotten* produce? Gamaliel assumes that it is because it is a large amount, in which case two sheaves making up the same amount would also be exempt. The Sages reply that it is because such a large sheaf is no longer in the category of a 'sheaf' but in the category of a 'pile' of produce.[26] The argument proceeds as follows:

Gamaliel suggests that if a 2-*seah* sheaf should be exempt from *forgotten* produce, then what about 2 sheaves of 1 *seah* each? The majority disagree, presumably on the basis of the first ruling in m.Pea.6.5. Gamaliel asks rhetorically, 'If there are more sheaves, does this make the farmer's case (that they were not actually forgotten), stronger or weaker?' The answer is 'Stronger, of course,' so Gamaliel says that the fact that the two *seah* were made up of two sheaves makes the case stronger than if it was made up of one sheaf. The majority reject this because they say that the one sheaf of two *seah* is excepted, not because it is exceptionally big, but because it can be regarded as a pile of produce, and not a sheaf.

Dating (2): Any debate by Gamaliel II is almost certainly after 70 CE, though not long after. The debate starts with a statement which appears to be a settled point accepted by both sides in the dispute, which is therefore likely to date from at least a generation before the debate. Both sides also appear to assume the ruling of 6.5 that two sheaves should be counted as *forgotten* though more sheaves strengthen the

---

[25] 6 *qab* equals 1 *seah*.
[26] A sheaf in a pile of produce can still be 'forgotten' (cf. 5.8—an undateable source), but not one which is as large as two *seahs*.

farmer's claim to them, which suggests that the ruling of 6.5 also dates from at least one generation previous.

t.Pea.3.8b (Z 3.13b): The man who gave thanks for forgetting a sheaf

It happened that: A certain pious man [or '*Ḥasid*']	מעשה בחסיד אחד
forgot a sheaf in the middle of his field	ששכח עומר בתוך שדהו
and said to his son:	ואמר לבנו
Go and offer for me	צא והקריב עלי
a bullock for a *burnt offering*	פר לעולה
and a bullock for a *peace offering*.	ופר לשלמים.
[His son] said to him: Father,	אמר לו, אבא,
why do you see [reason to] be joyful	מה ראית לשמוח
when you [fulfill] this commandment*1	במצוה זו
[more] than all the commandments	מכל מצות ה
spoken in Torah?*2	אמורות בתורה.
He said to him: All the commands	אמר לו כל מצות
which are in Torah the Omnipresent gave to us	שבתורה נתן לנו המקום
to [obey with] intent	לדעתנו,
[but] this one to [obey] without intent [i.e., accidentally].	זו שלא לדעתנו,
(For if we did [this] deliberately	שאילו עשינוה ברצון
before the Omnipresent,	לפני המקום
it is not possible for us to fulfill the command.)	לא באת מצוה זו לידינו

*1 Z reads בשמחת מצוה זו יותר 'in fulfilling this commandment more' instead of במצוה זו 'in [fulfilling] this commandment.'
*2 Z reads שבתורה 'which are in Torah' instead of האמורות בתורה 'spoken in Torah.'

Comments: A man who accidentally forgot a sheaf realized he had thereby accidentally fulfilled a commandment of the *forgotten* sheaf, which cannot be fulfilled deliberately because you cannot deliberately 'forget' something. The joy of this realization prompts him to thank God with two sacrifices, one for total consumption on the altar (the *burnt offering*) and one to share with his family and friends in a celebration meal (the *peace offering*).

The exceptional value of these sacrifices which he offered for this seemingly minor occurrence, puts this incident in the realm of story-telling. If an individual had really done this, it is unlikely that his name would have gone unmentioned.

Dating (11): This story cannot be dated reliably, partly because it is anonymous, but mostly because it is the type of *aggadic* 'sermon filler' which is likely to be made up. However, the incidental detail that he celebrated by means of offering sacrifices (rather than sponsoring something in the synagogue) puts the story in the time of the Temple. The story is more powerful if it is contemporary, because it is about a 'normal' person, and not a hero of the past, and so the person who invented it would not deliberately add an archaic feature concerning the Temple times.

The explanation at the end (which is translated in brackets) is probably an editorial addition. The story ends much more powerfully without this explanation.

This section is followed by a Scripture which the son quotes to his father, which was probably added later, and an exegesis which would have almost certainly been added later. The story is complete without the Scriptures and ends with a suitably arresting line. Therefore the original parable was something like this:

> A certain pious man forgot a sheaf in the middle of his field. He said to his son, "Go and offer two bullocks on my behalf, for a *burnt offering* and a *peace offering*." His son said to him, "Father, why are you more joyful at fulfilling this one commandment than all the other commandments in Torah?" He said to him, "God gave us all the commands in Torah to obey intentionally, but he only gave us this one to obey accidentally."

New Testament: The story is told as though it actually happened, but it is very similar to the form of many Gospel parables. It concerns 'a certain man,' without any details to tie it to an individual, and it unfolds a puzzling scenario about a man's strange behavior, which would have the listeners leaning forward to hear the explanation. The story builds up emotional tension by the huge size of the man's offering (comparable to the value of two tractors today), by the joyful celebration which is implied by the *peace offering*, which would have been large enough to make a feast for most of the village to share, and by the extreme joy which he exhibits. The reason for his joy, which is the solution to the whole puzzle, is given in the very last line, as in any good short story. An editor has felt the need to add an explanatory phrase after the story which helps the reader to understand it, but it spoils the ending somewhat. This is similar to the editorial activity which has 'spoiled' many of Jesus' parables. The story has a strong moral message which, as in most parables, is not stated explicitly. The moral is that God has allowed us to experience the joy of obeying commandments and we should thank him for that privilege.

m.Pea.6.7–7.2: Unharvested crop which cannot be *forgotten*

Summary of Mishnah: Harvest has not finished if there is more than two units of crop remaining, because they are too much to 'forget,' though they must be in the same field (6.7-9). Similarly a tree cannot be *forgotten* if it is noteworthy or if it has more than two *seahs* of produce (7.1-2). Some unharvested produce cannot be *forgotten*, such as produce which is not for human consumption, and perhaps root crops which are stored in the ground (6.10). You cannot argue that harvesting was incomplete when it was harvested badly, unless you *intended* to do an initial incomplete harvest (6.11).

Many of these rulings cannot be dated, but they appear to come from a later period when the principles of the schools of Hillel and Shammai were less important, and pragmatic issues were more important. The Hillelites rejected the Shammaite principle that produce could not be *forgotten* if it was significant in some way, and yet these rulings allowed a significant olive tree to be exempt, and R. Jose [T4] even allowed *any* olive tree to be exempt (m.Pea.7.1), presumably because the crop was too valuable. The last ruling in m.Pea.7.2, about unpicked olives, has an interpretative comment which is attributed to Meir in Mishnah and to the School of Shammai in the Jerusalem Talmud (y.Pea.7.2.VII). There is nothing to indicate that this was from a school debate, and so it is likely that Mishnah is correct, and the Jerusalem Talmud is due to a misreading of מאיר 'Meir' as שמאי 'Shammai.' There is no evidence that any of this section originated before 70 CE.

m.Pea.7.3: *Peret—separated* fruit

Summary of Mishnah: '*Separated*' fruit are individual grapes which fall off during harvest, before the bunch goes in the basket.

There is no evidence that any of this section originated before 70 CE.

m.Pea.7.4-8: *Olelot—defective* bunches of fruit

Summary of Mishnah: A bunch is '*defective*' if it has lost so many grapes that it lacks the general shape of a bunch (7.4). Is the farmer allowed to thin out *defective* bunches (7.5)? When the farmer does not harvest the crop for himself (if the whole crop is *defective*, or if he *dedicated* it, and perhaps in the fourth year rest for vines), there are no harvest *leftovers* for the poor (7.6-8).

The following traditions have elements (marked in bold) for which there is evidence of an origin before 70 CE:

m.Pea.7.6: Can the poor take any *fourth-year fruit*?

A *fourth [year] vineyard:*	כרם רבעי,
The School of Shammai says:	בית שמאי אומרים,
It does not have [liability to] an *added fifth*,	אין לו חומש,
and it does not have [liability to] *removal*.	ואין לו בעור.
And the School of Hillel says: It does.	ובית הלל אומרים, יש לו.
The School of Shammai says:	בית שמאי אומרים,
It does have [liability to] *separated* [fruit]	יש לו פרט
and it does have [liability to] *defective* [bunches]	ויש לו עוללות,
and the poor redeem [it] for themselves.	והעניים פודין לעצמן.

And the School of Hillel say: ,וּבֵית הִלֵּל אוֹמְרִים

It is all for the winepress.   .כֻּלּוֹ לַגַּת

Mishnaic parallel: m.MS.5.3; m.Ed.4.5

Comments: A *second tithe* can either be taken to Jerusalem and eaten there, or it can be redeemed at its *full value* plus an *added fifth* and the money spent in Jerusalem. An *added fifth* also applies to any *consecrated* produce such as *second tithe* or a *dedication*. *Removal* is the distribution or destruction of uneaten tithes (including *second tithes*) at *Pesach* (Passover) every fourth and seventh year.[27]

When a vineyard was planted, the first three years of crop was left unharvested and the *fourth-year fruit* was "holy" (Lev.19.23-25, *qodesh*, קֹדֶשׁ). The Hillelites regarded this crop as equivalent to *second tithe*, and the Shammaites regarded it as something unique from which the poor could take *separated* and *defective* fruit.

The Hillelites do not mention *second tithe*, but they say that it is liable to an *added fifth* and *removal*, which is true only for *second tithes*, and *fourth-year fruit* is dealt with more fully at the end of the tractate *Maaser Sheni* (*second tithe*).

Fourth-year harvest ends at the fifteenth of Shebat (the New Year for Trees, m.RH.1.1), and so there are at least a couple of months to use them before the time of *removal*. Because they are treated as *second tithe*, they are not liable for *separated* or *defective* fruit. The Hillelites therefore said that all the *fourth year fruit* went 'into the vat' (which is owned by the farmer, not by the poor), where it is made into wine which can be carried more easily to Jerusalem for consumption.

The Shammaites did not think that *fourth-year fruit* was liable for either an *added fifth* or *removal*. The only normal portion of produce which is not liable to either of these was the unconsecrated portion, but the *fourth-year fruit* is specifically called "holy," i.e., *consecrated*, at Leviticus 19.23. Other special *consecrated* produce such as *mixtures in a vineyard* (see m.Kil.4.5) or *firstfruits* could not be eaten by ordinary people, and so they were not subject to *separated* or *defective* fruit.

Therefore it appears that the Shammaites regarded *fourth-year fruit* as something unique. It could be redeemed (though only when it was made into wine, cf. t.MS.5.19) but not with the *added fifth*, and the harvest *leftovers* could be taken and redeemed by the poor.[28]

Dating (1): There is no reason to doubt that this represents the views of the schools before 70 CE. Neusner has pointed out that the form of these rulings is not

---

[27] These two features of '*Removal*' and 'Fifth' are also linked with *second tithe* at m.Dem.1.2. '*Removal*' is proscribed at m.MS.5.6-15.

[28] The '*added fifth*' is only paid if the original owner redeems the crop (cf. m.MS.4.3). This is presumably because the prohibition applies to the original owner, who would then be misappropriating it, so he has to pay the fine for this 'inadvertent' sin. If the original owner cannot redeem the crop (because only the poor can redeem it), there is no added 'Fifth.'

symmetrical, unlike most school disputes, so that the version preserved here is unlikely to be original.[29] He suggested that originally the dispute ended with something like "[They are liable to laws of *second tithe*] in all respects," instead of "It is all for the vat." This would make the two halves balance each other in a memorizable form:

A fourth [year] vineyard:
Shammaites:	It is not liable to an *added fifth* nor to *removal*.
Hillelites:	It is.
Shammaites:	It is not liable to *separated* nor *defective* nor *redemption*.
Hillelites:	It is liable to all [of them].

Although Neusner's suggestion makes the form more symmetrical, it is not completely symmetrical, and there is no reason why the final line should not contain the explanation for their differences ('because it is all put aside for the winepress').

The second ruling does not fit into the context in Mishnah, which is only dealing here with *defective* fruit. This suggests that the two rulings were already associated with each other, and the editor did not wish to break them up when the first ruling was inserted here.

m.Pea.7.8a: *Defective* bunches *dedicated* to the Temple

He who *dedicates* his [whole] vineyard:	המקדיש כרמו
Before one could identify	עד שלא נודעו
[any] 'defective' [bunches] in it,	בו העוללות,
no 'defective' [bunches go] to the poor.	אין העוללות לעניים.
When 'defective' [bunches] are identified in it,	משנודעו בו העוללות,
the 'defective' [bunches go] to the poor.	העוללות לעניים.
R. Jose [b. Halafta, T4] said:	רבי יוסי אומר,
One should give the value of their growth	יתנו שכר גדוליו
to the Holy [House].	להקדש.

Comments: Crops which were '*dedicated*' to the Temple were not liable for any harvest *leftovers* if they were *dedicated* when the *leftovers* became due (cf. m.Pea.1.6; 4.7-8). This ruling says that *defective* bunches became due as soon as they were recognizable as defective. So if someone *dedicates* a vineyard after the *defective* bunches are recognizable, the poor become owners of part of a *dedicated* crop.

R. Jose pointed out that this means the poor then become responsible for *dedications* from that part of the vineyard which they own. Therefore they should give to the Temple whatever growth occurs within the *defective* bunches which they own, from the time that the vineyard is *dedicated* to the time that the poor pick the

---

[29] *Traditions,* vol. 2, pp. 23-24, 59-60.

bunches. In practice this is impossible to measure or even to estimate, and, in any case, it was assumed that the poor would not pay tithes on any *leftovers* (cf. m.Pea.8.2-4). Therefore this comment is only of theoretical value, and it is not likely that anyone tried to enact it.

The parallel version in t.Pea.3.13 states the same principle in a different way: "He who *dedicates* his vineyard may not *dedicate defective* bunches, for a person cannot *dedicate* what he does not own."

Dating (9): The practice of '*dedication*' to the Temple places this ruling before 70 CE, as already discussed above (m.Pea.1.6; 2.8; 4.7-8), though there is no corroborating evidence in this tradition such as a reference to the Temple Treasurer. It is therefore possible that this is an instance of *dedication* after 70 CE, though there is no evidence that this was ever practiced.

The fact that R. Jose [T4] debated about *dedications* to the Temple shows that they still had an academic interest in it. But the ruling he proposed is more logical than practical. It is impossible to determine which grapes in a bunch had grown during the interval between *dedication* and picking, or to determine by how much they had grown. Jose suggests that the *value* of those later grapes should be calculated, and this should be paid by the poor to the Temple, but this calculation is almost equally impossible and would simply be a matter of guesswork. No guidelines are given as to how this guess should be made, and so it is unlikely that this was ever attempted. This whole idea looks like one which was stated as a theoretical solution without ever trying it out in practice. This is probably part of the same debate which is recorded in m.Meil.3.6 between two of Jose's contemporaries.

t.Pea.3.15 (Z 3.21): *Dedicated* vineyards are exempt from *forgotten* and *fourth year*

He who plants a vineyard [which is] *dedicated* [to the Temple]	הנוטע כרם להקדש,
is exempt from [the 3-year law of] *forefruit*	פטור מן הערלה
and from [the law of] the *fourth [year fruit]*	ומן הרבעי,
but is liable to the Sabbath Year.	וחייב בשביעית.
From when does a man have authority[*1]	מאימתי אדם רשיי
to harvest his vineyard?[*2]	לבצור כרמו
From when he knows [the nature of] the fruit	משיודע הפרי.
—when already the vineyard has became liable	שכבר נתחייב הכרם
to the growth of *defective* [bunches].	בגדולי עוללות.

[*1] רשיי is רשאי in Zuckermandel's edition (same meaning).
[*2] בשביעית 'in the Sabbath Year' is added after כרמו in Zuckermandel.

Comments: A vineyard whose future crops have already been *dedicated* to the Temple is exempt from *forefruit* and *fourth-year fruit* (see m.Pea.7.6), so it can be harvested and go straight to the Temple. However, the Sabbath Year restrictions apply as normal.

The second ruling says that you cannot start harvesting a vineyard until it is clear whether the bunches are going to be defective or not. A *defective* bunch is defined in m.Pea.7.4 as one which has neither 'shoulder' (rounded wide top) nor 'pendant' (cone shaped end). Once these can be recognized, the harvester will know which bunches to leave for the poor.

Dating (9): The practice of '*dedication*' to the Temple places this ruling before 70 CE, as already discussed above (m.Pea.1.6; 2.8; 4.7-8), though there is no corroborating evidence in this tradition.

There is no reason to date the second ruling at the same time, and so there is no way to determine whether or not the second half is pre-70.

m.Pea.8.1: The poor collect *leftovers* first

Summary of Mishnah: Those who are not poor may also go and collect harvest *leftovers*, but only after the poor have taken what they want.

Comments: The reason this is placed here is presumably that rich people might want to collect *defective* bunches, but they would not want to collect other produce which was less valuable or involved harder work. There is no evidence that any of this section originated before 70 CE.

m.Pea.8.2-4: The poor do not tithe the *poor tithe* or *leftovers*

Summary of Mishnah: A poor person who says that his food is already tithed is believed only if it is unprocessed food which is likely to be from harvest *leftovers* or from *poor tithe*. A Levite is always believed.

There is no evidence that any of this section originated before 70 CE.

m.Pea.8.5-7: How much *poor tithe* do you give someone?

Summary of Mishnah: Minimum portions of food which can be given to each poor person (unless you do not have enough for this minimum) (8.5). Up to half can be put aside for the poor of your own family (8.6). Poor people who are wandering from place to place are given enough for two meals, for a night's lodging, and an extra meal if it is a Sabbath. Local poor are given money for up to a week's food [two meals per day] from a communal fund (8.7).

The following traditions have elements (marked in bold) for which there is evidence of an origin before 70 CE:

m.Pea.8.7: Food for the wandering poor and for the local poor

One should not [give] less to the poor	אֵין פּוֹחֲתִין לְעָנִי
who moves from place to place	הָעוֹבֵר מִמָּקוֹם לְמָקוֹם
than a loaf [worth] a *pondion*	מִכִּכָּר בְּפוּנְדְּיוֹן,
from [wheat costing] four *seahs* for a *sela*.	מֵאַרְבַּע סְאִין בְּסֶלַע.
[If he stays for] the night,	לָן,
one should give him provisions for the night.	נוֹתְנִין לוֹ פַּרְנָסַת לִינָה.
[If he stays for] the Sabbath,	שַׁבָּת,
one should give him food for three meals.	נוֹתְנִין לוֹ מְזוֹן שָׁלֹשׁ סְעוּדוֹת.
Whoever possesses food for two meals	מִי שֶׁיֶּשׁ לוֹ מְזוֹן שְׁתֵּי סְעוּדוֹת,
must not take [anything] from	לֹא יִטּוֹל מִן
the '*bowl*' [i.e., soup kitchen].	הַתַּמְחוּי.
[Whoever possesses] food for fourteen meals	מְזוֹן אַרְבַּע עֶשְׂרֵה סְעוּדוֹת,
must not take [anything] from	לֹא יִטּוֹל מִן
the 'basket' [i.e., communal fund].	הַקֻּפָּה.
And [money for] the 'basket' is collected by two [people]	וְהַקֻּפָּה נִגְבֵּית בִּשְׁנַיִם,
and is distributed by three [people].	וּמִתְחַלֶּקֶת בִּשְׁלֹשָׁה.

Comments: This ruling implies a distinction between the itinerant poor and the local poor, which is made explicit in Tosefta (t.Pea.4.8f). The itinerant poor are given food for two meals, or three meals on a Sabbath, and shelter for the night if necessary. The local poor are helped from a communal fund, which later sources tell us was distributed every Friday night. The first half of this mishnah suggests that the itinerant poor were given food in the form of a loaf, which they could presumably beg from any householder, but the second half suggests that there was a central facility such as a soup kitchen where food was prepared for the poor. Probably the central soup kitchen was only organized in a town or large village.

Tosefta adds that the poor who go from house to house should be refused because they should go to the central facility instead, and that the local poor are provided with clothing as well as food (t.Pea.4.8—undateable). It also adds the principle that you provide a poor person with food and other things according to what they were accustomed to (t.Pea.4.10). As illustrations it gives a story concerning Hillel who gave a horse and a slave to an impoverished man of high standing. There is nothing to support the veracity or early creation of this story. Tosefta also says that Sabbath meals include fish and vegetables, which may be expressed in Mishnah in the difference between 'a loaf' on weekdays and 'food' on Sabbaths. It also says that in a town of mixed Jews and gentiles, they collected from both groups and gave to both groups (t.Git.3.13). These details from Tosefta may not represent the situation before 70 CE.

The Jerusalem Talmud tells a story about Eliezer ben Hyrcanus when he was appointed as an 'overseer' to collect and distribute food. Once he returned to his house and was told that a band of beggars had eaten and had praised him, but another time that some beggars had eaten and cursed him (presumably for his good fortune, or because they were dissatisfied in some way). Eliezer was more pleased the second time, because the curses would result in heavenly reward (y.Pea.8.7.III). It is accompanied by another story about Akiba who was also asked to be an 'overseer,' but his wife warned him that he would have to expect curses as his reward. These stories both suggest that the central food facility for beggars was actually at the home of one of the collectors.

Dating (?): None of this tradition can be positively dated before 70 CE, though it is illustrative of what we see in the New Testament, and there are other indications that it is an early tradition.

The biographical stories about Eliezer and Akiba must be treated with great caution, because much less care was taken about accuracy in non-*halakhic* material. Also, it is not certain that this story concerned Eliezer [T2], because two of the six extant editions of Yerushalmi say "Eleazar" [PA3].[30] However, the fact that the story about Eliezer/Eleazar comes immediately before the one about Akiba makes it more likely that it concerns someone from T2 than from PA3. These stories at least indicate that later rabbis thought that such collections were occurring at that time.

The quantity of food is about right for a poor person, and fits in with prices which come from the New Testament. Wheat costs one *sela* (which is four *denarii*) for four *seahs*, i.e., about one *denarii* per *seah*.[31] The loaf is made with wheat worth a *pondion*, which is a Roman coin worth an *ass* or one-twenty-fourth of a *denarius*.[32] Therefore, the poor person was to get a loaf made with one-twenty-fourth of a *seah* of wheat, worth one-twenty-fourth of a *denarius*, which would be a day's food for himself and any dependants. This is equivalent to the contribution for two meals defined at m.Pea.8.5, "half a *qab* of wheat," which is one-twelfth of a *seah*.[33]

These quantities fit in with the Gospels' story of the feeding of 5,000 men which would have cost 200 *denarii* (Mk.6.37; Jn.6.7), which at this reckoning would give each man a loaf for himself and his dependants. It also fits with the story of Hillel and

---

[30] Most MSS of Yerushalmi have "Eliezer" (אליעזר in Paris and London, or ליעזר in Venice and Leiden) though some have "Eleazar" (אלעזר in Vatican and Amsterdam). "Eliezer" is b. Hyrcanus [T2] while Eleazar in Yerushalmi is b. Pedat [PA3].

[31] One *sela* is worth four *denarii* (see m.MS.2.9).

[32] See Joachim Jeremias, *Jerusalem in the Time of Jesus: An Investigation into Economic and Social Conditions during the New Testament Period* (London: SCM Press, 1969), pp. 122-23. This exchange rate varied with subsequent inflation.

[33] Medieval rabbis debated whether the loaf was made with half a *qab* or whether it was made with quarter of a *qab* because half of the cost went to the baker—see *Yad Avraham* ad loc.

Ben Hé Hé where ten loaves can be bought for a *denarius*.[34] However, by the third century, after inflation devalued the Roman gold standard (a process which was started by Nero in 63 CE and continued throughout the second century), exchange rates had changed so much that R. Huna [BA2] said that the quantity in m.Pea.8.7 was about one-third more than the quantity in m.Pea.8.5 (y.Pea.8.7, I).[35]

New Testament: There are a few indications that the provisions for the poor, as described here, were already in place in New Testament times. The provision for the widows in Acts 6.1-6 appears to be a combination of the daily support for the itinerant poor and the longer-term support for the local poor.[36] The fact that they met together for a meal (rather than eating in their own homes) suggests that they were supported by means of a soup kitchen for itinerant poor, while the fact that people were selling farmland, and not just bringing in produce from farmland, suggests that they were building up a communal fund like that for the local poor. It may be that they did both—the soup kitchen for the converts among the pilgrims from the Diaspora, and the fund for those who lived in Jerusalem or who had settled there in order to be close to the Apostles.

The experience of the Apostles in Acts 6, who suffered complaint rather than thanks from those they were trying to help, is probably the common experience of anyone involved in this type of work, but it is significantly reflected in the similar experiences of R. Eliezer [T2] and R. Akiba [T3] (see Comments above).

The distinction between the itinerant poor (who were given enough for one day at a time) and the local poor (who were given enough for a week) may be the explanation for the curious phrase in the Lord's Prayer. "Give us today our daily bread" (Mt:6.11; Lk.11.3). The more normal prayer for food is "Bless to us, LORD our God, this year to our benefit, with all kinds of produce"[37]—i.e., the prayer of a farmer, for whom the food cycle is measured in a year. A poor person, provided for out of the community fund, had a food cycle of a week, but an itinerant poor person lived with a food cycle of only one day. Jesus and his band of followers lived as itinerant teachers, not as beggars, but they shared the same precarious daily food

---

[34] b.Hag.9b—though this detail is in a parable which has probably been added later, and which is not found in the version at m.Hag.1.6. For an analysis, see my *Techniques,* pp. 56-57. A *denarius* bought enough flour for twenty-four loaves, but half of the cost went to the baker.

[35] One solution which was proposed to explain this is that Deut.14.28-29 says 'you shall give the tithe to the poor,' which applies to giving from one's home as at 8.7, and Deut.26.12 says 'you shall leave the tithe for the poor,' which applies to giving from the threshing floor as at 8.5. This is found in the *Tosephot* (at b.Yeb.100a; b.Ned.84b; b.Hul.131a) as a citation from *Sifré,* but it is not found in any existing text of *Sifré* (see *Yad Avraham* re 8.5).

[36] Keith F. Nickle in *The Collection: A Study in Paul's Strategy* (London: SCM Press, 1966), p. 94 suggests that Acts 6.1-6 is "a combination of the two programmes" for the resident poor and the itinerant poor, but he does not detail what he means.

[37] The ninth of the Eighteen Benedictions in Palestinian and Babylonian versions.

cycle as itinerant beggars. This lifestyle is reflected in other sayings such as "the Son of Man has nowhere to lay his head" (Mt.8.20; Lk.9.58) and "consider the lilies" (Mt.6.28; Lk.12.27).

The criticism in the Tosefta (see Comments) of those who go from house to house may be reflected in Jesus' injunction to his disciples that they should accept the hospitality of one household and "not go from house to house" (Lk.10.7).

Collections for the poor were generally done at a local level, but the famine of 47/48 CE which affected the whole eastern Mediterranean needed a wider response. This allowed Paul to arrange a collection in advance among the churches for Christians in Jerusalem, and presumably there were similar collections among the synagogues. This is the same famine during which the King and Queen mother of Adiabene sent food to Jerusalem (t.Pea.4.18; see m.Pea.1.1 Dating). Jews from neighboring countries may have been expected to support the poor of Israel (see m.Yad.4.3 below).

The fact that Jews collected weekly for the poor is probably the reason why Christians also did so. It is noteworthy that 1 Corinthians 16.2 does not tell believers to bring the money to church, but to put it aside at home, so that it would be ready for Paul. This reflects the Jewish practice where the collectors would come to each house weekly, though Paul, of course, was not able to come weekly.[38]

m.Pea.8.8-9: Who is 'poor' enough for *poor tithe*?

Summary of Mishnah: Anyone is poor who owns less than 200 *zuz* (or *denarii*) of capital (excluding the value of his home and tools and anything which he holds for others such as a *ketubbah*) and has no income (8.8). Anyone who pretends poverty or disability to gain money will become poor or disabled before he dies. Similarly, accepting a bribe results in blindness (8.9).

There is no evidence that any of this section originated before 70 CE.

---

[38] De Lacey wonders why the Corinthians were asked to put aside money on a weekly basis. He considers whether wages may have been paid on a weekly basis, but there is no evidence for this, and there is frequent evidence for payment on a daily or monthly basis. He concludes that it is linked with the Christian Sunday, but only for lack of any other reason, and despite the fact that it was not brought to the church. Douglas R. De Lacey, "The Sabbath/Sunday Question and the Law in the Pauline Corpus" in Don A. Carson, ed., *From Sabbath to Lord's Day: A Biblical, Historical and Theological Investigation* (Grand Rapids: Zondervan Publishing House, 1982), pp. 160-95, esp. 184-85.

Related early traditions from other tractates

m.Yad.4.3: Poor man's tithe outside Israel

On that same day they said,	בו ביום אמרו,
"Ammon and Moab:	עמון ומואב
What [is the status of second tenth] on a Sabbath Year?"	מה הן בשביעית.
R. Tarfon [T3] prescribed, *"Poor tithe,"*	גזר רבי טרפון, מעשר עני.
and R. Eleazar b. Azariah [T2] prescribed,	וגזר רבי אלעזר בן עזריה,
"Second tithe."	מעשר שני.
R. Ishmael said,	אמר רבי ישמעאל,
"Eleazar b. Azariah	אלעזר בן עזריה,
it is for you [to give] evidence of the teaching	עליך ראיה ללמד,
for yours is the stricter [ruling];	שאתה מחמיר,
for all [who teach] the stricter [ruling]	שכל המחמיר,
it is for them [to give] evidence for the teaching."	עליו ראיה ללמד.
R. Eleazar b. Azariah said to him,	אמר לו רבי אלעזר בן עזריה,
"Ishmael, my brother,	ישמעאל אחי,
I did not change the **order of the years**	אני לא שניתי מסדר השנים,
[but] Tarfon, my brother, changed it;	טרפון אחי שנה,
and it is for him [to bring] evidence for the teaching."	ועליו ראיה ללמד.
R. Tarfon replied,	השיב רבי טרפון,
"Egypt is outside the Land [of Israel];	מצרים חוצה לארץ,
Ammon and Moab are outside the Land;	עמון ומואב חוצה לארץ,
just as those in **Egypt [give]**	מה מצרים
the *poor tithe* in the Sabbath Year,	מעשר עני בשביעית,
so those in Ammon and Moab [give]	אף עמון ומואב
the *poor tithe* in the Sabbath Year."	מעשר עני בשביעית.
R. Eleazar b. Azariah replied,	השיב רבי אלעזר בן עזריה,
"Babylon is outside the Land;	בבל חוצה לארץ,
Ammon and Moab are outside the Land;	עמון ומואב חוצה לארץ,
just as those in **Babylon [give]**	מה בבל
the *second tithe* in the Sabbath Year	מעשר שני בשביעית,
so those in Ammon and Moab [give]	אף עמון ומואב
the *second tithe* in the Sabbath Year."	מעשר שני בשביעית.
R. Tarfon said,	אמר רבי טרפון,
"Those in Egypt, because it is near,	מצרים שהיא קרובה,
were ordered [to give] *poor tithe*	עשאוה מעשר עני,
so that the poor of Israel [have] support	שיהיו עניי ישראל נסמכים
from it in the Sabbath Year,	עליה בשביעית,
so those in Ammon and Moab	אף עמון ומואב
which are near	שהם קרובים,
are ordered [to give] *poor tithe*	נעשים מעשר עני,
so that the poor of Israel [have] support	שיהיו עניי ישראל נסמכים

from them in the Sabbath Year."

R. Eleazar b. Azariah said to him,   אמר לו רבי אלעזר בן עזריה,

"You are like one who offers wealth   הרי אתה כמהן ממון,

and you [do] nothing   ואין אתה

except lose their souls.   אלא כמפסיד נפשות,

You would prevent the heavens   קובע אתה את השמים

from sending down dew and rain   מלהוריד טל ומטר,

as it is said [Mal.3.8],   שנאמר

'Will a man rob God?'   היקבע אדם אלהים

Yet you are robbing me.   כי אתם קובעים אותי

But you say, How have we robbed you?   ואמרתם במה קבענוך

The tithe and the *elevation offering*."   המעשר והתרומה.

R. Joshua [b. Hananiah, T2] said,   אמר רבי יהושע,

"I am like one who can reply   הריני כמשיב

for Tarfon, my brother   על טרפון אחי,

though not corresponding to his words.   אבל לא לעניין דבריו,

[In] Egypt [this is] a new practice   מצרים מעשה חדש

and [in] Babylon [this is] an old practice;   ובבל מעשה ישן,

and the decision before us is a new practice.   והנדון שלפנינו מעשה חדש,

One must decide the new practice   ידון מעשה חדש

from the new practice   ממעשה חדש,

and one must not decide the new practice   ואל ידון מעשה חדש

from the old practice.   ממעשה ישן,

The practice in Egypt [was decided by] the Elders.   מצרים מעשה זקנים

and the practice in Babylon [was decided by] the Prophets;   ובבל מעשה נביאים,

and the decision before us   והנדון שלפנינו

is a practice [decided by] the Elders.   מעשה זקנים,

One must decide a practice [decided by] the Elders   ידון מעשה זקנים

from a practice [decided by] the Elders;   ממעשה זקנים,

and one must not decide   ואל ידון

a practice [decided by] the Elders   מעשה זקנים

from a practice [decided by] the Prophets."   ממעשה נביאים.

They voted and concluded,   נמנו וגמרו,

"Those in Ammon and Moab tithe   עמון ומואב מעשרין

the *poor tithe* in the Sabbath Year."   מעשר עני בשביעית.

And when R. Jose son of the Damascene [T2] came   וכשבא רבי יוסי בן דורמסקית

beside R. Eliezer [b. Hyrcanus, T2]   אצל רבי אליעזר

in Lod, he said to him,   בלוד, אמר לו,

"What new [subject] was before them   מה חדוש היה לכם

in the School of *Midrash* today?"   בבית המדרש היום.

and he said to him,   אמר לו,

"They voted and concluded [that],   נמנו וגמרו,

Those in Ammon and Moab tithe   עמון ומואב מעשרים

the *poor tithe* in the Sabbath Year."   מעשר עני בשביעית.

R. Eliezer wept and said [Ps.25.14],	בכה רבי אליעזר
"The secret of the LORD for to those who fear him	סוד ה' ליראיו
and he will teach them his covenant."	ובריתו להודיעם.
Go and say to them,	צא ואמור להם,
"Do not be troubled by your voting,	אל תחושו למניינכם,
for I received from Rn. Johanan b. Zakkai [T1]	מקובל אני מרבן יוחנן בן זכאי,
which he heard from his rabbi	ששמע מרבו,
and his rabbi from his rabbi	ורבו מרבו
as a *halakhah* of Moses from Sinai	עד הלכה למשה מסיני,
that, 'those in Ammon and Moab tithe	שעמון ומואב מעשרין
poor tithe in the Sabbath Year.'"	מעשר עני בשביעית.

Comments: Within the Land, the *poor tithe* was given every third year and sixth year of the seven-year cycle, and this same tithe was consumed in Jerusalem as the '*second tithe*' on the other years, except for the Sabbath Year when no harvesting occurred. But what about outside the Land where the Sabbath Year crop *was* harvested? Should this tithe be a *second tithe* or a *poor tithe*? The *second tithe* had a higher sacramental value, but the *poor tithe* was more important socially. This matter had already been decided in Egypt (where they paid *poor tithe* in the Sabbath Year) and in Babylon (where they paid *second tithe* in the Sabbath Year), but it had not been decided in Ammon or Moab.

Food was much more expensive in Israel during the Sabbath Year, and the poor of Israel probably depended on the generosity of Jews in neighboring lands where they were allowed to harvest in the Sabbath Year. Householders had to distribute *poor tithe* before *Pesach* (Passover) in the Sabbath Year (this was the time of the *removal*—see Comments at m.Pea.7.6), and so the poor could expect nothing until the following harvest. This caused real hardship, which was recognized by the Roman rulers[39] and by *non-Jews* who jeered at the people who ate wild vegetables and the almost inedible wild endives.[40]

Tarfon argued that they should pay it as a *poor tithe* while Eleazar b. Azariah (who had become head of the Academy "on that same day," cf. m.Yad.3.5) argued vigorously that they should pay it as a *second tithe*. Joshua added arguments in favor of the *poor tithe*, and this won the vote. Finally Eliezer (who did not attend the debate because he was excommunicated at the time) said this agreed with a timeless oral tradition.

This is a fascinating insight into debates and how they were conducted. Eleazar, the newly appointed leader, suddenly found himself disagreeing with Tarfon, an older rabbi who was not always highly respected (cf. m.Ber.1.3). First he tried to wrong-

---

[39] Julius Caesar suspended taxes during Sabbath Years (Jos.*Ant*.14.202.320-28), and others probably followed this practice.
[40] See the discussion in *CRINT* 1.II.827 based on third-century material.

foot Tarfon by claiming that his view was a novelty, so Tarfon pointed out that this was already the practice in Egypt. Eleazar countered that his own viewpoint was followed by Babylon, which was probably more respectable in rabbinic circles than Egypt. Tarfon reminded them that Egypt's policy had been dictated by Jerusalem in the first place. He also suggested that Jerusalem had done this so that the poor of Israel could be supported by the Jews of neighboring countries. Eleazar clearly had no answer to this, so he replied with a vitriolic accusation that Tarfon was only interested in winning approval from the poor by bribing them with food stolen from God, and that this would result in their spiritual destruction and famine for the whole of Israel. Joshua stepped in to support Tarfon, saying that the Babylonian custom was decided by the Prophets whereas the Egyptian custom was decided recently by the Sanhedrin, so the Sanhedrin should make a similar decision now. This is a very strange argument, because it almost suggests that a decision of the Prophets is inferior to one by the Sanhedrin, but nevertheless it carried the day.

Eliezer wept when he heard about this debate, perhaps because of acrimony or perhaps because of the apparent denigration of the Prophets. His message suggests the latter, because he wanted to assure them that their decision was in line with a tradition which was even older than the Prophets.

Dating (5): None of the actual debate can be dated before 70 CE, of course. However, the debate assumes, as an established fact, that Egypt (and perhaps other countries of the Diaspora) collected an extra *poor tithe* in the Sabbath Year, and that at least part of this was used for supporting the poor in Palestine. It may also indicate that Jews in Egypt subjected themselves to rulings of the Sanhedrin in Jerusalem, though this is not certain because it may simply be a debating point and they may merely have been in agreement with Jerusalem on this point.

This debate assumes that the *poor tithe* takes the place of *second tithe* in the third and sixth year. This is contrary to non-rabbinic works which suggest that *poor tithe* and *second tithe* were both paid in these years (*Jub.*32.11; Jos.*Ant.*4.240-41; Tob.1.7-8; Tg.Ps.Jon.Deut.26.1-13), though the rabbinic practice is reflected in the Septuagint (Deut.26.12).

New Testament: The fact that Egypt was expected to give at least part of their *poor tithe* to Jews in Palestine makes Paul's collection fit naturally into normal Jewish expectations. It shows that his Jewish congregation would be used to contributing to such collections, and that Palestinian Jews would be used to receiving such collections. This does not mean that Paul was collecting *poor tithe*, because the fact that he called for a weekly collection would fit the pattern of collecting for a weekly "basket" for the poor (see m.Pea.8.7). However, it is likely that some believers who were practicing Jews would have regarded their contribution as equivalent to their *poor tithe*. .

Eleazar's accusation that Tarfon was 'the sort who gives money' (ממון, *mammon*) which results in "losing their souls" is similar to Jesus' use of the word *mammon* (Mt.6.24 // Lk.16.13) and similar to his message about losing one's soul (Mk.8.36 // Mt.16.26 // Lk.9.25), though Eleazar's words must be dated a couple of decades after 70 CE.

Summary and Conclusions

The concept of *corners* and other related *leftovers* for the poor certainly existed before 70 CE. There was no set minimum for *leftovers* donations, which was set as one-sixtieth soon after 70 CE. This meant that a farmer whose field was divided into several areas by natural borders, each of which was separately liable to *leftovers*, was likely to set aside more *corners* and forget more sheaves than a farmer who had a large field with only one border.

The earlier concept of *leftovers* (before it was defined as one-sixtieth) inspired the moral aphorism "There are three things which have no measure: *leftovers*, *firstfruits*, *appearance offerings*, and deeds of charity" (m.Pea.1.1), and the *'forgotten* sheaf' inspired a parable of rejoicing over fulfillment of a law which could only be fulfilled accidentally (t.Pea.3.8b).

Crops could be *dedicated* to the Temple for its upkeep and repairs (cf. comments on m.Pea.1.6; 2.8; 4.7-8; 7.8a). These *dedications* were probably handled by a local representative of the Treasurer (m.Pea.1.6; 2.8). Farmers tried to avoid paying tithes and the various forms of *leftovers* by *dedicating* their crops to the Temple and then redeeming them (m.Pea.2.7-8; 4.7-8). These donations benefited the Temple at the expense of the poor, but there is no hint of criticism for them. Although the farmers gained little financial advantage, they escaped the work of tithing and the inconvenience of allowing the poor to trample over their land.

There is other evidence of friction between the poor and the farmers. The farmers wanted to limit the amount of time the poor could walk over their fields (m.Pea.4.5 and possibly m.Pea.2.6). They also had the right to exclude the poor from fragile vineyards or trees (m.Pea.4.1-2—though this cannot be dated early with certainty). The poor, in turn, inconvenienced the farmer by demanding the right to glean underneath stacks of produce, and even took the case to court (m.Pea.5.1-3).

Some Shammaite rulings indicate that they were on the side of the poor (m.Pea.6.1a; 7.6) while others suggest that they were on the side of the farmers (m.Pea.6.1b-3, 5—though there are problems with both of these latter rulings, so they were probably on the side of the poor). This confusion did not tempt later generations to try and make the Hillelites appear to be on the side of the poor—they are portrayed as pragmatic and unbiased.

Support for the poor became institutionalized, with a daily provision for itinerant poor and a weekly provision for local poor (m.Pea.8.7). Jews in Egypt, and perhaps in other neighboring countries, were expected to help support Israel's poor, especially during the Sabbath Year (m.Yad.4.3). Paul joined in with this support, by means of a special collection which may have been related to the *poor tithe*.

Tractate *Demay*: Doubtfully Tithed Food

Definitions and Outline

Food which might or might not have been tithed was known as '*doubtful'* food or '*doubtfully tithed food'* (*demay*, דְּמַאי, 'doubtful'[1]), in contrast to '*certainly untithed food'* (*vadday*, וַדַּאי, 'certain'). Neither of these would be eaten by a pious Jew because they contained the *elevation offering* tithes which could only be eaten by a priest while in a state of *purity* (*toharah*, טָהֳרָה). Only *deconsecrated* food (*ḥullin*, חוּלִּין, 'profane,' i.e., food which was fully tithed so that none of it was due to the Temple or priesthood) or *doubtfully tithed food* which had been *corrected* (*metuqqanim*, מְתֻקָּנִים, 'adjusted') could be eaten by a pious nonpriest. The main concern of this tractate is how to recognize *doubtfully tithed food* and how to transform it into *corrected* food.

The *elevation offering* was separated in two parts called the *major elevation offering* and *minor elevation offering*. First the farmer separated for the *major elevation offering* (*terumah gedolah*, תְּרוּמָה גְדוֹלָה)—about one-fiftieth of the whole. This was such an important matter that even nonstrict Jews were scrupulous in separating this portion. *Doubtfully tithed food* may or may not have had the *first* and *second tithe* removed, but it was always assumed that the *major elevation offering* had been removed. Only *untithed* food still contained the *major elevation offering*.

The *minor elevation offering* (*terumah qetannah*, תְּרוּמָה קְטַנָּה) resided within the *first tithe* (the Levite's tithe), because the Levite was expected to give one-tenth of his tithe to the priests as an *elevation offering*. If the produce was *doubtfully tithed* (i.e., it was doubtful whether the *first tithe* had been separated), this *elevation offering* might still be present in the food. Therefore, just in case, pious Jews separated one-hundredth of any *doubtfully tithed food* and discarded it. It is this small *minor elevation offering* which is the main topic of the tractate of *Demay* because it is assumed throughout that the *major elevation offering* has been removed even from *doubtfully tithed food*. Only completely *untithed* food (*tebel*, טֶבֶל, i.e., 'liable [to tithing]') still contained the *major elevation offering*.

This tractate highlights the contrast between the Associates (*ḥaber*, pl. *ḥaberim*, חֲבֵרִים חָבֵר) and the Trusted (*neeman*, נֶאֱמָן) with the *impious* (*am ha-aretz*, עַם הָאָרֶץ). The former two can be trusted with regard to tithing and *purity* while the

---

[1] See various theories on the etymology of *demai* in Richard S. Sarason, *The Talmud of the Land of Israel;* vol. 3: *Demai* (Chicago: University of Chicago Press, 1993), pp. 307-8, n. 1.

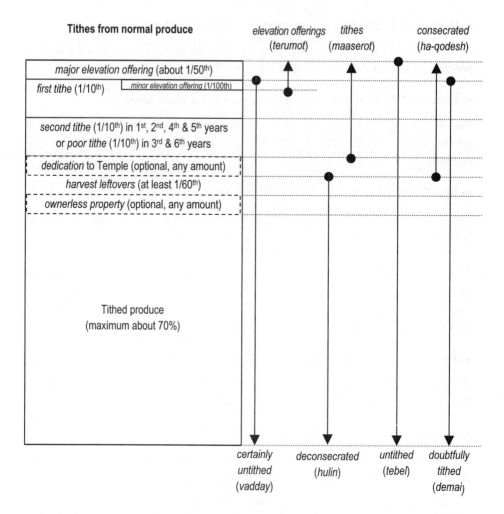

latter cannot. The meaning of *am ha-aretz* (literally 'people of the land') changed with time. In the OT it means 'the landed gentry' but by NT times it is used by the Pharisees to indicate those who do not keep their Oral Law, and after 70 CE it also came to be used as a term of abuse meaning something like 'ignoramus.' It does not indicate a class distinction because even a High Priest can be regarded as an *am ha-aretz* (cf. m.Hor.3.8).

m.Dem.1.1–2.1: What can be suspected of being *doubtful*?

Only cultivated food which is grown in the earth had to be tithed; therefore the same definition decides what is liable to *doubtful* status (though there are some exceptions).

m.Dem.2.2–4.2: Special circumstances re *doubtfully tithed food*

An Associate could be relied on to tithe properly while the *impious* could not. Poor people could be given *doubtfully tithed food* to eat.

m.Dem.4.3–5.2: How to recognize and process *doubtfully tithed food*

You need to physically separate only one hundredth—the amount of the *elevation offering* of the Levite's tithe. The other tithes can be dealt with by a statement or a payment.

m.Dem.5.3-11: *Doubtfully tithed food* from different sources

Sometimes one can make a single separation for food from two or more sources, but if the sources are too diverse, one has to make individual separations.

m.Dem.6.1-12: How farmers should tithe

Farmers were expected to separate off only the *major elevation offering* before they sold their produce, though if the recipient was not likely to tithe it fully, a conscientious farmer should do so.

m.Dem.7.1-6: When you cannot tithe *doubtfully tithed food* before eating

If you cannot tithe *doubtfully tithed food* during a meal, you may make the statement beforehand and silently leave a portion uneaten.

m.Dem.7.7-8: When tithes become *doubtful*

What to do if *deconsecrated* and *certainly untithed* food become mixed so that it is uncertain which portion contains the *elevation offerings*.

m.Dem.1.1–2.1: What can be suspected of being *doubtful*?

Summary of Mishnah: You do not have to tithe *doubtfully tithed food* if it grows wild (1.1), or if it is not used for human consumption, or if it was grown outside Israel (1.3-4). However, some food outside Israel should be assumed to have been grown in Israel and exported—i.e., pressed figs, dates, carobs, and white rice (2.1). The rules concerning tithing are not applied so strictly when tithing *doubtfully tithed food* (1.4); and *second tithe* which is separated from *doubtfully tithed food* is not subject to such strict rules as *second tithe* from *certainly untithed* food (1.2).

The following traditions have elements (marked in bold) for which there is evidence of an origin before 70 CE:

m.Dem.1.1a and t.Dem.1.1a: Uncultivated food is exempt from doubtful status

m.Dem.1.1a:

One should judge leniently the *doubtful* status of:	הקלין שבדמאי,
wild figs, jujube fruit, crab-apples	השיתין, והרימין והעוזרדין,
white figs, sycamore figs,	ובנות שוח, ובנות שקמה,
fallen dates	ונובלות התמרה,
late-grapes, capers.	והגופנין, והנצפה.
And in Judea, sumac berries,	וביהודה, האוג,
vinegar which is in Judea, and coriander.	והחומץ שביהודה, והכוסבר.

t.Dem.1.1a:

One should judge leniently the *doubtful* status of:	הקלין שבדמאיי,
wild figs, jujube fruit, crab-apples.	השיתין והרימין והעוזרדין
One should presume [that they are]	חזקתן
in all places, exempt,	בכל מקום פטורין,
but if they are guarded, they are liable.	ואם היו משתמרין חייבין

Comments: The rabbis were more lenient about some food than others. Mishnah does not explain why, but Tosefta explains that these are all uncultivated (i.e., they are "unguarded"). Food which grows wild is not subject to any tithes (m.Maas.1.1), so neither is it subject to *doubtful* status.

It is not clear why vinegar and sumac berries are exempt only if they are from Judea. Tosefta has a later undateable tradition that "at first, vinegar which [was made] in Judea was exempt, since it was presumed [to be made] from skins of grapes. Now, since it is presumed [to be made] from wine, it is liable." This suggests that it was not liable because of the Jewish habit of making vinegar from the discarded remains of winemaking, but that outside Judea they made it from wine, and that they later followed this practice also in Judea. The sumac berries were used for making dyes outside Judah, but it appears that they were also eaten by poor Jews when they were found growing wild.

Dating (1): R. Eliezer uses the principle in t.Dem.1.4 that 'guarded' food is never exempt because the fact that someone has fenced it off indicates that it is not simply growing wild. He refers to this principle as something which is universally accepted, so it must date from at least before 70 CE. This suggests that the first part of the ruling, as found in Tosefta, is pre-70.

The list of produce in Mishnah appears to have been gradually extended. The core list is probably that which is found in Tosefta. The process of gradual addition is especially evident at the end of the list, which is somewhat untidy. We would expect that "in Judea" would be followed either by a list of items grown in Judea, or that it would refer to only one item, but the second "in Judea" indicates that neither of these is the case. Probably the list grew in the following five stages:

1. wild figs, jujube fruit, crab-apples
2. white figs, sycamore figs, fallen dates, late-grapes, capers
3. in Judea, sumac berries
4. vinegar
5. which in Judea, coriander

The addition of "vinegar" referred to vinegar bought in Judea, like the preceding item, so there was no need at stage 4 to add the words "which is in Judea." But "coriander" was meant to refer to that which was purchased in Israel or outside, so the second "in Judea" had to be added after "vinegar." These untidy piecemeal additions suggest that there was a reluctance to disturb the order of the list, so that words had to be added to the end and not inserted.

m.Dem.1.3: Food not for eating or not from Israel is exempt

He who buys [grain] for seed or for cattle,	הלוקח לזרע ולבהמה,
flour for skins, oil for the lamp,	קמח לעורות, שמן לנר,
oil for lubricating utensils with it,	שמן לסוך בו את הכלים,
is exempt from *doubtful* status.	פטור מן הדמאי.
[Food] from Kezib and beyond	מכזיב ולהלן,
is exempt from *doubtful* status.	פטור מן הדמאי.
The *dough offering* of an *impious one*	חלת עם הארץ,
and [food which is] *tainted* [with *elevation offerings*]	והמדומע,
and [food] bought with *second tithe silver*	והלקוח בכסף מעשר שני,
and the remainder of a *meal offering*	ושירי המנחות,
are exempt from *doubtful* status.	פטורין מן הדמאי.
Spiced oil:	שמן ערב,
The School of Shammai obligate	בית שמאי מחייבין,
and the School of Hillel exempt.	ובית הלל פוטרין.

t.Dem.1.26-28 (Z 1.20): Some spiced oils and *meal offerings* are exempt

Spiced oil:	שמן ערב,
The School of Shammai obligate	בית שמיי מחייבין,
and the School of Hillel exempt.	ובית הלל פוטרין
R. Nathan said: Not thus.	אמר ר׳ נתן לא היו
The School of Hillel exempt	בית הלל פוטרין
[none] except only which is from spikenard	אלא בשל פלייטון בלבד
27) Others say in name of R. Nathan:	אחרים אומרים משום ר׳ נתן,
Obligated thus:	מחייבין היו
The School of Hillel, re oil of roses[*1]	בית הלל בשמן ורד ודנין
28) Recompense for *elevation offerings* and its *added fifth*	תשלומי תרומה וחומשה,
[if it is accidentally eaten by a nonpriest]	
and the *added fifth* of the *added fifth* [if that is eaten]	וחומש חומשה,

and the remainder of the *first sheaf*	,מוֹתַר הָעוֹמֶר
and of the *two loaves* [of *wave offering*]	,וּשְׁתֵּי הַלֶּחֶם
and the Loaves of the Presence	,וְלֶחֶם הַפָּנִים
and the remainder of a *meal offering*	,וּשְׁיָרֵי מְנָחוֹת
and the [voluntary] supplements to *firstfruits*.	וְתוֹסֶפֶת הַבִּכּוּרִים
R. Simeon b. Judah [T6] said	רִ׳ שִׁמְעוֹן בֶּן יְהוּדָה אוֹמֵר
in the name of R. Simeon [b. Yohai, T4]	מִשּׁוּם רִ׳ שִׁמְעוֹן
The School of Shammai obligate [these re *doubtful* status]	,בֵּית שַׁמַּי מְחַיְּיבִין
and the School of Hillel exempt.	.וּבֵית הִלֵּל פּוֹטְרִין
And concerning all [of them]—that which is designated	וְכוּלָן שֶׁקָּרָא שֵׁם
as *second tithe* [from] what belongs to this:*2	לְמַעֲשֵׂר שֵׁנִי שֶׁלָּהֶן
What has been done is done.	.מַה שֶּׁעָשָׂה עָשׂוּי

---

*1 Z has וורד 'and rose' for ודנין. ורד ודנין is a corruption of ῥόδινον, 'rose unguent' (Jastrow).

*2 Z has עֲלֵיהֶן 'elevated' for שֶׁלָּהֶן.

Comments: Both Mishnah and Tosefta have a list of items of food which are not subject to *doubtful* status—i.e., you do not have to remove the *elevation offering* of the *first tithe*, even if you cannot be sure that it has been removed. The parts of the lists which are given here contain some early elements. The rest of the list may or may not be early.

The list contains items of food which are not eaten by humans (cattle food, flour used for tanning, oil for burning, lubricating, or anointing), so there is no danger that a nonpriest will eat any *elevation offering* which remains in them. Food grown outside Israel ("beyond Kezib") is exempt from tithing (see m.Qid.1.9 which is dealt with in the chapter on *Orlah*[2]). Foods which had been given as offerings and become available as food can be assumed to be properly tithed, because even one of the *impious* would make sure that offerings were properly tithed.[3]

The schools debated whether anointing oil should be subject to *doubtful* status or exempt. Mishnah says only the Shammaites considered such oil to be liable—perhaps they feared that some may accidentally be imbibed, especially when it was used to clean your hands after a meal (cf. t.Ber.5.29). This would be akin to the ruling that oil with which a weaver lubricates his fingers is subject to *doubtful* status while the oil which is put on spun wool is not subject (m.Dem.1.4). This stricter policy is also seen in later debates about the Hillelite position, as seen in t.Dem.1.26, where later authorities say that Hillel only exempted certain oils—perhaps they were the ones used for anointing corpses which could not be imbibed accidentally.

Tosefta adds that the Schools also debated a longer list of possible exemptions, but this is unlikely (see Dating). It also adds that if anyone has designated *second*

---

[2] Placed at the end of the chapter on *Kilayim*.

[3] This principle is stated three times as a *baraytah* in y.Dem.2.2.I; 2.3.II; 5.1.

tithe and put aside the money for this (as described at m.Dem.4.3), and the item is then found to be on the list of exemptions, the *second tithe* cannot be revoked.

Dating (1): Three of the items in m.Dem.1.3 are shared with Tosefta (t.Dem.1.25 "flour for skins"; 1.26 "spiced oil"; 1.28 "remainder of a *meal offering*"), but they are dispersed within many more items which are not in Mishnah. It is likely that both Mishnah and Tosefta developed and enlarged the same source. Some of these developments or additions in Tosefta are concerned with matters which were of little interest after 70 CE, i.e., various meal offerings (the two loaves of *wave offering*, and the Loaf of the Presence). If we could be sure that these additions were made before 70 CE, then all the traditions which are shared by Mishnah and Tosefta would very likely also date from before 70 CE. However, these three items are already collected together in m.Zeb.9.5,[4] with "the remainder of a *meal offering*" which is in both Mishnah and Tosefta. So it is likely that the presence of "remainder of the *meal offering*" influenced the insertion of the others from that text, and it is quite possible that this took place long after 70 CE. Therefore it is not safe to conclude that the other additions are pre-70, although the "remainder of the *meal offering*" probably is pre-70 because there is no surrounding debate which would otherwise explain its inclusion.

Other items in this group which are shared by Mishnah and Tosefta are "oil with which the weaver lubricates his fingers" and "[oil] which the wool comber puts on the wool" (m.Dem.1.4; t.Dem.1.29). It is likely that these belong to the same set of traditions as the others in this group which Mishnah and Tosefta have in common, but we have seen that these common traditions may not be pre-70. It is likely that this pair belongs to a later period when oil was treated more strictly (see Comments).

The list in the Mishnah is much shorter and yet does not have the characteristics of an abbreviation of the list in Tosefta. It is therefore likely to be an earlier list. Some items in the list indicate a pre-70 origin—namely, the "spiced oil" (a school debate) and the "remainder of *meal offering*" (a Temple-based offering). Tosefta's attribution of the longer list to the schools (at the end of t.Dem.1.28) is not convincing. It looks 'tagged on' and secondary.

m.Dem.2.2–4.2: Special circumstances re *doubtfully tithed food*

Summary of Mishnah: A Trusted one or an Associate can be trusted with regard to tithing while the *impious* cannot (2.2). A Trusted one tithes all the food which he eats or sells or buys, and an Associate will not even sell anything to the *impious*, nor buy wet goods from them [because they are susceptible to picking up *impurity*]. An

---

[4] This lists items which come back from the altar for priests to consume. Cf. also m.Zeb.14.3.

Associate will not be a guest of the *impious* and will only let an *impious one* be a guest at his house in *pure* clothes [which the Associate supplies] (2.2-3).

You must not give *doubtfully tithed food* to a friend (3.3), though it is all right to give it to the poor or to your laborers, who may tithe it if they wish (3.1). If you discard substandard food which you own, you must first tithe it [in case someone eats it], even if you are returning it to the seller [he loses nothing, because it can now be sold as *deconsecrated* food, at a correspondingly higher price] (3.2).

Shopkeepers (who sell to the consumer) have to tithe what they sell just in case it is *doubtfully tithed*, though wholesalers do not (2.4-5). Bakers also have to remove the *elevation offering* of dough (Num.15.20-21—traditionally one-twenty-fourth for householders or one-forty-eighth for commercial bakers) (2.4). A Samaritan or one of the *impious* can be trusted not to contaminate tithed food, but food processed or stored by a gentile must be treated as *doubtfully tithed* (3.4). If you give *deconsecrated* food to be cooked by an innkeeper, or by your mother-in-law, they cannot be trusted, and you must treat the meal as *doubtfully tithed* (3.5-6).

If you are about to eat food on a Sabbath [when the work of tithing is prohibited] which might have been *doubtfully tithed*, you should find the vendor and ask him, and you may accept his word—but after the Sabbath you must tithe the remainder (4.1). If you are forced to eat a meal at the house of an *impious one* on a Sabbath, you may accept his word that it was not *doubtfully tithed*, but if the hospitality continues after the Sabbath, you must tithe your food (4.2).

The following traditions have elements (marked in bold) for which there is evidence of an origin before 70 CE:

m.Dem.2.2a: How to be a Trusted one

He who accepts [the obligations] upon himself	המקבל עליו
to be a Trusted one	להיות נאמן,
must tithe that which he eats	מעשר את שהוא אוכל,
and that which he sells	ואת שהוא מוכר,
and that which he buys,	ואת שהוא לוקח,
and he must not lodge with an *impious one.*	ואינו מתארח אצל עם הארץ.

Comments: A Trusted one is someone who can be trusted with regard to tithing. This means that it is safe to eat at his house on a Sabbath when you cannot tithe (see m.Dem.7.1). Lodging with an *impious one* would risk eating food which might not be tithed, and would risk contamination with *impurity*.

The following passage suggests that Associates carried out the requirements of being Trusted as well as further requirements which ensured that they avoided all *impurity*, so being a Trusted one was slightly easier than being an Associate.

Dating (2): The dating of this ruling depends on the dating of the following ruling about Associates. The ruling about Associates lists stricter requirements, without also listing the lesser requirements of the Trusted ones, which the Associates presumably also adhered to.[5] This suggests that the two rulings have to be read together, because the ruling about Associates depends on the ruling about Trusted ones. Therefore the ruling about Associates is either later or from the same time as the ruling about Trusted ones.

The single overlap between them ("must not lodge with an *impious one*") may indicate that the rulings originally had independent existences and that the ruling about Associates was an expansion of the ruling about the Trusted ones. This overlapping line was questioned by R. Judah in the second half of this mishnah, and the Sages defended it (though opinions are reversed in t.Dem.2.2). It is possible that R. Judah was trying to draw a clearer distinction between the Trusted ones (who kept tithing laws strictly) and Associates (who kept *purity* laws strictly). He was presumably wishing to remove the single overlap between the regulations for each group.

New Testament: The concept of 'faithfulness' or 'trustworthiness' (אֱמוּנָה, *emunah*), as found here, is completely different from the use of πίστις in the NT where it means 'faith' or 'trust,' except perhaps in James where there is some questioning of the faith-works dichotomy (Jas.2.14-26). The meaning of πίστις in Greek texts and papyri outside the NT is normally 'pledge, proof, commitment,' which is much closer to the meaning of *amanah* in the OT and rabbinic traditions. The verb *amen* (אָמֵן) does sometimes have the sense of 'to be trustworthy' (*niphal*) and 'to trust, believe in' (*hiphil*—e.g., m.Dem.7.1, below[6]), though usually it means 'to be strong, reliable, trustworthy.' Classical Greek literature also has a few examples of πίστις as 'faith' or 'trust,' but this meaning is only found commonly in the NT and in some other first-century Greek Jewish writings such as Philo, Josephus, and 4 Maccabees. However, in older Greek Jewish works such as the LXX, πίστις almost always translates *amanah*, which is perhaps why James appears to complain about the new meaning of the word, and why Hebrews continues to regard 'faith' as synonymous with 'proof, pledge' (Heb.11.1).[7] The Hebrew verb which does usually mean 'to believe in' or 'to trust' is *batah* (בָּטַח) which is translated in the LXX by ἐλπίζω 'to trust in' (e.g., Judg.9.26; 2Kgs.18.5, 30) or πείθω 'to believe in' (e.g., 2Kgs.19.10; Isa.12.2) but never by πιστεύω or πίστις. The verb *batah* continued to

---

[5] This principle is preserved as a *baraytah* (y.Dem.2.2.II; 2.3.II; 5.1.I), though this of course does not guarantee that it predates 70 CE.
[6] Cf. also m.Dem.7.3. Both these texts are concerned with tithing *doubtful food,* so they may be contrasting the person who they do not 'trust' with a Trusted one.
[7] The article in the *TDOT* contains further analysis of these issues.

have this meaning in rabbinic Hebrew (cf. the thirteenth of the Eighteen Benedictions).

m.Dem.2.3a: How to be an Associate

He who accepts [the obligations] upon himself	המקבל עליו
to be an Associate	להיות חבר,
he may not sell to an *impious one*	אינו מוכר לעם הארץ
wet or dry [produce]	לח ויבש,
and he may not buy wet [produce] from him	ואינו לוקח ממנו לח,
and he must not lodge with an *impious one*	ואינו מתארח אצל עם הארץ,
and he may not lodge him in his [own] clothes.	ולא מארחו אצלו בכסותו.

Comments: The 'Associates' were trusted to be careful with matters of *purity*, so a fellow Associate could eat or lodge with him, secure in the knowledge that his own *purity* would not be compromised. Wet produce or the clothes of a guest might carry *impurity*—cf. m.Hag.2.7: "The clothes of an *impious one* are [assumed to be] *impure* to Pharisees." As noted above, an Associate presumably also followed the requirements of being a Trusted one, which were lesser than those for being an Associate.

The requirement that an Associate should not sell any produce to the *impious* is presumably an effort to reduce any unnecessary meetings with the *impious* and the associated danger of *impurity*. This requirement would tend to produce ghettos of carefully observant Jews who bought and sold only among themselves. Associates were still allowed to purchase dry provisions from the *impious*, presumably because this would be necessary from time to time even if the ghetto contained producers of most types of food. However, it is also possible that not selling to non-Associates was an economic necessity, because if they had to tithe everything they sold (in case the purchaser did not tithe it) their produce would be 20 percent more expensive than someone who merely separated the *major elevation offering*. Only the Associates were willing to pay extra for produce which they knew was tithed.

The name 'Associate' was a normal term for a fellow or a friend, which became a technical term rather like 'brother' or 'comrade' today. The term 'comrade' has become firmly linked with socialist political parties, so it has ceased to be used as a normal word, but 'brother' is used by various religious and political groups to refer to their own members, and has therefore continued as a normal word. The term 'associate' also continued as a normal word,[8] which suggests that it was not used exclusively by one particular group. It may also suggest that this is an internal

---

[8] E.g., m.Ber.9.5c, talking about how to greet a friend in the street: "they decreed that when a man greets his associate, he should do so using the divine Name."

reference ('of us' not 'of them') just like 'brothers' are internal references in the NT and in the Dead Sea Scrolls.

Dating (2): This mishnah has little or nothing to do with tithing and is probably here because it is linked to the previous mishnah. The concept of Associates can be confidently dated back to before 70 CE because of the school debate concerning them (see t.Dem.2.12 below). The school debate assumes that the main requirements of an Associate concerns clothing and wet produce, as also in this mishnah. There would be a tendency to add to this list, especially with regard to tithing, and other matters of lifestyle (as R. Judah tried to do in m.Dem.2.3b), so it is likely that m.Dem.2.3a contains the original list of requirements.

It might be possible to argue that the lines "not sell to an *impious one* wet or dry" and "must not lodge with an *impious one*" were added at a later date, because they are not referred to in t.Dem.2.12. However, this is very unlikely, because the lines which *are* in t.Dem.2.12 are dependent on these lines:

> must not sell to **an *impious one*** wet or dry [produce]
>> and must not buy wet from **him**
> and must not be lodged with **an *impious one***
>> and not lodge **him** in his [own] clothes.

Unless the whole tradition was rewritten when these lines were imported, it is more likely that they are either older or of the same age as the ones attested to by the school debate.

This is confirmed by t.Maas.3.13 where Simeon b. Gamaliel refers to a school debate in which both schools agreed that "a man should sell a stack of grain or a basket of grapes or a vat of olives only to an Associate who prepares [food] in *purity.*" The substance of this school debate is missing, and only the area of agreement is noted; so, this tradition does not carry much weight by itself, but these two traditions help to confirm each other.[9]

New Testament: The attitude of the Pharisees in John is that "the multitude who do not know the law are accursed" (Jn.7.49). According to Luke, they did not regard Jesus as *impious* because some were willing to eat with him in their houses (cf. Lk.7.36, 39; 11.37; 14.1). However, in Matthew and Luke the first incident is the house of an ex-leper (Mt.26.6-13 // Mk.14.3-9), the second involves the Pharisees merely watching them eat (Mt.15.1-2 // Mk.7.1-5), and the third has no parallels. It may be significant that these meals in Matthew and Mark include his disciples, but in Luke, where Pharisees are hosts, the disciples are not mentioned.

---

[9] See also the discussion at m.Dem.6.6.

t.Dem.2.12 (Z 2.9c): How long before you trust an Associate?

How long before one should accept [an Associate]	עד מתי מקבלין
The School of Shammai says:	בית שמיי אומרים
For liquids, thirty days.	למשקין שלשים יום
For clothes, twelve months.	לכסות שנים עשר חודש
And the School of Hillel says:	ובית הלל אומרים
For both, thirty days.	זה וזה לשלשים יום.

Comments: There was a trial period during which someone who kept the restrictions could not be treated as an Associate. The Shammaites are characteristically more severe, saying that he has to show himself trustworthy for twelve months with regard to keeping clothes uncontaminated before he can be assumed to be trustworthy.

The use of the verb 'accept' (קִבֵּל, *qabal*) links this with both m.Dem.2.2a and 2.3a, which both start with "he who accepts [the obligations]." This tradition does not state whether it concerns the obligations of an Associate or a Trusted one, but the context in Tosefta is that of Associates—though this may not be significant, because the Tosefta says nothing about Trusted ones, and even the tradition of m.Dem.2.2 is related to Associates in t.Dem.2.2. However, the reference to "liquids" and "clothes" suggests that this refers to Associates.

This tradition shows that the Associates were not a separate group, like Shammaites or Hillelites, but they were a trusted group within both these schools, and presumably within other schools too. It also suggests that there was some mutual recognition of this status by each school, much like most churches recognize each other's baptism, even if they differ radically concerning the procedures for it.

Dating (1): There is no reason to doubt that this is a genuine school debate. This period of trial before you can be called an Associate is reminiscent of the period of initiation in the Qumran sect.

m.Dem.3.1: Who can be fed with *doubtfully tithed food*?

One may feed the [local] poor	מאכילין את העניים
with *doubtfully tithed* [food]	דמאי,
and the transient poor with *doubtfully tithed* [food]	ואת האכסניא דמאי.
Rn. Gamaliel used to	רבן גמליאל היה
feed his laborers *doubtful* [food],	מאכיל את פועליו דמאי.
Collectors of charity:	גבאי צדקה,
The School of Shammai says:	בית שמאי אומרים,
One should give tithed [food]	נותנין את המעושר
to him who does not tithe	לשאינו מעשר,
and non-tithed [food] to a tither.	ואת שאינו מעושר למעשר.
[This] will result in every man	נמצאו כל האדם
eating *corrected* [food].	אוכלין מתוקן.

But the Sages say:	,וחכמים אומרים
One should collect without a statement [about its status]	גובין סתם
and one should distribute without a statement;	,ומחלקין סתם
[if] he wishes to legitimate it, he must legitimate it.	.והרוצה לתקן, יתקן

Comments: Poor people may be fed with *doubtfully tithed food*.[10] This includes both the local poor and the transient poor who pass through or stay overnight. Rn. Gamaliel is even reputed to have fed his laborers with *doubtfully tithed food*. Shammaites say that *doubtfully tithed food* should be given only to those poor who are known to tithe properly, but the Sages (i.e., the majority) said that this was impractical, because food is collected without any statement about its status.

The Shammaite proposal appears to be completely impractical, as the response of the Sages points out. However, it is possible that their ruling dates from a time when central collections were less common. In small villages they did not always have official collectors, and the poor would be fed at whichever house they begged (see m.Pea.8.7). In this situation, the householder would decide what food to give to which poor, and so they could designate in the way that the Shammaites proposed.

Some translations have "billeted troops" instead of "transient poor." Although this is a perfectly possible translation of *akhsania* (אַכְסַנְיָא, 'unknown guests'), it is more likely that this ruling refers to the two classes of poor people—the local poor who are given provisions every week, and the transient poor who are fed every day at the home of the official collectors (see m.Pea.8.7).

Dating (1): There is no reason to doubt that the Shammaite ruling is genuine, though the Hillelite portion is missing. It is likely that the response of the Sages is a later explanation of the Hillelite ruling which would have been something like, "They give any food to any poor." This explanation made the Hillelite ruling redundant, so it was later omitted. It is unlikely that this school debate originally concerned "collectors of charity" but instead concerned something like "giving charity" (see Comments).

It is uncertain whether this is Gamaliel I [T1] or Gamaliel II [T2]. It is likely to be Gamaliel I because he is acting contrary to a ruling which was debated by rabbis in T4 (m.Dem.7.3), which says what a laborer should do if "he does not believe (מַאֲמִין, *maamin*) the employer." This is a pejorative way of suggesting that an employer may not have tithed his laborer's food, and shows that a good employer would certainly be expected to do so. The ruling of m.Dem.7.3 dates from the early second century, because it is disputed by rabbis in T4 (mid second century), which makes it unlikely

---

[10] The participle, which has the role of a present tense in Mishnaic Hebrew, can carry the force of a jussive or cohortative, so the opening phrase could mean "They should feed" or "They may feed." Similarly the saying of Shammai could mean "They may give" or "They should give." Because Mishnah contains mainly rulings, the participle usually means "should," but in this opening phrase the meaning of "may" fits better.

that Gamaliel II (who was an exemplary rabbi) would have been guilty of breaking this ruling. Therefore, this is likely to be a reference to Gamaliel I in whose day things were less regulated.

New Testament: The crowds of 5,000 and 4,000 men who ate the miraculous five loaves and seven loaves treated the food as *doubtful*, and therefore left twelve and seven baskets of broken-off fragments (κλάσματα). This detail is included in each account of these miracles in all four Gospels (Mt.14.20; 15.37; Mk.6.43; 8.8; Lk.9.17; Jn.6.12-13) and again when Jesus discusses the miracles with his disciples in the boat (Mk.8.19-20—though Matthew simply says 'baskets' in Mt.16.10). It is likely that these fragments were the *elevation offerings* which individuals had removed prior to eating the loaves—i.e., one-hundredth of each loaf, or three one-hundredths if they thought that the dough tithe needed to be removed too (see summary of m.Dem.2.2–4.2). These portions could not be eaten, but had to be destroyed if there was no priest available. The disciples picked the fragments up carefully, either to give them to a priest, or to destroy them so that no one would accidentally eat them.

m.Dem.4.3–5.2:   How to recognize and process *doubtfully tithed food*

Summary of Mishnah: A *poor tithe* does not need to be separated, but only designated (4.3), though a poor man can eat it if he is at the meal (4.4). An *elevation offering* cannot be separated on a Sabbath but only designated, though a priest may eat it if he is at the meal (4.4).

You cannot trust the *impious* to buy food from a trustworthy seller whom he chooses, though you can trust him to buy from a trustworthy seller whom you name (4.5). You can believe an unknown seller if he recommends someone else as trustworthy but not if he recommends himself (4.6-7).

To tithe *doubtfully tithed food*, you physically separate one-hundredth (the *elevation offering* of the Levites' *first tithe*) and verbally designate the rest of the *first tithe* and the *second tithe* (which you can redeem with money) (5.1). If it is bread, you physically separate a bit extra to include the *elevation offering* of the dough (5.1). If wholly untithed (i.e., even the *major elevation offering* is still present), you physically separate three-hundredths, which is the *major elevation offering* (one-fiftieth) plus the *minor elevation offering* of the *first tithe* (one-hundredth) (5.2).

The following traditions have elements (marked in bold) for which there is evidence of an origin before 70 CE:

m.Dem.4.3: The *poor tithe* from *doubtfully tithed food*

R. Eliezer [b. Hyrcanus, T2] said:
It is not necessary for a man to **designate**
the *poor tithe* from *doubtful* [produce].
But the Sages say:
He designates,
but it is not necessary to set it aside.

רבי אליעזר אומר,
אין אדם צריך לקרות שם
למעשר עני של דמאי.
וחכמים אומרים,
קורא שם
ואין צריך להפריש.

Comments: Normally when you tithe *doubtfully tithed food*, you physically separate the *elevation offering* of the *first tithe*, and then verbally designate the *first tithe* and *second tithe*, stating that it is to the north or south of the *elevation offering*. But what about the third and sixth years when you give *poor tithe* instead of *second tithe*? The majority say that you do exactly the same as for *second tithe* (i.e., designate it verbally, but leave it there), while Eliezer says that it is not even necessary to designate it.

It is not clear why Eliezer ruled in this way. The Jerusalem Talmud contains a long debate about this (y.Dem.4.5) which is based on an effort to harmonize this with a ruling by Rab [BA1] that "he who eats his produce when tithe for the poor has not been set aside from it has incurred the death penalty" (y.Qid.2.9, cf. b.Mak.16b). They argue that this would make even the poor tithe the *second tithe* properly, even if they don't tithe the *first tithe*. However, as they point out, this does not concur with the other ruling of Eliezer that "if they saw him setting aside the *second tithe*, [that person] is trusted [to have also set aside] the *first tithe*" (t.MS.3.16).

More likely, Eliezer was making the point that the designation of *poor tithe* was meaningless. When you designated *second tithe*, you put aside some money to represent its redemption, to make up for the fact that you did not actually set aside the *second tithes*. But *poor tithes* could not be redeemed in this way, so their designation had no practical value. From the reply of the Sages, it may be inferred that instead of merely designating the *poor tithe*, Eliezer actually set it aside and gave it to a poor person.

The normal process for tithing *doubtfully tithed food* would have been something akin to that found in m.Dem.4.5 and less fully elsewhere:

> He should *elevate* sufficient for the *elevation offering* of the [*first*] *tithe*, and say: "One hundredth of what is here will be on this side, [*first*] *tithe* and the rest of the [*first*] *tithe* is next to it, and the *second tithe* will be in the north (or south) of it and shall be redeemed with money."

This formula suggests that the *second tithe* was redeemed, but it may imply that the *first tithe* was not. This represents later practice and it may (or may not) represent practice before 70 CE. From this mishnah about Eliezer, we might expect that Eliezer would have put aside money for the *first* as well as the *second tithe*.

Dating (5): This ruling by Eliezer, who taught just after 70 CE, assumes the procedure of verbally designating *first* and *second tithes*, though it questions whether the *poor tithe* should be treated in the same way. This implies that the procedure of verbal tithing in this way was already practiced. We do not know exactly what the formula was, or even if there was a standard formula, but it was probably similar to this one.

    This is probably a continuation of the school dispute in t.MS.3.15 where the Hillelites say that you do not have to designate the *second tithe*, but the law followed the Shammaites who said that you have to designate them both even if the designation of the *second tithe* served no practical purpose.

m.Dem.5.3-11: *Doubtfully tithed food* from different sources

Summary of Mishnah: You must tithe each type of *doubtfully tithed food* separately, and even each loaf separately, unless you are sure it came from the same baker who used the same flour (5.3-4). If a poor man is given pieces of bread from several people, he must tithe each separately, though he does not have to tithe each date and fig separately—and similarly if you buy food from a poor man (5.5). If you buy food twice from the same merchant or householder you may assume both purchases came from the same source and tithe it all only once—unless the seller says it comes from different sources (5.6-7).

    Certainly untithed food from different sources can be tithed together, though you should only sell *certainly untithed* food in an emergency (5.8). You can even tithe together *certainly untithed* food from vendors as diverse as Israelites and Samaritans and gentiles (though Eliezer says Samaritan produce should always be regarded as *doubtfully tithed* and not as *certainly untithed*) (5.9).

    Food grown in a perforated pot is considered to be from the same source as food grown in the earth or in other nearby perforated pots, but food grown in unperforated pots are all separate sources (5.10).

    You cannot tithe *doubtfully tithed food* and *certainly untithed* food together. If you tithe *doubtfully tithed food* wrongly (e.g., when it is mixed with food from another source), the tithe has the status of *elevation offering*, but you must not give it to a priest until you have tithed the food again, correctly (5.11).

There is no evidence that traditions in this section predate 70 CE, though the following tradition gives some indication of pre-70 teaching.

m.Dem.5.9: Do the Samaritans tithe properly?

One should tithe the [produce] of Israelites   מְעַשְּׂרִין מִשֶּׁל יִשְׂרָאֵל
[to fulfill tithing] for [produce] of gentiles;   עַל שֶׁל נָכְרִי,

from that of gentiles for that of Israelites	מְשֶׁל נָכְרִי עַל שֶׁל יִשְׂרָאֵל,
from that of Israelites for that of Samaritans	מְשֶׁל יִשְׂרָאֵל עַל שֶׁל כּוּתִים,
from that of Samaritans for that of Samaritans.	מְשֶׁל כּוּתִים עַל שֶׁל כּוּתִים.
R. Eliezer [b. Hyrcanus, T2] prohibits	רִבִּי אֱלִיעֶזֶר אוֹסֵר
from that of Samaritans for that of Samaritans.	מְשֶׁל כּוּתִים עַל שֶׁל כּוּתִים.

Comments: Each item of *doubtfully tithed food* must be tithed for itself, or for an item from exactly the same batch of produce, but *untithed* food can be tithed together with food from a completely different source. This ruling shows how disparate those sources can be. For example, if a Jew bought a sack of grain which was grown in the Land by a gentile (which was *untithed*), and also had a sack of grain from his own harvest which he had not tithed, he could tithe his own grain twice, and thereby consider the gentile's grain to be tithed, or vice versa. This would not apply to produce which was grown outside the Land by a gentile, because this did not need to be tithed.

Samaritan food was, according to this ruling, assumed to be *untithed*. This did not imply that they did not tithe; it implied that they probably did not tithe food which they sold in Jewish markets. R. Eliezer said in t.Dem.5.22 that you could not make this assumption, and therefore the whole of Samaritan produce should be regarded as *doubtful*.

Dating (5): None of this tradition can be dated before 70 CE, but Eliezer's position represents the pre-70 ruling in m.Ter.3.9, which says that Samaritan tithing is valid. If their tithing is valid, then Samaritan produce must be *doubtful* and not *untithed*. This does not mean that Eliezer trusted the Samaritans to tithe properly—he is attributed with the saying that "One who eats bread [baked by] Samaritans is like one who eats pork" (m.Shebi.8.10).

Eliezer is not shown here as debating this ruling, and so there is no need to date the ruling before him or even contemporary with him. His position is simply stated by a later editor as opposing this ruling. Eliezer probably stated this position at the time of the edict of Rn. Gamaliel (probably II, T2) who tried to establish the principle that Samaritan pulse and grain were *doubtful* and all other Samaritan produce was *untithed*, though subsequent confusion made him revise this and state instead that all Samaritan produce was considered *certainly untithed* (t.Dem.5.24). This edict was probably prompted by the unilateral action of individual rabbis who treated Samaritan food as though it was *certainly untithed*, for example, Akiba in t.Dem.5.24.

In a later debate, R. Judah, R. Jose, and R. Simeon (all T4) tried to argue that you cannot tithe Israelite produce for Samaritans or gentiles, and vice versa (t.Dem.5.21), but R. Simeon of Shezuri recited an incident when R. Tarfon [T3] had allowed it (t.Dem.5.22).

m.Dem.6.1-12: How farmers should tithe

Summary of Mishnah: If you are a sharecropper (i.e., you rent someone's field for a proportion of the yield), you give the other owner their share, untithed (6.1). If you lease a field (i.e., you rent someone's field for a fixed sum), you pay your lease with *doubtful* produce of that field (i.e., only the *major elevation offering* is removed) (6.1), though if you pay with produce from another field, or if you lease it from a gentile, you tithe it fully (6.1-2).

If a provincial farmer sharecrops for an owner in Jerusalem, does he keep any of the *second tithe* [which is harder for the provincial person to spend] (6.4)?

If a Levite or priest sharecrops a field for a lay person, they divide up the *elevation offerings* with the lay person (though Eliezer says the Levite or priest keeps all the tithes due to them) (6.3), and if a lay person sharecrops for a Levite or priest, they keep all the *elevation offerings* (6.4). But in the case of olives [which is a much more valuable crop], you divide up the *elevation offerings* (6.5), and you sell them only to an Associate or to someone who is certain to tithe it (6.6).

If one joint owner tithes and the other does not (e.g., an Associate and his brother who is an *impious one*), then the one tithes only his own share (6.7-8). He can demand, "I will have the crop from this area and you from that," but he cannot demand, "I will have the oil and you have the wine [which is less valuable]" (6.8-9). (Though if a proselyte inherited an estate with his brother, he may demand, "You take the idols and wine and I will take the coins and produce" [6.10].)

You do not have to tithe any food grown outside Israel (assumed in 6.11). You can believe a seller who makes claims to his detriment (e.g., by saying his produce needs tithing), even if he subsequently says he was mistaken (6.11). If an Associate buys food for himself and (as a favor) for an *impious one*, he does not have to tithe the *impious one*'s food before handing it over [because he has not owned it]—unless he has already decided which food belongs to whom and it has become mixed up (6.12).

The following traditions have elements (marked in bold) for which there is evidence of an origin before 70 CE:

m.Dem.6.1a, 2a: When and how do tenant farmers tithe?

He who sharecrops a field from an Israelite,	הַמְקַבֵּל שָׂדֶה מִיִּשְׂרָאֵל,
from a gentile or from a Samaritan,	מִן הַנָּכְרִי וּמִן הַכּוּתִי,
should divide [the produce] before them.	יַחֲלֹק לִפְנֵיהֶם.
He who rents a field from an Israelite,	הַחוֹכֵר שָׂדֶה מִיִּשְׂרָאֵל,
elevates [the *elevation offering*] and gives [the rent] to him.	תּוֹרֵם וְנוֹתֵן לוֹ.
2a He who rents a field from a gentile	הַחוֹכֵר שָׂדֶה מִן הַנָּכְרִי,
tithes [*first* and *second tithes*] and gives [the rent] to him.	מְעַשֵּׂר וְנוֹתֵן לוֹ.

Comments: If you agree to work someone's field in return for a share of the produce,[11] you divide the produce before either of you start tithing. But if you rent it for a fixed sum, before paying the rent you must separate off the *major elevation offering*[12] if the owner is an Israelite, and remove the other tithes as well if the owner is a gentile.

This shows that a separation of the *major elevation offering* must always be made before produce leaves someone's ownership—before selling the produce or even paying for the rental of the farmland with it. The person who sharecrops never owns his partner's share, and so there is no need to separate the *elevation offering*. The Israelite owner can be trusted to complete the tithing process, but if the owner is a gentile (who does not tithe), the farmer must complete the tithing himself before payment.

The whole of the tractate *Demay* assumes that the *major elevation offering* has been faithfully separated, even by impious farmers. This assumption is also seen in rulings of Johanan b. Zakkai (t.Hag.3.36; cf. m.Hag.3.4) and of Eleazar b. Azariah [T2] (t.Maas.3.8—where the minor exceptions prove the rule). The rabbis did not regard the *impious* as untrustworthy with regard to the *major elevation offering*, but they could not be sure whether or not they had removed the *first* and *second tithes*.

Dating (2): The two parts of this ruling (1a and 2a) became separated by the insertion of a comment by R. Judah (1b) who adds a comment to a large number of the mishnahs in this tractate, almost like a running commentary.

This ruling is the basis of a ruling which R. Eliezer [T2] disputes in m.Dem.6.3:

> A priest or Levite who sharecropped a field from an Israelite [layman]: just as they divide the fully-tithed crop [i.e., the non-priests' portion], so they share the *elevation offerings* [i.e., the priests' portion]. R. Eliezer says: The tithes are also theirs, for that was the condition of their coming [to work the field].

The ruling says that a priest who sharecrops can keep the *elevation offering* for himself, and Eliezer adds that a Levite can keep the *first tithe*. Both rulings are based on the assumption that they would have stipulated this as part of the contract for working the land. This debate assumes that the rulings of m.Dem.6.1a, 2a are already established, so they must date before Eliezer, i.e., before 70 CE.

---

[11] The verb *qabal* (קָבַל, 'contract, rent') can be used for either sharecropping or for a fixed rental, but the presence of *hakaq* (חָדַק, 'share, divide') shows that sharecropping is intended here.

[12] The verb *taram* (תָּרַם) can mean 'to separate' generally, but also means specifically to separate the *terumah* (תְּרוּמָה) or *elevation offering*.

m.Dem.6.6: Only sell olives to someone who tithes properly

The School of Shammai says:	בית שמאי אומרים,
No man should sell olives	לא ימכור אדם את זיתיו
except to an Associate.	אלא לחבר.
The School of Hillel says:	בית הלל אומרים,
Also to someone who [is known to] tithe.	אף למעשר.
But the stricter [ones] of the School of Hillel used to	וצנועי בית הלל היו
follow the words of the School of Shammai.	נוהגין כדברי בית שמאי.

Comments: Olives could be used for food or processed into nonfood items such as lamp oil. They needed to be tithed only if they were used for food, and so it was left to the consumer to tithe them. The Associates, who normally sold food which was already tithed (m.Dem.2.2a), made sure that they sold untithed olives only to those who were known to tithe properly.

Olives exuded moisture when they were stored, which made them susceptible to *impurity*. Shammaites sold them only to Associates, who could be trusted not to contaminate them, as well as to tithe them properly. Hillelites, however, were willing to sell them to anyone who could be trusted to tithe them properly, without being sure that they would not contaminate them.

Tosefta said elsewhere that both schools would sell a vat of olives only to an Associate, because he knew how to prepare it in *purity* (t.Maas.3.13).[13] Jerusalem Talmud explains the contradiction by saying that the more lax ruling here at m.Dem.6.6 refers only to selling a few olives straight from the vat, before the moisture starts to exude (y.Dem.6.6.I).

Dating (1): There is no reason to doubt that this is a genuine school debate, especially as the Shammaite position is regarded as somewhat preferable to the Hillelite. The Hillelite opinion here is a little different from that in t.Maas.3.13 (despite the attempt at harmonization in y.Dem.6.6.I). It is more likely that the tradition here in m.Dem.6.6 is the original one, because t.Maas.3.13 is given in the name of Simeon b. Gamaliel (i.e., it is not part of the normal school source) and it is not in the normal form of a school debate (it is a short list of agreements between the Schools). Also, the fact that the t.Maas.3.13 makes the Hillelites agree with the Shammaite position which is somewhat praised here in m.Dem.6.6 makes it likely that this was changed in order to make Hillelite teaching accord with the later, stricter, practice of the majority.

---

[13] t.Maas.3.13: "R. Simeon b. Gamaliel said: The School of Shammai and the School of Hillel agree that a man should sell a stack of grain or a basket of grapes or a vat of olives only to an Associate who prepares [food] in cleanness."

m.Dem.7.1-6: When you cannot tithe *doubtfully tithed food* before eating

Summary of Mishnah: You cannot tithe on a Sabbath [because it is work] but you may make the statement of tithing before the Sabbath, then merely leave a portion on the plate or in the cup at the meal (7.1-2).

A laborer may wish to tithe the food which his employer gives him, but he should not, for this diminishes the amount of work he can do, and an employer is, in any case, supposed to tithe fully (7.3—though this was not the case in the early second century, as seen in 3.1).

If you cannot tithe before consuming (e.g., if you buy wine from a Samaritan vendor who may take offense) or if there are practical problems (e.g., you are in the schoolhouse or a field), you can make a statement of tithing (unobtrusively) and finish tithing that produce later (7.4), or tithe similar untithed produce at home later (7.5). Or, if there are two containers, you can designate one to be tithed later for both and eat from the other (7.6).

The following traditions have elements (marked in bold) for which there is evidence of an origin before 70 CE:

m.Dem.7.1: Eating *doubtfully tithed food* on a Sabbath

[If] one invites his associate to eat with him	הַמְזַמֵּן אֶת חֲבֵרוֹ שֶׁיֹּאכַל אֶצְלוֹ,
and he does not trust him about tithing	וְהוּא אֵינוֹ מַאֲמִינוֹ עַל הַמַּעַשְׂרוֹת,
he says on eve of Sabbath:	אוֹמֵר מֵעֶרֶב שַׁבָּת,
That which I am going to set aside	מַה שֶּׁאֲנִי עָתִיד לְהַפְרִישׁ
tomorrow, it will become [the *tithe of the first*] *tithe*	מָחָר, הֲרֵי הוּא מַעֲשֵׂר,
and the remainder of the [*first*] *tithe* is next to it.	וּשְׁאָר מַעֲשֵׂר סָמוּךְ לוֹ.
This [set-aside portion] which I have made into *tithe*	זֶה שֶׁעָשִׂיתִי מַעֲשֵׂר,
will become the *elevation offering* of the [*first*] *tithe;*	עָשׂוּי תְּרוּמַת מַעֲשֵׂר עָלָיו,
and the *second tithe* [is] on its north or south	וּמַעֲשֵׂר שֵׁנִי בִּצְפוֹנוֹ אוֹ בִדְרוֹמוֹ,
and [that] will be *deconsecrated* with coins.	וּמְחֻלָּל עַל הַמָּעוֹת.

Comments: If you eat a meal at the house of someone whom you do not completely trust with regard to tithing, you should regard the food as *doubtful*, and tithe it while you eat. This involves putting aside a hundredth of each type of food, saying a tithing formula over it (see m.Dem.4.3), and putting aside a small payment in place of the *second tithe*. It is not necessary to separate the *first tithe* or *second tithe* but they should be identified; so, this ruling says that the *first tithe* is that which is next to the minor *elevation offering* and the *second tithe* is north or south of the *first tithe* (i.e., next to it).

However, you cannot do this tithing at a Sabbath meal, because tithing is considered to be work which cannot be done on a Sabbath (m.Betz.5.2). You must therefore take care not to serve *doubtfully tithed food* on a Sabbath, and one of the three things which a husband asks his wife on a Sabbath eve is, "Have you tithed?" (m.Shab.2.7).

So what do you do if you are invited to a Sabbath meal at the house of someone who cannot be completely trusted with regard to tithing? This mishnah explains that you can do the tithing in advance, by reciting the formula for tithing on the eve just before the Sabbath begins, and then putting aside the money after the Sabbath ends.

It is difficult to know whether to translate the first line with the word 'associate' or 'Associate.' Although the word is *ḥaber* (חָבֵר), as in m.Dem.2.3a which says that an Associate always tithes properly, it may simply mean a 'friend,' as in m.Ber.9.5c. Also, when it says his friend is not someone whom he 'trusts' (מַאֲמִינוֹ, from אָמֵן *amen*), this may be a contrast with a Trusted one (cf. m.Dem.2.2a) or it may simply mean that he cannot trust him. The above translation assumes that neither word is used in its technical sense.

Dating (?): This passage is impossible to date, though the principle that food cannot be tithed on a Sabbath was already assumed by the first-century schools (m.Maas.4.2). This mishnah has been included here mainly because it illustrates the New Testament and it contains concepts which are known to be early while containing no concepts which are known to be late. The formula of tithing was already used, though not perhaps fixed (see m.Dem.4.3) and the Sabbath restrictions on tithing already existed (m.Betz.5.2 refers also to *dedicating*, i.e., offering something to the Temple, which was a pre-70 activity). This problem must have existed before 70 CE, though this solution cannot be definitely traced to before 70 CE.

It is possible that this was a Hillelite teaching which the Shammaites rejected, because this would explain why the Hillelites allowed all crumbs to be cleared away after a meal on the Sabbath while the Shammaites did not (see m.Shab.21.3). The crumbs might include some *elevation offering* which had been removed as a tithe, and so they had to be cleared in case they were accidentally eaten (cf. m.Dem.7.1).

If it could be shown that this mishnah was pre-70, then we would probably also include m.Dem.7.2 which starts "When his cup is filled up, he says . . ." and then repeats a version of a similar formula. This appears to be a continuation of m.Dem.7.1, though it is possibly a later addition which is reliant on it.

It is likely that the whole of m.Dem.7 is late, because it appears to be an appendix to m.Dem.5, just as m.Dem.6 is probably an appendix to m.Dem.2–3, because these chapters deal with issues which come out of these sections in the same order.[14] However, this does not mean that all the contents of these appendices are late.

---

[14] See Sarason, *The Talmud of the Land of Israel*, vol. 3: *Demai*, pp. 11-12.

New Testament: This problem of eating on a Sabbath with someone who cannot be trusted to tithe properly may be one of the reasons why Christians changed their day of worship from the Sabbath to Sunday. Christian worship always involved eating, whether it was bread and wine or a full meal. This matter of tithing *doubtfully tithed food* would make it very difficult for Christians who continued to be observant Jews to eat on a Sabbath with fellow Christians who were not observant Jews. If the food was completely untithed, the situation would become impossible, because there was no mechanism by which such food could be tithed in advance. The easiest solution might be to leave the meal until the evening of the Saturday, which the Jews would regard as the beginning of Sunday, though a more secure solution would be to meet on a Sunday instead.

This was not such a great problem in the Diaspora, because the Torah speaks only about tithing food from the Land (as assumed in m.Dem.6.11), but some foods, such as pressed figs, dates, carobs, and white rice, were assumed to originate in the Land (cf. m.Dem.2.1). Even if a pious Jew decided to avoid these foods, he could not avoid the wine, which was almost always from Israel in order to ensure that none had been offered to an idol while it was made (cf. 'New Testament' at m.Kil.4.5).

It is not clear in the NT when Christian worship moved to the Sabbath, and why. Paul tended to meet with Christians on a Sabbath (Acts 13.42, 44; 16.13). Christians are only recorded once at a meeting "on the first day of the week" (Acts 20.7-12), and this may simply have been the day when Paul was passing through. Although regular or weekly meetings are mentioned elsewhere (1Cor.16.2; Heb.10.25), it is only called "the Lord's Day" in one place (Rev.1.10). It is generally assumed that Sunday was chosen in order to celebrate the resurrection, but this is not stated explicitly and it does not form an explanation for this transition. Other attempts to explain the reasons for the transition are not convincing,[15] and so it is possible that the custom of meeting on Sundays is due to the problem of *doubtfully tithed food*.

---

[15] Max Turner and Douglas De Lacey both succeeded in demonstrating that this transition took place within the New Testament era, and not after it as Bacchiocchi has argued, but they failed to explain *why* the transition had occurred. Bacchiocchi argued that Christians moved to this day in order to distance themselves from the Jews during second-century persecutions. See Max M. B. Turner, "The Sabbath, Sunday, and the Law in Luke/Acts," in Don A. Carson, ed., *From Sabbath to Lord's Day: A Biblical, Historical and Theological Investigation* (Grand Rapids: Zondervan Publishing House, 1982), pp. 100-157; Douglas R. De Lacey, "The Sabbath/Sunday Question and the Law in the Pauline Corpus," in Don A. Carson, ed., *From Sabbath to Lord's Day*, pp. 160-95; Samuele Bacchiocchi, *From Sabbath to Sunday: A Historical Investigation of the Rise of Sunday Observance in Early Christianity* (Rome: Pontifical Gregorian University, 1977).

m.Dem.7.7-8: When tithes become *doubtful*

Summary of Mishnah: If *certainly untithed* food becomes mixed with *deconsecrated* produce or with *first tithes*, you remove an amount equivalent to all the *certainly untithed* food and the *elevation offering* of the tithed produce or *first tithes* as though they were *doubtfully tithed.*[16] If *deconsecrated* produce becomes mixed with *first tithes*, the *first tithes* do not become *doubtfully tithed* (7.7).

If you designated part of the produce as *first tithe* and then forgot which part, you separate enough portions so that you can be sure to separate one-tenth of the *first tithe*. For example, if you had ten rows of ten bottles and designated one row, but forgot which one, you take two bottles from diagonally opposite corners and then you are certain to have one-tenth of whatever row was designated (7.8).

There is no evidence that any of this section originated before 70 CE.

Summary and Conclusions

The Jewish population before 70 CE was divided into those who tithed properly and those who did not. The *impious* ('people of the land') were trusted to remove the *major elevation offering* (about one-fiftieth), because this tractate assumes that this portion was removed even from *doubtfully tithed food*. But they could not be trusted to tithe the food—i.e., remove the *first* and *second tithes*, which included the *minor elevation offering*.

There were various levels of trustworthiness with regard to tithing. Any person could be known as a 'tither'—i.e., they were generally known to tithe, but this was not proven and they might not always comply. Even some beggars were known to be tithers (m.Dem.3.1). The next level was a Trusted one, who could be assumed to always tithe anything he bought, or sold, or ate (m.Dem.2.2a). The highest level was an Associate, who not only could be trusted to tithe, but also to keep himself free of *impurity* (m.Dem.2.3a). This meant that it was safe to buy even wet goods from him, and to eat in his home without becoming *impure*. However, an *impious one* could not stay or eat in an Associate's home without changing into clothes which the Associate provided. Each school had their own system of recognizing Associates who had to go through different probationary periods (t.Dem.2.12).

We do not know if Samaritans tithed, and there was some confusion about this among Jews. Before 70 CE Jews assumed that Samaritans were like gentiles who did not tithe, so all their food was considered to be *certainly untithed* (implied in

---

[16] This is according to t.Dem.8.17. Mishnah is ambiguous and could also mean 'separate out the amount equivalent to the untithed and tithe it, then treat the tithed as *demai*.' See also the discussion in y.Dem.7.7-8.

m.Dem.5.9). Then Gamaliel II recognized that they often did tithe pulses and grain, and so he declared these to be *doubtful* (t.Dem.5.24), but Eliezer said all their food should be regarded as *doubtful* (t.Dem.5.22), which Gamaliel grudgingly accepted.

Observant Jews only sold untithed produce to someone who could be trusted to tithe it properly (m.Dem.6.6), or else they had to tithe it before selling it, which put their costs up by about 20 percent. This resulted in a system where observant Jews tended to buy and sell mainly among themselves, and Associates were expected to sell *only* to observant Jews (m.Dem.2.3a).

Any observant Jew would remove the *minor elevation offering* (one-hundredth of the whole) from *doubtfully tithed food*, just in case. You could do this during a meal by leaving the portion at the side of the plate and uttering a formula of tithing. You could not do this on a Sabbath (because it was considered work), but you could say the formula in advance before the Sabbath (m.Dem.7.1—though this may not have been customary before 70 CE). This difficulty meant that you should try never to have a Sabbath meal with someone who was not a Trusted one or an Associate. This would have caused great problems for early Christian communities, and perhaps the transition to Sunday worship was partially due to this.

Before 70 CE the problem of *doubtfully tithed food* was treated very seriously. Even tenant farmers, who were the poorest farmers, were instructed to remove the *major elevation offering* from the crop with which they paid their rent (m.Dem.6.1a, 2a), which must have been a great hardship. After 70 CE things appear to become even more strict. Some later rabbis tended to side with the stricter Shammaite rulings, especially concerning to whom they could sell untithed olives (m.Dem.6.6) and spiced oil (m.Dem.1.3), which later generations reinterpreted so narrowly that the Hillelite ruling became virtually identical to the Shammaite one (t.Dem.1.26-28). Sometimes, however, the Shammaite position was impractical, such as their ruling that *doubtfully tithed food* should only be given to beggars who tithe (m.Dem.3.1) or that Associates should be tested for twelve months (m.Dem.2.3a).

A large proportion of the mishnahs in this tractate consist of anonymous statements which are followed by a comment by R. Judah or another rabbi of T4 or occasionally T3 or T2. This suggests that the tractate existed in a fairly fixed form at the time of T2, and that there was a great deal of discussion and development at the time of T4. At some points the Tosefta may preserve an earlier form (see on m.Dem.1.1), though Tosefta also contains a great deal of later discussion which is not present in Mishnah, and so neither can be said to be earlier than the other. It appears that both Mishnah and Tosefta depend on a common core which has been added to more extensively in Tosefta.

Occasionally we can see the process by which new traditions were added to the old, in a piecemeal fashion, in an effort to leave the older text unchanged (see m.Dem.1.1a). In one place we can perhaps see how the Tosefta has added to the tradition by expanding one item using a list of similar items found in another tradition (see on m.Dem.1.3 which has expanded by a list in m.Zeb.9.5). All this shows a willingness to develop, but a reluctance to change the wording of older traditions.

Tractate *Kilayim*: Mixtures

Definitions and Outline

Torah taught that one may not have *mixtures* (כִּלְאַיִם, *kilayim*) of different plants, animals, or cloth in specific situations. One may not grow different plants together (Lev.19.19; Deut.22.9), harness different farm animals together for ploughing (Deut.22.10), cross-breed different cattle (Lev.19.19) or wear garments made from mingled wool and linen fibers (Lev.19.19; Deut.22.11). The rabbis extended these scriptural prohibitions by also forbidding *grafting* different plants together, growing plants *under and over* vines, *leading* farm animals together, interbreeding of *all* animals, and *mixing pieces* of wool and linen cloth rather than just *mixing* wool and linen fibers.

In this tractate, '*mixtures*' always refer to forbidden *mixtures* of heterogeneous kinds. The tractate deals first with *mixtures* of plants (m.Kil.1–7), then *mixtures* of animals (m.Kil.8), and finally *mixtures* of fibers in garments (m.Kil.9).

Most agricultural commandments applied only in the land of Israel, but the rabbis regarded the matter of *mixtures* as a universal principle which applied inside and outside Israel (see m.Orl.3.9; m.Qid.1.9).

m.Kil.1.1–2.5: *Mixtures* of plants

Different plants could not be grown in the same field with each other, but if they were sufficiently similar, they did not form *mixtures*. *Mixtures* have to be avoided at every stage of growing plants: grafting, sowing, and sowing after harvesting a different plant in the same field. They did not form *mixtures* if they were separated by a sufficient boundary or if there was insufficient mixing.

m.Kil.4.1–7.8: *Mixtures* in a vineyard

Vineyards are dealt with at extra length in Torah (Deut.22.9) and in this tractate. If vines form *mixtures* with a different plant, they are '*sanctified*' (קִדֵּשׁ, *qiddesh*, 'made holy, separate'—piel of קָדַשׁ) so that they cannot be eaten. Vines which are grown on trellises create extra problems of overhanging, measuring from their base and non-fruiting shoots.

m.Kil.8.1-6: *Mixtures* of animals

Animals form *mixtures* if they are yoked together or bred together.

m.Kil.9.1-10: *Mixtures* **in garments**

Torah prohibits *mixtures* of wool and linen but only in a garment.

Related texts: m.Sheq.1.2 re inspections and b.Men.40a re *tassels*

Agents inspect the fields for *mixtures*. The law of *tassels* is more important than prohibition of *mixtures*.

m.Kil.1.1-6: Which plants form *mixtures*?

Summary of Mishnah: A long list of pairs of plants which are very similar and do not form *mixtures*, so that they can be grown together (1.1-3), and another list of pairs which do form *mixtures* even if they are similar (1.4-5). This last list is joined to a list of animals which also form *mixtures* even if they are similar (1.6).[1]

The following traditions have elements (marked in bold) for which there is evidence of an origin before 70 CE:

m.Kil.1.1: Wheat and tares planted together

Wheat and tares	החטים והזונין
are not *mixtures* **together.**	אינם כלאים זה בזה.

Comments: 'Are not *mixtures*' means here, as throughout this tractate, that they are not *mixtures* of heterogeneous species, which is forbidden by Torah. This is the start of a list of pairs of species which are similar to each other and which either form '*mixtures*' together or they do not. The general principle is that plants which are clearly different from each other cannot be planted together, but plants which are similar may possibly be regarded as similar enough to grow together.

    Tares (i.e., darnel, rye grass, or vetch) look very similar to wheat while growing, but the seeds can cause poisoning in some circumstances. Therefore no farmer would deliberately grow these two together, but if some stray seeds fell on the field, it would be very difficult to weed them out until they are mature. This ruling may therefore be a pragmatic one.

Dating (2): This list of pairs of plants, which spans from m.Kil1.1-4, appears to have grown gradually. It is possible to discern some order in the items, starting with field crops such as wheat and barley (1.1a), then vegetable-plot crops such as beans, melons and lettuce (1.1b–1.2a), then herb-garden crops such as coriander, mustard

---

[1] This list of animals would fit better at m.Kil.8.5. It is probably here because it was part of a group of traditions which make up m.Kil.1.4-6, which all end "even though they are similar to one another, they are [considered] different from one another."

and garlic (1.2b–1.3), and finally trees (1.4). But there are too many items which are out of place to make this organization convincing, especially when two types of cowpea are separated by seven other pairs (at the end of 1.1 and the end of 1.2). A thematic order is only convincing in the last section which starts "And among trees. . . ." It is more likely that this list grew gradually over time, though additions were not always added strictly chronologically as indicated by the interjections of R. Judah [T4] and then R. Akiba [T3].

This supposition is supported by the repeated line "They are not *mixtures* together" which is found here after the first pair, and then repeated after the sixth, seventh, fourteenth, seventeenth, twentieth, and then after two final pairs of trees. This repeated line occurs at the end of each mishnah (i.e., the end of 1.1, 1.2, and 1.3) and before any interruption such as "R. Judah says . . ." (1.2), "R. Akiba added . . ." (1.3), and before the list of trees which *do* form *mixtures* (1.4). Therefore this line probably marked the end of each succeeding addition, and its presence after the first pair probably indicates that this pair once stood on its own. This suggests that this pair formed an older tradition which dates from a time when there were only one or a few such pairs.

The earliest dateable pair in the rest of the lists is "pears and crustaminum pears" in m.Kil.1.4, and this pair are also mentioned in a tradition in t.Kil.1.4:

> In the irrigated fields of Sepphoris they used to graft crustaminum pear [buds] onto pear [trees]. A certain student [once] found them [doing this]. He said to them, "You are forbidden [to do this]." They went and cut them [i.e., the buds] off, and they came and inquired at Yavneh. They [i.e., the Sages] said, "Whoever met you was none other than [one] of the students of the School of Shammai."

This tradition concerns an early time at Sepphoris when there were still disciples of the Shammaites. There are no known Shammaite teachers after 70 CE, so this must have been during the first generation following 70 CE. It appears that this pair of plants was the subject of a school debate, though perhaps a very late one.

It has been argued that the first pair of 'wheat and tares' was probably the oldest pair, and that the first dateable pair comes from just before or just after 70 CE. Therefore the first pair is likely to date from before 70 CE. However, there is too much conjecture in all this to give this conclusion a high degree of certainty.

New Testament: The parable of Wheat and Tares (Mt.13.24-30) takes for granted the fact that one may grow these two species in a single field, though one would not want to. The general theme of the parables of Matthew 13 is that there is a mixture of good and bad in the Kingdom. This theme is very clear in the parables of the Mustard Seed (vv. 31-32), the Leaven (v. 33), and the Dragnet (vv. 47-50), and it is present to a lesser extent in the parables of the Sower (vv. 3-23), the Hidden Treasure (v. 44), and the Pearl (vv. 45-46), in each of which the good is in the minority. The use of the pair 'wheat and tares' may have been a deliberate reference to a well-known example which was used for teaching the subject of *mixtures*. If the listeners understood this, Jesus' message would have conveyed something like: "The Pharisees attempt to avoid all *mixtures*, but a strange mixture is allowed in the Kingdom in order to help more outsiders to enter."

m.Kil.1.7–2.5: Farming with *mixtures* of plants

Summary of Mishnah: You must not graft different plants together (1.7-8) or grow root plants under vines (1.9) or sow different plants together (1.9) though a small amount of different seeds may be permitted (2.1-2). If you rotate crops, you must be careful to plough in the former crop completely before sowing with a different one (2.3-5).

The following traditions have elements (marked in bold) for which there is evidence of an origin before 70 CE:

m.Kil.1.7: Grafting onto a different plant

One should not graft	אֵין מְבִיאִין
a tree onto a tree	אִילָן בְּאִילָן,
a vegetable onto a vegetable	יָרָק בְּיָרָק,
and not a tree onto a vegetable	וְלֹא אִילָן בְּיָרָק,
and not a vegetable onto a tree.	וְלֹא יָרָק בְּאִילָן.
R. Judah [b. Illai, T4] permits	רַבִּי יְהוּדָה מַתִּיר
[grafting] a vegetable onto a tree.	יָרָק בְּאִילָן.

Comments: Torah did not specifically forbid grafting different plants together, but the Sages presumably felt that the same principle applied. This ruling did not mean that no trees could be grafted, but one was not permitted to graft trees which formed forbidden *mixtures*. For example, the dispute in t.Kil.1.4 (cited at m.Kil.1.1 above) concerned whether a crustaminum pear could be grafted onto a normal pear tree, which mishnah says is an allowable pair (m.Kil.1.4).

R. Judah allowed grafting of a vegetable onto a tree, which involved grafting two very dissimilar plants together. He presumably also allowed the grafting of similar plants together, like a tree to a tree and vegetable to a vegetable. In other words, R. Judah disputed that grafting fell into the area of forbidden *mixtures*. Later rabbis found this disagreement so surprising that they assumed Judah and the majority meant different types of grafting. They assumed that Judah allowed the grafting of a stem onto a branch or trunk, while the anonymous majority was prohibiting the splicing together of two fruiting bodies in order to produce a hybrid plant (y.Kil.1.7.I).

However, the other discussions about this in Mishnah and Talmud assume that one may not graft a vegetable onto a tree.

Dating (2): The tradition in t.Kil.1.4, which comes from the generation immediately after 70 CE (see Dating at m.Kil.1.1), assumes that some trees can be grafted to each other and some cannot. This principle that trees which are different cannot be grafted onto each other must therefore date back to before 70 CE.

However, we do not know when this one ruling (grafting a tree to a tree) was expanded into four prohibitions (vegetable to a vegetable, vegetable to a tree, and tree to a vegetable). The extra three could be said to be implied in the single prohibition of grafting a tree to a tree. Presumably these four had already been stated by the time of Judah b. Illai who disputed at least one of them.

New Testament: The concept of grafting a tree to a tree is used by Paul as an illustration of how the gentiles will become one with Judaism (Rom.11.17-25). It is likely that he has a Jewish readership at least partially in mind, because immediately before this he also refers to Jewish concepts such as *firstfruits* and contamination from 'the lump' (i.e., of leaven, in v. 16). He is therefore implying that the gentiles and the Jews are very similar, so that they can be grafted together without forming forbidden *mixtures*.

m.Kil.2.6: The distance between furrows of different plants

He who wishes to make his field [with]	הרוצה לעשות שדהו
row [on] row of every kind:	מֵשֶׁר מֵשֶׁר מכל מִין,
The School of Shammai says:	בית שמאי אומרים,
[Make rows as wide as] three furrows	שלשה תלמים
which are for ploughing.	של פתיח.
And the School of Hillel says:	ובית הלל אומרים,
[Make rows as wide as] the fullness	מלא
of the yoke of Sharon.	העול השרוני.
And the words of these are close	וקרובין דברי אלו
to being like the words of the others.	להיות כדברי אלו.

Comments: What is the minimum gap between rows of different plants in order to avoid forming forbidden *mixtures*? Either three normal furrows or a single wide furrow—Sharon was a wide fertile plain, and so the ploughs used there were probably wider than normal.

Dating (1): There is no reason to doubt that this represents a genuine school debate. A later comment says that these both amount to about the same. If this is true, it suggests that these rulings were not the result of a dispute in the schoolhouse, but a practical rule which was given to farmers by the two schools independently, and which were later codified in the schoolhouse. By the time that they were discussed in the schoolhouse, they were both sufficiently established to remain as distinct rulings, despite the fact that they represented no practical difference.

m.Kil.2.6–3.7: Separating *mixtures* of plants

Summary of Mishnah: To avoid different plants forming *mixtures*, you must separate them by a specific distance (2.6) or by a boundary such as a wall or uncultivated land (2.8). Plants can be closer if the plots are owned by different people (2.7) or there is only a small amount of one plant (2.9-10). Most plants may overshadow another without forming *mixtures*, except for Greek gourds and perhaps others [which project and become intertwined with other plants] (2.11), and vines (see later).

These principles are then worked out in practical examples. With careful planning, a small vegetable garden can hold five species, or even thirteen if there is a raised border (3.1-2, cf. 2.6). The problem of a field which protrudes into another can be dealt with (3.3, cf. 2.7), as well as the various problems of planting gourds near other plants (3.4-6, cf. 2.11).

There is no evidence that any of this section originated before 70 CE.

m.Kil.4.1–5.8: Vineyards

Summary of Mishnah: Vineyards are discussed separately in this tractate, just as they are in Torah (plants in fields are discussed only in Lev.19.19 while vines are discussed only in Deut.22.9). The concept of a different plant being '*sanctified*' by a vine (i.e., made prohibited for eating) is found only with regard to vines, both in Torah and in rabbinic rulings.

You can grow plants without forming *mixtures* both in bare ground in the middle of a vineyard (4.1) and around the edge (4.2-3), and between the rows (4.8-9) if these areas are all large enough, or if they are separated by a fence (4.3-4), unless there are too many gaps in the fence (4.4). What is the minimum size of a 'vineyard' (4.5-7); and what is the minimum plant density of a 'vineyard' (5.1-2)? Can you grow other plants in the ditch which is used as a winepress, or in the ground under the watchtower (5.3-4)?

A single group of other plants can '*sanctify*' up to forty-five vines (5.5) which might also include wild plants (5.8). However, the vines are safe from other plants if you promise "When I find them I will remove them" (5.6) or if the seeds were blown there without you seeing and you do not let them fruit (5.7).

The following traditions have elements (marked in bold) for which there is evidence of an origin before 70 CE:

m.Kil.4.1: Distances in the middle and edge of a vineyard

The bald [middle] of a vineyard:	קרחת הכרם,
The School of Shammai says:	בית שמאי אומרים,
Twenty-four cubits	עשרים וארבע אמות.
And the School of Hillel says:	ובית הלל אומרים,
Sixteen cubits.	שש עשרה אמה.
The encircling [edge] of the vineyard:	מחול הכרם,
The School of Shammai says:	בית שמאי אומרים,
Sixteen cubits	שש עשרה אמה.
and the School of Hillel say:	ובית הלל אומרים,
Twelve cubits.	שתים עשרה אמה.
And what is the 'bald of a vineyard'?	ואיזו היא קרחת הכרם.
The [part of] the vineyard which is bare	כרם שחרב
in its middle.	מאמצעו,
If there are not sixteen cubits	אם אין שם שש עשרה אמה,
one must not sow seed there.	לא יביא זרע לשם.
[But if] there are sixteen cubits	היו שם שש עשרה אמה,
one should allocate it work-space	נותנין לה עבודתה,
and sow [in] the remainder.	וזורע את המותר.

Comments: These traditions use obscure terminology which later editors felt it was necessary to expound. The 'bald of a vineyard' is explained here as a bare patch in the middle, and the 'circle of a vineyard' is similarly explained in the next mishnah (m.Kil.4.2) as the area between the vineyard and its fence. The comments assume that one follows the Hillelite interpretation, as was usual.

This caution over planting in the middle and round the edge, inside the wall of a vineyard, is because a single plant can '*sanctify*' several rows of vines (see m.Kil.4.5). But the measurements are much larger than one might expect. The normal distance between a vine and other plants is only four cubits—about two meters (see m.Kil.4.5)—and yet these measurements demand that the space in the centre is at least sixteen cubits in diameter and that the edge should be at least twelve cubits away from the fence. The later commentators say that the measurement includes a minimum sowing area of other plants.

Perhaps this extreme caution is due to a concern over appearances, especially round the edge of a vineyard. Elsewhere this tractate also has rulings which are for appearance's sake, at m.Kil.3.5 ("the Sages prohibited this only for the sake of appearances") and m.Kil.9.2 ("silk and bast-silk have no law of *mixtures*, but are forbidden for the sake of appearance").

Dating (1): There is no reason to doubt that this was a genuine school debate, especially as later editors felt the need to explain the meaning of the obscure language.

New Testament: Paul counsels against doing things which have the appearance of disobeying the law, in 1 Thessalonians 5.22, "avoid all appearance of evil." This is not a form of hypocrisy, but it is to prevent others thinking that such infringement does not matter.

The fig tree which a man planted in his vineyard (Lk.13.6) was presumably planted in a bare patch in the center, as described here.

m.Kil.4.5: How many vines are 'sanctified' by different plants?

He who plants a row of five vines:	הנוטע שורה של חמש גפנים,
The School of Shammai says:	בית שמאי אומרים,
[It is considered to be] a vineyard.	כרם.
And the School of Hillel says:	ובית הלל אומרים,
It is not [considered to be] a vineyard,	אינו כרם,
unless there are two rows there.	עד שיהו שם שתי שורות.
Therefore:	לפיכך,
He who sows [with different plants]	הזורע
[less than] four cubits near the vineyard:	ארבע אמות שבכרם,
The School of Shammai says:	בית שמאי אומרים,
He *sanctified* one row [of vines].	קדש שורה אחת.
And the School of Hillel says:	ובית הלל אומרים,
He *sanctified* two rows [of vines].	קדש שתי שורות.

Mishnaic parallel: m.MS.5.2

Comments: The significance of the first set of rulings is determined by the second set of rulings. If the minimum size of a vineyard is two rows of vines, then the minimum which is spoiled by forbidden *mixtures* is also two rows. Both schools work on the assumption that the minimum permitted distance between a vine and different plants is four cubits.

The concept of '*sanctifying*' comes from Deuteronomy 22.9, "You shall not sow your vineyard with *mixtures*, lest the fruit of the seed which you have sown and the fruit of your vineyard are *sanctified* (תִּקְדַּשׁ, *tiqdash*)." This is a special sense of the verb *qadash* (קְדַשׁ, 'to sanctify, make holy'), which has to be understood here as 'make prohibited.' In practice, if either plant which formed *mixtures* with a vine had fruited before the *mixture* was spotted and corrected, it was burnt (m.Kil.5.7). This means that the produce in a *mixture* with vines should be treated as *consecrated* (קֹדֶשׁ, *qodesh*)—i.e., belonging to the Temple or priest.

This '*sanctification*' resulted in an important practical difference between vines and other plants. When other plants were found to form *mixtures*, the food derived from those plants could still be eaten or sold, but when vines were *'sanctified'* by *mixtures* their produce could not be eaten or sold (see m.Kil.8.1). Rulings concerning *mixtures* applied outside Israel as well as inside (see Definitions and Outline above). This meant that it was risky to drink wine which had been produced by gentiles, who were not concerned about *mixtures*.

Dating (1): There is no reason to doubt that these were both genuine school debates, though the explanation "unless there are two rows there" and the linking "therefore" were probably added late.

New Testament: The 'weak' Christians in Rome who did not eat meat or drink wine (Rom.14.21) are probably avoiding things which might have been offered to idols (for meat see 1Cor.8.4; 10.28; Acts 15.29; Rev.2.14 and for wine see m.Dem.6.10; m.AZ.2.3-4; etc.).[2] Although it was risky to drink gentile wine in case it had been contaminated by *mixtures*, this was not regarded as a problem worth worrying about, because gentile wine was avoided in case it had been used as an offering. This risk is even ignored in m.AZ.4.11, which discusses the theoretical situation where a Jew prepared gentile wine in a state of *purity* and left it unmarked in his *domain* where Jews might drink it—they decide that it is permitted to Jews.

t.Kil.3.17 (Z 3.14b): What is the status of a caper bush?

[What is the status of] caper?	צָלָף,
The School of Shammai says:	בֵּית שַׁמַּאי אוֹמְרִים,
[It forms] *mixtures in a vineyard**	כִּלְאַיִם בְּכָרֶם.
And the School of Hillel says:	וּבֵית הִלֵּל אוֹמְרִים,
It does not [form] *mixtures* [in a *vineyard*].	אֵין כִּלְאַיִם
They both agree that:	אֵלּוּ וְאֵלּוּ מוֹדִים
It is liable to *forefruit*.	שֶׁחַיָּיב בְּעָרְלָה.

---

* Z does not have בכרם 'in a vineyard,' probably because it is not necessary in the context.

Comments: Many such traditions probably existed at some time, which were replaced by lists such as in t.Kil.3.12-16. This tradition probably remained intact because it links together two rulings, about the status with regard to *mixtures* and *forefruits* (the first four years of fruit in Lev.19.23-24).

Dating (1): Mishnah lists a few plants which form *mixtures in a vineyard* (in m.Kil.5.8), though Tosefta adds many more. They are added both anonymously and

---

[2] Many other references are often listed, but some refer to avoiding meat or wine in a time of mourning (Dan.10.3; T.Reub.1.10; T.Jud.15.4), and some to not consuming meat or wine which comes from the table of pagan worshipper, where a portion would have been offered to a god before the meal (Dan.1.3-16; Gk.Est.14.17; *Jos.Asen.*8.3).

in the name of various post-70 authorities. Although this tradition is at the end of the list in Tosefta, this position does not indicate that it was added last. It was probably listed last because it ends with a reference to *forefruit*, which would break up the list if it was put in the middle.

m.Kil.5.3: Sowing in a ditch, a winepress, or under the watchtower

A trench which passes through a vineyard,	חריץ שהוא עובר בכרם
[having] a depth of ten [handbreadths]	עמוק עשרה
and a width of four [handbreadths]:	ורחב ארבעה,
R. Eliezer b. Jacob [I T2 or II T4] says:	רבי אליעזר בן יעקב אומר,
If it was dividing from the top of the vineyard	אם היה מפולש מראש הכרם
to its end, this is regarded as	ועד סופו, הרי זה נראה
[extending] between two vineyards	כבין שני כרמים
and **one should sow seed within it.**	וזורעים בתוכו.
And if not, it is regarded as a winepress.	ואם לאו, הרי הוא כגת.
And the winepress which is in a vineyard	והגת שבכרם
[having] a depth of ten [handbreadths]	עמוקה עשרה
and a width of four [handbreadths]:	ורחבה ארבעה,
Eliezer (b. Hyrcanus [T2]) says:	רבי אליעזר אומר,
One should sow seed within it.	זורעים בתוכה.
But the Sages **prohibit** [it].	וחכמים אוסרים.
A watchtower which is in the vineyard	שומרה שבכרם
[having] a height of ten [handbreadths]	גבוהה עשרה
and a width of four [handbreadths]:	ורחבה ארבעה,
One should sow seed within it.	זורעין בתוכה.
But if there was an overhang [of vines]	ואם היה שער
intertwined, it is **prohibited**.	כותש, אסור.

Comments: Can different plants be grown in the gaps in a vineyard which are formed by a ditch, the winepress, and the watchtower? They decide that if these gaps are at least ten handbreadths high (about one yard) and four handbreadths wide (about one foot), there is sufficient distance from the vine. These measurements are based on a generally accepted definition of a barrier for a vineyard (cf. m.Kil.4.3).

The 'watchtower' could be translated a 'watchman's hut' or anything similar. The justification for 'watchtower' comes in the term 'overhang' (*shear*, שער). A wide watchtower would have a significant piece of land underneath it.

Dating (2): The tradition, as we have it, is interspersed with the comments of later rabbis and it is difficult to reconstruct the original rulings. The measurements may (or may not) have been added later, based on the definitions of a 'ditch' in m.Kil.4.3. We have only the ruling of Eliezer b. Jacob for the first matter and only an anonymous ruling for the last, but for the middle one we have both 'Eliezer' and the 'Sages.'

It might be assumed that 'Eliezer' is a shorthand for Eliezer b. Jacob who appeared just before, but their rulings contradict each other. Eliezer b. Jacob says that sowing in a ditch is allowed if it extends beyond the vineyard, but a shorter ditch should be treated like a winepress. This implies that sowing would not be allowed in a winepress, but 'Eliezer' says that it is. Therefore it is likely that 'Eliezer' is Eliezer b. Hyrcanus (who is normally known simply as 'Eliezer'). There were two rabbis known as Eliezer b. Jacob, but if both of these Eliezers were debating these matters at same time, as seems likely, then this is Eliezer b. Jacob I, who was contemporary with Eliezer b. Hyrcanus. They were both active just after 70 CE, and so the original rulings must date from before 70.

If we assume that the Sages represent the original ruling with regard to a winepress (i.e., they did not allow sowing), this would imply that they did allow it in a ditch. If that is so, in what way was Eliezer b. Jacob different? Probably he added the definition which distinguished a ditch from a winepress. This meant that he did not change the ruling of the majority, so their ruling did not need to be recorded separately.

The logic behind these rulings is probably that a ditch could be considered to be something separate from the vineyard, whereas a winepress could not. If this is so, then it is also likely that the Sages prohibited sowing under a watchtower. Later, when the simple logic of the original rulings disappeared under the details of measurements and definitions, they were able to explain away the prohibition of sowing under the watchtower as something which only applied if the struts were used as a vine trellis.

New Testament: The parable of the vineyard owner describes the components of a vineyard in very similar terms: "He planted a vineyard, and set a hedge around it and dug a pit for the winepress and built a tower" (Mk.12.1 // Mt.21.33).

m.Kil.6.1–7.8: Vine trellises

Summary of Mishnah: Vines can be grown up the side of a fence or the side of a ditch (6.1, 3), or through non-fruit-bearing or barren trees (6.3, 5). You must leave a specific gap between the trellis and other plants (6.1), which is more if they overhang (6.2-4). You *may* plant within large gaps in the trellis (6.6-7) and near non-fruiting portions of vine (6.8-9) though not near withered portions (7.2) nor over buried vine shoots (7.1-2—unless it goes through the stony layer under the soil, 7.1), but you *should* not (7.3). Similarly you *may* carry an unperforated pot of a different plant through a vineyard, but you *should* not (7.8). If someone lets his vine overshadow another person's plants, does this '*sanctify*' them (7.4-5)? If you find vines over plants, you should cut them down immediately, even during a *ordinary festival day* (7.6-7).

The following traditions have elements (marked in bold) for which there is evidence of an origin before 70 CE:

m.Kil.6.1: The minimum size and distance for a vine trellis

What is a [vine] trellis?	אֵיזֶהוּ עָרִיס.
He who plants a row of five vines	הַנּוֹטֵעַ שׁוּרָה שֶׁל חָמֵשׁ גְּפָנִים
by the side of a fence,	בְּצַד הַגָּדֵר
which has a height of ten handbreadths,	שֶׁהוּא גָבוֹהַ עֲשָׂרָה טְפָחִים,
or by the side of a trench	אוֹ בְּצַד חָרִיץ
which has a depth of ten handbreadths	שֶׁהוּא עָמוֹק עֲשָׂרָה טְפָחִים
and width of four [handbreadths].	וְרֹחַב אַרְבָּעָה,
One should allocate it a workspace of	נוֹתְנִין לוֹ עֲבוֹדָתוֹ
four cubits.	אַרְבַּע אַמּוֹת.
The School of Shammai says:	בֵּית שַׁמַּאי אוֹמְרִים,
One should measure four cubits	מוֹדְדִין אַרְבַּע אַמּוֹת
from the stem of the vines to the field.	מֵעִקַּר הַגְּפָנִים לַשָּׂדֶה.
And the School of Hillel says:	וּבֵית הִלֵּל אוֹמְרִים,
[They measure] from the fence to the field.	מִן הַגָּדֵר לַשָּׂדֶה.
R. Johanan b. Nuri [T3] said:	אָמַר רַבִּי יוֹחָנָן בֶּן נוּרִי,
All err, who say this.	טוֹעִים כָּל הָאוֹמְרִים כֵּן,
Unless there are four cubits	אֶלָּא אִם יֵשׁ שָׁם אַרְבַּע אַמּוֹת
from the base of the vines to the fence	מֵעִקַּר גְּפָנִים וְלַגָּדֵר,
one should allocate to it its workspace,	נוֹתְנִין לוֹ אֶת עֲבוֹדָתוֹ,
and he seeds the remainder.	וְזוֹרֵעַ אֶת הַמּוֹתָר.
And how much is the workspace of a vine?	וְכַמָּה הִיא עֲבוֹדַת הַגֶּפֶן.
Six handbreadths on all sides.	שִׁשָּׁה טְפָחִים לְכָל רוּחַ.
R. Akiba [T3] says: Three [handbreadths].	רַבִּי עֲקִיבָה אוֹמֵר, שְׁלֹשָׁה.

Comments: Vines were trailed over fences, over trees, or down trenches to give them access to more light. The significance of the definition is that even the Hillelites agree that a single row in a trellis can form a vineyard (unlike free-standing vines in m.Kil.4.5).

With respect to the minimum distance to other plants, the Shammaites treated them the same as free-standing vines, while the Hillelites were more generous and allowed measurement to start at the fence rather than at the stem of the vines.

The following contrary definitions are not explained, but one might surmise the following reasoning. If they followed the Hillelite ruling, the stem might be more than four cubits from the fence, in which case they would be planting around the base of the vine. Johanan solved this by saying that the workspace was measured from the fence only if the vines were less than four cubits from the fence. But if the workspace was four cubits (as assumed by the schools), this still meant that one could sow right up to a vine stem which was exactly four cubits from the fence. To solve this problem, the workspace was increased to '6 cubits on all sides.' The 'all sides' probably referred to the fence, but if it referred to the plant, Akiba realized that he only needed to allow three cubits on all sides to avoid *mixtures*.

The first part of this mishnah defines a trellis and ends with an ambiguous "width of four." In the context of the first part, this presumably means the trench has a minimum width of four handbreadths, but in the context of the following part, it may refer to the minimum gap of four cubits to prevent *mixtures*. It is more likely that it was linked with the following part at a later date, so "four [handbreadths]" is correct.

Dating (1): There is no reason to doubt that the school tradition is genuine, especially as the later rabbis followed neither ruling. They were very unlikely to invent a tradition which was opposed to the majority practice. The definition of a trellis at the beginning probably also dates back to the school debates, because it uses wording which is very similar to the debate in m.Kil.4.5, and it is possible that it has been derived from a similar debate. The final ruling about the size of vine workspace may relate to the measurement which is assumed in the opinion of Hillel in t.Kil.4.11 (see below), though the actual figure given there is uncertain.

Therefore it is likely that this was originally a group of two school disputes, but only the Hillelite part of the first has survived. It also became interspersed with later comments. The adoption of the Akiban view instead of the Hillelite "four handbreadths" probably prompted the disappearance of the attribution to the Hillelites, because it was difficult for Akiba to take precedence over the highly respected Hillelites.

m.Kil.7.1 and t.Kil.4.11 (Z 4.9): An underground vine shoot

m.Kil.7.1:

He who bends a vine [shoot] into the ground:	הַמַּבְרִיךְ אֶת הַגֶּפֶן בָּאָרֶץ,
If there is not soil over it	אִם אֵין עָפָר עַל
to a height of three handbreadths	גַּבָּהּ שְׁלֹשָׁה טְפָחִים,
one should not sow seed over it	לֹא יָבִיא זֶרַע עָלֶיהָ,
even if he bends it [under the soil]	אֲפִילוּ הִבְרִיכָהּ
through a gourd [shell] or a pipe.	בִּדְלַעַת אוֹ בְּסִילוֹן.
He who bends [the vine shoot] through stones	הִבְרִיכָהּ בְּסֶלַע,
even if there was soil	אַף עַל פִּי שֶׁאֵין עָפָר
only to the height of three finger-breadths	עַל גַּבָּהּ אֶלָּא שָׁלֹשׁ אֶצְבָּעוֹת,
it is permitted to sow seed over it.	מוּתָּר לְהָבִיא זֶרַע עָלֶיהָ.
The 'knee' of the vine [where it is bent into the soil]:	הָאַרְכּוּבָה שֶׁבַּגֶּפֶן,
One does not measure it except	אֵין מוֹדְדִין לָהּ אֶלָּא
from the second root [where it surfaces again].	מִן הָעִקָּר הַשֵּׁנִי.

t.Kil.4.11 (Z 4.9):

He who bends a vine [shoot] into the ground:	הַמַּבְרִיךְ אֶת הַגֶּפֶן בָּאָרֶץ,
If there is no height of soil on [top of] it	[אִם אֵין] עַל גַּבָּיו עָפָר
except whatever it has	אֶלָּא כָּל שֶׁהוּא,
one is permitted to seed on both sides	מוּתָּר לִזְרוֹעַ מִיכָּן וּמִיכָּן
but it is prohibited to seed on [top of that] height.	וְאָסוּר לִזְרוֹעַ עַל גַּבָּיו.
He who bends [the vine] which is through stones	הַבְרִיכָהּ שֶׁבַּסֶּלַע,
even if over it was soil	אַף עַל פִּי שֶׁאֵין עָפָר
only to the height of two finger-breadths	עַל גַּבָּיו אֶלָּא שְׁתֵּי אֶצְבָּעוֹת,
it is permitted to seed on [top of that] height	מוּתָּר לִזְרוֹעַ עַל גַּבָּהּ
—the words of R. Meir [T4].	דִּבְרֵי רִ׳ מֵאִיר.
R. Jose (b. Halafta) [T4] says	רִ׳ יוֹסֵה אוֹמֵר
[the height must be] three finger-breadths.	שָׁלֹשׁ אֶצְבָּעוֹת
Rn. Simeon b. Gamaliel [II T4] says:	רַבָּן שִׁמְעוֹן בֶּן גַּמְלִיאֵל אוֹמֵר
The School of Shammai says:	בֵּית שַׁמַּי אוֹמְרִים
Ten cubits[1]	עֶשֶׂר אַמּוֹת
And the School of Hillel say:	וּבֵית הִלֵּל אוֹמְרִים
Six handbreadths.[2]	שִׁשָּׁה טְפָחִים

[1] Variant: "Ten handbreadths."
[2] Variant: "Ten handbreadths."

Comments: One way to propagate vines was to bury a shoot and let it take root and start growing at a new location. Could one grow other plants in the soil on top of a buried shoot? Mishnah said Yes, if there was enough soil above the shoot, while Tosefta said No, but you may plant to either side of the shoots. Both rulings contain a line saying that it is prohibited, and this may have been the original ruling which was later changed in two different ways. This 'original' ruling is also attested by R. Jeremiah [PA4] in the name of R. Hiyya b. Abba [II PA3] in the Jerusalem Talmud where this discrepancy is being debated (y.Kil.7.1.I).

One was not allowed to plant over the top of buried shoots even if one encased the shoot in a gourd shell or a pipe, but one might possibly be allowed to sow over a shoot which was shielded by stone. Mishnah and Tosefta agree that only two or three finger-breadths of soil are needed over stone, though Simeon recalls a school dispute where the Hillelites say that the soil must be at least six handbreadths (i.e., twenty-four finger-breadths) and the Shammaites say it must be ten cubits. The Hillelite ruling is presumably based on the ruling that vines have a workspace of "six handbreadths on all sides" (m.Kil.6.1), and the Shammaite ruling demands an impossible depth of soil so they are saying, in effect, that even stone does not insulate plants from a vine shoot growing underneath.

Dating (1): Although Simeon is speaking in the mid second century, the school dispute which he presents is still likely to be genuine, because it retains the normal form of an uninterpreted school debate, without any explanations or glosses added.

However there is great uncertainty over the measurements, and these may well have been altered. It will be argued below that the original measurements were four handbreadths and ten cubits.

It appears that there was lot of debate in this area, and perhaps a lot of pressure by farmers who wanted to be able to sow on top of vine shoots. The original ruling was probably that one could not sow on top of vine shoots, unless they were insulated by stone, and even then there had to be four handbreadths (i.e., one workspace) of soil above the stone. This was the Hillelite view, and the Shammaites agreed, except that they did not accept the exception for insulation by stone.

The Shammaite measurement of 'ten cubits' did not balance well with the Hillelite measurement of 'four handbreadths,' because they were both different measurements and different numbers. A striving after easy memorization (or perhaps errors due to poor memorization) tended to either change the Hillelite measurement to 'one cubit' (i.e., six handbreadths) or the Shammaite measurement to 'ten handbreadths'. Therefore it was either "Shammaites ten cubits; Hillelites one cubit" or "Shammaites ten handbreadths; Hillelites four handbreadths". The Hillelite measurement became fixed at six handbreadths (i.e., one cubit) probably because this concurred with the width of a workspace in m.Kil.6.1. The others remained as variant readings.

Later it was decided that three handbreadths of soil *could* insulate the buried shoots. This measurement is probably based on the workspace of a vine, which is "six handbreadths on all sides" according to the Hillelites but "three" according to Akiba (m.Kil.6.1). It is likely that the Akiban view was adopted as correct with regard to buried shoots, and that this was transferred from the height of soil over stone to the height of soil over the shoots themselves.

We do not know when or how this change came about, which allowed sowing three handbreadths above a buried shoot, but when it did, they had to change the rulings about burying under stone. If three handbreadths of soil were sufficient insulation, then even the tiniest amount of soil was sufficient on top of insulation by stone. This conclusion had been reached by the mid second century when Meir and Jose disagreed only about how little soil was needed. The ruling "three finger-breadths" is reported anonymously in Mishnah, but it is attributed to R. Jose in Tosefta in order that it can be debated and refuted.

m.Kil.8.1-6: *Mixtures* of animals

Summary of Mishnah: This section starts with a short summary of the whole subject of *mixtures* which one would expect to find at the beginning of this tractate as an introduction (8.1).

Different animals may not be bred together (8.1), harnessed into a plough together, or even led together (8.2), and the punishment is forty lashes (8.3). This includes horses with asses (8.4) and asses with asses or mules with mules unless they share the same mother (8.3-4). Any animal can pull or be led with a man (8.6b), unless it is a 'wild man,' which is considered to be a type of animal (8.5a). The concept of a 'wild man' initiates a digression about which animals are wild (8.5b-6a).

The following traditions have elements (marked in bold) for which there is evidence of an origin before 70 CE:

m.Kil.8.1: Introductory summary of *mixtures*

Mixtures of the vineyard are prohibited	כלאי הכרם אסורין
from seeding and from maturing	מל זרוע ומל קים,
and are prohibited from making profit.	ואסורין בהנאה.
Mixtures of seeds are prohibited	כלאי זרעים, אסורים
from seeding and from maturing	מל זרוע ומל קים,
but are permitted for eating,	ומותרין באכילה
and [therefore], much more so, for making profit.	וכל שכן בהנאה.
Mixtures in garments are permitted	כלאי בגדים מותרין
in every thing	בכל דבר,
except they are prohibited from being worn.	ואינן אסורין אלא מללבוש.
Mixtures of cattle are permitted	כלאי בהמה מותרים
to be reared and matured	לגדל ולקים,
except they are prohibited from copulating.	ואינן אסורים אלא מל הרביע.
Mixtures of cattle are prohibited	כלאי בהמה אסורים
[from ploughing] with each other.	זה בזה.

Comments: This could act as an introduction to the whole subject of this tractate, and perhaps it did at one time (see Dating). Forbidden *mixtures in a vineyard* are prohibited in every way, but *mixtures* of other plants are only forbidden while they are growing. If other plants have been grown in *mixtures* (by gentiles), one is permitted to buy and sell them and to eat them, but wine must always be made from vines which are free of *mixtures*.

Garments which form *mixtures* can be kept together and are only prohibited from actually being worn. Similarly, animals which form *mixtures* can be kept together and even reared from young, but they cannot be allowed to interbreed.

If we ignore the last sentence ("*mixtures* of cattle are prohibited with each other"), which is probably a late addition (see Dating), this tradition forms a highly edited and unified whole. The first two and the last two share very similar forms, and the two pairs are linked by the first and last set of stipulations, "from seeding and from growing" and "to be reared and grown". The reason this tradition has been placed here is probably so that it can act as a transition from the section on plants (chapters 1–7) to the section on animals (chapter 8).

The different subject areas of *mixtures*, as found in the tractate, are also listed in this introduction, though in a slightly different order:

Order in tractate:	Order in m.Kil.8.1:
Plants in general	Vineyards
Vineyards	Plants in general
Animals	Garments
Garments	Animals

The order in the tractate is more logical (general plants before vineyards and farm animals after farm plants), and the rulings could have easily been rearranged without losing any meaning or force, but the editor(s) chose not to change the order.

Dating (2): This tradition contains necessary details which are not mentioned in the different sections of this tractate. Nowhere in the section on plants does it say that *mixtures* can be allowed to be eaten and or that vines are different in that they may not be used for profit, though this might be implied in the references to 'fruit' (m.Kil.2.5; 6.5) and to '*sanctifying*' (which is never defined). Nowhere in the section on garments does it define the prohibition on 'being worn,' though one might deduce this as the unifying factor in the list of prohibitions which are listed. Nowhere in the section on animals is there any mention of the prohibition of interbreeding.[3] All this suggests that this tradition in m.Kil.8.1 was originally an introduction to the whole subject, perhaps at the beginning of the tractate, so that individual sections did not have to mention details which the introduction had already stated.

Therefore, this tradition is one of the earliest parts of this tractate. We cannot know if it predates the school debates, because the details which it contains, which are so obviously missing from the rest of the tractate, would not normally be found in the highly abbreviated school debates in any case. It can, however, be dated to the earliest collections of *halakhah*, before Akiba's first Mishnah in the early second century; and the principles, which are undisputed in this tradition, must date much earlier still.

The editor(s) chose to make as few changes as possible. Although this introduction deals with the subject of garments, between that of plants and animals, the editors did not feel able to cut out these lines when they decided to employ it as a transition instead of an introduction to the tractate. Also, when they wanted to add a reference to ploughing and leading, they tacked it on the end as a separate ruling with as few words as possible.

Curiously, this introduction says nothing about *mixtures* of animals pulling a plough together. The last ruling simply says "*mixtures* of cattle are prohibited with

---

[3] Neusner and Danby both translate m.Kil.8.5a as though this refers to mating of mules, but there is nothing in the text to indicate this, and the parallel ruling in t.Kil.5.6 clearly relates to mules pulling together ("as one").

each other." Most translators relate this to interbreeding, assuming that it is an explanation of the preceding "*mixtures* of cattle . . . are prohibited from copulating." This perhaps needed an explanation because it could be ambiguous—it appears to forbid breeding and not just interbreeding. However, this same construction is used throughout this tradition without requiring any similar explanation (e.g., "*mixtures* of seeds are prohibited from seeding and from growing"). It is more likely that this last ruling was a somewhat clumsy attempt by a later editor to add some reference to ploughing and leading, in as few words as possible. The highly abbreviated phrase makes sense in the context, because the next mishnah ends with "to plough with them or lead them" (m.Kil.8.2), but it is obscure when it is read in isolation.

Another curious feature is that this introduction only mentions the prohibition of interbreeding "cattle" (בהמה, *behemah*), as in Torah (Lev.19.19). Perhaps the concept of prohibiting the interbreeding of wild animals was a later theoretical concept—it is certainly impractical to try and enforce it! Later Amoraim still discussed the justification for spreading this prohibition beyond cattle (y.Kil.1.7.IV). This wider prohibition is only present in Mishnah by implication. It is implied in the list of animals in m.Kil.1.6, which almost certainly refers to animals which may not be interbred, because it lists wild animals which cannot be yoked, such as a fox and deer. Also, it is implied every time there is a prohibition of yoking animals together, because 'to yoke together' was a common way of referring to marriage. Indeed, the term 'to be unyoked' occurs so regularly in legal documents that it can be regarded as a technical term for divorce.[4] This does not mean that 'yoking together' was regarded as a direct reference to breeding (otherwise m.Kil.8.6 would allow the interbreeding of men with wild animals), but there was a clear link in people's minds between these two concepts. This explains why the later traditions based on chapter 8, in Tosefta and the Jerusalem Talmud, discuss interbreeding throughout.

Paul uses a metaphor which relies on the equivalence of 'yoking' and 'marriage' (see below), which suggests that the equivalence of 'yoking' and 'breeding' was already part of normal thinking. This would confirm the idea that a prohibition of interbreeding would be implied by the text of Mishnah in the minds of most first-century rabbis.

New Testament: The ruling that one should not be 'unequally yoked with unbelievers' (2Cor.6.14) appears to be based on the principle of prohibiting *mixtures*, as a metaphorical way of saying that mixing a believer and unbeliever is like trying to

---

[4] This concept is represented by a group of words, which are all used in divorce certificates: ἀποζυγή, ἀποζεύγνυμαι, διαζεύγνυμαι, διαζεύγνυμι and διαζύγιον. The verb ζεύγνυμι (yoke, join together) is often used for joining in wedlock, and the noun ζεῦγος (yoke of beasts, pair) often refers to a married couple. See D. Instone-Brewer, "1 Corinthians 7 in the Light of the Jewish Greek and Aramaic Marriage and Divorce Papyri," *Tyndale Bulletin* 52 (2001): 227-45, esp. p. 240.

plough with an ox and an ass. Some commentators see this as a prohibition of a mixed business partnership and others as a prohibition of a mixed marriage. In favor of the latter, Paul gives a similar ruling in another epistle to the Corinthians, using different words. He told widows (who had complete freedom of choice about whom they could marry) that they should only marry "in the Lord" (1Cor.7.39), though of course he forbids believers to divorce their unbelieving spouse (1Cor.7.12-13). As mentioned above (Dating), the term 'to be unyoked' was a technical term for divorce.

m.Kil.9.1-10: *Mixtures* in garments

Summary of Mishnah: The *mixtures* prohibition only involves wool and linen [i.e., fibers of flax] (9.1) though silk is included for appearance's sake (9.2). Cloth made from a majority of camel hair and some wool fibers or a cloth made from a majority of hemp with some flax are not subject to this prohibition of *mixtures* (9.1). The prohibition only applies to garments, which does not include covered cushions because your skin does not touch them (9.2) but does include towels (9.3) and bags and unworn garments if you carry them (9.4-5) but not if you do not carry them (9.6). You should even examine shoes for any *mixtures* (9.7).

Scripture only forbade the *mixtures* of wool and linen *fibers* (9.8) but this can be extended to wool and linen pieces which are sewn together (9.9-10).

The following traditions have elements (marked in bold) for which there is evidence of an origin before 70 CE:

m.Kil.9.3: Towels can sometimes be 'garments'

Wrappers of the hands [i.e., hand towels],	מטפחות הידים,
wrappers of the scrolls [i.e., scroll covers],	מטפחות הספרים,
wrappers of drying [i.e., bath towels]	מטפחות הספג,
are not included in the category of *mixtures*.	אין בהם משום כלאים.
R. Eliezer (b. Hyrcanus) [T2]*1 prohibited.	רבי אליעזר אוסר.
And wrappers of barbers*2 [i.e., barbers' towels]	ומטפחות הספרים,
are prohibited by the category of *mixtures*.	אסורות משום כלאים.

*1 Some eds.: אלעזר Eleazar, i.e., b. Shammua [T4]
*2 This has exactly the same consonants as 'scrolls,' but it is traditionally pointed differently—"the scrolls" is הַסְּפָרִים, *hasspharim* while "the haircuts" is הַסַּפָרִים, *hasaparim*.

Comments: A towel which is placed on one's shoulders while hair is cut is included in the 'garments' which are subject to the restrictions of *mixtures*. R. Eliezer derived a number of other rulings from this one, either by wordplay (*hassepher* 'scroll' and *hassepag* 'drying' have a similar sound to *hasapar* 'haircuts') or by logic (bath towels and hand towels have a similar function to barbers' towels). This shows that the concept of 'garments' has already been widened to include anything which covers a person. The reason for including scrolls is uncertain. It is probably due to the extreme similarity of the words 'the scrolls' (הַסְּפָרִים, *hassepharim*) and 'the barbers' (הַסַּפָּרִים, *hassaparim*), but it may also be because Torah scrolls are sometimes like people (e.g., they have to be rescued from fire even on a Sabbath, m.Shab.16.1), or because the Torah covering may cover someone's hand during a synagogue service.

Dating (2): Chronologically, the last part of this mishnah is the earliest. This anonymous ruling was used by Eliezer to derive a series of three further rulings, with which the majority disagreed. This mishnah records first the decision of the majority, then the opinion of Eliezer, and finally the ruling which started it all.

Tosefta has the same tradition, but then records the opposite in the name of R. Judah: "R. Judah says, 'R. Eliezer permits and Sages prohibit.' " If Eliezer's rulings are based on the anonymous ruling which follows, then R. Judah's version is incorrect. R. Judah's version probably arose to explain the strange order in which the stages of this debate are recorded in this mishnah.

The attribution to Eliezer is doubtful. Not only are there variants which attribute this to Eleazar Shammua [T4] (though confusion between these two is common), but also it is unusual for Mishnah to be exegeted in this way at such an early date. The exegesis is based at least partly on wordplay, which is usually reserved for Scripture before Amoraic times.

m.Kil.9.8: Mixtures of threads woven together

There is no prohibition in the category of *mixtures*	אין אסור משום כלאים
except for spun and woven [materials],	אלא טווי וארוג,
as it is said [in Deut.22.11]:	שנאמר
"You shall not wear *shaatnez*."	לא תלבש שעטנז,
[Shaatnez] is something which is	דבר שהוא
combed and spun and twisted.	שוע טווי ונוז.

Comments: Torah said that "You must not wear *shaatnez* of wool and linen together" (Deut.22.11) but *shaatnez* is an obscure word. This tradition gives an etymology based on a merging of three words: *shua* (שׁוּעַ 'comb'), *tené* (טְוִי 'spin') and *nuz* (נוז 'weave'). According to this, the forbidden *mixtures* are wool and linen fibers which are woven together.

Dating (2): The next rulings in Mishnah (m.Kil.9.9-10) assume that it is also prohibited to sew anything made of wool to anything made of linen, such as edgings, bands, patches, or labels. The tradition here in m.Kil.9.8 does not include sewing, and appears to specifically exclude anything except spinning or weaving together.

Therefore it seems that the prohibition of sewing was a later development. This development had already taken place before 70 CE, because the school dispute in b.Men.40a (see Related Texts below) assumes that the sewing of *tassels* to a linen garment forms *mixtures*. Therefore the tradition here in m.Kil.9.8 dates from before 70 CE.

t.Kil.5.27 (Z 5.14b): Garments of the High Priest contain *mixtures*

Garments of the High Priest:	בגדי כהן גדול
He who goes in them outside [the Temple]	היוצא בהן למדינה
is liable [to *mixtures* of linen and wool in the garments]	חייב
but in the Sanctuary, whether approaching [to serve],	ובמקדש בין לשרת
or whether not approaching [to serve],	ובין שלא לשרת
one is exempt because [they are those]	פטור מפני
which are seemly for [Temple] service.	שהן ראוין לעבודה.

Comments: The High Priest wore five garments which the ordinary priest did not wear, all of which contained mixtures of linen and wool—the undergirdle (Exod.28.39; 39.29), the ephod (Exod.28.6-12; 39.2-7), the breastplate (Exod.28.15-30; 29.8-21), the robe of the ephod (Exod.28.31-35; 39.22-26) and the 'crown' or 'plate' of the miter (Exod.28.36-38; 39.30-31). The priests' clothes did not contain any *mixtures*.[5] This tradition points out that such *mixtures* are permitted, but only in the Temple.

Dating (8): This may merely be a meditation on the High Priest's garments, dating from a time after the destruction of the Temple. It follows a comment in t.Kil.5.26 that "the garments of the high priest are not subject to [the laws of] *mixtures*." This tradition is inserted in order to explain that the High Priest's garments did in fact contravene the law of *mixtures*.

However, the editor(s) of Tosefta could have stated this fact in a much more straightforward manner, because this tradition merely *implies* that a High Priest's garments contravene *mixtures*. Therefore it is more likely that they inserted a tradition which already existed, which was not ideal but which served the purpose. This tradition is also particularly practical in its rulings, which may suggest that it does date from Temple times. The High Priest was known to only wear these special garments inside the Holy of Holies on the Day of Atonement, and the rest of the time he wore "a more plain habit" (Jos.*Wars*.5.237). Therefore it is likely that the Tosefta has inserted a genuine pre-70 tradition rather than inventing something to suit its need.

---

[5] Some later traditions assume that the High Priest's girdle was also worn by priests (b.Hul.138a; b.Yom.12a) though others disagreed (b.Yom.6a).

Related early traditions from other tractates

m.Sheq.1.2: Inspecting the land for *mixtures*

R. Judah [b. Illai, T4] said:	אָמַר רַבִּי יְהוּדָה,
In former times they used to uproot them	בָּרִאשׁוֹנָה הָיוּ עוֹקְרִין
and throw them before [the owners].	וּמַשְׁלִיכִין לִפְנֵיהֶם.
When the transgressors increased	מִשֶּׁרַבּוּ עוֹבְרֵי עֲבֵרָה,
they used to uproot them	הָיוּ עוֹקְרִין
and threw them on the roads.	וּמַשְׁלִיכִין עַל הַדְּרָכִים,
They *decreed* that it shall be [declared as] *ownerless*	הִתְקִינוּ שֶׁיְּהוּ מַפְקִירִין
each entire field [where mixtures were found].	כָּל הַשָּׂדֶה כֻּלָּהּ.

Comments: When the majority willingly obeyed the law of *mixtures*, they would personally visit the owner of any offending field. However, when this became too common, they would simply throw the evidence on the road, for all to see. Later, when the rabbis had more authority, they even declared the field *ownerless* so that anyone could help themselves to the produce. The previous mishnah in *Sheqalim* says that they went to inspect the fields every year on the first of Adar, which is about 6 weeks before harvest.

Dating (9): This is very difficult to date early because the earliest source comes from R. Judah in the mid second century. The only way to date it is by the form which it shares with a few other traditions which may indicate that they originally formed a single group of traditions. These others are found at m.Sot.9.9 and m.Shebi.4.1:

In former times (בָּרִאשׁוֹנָה) they said: A man may gather wood, stones or grass from his own field, just as he gathers from the [field] of his associate, [but only gathering] the large ones. When transgressors increased (מִשֶּׁרַבּוּ עוֹבְרֵי עֲבֵרָה), they *decreed* (הִתְקִינוּ) that one should gather only from the field of another. . . . (m.Shebi.4.1)

When murderers increased (מִשֶּׁרַבּוּ) the rite of breaking the heifer's neck was abolished. . . . When adulterers increased (מִשֶּׁרַבּוּ) the application of the waters of jealousy ended. And R. Johanan b. Zakkai [T1] ended them. (m.Sot.9.9)

The passage at m.Shebi.4.1 cannot be dated with any certainty, except with reference to this same group. The passage at m.Sot.9.9 claims that the tradition goes back to Johanan b. Zakkai in the time of the Temple. This is probably authentic, because both of these rites would have ended at 70 CE without the need for any rulings, and so decisions to end them must predate 70 CE.

It is unlikely that later generations would invent the idea that some OT rites were abolished before such establishment was necessitated by the destruction of the Temple, unless the purpose was to show how evil that generation was. However, the other traditions which appear to speak about this "increase" in wickedness seem to trace the rot to the period after the destruction of the Temple. This mixture suggests that there is no 'message' in these texts, but merely a collection of traditions about the increase in evil.

When we take all these traditions altogether, the best we can say is that two of them (at m.Sot.9.9) are likely to reflect rulings which predated 70 CE, and the others reflect situations which fit into a pre-70 context. Two undateable rulings might be said to reflect a later nostalgia about a willingness to obey the law in the past which is contrasted with enforced law keeping in the present. In the past they could be trusted to gather wood without clearing a field, and there were so few transgressions of the law of *mixtures* that they could confront each individual, but now they have to use other means to minimize transgressions. The other two in m.Sot.9.9 reflect the opposite view, that a previous generation became so lawless that certain Temple rites had to be abolished.

The term "in former times" (*barishonah*, בראשונה, cf. *bereshit* בראשית, "in the beginning") is used variously, including as a reference to times before 70 CE (see m.Git.4.2).

It is possible that the date of the first of Adar (see Comments) is pre-70 because this date is linked to the time when the Temple tax was announced (see m.Sheq.1.1).

New Testament: Various saying of Jesus reflect the same contrast which we find in these traditions—a society where the majority keep the laws of tithing and agriculture, but a growing number were neglecting issues of morality. Jesus expressed consternation at those who gave increasing attention to obeying what he considered to be minor aspects of the law while ignoring the increase in adultery and perhaps murder. He criticized those who tithed herbs (Mt.23.23; cf. Lk.11.42), washed the outside of vessels (Mt.23.25; Lk.11.39), fasted twice a week (Lk.18.12), washed hands (Mt.15.20; Mk.7.2-5; Lk.11.38), and yet acted like those who murdered the prophets (Mt.23.29-35; Lk.11.47-51), and were part of the "adulterous and sinful generation" (Mt.12.39; 16.4). At least two and perhaps three of the few women mentioned in the Gospels were prostitutes (the Samaritan, the one 'caught in the act,' and the woman who anointed his feet), which suggests that this was a large and growing problem.

m.Ed.4.10: Linen garments are allowed woollen *tassels*

Our rabbis taught [this *baraytah*]:	:תנו רבנן
Linen [garment. Does one wear it] with *tassels*?	סדין בציצית
The School of Shammai [rule it] exempt [from *tassels*]	,בית שמיי פוטרין
and the School of Hillel [rule it] liable [to *tassels*].	,ובית הלל מחייבין
And the *halakhah* is according to the words of	והלכה כדברי
the School of Hillel.	בית הלל

Comments: Since *tassels* were normally made of wool, should one attach them to linen garments? The School of Hillel said that the law of the *tassels* was more important, and the School of Shammai said the law of *mixtures* was more important. Midrash Tannaim (re Deut.22.12) said that the School of Hillel used the maxim that a positive command (to wear *tassels*) should always outweigh a negative command (to not wear a *mixture*), while the Shammaites pointed out that in Scripture (Deut.22.11f) the negative command (to not mix) precedes the positive one (to add *tassels*).

Dating (1): The fact that this school dispute is recorded in Eduyyot but nowhere else in Mishnah or Tosefta is very unusual. However, it is transmitted with unhelpfully extreme abbreviation which was typical of records of school disputes, and so it is likely to be genuine. If it had been constructed in order to supply the basis for a *halakhah*, it would likely be less obscure.

The comment that *halakhah* follows Hillel is strange, because one would normally assume this to be the case. Perhaps doubt was created by the strong Shammaite argument. This helps to suggest that this argument was added relatively early, but not necessarily before 70 CE.

Later rabbis ruled that linen night clothes were not allowed to have a *tassel*, because it was not compulsory to put *tassels* on night clothes, so the command of *tassels* could not overrule the command of *mixtures* in this case (b.Shab.25b—a story re R. Judah b. Illai [T4]).

Summary and Conclusions

The rabbis extended the Torah prohibitions of *mixtures* to include grafting, growing under and over other plants, leading animals, even wild animals and *mixtures* of pieces of cloth. They applied these restrictions outside as well as inside Israel (m.Orl.3.9; m.Qid.1.9).

An older introduction to this Mishnah tractate is preserved at m.Kil.8.1. This includes several principles which are necessary for understanding the various sections.

The section on plants has a long list of similar plants which are considered different or sufficiently similar to each other to grow together without forming *mixtures*. This list started to grow before 70 CE, with at least one pair of plants (m.Kil.1.1) and one pair of trees (t.Kil.1.4). Grafting between different plants was already forbidden (m.Kil.1.7), though Scripture was silent on this.

The rabbis took *mixtures* in fields very seriously, patrolling the field on the first of Adar (m.Sheq.1.1), and if they found *mixtures*, they uprooted them and took proof to the owner (m.Sheq.1.2). Distances between rows of different plants on small holdings were defined in very practical ways in terms of furrow widths, which farmers would understand easily (m.Kil.2.6). However, distances between different plants and vines (which would be grown on larger plots of land) were defined by a number of exact measurements. These measurements were still developing and changing after 70 CE (m.Kil.6.1) especially with regard to sowing on top of underground shoots, where the *halakhah* was considerably relaxed after 70 CE (m.Kil.7.1), and perhaps with regard to sowing in wine presses and under watch towers (m.Kil.5.3)

The descriptions of vineyards are very similar to the descriptions in the New Testament, including a dugout winepress, a watch tower (m.Kil.5.3), a surrounding fence or hedge and an area in the center for different plants (m.Kil.4.1). Vines which were spoiled by *mixtures* were '*sanctified*' but there is no indication that this ever meant that they were actually offered to the Temple. They were simply destroyed, even in the time of the Temple, probably by burning (cf. m.Kil.5.7). This was an extremely significant matter, especially for Hillelites who said that the minimum amount to be destroyed was two rows of vines (m.Kil.4.5). The list of plants which caused *mixtures* with a vine was starting to grow before 70 CE (t.Kil.3.17).

The misplaced 'introduction' to the tractate (m.Kil.8.1) is the only place in the Mishnah which mentions interbreeding (though it may be implied in m.Kil.1.6), and it only speaks about interbreeding farm animals. After 70 CE, wild animals were specifically excluded from the prohibition of ploughing together, but were included in the prohibition of interbreeding.

Mixtures of wool and linen in Scripture were known to refer only to cloth which was woven from both fibers (9.8), but by 70 CE it was expanded to include pieces of wool and linen which were sewn together (b.Men.40a). The definition of 'garment' was already starting to change from something which one wore to something which might incidentally touch or cover one (m.Kil.9.3). Exceptions were allowed for the High Priest's garments (t.Kil.5.27) and *tassels* (b.Men.40a).

The overall structure of this tractate was probably determined by Scripture. The major passage is Deuteronomy 22.9-11 which discusses vines, animals ploughing, and then garments. The shorter text in Leviticus 19.19 discusses cattle breeding, plants in fields, and then garments. This tractate is based on the order in the major passage, into which it inserts subjects from the minor passage. Therefore it discusses plants in a field with vines (as two large and separate sections, m.Kil.1-3 and 4-7), then cattle breeding with animal ploughing (m.Kil.8), and then garments (m.Kil.9).

This tractate is highly edited, with a clear structure and almost no material which is outside the topic of the tractate (only m.Kil.8.5b). Nevertheless, where the development of the tractate is evident, it shows an unwillingness to change earlier traditions. The editing process consisted of changing the order of older traditions and inserting new material.

For example, m.Kil.3.1-7 is a series of applications of three principles which are laid out in m.Kil.2.6-11 in the same order—minimum spacing (2.6 applied in 3.1-2), protruding corners (2.7 applied in 3.3), and gourds (2.11 applied in 3.4-7). This is not a commentary as such because there is no application of boundaries (2.8) or patches (2.9-10). It is significant that these three applications have not been inserted at the point where the corresponding principles are stated and where they would fit very naturally. This probably indicates that the passage with the principles (2.6-11) already formed a tradition which later editors did not feel free to break up. For similar reasons, a mishnah about animals (m.Kil.1.6) was permitted to remain in the middle of rulings about plants, because it was part of a group of traditions which all end with the same phrase (m.Kil.1.4-6).

Another use of older traditions which have not been edited is m.Kil.8.1. This was probably originally a summary introduction for the whole subject, but it was employed by the editors to form a transition from the section on plants (chapters 1–7) to the section on animals (chapter 8), because it starts with plants and ends with animals. This tradition has been kept unchanged, even though a summary about garments exists in the middle of 8.1 where it is out of place when it is used as a transitional passage.

Tractate *Shebiit*: Sabbath Year

Definitions and Outline

Torah said that in the Sabbath Year (*shebiit*, שְׁבִיעִית) the Land had to have a *release* (*shemittah*, שְׁמִטָּה), during which no one could cultivate the land, and any produce which grew by itself could be eaten by the poor or by animals (Exod.23.10-11; Lev.25.2-7). God promised that the harvest would be three times the normal size in the sixth year, so that they would have sufficient food during the Sabbath Year when they could not harvest or prepare the land, and during the first year of the next cycle while they waited for the crops to grow (Lev.25.20-22). After every seven Sabbath Years they were to have a Jubilee when, in addition to these Sabbath Year regulations, land property reverted to its original owners (Lev.25.8-17; Num.36.4).

Torah specifically forbade sowing, reaping, pruning, and picking grapes, to which the rabbis added other prohibitions such as ploughing, planting, fertilizing, clearing, watering, and storing. Some produce was exempt because it was not 'food.' The rabbis defined the Sabbath Year produce as *ownerless* (*hephqer*, הֶפְקֵר— m.Shebi.9.4),[1] because it could be gathered by anyone as food. Storage of food was restricted by the time of *removal* (*biur*, בִּיעוּר, which was the time when uneaten Sabbath Year produce which had been gathered had to be *removed* from your house, because it was no longer available in the fields. To leave it in your house after this time would imply that you were storing it, and not just using it.

Much of this tractate concerns the exact time when the Sabbath Year regulations come into force, and when they ended, for various activities such as tending the soil and plants in the previous year, gathering and *removal* of food during the Sabbath Year, and purchasing the new crop in the following year. This concern is reflected in the repeated phrase "until what time" or "from what time" (1.1; 2.1; 3.1; 4.7, 10; 5.5; 6.4; and perhaps 9.7).

The Sabbath Year *release* was also extended to anyone who had a loan, so all loans were cancelled (Deut.15.1-3). This caused practical problems, and so there were ways around this regulation, especially Hillel's *prozbul* (פְּרוֹזְבּוּל from πρὸς βουλῇ 'via a court') and later distinctions between a 'loan' and a 'debt' (which was not subject to *release*).

---

[1] This was also stated by the houses outside this tractate in m.Pea.6.1; m.Ed.4.3.

There is considerable evidence that the restrictions of the Sabbath Year were widely practiced in the first century.[2] Herod's siege of Jerusalem in 37 BCE lasted only fifty-five days because "a Sabbatical year happened to fall at that time" (Jos.*War*.14.475).[3] A certificate of lending has been found which was drawn up "in this Year of *Release*" dated 55/56 CE.[4] Julius Caesar and perhaps Alexander the Great exempted the Jews from taxes during the Sabbath Year,[5] and this continued until the Bar Kokhba Revolt.[6] Toward the end of the Sabbath Year, there was real fear of starvation among the poor, who were reduced to eating the normally inedible endives.[7] Because of this, even the Tosefta admits that "the Sages prescribed only such rules as they could enforce" (t.Shebi.3.11, 13).

The two definite dates above imply that the Sabbath Years during the New Testament eras were:

2/1 BCE, 6/7 CE, 13/14 CE, 20/21 CE, 27/28 CE—before the ministry of Jesus
34/35 CE—when the church had difficulty feeding its poor (t.Shebi.4.5b)
41/42 CE—when Agrippa I took part in a Sabbath Year ceremony (m.Sot.7.8)
48/49 CE—following a famine; Paul arranged a collection (m.Pea.8.7)
55/56 CE, 62/63 CE, 69/70 CE—the year before the destruction[8]

There is little evidence that a Jubilee was ever practiced during the Second Temple period (the best evidence in m.Arak.7.1 is equivocal) and it is very unlikely that it was practiced after 70 CE (see m.Bek.8.10, discussed at the end of this chapter).

m.Shebi.1.1–2.10: Activities before the Sabbath Year

Ploughing an orchard at the end of the sixth year was regarded as benefiting the cultivation of the Sabbath Year produce, and so you could only plough up to the end of the grain harvest, i.e., until *Shabuot* (Pentecost). Tending a field, however, can carry on until the start of the Sabbath Year, except for activities which clearly benefit

---

[2] See Ben Zion Wacholder, "Calendar of Sabbatical Cycles during the Second Temple and the Early Rabbinic Period," *Hebrew Union College Annual* 44 (1973): 153-96.

[3] This means the Seventh Year started in Tishri of 38 BCE, though other comments by Josephus suggests that it may have been in the year following the seige—see Wacholder, "Calendar," pp. 166-67.

[4] The actual date is "year two of Nero"—see the discussion in Wacholder, "Calendar" pp. 169-71. The text is found in *DJD* II #18, pp. 100-104.

[5] Jos.*Ant*.14.202, 320-28; 11.338.

[6] *CRINT* 1.II.826.

[7] See the discussion in *CRINT* 1.II.827 based on third-century material.

[8] The classic work of Benedict Zuckermann ("Ueber Sabbatjahrcyclus und Jobelperiode," *Jahresbericht des jüdische-theologischen Seminars "Fraenckelscher Stiftung,"* Breslau, 1857) agrees with later rabbinic tradition that the Second Temple fell during a Seventh Year like the first, but Wacholder argues convincingly that it was actually the year after a Seventh Year ("Calendar," pp. 171-76).

the next crop, such as ploughing. You can plough only up to the end of the grain harvest, i.e., until *Pesach* (Passover).

m.Shebi.3.1–5.9: Activities during the Sabbath Year

Some activities during the Sabbath Year inadvertently benefit the wild crop or the soil. For example, if animals graze they add manure, or if the farmer builds a wall he might remove stones. How much of these activities are allowed before they are considered to be beneficial? Produce can be gathered by anyone as food during the Sabbath Year, but it cannot be harvested. You must not gather it too early, before it is ripe, otherwise you stop it becoming 'food.' You must not use tools to gather it, otherwise it is being 'harvested.'

m.Shebi.6.1–9.9: Using Sabbath Year produce

Sabbath Year produce can be eaten until the time of the *removal*, which varied according to the time when each type of food was no longer available in fields in one's locality. Some trading could take place with produce which was not for human or animal consumption or for dyeing. Also one could sell ad hoc quantities of surplus gathered food.

m.Shebi.10.1-9: Loans in the Sabbath Year

Loans were *released* by the Sabbath Year, but not debts, and not loans to a court. Hillel allowed any loan to be made via a court by the legal process of *prozbul*.

Related texts: m.Sot.7.8 re Agrippa and m.Bek.8.10 re Jubilees

Agrippa I may have taken part in a ceremony at the end of a Sabbath Year, but it is unlikely that any Jubilee was celebrated.

m.Shebi.1.1-8: Tending orchards before the Sabbath Year

Summary of Mishnah: You can plough an orchard while it continues to benefit the sixth year fruit, i.e., until *Shabuot* (Pentecost) (1.1), and you can plough a field until the beginning of the grain harvest, i.e., until *Pesach* (Passover) (2.1). When you plough an orchard [between Passover and Pentecost], you must plough only around individual trees (1.2) and only if they are fruit trees (1.3), or you can plough the whole orchard if the trees are dense enough (1.2, 4-5). If they are saplings which will not provide produce during the next year (1.8), you may plough up until the New Year (1.6-7). You may also plough a field [after Passover] if you intend to plant melons or gourds [which are planted late and grow quickly] (2.1).

The following traditions have elements (marked in bold) for which there is evidence of an origin before 70 CE:

m.Shebi.1.1: Ploughing an orchard

Until what time should one plough	עד אימתי חורשין
a field of trees [i.e., an orchard]	בשדה האילן
before the Sabbath Year?	ערב שביעית.
The School of Shammai says:	בית שמאי אומרים,
All the time that it benefits the [sixth-year] fruit.	כל זמן שהוא יפה לפרי.
And the School of Hillel says:	ובית הלל אומרים,
Until the Assembly [Day of Pentecost].	עד העצרת.
And the statement of these are close	וקרובין דברי אלו
to being like the statement of the others.	להיות כדברי אלו.

Comments: Both schools agreed that you should not plough around fruit trees after the sixth-year fruit harvest, because otherwise you would be benefiting only the Sabbath Year harvest. They had different ways of defining the latest date—the Hillelites preferred a specific date, while the Shammaites defined it with reference to the reason behind the ruling.

The Assembly in Torah was the last day of a feast—of *Sukkot* (Tabernacles, Lev.23.36; Num.29.35) or *Pesach* (Passover, Deut.16.8) or *Shabuot* (Pentecost, Num.28.26). In rabbinic traditions it is usually the latter, so it is a name for the final great day of that feast, the Day of Pentecost (cf. m.Bek.9.5).[9]

Dating (1): There is no reason to doubt that this represents the rulings of the schools before 70 CE. A later editor has commented that these rulings are, in practical terms, very similar. This editorial comment may have been part of the source which was used by the Mishnah, and so it may also date from before 70 CE, but this is not certain. The fact that both rulings were retained in this form, even though they were almost identical, suggests that they originated in communities and became well established before the matter was debated by the schools. After 70 CE, this ruling was changed to allow ploughing up to the end of the year (see Dating at m.Shebi.2.1).

The rest of this section (m.Shebi.1.2-8) is likely to date from the generation immediately after 70 CE, but this is uncertain. This likelihood is indicated by the fact that the last part of it (2.8) is based on a debate between R. Eleazar b. Azariah and R. Joshua b. Hananiah (both T2, end of first century). Their debate is on a matter which presupposes almost all the preceding rulings in m.Shebi.1.2-7. They debate the definition of 'saplings' which presupposes the distinction between an orchard of saplings and of mature trees (m.Shebi.1.6-7), and these rulings in turn presuppose the

---

[9] See also m.Bik.1.10; m.BB.6.3; m.Ed.2.10.

ruling about ten trees (m.Shebi.1.4), which in turn presupposes the question about the definition of an orchard (m.Shebi.1.2). The fact that their debate presupposed these other rulings does not mean that these other rulings date from a previous generation, because they are not referring to any of these previous decisions as unquestionable— they merely refer to the principles which were discussed in these previous rulings. Therefore it is possible that the whole of this section (m.Shebi.1.2-8) was a product of the T2 generation and that it does not date from before 70 CE.

It may be possible to regard much of this section (m.Shebi.1.2-8) as pre-70 on the basis of some later rabbis who regarded the ruling about "ten saplings" (1.6) as a "*halakhah* of Moses from Sinai" (b.MK.3b, Johanan [b. Nappaha, PA2], late third century). If we regard this to mean that this ruling dates back to before 70 CE, then this would also establish an early date for 1.4 (on which 1.6 relies) and 1.2 (on which 1.4 relies). However, this attribution to Moses merely means that Johanan's generation could not recall its origin, so that it *might* be as early as pre-70.

m.Shebi.2.1-10: Tending fields before the Sabbath Year

Summary of Mishnah: Torah prohibits only sowing, reaping, pruning, and picking grapes. The rabbis added related prohibitions such as ploughing, which was prohibited once the sixth-year crop was harvested (2.1). Other rabbinic additions included fertilizing and hoeing (2.2), removing stones and thinning branches (2.3), protecting them with oil or shelters (2.4), oiling or piercing figs (2.5), and drying out gourds (2.10). Most of these were allowed until the New Year though some activities were prohibited thirty days before the New Year because they result in the growth of new plants. This latter group included planting or grafting partially grown plants (2.6), and planting late crops such as rice or beans which can be harvested in the Sabbath Year if they rooted in the sixth (2.7-8), though you may not water them (2.9).

This section collects virtually all the rulings concerning the Sabbath Year which contain the phrases "until the New Year" (2.2-5) or "before the New Year" (2.6-10). These phrases occur elsewhere in this tractate only at 1.6-7 and in a relatively late comment in 7.2 (Meir, T2). It is possible that 2.2-10 already formed a collection before it was joined to 2.1 by the influence of the similar reference to melons and gourds in 2.1 and 2.2.

Dating: None of this section after the first mishnah can be dated before 70 CE, and only one of these rulings (m.Shebi.2.3) can be dated to T2, the late first century. Therefore it is likely that these rabbinic restrictions, which were added to the biblical restrictions, did not come into force until after this time. The only exception is the ploughing of orchards in m.Shebi.2.1.

The following traditions have elements (marked in bold) for which there is evidence of an origin before 70 CE:

m.Shebi.2.1: Ploughing a field

Until what time should one plough	עד **אימתי** חורשין
a field of white [i.e., a grain field]	בשדה הלבן
before the Sabbath Year?	ערב שביעית.
Until the [soil's] moisture is gone.	עד שתכלה הלחה,
All the time when the sons of men plough	כל זמן שבני אדם חורשים
in order to plant cucumbers or gourds.	לטע במקשאות ובמדלעות.
R. Simeon [b. Yohai, T4] said:	אמר רבי שמעון,
You have put the Law	נתת תורת
for each individual into his hands.	**כל אחד ואחד** בידו,
Instead: **A field of white [i.e., a grain field]**	אלא בשדה הלבן
until *Pesach* (Passover),	עד הפסח,
and a field of trees [i.e., an orchard]	ובשדה האילן
until the Assembly [Day of Pentecost].	עד עצרת.

Comments: When can you continue to plough a grain field without benefiting only the Sabbath Year's crop? Some (probably the Shammaites—see below) said up to the time when there would be no more benefit to this year's crop of grain or even the late maturing crops like gourds. Others (probably the Hillelites) gave the specific date of Passover, which was the time of the grain harvest.

Dating (1): It is very likely that this tradition preserves the core of a school debate, which we might reconstruct as follows:

> Until what time do they plough a grain field before the Sabbath Year?
> Shammai: All the time during which people plough in order to plant cucumbers or
>   gourds.
> Hillel: Until Passover.

This is very similar to the school debate at m.Shebi.1.1:

> Until what time do they plough an orchard before the Sabbath Year?
> Shammai: All the time that it benefits the [sixth-year] fruit.
> Hillel: Until the Assembly [Day of Pentecost].

We cannot be certain whether the Shammaite ruling was "Until the [soil's] moisture is gone" or "All the time during which people plough in order to plant cucumbers or gourds." The second agrees more with the form of the Shammaite ruling in m.Shebi.1.1 ("All the time . . .") and it uses the same logic as m.Shebi.1.1 because it bases the argument on the reason for the prohibition.

The end of Simeon's ruling appears to be a quotation of a summary of the Hillelite rulings, which would have been the accepted majority teaching after 70 CE. These rulings did not remain the majority teaching for very long, because Rn. Gamaliel II [T2, soon after 70 CE] overruled them, according to a tradition in b.MK.3b (cf. t.Shebi.1.1):

> What is meant by 'the days [of restriction] prior to New Year'?—According to what we learned: 'Up to what date may ploughing be done in a tree field [orchard] in the pre-sabbatical year? The School of Shammai says, As long as it is for the benefit of the fruit; the School of Hillel says, Up to the Assembly [Day of Pentecost]; and the [practical effect of] one ruling is much the same as that of the other. And up to what date may they plough a "white field" in the pre-sabbatical year? Up to when the moisture gives out and as long as people until for planting their cucumber and gourd beds. Said R. Simeon: If that is so, you have handed over the Torah for every individual to determine for himself the right time! No: [I say], a white field [i.e., grain field, they may until] up to Passover and a tree field [i.e., orchard] up to the Assembly [Day of Pentecost].' (And the School of Hillel says: Up to Passover.)
>
> And R. Simeon b. Pazzi reported in the name of R. Joshua b. Levi who had it from Bar Kappara that Rabban Gamaliel and his Courthouse took a vote on these two [terminal] periods and abrogated them.

This tradition assumes that the restrictions for ploughing both orchards and fields have originated with the schools, as argued here. It also says that these restrictions were removed by Gamaliel II, though it is only later reported by Simeon b. Pazzi [PA3, end of third century]. If these restrictions were removed soon after 70 CE, the summary at the end of this mishnah must date from before 70 CE. It is very likely that this tradition in b.MK.3b is accurate because it was the cause of great embarrassment (as discussion which follows in b.MK.3b indicates) due to the fact that a later court overruled an earlier court which was normally regarded as superior to it.

New Testament: The term 'sons of man' (*bené adam*, בְּנֵי אָדָם) occurs about twenty times in Mishnah, sometimes in pre-70 sources like this, and always means 'ordinary people.' The singular *ben adam* (בֶּן אָדָם) or Aramaic *bar enash* (בַּר אֱנָשׁ) is used much less often, and never in Mishnah. The nearest parallel to the Gospel ὁ υἱὸς τοῦ ἀνθρώπου (*ho huios tou anthproopou*, 'the son of man' or 'the Son of Man') is the Aramaic with an article, *bar enasha*. There has been a great deal of debate by New Testament scholars about a few relatively late rabbinic traditions where this phrase is used as a self-reference. Vermes argued that this phrase was an exclusive self-reference in which the speaker referred only to himself. Casey argued that it was a self-reference in which the speaker identifies himself with all the rest of humanity. Lindars argued that it was a self-reference to oneself and to anyone within one's own class, even if there is only one person in this class.[10]

Jesus' phrase in John 4.35 'the fields are white to harvest' sounds natural and idiomatic in the light of this mishnah.

t.Shebi.1.5 (Z 1.6): Watering saplings until the New Year

One may water saplings	משקין את הנטיעות
until *Rosh ha-Shanah* (New Year).	עד ראש השנה.
R. Joseh b. Kippar [T3]says*	רבי יוסה בן כיפר אומר
in the name of R. Eliezer [b. Hyrcanus, T2]:	משום רבי אליעזר
The School of Shammai says:	בית שמאי אומרים
He waters the foliage	משקה על הנוף
and it goes down to the root.	ויורד על העיקר
The School of Hillel says:	בית הלל אומרים
[He waters both] the foliage	על הנוף
and the root.	ועל העיקר
The School of Hillel said to the School of Shammai	אמרו בית הלל לבית שמאי
If you permit him [to water] part,	אם אתה מתיר לו מקצת
permit him [to water] the whole.	התר לו את הכל,
If you do not permit him [to water] the whole,	אם אין את מתיר לו את הכל
do not permit him [to water] the part.	אל תתיר לו מקצת.

*Z reads רבי יוסי, R. José.
Mishnaic parallel: m.Shebi.2.4

Comments: Both schools agree that saplings may be kept watered after *Shabuot* (Pentecost) and before the New Year which begins the Sabbath Year, but you are not allowed to improve the ground by watering it. The Shammaites say that one may water the foliage, and let the water drip down to the roots, while the Hillelites say that one may also water the roots directly.

This implies that watering the land or any other crops was forbidden during the Sabbath Year, and probably after harvest in the sixth year, because they appear to be making a special exception for saplings.

Dating (1): There is no reason to doubt that this is a genuine school dispute, though the overly long explanation which follows has been added later.

Later, R. Eliezer b. Zadok [II, T5] allowed the watering of sapling foliage during the Sabbath Year (m.Shebi.2.4).

---

[10] Geza Vermes, "Present State of the 'son of man' Debate," *Journal of Jewish Studies* 29 (1978): 23-134; Maurice Casey, "Corporate Interpretation of 'one like a son of man' (Dan 7:13) at the Time of Jesus," *Novum Testamentum* 18 (1976): 167-80; Barnabas Lindars, *Jesus Son of Man: A Fresh Examination of the Son of Man Sayings in the Gospels* (London: SPCK; Grand Rapids: Eerdmans, 1983).

t.Shebi.2.6a (Z 2.5a): Plants which continue to grow after New Year

Rn. Simeon b. Gamaliel [II T4] said:	אמר רבן שמעון בן גמליאל
The School of Shammai and the School of Hillel were not divided	לא נחלקו בית שמאי ובית הלל
concerning mature [produce]	על הגמור
that it is [tithed according] to the previous [year]	שהוא לשעבר,
and concerning that which is not budding	ועל שלא הנץ
that it is [tithed according] to the coming [year].	שהוא לעתיד לבא,
Concerning what were they divided?	על מה נחלקו
Concerning **that which forms pods,**	על התורמל,
for **the School of Shammai says:**	שבית שמאי אומרים
[It is tithed according] to the previous [year]	לשעבר,
and **the School of Hillel says:**	ובית הילל אומרים
[It is tithed according] to the coming [year].	לעתיד לבא

Tosefta parallel: t.Maas.1.5

Comments: When plants are planted in one year and mature in another, one tithes according to the year in which the fruit was actually growing (this is in accord with m.Shebi.5.1). The only problem is fruit with pods, like gourds, which mature for a long period extending from the end of one year to the beginning of the next (cf. m.Shebi.2.10).

Most tithes remain the same throughout the first six years of the seven-year cycle, except for the *poor tithe* which replaces the *second tithe* in the third and sixth years (see tractate *Peah*). In the Sabbath Year there are no tithes except for the *elevation offering*.[11]

Dating (1): There is no reason to doubt that this was a genuine school dispute, though the original introduction has been vastly extended, perhaps by Simeon b. Gamaliel himself. It is not clear if this Simeon b. Gamaliel is I [T2] or II [T4] but the latter is much more likely because the first left very few traditions.

Soon after 70 CE a distinction was made between the fruit of trees and vegetables. Vegetables were tithed according to the year in which they matured (m.Bik.2.6), and trees were presumably tithed according to the year in which the fruit starts growing.

m.Shebi.3.1–4.6: Tending fields during the Sabbath Year

Summary of Mishnah: Dung can be moved to a field for storage, but not in order to fertilize the field; therefore put dung in fields only after the Sabbath Year growing

---

[11] This is not made clear in Mishnah, but it is implied by m.Shebi.9.9 which says that the *elevation offering* of dough has to be removed in the Seventh Year.

season (3.1) and pile it up in heaps (3.2-3). Grazing animals must be kept in an enclosure so that they do not fertilize the whole field (3.10).

Stones can be quarried or built into a wall, but you may not improve a field by removing stones; therefore, quarry only if there is a large amount of stone (3.5), and remove only very large stones or stones on top of other stones (3.6, 7, 9) or stones very near the wall (3.8) or stones in a neighbor's field (3.6). You may dig a foundation for a wall, but you may not dig a field; therefore leave the extracted top soil in piles (3.10). You may gather fuel, but you may not clear rubbish from a field; therefore, gather only large pieces of wood or gather it from a neighbor's field (4.1). It is not forbidden to clear thorns (4.2).

If a field was fertilized or cleared during the Sabbath Year, it may not be cultivated the next year, but may you eat its Sabbath Year produce? Gentiles may harvest and prepare fields during the Sabbath Year, and Israelites may help them or lease the field the following year.

You may cut down trees for wood, but you may not prepare land for planting. Therefore, you should not dig out the roots if you fell an area of trees. But what if you cut down individual trees within an orchard (4.4)? You should not encourage new growth during the Sabbath Year by treating a tree stump (4.5) or by cutting near the buds when gathering vine or reeds for weaving (4.6).

The following traditions have elements (marked in bold) for which there is evidence of an origin before 70 CE:

m.Shebi.4.1: Produce from a field which was not neglected

In former times they used to say:	בראשונה היו אומרים,
A man may gather wood or stones	מלקט אדם עצים ואבנים
or grass from within his own [field]	ועשבים מתוך שלו,
similar to the way in which he gathers	כדרך שהוא מלקט
from within [the field] of his associate,	מתוך של חברו,
[from which he gathers only] the large ones	את הגס הגס.
[which are suitable for building with or burning].	
When the transgressors increased	משרבו עוברי עברה,
they *decreed* that this one gathers [only]	התקינו שיהא זה מלקט
from within [the field] of that one [his associate]	מתוך של זה,
and that one gathers [only]	וזה מלקט
from within [the field] of this one,	מתוך של זה,
[though] this must not [be done] as a favor,	שלא בטובה,
and he does not, needless to say,	ואין צריך לומר
provide them food [in payment].	שיקצץ להם מזונות.

Comments: You may gather fuel (wood or dry grass) or stones from a field, but you may not improve a field. In the early days they could trust farmers to gather these without being so meticulous that you end up improving the field, but later they had to say that you can only gather them from someone else's field, so that you would not be tempted to improve the field while gathering. And of course you should not agree to reward someone who improves your field.

Dating (9): This tradition is very difficult to date, but its form provides a clue, albeit a relatively unreliable one. The form "When transgressors increased" is seen in other early traditions in m.Sot.9.9 and m.Sheq.1.2—see the discussion at the end of *Kilayim*.

This tradition is also related to the school dispute of m.Shebi.4.2 by the word 'as a favor' (בטובה). These two traditions may have been attached to each other before the tradition in m.Shebi.4.2a was added and separated them.

In later times the use of Sabbath Year grass for fuel was looked down on—cf. m.Shebi.8.11:

> A bath which was heated by straw or stubble of the Sabbatical year: it is permissible to bathe in it. But someone who is highly regarded, will not bathe [in it].

m.Shebi.4.2: Produce from a field which was not neglected

A field which has been cleared [of weeds during a Sabbath Year]	שדה שנתקוצה,
may be seeded	תזרע
in [the year] following the Sabbath Year.	במוצאי שביעית.
[A field] which has been improved [by ploughing]	שנטיבה
or has been enclosed [for grazing during a Sabbath Year]	או שנדירה,
may not be seeded	לא תזרע
in [the year] following the Sabbath Year.	במוצאי שביעית.
A field which has been improved	שדה שנטיבה,
[by ploughing during a Sabbath Year]:	
The School of Shammai says:	בית שמאי אומרים,
One may not eat	אין אוכלין
its produce in the Sabbath Year.	פרותיה בשביעית.
And the School of Hillel says:	ובית הלל אומרים,
One may eat [its produce in the Sabbath Year].	אוכלין.
The School of Shammai says:	בית שמאי אומרים,
One may not eat	אין אוכלין
produce of the Sabbath Year	פרות שביעית
[which was given by the owner] as a favor.	בטובה.
And the School of Hillel says:	ובית הלל אומרים,
One may eat [what was given] as a favor	אוכלין בטובה
and what was not [given] as a favor.	ושלא בטובה.
R. Judah [b. Illai, T4] says:	רבי יהודה אומר,
Change the statements	חלוף הדברים,
This [is] from the lenient [rulings] of the School of Shammai	זו מקולי בית שמאי

and from the severe [rulings] of the School of Hillel.   .ומחומרי בית הלל

Mishnaic parallel: m.MS.5.1

Comments: What do you do if land has been improved, contrary to the Sabbath Year regulations? If there was a severe breach of the regulations, you may not plant anything in the following year, and you may not gather anything which grows in it during the Sabbath Year, though the Hillelites say that you may accept such produce if the farmer gives it to you.

If a field was "cleared" (from *qavatz,* קָוַץ, 'to shrink, dry up'; niphal 'to be cleared'), this was a minor breach of the regulations, and if it was "improved" (from *tob,* טוֹב, 'to be good, valuable'; nithpael 'to be improved'), this was a major breach. The definitions of "clear" and "improve" are not given here, and later traditions debate their meanings. Tosefta thinks that "improve" means to plough more often than in a normal year (t.Shebi.3.10), and the Jerusalem Talmud thinks that "clear" means removing thorns (y.Shebi.4.2 I). The enclosure of land implies that animals were grazed on it, so it was fertilized by their dung.

It is likely that the original meaning of "improve" was to plough, and "clear" meant to do anything short of ploughing, because the subject of ploughing was a matter of dispute at the time. It is clear from b.MK.3b that the schools were responsible for extending the no-ploughing rule to the time after the harvest of the sixth year (a ruling which was reversed at Yavneh—see m.Shebi.2.1). It is possible that they were also responsible for introducing the prohibition of ploughing, which was not specifically mentioned in Torah.

These rulings must have created great hardship for the poor who wished to be pious. The Shammaites were willing to enforce this prohibition by forbidding the eating of any food grown on land which had been ploughed during the Sabbath Year. They included both food which had been gathered from such land, and food which had been harvested by the non-pious owner of the land, even if it was given to you as a gift. The Hillelites allowed the eating of this food, but not its purchase—it had to be acquired as a 'favor'. However, this term 'favor' may be a technical reference to transactions in the market which managed to avoid Sabbath Year restrictions by paying with "favors"—see m.Shebi.8.3.

Judah remembered the rulings in reverse, and says they should be listed among the few times when Hillelites were stricter than the Shammaites (see such lists at m.Ed.4.1–5.5).

Dating (1): There is no reason to doubt that the school disputes originated before 70 CE, though two phrases have been added, as discussed below.

Tosefta has an anonymous tradition that Shammai the Elder [1st C BCE] wanted to forbid even the seeding of a field after a Sabbath Year when it had been "improved," but he did not have sufficient influence over the farmers to implement this ruling:

Shammai the Elder says: If the time were right, I would prescribe concerning [such a field] that it may not be sown. The court which succeeded him prescribe concerning [such a field] that it may not be sown. (t.Shebi.3.10).

This tradition may or may not be accurate, but it demonstrates the belief that the schools could not always implement the law as they wished. It fits in with what we know about the Shammaite position, though by the time that it was implemented, the meaning of an "improved" field had changed to that of a field which is ploughed *more* times in a Sabbath Year than in a normal year. In the days of Shammai it probably meant simply a field which was ploughed.

It is possible that the second school dispute (about food from a ploughed field given as a "favor") was a later development based on the first ruling, because there appears to be a play on words between "improve" and "favor" (both from *tob*, טוב, 'to be good'). It is possible that this development comes from after 70 CE, when they enforced the ruling about seeding after ploughing, but it is more likely that it originated before 70 CE, because it does not produce a ruling which was followed by future generations.

The original form of the second half was very memorable. If we remove "the School of X says" (because these are always in the same order, so they did not need to be memorized), we have two rulings which are linked by a similar sounding word:

A field which was improved: (*nittaybah*, נִטַּיְבָה)
One may not eat
One may eat.
One may not eat by favor (*betobah*, בְּטוֹבָה)
One may eat by favor

A few phrases were added later to clear up ambiguities. The two phrases "produce of the Sabbath Year" became necessary when these school disputes were placed next to the ruling which concerned the year "following the Sabbath Year." Someone then noted that the second Hillelite ruling might conceivably be taken to contradict the first, because it might mean you can *only* eat by favor (i.e., only what the farmer gives you), while the first ruling implied that you have the right to eat *anything* from the field, so the phrase "and which is not by favor" was added to confirm that you can eat anything.

This mishnah shows that the principle of improving a field was already recognized by 70 CE, but the details about what activities constituted improvement (manure in m.Shebi.3.1-4, and removing stones in m.Shebi.3.5–4.2) had not yet been defined. The earliest dateable material in m.Shebi.3.1–4.2 is T2, end of the first century (3.3, 10).

The comment after Judah's correction is interesting because it appears to be concerned with textual criticism. It points out that if these rulings were reversed (as Judah asserts), then the Shammaites would take the lenient position and the Hillelites the severe, which is unusual. This comment is pointing out either a reason why the mix-up occurred (because someone thought it was unusual and 'corrected' it) or it is pointing out a reason why Judah's version is correct (because the more difficult version is more likely to be correct). This may, therefore, be a very early example of the textual-critical principle that one should prefer the more difficult reading. However, it is more likely that it is merely pointing out that this reversal puts these rulings among the group of severe Hillelite rulings (as collected at m.Ed.4.1–5.5).

New Testament: These regulations caused great problems for the poor, and even for the wealthy if the sixth-year harvest failed, as in 47/48, when Paul organized a collection for the Palestinian Christians. Paul was able to predict that the effects of this famine would extend into the next year in Palestine, because of the Sabbath Year regulations. This explains why Paul was able to arrange his collection in advance, over a period of several months, and why the famine relief could come into Israel from outside the land, even though it was a worldwide famine (Acts 11.27-30).

m.Shebi.4.4: Clearing trees in the Sabbath Year

He who thins among olive trees [in the Sabbath Year]	הַמַּדֵּל בַּזֵּיתִים,
The School of Shammai says:	בֵּית שַׁמַּאי אוֹמְרִים,
He may cut them down.	יָגוֹם.
And the School of Hillel says:	וּבֵית הִלֵּל אוֹמְרִים,
He may uproot them.	יְשָׁרֵשׁ.
And they agree concerning leveling [the orchard]	וּמוֹדִים בְּמַחְלִיק
[that they] only cut them down [without uprooting them].	עַד שֶׁיָּגוֹם.
And who is he who thins?	אֵיזֶה הוּא הַמַּדֵּל,
—[the one who thins] one or two [trees].	אֶחָד אוֹ שְׁנַיִם.
[And who is] he who levels?	הַמַּחְלִיק.
—[the one who thins] three [trees] beside each other.	שְׁלֹשָׁה, זֶה בְּצַד זֶה.
To whom do these words apply?	בַּמֶּה דְבָרִים אֲמוּרִים,
—[to him who] clears his own [orchard].	מִתּוֹךְ שֶׁלּוֹ.
But [he who] clears [the orchard] of his neighbor	אֲבָל מִתּוֹךְ שֶׁל חֲבֵרוֹ,
even if he levels it, he may uproot [the trees].	אַף הַמַּחְלִיק, יְשָׁרֵשׁ.

Comments: You may not prune fruit trees, or clear a field for cultivation, but you may cut down trees for wood. The Shammaites do not allow you to uproot them, because this would be similar to preparing the field, though the Hillelites allow you to uproot one or two trees together, but not more. You may do this for a neighbor because you would not clear his field altruistically, and so you must be doing it in order to gather wood.

Dating (1): There is no reason to doubt that the school dispute is accurate, though the notice of agreement (the case of someone who levels an orchard) may well have been added later. The definitions have almost certainly been added later.

m.Shebi.4.7–5.9: Gathering Sabbath Year produce

Summary of Mishnah: You may not gather fruit from trees until they are fully ripe, but you may consume them in the field before this time (4.7-9). You may not cut down fruit-bearing branches [for firewood] until after this time of gathering (4.10). Figs which appear in the Sabbath Year and which take more than one year to ripen (such as white figs) are subject to Sabbath Year regulations when they ripen (5.1).

When arum roots have been gathered, you may store them under soil, as normal, but you may not plant them, and so you must bury them in a large pile together (5.2). If individual plants matured in the sixth year and were left buried you may harvest them during the Sabbath Year (5.3-4) even with tools (5.4), and they can be sold immediately (5.5). If they had grown new leaves during the Sabbath Year, which the poor had not gathered, does the farmer owe the poor anything (5.3)? If onions which were left in the ground during the *seventh year*, grow new dark green leaves during that year, they are forbidden (6.3).

Farming tools cannot be used in the Sabbath Year, or even sold (5.6), but oil or wine containers can be sold which might be used for gathered produce (5.7), and other implements which could be used for non-farming purposes (5.8). What about a ploughing heifer (5.8)? These restrictions do not apply outside the Land (5.7) or to gentiles (5.7, 9). You may lend kitchen implements to a nonobservant neighbor, though you may not prepare food with the neighbor; and similarly, an Associate's wife may lend implements to the wife of an *impious one*, and may work with her, but not with wet food [which can pass on *impurity*] (5.9).

The following traditions have elements (marked in bold) for which there is evidence of an origin before 70 CE:

m.Shebi.4.10: Cutting off fruit-bearing branches

At what time should one not cut	מאימתי אין קוצצין
[fruit] trees in a Sabbath Year?	האילן בשביעית.
The School of Shammai says:	בית שמאי אומרים,
[The rule for] all trees: when they put out [leaves].	כל האילן משיוציא.
And the School of Hillel says:	ובית הלל אומרים,
[For] carob: when [the branches] hang down	החרובין משישלשלו,
and [for] vines: when their [grapes form] seed	והגפנים משיגרעו,
and [for] olives: when they bud	והזיתים משינצו,
and [for] the rest [of]	ושאר
all trees: when they put out [leaves].	כל האילן משיוציא.
And [for] all trees:	וכל האילן,
When it came to the time of tithing,	כיון שבא לעונת המעשרות,
the remainder may be cut down.	מותר לקצצו.

How much [fruit] is on an olive tree	כמה יהא בזית
that one should not cut it down?	ולא יקוצנו.
A *roba* [i.e., a quarter *qab*]	רובע.
R. Simeon b. Gamaliel [II, T4] says:	רבן שמעון בן גמליאל אומר,
Each is according to [the quality of] the olives.	הכל לפי הזית.

Comments: Fruit trees can be cut for their wood during a Sabbath Year, but not during the period when they are bearing fruit because you might prevent this fruit from being gathered. The Hillelites restricted this to the time when the fruit was optimally ripe, and had different definitions of this period for different trees. The Shammaites extended this period to any time when the branches bore fruit, both before and after (which would concur with the principle at t.MS.5.18).

It will be argued below that the original ruling said simply that you cannot cut down the branch while it bore ripe fruit. A later addition made it mean that you cannot cut down a branch after the time of budding and before the fruit would be liable to tithes in a normal year—i.e., at the end of harvest. An even later ruling says that you may cut down a branch if it does not have much fruit.

Dating (1): There is no reason to doubt that this was a genuine school debate. The ruling about tithing has been added to indicate when the period of no cutting ends. Without this added comment, the school rulings describe the time when a branch cannot be cut, but when the comment about tithing is added, these rulings become descriptions of the *start* of the time when a branch cannot be cut. Some undateable later traditions assume that "hang" and "drip" refer to the fruit itself (m.Shebi.4.7-8; y.Shebi.4.10 I-II).

The ruling that you may cut down a branch which has little fruit dates from a time before Simeon b. Gamaliel [II, T4, mid second century], but this cannot be dated back to before 70 CE.

m.Shebi.5.4: Digging up arum lily roots

Arum which [grew] before the Sabbath Year	לוף של ערב שביעית
which were gathered in the Sabbath Year	שנכנס לשביעית,
and this [also applies to] summer onions	וכן בצלים הקיצונים,
and this [also applies to] madder	וכן פואה
which [is growing on] fertile [soil]	של עדית,
The School of Shammai says:	בית שמאי אומרים,
One may uproot them	עוקרין אותן
with rakes which [are made of] wood.	במארופות של עץ.
And the School of Hillel says:	ובית הלל אומרים,
... with spades which [are made of] metal.	בקרדומות של מתכת.
And they agree concerning madder	ומודים בפואה
which [is growing] on the sides [of hills]	של צלעות,

that one may uproot them	שעוקרין אותה
with spades which [are made of] metal.	בקרדומות של מתכת.

Comments: Arum produces a root which is edible when it is cooked, but it takes three years to mature (cf. m.Kil.2.5), and it can be left in the ground to be dug up later. This means that the roots which grew in the sixth year can be dug up during the Sabbath Year and eaten. However, by digging them up, you might be contravening the rabbinic additions to the Sabbath Year regulations which forbid the use of the normal harvesting tools for gathering food (m.Shebi.5.6, 8) and which forbid improving the land by ploughing or digging (m.Shebi.4.4). Both schools allowed people to dig them up, but the Shammaites said you had to use a wooden rake, which was not a normal harvesting tool for roots, and which would not disturb the soil as much as a spade.

This ruling was also applied to other roots which have a long growing period, such as summer onions and madder. Madder roots were normally used to produce a contraceptive and a dye, but perhaps they were eaten by the poor in the Sabbath Year.

Even the Shammaites agreed that you could use a metal spade to dig up roots which grew in the side of hills, where the soil was very stony.

Dating (1): There is no reason to doubt that this was a genuine school debate, though it is difficult to date the additions concerning onions and madder. There would be little reason for rabbis after 70 CE to add the ruling that metal spades can be used in stony ground, because the Hillelite ruling would by then have become normative; so, it is likely that this addition is pre-70, though this is not certain.

New Testament: Arum is the Palestinian lily, or Solomon's Lily,[12] which is named after Jesus' saying, "Consider the lilies of the field . . . even Solomon in all his glory was not arrayed like one of these" (Mt.6.28-29; Lk.12.27). Jesus said this in the context of speaking about anxiety concerning clothing and food. He was not just pointing to a pretty flower, but to a major source of food for the poor.

The arum was the only crop which could be harvested and sold throughout the Sabbath Year (though the summer onion was also available for a short period). After Passover (the end of the grain harvest time) and Pentecost (the end of the fruit season), when everyone was obliged to *remove* these foods from their homes (see m.Shebi.9.5), the arum would have been virtually the only local food on sale.

---

[12] *Arum palestinum*, or black calla, or Solomon's lily—see Yehuda Feliks, *ha-Hakla'ut be-Erets-Yisra'el bi-yeme ha-Mikra, ha-Mishnah veha-Talmud (Agriculture in the Land of Israel in the Period of the Bible, Mishnah and Talmud)* (Jerusalem: R. Mas, 1990). See Mordechai Rabinovitch et al., *Seder Zeraim* IIIb, Tractate *Sheviis*, Artscroll Mishnah series (New York: Mesorah Publications, 1984), p. 118. The name 'lily' is something of a misnomer for this plant because it is in the family *Araceae*, not *Liliacae*.

Rich people would have stocks of grain and other dried food from the sixth year, but poor people would have to gather what they could and buy what they could in the market. Up until Pentecost, the poor could gather other food from the field, but after Pentecost they would be reliant on what they could buy in the market, and arum would be virtually the only local food on sale.

In the second year of the seven-year cycle, the poor would be even more reliant on arum. This was the most difficult year of the cycle for poor people, because the last *poor tithe* was three years previous. They were given the *poor tithe* in the third and sixth years, and they were allowed to help themselves to what grew wild during the Sabbath Year (though they had to compete with the rest of the population for this meagre crop). But in the first, second, fourth, and fifth years they had to rely on the harvest *leftovers* and charity, and the second year was the one which was furthest removed from a year of *poor tithe*.

However, during the second year they were allowed to dig up arum roots. Since these took three years to mature (m.Kil.2.5), the Sabbath Year arum was coming to maturity during this year. Most other plants were freely available *during* the Sabbath Year, but because of the long maturation, arum was not free to the poor during the Sabbath Year (though it was sold in the market, which was important to them). But this did mean that it was freely available during the difficult second year.

For these reasons, the arum root must have been a lifesaver for many poor people, both during the Sabbath Year and more especially during the second year of the cycle. It is significant that Jesus pointed to this plant to illustrate God's care for the poor. It is likely that Jesus gave this teaching during a second year of the cycle in 29/30 CE, which was probably the first year of his ministry.

m.Shebi.5.8: Providing agricultural tools in the Sabbath Year

The School of Shammai says:	בית שמאי אומרים,
One must not sell to anyone	לא ימכור לו
a heifer which ploughs, in the Sabbath Year.	פרה חורשת בשביעית.
And the School of Hillel permits [it],	ובית הלל מתירין,
because he is able to slaughter it.	מפני שהוא יכול לשחטה.
One may sell to someone	מוכר לו
produce [suitable for planting] in the time of sowing.	פרות בשעת הזרע,
And one may lend to someone a *seah* [measure]	ומשאיל לו סאתו
even if he knows that	אף על פי שהוא יודע
he has a granary [with grain which needs measuring].	שיש לו גורן,
And one may split coins [i.e., make change] for someone	ופורט לו מעות
even if he knows that	אף על פי שהוא יודע
he has laborers [to pay wages to].	שיש לו פועלים.
And [in] all of these [cases],	וכולן,
when [they declare intentions] explicitly,	בפרוש,

they are prohibited.   אסורין.

Comments: Ploughing was prohibited during the Sabbath Year, so the Shammaites forbade the selling of a ploughing heifer during this time. The Hillelites allowed it because the heifer might be slaughtered as a *peace offering* and then shared with your family and friends (cf. m.Shebi.10.2), though it would be unusual to slaughter a heifer which had been trained to plough. Therefore this ruling presents an extreme example, saying that even if there was the remotest possibility that there was an innocent reason for the sale, it should be allowed and therefore all other such sales were also allowed.

Similarly you may sell fruit which contains seeds which could be sowed, or lend someone a container which could be used for measuring out grain for selling, or change coins into smaller values which could be used to pay farm workers. But if the person admitted he was going to break the Sabbath Year regulations with the seeds, measure, or money, you should refuse.

Dating (1): There is no reason to doubt that the school debate is genuine, though the form is perhaps altered. The expected form would be:

> Selling a ploughing heifer in the Sabbath Year:
> The School of Shammai forbids.
> And the School of Hillel permits,
> because he is able to [use it] for slaughter.

It is possible that the Hillelite explanation has been added later, though this is unlikely because their ruling has very little force without some kind of justification.

The further examples were certainly added later, and probably after 70 CE. They may have resulted from exegetical meditations on the school debate rather than from actual cases. This is indicated by the wordplays between the school debate which concerned a "heifer" (*parah*, פָּרָה) and the first and last additional cases which concerned "fruit" (*pérot*, פֵּירוֹת) and money which was "split" (*poret*, פּוֹרֵט).

t.Shebi.4.5b (Z 1.3b): Selling a field during the Seventh Year

The School of Shammai says:	בית שמאי אומרים,
They must not sell	לא ימכור
to anyone [who is suspected of breaking the Law],	לו
a field during the Sabbath Year.	שדה בשביעית,
And the School of Hillel permits [it].	ובית הלל מתירין.

Comments: You are not allowed to sell one's land during the Sabbath Year to someone who would cultivate it, but what if it was not certain that the buyer would cultivate it? The Hillelites give the benefit of the doubt, as they do on other occasions (cf. m.Shebi.5.8).

Dating (1): There is no reason to doubt that this represents a genuine school dispute, but it has lost its introduction and ending. The introduction was made superfluous in the Tosefta by the preceding ruling: "They [may] not sell produce of the Sabbath Year to him who is suspected [of breaking the law] of the Sabbath Year. . . ." This supplied the concept of someone who is suspected of breaking the Sabbath Year regulations. The original dispute was probably:

> Selling a field to one suspected of [breaking regulations of] the Sabbath Year:
> The School of Shammai forbid.
> And the School of Hillel permit.

New Testament: Selling a field in Israel during or just before the Sabbath Year was a foolish transaction, because you would not get a good price for it. This makes it doubly remarkable that believers were willing to sell their land to support the poor in Acts 4.34, which probably occurred just before or during a Sabbath Year. The most likely date for Jesus' crucifixion was 33 CE though this is still very uncertain.[13] This means that the first Sabbath Year would start about sixteen months after the first Pentecost. Given that Acts 4 is likely to cover a period of several months, the selling of land by believers at the end of the chapter would take place in or just before the Sabbath Year.

Some other details in Acts 4–6 may also indicate that this was a Sabbath Year. It would explain why it was necessary to raise so much money to support the poor. there was very little food available, especially in the city. It would also explain why Ananias thought he might get away with saying that his land was sold for much less than it was worth (Acts 5.1-4): land was undervalued if you sold it with the stipulation that it could not be cultivated until the end of the Sabbath Year. However, if Ananias ignored such scruples, he would get a much better price for it, which he did not declare. Peter did not criticize him for this non-*halakhic* behavior but for lying about the price. As the year continued, and food shortages got worse, the church may have had to impose some kind of rationing among their poor, which might be the origin of the disputes between the Greek- and Aramaic-speaking widows in Acts 6.

m.Shebi.6.1–7.7: Produce which is liable to *removal*

Summary of Mishnah: In gentile areas, you may both cultivate the land and eat the produce without restriction [i.e., harvest it, buy and sell it, and eat it beyond the time of *removal* (cf. 9.2)], while in the Land proper you may not cultivate or eat it [without

---

[13] For a good overview and strong case for 33 CE see Colin J. Humphreys and W. G. Waddington, "A Lunar Eclipse and the Date of Christ's Crucifixion," *Tyndale Bulletin* 43 (1992): 331-51.

these restrictions] (6.1). In the land settled by Joshua but not resettled by Ezra [north of Tyre?—the place names are obscure], you may not cultivate but you may eat [without these restrictions] (6.1). In Syria you may not harvest, but you may process harvested food (6.2).

Food can be bought and sold in the year after the Sabbath Year only when the harvest of that type of food has started (6.4) [because otherwise you would be buying food which had been gathered in the Sabbath Year]. Food which may not be sold in Israel may not be exported for sale (6.5), and *elevation offerings* from outside Israel may not be imported to Israel (6.6).[14]

Sabbath Year regulations apply to all produce which is used as food for humans or animals or which is used as a dye (7.1, 2, 3). This produce, and any money from its sale, are also subject to the rule of *removal* (7.1). Plants which remain in the ground during the Sabbath Year are not subject to *removal* (7.2), and branches of trees which do not wither [so they are always available] are not subject to *removal* (7.5). Spices are subject to *removal* but perhaps not Balsam (7.6). Sixth-year produce which is mixed with Sabbath Year produce becomes liable to Sabbath Year regulations if flavor is imparted to it (7.7).

You may not do business with Sabbath Year produce, but your son can sell a surplus which you gathered (7.3), just as individuals can sell substandard produce which they happen to have, though not as a regular trade (7.4).

There is no firm evidence that any traditions in this section predate 70 CE, though related concepts were recognized before 70 CE. The concept of *removal* was certainly recognized before 70 CE (see m.Shebi.9.5), and the principle about imparting flavor (as at 7.7, see m.Ter.10.5). Also, despite the tradition in m.Hal.2.2,[15] food from outside Israel could be imported and sold because the Sabbath Year did not apply there (see m.Yad.4.3 which is dealt with at the end of *Peah*). Syria was already a special case, as discussed in the following section.

The following traditions have elements (marked in bold) for which there is some evidence of an origin before 70 CE:

---

[14] The reason for this is uncertain. Jerusalem Talmud suggests it is because it is the responsibility of the priest to collect the *elevation offerings*, and they would not be willing to go outside the Land to do so. This unlikely explanation is given merely to solve a contradiction.

[15] "[Produce grown in] foreign soil, which was brought on a ship to the Land [of Israel] is subject to tithes and [the laws of] the Sabbatical year." This predates R. Judah [b. Illai, T4] who finds a way round it, and it appears to be based on the pre-70 principle of giving a dough offering of bread made from imported grain (m.Hal.2.1). All this suggests that it was a Yavnean ruling.

m.Shebi.6.2: Sabbath Year in Syria

One may work with picked [produce] in Syria	עושין בתלוש בסוריא,
but not with attached [i.e., unharvested produce].	אבל לא במחובר.
One may thresh or winnow or tread	דשין וזורין ודורכין
or bind [into bundles],	ומעמרין,
but one may not reap nor cut off [grapes]	אבל לא קוצרין ולא בוצרין
nor pick olives.	ולא מוסקין.
R. Akiba [T3] said a general [rule]:	כלל אמר רבי עקיבה,
Any [work] which is similar to what is permitted	כל שכיוצא בו מותר
in the Land of Israel,	בארץ ישראל,
one may work [in that way] in Syria.	עושין אותו בסוריא.

Comments: Jewish farm workers in Syria could not break the Torah regulations (i.e., no reaping, pruning, or picking), but if gentiles had already done this work, they could join in with other harvesting activities which were not mentioned in Scripture. This is similar to the ruling of R. Judah [T4] about tithing crops grown in Syria, who said that a Jew should let gentiles do the harvesting (m.Maas.5.5).

Dating (2): The dating of this is difficult, but we have a clue in a debate at the end of the first century:

Israelites who sharecropped for gentiles in Syria:
R. Eliezer [b. Hyrcanus, T2, says] their produce is liable to tithes and Sabbath Year.
And Rn Gamaliel [I, T1] exempts [them]. (m.Hal.4.7).

Eliezer is responding to an accepted ruling by Gamaliel I[16] and both appear to be commenting on the more general rule in m.Shebi.6.2 which applied to all Jews in Syria, from farm workers to farm owners. Strictly speaking, it was difficult for Jew who owned a farm in Syria to use m.Shebi.6.2 to get round the laws of the Sabbath Year, because he would have to employ gentiles to start the harvesting process but he could not actually *ask* them to break the Law. He would have to hope that the gentiles would start the harvesting without being asked. This left a potential loophole for some sharecroppers who had gentile partners, because the partner would start the work without being asked, and then the Jew could join in with processing the crop and selling it. Eliezer wanted to plug this loophole while Gamaliel was happy to leave it.

---

[16] See the discussion at m.Hal.4.7.

m.Shebi.8.1–9.1: Commerce and use of Sabbath Year produce

Summary of Mishnah: Sabbath Year produce can be used for emollients or wood [which can be bought and sold] unless that produce is normally used only as human food (8.1). Sabbath Year produce which is normally food, drink, or anointing or lamp fuel can be used, but only for these purposes (8.2). You may not sell Sabbath Year food as a business, or process them with business equipment such as a vat (8.6), but you can sell ad hoc quantities (8.3). Money from such sales cannot be used to pay a wage or pay for a service, but it can be given as a free gift or as a reward in thanks for something (8.5). You can reward someone who gathers Sabbath Year produce for you, but not as an agreed payment (8.4).

Sabbath Year produce retains its status even if it is cooked in non-Sabbath Year oil (8.7) or if it is sold or exchanged (8.8), and the items exchanged or bought with the proceeds also have Sabbath Year status (8.7). You should not use such proceeds for buying slaves, land, *impure* animals or offerings for *impurity*, and you should not use Sabbath Year oil to rub a hide (8.9), though you may (if you are undiscerning) use Sabbath Year straw to heat a bath (8.11). If you *misuse* any Sabbath Year produce, you must purchase replacement produce (8.8, 9).

Crops which grow wild or after-growths of cultivated crops which grew by themselves during the Sabbath Year can be bought and sold during the Sabbath Year; this was forbidden in the mid second century (9.1).

The following traditions have elements (marked in bold) for which there is evidence of an origin before 70 CE:

m.Shebi.8.3: Selling produce gathered in the Sabbath Year

One should not sell produce of the Sabbath Year	אֵין מוֹכְרִין פֵּרוֹת שְׁבִיעִית,
not by measure [of volume]	לֹא בְמִדָּה,
nor by weight	וְלֹא בְמִשְׁקָל,
nor by number	וְלֹא בְמִנְיָן,
and [one may not sell] figs by number	וְלֹא תְאֵנִים בְּמִנְיָן,
and [one may not sell] vegetables by weight.	וְלֹא יָרָק בְּמִשְׁקָל.
The School of Shammai says:	בֵּית שַׁמַּאי אוֹמְרִים,
Also [one may] not [sell] bunches.	אַף לֹא אֲגֻדּוֹת.
And the School of Hillel says:	וּבֵית הִלֵּל אוֹמְרִים,
That for which it is normal to bunch in the home	אֶת שֶׁדַּרְכּוֹ לֶאֱגוֹד בַּבַּיִת,
one may bunch them in the market.	אוֹגְדִין אוֹתוֹ בַּשּׁוּק,

For example, leeks and spring onions.[17]   כגון הכרשין ונץ החלב.

Comments: Food could not be harvested and sold as a business in the Sabbath Year, but food which had been gathered could be sold if it was surplus to one's needs, as in the undateable ruling in m.Shebi.7.3:

> He may not gather vegetables from the field and sell them in the market, but he may gather and his son sell them for him; if he gathered for himself and some were left over, these he may sell.

Whatever the date of this ruling, it is clear that there were ways around the restrictions so that there was some food for sale in the market, at least until the time of *removal* (see m.Shebi.9.5). The early tradition in t.Shebi.6.19 (see below) shows that Hillelites were willing to sell gathered food in the market.

This pre-70 ruling makes clear that when food was being sold in the Sabbath Year, everything was done to avoid the appearance of doing 'business.' Therefore people could not sell food by a set price for specific quantities. Instead they 'gave' food to people in the market, who in turn 'gave' them some money. This was allowed, so long as it was not a business transaction but an exchange of gifts. The fine line between these two types of transaction is illustrated in another undateable ruling in m.Shebi.8.4:

> Someone says to a laborer: "Here is an *issar* [i.e., a coin] for you, and gather vegetables today for me"—his payment is allowed. [But if he says]: ". . . gather vegetables today for me, in return for it"—his payment is forbidden.

It is likely that they called this type of transaction "by favor" (*betobah*, בְּטוֹבָה), as used in m.Shebi.4.2. Those who ignored these legal restrictions and transacted business in a more normal way were called 'sinners' (m.Shebi.9.9).

The normal way to measure grain and oil was by volume (dry volumes based on the *seah* and wet volumes based on the *log*), while the normal way to sell vegetables and figs was by weight and by number respectively (as indicated in this tradition).

Dating (1): There is no reason to doubt that the school debate about bunches is genuine, but it is difficult to decide if the anonymous rulings about volume, weight, and number are earlier or later than it.

It is possible that the school debate came first, and that later Sages wanted to make sure that the Hillelite position was not expanded to allow all forms of measurement. However, it is equally likely that the schools agreed that the other forms of measurement were forbidden, but they only disagreed concerning bunches.

---

[17] The plant translated here as "spring onions" (*netz hehalab*, נֵץ הֶחָלָב, 'milky flowers') is difficult to identify with certainty. They may be ornithogalum or Star of Bethlehem, the star-shaped flowers of which are very similar to those of wild garlic and some spring onions.

This seems more likely because wording of the Shammaite ruling suggests that it was preceded by something which both schools agreed with, because it starts "Also...." This makes the Hillelite position fit with their other decisions that if an innocent explanation can be found, you should not assume that something has been done in order to break the Sabbath Year law—e.g., selling a ploughing heifer which *could* be sacrificed (m.Shebi.5.8).

The rulings about volume, weight, and number appear to be presented in two different ways. First there is an absolute ban on the use of all three, and then the use of weight is restricted to weighing vegetables, and the use of number is restricted to figs. Ostensibly these are simply describing the way that vegetables and figs are normally measured, but this may have provided a loophole so that grain could be measured by weight and vegetables could be measured by number. In other words, you may use measurements in the Sabbath Year which are not normally used in business. This suggests that these further refinements may have been added later, and may not therefore be pre-70.

t.Shebi.6.19 (Z 6.11a): Selling Sabbath Year produce for coins

The School of Shammai says:	בית שמאי אומרים
One should not sell produce	אין מוכרין פירות
of the Sabbath Year for coins.	שביעית במעות
Instead [exchange it] for [other] produce	אלא בפירות
so that he may not buy a spade with it.	כדי שלא יקח בהן קרדום
And the School of Hillel permits [it].	ובית הלל מתירין

Comments: Sabbath Year produce which had been gathered in one field could be exchanged for produce which was gathered by someone else in another field, but the Shammaites said it should not be exchanged for coins which might be used to buy other commodities.

The example of a 'spade' may suggest that Shammai implied that it might be spent on a tool which would be used to break the Sabbath Year regulations (cf. m.Shebi.5.4) or they might mean anything which was inedible, which would not inherit the restrictions of Sabbath Year produce (cf. m.Shebi.8.7).[18]

Dating (1): There is no reason to doubt that this was a genuine school dispute. The first line is the same as that in another school dispute in m.Shebi.8.3, to which it was probably related. The explanation was probably added later, and may not reflect the original reasons of the Shammaites. If they originally made this restriction in order to prevent the purchase of non-food items, this would be in line with later rulings (such as m.Shebi.8.7), and later generations did not generally want to show themselves

---

[18] Newman's translation in Neusner's edition follows this idea.

following Shammaite rulings. The explanation which is given is probably influenced by m.Shebi.5.4 where the Hillelites allow the use of metal 'spades' to dig up arum, while the Shammaites allow only wooden rakes.

t.Shebi.7.6 (Z 7.3c): Selling Sabbath Year food for peace offerings

[Produce of the] Sabbath Year:	שביעית
One should not buy with it	אין לוקחין בה
sacrifices of *peace offerings*,	זבחי שלמים,
which is not so with *second tithes*.	מה שאין כן במעשר שני.

Comments: You cannot buy a *peace offering* with money exchanged for produce of the Sabbath Year, though you can do so with money exchanged for *second tithes*. The probable reason is that part of the *peace offering* can be eaten only by a priest (Lev.7.30-36), while the Sabbath Year produce should be available to everyone (Lev.25.6), and there was no comparable regulation concerning *second tithes*.

Dating (8): The reference to *peace offerings* suggests this originates from the time of the Temple. It is possible that this was a post-70 comparison between the Sabbath Year and *second tithe* regulations, but it serves little purpose. More likely, it was one of those minor regulations of the Second Temple period which fell into obscurity—it is not found in Mishnah, nor commented on in the Talmud.

This ruling suggests that there was already a principle that the status of Sabbath Year produce is inherited by whatever it is exchanged for. This principle is stated in an undateable tradition in m.Shebi.8.7b:

> The last [produce obtained by a series of exchanges] is liable to [the regulations of] the Sabbath Year, and the [original Sabbath Year] produce itself [remains] forbidden.

m.Shebi.9.2-9: *Removal* of Sabbath Year produce

Summary of Mishnah: The *removal* of Sabbath Year produce from your home must take place when that food is no longer available in your locality (9.3-4). The localities are defined as three subregions of each of the three regions of Judea, Galilee, and Transjordan (9.2). What do you do if different types of produce have been mixed together (9.5)? Fresh herbs are *removed* when the dry season comes and dried plants are *removed* when the wet season comes (9.6)—"until the rains" means "until the second rainfall [of the year]" (9.7).

When you *remove* Sabbath Year produce, you keep enough for three meals for your household and offer the rest to any poor people who (after the mid second century) were allowed to continue eating this produce (9.8—cf. Mekh. re

Exod.23.11). If you are given Sabbath Year produce [after the time of *removal*] should you give it to those who eat it sinfully (9.9)?

The following traditions have elements (marked in bold) for which there is evidence of an origin before 70 CE:

m.Shebi.9.5: *Removal* when a crop disappears from the field

He who pickles three [types] of pickle	הכובש שלשה כבשים
in one jar:	בחבית אחת,
R. Eliezer [b. Hyrcanus, T2] says:	רבי אליעזר אומר,
One may eat until the first	אוכלין על הראשון.
[time of *removal* occurs for of any of the pickled vegetables].	
R. Joshua [(b. Hananiah, T2] says:	רבי יהושע אומר,
[One may eat] even until the last	אף על האחרון.
[time of *removal* occurs for all the pickled vegetables].	
Rabban Gamaliel [II, T2] says:	רבן גמליאל אומר,
[When] each [type of vegetable] disappears	כל שכלה מינו
from the field [i.e., their time of *removal* occurs],	מן השדה,
one should eliminate that type from the jar.	יבער מינו מן החבית,
And the *halakhah* is according to his words.	והלכה כדבריו.
R. Simeon [b. Yohai, T4] says:	רבי שמעון אומר,
[For] all vegetables [there is] one [time of] *removal*.	כל ירק, אחד לבעור.
One may eat purslane until	אוכלין ברגילה עד
[the long-living] oxygarum[19] disappears	שיכלו סגריות
from the valley of Bét Netophah.	מבקעת בית נטופה.

Comments: When individual types of food are no longer available in the field, so that they cannot be 'gathered,' you should no longer keep such food in the home, because this would count as storage. Therefore the time of *removal* for different types of food is at different times. However, what happens if different types of food are mixed together, such as in a jar of mixed pickles? Eliezer said the mixed pickle can only be eaten until the *removal* of the first of the ingredients, but Joshua extended this to the *removal* of all of the ingredients. Later, Simeon simplified all this by saying there was only one time of *removal* for all vegetables, which occurs when the latest vegetable (the oxygarum in the moist soil near Bethlehem) is no longer available.

Dating (5): Although this debate does not date from before 70 CE, the principle that you can eat gathered food only until it disappears from the field is assumed as an established ruling by all three of these T2 debaters, so it was established at least before 70 CE.

---

[19] סְגְרִיּוֹת is from אָבְסִיגָרִיּוֹת, ὀξύγαρον.

By the mid second century the rabbis had decided that the poor may eat Sabbath Year produce after the time of *removal* (m.Shebi.9.8; t.Shebi.8.1-2—both sides in this dispute agree that the poor may eat it, but R. Jose [b. Halfta, T4] says that the rich should also be allowed to eat it). We cannot know when this concession was introduced, but it was not in place during the time of Eliezer b. Hyrcanus, because his debate in m.Shebi.9.9 indicates that Sabbath Year produce cannot simply be given to a poor person after the time of *removal*.[20] Eliezer argued that if you inherited or were given such produce, you could give it away to whoever was willing to eat it, but the Sages call these people 'sinners.' If the poor had been allowed to eat it, Eliezer or the Sages would have suggested giving it to them.

m.Shebi.10.1-9: Loans in the Sabbath Year

Summary of Mishnah: The Sabbath Year is a *release* for loans but not for unpaid bills or unpaid wages (10.1) or unpaid fines, or any loans which are collectable by a court (10.2). Hillel introduced the *prozbul* to make loans payable through a court (10.3). A *prozbul* is written by the lender, and is valid for every subsequent loan he makes (10.4-5). A *prozbul* is only for loans with land as security, though the land can be a trivial size (10.6) and perhaps even as small as a beehive (10.7).

In the Sabbath Year you must say to a creditor, "I cancel the loan," though the lender may decide nevertheless to pay it (10.8)—an action which pleases the Sages (10.9).

The following traditions have elements (marked in bold) for which there is evidence of an origin before 70 CE:

m.Shebi.10.3: Origin of the *prozbul* (loans via the court)

A *prozbul* is not *released* [in the Sabbath Year].	פרוזבול, אינו משמט.
This is one of the things	זה אחד מן הדברים
which Hillel the Elder *decreed*.	שהתקין הלל הזקן,
When he saw that the people held back	כשראה שנמנעו העם
from lending to each other	מלהלוות זה את זה
and transgressed against what is written	ועוברין על מה שכתוב
in the Torah [Deut.15.9]:	בתורה
"Guard yourself lest there will be a	השמר לך פן יהיה
a base thought in your heart"	דבר עם בלבד בליעל

---

[20] The mishnah does not actually state that it concerns the time after the *removal*, but its context in Mishnah and the logic of the debate suggests this. Jerusalem Talmud discusses other possibilities such as the idea that Eliezer rejected giving away any Seventh Year produce as a gift because he was a Shammaite (y.Shebi.9.9).

and following   ,וגומר
[i.e., ". . . saying, The Sabbath Year is near, the Year of Release"],
Hillel *decreed* the *prozbul.*   התקין הלל פרוזבול.
(Mishnaic parallel: m.Git.4.3; cf. Sif.Deut.113; Mid.Tann. p. 80)

Comments: The *prozbul* is literally 'via the court' in Greek, transliterated into Hebrew (פְּרוֹזְבּוּל, πρòς βουλἡ). All loans were cancelled by the *release* of the Sabbath Year, but this could produce hardship because people were unwilling to make loans when the Sabbath Year approached. Therefore Hillel invented a procedure by which a loan could be made via a court so that, strictly speaking, the money was owed to the court. Court loans remained valid in a Sabbath Year, so this was a way of securing repayment even if the loan was made near the Sabbath Year. The next mishnah describes how this worked.

Dating (1): The only phrase which occurs in all the early parallel versions is "Hillel *decreed* the *prozbul.*" This is very likely to originate before 70 CE. The explanations in the form of the story about Hillel and the scriptural basis were probably added later. Both of these give the same reason in a different form—i.e., a pragmatic solution to a practical problem, which was inspired by necessity rather than by Scripture. Despite the late origin of these explanations, it is likely that they represent the real reason behind this ruling.

m.Shebi:10.4: Wording of the *prozbul*

This is the essence of the *prozbul*:   ,זהו גופו של פרוזבול
A bond [made by] me before you,   מוסר אני לכם
Mr. so-and-so and so-and-so,   איש פלוני ופלוני
the judges which are in the place so-and-so,   ,הדינים שבמקום פלוני
that, every obligation which is [owed] to me,   ,שכל חוב שיש לי
that I may collect it at any time which I wish.   .שאגבנו כל זמן שארצה
And the judges sign below   ,והדינים חותמין למטה
or the witnesses.   .או העדים

Comments: The *prozbul* is a written deed which says that any loan which is owed to this person can be collected from the judges—i.e., from the court. When this is accepted by the judges, it effectively means that they have made themselves liable to pay the loan, so that the loan is owed to the court. A court is not subject to the Sabbath Year regulations, so this means the loan does not expire at the Sabbath Year.

This deed is effective for every loan made to this individual after the date that it is signed, and so it cannot be applied retrospectively to a debt which is about to expire (m.Shebi.10.5).

Dating (2): It is likely that this wording is original, because it does not mention a restriction about security which was introduced before the time of R. Eliezer (b. Hyrcanus) [T2, just after 70 CE]—see m.Shebi.10.7.

m.Shebi.10.7: A *prozbul* requires security

A beehive [as security for *prozbul*]:	כורת דבורים,
R. Eliezer [b. Hyrcanus, T2] says:	רבי אליעזר אומר,
Behold, it is like **land** and one should write	הרי היא כקרקע, וכותבין
a *prozbul* on [the basis of] it	עליה פרוזבול,
and one does not receive *impurity*	ואינה מקבלת טומאה
[while it remains] in its place	במקומה,
and one extracting [honey] from it on a Sabbath	והרודה ממנה בשבת,
is liable [for violating the Sabbath rest].	חייב.
But the Sages say:	וחכמים אומרים,
It is not like land and one should not write	אינה כקרקע, ואין כותבין
a *prozbul* on [the basis of] it,	עליה פרוזבול,
and one does receive *impurity*	ומקבלת טומאה
[while it remains] in its place	במקומה,
and one extracting [honey] from it on a Sabbath	והרודה ממנה בשבת,
is exempt [from violating the Sabbath rest].	פטור.

Comments: This summarizes a series of disputes between Eliezer and the majority concerning beehives. The only matter of interest in this tractate is that Eliezer considered a beehive to be equivalent to land, so that it could be used as security for a loan covered by a *prozbul*. The other matters are recorded because the editor(s) did not want to remove parts of the tradition.

It appears that *prozbul* loans had to be based on security. This is understandable, because the deed of *prozbul* is effectively a loan guarantee by the judges, so if there was no security they would become personally responsible for covering any non-payment. It also appears that the only type of security which was acceptable was land, because the beehive could not be accepted as security for a *prozbul* unless it could be regarded as 'land.' This is also understandable because it means that the judges need not worry about the security disappearing one night along with the creditor.

The problem with demanding this security is that poor people still cannot get a loan, because they do not own any land. This may be the reason why Eliezer wanted to extend the definition of 'land' to include a beehive.

Dating (5): Both Eliezer and the majority of Sages assumed that a *prozbul* required 'land' as security, even though Eliezer wanted to stretch the definition of 'land' as far as possible. This means that such security had already become a fixed necessity soon after 70 CE, and that it must have been introduced before 70 CE. This necessity went against Hillel's wish to provide a way for poor people to get a loan close to the

Sabbath Year. This helps to confirm that Hillel's motive, as expressed in m.Shebi.10.3, is likely to be accurate. It also helps to confirm that the wording in m.Shebi.10.4, which does not mention any requirement for security, is also early.

The later summary at the end of m.Shebi.10.2 summarizes the *prozbul* clearly, in a way that these early traditions do not:

One who lends [money] for security and one who hands over his bonds to a court, [such loans] are not *released* [by the Sabbath Year].

New Testament: This requirement for security, even for a loan which is specifically designed to help poor people, illustrates the type of climate which Jesus was addressing when he said: "Even sinners lend to sinners . . . but [you should] lend expecting nothing in return" (Lk.6.34-35).

The parable of the man who demanded the immediate return of his loan may also be related to a coming Sabbath Year (Mt.18.21-34). If he allowed the lender to delay long enough, he could lose his money, and so there was an urgency in his demands.[21] By putting him in jail, he may have converted personal loan into a criminal debt, like someone who owed a fine to the court. This may have been another way of making the debt the property of the court and thereby circumventing the law of the Sabbath Year *release*.

Related early traditions from other tractates

m.Sot.7.8: Agrippa in the Sabbath Year Temple ceremony

The passage about the king—How [was it carried out]?	פרשת המלך כיצד,
At the end of the *holyday*,	מוצאי יום טוב
the first [day] of the Feast [*Sukkot*, Tabernacles],	הראשון של חג,
in the eighth [year, i.e.,] at the end of the seventh,	בשמיני במוצאי שביעית,
they make him a platform of wood	עושין לו בימה של עץ
in the [Temple] Court, and he sits in it	בעזרה, והוא יושב עליה,
as it is said [Deut.31.10]:	שנאמר
"At the end of seven years in the appointed . . ."	מקץ שבע שנים במעד וגי'.
The Officer of the Assembly carries	חזן הכנסת נוטל
the Scroll of the Torah and gives it	ספר תורה ונותנה
to the Head of the Assembly,	לראש הכנסת,
and the Head of the Assembly	וראש הכנסת
gives it to the Deputy [of the priests],	נותנה לסגן,
and the Deputy [of the priests]	והסגן
gives it to the High Priest,	נותנה לכהן גדול,
and the High Priest gives it to the King,	וכהן גדול נותנה למלך,

---

[21] This was proposed by Justin Hardin in a personal communication.

and the King stands and receives [it]	וְהַמֶּלֶךְ עוֹמֵד וּמְקַבֵּל
and he reads it seated.	וְקוֹרֵא יוֹשֵׁב.
King Agrippa stood and received [it]	**אַגְרִפַּס הַמֶּלֶךְ עָמַד וְקִבֵּל**
and recited it standing,	**וְקָרָא עוֹמֵד,**
and the Sages praised him [for it].	וְשִׁבְּחוּהוּ חֲכָמִים.
And when he reached [Deut.17.15]	**וּכְשֶׁהִגִּיעַ**
to You shall not set over you a gentile . . .	**לְלֹא תוּכַל לָתֵת עָלֶיךָ אִישׁ נָכְרִי,**
tears streamed from his eyes.	**זָלְגוּ עֵינָיו דְּמָעוֹת.**
They said to him:	**אָמְרוּ לוֹ,**
Do not be afraid Agrippa,	**אַל תִּתְיָרֵא אַגְרִפַּס,**
you are our brother	**אָחִינוּ אָתָּה,**
you are our brother, you are our brother.	**אָחִינוּ אַתָּה, אָחִינוּ אַתָּה,**
And he recites from the beginning [Deut.1.1]:	וְקוֹרֵא מִתְּחִלָּה
"These are the words to Hear" [Deut.6.4]	אֵלֶּה הַדְּבָרִים עַד שְׁמַע,
then "Hear . . ." [Deut.6.4-9],	וּשְׁמַע,
and "It shall be, if you carefully . . ." [Deut.11.13-21],	וְהָיָה אִם שָׁמֹעַ,
"You shall surely tithe . . ." [Deut.14.22-28]	עַשֵּׂר תְּעַשֵּׂר,
"When you have finished tithing . . ." [Deut.26.12-15]	כִּי תְכַלֶּה לַעְשֵׂר,
and the passage of the king [Deut.17.14-20]	וּפָרָשַׁת הַמֶּלֶךְ,
and the blessings and the curses [Deut.27.15-26]	וּבְרָכוֹת וּקְלָלוֹת,
until [he] finishes the whole passage.	עַד שֶׁגּוֹמֵר כָּל הַפָּרָשָׁה.
The blessings with which the High Priest	בְּרָכוֹת שֶׁכֹּהֵן גָּדוֹל
blessed them [as listed in m.Sot.7.7],	מְבָרֵךְ אוֹתָן,
the king blesses them,	הַמֶּלֶךְ מְבָרֵךְ אוֹתָן,
except he gave the [blessing] concerning pilgrimages	אֶלָּא שֶׁנּוֹתֵן שֶׁל רְגָלִים
instead of the [blessing] concerning pardon for sin.	תַּחַת מְחִילַת הֶעָוֹן.

Comments: The Sabbath Year officially finishes with a ceremony at the end of *Sukkot* (Tabernacles) in the following year. This is when the next year's harvest has finished, and all foods can be bought and sold again in the markets. The ceremony includes a long series of readings by the king in the Temple Court. The account says that the king sits to read, but it is interrupted by a tradition that when King Herod Agrippa I read, he remained standing, and he wept because of his Edomite father, though his mother was Jewish.

Dating (10): Ben Zion Wacholder discusses this incident at length, especially with regard to the date of the Sabbath Year.[22] He thinks it impossible that this would be Agrippa II because he never governed Jerusalem and he either could not or would not read Hebrew. Agrippa I ruled Galilee and Peraea from 39 CE, and Claudius added Judea and Samaria to his kingdom in 41 CE, which he ruled until his death in 44 CE.

---

[22] m.Sot.7.8. See the discussion in Wacholder, "Calendars," pp. 167-69.

Wacholder argues that the Sabbath Year could not have been 40/41 CE, as previously thought, because Josephus notes that the Jews who were protesting Caligula's order to place his statue in the Temple in late 40 CE were so intent on their protest that they were willing to neglect their fields.[23] Instead, he says that 41/42 CE was a Sabbath Year, which means that this occurred in *Sukkot* (Tabernacles) of 42 CE. The assassination of Caligula in January 41 CE just before the statue of the emperor was going to be transported to Jerusalem for erection in the Temple, must have been seen as an answer to fervent prayers in Israel. It is likely that this was especially on their minds when Agrippa read out the passages about the king at this ceremony.

Later rabbinic traditions add other less probable stories about Agrippa's piety,[24] but they were probably inspired by this one, and they should not influence our dating of this tradition. This tradition has clearly been inserted into the description of the Temple ceremony, because it interrupts the flow of the description. It is slotted in where it mentions that the king sits to read, because Agrippa chose to stand. Immediately after the final "and you are our brother" the description of the ceremony restarts where it was interrupted. The comment "and the Sages praised him" looks like something which was added later to explain that even though Agrippa did not act correctly, it was nevertheless praiseworthy. The fact that it was added does not mean that it was later. It looks as though it was already a fixed tradition which was mentioned here because it appeared to contradict the description of what normally happened. The comment "and the Sages praised him" acts to harmonize two accounts which were already fixed.

It is difficult to decide if this definitely represents a historical occurrence, but it fits in with the character of Agrippa I who was, as Wacholder says, "shrewd and subtle, pious where piety was called for, . . . quite capable of shedding tears to elicit a reply that would ease the un-Jewish reputation of the Herodian princes."[25]

The description of the Temple ceremony may also date from before 70 CE, but this is difficult to establish.

New Testament: The "platform" which they built for Agrippa is a *béma* (βῆμα transliterated into Hebrew as *bimah*, בִּימָה). This was the name of an official platform or seat of honor which was in the center of all Graeco-Roman cities, where public officials or visiting rulers would make public proclamations or hold trials. It is used in the NT for the judgment seat of Pilate (Mt.27.19; Jn.19.13), Herod Agrippa I

---

[23] *Ant.*18.271: "Falling on their faces and baring their throats, they declared that they were ready to be slain. They continued to make these supplications for forty days. Futhermore, they neglected their fields, though it was time to sow the seed"; cf. *War.*2.200. This would indicate December, but Philo *Legat.*249 says that "the wheat crop was just ripe and so were the other cereals," which would indicate something like April/May.

[24] e.g. m.Bik.3.4; b.Pes.107b.

[25] Wacholder, p. 169.

(Acts 12.21), Gallio (Acts 18.12, 16-17), Festus (Acts 25.6, 10, 17), and of Christ (Rom.14.10; 2Cor.5.10).

The incident concerning the statue of Caligula may have been what prompted the Thessalonians to expect the imminent return of Christ (1Thes.4.11–5.10) after the "man of lawlessness ... exalts himself above every so-called god or object of worship, so that he takes his seat in the Temple" (2Thes.2.3-4; cf. Mk.13.14 // Mt.24.15). The near-fulfillment of this prophesy in 41 CE must have increased the expectation of many believers.

m.Bek.8.10: What reverts to the original owner in Jubilees?

These [matters] do not revert in Jubilee:	אלו שאינן חוזרין ביובל,
The [inheritance of] the *firstborn*,	הבכורה,
and of him who inherits from his wife	והיורש את אשתו,
and of him who levirately marries	והמיבם
the wife of his brother.	את אשת אחיו.
And what is given [as a gift]	והמתנה,
—the words of R. Meir [T4].	דברי רבי מאיר.
And the Sages say:	וחכמים אומרים,
A gift is equivalent to a sale.	מתנה כמכר.
R. Eliezer [b. Hyrcanus, T2] says:*	רבי אליעזר אומר,
They all revert in Jubilee.	כולן חוזרין ביובל.
R. Johanan b. Beroka [T3] says:	רבי יוחנן בן ברוקא אומר,
He who inherits from his wife:	היורש את אשתו,
It must revert to the sons of her family	יחזיר לבני משפחה
and he deducts for them	וינכה להם
[some] of the compensation payment.	מן הדמים.

*Variant: אלעזר Eleazar [b. Shammua, T4].

Comments: When the Year of Jubilee came and property had to revert to the original owners, there were some exceptions. This may be based on the concept that the property reverts back to the original families, not to individuals (Lev.25.11), and that property which is inherited from a wife has not moved from one family to another. However, the silence concerning property inherited by the wife from a husband suggests that this is based on a strict interpretation of "to his family" (אל משפחתו, Lev.25.11)—i.e., it reverts to "his" family but not to "her" family. Johanan replies to this interpretation by saying it reverts to the males in *her* family, though the husband does not have to hand over the land—he only has to pay them some compensation.

Dating (2): None of this is likely to be pre-70. The only reason for dating the first section early is the comment by Eliezer, and it is more likely that this should read "Eleazar [b. Shammua, T4]."[26] This reading would fit in with the debate at the time of Johanan [T3] and with the growing debate about Jubilees in the middle and late second century.

It is unlikely that Jubilees was ever celebrated in the Second Temple period and the later rabbis were in general agreement that it had not been celebrated (y.Shebi.10.3.II), though the ruling in m.Arak.7.1 may suggest that there was a memory of its celebration in Temple times and it may have been kept at Qumran (cf. 1QS.10.6-8). There were some significant discussions in the mid second century about the details of Jubilees (esp. m.Arak.7.1–9.1), but later rabbis could not even decide whether it should be every forty-ninth year (i.e., at the same time as the Sabbath Year) or every fiftieth year (i.e., after the normal Sabbath Year),[27] which confirms that they had not been celebrating it.

New Testament The only possible reference to a Jubilee in the NT is Jesus' reading from Isaiah 61 in the Nazareth synagogue, which ends with "to proclaim the acceptable year of the Lord" (Isa.61.2; Lk.4.19). It is likely that Isaiah had an eschatological Jubilee in mind, and this may have been Jesus' thought too, but it is fairly certain that he was not referring to any present-day Jubilee. This reference to a Jubilee in the context of a messianic message may have prompted many of the congregation to consider a chronology such as that of the Qumran community, as in Jubilees, and which may have ended with the coming of a messiah at about this time.[28]

---

[26] As also at m.Arak.7.4; 9.1, which also debate the Jubilee.

[27] R. Judah argued for a forty-nine-year cycle while the majority argued for a fifty-year cycle— b.Ned.61a; b.RH.9a; b.Arak.12b; 24b; 33a. For a brief discussion and other references, see Wacholder, p. 154; fuller details in Shmuel Safrai, "Jubilee in the Second Temple Period," *Encyclopaedia Judaica*, 16 vols. (Jerusalem: Keter Publishing House, 1972), cols. 578-82.

[28] Roger Beckwith has argued persuasively that this chronology was found in the Damascus Document, the Melchizedek Document, and the Testament of Levi, which means that it was probably widespread outside the Qumran sect. They divided time into ten decades of Jubilees (i.e., periods of 490 years, based on Dan.9.24-27) and said that the Era of Wickedness would finish at the end of the eighth decade of Jubilees. The Messiah(s) would come at this time (CD.6.10, 14; 12.23-24; 14.19; 15.7, 10). Depending on how this is calculated (on the basis of T.Levi.17.10-11), they expected the Messiah(s) somewhere between 3 BCE and 2 CE. See Roger T. Beckwith, *Calendar and Chronology, Jewish and Christian: Biblical, Intertestamental and Patristic Studies*, Arbeiten zur Geschichte des antiken Judentums und des Urchristentums 33 (Leiden: Brill, 1996), pp. 218-32.

Summary and Conclusions

This tractate is based on a substantial core of school disputes with dated traditions coming mainly from T2 and T4. An early structure of the tractate was based on the repeated phrase "until what time" or "from what time" (1.1; 2.1; 3.1; 4.7, 10; 5.5; 6.4). If a couple of these are omitted (4.10 and 5.5),[29] this produces a plausible list of subject headings for the tractate:

1.1 Ploughing an orchard
2.1 Ploughing a field (and other matters of tending a field before the Sabbath Year)
3.1 Taking out manure (and other matters of tending a field during the Sabbath Year)
4.7 Eating the fruit of trees (and other matters of gathering food during the Sabbath Year)
6.4 Buying vegetables (and other commerce which is permitted during the Sabbath Year)

Of these headings, the only ones which can be argued to date back to before 70 CE are 1.1 and 4.10, so it is likely that the others were created in the early second century and deliberately based on the style of 1.1.

The pre-70 material shows that the Sabbath Year restrictions in Torah had already been extended to include ploughing, watering, and storing. Ploughing was forbidden in fields after the sixth-year harvest at *Pesach* (Passover) (m.Shebi.2.1) and in orchards after the harvest at *Shabuot* (Pentecost) (m.Shebi.1.1), though after 70 CE this was soon changed so that ploughing was allowed up to the New Year. Watering was allowed for saplings up to the New Year (t.Shebi.1.5), which implies that it was forbidden for other plants probably after their harvest. Storing was forbidden after the plants were no longer available in the fields, and this was marked by the *removal* of those plants from houses (m.Shebi.9.5).

Ploughing is a recurring theme in the school disputes, probably because this restriction was the first of the rabbinic additions to the biblical Sabbath Year regulations, and the variety of rulings indicate that they had difficulty imposing it. Although both schools agreed that no ploughing should be allowed after the sixth-year harvest, they had different ways of imposing this ban. The Shammaites forbade anyone eating food which had been grown on a ploughed field (m.Shebi.4.2) and wanted to forbid the sale of food grown in such fields in the following year too, but could not impose this (t.Shebi.3.10). Both Schools discouraged the sale and purchase of ploughing heifers (m.Shebi.5.8) and tools such as spades (t.Shebi.6.19), or the selling of a field to someone who would plough it (t.Shebi.4.5b), though Hillelites

---

[29] 4.10 is 'Cutting down a fruit-bearing tree' (in a T1 tradition) and 5.5 is 'buying arum' (in a T4 tradition). 'Cutting down trees' is part of the preceding subject ('eating fruit of trees'), and 'buying arum' is displaced, in a group of sayings about arum.

allowed these sales if it was not certain that the buyer would break the law. They both stopped people from turning over a field by digging up tree roots, though the Hillelites allowed one or two tree roots to be dug (m.Shebi.4.4).

Selling of produce was another practice which the schools had difficulty banning because it was inevitable that someone living next to a vegetable field would want to exchange gathered goods with someone living next to a grain field, if only for a balanced diet, and the market was the most convenient place to do this. The Shammaites tried to ban the exchange of gathered food for coins (t.Shebi.6.19) and to force people to use barter instead. The Hillelites allowed exchange of goods for money, so long as this was not done in a commercial way—i.e., they did not use commercial methods of measuring (m.Shebi.8.3). In other words, you could exchange goods for money or for other goods as a 'favor' (m.Shebi.4.2), but not as a commercial transaction (cf. m.Shebi.8.4). Anything which you obtained by exchange retained the restrictions of Sabbath Year produce (t.Shebi.7.6).

All food which grew by itself was available for anyone to gather during the Sabbath Year, and this should not be prevented even by cutting branches for wood (m.Shebi.4.10). A few plants, such as arum and late onions, were not available because they started maturing during the previous year (t.Shebi.2.6a), and these plants could be harvested and sold in the Sabbath Year (m.Shebi.5.4), along with expensive imported food (m.Yad.4.3). However, this also meant that their Sabbath Year crop could be gathered whenever it matured (t.Shebi.2.6a), during the next year (in the case of late onions) or during the second year (in the case of arum—cf. m.Kil.2.5).

The *release* of loans caused problems for poor people who could not get a loan near the Sabbath Year, so Hillel *decreed* the *prozbul* which allowed loans to be made through the courts (m.Shebi.10.3-4). This meant, in effect, that the judges were guarantors of the loans, and so this was soon restricted to secured loans (m.Shebi.10.7), even though this made such loans unusable by the poor for whom the system was invented.

External sources indicate that the Sabbath Year regulations were widely enforced during the whole first century, and two dateable sources indicate a timetable for them. The year 29/30 CE, which was probably the first year of Jesus' ministry, was a second year in the cycle when arum was freely available to the poor, which made his comments about arum lilies particularly appropriate. A Sabbath Year occurred soon after the early church had started (34/35 CE) which necessitated heroic generosity in order to support the poor of the church. Another Sabbath Year followed the famine of 47/48 CE, and so Paul was able to predict that Palestinian Christians would need a collection to help them cope.

It is likely that there was a Temple ceremony of readings and blessings at the end of the harvest in the year after the Seventh, and it is possible that King Agrippa I took part in this. It is possible that the Jubilee was never celebrated in the Second Temple period.

Tractate *Terumot*: Elevation Offerings

Definitions and Outline

Torah said that the people should *elevate* (*taram*, תָּרַם, from רוּם, 'to rise') an *elevation offering* (*terumah*, תְּרוּמָה, 'an elevation, removal, separation') for the priests (Num.18.8-11, 19, 24-32; Deut.18.4). This is often translated a 'heave offering,' following Tyndale and popularized in the King James version, but '*elevation offering*' is more accurate and helps to convey both the sense of 'separation' and 'holiness.' Torah did not specify a quantity, but the rabbis considered about one-fiftieth was correct for the *elevation offering* of produce.

The *elevation offering* had to be given to a priest, though very small quantities could simply be destroyed to prevent nonpriests from eating it. *Elevation offerings* from the Temple sacrifices could only be eaten by males in the Temple (Num.18.9-10), but *elevation offerings* from crops (the first separation of one-fiftieth and the tithe of the Levites' tithe) could be eaten in *purity* (*toharah*, טָהֳרָה) at home by the priests and their whole families (Num.18.11, 19, 31). Deliberate wrongful consumption of *elevation offerings* was liable to death (Num.18.32), but accidental consumption was liable only to replacement by the *full value* (*qeren*, קֶרֶן) plus an *added fifth* (*ḥomesh*, חֹמֶשׁ) (Lev.5.15-16).

If a portion of *elevation offering* accidentally fell into *deconsecrated* produce, the status of *elevation offering* taints (*dama*, דָּמַע, 'to mix') the rest of the produce which must thereafter be treated like *elevation offering*. However, if it fell into a large quantity of *deconsecrated* produce which is more than 100 times the quantity of the *elevation offering*, this '*neutralizes*' (*olah*, עָלָה, 'raises') the *elevation offering*.

m.Ter.1.1–4.6: Elevating *elevation offerings*

Only those who are responsible and capable may separate *elevation offerings*. They must be separated from the same or very similar produce. You must intend to separate, and you must separate a suitable amount.

m.Ter.4.7–5.9: *Neutralizing elevation offerings*

Elevation offering status is *neutralized* if it falls into normal food more than 100 times as large.

m.Ter.6.1–8.12: Restoring *elevation offerings*

If nonpriests accidentally consume an *elevation offering*, they have to repay the *full value* plus an *added fifth*. Liquids and fruit may be spoiled by snake venom and other things.

m.Ter.9.1–11.10: *Tainting* with *elevation offerings*

Elevation offering status can be conferred by flavor imparted during cooking or pickling, but tiny amounts of *elevation offering* can be ignored.

Related texts: m.MS.2.3-4 re fenugreek and vetches

Must these non-food *elevation offerings* be consumed in *purity*?

m.Ter.1.1-3, 6: Who may *elevate*?

Summary of Mishnah: *Elevation offering must* not be *elevated* by those who are not counted as responsible for fulfilling the law—but if they do, it is *invalid* (1.1-3)—and *should* not be *elevated* by those who are incapacitated—but if they do, it is *valid* (1.6). [This distinction between valid and invalid recurs throughout the larger section of m.Ter.1.1–4.6.]

The following traditions have elements (marked in bold) for which there is evidence of an origin before 70 CE:

m.Ter.1.1: Five kinds of people may not elevate elevation offerings.

Five [kinds of people] must not *elevate* [*elevation offering*]	חמשה, לא יתרומו,
and if they [have already] *elevated* [*elevation offering*],	ואם תרמו,
they have not *elevated* [valid] *elevation offering*.	אין תרומתן תרומה.
The *deaf-mute* and the *imbecile* and the minor	החרש, והשוטה, והקטן,
and he who *elevates* that which is not his;	והתורם את שאינו שלו.
a gentile who *elevates*	נכרי שתרם
that which is an Israelite's,	את של ישראל,
even if it was with his permission:	אפילו ברשות,
He has not *elevated* [valid] *elevation offering*.	אין תרומתו תרומה.

Comments: If these five types of people separate a portion of produce with the intention of *elevating elevation offering*, the portion they have *elevated* retains the status of ordinary produce. The first three are not responsible under the law, and the latter two are not legally responsible for the produce they are *elevating*.

The "*deaf-mute, imbecile,* and minor" are commonly listed together as those who are not held responsible for fulfilling the Commandments. The deaf (*ḥeresh*, חֵרֵשׁ,

'closed up') is translated "*deaf-mute*" because, as m.Ter.1.2 states, the rabbis normally assumed that a deaf person cannot speak. Simeon b. Gamaliel [II?] in Tosefta 1.1 debates whether a *deaf-mute* can have understanding—it is acknowledged that one who has become a *deaf-mute* can signal his intentions, though this is by writing, not by speaking. An *imbecile* is defined in t.Ter.1.3 (which is undateable) as "One who goes out alone at night, and who sleeps in a graveyard and who rips his clothing and who loses what is given to him."

The phrase "that which is not his" is expanded here to suggest that it means a gentile worker who separates *elevation offering* for his Israelite master. Other possible meanings which are explored are that a thief might *elevate* what is still being sought by its rightful owner (t.Ter.1.6) or that one might use harvest *leftovers* as *elevation offering* (m.Ter.1.6).

Dating (2): This list of five people who may not *elevate* was strongly linked to the school debate of m.Ter.1.4 at a very early stage. This is seen by the fact that the first two sections ("Who may *elevate*?" and "From what can you *elevate*?") occur in two versions, a short one in m.Ter.1.1-5 and a much expanded one in m.Ter.1.6–3.2. The short version contains mainly early material, and the longer one contains mainly later material. The two versions both cover the same two subjects, and so we would expect the two sections on "Who may *elevate*" to be next to each other followed by the two sections on "From what can you *elevate*." The fact that the two early sections are kept together suggests that the traditional link between them was already very strong by the second century, and so they added later material on to the end of them instead of inserting it between them. This did not prevent later generations from inserting material into the early version, such as the comment by Judah [T4] in m.Ter.1.3 on the definition of a minor, which would be out of place elsewhere.

It is impossible to decide which parts of this material are from before 70 CE. The earliest portion probably just concerned the *deaf-mute*, *imbecile*, and minor, to which was first added "he who *elevates* that which is not his," and then the "gentile" was added as an example of this. The concept of nonvalid *elevation offering* is already present in the earliest portion and is later repeated when the "gentile" was added and finally when the introduction about "five" was added. This introduction was necessary to make a clear distinction with m.Ter.1.6 where another five are listed who *should* not *elevate* though their *elevation* is nevertheless valid.

t.Ter.1.1a: *Deaf-mutes* can supervise pure things, but not *elevation offerings*

R. Judah [b. Illai, T4] says:	רבי יהודה אומר
A *deaf-mute* who *elevated* [*elevation offering*]:	חרש שתרם
He *elevated* [valid] *elevation offering*.	תרומתו תרומה.
R. Judah said: It happened that:	אמר רבי יהודה מעשה
The sons of R. Johanan b. Gudgada [T1]	בבניו של רבי יוחנן בן גודגדה

who were *deaf-mutes*,	שֶׁהָיוּ חֵרְשִׁים,
and it used to be that all the *pure* things	וְהָיוּ כָל טָהֳרוֹת
[which were] in Jerusalem *	יְרוּשָׁלַיִם
were prepared under their management.	נַעֲשִׂין עַל גַבָּם.
They said to him: [Do you argue] from this evidence?	אָמְרוּ לוֹ מִשָּׁם רְאָיָה
The *pure* things do not require intention,	שֶׁהַטָּהֳרוֹת אֵין צְרִיכוֹת מַחֲשָׁבָה
and can [therefore] be prepared under the management of	וְנַעֲשׂוֹת עַל גַבֵּי
a *deaf-mute*, an *imbecile* or a minor;	חֵרֵשׁ שׁוֹטֶה וְקָטָן,
[but] *elevation offering* and tithes	תְּרוּמָה וּמַעֲשְׂרוֹת
require intention [in order to be valid].	צְרִיכִין מַחֲשָׁבָה

* Z reads שֶׁבִּירוּשָׁלַיִם, 'which were in Jerusalem'

Comments: Judah argues (against m.Ter.1.1) that although a *deaf-mute* should not *elevate elevation offerings*, what he *elevates* should nevertheless be treated as *elevation offerings*. His evidence is a *baraytah* concerning some *deaf-mutes* who apparently looked after items of levitical *purity* in Jerusalem. His argument is refuted by pointing out that such work does not need 'intention'—i.e., it can be done mechanically, without understanding or decision, so it does not need to be done by someone who is legally responsible—unlike the *elevation* of an *elevation offering*.

Tosefta goes on to debate whether a *deaf-mute* can have understanding—it is acknowledged that one who has become a *deaf-mute* can signal his intentions by writing.

Dating (3): The tradition reported by R. Judah is introduced as a *baraytah* with the characteristic formula "It happened that. . . ." This is a relatively early attribution for a *baraytah,* and those who questioned Judah's conclusion did not question the authenticity of this tradition, so there is no reason to doubt that it is genuine. We know almost nothing about Johanan b. Gudgada. His purity is famed in m.Hag.2.7 (though this is likely to be a late honorific tradition), and a few rulings are preserved in his name (m.Yeb.14.2 // m.Git.5.5 // m.Ed.7.9). It may be significant that his rulings include one about a stolen *sin offering*, and one about the divorce rights of a *deaf-mute* girl. This helps to confirm that he was active in the Temple era and may indicate that he had a special interest in Temple offerings and *deaf-mutes* (which would be the case if he had *deaf-mute* sons).

t.Ter.1.6 (Z 1.6a): Thieves can offer tithes and dedications

A thief and a mugger and an extortionist:	הַגַּנָּב וְהָאַנָּס וְהַגַּזְלָן
What they *elevate* is [valid] *elevation offering*,	תְּרוּמָתָן תְּרוּמָה,
and what they tithe [are valid] tithes,	וּמַעְשְׂרוֹתָן מַעֲשְׂרוֹת,
and what they *dedicate* is a [valid] *dedication*.	וְהֶקְדֵּשָׁן הֶקְדֵּשׁ.
If the owners were [still] pursuing	אִם הָיוּ בְעָלִים מְרַדְּפִין
after them [to recover their stolen goods]:	אַחֲרֵיהֶם

What they *elevate* is not [valid] *elevation offering*	אֵין תְּרוּמָתָן תְּרוּמָה,
and what they tithe [are] not [valid] tithes	וְאֵין מַעְשְׂרוֹתָן מַעַשְׂרוֹת,
and what they *dedicate* is not a [valid] *dedication*.	וְאֵין הֶקְדֵּשָׁן הֶקְדֵּשׁ.
Owners of houses of terrorists	בַּעֲלֵי בָתֵּי סִיקְרִיקוֹן
[confiscated by the government and owned illegally]:	
What they *elevate* is [valid] *elevation offering*	תְּרוּמָתָן תְּרוּמָה,
and what they tithe [are valid] tithes,	וּמַעְשְׂרוֹתָן מַעַשְׂרוֹת,
and what they *dedicate* is a [valid] *dedication*.	וְהֶקְדֵּשָׁן הֶקְדֵּשׁ.

Comments: You can *elevate elevation offering*, tithes, and a *dedication* from anything which you own. This includes stolen property if the original owner has given up trying to reclaim it, and property which is 'stolen' by the Romans.

The "terrorists" are the *siqaricon* (סִיקְרִיקוֹן) whose property was confiscated by the Romans and given to loyal supporters. Later rabbis ruled that someone who buys property which has been confiscated in this way should also pay one quarter of the value to the original owner. This suggests that they believed the original owner still had a legitimate claim to the property. This practice of confiscating homes was already occurring in the time of the Temple (cf. m.Bik.1.2).

The ruling is cited here to illustrate the rule that you can *elevate elevation offerings* only from what you own (m.Ter.1.1).

Dating (9): The reference to a "*dedication*" may indicate this is an early tradition, because in Mishnah this always implies a *dedication* to the Temple. However, this triad (*elevation offerings*, tithes, and *dedications*) commonly occur together. They are occasionally referred to collectively as "the *consecrated*" (*ha-qodesh*, הַקֹּדֶשׁ cf. m.Ter.6.5), but this appears to be a late term and usually all three are listed. Therefore the occurrence of "*dedication*" may not be significant, because it may simply be present in order to complete the list which forms this category.

This tradition may be related to m.Ter.3.9 where the same phrases are used concerning gentiles and Samaritans, who can also present valid *elevation offerings*, tithes, and *dedications*.

t.Ter.3.1 (Z 3.1a): Why the drunk cannot elevate *elevation offerings*

For what reason did it say	מִפְּנֵי מָה אָמְרוּ
a mute [person] may not *elevate* [*elevation offering*]?	אִלֵּם לֹא תָרוֹם.
Because he is not able to [say the] blessing.	מִפְּנֵי שֶׁאֵין יָכוֹל לְבָרֵךְ.
For what reason did it say	מִפְּנֵי מָה אָמְרוּ
a blind [person] must not *elevate* [*elevation offering*]?	סוֹמָא לֹא יִתְרוֹם,
Because he is not able to distinguish	מִפְּנֵי שֶׁאֵין יָכוֹל לְבוֹר
the fine [quality produce] from the bad.	אֶת הַיָּפֶה מִן הָרָעָה.
For what reason did it say	מִפְּנֵי מָה אָמְרוּ
a drunk [person] must not *elevate* [*elevation offering*]?	שִׁכּוֹר לֹא יִתְרוֹם,

Because he does not have [enough] understanding.	מִפְּנֵי שָׁאֵין בּוֹ דַעַת.
Even if he is drunk*	אַף עַל פִּי שְׁכוּר,
what he purchases is a [valid] purchase	מִקְחוֹ מִקָּח
and what he sells is a [valid] sale	וּמִמְכָּרוֹ מִמְכָּר
and what he vows is a [valid] vow	וְנִדְרוֹ נֶדֶר
and what he *dedicates* is a [valid] *dedication*	וְהִקְדֵּשׁוֹ הֶקְדֵּשׁ
and what he gives [as a gift] is a [valid] gift.	וּמַתְּנָתוֹ מַתָּנָה.
[If] he committed a transgression	עָבַר עֲבֵרָה
for which he is liable to a *sin offering*,	שֶׁחַיָּיב עָלֶיהָ חַטָּאת
one should hold him liable (for the *sin offering*),	מְחַיְּיבִין אוֹתוֹ (חַטָּאת),
[and if he committed a transgression for which he is liable to] stoning,	סְקִילָה
one should hold him liable for stoning.	מְחַיְּיבִין אוֹתוֹ סְקִילָה.
The general principle which is from this matter:	כְּלָלוּ שֶׁל דָּבָר,
A drunk [person], behold he is	שְׁכוּר הֲרֵי הוּא
like a fully aware [person] in all matters.	כְּפִקֵּחַ לְכָל דָּבָר.

* Z reads אַף עַל פִּי שֶׁאָמְרוּ שִׁיכּוֹר 'Even if it says he is drunk.'

Comments: This is part of a commentary on m.Ter.1.6 which says that *elevation offering* should not be *elevated* by the mute, drunk, naked, blind, or one who has had a nocturnal emission. Tosefta Ter.3.1-2 asks for the reason for each in a different order (mute, blind, drunk, nocturnal emission, naked). The reasons given for the mute, nocturnal emission, and naked are that they cannot recite the blessing, and the reason for the blind and the drunk is that they cannot pick out the best (cf. m.Ter.2.6).

The tradition about the legal status of a drunk is inserted into the middle of these after the explanation about the drunk. It appears to be part of an argument against this explanation, pointing out that a drunk is considered responsible under law in every other respect. Presumably the editor(s) of Tosefta were either not concerned about this contradiction or (more likely) they decided that although he was legally responsible, this did not mean that he was capable.

Dating (8): The commentary on m.Ter.1.6 is probably later than 70 CE (see Dating at m.Ter.1.1), and so the commentary is certainly later than 70 CE. The tradition about the legal status of the drunk is cited as an accepted ruling (or series of rulings) in order to derive a general principle from it (or them), and the fact that it contains references to a *dedication* to the Temple, a *sin offering,* and punishment by stoning tends to suggest an early origin, though none of these references are decisive.

This is an example of a commentary in Tosefta on a passage which is found only in Mishnah. Examples like this are the main evidence for thinking that Tosefta was the first commentary on Mishnah, or that Tosefta was a repository of traditions which were excluded from Mishnah. However, Tosefta also includes a large number of traditions which *are* in Mishnah and traditions which are not commentaries on anything in Mishnah, and so the relationship between the two is difficult to determine.

m.Ter.1.4-5, 1.7–3.2: From what can you *elevate*?

Summary of Mishnah: You *must* not *elevate* a processed crop for an unprocessed crop (1.4), or for crops which are different in other ways (1.5), or from a different species (2.4). You *should* not *elevate* for a crop which is similar but not identical (1.8–2.1), though you may *elevate* similar crop of higher value (2.4-6). If *elevated* crop is found to be spoiled, it is still valid (though it does not *taint* non-*elevation offering*—3.2) but you must *elevate* again (3.1).

Elevation offering must not come from harvest *leftovers* or tithes (1.5). You do not use measures to *elevate* (1.7). If you *elevated* unintentionally, it is not valid, as with other unintentional acts (2.2-3).

The following traditions have elements (marked in bold) for which there is evidence of an origin before 70 CE:

m.Ter.1.4: Do not *elevate* crop on behalf of the processed product

One should not *elevate* [*elevation offering of*]	אֵין תּוֹרְמִין
olives for olive oil	זֵיתִים עַל הַשֶּׁמֶן,
nor of grapes for wine.	וְלֹא עֲנָבִים עַל הַיַּיִן.
And if they did *elevate* [in this manner]:	וְאִם תָּרְמוּ,
The School of Shammai says:	בֵּית שַׁמַּאי אוֹמְרִים,
The *elevation* **for these** [products]	תְּרוּמַת עַצְמָן
was [inherent] **within them** [the fruits].	בָּהֶם.
And the School of Hillel says:	וּבֵית הִלֵּל אוֹמְרִים,
One has not *elevated* [valid] *elevation offering.*	אֵין תְּרוּמָתָן תְּרוּמָה.

Mishnaic parallel: m.Ed.7.2

Comments: You have to *elevate elevation offering* from the same or similar produce, and this tradition helps to define what is not 'similar.' If you *elevate* from something which is not similar enough, should you treat the *elevation* as valid *elevation offering* or as *deconsecrated* produce? The School of Shammai says that if one *elevated* olives for oil, the olives could be said to contain the oil which is due. The School of Hillel says that it is not valid *elevation offering* at all; it can be treated as normal produce.

The problem concerned whether to take the grapes and olives to Jerusalem or the processed wine and oil which is made from them. The latter was much easier to carry and it did not need to be taken so quickly before the fruit spoiled. This issue has further ramifications, as debated in m.Ter.1.8 and t.Ter.3.14a; t.Ter.3.12 (see below).

Dating (1): There is no reason to doubt that this is a genuine school debate. This is the earliest evidence for a distinction between valid and invalid *elevations*, which is the basis for much of the first half of this tractate (m.Ter.1.1–4.6). One or both of the phrases "they have *elevated* [valid] *elevation offering*" and "one has not *elevated* [valid] *elevation offering*" occurs in almost all the mishnahs in this section.

The practical concerns, about carrying *elevation offerings* to Jerusalem, stopped being an issue after 70 CE when *elevation offerings* could be given to any local priest. Before 70 CE it is likely that *elevation offerings* had to be taken to the Temple which sold them to the priests, unless they originated outside Israel (see Comments at m.Ter.5.1).

t.Ter.3.16 (Z.3.15): Some processed crops may be *elevated* for crops

He who *elevates* [*elevation offering*]	התורם
for grapes [destined] for the market*¹	ענבים לשוק
and is going to make them into raisins,	ועתיד לעשותן צימוקים
[or *elevates elevation offering* for] figs	תאנים
and is going to make them into dried figs	ועתיד לעשותן גרוגרות,
[or *elevates elevation offering* for] pomegranates	רמונים
and is going to make them into split [pomegranates]:*²	ועתיד לעשותן פרד
[They are valid] *elevation offering*.	תרומה
and it is not necessary to *elevate* a second time.	ואין צריך לתרום שניה.
R. Eliezer [b. Hyrcanus, T2] says:	רבי אליעזר אומר
The School of Shammai says:	בית שמאי אומרים
It is not necessary to *elevate* a second time.	אין צריך לתרום שניה,
And the School of Hillel says:	ובית הלל אומרים
It is necessary to *elevate* a second time.	צריך לתרום שניה.
The School of Hillel says to the School of Shammai:	אמרו בית הלל לבית שמאי
Behold, it says [in Num.18.27]:	הרי הוא אומר
"[And you shall say to the Levites . . . Your *elevation offering* will be counted for you as grain from the threshing floor]	
and as fullness from the winepress."	וכמלאה מן היקב
This one has not *elevated* from the winepress.	לא תרם זה מן היקב.
The School of Shammai says to them:	אמרו להם בית שמאי
Behold it says [in Lev.27.30]	הרי הוא אומר
"And all the tithe	וכל מעשר וגו׳,
[of the land, from the seed of the land, from the fruit of the tree, is for the Lord, holy to the Lord]."	
If you say	אם אומר אתה
it is necessary to *elevate* a second time	צריך לתרום שניה
[you imply that] even this one has not [fulfilled the requirement]	אף זה לא

to become "holy to the Lord."

קַיָּם קֹדֶשׁ לֹה:

---

*1 Z omits 'for the market.'

*2 Z reads כְּרִי 'hollowed' or 'pierced' [pomegranates].

Comments: This starts with an anonymous definition of what is 'similar' in terms of valid *elevations* (as already discussed in m.Ter.1.4). Eliezer recites a school debate in which this anonymous position is represented by Shammaites, and he (or a later editor) adds exegetical support for both schools. The Hillelites are following the same principle as found in m.Ter.1.4 that the product of *elevation offering* should be presented rather than the crop from which that product was produced.

The Hillelites would argue that although Numbers 18.27 says that one thing can be *elevated* on behalf of another, this case is different because Numbers 18.26-27 is concerned with the *elevation offering* of the Levite's tithe. The Shammaites would argue that if you said a second *elevation* was necessary, this implied that the first *elevation* was completely invalid and it was not *consecrated* at all. This would contradict Leviticus 27.28-30 which says that "Any devoted thing which a man devotes to the Lord . . . shall be redeemed . . . [which includes] all the tithe of the land . . . it is holy to the Lord." The Shammaites appear to argue from this that once something has been *elevated* it is *consecrated*, even if the *elevation* was technically faulty.

Dating (2, 1): The fact that the opening tradition is presented anonymously suggests that it was already established when Eliezer chose to comment on it. It is not clear whether Eliezer wants to cast doubt on it by showing that it was based on a Shammaite ruling, or whether he wants to remind us that the Shammaites had some worthy rulings. He makes no comment in favor or against the ruling, and so he is probably just wishing to establish the origin of the ruling.

The exegeses are almost certainly added later, and they may or may not represent the actual reasoning of the schools.

m.Ter.1.5: Do not *elevate* from what does not belong to you

One may not *elevate* [*elevation offering*]	אֵין תּוֹרְמִין
from *gleanings* or from *forgotten* [harvest produce]	מִן הַלֶּקֶט וּמִן הַשִּׁכְחָה
or from *corner* [crop left at harvest for the poor]	וּמִן הַפֵּאָה
or from [property which has been declared] *ownerless*	וּמִן הַהֶפְקֵר,
and not from *first tithe*	וְלֹא מִמַּעֲשֵׂר רִאשׁוֹן
from which the *elevation offering* is removed,	שֶׁנִּטְּלָה תְרוּמָתוֹ,
and not from *second tithe*	וְלֹא מִמַּעֲשֵׂר שֵׁנִי
or a *dedication* which is redeemed.*	וְהֶקְדֵּשׁ שֶׁנִּפְדּוּ,
And [one may] not [*elevate*] from what is liable	וְלֹא מִן הַחַיּוּב
[for *elevation offering*] for what is exempt [from it],	עַל הַפָּטוּר,
and [one may] not [*elevate*] from what is exempt	וְלֹא מִן הַפָּטוּר

[from an *elevation offering*] for what is liable [for it],	עַל הֶחָיוּב,
and not from picked [produce] for unpicked,	וְלֹא מִן הַתָּלוּשׁ עַל הַמְחוּבָּר,
and not from unpicked [produce] for picked,	וְלֹא מִן הַמְחוּבָּר עַל הַתָּלוּשׁ,
and not from new for old [i.e., last year's],	וְלֹא מִן הֶחָדָשׁ עַל הַיָּשָׁן,
and not from old for new [i.e., this year's],	וְלֹא מִן הַיָּשָׁן עַל הֶחָדָשׁ,
and not from the fruit of the Land	וְלֹא מִפֵּרוֹת הָאָרֶץ
for the fruit of outside the Land,	עַל פֵּרוֹת חוּצָה לָאָרֶץ,
and not from fruit of outside the Land	וְלֹא מִפֵּרוֹת חוּצָה לָאָרֶץ
for fruit of the Land.	עַל פֵּרוֹת הָאָרֶץ.
And if one *elevated* [in the ways prohibited above],	וְאִם תָּרַם,
one has not *elevated* [valid] *elevation offering*.	אֵין תְּרוּמָתָן תְּרוּמָה.

*Some editions read "not redeemed."

Comments: The first half says you should not make the *elevation offering* from produce which does not properly belong to you, such as the harvest *leftovers* and tithes or even from produce which was *consecrated* and redeemed (though some editions have the more understandable "not redeemed"). The second half is a further definition of how 'similar' the two sets of produce must be in order to provide *elevation offering* from one for the other. All of these practices produce invalid *elevation offering*. Produce which is not liable is that which has not yet grown by one third (m.Ter.9.1). 'Old' produce is from the year before the waving of the *first sheaf*, and 'new' is from after.

Dating (9): The only clue that any of this dates from before 70 CE is the mention of a *dedication*, which always refers in Mishnah to a *dedication* to the Temple. However, this mention of *dedication* may simply be part of the often-used list of *elevation offerings*, tithes, and *dedications*, or the often-used phrase "a *second tithe* or *dedication* which is redeemed" (see Dating at m.Ter.6.5).

Even if the first section does date from before 70 CE, there is no reason to believe that the second section dates from the same time. The two have been put together in one mishnah only because of the summary statement at the end which the editor(s) wanted to apply to both. Most of the details in the second section ('picked . . . unpicked . . . new . . . old') are repeated in m.MS.5.11, but it is uncertain where they occurred originally.

t.Ter.2.5 (Z.2.4b): You can *elevate* from one variety for another

[If] he had **black figs and white [figs]**	הָיוּ לוֹ הַתְּאֵנִים שְׁחוֹרוֹת וּלְבָנוֹת
inside his house,	בְּתוֹךְ בֵּיתוֹ,
or similarly, two types of wheat,	וְכֵן שְׁנֵי מִינֵי חִטִּים
one should *elevate* [*elevation offering*] and tithe	תּוֹרְמִין וּמְעַשְׂרִין
from this [kind] for that [kind].	מִזֶּה עַל זֶה.
R. Isaac [T5] says in the name of	רַבִּי יִצְחָק אוֹמֵר מִשּׁוּם

R. Eleazar [b. Shammua, T4]:*	רבי אליעזר
The School of Shammai says:	בית שמאי אומרים
[They are] not [valid] *elevation offerings*	אין תורמין,
But the School of Hillel says:	ובית הלל אומרים
[They are valid] *elevation offerings.*	תורמין.

*Z reads Eliezer and some editions of b.Hul.136b read Illai.

Comments: Hillelites say that you may *elevate elevation offerings* from one species for another of the same kind of plant.

Dating (1): There is no reason to doubt that this is a genuine school debate, even though its route of transmission has gone through two hands. The introduction to this debate is, however, very uncertain. This introduction debate was probably transmitted originally as simply "black and white figs," which was first expanded to "If he has . . . in his house" to emphasize that he has to *own* both types, and it was then extended to two species of wheat.

There is a debate about whether black and white figs *neutralize* each other at m.Ter.4.8-9 between R. Eliezer b. Hyrcanus [T2] and R. Joshua b. Hananiah [T2], where Eliezer sides with the Shammaites. This may help confirm that this school debate already existed.

t.Ter.2.14a: You can *elevate* produce which has not grown one third

One should not *elevate* **[elevation offerings] from**	אין תורמין מן
produce which has not	התבואה שלא
reached a third [of its growth].	הביאה שליש.

Comments: In general, plants which have not grown by one third will not be ready for harvesting, and so the food produced from them will be inferior. This ruling may therefore be related to the idea that an *elevation offering* must not be offered from second-rate produce (m.Ter.3.1).

Dating (2): This ruling is assumed by Eliezer [T2] in m.Hal.1.3 with regard to the *dough offerings* (which are a form of *elevation offering*).

t.Ter.3.12 (Z.3.11): Tithing before the impurity of treading grapes

From when should one *elevate*	מאימתי תורמין
[the *elevation offering* of the wine from] the vat?	את הגת,
From when they tread them	משיהלכו בה
this way and that [lit., 'warp and woof'.]	שתי וערב.
From when should one let it become *impure?**1	מאימתי מטמין אותה,
The School of Shammai says:	בית שמיי אומרים
From when one removed the *first tithe.*	משיינטל מעשר ראשון.

The School of Hillel says:
From when one removed the *second tithe*.[*2]

Judah [b. Illai, T4][*3] said: The *halakhah* is
according to the words of the School of Shammai
but the conduct of the majority
is according to the words of the School of Hillel.
And the Sages say:
One should extract the *elevation offering* and tithes[*4]
and let the vat become *impure* after that.[*1]

בית הלל אומרים
משיינטל מעשר שני.
אמר רבי יהודה הלכה
כדברי בית שמאי
אלא שנהגו הרבים
כדברי בית הלל
וחכמים אומרים
מוציאין תרומה ומעשרות
ומטמין את הגת מיד.

[*1] Z reads מטמאין which is the normal spelling.
[*2] y.Ter.3.4.IV reverses these opinions.
[*3] y.Ter.3.4.IV says R. Jose [b. Halafta, T4].
[*4] y.Ter.3.4.IV says "*elevates elevation offering* and *elevation offering* of the tithe."

Comments: Treading grapes imparts *impurity* (cf. m.Ter.3.4), and so the *elevation offering* and tithes must be removed before this, though the Shammaites say that the *second tithe* does not have to be *pure*. This is probably partly because the householder consumes this himself, and mostly because it is impractical to carry the bulky uncrushed grapes to Jerusalem instead of the wine. The majority of the people followed the easier Hillelite ruling but the majority of the scholars (the Sages) followed the Shammaite ruling.

Dating (1): There is no reason to doubt that this is a genuine school debate, though the rulings may have become reversed. The Jerusalem Talmud reverses the rulings, and m.Pea.7.6 suggests that the Hillelites allowed *second tithe* grapes to be turned into wine, though t.Ter.3.14a agrees with t.Ter.3.12 (see below). In both cases, the Sages follow the Shammaite viewpoint because in Tosefta they say that before defiling the grapes one has to extract the "tithes" (i.e., both the *first* and *second tithe*), and in the Jerusalem Talmud (where the rulings are reversed) they say that one can make it *impure* after removing the *elevation offering* of the tithe (i.e., from the *first tithe*).

It is more likely that the majority would follow the easier ruling, which would mean that the Tosefta is correct. The Jerusalem Talmud implies that the majority carried the undefiled grapes to Jerusalem, and adds a comment by Simeon [b. Yohai, T4] that this would not apply after the Temple was destroyed, presumably because all of the *second tithe* was redeemed and therefore the state of *purity* did not matter. This comment probably helps to explain why the confusion arose—because the practical application no longer mattered and the ruling became much less important.

The existence of this ruling about defilement of trodden grapes suggests that they also debated whether or not one may *elevate* wine for trodden grapes, which is probably the debate in t.Ter.3.14 (see below).

The ruling here appears to contradict m.Ter.1.4 where the Hillelites say that wine can be *elevated* as *elevation offerings* on behalf of grapes. It also partly contradicts t.Ter.3.14a where the Shammaites say that you may *elevate* wine for grapes, though this is not strictly correct, and so you should *elevate* properly when the mistake is found. These contradictions may be the reason why the two Tosefta rulings were not included in Mishnah.

m.Ter.1.8 & t.Ter.3.14a (Z.3.13): *Elevate* grapes after treading them

One should not *elevate* [elevation offering from] oil	אֵין תּוֹרְמִין שֶׁמֶן
for olives which have been crushed,	עַל זֵיתִים הַנִּכְתָּשִׁין.
nor **wine for grapes which have been trodden;**	וְלֹא יַיִן עַל עֲנָבִים הַנִּדְרָכוֹת
and if one *elevated* [elevation offering in these ways]	וְאָם תָּרַם,
one has *elevated* [valid] elevation offering	תְּרוּמָתוֹ תְּרוּמָה,
but one should return and *elevate* [again].	וְיַחֲזוֹר וְיִתְרוֹם.
The first [elevation] taints	הָרִאשׁוֹנָה מְדַמַּעַת
[with the status of *elevation offering*] by itself	בִּפְנֵי עַצְמָהּ,
and [nonpriests] are liable	וְחַיָּיבִין
to an *added fifth* for [accidentally eating] it	עָלֶיהָ חוֹמֶשׁ,
but [these things are] not so for the second [elevation].	אֲבָל לֹא שְׁנִיָּה.
[The following is only in Tosefta.]	
and it is necessary to remove from it	וְצָרִיךְ לְהוֹצִיא עֲלֵיהֶן
elevation offerings * and tithes.	תְּרוּמוֹת וּמַעְשְׂרוֹת.
Rabbi Jose [b. Halafta, T4] says:	רַבִּי יוֹסֵי אוֹמֵר
The School of Shammai says:	בֵּית שַׁמַּאי אוֹמְרִים
One should *elevate* [in this way].	תּוֹרְמִין,
But the School of Hillel says:	וּבֵית הִלֵּל אוֹמְרִין
One should not *elevate* [in this way].	אֵין תּוֹרְמִין.
They agree that one who *elevates*	מוֹדִים שֶׁאָם תָּרַם
it is necessary [for him] to *elevate* a second time.	שֶׁצָּרִיךְ לִתְרוֹם שְׁנִיָּיה.

* Z reads תְּרוּמָה, '*elevation offering*.'

Comments: If you delay *elevating elevation offering* until olives or grapes have been turned into oil and wine, this *elevation offering* is valid but (after realizing your mistake) you should make another *elevation* from the olives and grapes themselves. However, only the first *elevation* has the full status of *elevation offering*, and the second has to be tithed like normal produce. Tosefta adds that the Shammaites allowed *elevation* from the oil or wine, but they both agreed that a second *elevation* should also be made.

Dating (1): The portion which is only in Tosefta consists mainly of the school dispute, which contradicts m.Ter.1.4—see Dating re t.Ter.3.12. The Amoraim in the Jerusalem Talmud are very aware of this contradiction and they propose a couple of solutions but do not appear to be convinced by them (y.Ter.1.8). This contradiction makes it unlikely that this school debate is an invention, though its meaning may have been changed by citing it in this context.

The heading to the school dispute is uncertain, because it could be related to "*elevating* oil for crushed olives" or "*elevating* wine for trodden grapes." The latter seems likely because this would supply a ruling which is implied in t.Ter.3.12 (see below). This tradition probably started as a ruling about oil, to which the ruling about wine was added. This prompted Jose to add the school debate about wine. It is possible that the rulings have become reversed, because the Shammaite ruling is similar to the Hillelite ruling in m.Ter.1.4 where they allowed the *elevation* of wine on behalf of grapes.

The concept of a second *elevation* cannot be traced before 70 CE though it probably originated as a compromise soon after. It occurs also at m.Ter.1.9 in a later development of this tradition, at m.Ter.3.1 in an undateable tradition about cucumbers, and at m.Ter.4.3 in another later development of a school debate. This is a later development of the distinction between valid and invalid *elevations*. If the *elevation* was neither fully valid nor fully invalid, they ruled that it was valid but the *elevation* had to be repeated. This new concept of a second *elevation* probably originated with this ruling about wine, concerning which there was so much confusion (see t.Ter.3.12 above). The concept is already becoming complex in Mishnah, where some cases result in a first *elevation* which has full *elevation offering* status (as here and m.Ter.4.3) and others where neither have this status (as in m.Ter.3.1).[1]

The second *elevation* is stated as though it was a generally accepted solution to the school dispute. This solution would have been impractical in most situations, because by the time the mistake has been discovered (or, by the time a passing rabbi has pointed it out), all the olives or grapes would have been processed. It was probably an academic solution which was only later applied in the real world by those who decided beforehand to make two *elevations*.

By Amoraic times (as described in the debates at y.Ter.1.8) some said that a second *elevation* should always take place and others said that it was optional, but there was general confusion about the reason for a second *elevation*. They appeared to be ignorant of the practical problems of transporting untrodden grapes or unpressed olives (see Comments at m.Ter.1.4). These problems disappeared after 70 CE and

---

[1] It is possible that m.Ter.3.1 is saying that the second separation has full *elevation offering* status, if the end is understood as meaning "But [all this applies] thus for the second"—i.e., the stipulations which do not apply to the first separation (contaminating with *elevation offering* status and the requirement of an *added fifth*) *do* apply to the second, which is the reverse of the situation in m.Ter.1.8. The traditional way to understand appears in Danby's translation: "and so too it is with the second," which implies that the first and second separation are treated identically.

were never specifically mentioned in Mishnah (though see the Comments at m.Ter.5.1), and so the Amoraim did not take them into account.

m.Ter.3.3–4.6: How does one *elevate*?

Summary of Mishnah: If someone *elevates* for you and you also *elevate* for yourself, are they both valid *elevation offerings* (3.3-4)? *Elevation* has occurred when the owner has stated his intention, not when he carries it out (3.5). The order of tithing should be *firstfruits, elevation offering, first tithe, second tithe* (3.6-7). If one intends to say "*elevation offering*" but says something else, it is invalid, as with similar mistakes (3.8). A gentile can validly separate tithes (3.9).

One does not need to *elevate* for the whole store at once (4.1), but one should only eat the proportion which is already tithed (4.2). You should measure how much remains to be tithed after the end of each of the three crops (4.6). You should *elevate* between a sixtieth and a fortieth or perhaps a thirtieth (4.3). If a servant has no exact instructions, he *elevates* an average of a fiftieth (4.4). How much is the maximum (4.5)?

The following traditions have elements (marked in bold) for which there is evidence of an origin before 70 CE:

m.Ter.3.9: Gentiles and Samaritans can tithe and elevate

A gentile and a Samaritan:	הנכרי והכותי,
They *elevate* [valid] *elevation offering*	תרומתן תרומה,
and they tithe a [valid] tithe	ומעשרותיהן מעשר,
and they *dedicate* a [valid] *dedication*.	והקדשן הקדש.
R. Judah [b. Illai, T4] says:	רבי יהודה אומר,
A gentile has no *fourth[-year]* vineyard	אין לנכרי כרם רבעי.
but the Sages say: He has.	וחכמים אומרים, יש לו.
The *elevation offering* of a gentile	תרומת הנכרי,
taints [other produce with the status of *elevation offering*]	מדמעת,
and [nonpriests] are liable to an *added fifth* for [eating] it,	וחייבין עליה חומש.
but R. Simeon [b. Yohai, T4] exempts it.	ורבי שמעון פוטר.

Comments: Tithes and *dedications* (i.e., gifts to the Temple) from gentiles and Samaritans can be accepted as valid though they were later increasingly rejected. According to t.Ter.1.6 even a thief could give valid *elevation offerings*, tithes, or *dedications* from the goods which he had stolen, but it is questionable that this is a pre-70 tradition (see m.Ter.1.1).

Dating (8): The reference to *dedications* may suggest an origin before 70 CE though it may merely be part of the frequently used list of '*elevation offering*, tithes, and *dedications*' (see Dating at m.Ter.6.5). Additional evidence for an early date comes from the edict of Gamaliel II, which was published during the generation following 70 CE, saying that all Samaritan produce should be regarded as *certainly untithed* food. This edict implies that before this time Samaritan produce was treated as *doubtfully tithed* (t.Dem.5.24; see m.Dem.5.9), which means that at least some Samaritans were assumed to tithe their produce properly. According to t.Dem.5.24 Gamaliel appears to have made this edict reluctantly when he found that individuals like Akiba were already treating Samaritan produce as *certainly untithed* food:

> It happened that: Our rabbis entered Samaritan towns along the road. They brought vegetables before them. R. Akiba hurried to tithe them as *certainly untithed* food. R. Gamaliel [II] said to him: How are you so bold as to transgress the words of your associates, or who gave you permission to tithe? He [Akiba] said to him: And am I establishing a *halakhah* in Israel?—I have [merely] tithed my own vegetables. He (Gamaliel) said to him: Know that you have established a *halakhah* in Israel by tithing your own vegetables. And when R. Gamaliel came among [the Samaritans] he declared their grain and pulse to be *doubtfully tithed food* and the rest of their produce to be *certainly untithed* food. And when R. Gamaliel came back among them, he saw that matters were in disarray, and he declared all of their produce to be *certainly untithed* food. (t.Dem.5.24).

Although this is a biographical story, and therefore suspect with regard to dating because stories were not subject to such stringent care, it is unlikely that someone would have made up a story which appears to be critical of both Akiba and Gamaliel. Akiba is rightly criticized for taking the law into his own hands and acting against the ruling of the majority, and Gamaliel is seen to be fudging the issue by giving in to rabbis like Akiba and then causing extra confusion by making a half-hearted ruling.

The traditions of Judah appear to have been added by a later editor, because the inclusion of the unrelated ruling about the gentile's *fourth-year vineyard* suggests that this was so tightly linked with the ruling about the gentile's *elevation offering* that the editor did not feel able to divide them up. This suggests that this comment was not written as a commentary to an early version of m.Ter.3.9, because otherwise it would not be linked with the matter of the *fourth-year fruit* (which is dealt with at m.MS.5.1-5). R. Judah makes so many comments on individual mishnahs that they sometimes appear to form a commentary which has been added to an earlier Mishnah. However, this tradition may indicate that a later editor added Judah's comments to the individual mishnahs at a later date from another source.

m.Ter.4.3: Average elevation of *elevation offering* is one-fiftieth

The measure of *elevation offering*:	שָׁעוּר תְּרוּמָה,
A generous person [lit., 'of beautiful eye'],	עַיִן יָפָה,
one-fortieth.	אֶחָד מֵאַרְבָּעִים.

The School of Shammai says:	בית שמאי אומרים,
One-thirtieth.	משלשים.
And the average [man], a fiftieth	והבינונית, מחמשים.
and the mean [man], a sixtieth.	והרעה, משישים.
[If] one *elevated* [*elevation offering*]	תרם
and it came up in his hand [as] one-sixtieth,	ועלה בידו אחד מששים,
it is [valid] *elevation offering*	תרומה,
and it is not necessary to *elevate* [again].	ואינו צריך לתרום.
[If] he reverted and added [more],	חזר והוסיף,
[the second *elevation*] is liable to tithes.	חייב במעשרות.
[If] it came up in his hand as a sixty-first,	עלה בידו מששים ואחד,
it is [valid] *elevation offering*	תרומה,
but he must revert and *elevate* [again]	ויחזור ויתרום
according to what he is accustomed to do,	כמו שהוא למוד,
by measure [of volume]	במדה
or weight or number [which is normally prohibited].	ובמשקל ובמנין.
R. Judah [b. Illai, T4] says:	רבי יהודה אומר,
[He may] even [*elevate* from] that which is not	אף שלא מן
nearby [i.e., from a different batch].	המוקף.

Comments: Torah does not specify the quantity of *elevation offering* but an average is one-fiftieth. You are not allowed to use a measure when *elevating* (see m.Ter.1.7), though presumably you are allowed to use a measure afterward to see how much has been *elevated*. If you want to add more, you can do so, and you *should* do so if there was less than one-sixtieth. For the second *elevation*, you can use a measure, and because this second *elevation* is not real *elevation offering*, you should tithe it like normal produce.

In t.Ter.5.3 the quantities are slightly different:

The School of Shammai say: Generous thirtieth; average fortieth; mean fiftieth.
The School of Hillel say: Generous fortieth; average fiftieth; mean sixtieth.

In t.Ter.5.8 the origin of fiftieth is found (anonymously) in Num.31.30:

And from the people of Israel's half, you shall take one drawn out of every fifty [of the persons, oxen, asses and of the flocks, of all the cattle and give them to the Levites who have charge of the tabernacle of the Lord].

Dating (1): There is no reason to doubt that the schools did set an average quantity for *elevation offerings*, but it is now unclear exactly what that quantity was. The tradition in m.Ter.4.3 is more likely to be correct, because it shows the Shammaite ruling as the one which was followed (which is unusual). The tradition in t.Ter.5.3 reverses this to the more normal situation that later generations followed the Hillelites.

A scriptural basis for one-fiftieth was later found in Num.31.30 and for one-sixtieth in Ezekiel 45.13 (t.Ter.5.8, attributed to R. Jose b. Halafta [T4]). The concept of the second *elevation* is probably a little later than 70 CE (see m.Ter.1.8). Later rabbis, starting with Eliezer b. Hyrcanus [T2], allowed progressively larger *elevations* of *elevation offerings* (cf. m.Ter.4.5).

m.Ter.4.7–5.9: *Neutralizing elevation offerings*

Summary of Mishnah: If one part of *elevation offering* falls into a hundred parts or more of normal produce, it is *neutralized* (4.7), even if the produce is slightly different (4.8-10), and even if the hundred parts are spread between two containers (4.12-13). If one can remove the *elevation offering* by skimming it off the surface, one should do so (4.11). If it is not *neutralized*, it all becomes *elevation offering*, though one treats different mixtures in various ways (5.1). Is *impurity neutralized* in the same way (5.2-4)?

Produce which becomes *elevation offering* by such mixing can also *taint* other produce, but only proportionately (5.5-6). Repeated *tainting* does not increase the proportion of the *elevation offering*, unless it occurs before the *elevation offering* is *elevated* from the mixture (5.7-8) [which implies that when produce becomes *tainted*, one *elevates* a hundredth as if it was *doubtfully tithed*]. If the mixture increased or decreased in volume when processed, its status remains the same, but if one accidentally added unprocessed crop to it and made it more than a hundred parts, it becomes *neutralized* (5.9).

The following traditions have elements (marked in bold) for which there is evidence of an origin before 70 CE:

m.Ter.4.7: *Elevation offering* is *neutralized* by one hundred parts

R. Eliezer [b. Hyrcanus, T2] says:	רבי אליעזר אומר,
Elevation offering is neutralized	תרומה עולה
by a hundred and one [parts of *deconsecrated* produce].	באחד ומאה.
R. Joshua [b. Hananiah, T2] says:	רבי יהושע אומר,
[It is *neutralized* by] a hundred and more,	במאה ועוד,
and this 'more' has no measure.	ועוד זה, אין לו שעור.
R. Jose b. Meshullam [T5] says:	רבי יוסי בן משולם אומר,
'And more' [is] a *qab* per hundred *seahs*,	ועוד, קב למאה סאה,
[i.e.,] a sixth [of *elevation offering*] *tainting* it.	שתות למדמע.

Comments: *Elevation offering* is *neutralized* by more than one-hundredth part of *deconsecrated* produce, but how much more? Eliezer says one more, Joshua says the tiniest bit more, but Jose says at least one-sixth of one part (a *qab* is one sixth of a *seah*).

Dating (5): None of this tradition goes back to before 70 CE, but both Eliezer and Joshua assume that *elevation offering* is *neutralized* by one part in a hundred, which means that this principle was already established before 70 CE.

The origin of this principle is unknown, but it may be based on the tithe of the Levites' tithe (i.e., one-hundredth of the original), which was regarded as *elevation offering*. This was the only measurement of *elevation offering* defined by Torah (in Num.18.26), and it was part of everyday life because it was the portion which was removed from *doubtfully tithed food*.

In most rulings about *neutralizing*, they simply refer to falling into "one hundred" parts rather than "one hundred and one" or "one hundred and more" (e.g., the School debate in m.Ter.5.4, but also in later debates such as with Eliezer [T2] in m.Ter.5.2). It is possible that "one hundred" was an earlier position which was succeeded by "more than one hundred" just before 70 CE, but it is more likely that "one hundred" was a shorthand for "more than one hundred".

m.Ter.5.1: *Elevation offering* in less than one hundred parts of *pure* or *impure*.

A *seah* of *impure elevation offering* which fell	סאה תרומה טמאה שנפלה
into less than a hundred [parts of]	לפחות ממאה
deconsecrated [produce]	חולין,
or into *first tithe*	או למעשר ראשון,
or into *second tithe*	או למעשר שני,
or into a *dedication* [to the Temple]	או להקדש,
either *impure* or *pure*:	בין טמאין בין טהורים,
[The whole *tainted* produce] must rot.	ירקבו.
And if that "*seah*" is *pure*:	ואם טהורה היתה אותה הסאה,
It must be sold to the priests	ימכרו לכהנים
at the [low] price of *elevation offering*	בדמי תרומה,
minus the *valuation* of that seah.	חוץ מדמי אותה סאה.
And if it fell "into *first tithe*,"	ואם למעשר ראשון נפלה,
he must designate it [lit., call it by the name]	יקרא שם
as *elevation offering* of the tithe.	לתרומת מעשר.
And if it fell "into *second tithe*"	ואם למעשר שני
or "into a *dedication*"	או להקדש נפלה,
behold, it must be redeemed.	הרי אלו יפדו.
And if that "*deconsecrated* [produce]" was *impure*:	ואם טמאים היו אותן החולין,
It must be eaten as crumbs or parched,	יאכלו נקודים או קליות,
or it must be kneaded with fruit juice,	או ילושו במי פרות,
or it must be distributed into [small pieces of] dough	או יתחלקו לעסות,
such that there will not be there	כדי שלא יהא במקום

one egg-size [piece of produce].   .אֶחָד כְּבֵיצָה

Comments: The three rulings in m.Ter.5.1 deal with *elevation offering* which falls into less than one hundred parts of normal produce in varying combinations of *pure* and *impure*.

1. **Impure** elevation offering **falling into** deconsecrated produce (**pure or impure**).
2. **Pure** elevation offering **falling into pure** deconsecrated produce.
   (Although we are not told that it falls into pure produce, it cannot be impure because otherwise one could not sell it to priests.)
3. Elevation offering (**pure**) **falling into impure** deconsecrated produce.
   (Although we are not told that this elevation offering is pure, it must be because otherwise it would be forbidden to priests (see m.Ter.5.4), and because otherwise it would overlap with number 1. This is also assumed in y.Ter.5.1.V.)

If *impure elevation offering* fell into normal *deconsecrated* produce which is too little to *neutralize* it, the whole becomes *impure elevation offering* and must be left uneaten by anyone. If *pure elevation offering* fell into it, it all becomes *elevation offering*, though if it fell into *second tithe* or a *dedication,* one should also redeem it with money. If *.pure elevation offering* fell into *impure* produce (which can only be eaten in tiny quantities diluted by other food), it should be eaten in tiny quantities (presumably by a priest, though this is not stated here). This last ruling is difficult, because the resultant mixture would presumably be *impure elevation offering*, which may not be eaten by anyone because *elevation offering* can only be eaten by priests in a state of *purity*. But instead of treating it as *impure elevation offering*, it is treated as a hybrid of *pure elevation offering* (which is eaten by priests) and *impure* food (which is eaten in tiny quantities).

The second ruling gives us an interesting insight into what actually happened to *elevation offerings*, because it says that one should "sell it to priests at the price of *elevation offerings*, minus the *valuation* of that [one] *seah*." This implies that *elevation offerings* had a market value and that this value was lower than normal produce. The value was probably lower because only priests could eat it and so there was less demand for it.

How did *elevation offerings* attain a market value, and where were they on sale? The sale of produce which was *tainted* with *elevation offerings* would not be sufficient to establish a market value for *elevation offerings* because this was a relatively rare accident, and so the market must have existed already. Nonpriests did not sell *elevation offerings* because they were meant to be part of their tithes. That is the reason why the one *seah* of *elevation offering* which fell in is deducted from the resale value of the *tainted* hundred *seah*s—because this portion should be a free offering. Priests would be allowed to sell *elevation offerings* to each other, but this would have been a time-consuming way to distribute the *elevation offerings*. It is therefore likely that the market for *elevation offerings* was established by the Temple as a way to distribute them.

This makes it likely that the Temple received *elevation offerings* on behalf of the priests and then sold them to the priests at a low price. This practice is mirrored in the rulings about *dough offerings* (cf. m.Hal.4.10). After the Temple was destroyed, *elevation offerings* and *dough offerings* were given directly to a priest, and the sale of *elevation offerings* was much less common. This may be why the Amoraim are confused by the mention of this market value when they debated this passage[2] and why they could not work out the reason for wanting to *elevate* oil and wine rather than the bulky and heavy olives and grapes.[3]

Dating (9): The reference to a *dedication* to the Temple in the first ruling may suggest an origin before 70 CE but it may merely have been included because many rulings which relate to *second tithes* also relate to a *dedication*. This is especially the case with the phrase "a *second tithe* or *dedication* which is redeemed" which occurs frequently in Mishnah and especially in this tractate (m.Ter.1.5; 6.5; 8.2; cf. 5.1; 9.4), and so the phrase might be used in a later ruling even though part of it was no longer applicable. However, the phrase here is significantly different, and so this would not be an explanation for its inclusion.

The following rulings in m.Ter.5.1 appear to be framed as a commentary on the first set. They cite words from the first ruling, as seen by the use of "that (אותה) *seah*," and "that *deconsecrated* [produce]," and by the unusual word order at times— especially the verb 'fell' which twice occurs after a quote from the first ruling rather than near the beginning of the sentence as normal. It is possible that this commentary started as an expansion of the first ruling's phrase "either *impure* or *pure*."

Both the first ruling and the last ruling of m.Ter.5.1 are cited during a debate in m.Ter.5.2 involving Eliezer b. Hyrcanus [T2], which suggests that they were all established rulings by the time of Eliezer and that they thus date from before 70 CE. The first ruling predates the following rulings by at least a generation, which may suggest that it comes from the time of the schools. The first debate appears to be cited by the Shammaites in m.Ter.5.4 which helps to confirm this conclusion.

The concept of allowing the consumption of *impure* produce in quantities of an egg's bulk or less dates back to the time of the schools or even earlier (cf. m.Orl.2.4-5).

---

[2] R. Hanina bar Hama [PA1] in y.Ter.5.1.IV.

[3] The majority wanted to avoid carrying the unprocessed grapes and olives to Jerusalem (see Comments re m.Ter.1.4), but the Amoraim could not understand why they wanted to separate oil and wine. They suggested that perhaps it was to save the priests the work of processing them, or that the amount separated did not look so generous after it had been processed, but they find problems with both of these suggestions, especially the fact that this rule did not apply to grain (y.Ter.1.4.I).

m.Ter.5.2: *Elevation offering* in one hundred parts or more of *pure* or *impure*

[If] a *seah* of *impure elevation offering* fell	סאה תרומה טמאה שנפלה
into the middle of a hundred [parts of]	לתוך מאה
deconsecrated [produce] [which is] *pure*:	חולין טהורין,
R. Eliezer [b. Hyrcanus, T2] says:	רבי אליעזר אומר,
It is *elevation offering* and it is burned,	תרום ותשרף,
for I declare:	שאני אומר,
"The *seah* which fell [into the hundred]	סאה שנפלה היא
is the [same] *seah* which is raised up."*	סאה שעלתה.
But the Sages say: **It is raised up***	וחכמים אומרים, תעלה
and is eaten as crumbs or parched,	ותאכל נקודים או קליות,
or kneaded with fruit juice,	או תלוש במי פרות,
or distributed into [small pieces of] dough,	או תתחלק לעסות,
such as there will not be in the place [i.e., in a meal]	כדי שלא יהא במקום
one egg-size [piece of produce].	אחד כביצה.

* "raised up" could be translated "is *neutralized*".

Comments: The two rulings in m.Ter.5.2-3 deal with *elevation offerings* which fall into one hundred parts or more of normal produce in varying combinations of *pure* and *impure*.

1. **Impure** elevation offering **falling into pure** deconsecrated produce (m.Ter.5.2).
2. **Pure** elevation offering **falling into impure** deconsecrated produce (m.Ter.5.3).

There is no need to deal with *pure* falling into *pure*, or *impure* falling into *impure*, because in these cases there is no change in the nature of the *elevation offering*.

These rulings show what happened in practice when *elevation offering* was *neutralized* by falling into a hundred or more parts of *deconsecrated* produce. The owner immediately lifted out the quantity which had fallen in and *elevated* it as *elevation offering* anew.

Eliezer argued that what one lifts out should be regarded as the same produce which one dropped in, and so if one dropped in *impure elevation offering* one should treat it as such and burn it. The Sages argued that the *impurity* has been diluted, so that it is like the hybrid *elevation offering* of the third ruling of m.Ter.5.1 and should therefore be treated in the same way as prescribed there.

This practice of 'lifting out' the *elevation offering* which fell in is probably the reason why the word that is used when *elevation offering* is '*neutralized*' is *olah* (עָלָה, literally 'raised'). Another derivation for this word may be the lower market value for produce which is *tainted* by *elevation offering*, so that if the *elevation offering* is *neutralized* and some *elevation offering* is *elevated* again, then the value of the *tainted* produce is raised (see m.Ter.5.1).

Dating (5): All of this debate took place in the generation following 70 CE, but both sides assume that one lifts out replacement *elevation offering* when a mixture is formed. This practice must therefore predate 70 CE.

m.Ter.5.4: *Impurity* of *elevation offering* is not *neutralized*

A *seah* of *impure elevation offering*	סאה תרומה טמאה
which fell into a hundred *seahs*	שנפלה למאה סאה
of *pure elevation offering*:	תרומה טהורה,
The School of Shammai prohibits [it to a priest]	בית שמאי אוסרים,
but the School of Hillel permits it.	ובית הלל מתירין.
The School of Hillel said	אמרו בית הלל
to the School of Shammai:	לבית שמאי,
Since *pure* [*elevation offering*]	הואיל וטהורה
is prohibited to nonpriests	אסורה לזרים
and *impure* [*elevation offering*]	וטמאה
is prohibited to priests,	אסורה לכהנים,
it follows that just as *pure* is *neutralized*,	מה טהורה עולה,
so also *impure* can be *neutralized*.	אף טמאה תעלה.
The School of Shammai said to them: No!	אמרו להם בית שמאי, לא,
If he can *neutralize* ([using] *deconsecrated* [produce]	אם העלו החולין
[which is regarded] leniently	הקלין
[and is] permitted for nonpriests)	המותרין לזרים,
pure [*elevation offering*],	את הטהורה,
[surely] he can *neutralize* ([using] *elevation offering*	תעלה תרומה
[which is regarded] seriously	החמורה
[and is] prohibited to nonpriests)	האסורה לזרים,
impure [*elevation offerings*]?	את הטמאה.
After they [the Shammaites] had yielded [to the Hillelites]	לאחר שהודו,
R. Eliezer [b. Hyrcanus, T2] says:	רבי אליעזר אומר,
Let it be raised and burned.	תרום ותשרף.
And the Sages say:	וחכמים אומרים,
It is nullified by smallness.	אבדה במעוטה.

Comments: This tradition investigates yet another permutation which has not been covered in m.Ter.5.1-3: *impure elevation offering* falling into *pure elevation offering*. The Hillelites argued that *impurity* can be neutralized just like the status of *elevation offering*. The Shammaites say that if *deconsecrated* produce can neutralize something which is *pure* (as in m.Ter.5.1), then how can one say that *elevation offering* can neutralize something which is *impure*? After the Shammaites had agreed (or perhaps when they lost their majority after 70 CE),[4] Eliezer came to the same conclusion but with a different argument (as seen in m.Ter.5.2).

Dating (1): There is no reason to doubt that this was a genuine school debate, especially as it appears to provide the background for Eliezer's dispute in m.Ter.5.2 and to be related to the first (and earliest) ruling in m.Ter.5.1.

The explanations given by the schools for their positions are likely to reflect their reasoning accurately, especially as the Shammaites appear to have a strong case. However this explanation was almost certainly added later, and probably after 70 CE. This school debate is carried on at greater length at t.Ter.6.4, but that expansion is almost certainly later than 70 CE.

New Testament: The terms used for 'permit' and 'prohibit' usually occur separately, in the form "so-and-so rules such-and-such but so-and-so permits/prohibits it." This tradition is unusual in that both terms occur together. The literal meaning of these terms are 'release' or 'loose' and 'tie' or 'bind,' so it is very likely that these are the precise terms behind the sayings in Matthew about 'loosing and binding' (Mt.16.19; 18.18).

m.Ter.6.1–8.3: Wrongful consumption of *elevation offerings*

Summary of Mishnah: If a nonpriest unintentionally consumes *elevation offering*, he repays the owner the *full value* (who must accept it) plus an *added fifth* of the value to any priest (6.1-3). The repayment is by the person who ate or offered the food to a guest (or twice as much if he stole it—6.4, cf. Exod.22.7), but the *added fifth* is paid by the person who actually ate it (6.3-4). You repay with *deconsecrated* food (6.1) of the same type or better, though later they said it must be exactly the same (6.6). You do not repay with harvest *leftovers* or tithes or *dedications* (6.5). This *deconsecrated* food gains the status of *elevation offering* which the priest cannot refuse (6.1).

The *added fifth* is not paid by someone who eats intentionally (7.1), a daughter of a priest who becomes ineligible (7.2), a minor or slave or someone who eats *elevation offering* originating outside Israel or a very small quantity (7.3). When the *added fifth* is not paid, the repayment does not become *elevation offering* and the priest does not need to accept it (7.1, 3, 4). Is it paid by a wife or slave of a priest or by a priest who has become ineligible (8.1)? If you are eating *elevation offering* when you become

---

[4] Or perhaps the Hillelites agree with the Shammaites—this possibility is debated at y.Ter.5.4 on the basis that Eliezer was a Shammaite (which is very questionable) who here yields to the Hillelite view.

ineligible, should you swallow or spit (8.2)? Similarly, what if you are eating something when it became liable for tithing (8.3)?

If you are uncertain which container holds *elevation offering*, you may assume it is one from which you have not eaten (7.5) or one which did not spill into other food (7.6), or one with which you did not sow (7.7).

The following traditions have elements (marked in bold) for which there is evidence of an origin before 70 CE:

m.Ter.6.4 and t.Ter.7.8a: Stolen *elevation offerings* and *dedications*.

m.Ter.6.4

He who steals [some] *elevation offering*	הגונב תרומה
but does not eat it	ולא אכלה,
recompenses a recompense of double	משלם תשלומי כפל
the *valuation* of the *elevation offering*.	דמי תרומה.
[He who unintentionally] ate it,	אכלה,
recompenses two *full values* **and an** *added fifth;*	משלם שני קרנים וחומש,
[one] *full value* **and an** *added fifth* **[is paid]**	קרן וחומש
from *deconsecrated* **[produce]**	מן החולין,
and [the other] monetary *full value*	וקרן דמי
[from] *elevation offering*.	תרומה.
[If] he stole [some] *elevation offering* **of dedication**	גנב תרומת הקדש
and [unintentionally] ate it,	ואכלה,
he recompenses two *added fifths* **and a** *full value,*	משלם שני חמשים וקרן,
for with a *dedication* **there is no**	שאין בהקדש
recompense of double.	תשלומי כפל.

t.Ter.7.8a:

He who steals [some] *elevation offering* **of dedication**	הגונב תרומת הקדש
and does not eat it	ולא אכלה,
recompenses the *full value*	משלם את הקרן
but he does not recompense the *added fifth*	ואינו משלם את החומש,
but double [recompense] is not with this [type of theft]	וכפל אין בה,
as it is said [Exod.22.9(8)]:	שנאמר
"he shall recompense double to his neighbor"	ישלם שנים לרעהו,
but not for what is *dedicated* [to the Temple].	ולא להקדש.
[But if he who steals it unintentionally] eats it,	אכלה,
he recompenses two added *fifths* **[and a** *full value*].*¹	משלם שני חומשין,
The *full value* **and [first]** *added fifth*	קרן וחומש
[he provides] from *deconsecrated* **[produce]**	מן החולין,
and it becomes holy like *elevation offering*.	והן נעשין קדש כתרומה.
The *full value* **he gives to the [Temple] Treasurer**	קרן נותן לגזבר
and the [first] *added fifth to* **the [original] owners.**	וחומש לבעלים.

The *full value* is [liable to the law of] *misuse*.	בקרן זה מועלין,
The *added fifth* is not [liable to] *misuse*.	בחומש זה אין מועלין.
The second *added fifth*	חומש שני
[he provides from] *elevation offering*	תרומה
or with *valuation of the elevation offering*;*²	ודמיי תרומה,
he gives [it] to the [Temple] Treasurer	נותן לגזבר
and the [first] *added fifth* to the [original] owners.*³	וחומש לבעלים.

---

*1 Z reads שני קרנים וחומש 'two *full values* and an *added fifth*.
*2 Z omits this line.
*3 This unnecessary repetitive last line is missing from some editions.

Comments: There was such a strong taboo against eating *elevation offerings* that even a thief was assumed to avoid it, and even a thief was expected to separate *elevation offerings* from what he had stolen (cf. t.Ter.1.6). The general principles are that if you eat *elevation offering* unintentionally you recompense with the *full value* plus an *added fifth,* and if you steal something you pay double as recompense.

Therefore if a thief stole some produce and then found out that it was *elevation offering*, or that it was completely untithed so that it still contained the *elevation offering*, what should he do? If he had not eaten it he would have been liable to pay double recompense of the *full value* (Exod.22.9[8])—though it is unlikely that he would do so and this comment was probably appended merely in order to state the general principle. In practice the thief would simply hand in the portion which was *elevation offering* or (more likely) destroy it. But what if he had eaten it? Then, as well as paying double recompense because it was stolen, he should also pay an *added fifth* because it was eaten.

However, if someone stole and ate a *dedicated* crop which had not been tithed, this included the *elevation offering* of a *dedication*, and this was doubly *consecrated*—once as an *elevation offering* and again as a *dedication*. Therefore, if he ate it accidentally he should pay not only the *full value* twice (because it was stolen) but also the *added fifth* twice—one to a priest because it was an *elevation offering* and one to the Temple because it was a *dedication*.

Tosefta pointed out that in fact a thief cannot pay the *full value* twice for a stolen *dedication* because the recompense has to be paid to your "neighbor" (according to Exod.22.9[8]) and a *dedication* belongs to God or the Temple, and not to a person.

Dating (8): The references to a '*dedication*' (which always means a *dedication* to the Temple in the Mishnah) suggests a context before 70 CE. Although references to '*dedication*' can sometimes occur in later debates, especially when it is part of a common phrase such as "*second tithe* or *dedication*," it clearly stands on its own in this tradition, and the reference to the Temple Treasurer (cf. m.Pea.1.6; 2.8; 4.8) confirms this. The concept of paying recompense for unintentionally eating some *elevation offering* already occurred before 70 CE, because it is assumed to be an established practice by Eliezer b. Hyrcanus [T2] in m.Ter.6.6. The Scripture proof from Exodus 22 may have been added later.

This debate confirms the meaning of "*dedication*" as 'a *dedication* to the Temple' because one of the *added fifth*s for the *elevation offering* of *dedication* is paid to the Temple, as an indication of the Temple's ownership of it. The Jerusalem Talmud continues to speak about paying this *added fifth* to the Temple (y.Ter.6.4 where it is affirmed by R. Yannai and R. Kahana) which implies that they still understood it to mean 'a *dedication* to the Temple.'

m.Ter.6.5: Recompense for accidentally eating some *elevation offering*

One should not recompense [accidentally eaten *elevation offering*]	אֵין מְשַׁלְּמִין
from *gleanings* or from *forgotten* [harvest produce]	מִן הַלֶּקֶט וּמִן הַשִּׁכְחָה
or from *corner* [crop left at harvest for the poor]	וּמִן הַפֵּאָה
or from [property which has been declared] *ownerless*	וּמִן הַהֶפְקֵר,
and not from *first tithe*	וְלֹא מִמַּעֲשֵׂר רִאשׁוֹן
from which the *elevation offering* is removed,	שֶׁנִּטְּלָה תְרוּמָתוֹ,
and not from *second tithe*	וְלֹא מִמַּעֲשֵׂר שֵׁנִי
or a *dedication* which is redeemed.	וְהֶקְדֵּשׁ שֶׁנִּפְדּוּ,
For the *consecrated* thing does not redeem	שֶׁאֵין הַקֹּדֶשׁ פּוֹדֶה
the *consecrated* thing.	אֶת הַקֹּדֶשׁ,
—the words of R. Meir [T4].	דִּבְרֵי רַבִּי מֵאִיר.
But the Sages permit in these [cases].	וַחֲכָמִים, מַתִּירִין בְּאֵלּוּ.

Comments: If you accidentally eat some *elevation offering* (or other *consecrated* food such as tithes or *dedication*), you pay recompense for it (see previous Comments). You must not pay this recompense from what you do not own, such as harvest *leftovers* (which belong to the poor) or from *consecrated* produce (which belongs to the priests or Temple). This is exactly the same list which defines the produce from which one cannot *elevate elevation offerings* in the first place (m.Ter.1.5).

Meir's saying contains a word which can be pointed in two ways: *ha-qodesh* "the *consecrated* thing" (הַקֹּדֶשׁ) or *heqdesh* "a *dedication*" (הֶקְדֵּשׁ). Some translators have followed the latter pointing which is influenced by the occurrence of the word "*dedication*" (*heqdesh*) in the previous line.[5] However, the first translation is much better because a "*consecrated* thing" can include *elevation offerings*, tithes, and *dedications* (see the chart in the introduction to *Demay*). This pointing is confirmed by the fact that the second half of Meir's saying (אֶת הַקֹּדֶשׁ) appears to be cited from

---

[5] English translations which use "dedication" include Blackman and Danby. Alan Avery-Peck in Neusner's edition translates "consecrated."

Lev.22.14 which is also cited in the next mishnah (m.Ter.6.6) and which is pointed *ha-qodesh*.

Dating (9): The term "*consecrated* thing" (*ha-qodesh*, הַקֹּדֶשׁ) occurs rarely. Instead of using this collective term, many rulings list the *consecrated* things (*elevation offerings*, *tithes*, and *dedications*). This means that the occurrence of the term '*dedication*' is not very significant in such traditions, because even after 70 CE (when no one *dedicated* goods, except by accident), it would still be traditional to include it in such lists. The phrase "*Second tithe* or *dedication* which is redeemed" also occurs frequently in Mishnah and especially in this tractate (m.Ter.1.5; 6.5; 8.2; cf. 9.4) and it is likely that this phrase remained in use after *dedications* had ceased.[6] There is nothing else in this tradition to suggest that it dates from before 70 CE.

m.Ter.8.2b: If you find you are eating unlawful food, spit it out

[If they said to him] "You were *impure*	טמא היית
[when you began eating *elevation offering*]"	
or "The *elevation offering* was *impure*,"	וטמאה היתה תרומה,
or [if] it became known that [the food he is eating]	או נודע שהוא
was *untithed*, or *first tithe*	טבל, ומעשר ראשון
from which *elevation offering* is not removed,	שלא נטלה תרומתו,
or *second tithe* or *dedication*	ומעשר שני והקדש
which has not been redeemed,	שלא נפדו,
or he tastes the taste of insect*	או שטעם טעם פשפש
in the middle of his mouth,	לתוך פיו,
behold, this one must spit [it out].	הרי זה יפלוט.

*The rare word פשפש refers to the mashed insides of insects, the taste or smell of which
    was familiar in a society which ate locusts.

Comments: This follows a discussion about whether you should spit or swallow when you discover that you are no longer permitted to eat the *elevation offering* which is in your mouth (m.Ter.8.1-2a). The tradition here (m.Ter.8.2b) says that you should always spit out food if you discover that you had not been permitted to eat it in the first place.

Dating (9): The reference to a *dedication* to the Temple may indicate a pre-70 date, but it is possible that it is included here merely as part of the common phrase "*second tithe* or *dedication* which is (not) redeemed" (cf. Dating at m.Ter.6.5). This tradition occurs immediately after a debate between R. Eliezer (b. Hyrcanus) [T2] and

---

[6] E.g. at t.Ter.10.2 where it is used by R. Jacob b. Korshai [T4] in the name of Dosa [b. Harkinas, T2]: "The same restrictions which apply to the eating of [refuse of produce in the status of] *elevation offering* apply to untithed produce, *first tithe* from which [its] *elevation offering* has not been separated, and *second tithe* or *dedication* which has not been redeemed."

R. Joshua (b. Hananiah) [T2], though this does not mean that it dates from the same time.

m.Ter.7.2: When a priest's daughter cannot eat *elevation offering*

The daughter of a priest who married an Israelite	בת כהן שנשאת לישראל
and after this [unintentionally] ate	ואחר כך אכלה
elevation offering recompenses the *full value*	תרומה, משלמת את הקרן
but she does not recompense the *added fifth*.	ואינה משלמת את החומש.
And [if she commits adultery] her death is by burning.	ומיתתה בשרפה.
[If] she marries one from all those [who are]	נשאת לאחד מכל
ineligible [to marry into a priest's family,	הפסולין,
and then she eats *elevation offering*],	
she recompenses the *full value* and the *added fifth*.	משלמת קרן וחומש.
And [if she commits adultery] her death is by strangling	ומיתתה בחנק.
—the words of R. Meir [T4].	דברי רבי מאיר.
And the Sages say: For both [of them],	וחכמים אומרים, זו וזו
one should recompense the *full value*	משלמות את הקרן
and one should not recompense the *added fifth*;	ואינן משלמות את החומש,
and their death is by burning.	ומיתתן בשרפה.

Comments: A priest's family could eat *elevation offerings* of produce at home, but when a priest's daughter married a nonpriest she was no longer counted as part of a priest's family (Lev.22.12). However, if she accidentally ate *elevation offering*, perhaps while visiting her family, she was not as guilty as a nonpriest, and so she did not pay the *added fifth*. Meir felt that if she had married someone who was ineligible to marry into a priest's family (such as an *illegitimate*), she no longer had any connection to her family, and so she should pay the *added fifth*, but the majority (the 'Sages') disagreed with the idea of this distinction.

Torah said that an adulterous priest's daughter should be punished by burning (Lev.21.9), and a woman who was found to be a non-virgin on her wedding night should be punished by stoning (Deut.22.21), but the form of death for other adulterous women was not prescribed. In m.San.11.1 there is a list of crimes which are punished by strangling, and their only shared characteristic is the silence in Torah about the form of death for these crimes. This list does not include an adulteress (though it includes an adulterer) but this tradition here suggests that adulteresses could be included.

Dating (2): The debate started by Meir is clearly late, but the tradition which he is debating predates Eliezer b. Hyrcanus [T2] because Eliezer assumes this to be an established ruling in m.Ter.8.1. Therefore it predates 70 CE.

The detail about death by burning is less certain, because it may have been added after Meir introduced his debate. However, the process of burning a priest's daughter is attested in a *baraytah* preserved by Eliezer b. Zadok in m.San.7.2, where the practical details of such burning are discussed. It is uncertain whether this is Eliezer b. Zadok I [T2] or II [T5], but the Babylonian Talmud assumes he is the earlier and that he is remembering what happened in the days when the Sadducees ruled the Sanhedrin before 70 CE (b.San.52b). Therefore it is reasonable to assume that this was part of this debate, or at least that it is not anachronistically attached to it.

New Testament: The proposed stoning of the adulteress in John 8 has often been regarded as unhistorical, despite the fact that it is difficult to think of who would have invented it because it flies in the face of the strict moral teachings of the church. Roger David Aus has made a good defense for its historicity.[7] He points out that although the Jews had lost the formal right to execute criminals,[8] zealots in the Temple were known to execute people on the spot (m.San.9.6). If this event is historical, one has to wonder whether adulteresses were executed by stoning or strangling.

Most other commentators assume that the crowd envisioned in John 8 was simply a mob. As pointed out above, the Torah is silent on the mode of death for an adulteress, and although the rabbis assumed one should use strangulation in these cases, this was not certain. It is therefore likely that a mob would use the mode prescribed in Torah for the similar crime of being found to have been unfaithful before marriage (Deut.22.21). However, the reality of the situation is probably that there were few if any instances of the death penalty for adultery,[9] and so the mob would not be familiar with the rabbinic law on this matter (if they cared).

---

[7] "Caught in the Act," in *Walking on the Sea and the Release of Barabbas Revisited* (Atlanta: Scholars, 1998), esp. pp. 1-26.

[8] According to the Babylonian Talmud, the death penalty was abolished soon after 30 CE ("forty years before the destruction of the Temple," b.Shab.15a; b.AZ 8a). The reference to "forty years before the destruction of the Temple" may be figurative, because several other events are dated to this point (b.Yom:39a; cf. b.RS 31b). However, it is significant that there is no record of official death penalties, and rabbinic literature argues strongly against the use of the death penalty (b.Nid:44b-45a; m.Yeb.1.3), presumably partly because of their inability to carry it out.

[9] Some rabbinic rulings would make no sense if the death penalty were carried out for adultery, e.g., the rule that an unfaithful wife cannot marry her lover (m.Sot.5.1) and that if such a marriage took place, they had to divorce (m.Yeb.2.8). Josephus's casual assertion that the penalty for adultery was death is probably an antiquarian note rather than a record of experience (*C.Apion.*2.25). See the discussions in Louis M. Epstein, *Sex Laws and Customs in Judaism,* pp. 201-2, 210-11; I. Abrahams, *Studies in Pharisaism and the Gospels,* p. 73.

m.Ter.8.4-12: Spoiled food

Summary of Mishnah: Water, wine, and milk must be covered to prevent possible contamination by snakes and other reptiles (8.4), though large bodies of water may dilute it sufficiently (8.5), and any fruit or animals with snake bites must not be eaten (8.6). A sieve will protect from snakes but not from other *impurity* (8.7). If it was already uncovered, should one protect it (8.8)? And if it is spilling, should one try to rescue some (8.9-10)? Even if a gentile threatens to render *impure* all your *elevation offerings*, you should not give him one (8.11), and similarly if they threaten your women (8.12).

The following traditions have elements (marked in bold) for which there is evidence of an origin before 70 CE:

m.Ter.8.4: Uncovered drinks are spoiled by reptiles

Wine which [has the status of] *elevation offering*,	יין של תרומה
which is uncovered:	שנתגלה,
It must be poured away [lest it has been spoiled].	ישפך.
And it is self evident [lit., 'not necessary to say']	ואין צריך לומר
that [this also applies] to *deconsecrated* [wine].	של חולין.
Three [types of] liquid	שלשה משקין,
are prohibited if they have been uncovered:	אסורין משום גלוי,
water and wine and milk,	המים והיין והחלב.
but all other liquids are permitted.	ושאר כל המשקין, מותרין.
How long [do they have to] remain [uncovered]	כמה ישהו
to be prohibited?	ויהיו אסורין,
[Long enough] so that a reptile can come	כדי שיצא הרחש
from a nearby place and drink.	ממקום קרוב וישתה.

Comments: Wine can be spoiled if it is uncovered long enough for a snake or other reptile to deposit poison in it while drinking from it. This only applied to the three liquids which creatures liked to drink.

Dating (2): A debate by Eliezer b. Hyrcanus [T2] in m.Ter.8.8 assumes the opening ruling and debates whether it is worth moving vulnerable liquids to a safer place. Therefore the opening ruling was already established in Eliezer's time, and so it predates 70 CE.

The rest of this mishnah is a commentary on that ruling. First it argues that this should also apply to *deconsecrated* wine. Then at a later date someone added that it applies to the standard three liquids. Then at the same time or later someone added that the minimum time is long enough for a reptile to drink from it and hide again.

m.Ter.8.6: Beware of snake bites in fruit or animal carcasses

[If you find] perforations [by animals such as snakes] in **figs or grapes**	נִקּוּרֵי תְאֵנִים וַעֲנָבִים
or cucumbers or gourds	וְקִשּׁוּאִין וְהַדְּלוּעִין
or watermelons or squash,	וְהָאֲבַטִּיחִים וְהַמְּלָפְפוֹנוֹת,
even as much as a *kikar* [a huge weight],	אֲפִילוּ הֵם כִּכָּר,
[it is] one and the same for big or small,	אֶחָד גָּדוֹל וְאֶחָד קָטָן,
one and the same for picked or unpicked,	אֶחָד תָּלוּשׁ וְאֶחָד מְחוּבָּר,
[and for] anything which has moisture in it:	כָּל שֶׁיֵּשׁ בּוֹ לֵחָה,
[It is] prohibited [for eating].	אָסוּר.
And [an animal] bitten by a snake is prohibited,	וּנְשׁוּכַת הַנָּחָשׁ, אֲסוּרָה,
because [it is] a danger to lives.	מִפְּנֵי סַכָּנַת נְפָשׁוֹת.

Comments: Any food which contains moisture could be contaminated by snake venom without the eater being aware, and so puncture marks meant the food must be thrown away.

This ruling has nothing to do with *elevation offerings* but it follows on from the ruling in m.Ter.8.4 about not using spoiled food for *elevation offerings*.

Dating (2): The rejection of punctured figs and grapes is assumed by Eliezer b. Hyrcanus [T2] in a *baraytah* in y.Ter.8.7.II:

> It is taught: R. Eliezer says: A person may eat figs or grapes at night [when it is too dark to see puncture marks] and he need not be apprehensive, for it is said [in Ps.116.6]: *"The Lord preserves the simple."*

The genuineness of this *baraytah* is uncertain because this saying verges on *aggadah* rather than *halakhah*—and so there may have been less care taken with regard to transmission—and because it is not recorded anywhere in Mishnah or Tosefta.

The fact that Eliezer refers only to figs and grapes rather than the complete list or the generic description ("anything which has moisture in it") may suggest that he knew this ruling before all the other details were added.

t.Ter.7.11 (Z.7.11-12): Food spoiled by insects

R. Joshua [b. Hananiah, T2] says	רַבִּי יְהוֹשֻׁעַ אוֹמֵר
Blood [of an insect] which is on a loaf:	דַּם שֶׁעַל הַכִּכָּר,
He rubs [off the bread at] its place [where the blood is seen]	גּוֹרֵר אֶת מְקוֹמוֹ
and eats the remainder.	וְאוֹכֵל אֶת הַשְּׁאָר.
[If] it is found between his teeth,	נִמְצָא בֵּין שִׁנָּיו,
he brushes it [off] and does not agonize [about it].	מְשַׁפְשְׁפוֹ וְאֵינוֹ חוֹשֵׁשׁ.
He who eats a grain worm or an ant	הָאוֹכֵל הַדִּירָה וְאֶת הַנְּמָלָה
or a louse which is in produce, is liable.	וְאֶת הַכִּינָה שֶׁבַּתְּבוּאָה חַיָּיב.
[Or] a mite which is in lentils	אֶת הַזִּיז שֶׁבָּעֲדָשִׁין,
or gnats which are in pods	וְאֶת יַתּוּשִׁין שֶׁבַּכְּלִיסִין

or worms which are in dates	וְאֶת הַתּוֹלָעִין שֶׁבַּתְּמָרִים
or which are in dried figs, he is exempt [if he eats them].	וְשֶׁבַּגְּרוֹגְרוֹת פָּטוּר.
[If] he set it aside [i.e., removed any of the above creatures from food]	פֵּרְשׁוּ
and returned it [to the food], he is liable.	וְחָזְרוּ, חַיָּב.
[If one ate] worms which are in tree roots	אֶת הַתּוֹלָעִין שֶׁבְּעִיקְרֵי אִילָנוֹת,
or the leech which is in vegetables, he is liable.	וְאֶת הַקְּפָּא שֶׁבְּיָרָק חַיָּב.
Gnats which are in wine or in vinegar,	יַבְחוּשִׁין שֶׁבַּיַּיִן וְשֶׁבַּחוֹמֶץ,
behold, these are permitted.*1	הֲרֵי אֵלּוּ מוּתָּרִין.
If he filtered [them out of the wine]*1	אִם סִינְּן,
behold, these are prohibited.	הֲרֵי אֵלּוּ אֲסוּרִין.
R. Judah [b. Illai, T4] says:	רַבִּי יְהוּדָה אוֹמֵר
He who strains wine or vinegar*2	מְסַנְּנִין אֶת הַיַּיִן וְאֶת הַחוֹמֶץ,
or he who blesses the Sun	וְהַמְּבָרֵךְ עַל הַחַמָּה
Behold, this is another way [i.e., heresy].	הֲרֵי זֶה דֶרֶךְ אַחֶרֶת.

*1 Z omits this line.
*2 Some editions read הַמְפַנִּין 'cleans out' for מְסַנְּנִין.

Comments: What should you do if there is small creature in your food? Some creatures matter more than others. The common factor for those which do not matter appears to be the fact that one cannot necessarily see them—they are hidden inside a pod or a fig, etc. (cf. y.Ter.8.3.II). Worms which live inside tree roots do not share this exemption perhaps because the roots are boiled and mashed, so that the creature would become visible.

The main exception to this principle is a gnat in wine or vinegar (i.e., cheap soured wine). You can strain out the wine, but if you see a gnat while you are drinking, you can ignore it. R. Judah says you *must* ignore it and removing it is as heretical as praying to the sun. Presumably he is concerned because picking out a gnat and flicking it to the ground was similar to the performance of a *libation offering*, as carried out by most gentiles when they drank wine. Therefore someone might see it and think that a Jew was giving a *libation offering* to the emperor, or someone might pretend to pick out a gnat to cover up the fact that he *was* giving a secret *libation offering*.[10]

Why was there any need to prohibit someone from returning a strained gnat back into wine? When wine was strained to remove the lees, they were often kept for making very cheap wine by flavoring water with the lees (cf. t.Ter.10.12, below). This ruling said that you may not make cheap wine by mixing the lees with water and then sieving it, because this would be re-adding any gnats which had been removed. Therefore one had to slowly run water through the lees in the sieve, so that the water

---

[10] Later Talmudic commentators felt that it was heretical to remove a gnat because it had been blessed when the wine was blessed, and it was of the same substance as the wine. This view may have been based on the belief that gnats were spontaneously generated within wine.

was flavored but none of the gnats entered the water even temporarily. This method transmitted much less flavor to the water than mixing the lees and then filtering them out again.

Dating (9): On the internal evidence of this tradition, none of it can be dated before 70 CE, though the tradition of Joshua b. Hananiah, who taught just after 70 CE, suggests that these matters were important before 70 CE, and that the details were not yet definite.

It is difficult to know how much of this tradition can be dated back to Joshua. The ruling about blood on bread is certainly his, and probably the one about blood on teeth, and possibly the first two lists of creatures which one can or cannot ignore. However it is very unlikely that the supplementary list of root worms and leeches or the ruling about gnats in wine can be attributed to him.

The ruling about gnats in wine was probably added later as an example to illustrate the strange ruling that you cannot remove creatures and then return them to the food. This very unlikely occurrence makes sense with regard to wine lees, as explained in the Comments above. Therefore the more general ruling about not returning a removed creature was probably based on this older specific ruling.

The ruling about gnats in wine includes the prohibition of gnats in lees, which meant that people had to pour water through the lees in a sieve in order to flavor the water. This practice already occurred in the Temple period (see t.Ter.10.12 below, though the dating is not certain). If this ruling had not been in place, people would have mixed the lees with water and then refiltered it, which would have given much more flavor to the water. The early date also gains some confirmation from the Gospel reference to straining gnats (see New Testament below).

The removal of a gnat while drinking was called a heresy by Judah in the mid second century. This may have been a prohibition which he initiated, or he may have been emphasizing a traditional ruling because of the increasing pressures for Jews to conform to pagan customs in his day.

New Testament: Jesus criticized those rabbis who "strain at a gnat and swallow a camel" (Mt.23.24), by which he presumably means that they were more concerned about tiny matters of the law than the greater matters of morality.[11] This ruling about gnats must have been particularly irksome to the poor people who made the very cheap wine from the lees, and which was much more difficult when you had to use

---

[11] This is one of a series of examples where Jesus brings a moral message out of a *halakhah*, which is discussed by Menahem Kister in "Law, Morality, and Rhetoric in Some Sayings of Jesus," in *Studies in Ancient Midrash*, ed. James L. Kugal (Cambridge, Mass.: Harvard University Center for Jewish Studies, 2001), vol. 2, pp. 145-54, esp. pp. 148f. Other *halakhot* which he discusses include 'purifying inside a vessel', and 'what goes into your mouth.'

the cumbersome method of pouring water through the lees. Jesus may have had in mind the social consequences of this *halakhic* ruling.

m.Ter.9.1–11.5: Food produced from *elevation offerings*

Summary of Mishnah: If you sow with *elevation offerings*, you should plough it up unless you intended to sow it, or unless it has already grown by one-third (9.1). In that case you let it grow but treat the whole harvest as *elevation offerings*. Harvest *leftovers* and tithes of this produce are sold by the poor and Levites as *elevation offerings,* and they keep the money (9.2-3). This does not happen if you re-sow this produce, or if you sow from other *consecrated* crops (9.4), unless the seed remains intact (9.5-6), or if you sow *impure elevation offering* sapling seed (9.7).

Elevation offering taints food which it is cooked with only if it imparts flavor or leaven (10.1-5). Fenugreek stalks must be considered alongside the seeds in this matter (10.5) and other matters (10.6). Crushed olives are *tainted* by *elevation offerings*, but not whole olives (10.7). What proportion of *impure* fish *taints* pickling brine (10.8)? *Impure* locusts do not *taint* their brine (10.9). Food is not *tainted* when pickled with any *elevation offerings* except leeks (10.10), or when boiled with any *elevation offerings* except beets or meat (10.11), though the liquid pickle or broth is restricted to priests (10.12). You may not use *elevation offering* in a process which makes it inedible (11.1).

Do juices made from *elevation offering* inherit this status (11.2)? No, because these do not pass on *impurity* (11.2) and anyway you may not make them from *elevation offerings* (11.3). Parts of an *elevation offering* such as stalks and bran are allowed to nonpriests if they are thrown out, though he may not throw out the coarse sieving of fine flour (11.4-5).

The following traditions have elements (marked in bold) for which there is evidence of an origin before 70 CE:

m.Ter.9.4: Crops grown from *consecrated* food

That which grows from *elevation offering*	גדולי תרומה,
[has the status of] *elevation offering*,	תרומה.
and the growth from [the seeds of this] growth	וגדולי גדולין,
[has the status of] *deconsecrated* [produce].	חולין.
But, that which is *untithed*	אבל הטבל
or *first tithes*	ומעשר ראשון
or after-growths of the Sabbath Year	וספיחי שביעית
or *elevation offerings* [from] outside the Land	ותרומת חוצה לארץ
or [food] *tainted* [with *elevation offering*]	והמדומע
or firstfruits	והבכורים,

—their growths are *deconsecrated*.	גְּדוּלֵיהֶן, חֻלִּין.
Growths from a *dedication* or *second tithe*	גְּדוּלֵי הַקֹּדֶשׁ וּמַעֲשֵׂר שֵׁנִי,
—[their growths are] *deconsecrated*	חֻלִּין,
and one redeems them	וּפוֹדֶה אוֹתָם
at the time they are sown.	בִּזְמַן זַרְעָם.

Comments: If seed which has the status of *elevation offering* is sown, the crop which grows from it also has the status of *elevation offering*. But if seed from this crop is grown, the status of *elevation offering* is not passed on to the next crop. Other *consecrated* produce does not pass on its status in this way, though a *dedication* or *second tithe* should be redeemed if it has been sown.

Dating (9): Although this contains a reference to a *dedication* to the Temple, this may merely have been included because of the frequent phrase "*second tithe* or *dedication* which is redeemed" (cf. Dating at m.Ter.6.5). It may be significant that this tradition reverses the normal order to "*dedication* or *second tithe*" because this may possibly indicate that the inclusion of "*dedication*" is more than just a conventional mention of an anachronistic custom.

m.Ter.10.5: *Tainting* by fenugreek

[*Consecrated*] fenugreek which fell into the middle of	תִּלְתָּן שֶׁנָּפְלָה לְתוֹךְ
the vat of [*deconsecrated*] wine:	הַבּוֹר שֶׁל יַיִן,
When it is *elevation offering* or *second tithe*:	בַּתְּרוּמָה וּבְמַעֲשֵׂר שֵׁנִי,
If the seed is [by itself, without the stalk]	אִם יֵשׁ בַּזֶּרַע
able to give flavor [to the wine]	כְּדֵי לִתֵּן טַעַם,
[then the wine takes on the status of the fenugreek].	
but not [if it flavors it by means of] the stalk.	אֲבָל לֹא בָעֵץ.
When it is by Sabbath Year [produce]	בַּשְּׁבִיעִית
or by *mixtures of the vineyard*	וּבְכִלְאֵי הַכֶּרֶם
or a *dedication* [to the Temple]:	וְהַקֹּדֶשׁ,
If the seed with the stalk is	אִם יֵשׁ בַּזֶּרַע וּבָעֵץ
able to give flavor [to the wine]	כְּדֵי לִתֵּן טַעַם.
[then the wine takes on the status of the fenugreek].	

Comments: Fenugreek seeds were used to flavor food and add a pleasant smell to hay or hair (by putting it in shampoo), but the stalks were not normally eaten or used. However, if the *elevation offering* is *elevated* before the seeds are extracted, the stalks also take on the status of *elevation offering*, though they cannot impart this status. However, when the fenugreek has other types of *consecrated* status which does not depend on it being consumed by priests, the stalks *can* impart their status. The "*mixtures of a vineyard*" is the type of mixture which results in crops being '*sanctified*' (see m.Kil.4.1–5.8).

Tainting by fenugreek was potentially much more serious than *tainting* by other produce, because it could *taint* dissimilar produce. If beans fell into corn, they could be picked out with certainty, and *tainting* only happened when corn fell into corn or beans into beans, because the original *elevation offering* could not be identified. However, if fenugreek fell into wine and flavored it, then the whole vat became *elevation offering*, and this *tainting* was not limited to one hundred parts of *deconsecrated* produce (cf. m.Orl.2.4).

Dating (8): The reference to fenugreek which is *dedicated* suggests that this ruling originated before 70 CE. We know from m.MS.2.3-4 that the schools debated the role of fenugreek as *elevation offering,* and this ruling may be a result of those disputes. Although it is listed here alongside *elevation offering* and *second tithe*, the phrasing of this ruling does not appear to be influenced by either the frequently used list of "*elevation offering*, tithes, and *dedications*" or the frequently used phrase "*second tithe* and *dedication* which is redeemed" (cf. Dating at m.Ter.6.5).

m.Ter.10.9: Pickling brine is not *tainted* by *unclean* locusts

Impure locusts which were pickled	חגבים טמאים שנכבשו
with *pure* locusts:	עם חגבים טהורים,
[They] have not invalidated the [pickling] brine.	לא פסלו את צירם.
R. Zadok [I T2 or II T5] testified	העיד רבי צדוק
about the brine of the *impure* locusts	על ציר חגבים טמאים,
that it is *pure*.	שהוא טהור.

Mishnaic parallel: m.Ed.7.2

Comments: Brine can be reused after pickling *impure* locusts, though not after pickling *impure* fish (m.Ter.10.8). Presumably this is because the outer casing of the locusts stop them from flavoring the brine.

Dating (2): Zadok is not making a ruling but testifying to it without attributing it to a specific authority. This suggests that it was a traditional ruling or that he had forgotten who had originated it. Either way, it dates from at least a generation before Zadok. If this is Zadok I, the ruling is pre-70, but if this is Zadok II it is very probably later. The context of this same testimony of Zadok in m.Ed.7.2 suggests that it is Zadok I, because it is listed among other rulings which date from T2, and the rulings of Zadok concerning *purity* in m.Ed.3.8 are commented on by Akiba in m.Kel.12.5, which means that those rulings must be from Zadok I. All this helps to suggest that this ruling is testified by Zadok I.

This tradition is out of place in this tractate because it does not mention *elevation offerings*. It is part of a group of traditions about pickling brine (m.Ter.10.7-10), the first and last of which concern *elevation offerings*. It is unclear whether these traditions were already traditionally linked together and were inserted as an intact group into this tractate or whether the presence of two traditions about brine and *elevation offerings* (m.Ter.10.7, 10) attracted the other two.

New Testament: John the Baptist's food of "locusts and wild honey" (Mt.3.4 // Mk.1.6) was not noteworthy for being unusual but for being unprocessed.

m.Ter.11.5: *Uneaten* portions of *consecrated* food

Fruit stones* of an *elevation offering*,	גרעיני תרומה,
during the time in which [the priest] keeps them,	בזמן שהוא מכנסן,
are prohibited [to a nonpriest].	אסורות.
But if he throws them out, they are permitted.	ואם השליכן, מותרות.
And similarly, bones of *consecrated* [sacrifices],	וכן עצמות הקדשים,
during the time in which [the priest] keeps them,	בזמן שהוא מכנסן,
they are prohibited [to a nonpriest].	אסורין.
But if he throws them out, they are permitted.	ואם השליכן, מותרין.
Crushed [coarse bran] [from *elevation offerings*]	המורסן
is permitted [to nonpriests].	מותר.
Fine bran which is [from *elevation offering* of] fresh [crop]	סובין של חדשות
is prohibited [to a nonpriest],	אסורות.
but [fine bran] which is from old [crop]	ושל ישנות
is permitted to them.	מותרות.
And [the priest] treats *elevation offering*	ונוהג בתרומה
according to the way in which he treats	כדרך שהוא נוהג
deconsecrated [produce, regarding what he throws out].	בחולין.
One who sifts fine flour [so finely that there only remains]	המסלת
a *qab* or two *qabs* [of fine flour] from a *seah*,	קב או קבים לסאה,
must not destroy the remaining [4 or 5 *qabs*]	לא יאבד את השאר,
but must put it in a hidden place.	אלא יניחנו במקום המוצנע.

*Or perhaps 'residue,' lit., 'drops,' 'shavings' occasionally used for 'kernels' or 'fruit stones.'

Comments: Parts of *elevation offering* food which are discarded can be eaten by nonpriests. This includes anything from stones and bones, which would be discarded by any priest, to coarse or older flour, which would be discarded only by a well-off priest. Each priest acts with *elevation offerings* as he normally acts with other food. If the discarded food is too good (such as the remainder after very fine sieving), it is not given to nonpriests but it is hidden and left to rot.

Dating (2): The "*consecrated*" things eaten by the priests are the Temple sacrifices, and there is no reason to add this type of regulation after 70 CE. It is difficult to know whether this has been used as an illustration of a later regulation, or as the basis for later expansion, or how else this might belong with these rulings. Probably the rules about stones and bones were originally linked, and the rest were added later. First the coarse and fine bran, then the caveat about older bran, then the wide variety of practice was united by "according to his normal practice," and finally the caveat was added about good food which is discarded.

This issue was still being debated immediately after 70 CE by Dosa [b. Harkinas, T2] (m.Ter.11.5; m.Ed.3.3) though he appears to want to make the innards of melons and the outer leaves of vegetables automatically available to nonpriests, instead of waiting until they throw them out. He appears to be basing his reasons on m.Ter.11.5 which must therefore predate 70 CE.

t.Ter.10.12: Products from the filtered lees of *consecrated* wine

The filtered lees of *elevation offering* [wine]:	שמרים של תרומה,
The first and second [straining of water through the lees]:	ראשון ושיני
[The resultant flavored water] is prohibited [to nonpriests],	אסור,
but [water of the] third [straining is permitted [to nonpriests].	ושל ישי מותר.
R. Meir [T4] says:	רבי מאיר אומר
The third*1 [straining is prohibited] when it gives flavor.	של ישי בנותן טעם.
[The filtered lees of] *second* [tithe]:*2	שיני,
The first*3 [straining of water through the lees]:	ראשון
[The resultant flavored water] is prohibited [to nonpriests],	אסור
but [water of the] second*4 [straining] is permitted.	ושיני מותר.
R. Meir [T4] says:*5	רבי מאיר אומר
The second*6 [is prohibited] when it gives flavor.	שיני בנותן טעם.
And [filtered lees]*7 of a *dedication*:	ושל הקדש,
The first and second and third [straining of water]:	ראשון ושיני ושל ישי
[The resultant flavored water] is prohibited [to nonpriests],	אסור,
but [water of the] fourth [straining] is permitted.	ורביעי מותר.
R. Meir [T4] says:	רבי מאיר אומר
The fourth [is prohibited] when it gives flavor.	רביעי בנותן טעם.

*1 Z has שיני 'second.'
*2 Z has ושל מעשר, 'And [that] which is of a tithe.' If both are conflated it reads, 'And that which is of *second tithe*.'
*3 Z adds ושני, 'and the second.'
*4 Z has של ישי, 'the third.'
*5 Z has ורבי יהודה, 'And R. Judah [b. Illai, T4].'
*6 Z omits 'The second.'
*7 Z adds חדש, 'new' i.e., of new wine (?).

Comments: The filtered lees were a valuable part of the wine, which a purchaser may be entitled to when he bought wine (cf. m.BM.4.11). It could be used to make a flavored cordial by pouring water through it in a sieve, though one was not allowed to mix it with water to get more flavor out (see Comments at t.Ter.7.11). If the lees were from *elevation offerings* or *second tithes* or *dedications*, the water flavored by the lees gained the status of the lees for the first or even up to the third lot of water poured through it. Meir said it always gained the status of the lees until no more flavor was gained from them.

Dating (9): The only reason for dating any of this tradition before 70 CE would be the mention of a *dedication*. It is likely that this reference to a *dedication* has been added onto an existing tradition, because it looks as if it is out of place. One would expect the rulings to be presented in the order of "one," "two," and then "three" strainings which were prohibited (or the reverse), but instead the order is "two," "one," and then "three" strainings. This suggests that the last one, concerning a *dedication*, was added later. It is impossible to say whether it was added because the problem of a *dedication* came up in case law (i.e., before 70 CE), or because a later editor added it in order to make the ruling more complete.

m.Ter.11.6-10:   *Elevation offering* containers and non-food items

Summary of Mishnah: Emptied containers of *elevation offerings* can be cleaned out as normal (11.6-7). One can ignore up to three drops of liquid without treating it as *elevation offering*. One can ignore a sixty-fourth of a log of *elevation offering* from *doubtfully tithed food* and not bother to take it to a priest (11.8). *Elevation offering* vetches can be fed only to a priest's cow, and *elevation offering* oil can be burned only for the benefit of a priest (11.10).

There is no evidence that any of this section originated before 70 CE.

Related early traditions from other tractates

m.MS.2.3-4: Consumption of *consecrated* fenugreek and vetches

Fenugreek which is [in the status of] *second tithe*	תלתן של מעשר שני,
is eaten when freshly sprouting.	תאכל צמחונים.
And [fenugreek] which is [in the status of] *elevation offering*:	ושל תרומה,
The School of Shammai says:	בית שמאי אומרים,
Everything is done with it in *purity*	כל מעשיה בטהרה,
except shampooing [with it].	חוץ מחפיפתה.
But the School of Hillel says:	ובית הלל אומרים,
Everything can be done with it in *impurity*	כל מעשיה בטומאה,
except soaking it.	חוץ משריתה.
4) Vetches of *second tithe*,	כרשיני מעשר שני,
must be eaten when freshly sprouting,	יאכלו צמחונים,
and they enter Jerusalem and they may leave.	ונכנסין לירושלים ויוצאין.
[If they become] *impure*, R. Tarfon says:*	נטמאו, רבי טרפון אומר,

It must be distributed into [small pieces of] dough.	יתחלקו לעסות.
But the Sages say: It must be redeemed.	וחכמים אומרים, יפדו.
And [vetches] which [are in the status of] *elevation offering*:	ושל תרומה,
The School of Shammai says:	בית שמאי אומרים,
They are soaked and crushed in *purity*	שורין ושפין בטהרה,
and [can be] fed [to cattle] in *impurity*.	ומאכילין בטומאה.
And the School of Hillel says:	ובית הלל אומרים
They are soaked in *purity* and [can be] crushed	שורין בטהרה, ושפין
and fed [to cattle] in *impurity*.	ומאכילין בטומאה.
Shammai says: They must eat them dry.	שמאי אומר, יאכלו צריד.
R. Akiba [T3] says:	רבי עקיבה אומר,
Everything is done with it in *impurity*.	כל מעשיהן בטומאה.

*Some editions read שִׁמְעוֹן, 'Simeon.'
Mishnaic parallel: m.Ed.1.8 // m.Ter.2.4b

Comments: Fenugreek can be used to flavor food or scent hair, while vetches can be eaten or fed to cattle. When they have the status of *second tithe* they should be eaten, but when they are in the status of *elevation offering* the priests can consume them in any way. The Shammaites say that the priests need not be in a state of *purity* if they do not eat them, but the Hillelites say that a state of *purity* is not needed at all, though one may not be in a state of *impurity* when preparing it with water, because the wet food will pass on the *impurity*.

The Hillelites are effectively letting the priests ignore the *elevation offering* status of fenugreek and vetches. This may indicate that they did not feel the need to tithe spices or food which was normally fed to animals. This was presumably based on the argument that neither of these were "food". This may concur with the Hillelite ruling that spiced oil was exempt from *doubtful* status (m.Dem.1.3). Later generations from the mid second century did *elevate elevation offerings* from spices.[12]

As pointed out in the Comments to m.Ter.10.5, the practical consequences of making fenugreek into an *elevation offering* could be dire, if it fell into a pot of other produce. This presumably applied to any other spice which was used as a flavoring.

[12] Cf. m.Ter.10.12; m.Orl.2.15; m.Zeb.10.7; m.Uq.3.4-5; and a later comment which prefaces the school debate in m.Orl.2.4, which is commented on in m.Orl.2.6. A debate between the Sages and Eliezer b. Hyrcanus [T2] in m.Maas.4.5 may indicate that the Sages wished to avoid tithing spices, but their motive is not clear. According to an undateable tradition in Tosefta they used to keep different types of *elevation offering* strictly separate, which would have made it very difficult in practice for each person to separate herbs because of the large number of separate containers: "After the destruction of Judea (quickly may it be rebuilt), they began to mix together different types of grain and different types of pulse, but not grain with pulse nor pulse with grain" (t.Ter.10.15). This suggests that the tithing of herbs coincided with a relaxation of this ruling about keeping different types separate.

Dating (1): There is no reason to doubt that these school debates are genuine, especially as later rabbis appear to follow the spirit (if not the letter) of Shammaite rulings in this area. The rulings about eating fenugreek and vetches as *second tithe* are probably later, because these rulings assume that these herbs and animal food *should* be treated as "food" (contra the Hillelite principles).

The comment by "Shammai" is almost certainly a later addition to explain why the Shammaites allowed vetches to be fed in *impurity* whereas they wanted everything to be done in *purity*. The proposed solution is that the Shammaites assumed the vetches would be fed in a dried state, so that there would be no liquid to spread the *impurity*.

New Testament: Jesus criticized some Pharisees for tithing mint and other spices (Mt.23.23 // Lk.11.42). It is possible that he is here in agreement with the Hillelites who did not tithe spices. Jesus may have shared the practical concerns of the Hillelites, though the Gospel writers portray Jesus as highlighting minute adherence to tithing laws while weightier moral matters were being neglected.

Summary and Conclusions

Torah deals with *elevation offerings* of sacrifices which had to be eaten in the Temple and with *elevation offerings* of produce which could be eaten by priests at home. This tractate is concerned only with the non-Temple *elevation offering*, from which one might conclude that this tractate reflects only the concerns of post-70 Judaism. However, Mishnah deals with the *elevation offerings* of sacrifices elsewhere —in the relevant tractates of the *order Qodashim* (Sacrifices) — and the fact that the present tractate is found in the *order Zeraim* (Agriculture), means that we should not be surprised if its remit only concerns the *elevation offerings* of farm produce.

The first half of this tractate is concerned with valid and invalid *elevation offerings* (m.Ter.1.1–4.6). The first two subjects covered in this unit appear in two sections of material with the older material following the earlier.

	mainly early:	mainly late:
Who may *elevate*?	1.1-3	1.6
From what can you *elevate*?	1.4-5	1.7–3.2

This suggests that 1.1-5 formed an early traditional unit, and that by the time later editors added more traditions, they did not feel able to split it up and insert the new material into the appropriate places. So, they simply appended it. This conclusion is not certain because the order of the material could simply be due to the misplacement of the one mishnah 1.6. However, if we accept the material as presented, it appears that 1.6 onward was added to 1.1-5 in the early or mid second century and then late second century editors inserted additional material into individual mishnahs in both the early and later sections wherever they were most appropriate.

Some of the traditions which are included here are very difficult to date (m.Ter.1.5; 5.1; 6.5; 8.2b; 9.4; t.Ter.1.6; 10.12; and 7.11 which depends on 10.12) because although they refer to making a *dedication* to the Temple, it is possible that the term "*dedication*" was included in rulings which originate after 70 CE. The practice of *dedication* almost certainly ceased after 70 CE (see the Introduction re Dating) but the word is used in a couple of legal phrases which may have continued to be used in new rulings after 70 CE (see Dating at m.Ter.6.5).

Torah did not state how much *elevation offering* should be given, but an average of about one-fiftieth was decided very early. Unlike harvest *leftovers*, for which the amount was completely undefined in the earliest stratum of Mishnah (cf. m.Pea.1.1), there is no tradition in this tractate that suggests the amount of *elevation offering* is completely undefined, though the undateable ruling that measuring instruments were disallowed may hark back to such days (m.Ter.1.7).

Elevation offering could be eaten only by priests and their families (m.Ter.7.2), and the penalty for eating them deliberately was death (Num.18.32). It is assumed in this tractate that no nonpriest ever ate it deliberately although a punishment was prescribed for it (m.Hal.1.9; m.Bik.2.1; cf. m.Shebi.8.10 concerning *dough offering*). If someone accidentally ate some *elevation offering*, they restored the amount eaten plus an *added fifth*. It was expected that even thieves would sometimes do this (m.Ter.6.4; and t.Ter.7.8a). When the priests threw out portions of *elevation offering* which they considered inedible, nonpriests could then eat it with impunity (m.Ter.11.5).

Elevating elevation offerings was regarded as a religious act and not just a mechanical act. Before 70 it was already ruled that it could be performed only by those who were capable of acting responsibly in legal matters (i.e., not by a *deaf-mute, imbecile,* or a minor—m.Ter.1.1), and some time after 70 CE the act of elevation was further restricted to those who were capable of making the blessing and those who could act with discernment (m.Ter.1.6, cf. t.Ter.3.1). There is no evidence that the blessings which accompanied the *elevation* of *elevation offerings* were used before 70 CE.

It is assumed in this tractate, as in *Demay*, that every Jewish farmer could be relied on to separate *elevation offerings* from their produce before selling it. It is even assumed that valid *elevation offerings* were separated by Jewish thieves (t.Ter.1.6; m.Ter.6.4; and t.Ter.7.8a), by gentiles, and by Samaritans (m.Ter.3.9). Before 70 CE it was generally assumed that Samaritans separated *elevation offerings*, though they were not trusted to do so after 70 CE (see Comments at m.Ter.3.9). The fact that at least some thieves were expected to be concerned about *elevation offerings* suggests that this taboo was based as much on fear as on personal concerns about morality.

The early material in this tractate tends to be concerned with specific practical problems which later became generalized principles such as 'only *elevate elevation offering* from identical or similar produce' (see m.Ter.1.7–3.2; cf. t.Ter.2.5). The problem of carrying *elevation offerings* to Jerusalem meant that it was easier to take products such as wine and dried figs than to take produce such as grapes or fresh figs. The Hillelites argued that one should take these products to Jerusalem rather than the produce (m.Ter.1.4; t.Ter.3.16), though the Hillelites also said that the grapes themselves had to be taken before they were made *impure* by treading them (t.Ter.3.14a). This confusion, which is compounded by yet more contradiction and various versions in t.Ter.3.12, suggests that the issue was not understood very well by later generations for whom this was no longer of practical concern.

A very pressing practical problem arose when *elevation offerings* were accidentally dropped into *deconsecrated* offerings of the same kind, so that the *elevation offering* could not be extracted with certainty. In this situation the whole container of produce was *tainted* and had to be treated as *elevation offering*, though by 70 CE they had instituted the principle that an *elevation offering* was *neutralized* if it fell into a volume a hundred times as large as itself (m.Ter.4.7). In that situation they simply *elevated* new *elevation offering* from the mixture (see Comments at m.Ter.5.2). *Impurity* could *taint* in the same way (m.Ter.5.1-2) though only the Hillelites thought that it could be *neutralized* (m.Ter.5.4). Crops grown from *elevation offering* seed also inherited the *elevation offering* status (m.Ter.9.4).

Another practical problem before 70 CE concerned spices such as fenugreek which could flavor a whole vat of wine if it was dropped in (m.Ter.10.5). The Hillelites took a practical view and did not really regard fenugreek as having *elevation offering* status (m.MS.2.3-4). It is possible that they were not keen on tithing spices, though this can only be inferred from hints because later rabbis did tithe spices (see Comments at m.MS.2.3-4). *Impurity* was also spread by flavor (cf. m.Ter.10.9).

Elevation offerings (and other food) can be spoiled by reptiles drinking from an uncovered pot (m.Ter.8.4) or puncturing fruit (m.Ter.8.6) or by insects inside the food (t.Ter.7.11). A ruling about gnats which were strained out of wine (t.Ter.7.11) has the consequence of not allowing the mixing of the lees with water to make cheap cordial. Instead, you have to pour the water through the lees in a sieve (t.Ter.10.12), which is much less efficient at imparting the flavor.

There are scant references to how, in practice, *elevation offerings* were distributed before 70 CE, but a few hints suggest that they were taken to Jerusalem and sold to priests by the Temple (cf. Comments at m.Ter.5.1 and at m.Hal.4.10-11; see also m.Sheq.5.4 which refers to selling drink offerings to priests). They might also have been taken to regional collecting points where Temple Treasurers had an office (cf. m.Pea.1.6; 2.8). This may explain why *elevation offerings* from outside Israel (which probably were not brought to Jerusalem) had a lower status (cf. m.Ter.7.3; 9.4). After the destruction of the Temple, *elevation offerings* continued to be given to local priests (cf. m.Bik.2.3; t.Hag.3.33; b.Pes.72b-73a) and the principles involved in *elevating elevation offerings* continued to evolve.

Tractate *Maaserot*: Tithes (First Tithe)

Definitions and Outline

Torah said that the Levites should be given a tithe in exchange for their service (Num.18.21) and in compensation for not inheriting land (Num.18.23-24). This tractate is concerned with this Levites' tithe, which was known as the tithe (*maasar*, מַעֲשֵׂר) or the '*first tithe*' (*maaser rishon*, מַעֲשֵׂר רִאשׁוֹן)—which is the name of this tractate in the Tosefta. This tithe consisted of "the tithe of the land, whether of the seed of the land or the fruit of the tree" (Lev.27.30) and the tithe of "the herds and flocks" (Lev.27.32).

The *first tithe* of "the herds and flocks" is not dealt with in this tractate and it is only dealt with briefly in the tractate on *firstborn* animals (m.Bek.9.1-8), though it is also referred to elsewhere in Mishnah (m.Hag.1.4; m.Tem.1.6). Tithes of animals did not concern the general public because farmers paid the tithe with a whole animal (cf. m.Bek.9.7), and therefore a consumer would not be in danger of buying untithed meat. The *first tithe* of fruit, seed, and vegetables ("corn of the threshing floor, and fullness of the winepress"—Num.18.27) was, in contrast, of great concern to all consumers, because produce was often sold untithed, and so every individual was responsible to tithe the food which they bought in the market.

This tractate is only concerned with produce which is called *untithed* food (*tebel*, טֶבֶל)—which is produce with the *major elevation offering* removed but which is still liable to the rest of the tithing process. It is assumed in this tractate that the *major elevation offering* tithe was always removed by the farmer (with a few possible exceptions which prove the rule—t.Maas.3.8), and this same assumption is found in other tractates (especially *Demay* and *Terumot*).

m.Maas.1.1-7: When you should tithe

The rabbis inferred from Torah that tithing was something which was done to food which is harvested from the land. Therefore the time when a crop could be tithed spanned from the time when it was ready for harvesting (i.e., when it became food) to the last stage of processing it into its edible form.

m.Maas.2.1–3.10: When you may eat *untithed* food

The Law said "Do not muzzle an ox while it is treading out the grain" (Deut.25.4), from which the rabbis inferred that any worker could eat untithed produce during all the time that it was being processed in a public place. This includes anyone who eats a *snack* (*aray*, עֲרַאי, 'incidental [meal]') from produce drying in a public courtyard, from food on its way to market, or from food which is on its way home from the field or market.

m.Maas.4.1–5.8: Produce which might not need tithing

There were grey areas in various definitions: What is 'food'? When does tithing start (does it start when you decide that you will do it, or when you actually start to do it)? What is the last stage of processing various types of food?

m.Maas.1.1-7: The earliest and latest time to tithe

Summary of Mishnah: Crops *can* be tithed [for an *elevation offering*] from the time they become edible (1.1), which is different for different types of fruit (1.2-3) and vegetables (1.4). Crops *must* be tithed after the last stage of harvesting or storing (1.5-8). Until then you can take a random *snack* without tithing it. The very last stage is usually when you take it home or to market (1.5).

The following traditions have elements (marked in bold) for which there is evidence of an origin before 70 CE:

t.Maas.1.1a (Z.1.1): Produce becomes *untithed* at the end of processing

[What is] the "threshing floor" stage for tithing?	גרנן למעשרות
It becomes liable as a category of *untithed*	לחייב עליו משם טבל
at the completion of its processing	משתיגמר מל אכתו
and the process of gathering.	ומל אכת מכנסתו.

Comments: Torah said that *elevation offering*s are separated at the "threshing floor" (*goren*, גֹּרֶן, Num.18.27), and this ruling tries to define what that means. You are not liable for tithing until the last stage of harvest was completed, which included all the work of processing and gathering the produce. This meant that until that time one could eat the produce without removing the *first* and *second tithes*. This useful general statement is only found in Tosefta though it is implied in Mishnah.

Both Mishnah and Tosefta also discuss the earliest stage at which food becomes *'untithed'*—i.e., liable for tithes. This is, generally speaking, the time when it becomes edible—i.e., when it becomes 'food.' But why would someone want to know the earliest stage? The rest of t.Maas.1.1 explains that some produce is 'food' at an early stage but can be left to grow in order to produce seeds for planting, and so it is only liable for tithing at that early stage.

Dating (?): There is no reason to believe that this general statement predates 70 CE, but the principle certainly does. The concept that liability to tithing is defined by harvest is relied on as a generally accepted principle by Eleazar b. Azariah [T2] just after 70 CE (m.Maas.5.1), and the concept that the latest time is the last stage of processing is assumed in the pre-70 tradition in t.Maas.1.7 (see below).

m.Maas.1.5: When exactly is the last stage of processing?

What is the "threshing floor" stage for tithing?	אֵיזֶהוּ גָרְנָן לַמַּעַשְׂרוֹת,
Cucumbers and gourds:	הַקִּשּׁוּאִים וְהַדְּלוּעִים,
When they are trimmed.	מִשֶּׁיְּפַקְּסוּ.
But if one does not trim [them]:	וְאִם אֵינוּ מְפַקֵּס,
When they are stacked in a heap.	מִשֶּׁיַּעֲמִיד עֲרֵמָה.
[other cases]	
In what [circumstances] do these rulings apply?	בַּמֶּה דְבָרִים אֲמוּרִים,
When bringing them to the market.	בְּמוֹלִיךְ לַשּׁוּק.
But when bringing them to his home	אֲבָל בְּמוֹלִיךְ לְבֵיתוֹ,
he eats a *snack* from them [without tithing]	אוֹכֵל מֵהֶם עֲרַאי
until he reaches his home.	עַד שֶׁהוּא מַגִּיעַ לְבֵיתוֹ.

Comments: This is the start of a list of different definitions for the stage at which different crops become *untithed*—i.e., when they become liable for *first* and *second tithes*. The examples follow the general principle in t.Maas.1.1 that the produce becomes *untithed* either at the last stage of processing or at the last stage of storage, whichever is later. The list of other crops is omitted here. This list carries on to the end of m.Maas.1.8, though it is interrupted with comments such as the general principle recorded here at the end of m.Maas.1.5.

This general principle says that the last stage of storage is normally when the produce is brought into the home or when it reaches the market where it is to be sold. The implication of this is spelled out: until that time anyone can eat a *snack* from the produce without regarding the food as *untithed* or *doubtful*.

Dating (?): There is no reason to date any of this specific tradition before 70 CE, though the principles certainly did exist then (see t.Maas.1.1 above).

The first item in the list is likely to be early, because later parts of a list are generally added at the end, in order to preserve the traditional form of a text without fresh insertions[1]—though this did not stop later rabbis from inserting other comments such as the general statement recorded here. One item later in the list (about a vat, at the start of m.Maas.1.7) is witnessed to by a pre-70 tradition in t.Maas.1.7 (see below), and so it is likely that at least part of the list was already accumulating before 70 CE. However, it is possible that this rule about a vat was a later generalized rule based on the tradition in t.Maas.1.7.

---

[1] Cf. the discussion of m.Pea.2.1.

The concept of allowing incidental *snacks* without tithing was already regarded as an established ruling by the schools before 70 CE[2] and by Johanan b. Zakkai [T2] and Eliezer b. Hyrcanus [T2] just after 70 CE.[3]

t.Maas.1.7 (Z 1.7-8a): Tithing wine which is dedicated and redeemed

He who *dedicates* a vat [of wine to the Temple]	המקדיש את הבור
before drawing or skimming [it]	עד שלא שילה וקיפה,
and having drawn and skimmed [it]	ומששלה וקיפה
the [Temple] Treasurer came	בא גזבר
and he [who *dedicated* it] redeemed it:	ופדאו
He is liable [to pay tithes on the vat of wine].	חייב.
He who *dedicated* [a vat of wine]	הקדישו
before drawing or skimming [it]	עד שלא שילה וקיפה,
and the [Temple] Treasurer came	ובא גזבר
and he drew and skimmed [it]	ושילה וקיפה
and after this he redeemed it:	ואחר כך פדאו,
It is agreed [in m.Pea.4.7] that:	הואיל
"And at the time of its liability [it was] exempt"[*1]	ובשעת חובתו פטור,
[so it is] exempt.[*2]	פטור.
"Wine having been skimmed:	היין משיקפה.
Even if he skimmed [it]	אף על פי שקיפה,
he [may still] collect from the upper vat	קולט מן הגת העליונה
and from the pipe, and drink [without tithing]." [m.Maas.1.7a]	ומן הצינור, ושותה.

[*1] Mishnah text reads: שבשעת חובתה היתה פטורה, 'for at the time it [was] liable it was exempt.'
[*2] Missing from Z.
Mishnaic parallel: m.Pea.4.8

Comments: Whoever owns the vat at the time that it becomes liable to tithing is responsible for the tithing. If the Temple owns it at that time, no tithing takes place because Temple goods are not subject to tithes. So if the owner *dedicates* a vine crop and then redeems it back (by paying its *full value* plus an *added fifth*), he does not need to pay tithes if the Temple owned it at the time it became liable to tithes. Two passages are quoted from Mishnah to substantiate this ruling.

Dating (8): The reference to *dedication* and especially to the action of the Temple Treasurer suggests that this ruling originated before 70 CE. The quotations from Mishnah were probably added some time later, when the reverence for oral *halakhah* had grown considerably, so that a point could be proved simply by showing that it

---

[2] m.Maas.4.2 // t.Maas.3.2.
[3] Yohanan b. Zakkai in t.Maas.2.1 and Eliezer b. Hyrcanus in m.Maas.2.4 // t.Maas.2.2; m.Maas.4.3.

agreed with these traditions. It is likely that the first citation from m.Pea.4.7 was added first, and that the longer citation was added later, either in corroboration or merely as the next *halakhah* to be dealt with in this tractate.

It is interesting that the citation of m.Pea.4.7 is considerably different from the form in which it is preserved in Mishnah. The changes are not likely to be due to the editor(s) of the Tosefta because otherwise they would have removed the opening *vav* which does not fit into the context. Therefore it is likely that they have quoted the tradition in the form that they had it. This indicates that the exact wording of such traditions was not fixed.

m.Maas.2.1-4: Eating *untithed* food before reaching home

Summary of Mishnah: You can accept the gift of a random untithed *snack* in the market (2.1), but if you take it into a home, the owner of the home is responsible to tithe it (2.1-2). The trader can eat *snacks* from it until he reaches the final marketplace or his lodgings (2.3). Eliezer [T2] does not allow these random *snacks* after tithing has started but the Sages allow them until tithing has finished, except for figs (2.4).

The following traditions have elements (marked in bold) for which there is evidence of an origin before 70 CE:

m.Maas.2.3: This ruling about random *snacks* being allowed on a journey until you reach your Sabbath lodging, which is attributed to Meir [T3] in Mishnah, is attributed to Hillel by Judah [b. Illai, T4] in t.Maas.3.4. However, there are good reasons to doubt that this is an accurate attribution because it is a series of three rulings to which Judah has added "Hillel himself used to forbid it," without any citation of the actual tradition of Hillel. The first one is attached to a Hillelite ruling (m.Maas.4.2 // t.Maas.3.2) then the next two are attached to a ruling of Judah (m.Maas.4.2 // t.Maas.3.3) and to this ruling of Meir. It is likely that the phrase first became attached to the Hillelite ruling in t.Maas.3.2 in order to give added weight to a ruling where the Shammaites would otherwise have a better case, and then it became copied onto the next two rulings in Tosefta.

m.Maas.2.4: Snacks after tithing has started but not finished

Produce from which [*elevation offerings*] have been *elevated*	פרות שתרמן
when the processing is not [yet] complete:	עד שלא נגמרה מלאכתן,
R. Eliezer [b. Hyrcanus, T2] prohibits	רבי אליעזר אוסר
eating a *snack* from it [without tithing it]	מלאכול מהם עראי.
But the Sages permit [it],	וחכמים מתירין,
except from a basket of figs.	חוץ מכלכלת תאנים.
A basket of figs	כלכלת תאנים

from which [*elevation offerings*] are *elevated*:
R. Simeon [b. Yohai, T4] permits [a *snack* from it]
but the Sages prohibit [it].

שׁתּרמה,
רבי שׁמעון מתיר,
וחכמים אוסרין.

Comments: Farm workers could, like the ox in Deuteronomy 25.4, take a *snack* from the food which they were working on before it was tithed. But did this right extend beyond the time that tithing started? The first tithing was the *elevation* of *elevation offerings,* and then the *first* and *second tithes* were separated. From this tractate we see that tithing could start when harvest began and could finish when the last stage of processing had been completed.

Most people would process the *elevation offerings* at the same time as *first* and *second tithes.* Although it was *possible* to separate *elevation offerings* from the harvested produce before it was measured because *elevation offerings* were unmeasured, in practice people were keen to make sure that the amount was about one-fiftieth of the harvested produce (see discussions at m.Ter.4.3). Also, *elevation offerings* were not separated until processing had finished, because unprocessed food could not be separated on behalf of processed food (see m.Ter.1.4—with the possible exception of grapes, cf. m.Ter.1.8), and so they would be *elevated* at the same time as *first* and *second tithes* were removed.

After 70 CE, however, they no longer took *elevation offerings* to the Temple or other collection points in market towns where the Temple Treasurer had a representative, but instead they could give their *elevation offerings* to any local priest.[4] This meant that they did not need to carry this portion of their produce to the market. The *first* and *second tithe* could also be distributed at home to a local Levite and to the poor, or redeemed for cash which could be carried to the Temple, and so there was no need to carry these to the market either. But in practice most farmers never removed the *first* and *second tithes* even if they were still faithful with regard to *elevation offerings.* This is clear from the universal practice of treating food from the market as *doubtful.* This meant that purchasers assumed that the *elevation offerings* had been separated but that the *first* and *second tithes* had not been removed.[5]

Therefore, after 70 CE, many farmers would have separated the *elevation offerings* as soon as they had finished processing the crop, but the *first* and *second tithes* would not be removed until a diligent householder took the produce home and tithed it themselves.

Dating (5): Eliezer probably represents the old status quo, where the tithing of the *elevation offering* took place at the same time as the *first* and *second tithes.* The separation of these two tasks after 70 CE, which also encouraged the neglect of *first* and *second tithes*, was difficult for him to accept. One way of complaining against

---

[4] See the conclusions to *Terumot* which suggests that this was the practice before 70 CE.
[5] See the introduction to the tractate *Demai.*

this was to refuse the right of *snacks* after tithing had started by separating the *elevation offering*.

The Sages disagreed with Eliezer and there was a progressive time gap between the separation of *elevation offerings* and other tithes. This tractate shows that people gradually extended the right of *snacks* on untithed food from the time that the harvest was brought home, to the time that it was taken to market, to the time that a purchaser took it home, and finally to the time when it was presented as a meal. This gap was already growing during the time of the Temple, as seen by the debate in m.Maas.4.2, but it became much more important after 70 CE.

The application of the law of an ox to a farm worker was based on the principle that an 'ox' in Scripture is a reference to anyone who works on a farm. This is the basic assumption behind much of the tractate *Baba Qamma*, and is seen in the early traditions of b.San.19ab and m.Yad.4.7. The reasoning behind this assumption is not stated anywhere, but it was probably derived by the rule of *Qal vaHomer* ('major and minor') by saying that: If an ox has this right, then surely a human worker (who is more important) also has this right, and if a worker has this right, then surely his employer also has this right.

New Testament: The rule that a church worker has a right to wages was based on the principle that he is like an ox (1Cor.9.9-11; 1Tim.5.17-18). In the light of the way that Jewish laws concerning an ox applied also to human workers, it is likely that this was regarded as a literal exegesis, and not as allegory.[6]

m.Maas.2.5-6: Eating *untithed* food which you paid for

Summary of Mishnah: Random *snacks* of figs are permissible if you eat them one by one, even if you have paid for them (2.5), and you can eat other produce bit by bit (2.6) [before you reach home].

There is no evidence that any of this section originated before 70 CE.

m.Maas.2.7–3.3: Eating *untithed* food given as payment

Summary of Mishnah: A worker can eat untithed food while harvesting because Scripture gives him privileges [because he is like the ox in Deut.25.4] (2.7), but he can eat only the type of food which he has harvested (2.8).

---

[6] See my "1 Corinthians 9.9-11: A Literal Interpretation of 'Do Not Muzzle the Ox,'" *New Testament Studies* 38 (1992): 554-65.

A family can eat untithed figs drying in their courtyard (3.1) [because they are not yet brought into the house]. If the employees pay their own board, they pay their own tithes for meals which they eat from the courtyard (3.1) or the field (3.2-3), but if food is part of their wages [the employer pays their tithes], only random *snacks* can be taken (3.3). *Snacks* are not 'random' if you make a collection of them first (3.2-3, 8).

There is no evidence that any of this section originated before 70 CE.

m.Maas.3.4-10: Eating *untithed* food found in a public place

Summary of Mishnah: Produce which is 'found' on the road is like stolen produce—it is liable for tithing if it has reached the last stage of harvesting (3.4). Food from a courtyard which is closed to outsiders is not exempt from tithing (3.5). Roofs, porticoes, or balconies adjoining a courtyard have the same status as the courtyard (3.6). Storage huts which are not lived in constantly are exempt (3.7). Trees (and other plants) growing in a courtyard are exempt though one cannot collect the produce [for a meal] (3.8-9)—though perhaps you can have a whole cluster of grapes or a whole melon if you only eat one grape or one slice of melon at a time (3.9) Branches of trees growing into a courtyard are treated according to where the roots are, as also with other laws (3.10).

There is no evidence that any of this section originated before 70 CE.

m.Maas.4.1-5a: Produce which might not be fully processed

Summary of Mishnah: Produce which is only *partially* processed in the field, or which is processed as non-food can be eaten untithed as a *snack* (4.1), but not food one *intended* to tithe (4.2). Partially processed food can be eaten as a *snack* but not if you process it further (e.g., by salting it) so that the remainder cannot be returned to the store (4.3). You can drink wine untithed at the press unless you mix in hot water (4.4) [because this indicates preparation as a meal—cf. y.Maas.4.4]. You can husk barley or wheat [as an untithed *snack*] but only one kernel at a time (4.5a).

The following traditions have elements (marked in bold) for which there is evidence of an origin before 70 CE:

t.Maas.3.10 // m.Maas.4.5a: This tradition about rubbing the husk off wheat on a Sabbath (which provides insights into the Gospel story) is related to the school debate at m.Betz.1.8 by which it can be dated, and so it is discussed in tractate *Bétzah*.

m.Maas.4.2: *Snacks* after intending to tithe produce

Children who stored [untithed] figs	תִּינוֹקוֹת שֶׁטָּמְנוּ הַאֲנִים
for [eating on] the Sabbath	לְשַׁבָּת,
but [then] they forgot to tithe them [before the Sabbath started]:	וְשָׁכְחוּ לְעַשְׂרָן,
They must not eat [the figs]	לֹא יֹאכְלוּ
[even] after the Sabbath [ended]	לְמוֹצָאֵי שַׁבָּת
[even as a *snack*] until they are tithed.	עַד שֶׁיְּעַשְׂרוּ.
A basket [of untithed provisions for] the Sabbath:	כַּלְכַּלַּת שַׁבָּת,
The School of Shammai exempts	בֵּית שַׁמַּאי פּוֹטְרִין,
[it from tithing for *snacks* before the Sabbath]	
and the School of Hillel obligates [it].	וּבֵית הִלֵּל מְחַיְּבִין.
R. Judah [b. Illai, T4] says:	רַבִּי יְהוּדָה אוֹמֵר,
Also, he who gathers a basket [of provisions]	אַף הַלּוֹקֵט אֶת הַכַּלְכַּלָּה
to send to his associate:	לִשְׁלֹחַ לַחֲבֵרוֹ,
He must not eat [*snacks* from it] until it is tithed.	לֹא יֹאכַל עַד שֶׁיְּעַשֵּׂר.

Mishnaic parallel: m.MS.4.10

Comments: The school dispute concerns someone who put food aside for the Sabbath meal, which indicated that they intended to eat this food as part of a meal (and not as a *snack*) and therefore that they intended to tithe it some time before the Sabbath (because the work of tithing cannot be performed on the Sabbath). If they then wanted to eat a *snack* from that food before it was tithed (which would normally be acceptable), the Hillelites said this would be wrong because they have already intended to tithe that collection of food.

The first part of this mishnah extends the limits of the Hillelite ruling to its extremes. What if the person was below legal age? And what if the collection of food did not constitute a meal but was something like figs which were often eaten as a *snack* between meals? What if they didn't fulfill their intention because they forgot? The Hillelite ruling still applies even in these extreme circumstances, because they had nevertheless intended to tithe it for the Sabbath. R. Judah adds that even if you intended to give it to someone else (so that you intended that they, and not you, would tithe it), it was still liable to tithes because you intended that it would be tithed.

Dating (1): There is no reason to doubt that the school dispute is authentic, especially as the Hillelite argument depends on intention, which was a favorite basis for their reasoning. At a later time, R. Judah felt it was necessary to bolster this rather weak Hillelite argument by saying that "Hillel himself used to forbid it" (t.Maas.3.2—see m.Maas.2.3 after the Summary of m.Maas.2.1-4).

Logically the School dispute comes before the ruling about children, because although the ruling about children is recorded first in this mishnah, it makes no sense without assuming the Hillelite ruling to be correct. Possibly the ruling about the children was recorded first and the school dispute was added in order to provide an explanation for it. In the highly abbreviated form of both of these rulings, neither is understandable without the other and without the context of tithing and *snacking*. It is likely that the ruling about children is post-70 because it assumes the Hillelite ruling to be correct.

This school dispute is very important in the tractate of *Maaserot* because it is the only tradition from before 70 CE which has retained what was probably its original form. There are a few other possible references to the schools[7] but they are all reported by later authorities. However, even here it is likely that the School material has been added to the post-70 tradition about children. Nevertheless, it confirms that before 70 CE they already allowed tithing to be delayed until the person who was going to eat it brought it into their home (or perhaps to their table), and that *snacking* was allowed from untithed produce. The practice of *snacking* is not specifically mentioned in this tradition, but it would not make sense without it, and so it may legitimately be inferred.

m.Maas.4.5b–5.8: Produce which might not be food

Summary of Mishnah: You do not need to tithe herbs which you intended for non-food even if you eat them (4.5a), and you do not need to tithe parts of herbs which are not normally eaten (4.6). Produce is not tithed until harvest time [when it becomes food], even if it is sold, or picked for a friend prior to harvest, or uprooted for replanting (5.1), unless they are root crops which are already edible (5.2) or unless the unharvested food is sold to someone who cannot be trusted to tithe it (5.3-4). If you buy an unharvested field in Syria, you must tithe the produce when you harvest it, but if it is already partially harvested, then you have bought it after 'harvest time' so the late ripening produce need not be tithed (5.5). If you make cordial from steeping grape pulp, does this require tithing (5.6)? Grain found in anthills next to untithed stores needs tithing (5.7). Types of produce which grow only outside Israel do not need tithing [even when you do not know their provenance], and types of seeds which are not normally eaten do not need tithing, even if they are eaten.

The following traditions have elements (marked in bold) for which there is evidence of an origin before 70 CE:

---

[7] t.Maas.3.10 // m.Maas.4.5a. Possibly also the two other traditions of which R. Judah says, "Hillel himself used to forbid it" (m.Maas.4.2 // t.Maas.3.2 and m.Maas.4.2 // t.Maas.3.3), but see the comments at the Summary of m.Maas.2.1-4.

m.Maas.4.5b: Tithing leaves and seeds of herbs

Coriander which [the farmer] sowed	כוסבר שזרעה
for [producing] seed [for future sowing]:	לזרע,
The leaves may be exempt [from tithes if they are eaten].	ירקה פטור.
[If] he sowed it for the leaves [to be eaten as a herb]:	זרעה לירק.
The seeds and leaves should be tithed.	מתעשרת זרע וירק.
R. Eliezer [b. Hyrcanus, T2] says: Dill:	רבי אליעזר אומר, השבת
the seeds and leaves and pods should be tithed,	מתעשרת זרע וירק וזירין.
But the Sages say:	וחכמים אומרים,
Nothing should be tithed [for both] seeds and leaves	אינו מתעשר זרע וירק
except cress and field-rocket alone.	אלא השחלים והגרגיר בלבד.

Comments: If a herb is sown for producing seed for future planting, its crop is not 'food,' and so it is not subject to tithing. If it is grown for both seeds and leaves, they were both tithed. Eliezer extends this to pods in the case of dill, because they are edible (cf. b.AZ.7b). The Sages say that only one part of a plant should be tithed, though they (or a later editor) have two exceptions.

Although these are only herbs, they could form valuable crops, and so their tithing was economically important to the large growers.[8] But for the householders who grew small patches of herbs or vegetables between their other crops,[9] this matter of tithing must have seemed very tedious. The Sages appear to be making a practical point that a large crop is grown for one thing or another—either it is harvested at the time that the leaves are best for eating, or it is harvested at the time the seeds are ready, and so you should tithe it according to the economic purpose of the crop. Small householders may attempt to put by the seeds for replanting, and the Sages would ignore this.

Dating (5): The first ruling is also found in Tosefta though the middle section is different.

> **Coriander which [the farmer] sowed for [producing] seed [for future sowing],** but his intention concerning it (וחשב עליה) [changed to growing it] for the leaves: **the seeds and leaves must be tithed.** (t.Maas.3.7)

Both versions appear to be attempts to explain why this ruling should be allowed to contradict the ruling of the Sages (the majority accepted ruling) that nothing is tithed

---

[8] Cf. b.Git.57a: 'Kefar Shihlayim was so named because they made their living from *shihlayim* [watercress].' This may well be guesswork by a later generation, because the Jerusalem Talmud says: 'Kefar Shihlayim was so named because they reared their children as carefully as *shihlayim* [watercress]' (y.Taan.4.5.XIII, 69a). However, both versions are based on the assumption that watercress is a valuable crop, and so this is likely to have also been true in earlier generations.

[9] Cf. m.Pea.3.2 where Akiba [T3] says that each small plot of herbs sown between other crops must be treated separately concerning *Peah*.

for both seeds and leaves.[10] Tosefta says that it represents a special case where the farmer originally planted the crop with the intention of harvesting only the seeds for replanting, but he changed his mind and decided that he would harvest the leaves as well. Mishnah converts it into two rulings for the two situations, where the farmer intended only to harvest the seeds but actually harvested the leaves as well, and where the farmer intended to harvest the leaves (and, presumably, the seeds). The Mishnah version makes more sense but it also clashes more obviously with the ruling of the Sages. It is therefore likely that the Tosefta contains a later version because it managed to harmonize more effectively with the Sages by presenting the situation as a special case which acts as a caveat or exception to the general rule by the Sages.

The fact that the editors of both Mishnah and Tosefta have felt constrained to include this difficult ruling suggests that it was already firmly accepted so that even the ruling of the Sages could not displace it. In order to incorporate this ancient ruling, they had to add an interpretation which removed the contradiction. Eliezer's ruling appears to refer to the wording of this ancient ruling when he says "the seeds and leaves *and pods* must be tithed" (Eliezer's addition in italics). Therefore it is likely that there was a ruling before 70 CE which read:

> Coriander which was sowed for seed: the seeds and leaves must be tithed.

It is possible that dill was tithed before 70 CE because Nahum the Mede is attributed with a ruling very similar to Eliezer's, though the rabbis did not give it the same weight as a ruling by a recognized scholar (see b.AZ.7b).

There was a great deal of further debate about different herbs soon after 70 CE and in the early second century (as seen in this mishnah and the following one) which was probably inspired by this ruling. The schools debated whether or not fenugreek, which cannot be regarded as food but which can be used to flavor food, should be subject to *elevation offering* tithes (m.MS.2.3-4). This ruling in *Maaserot* is less difficult to decide because these herbs can clearly be called 'food.' It is likely that the debate about tithing herbs which can be regarded as food predated the more difficult debate about herbs which could only be regarded as flavorings. This is a further indication that at least some of these debates about herbs originate before 70 CE.

New Testament: Jesus criticized those who tithed herbs (Mt.23.23; cf. Lk.11.42). Although the majority of the debates about herbs took place after 70 CE, the origins of this series of debates can be traced back before 70 CE. Small farmers who grew a variety of crops in their vegetable gardens for their own use[11] would have found such debates extremely difficult. Not only did it cause them to worry about whether their

---

[10] This contradiction is acknowledged and discussed by the Jerusalem Talmud, y.Maas.4.5 V, 51b.

[11] Cf. the herb garden growing thirteen different species of vegetables and herbs in m.Kil.3.1-2.

crops should be tithed or not, but it also introduced the huge practical problem of where to store all the tiny portions of tithe, because each different type had to be stored separately. This kind of ruling made sense for commercial growers, but Jesus complained on behalf of the common people that they were being oppressed by such rules.

Summary and Conclusions

There is very little in this tractate which is early, and the few early portions appear to have been cited in order to explain later rulings. Therefore the whole of this tractate appears to originate after 70 CE. Nevertheless, this tractate gives some valuable insights into tithing before 70 CE.

This tractate is supposedly about the *first tithe*, because it occurs after the tractate on *elevation offerings* and before the tractate on the *second tithe*, and because its title in Tosefta is *"first tithe."* However the title in Mishnah, 'tithes,' conveys the real subject which is the payment of both *first* and *second tithes*. In particular, this tractate is concerned with the questions of *when* and *whether* a consumer needs to tithe food grown from plants. There is very little discussion of the role of the farmer in tithing (except to say when his *untithed* food may be eaten), and there is no discussion of tithing animals (which is done by the farmer).

Tithing *can* start as soon as produce becomes edible, because it can then be classed as food. Only *elevation offerings* can be separated at this stage, because they are unmeasured, because *first* and *second tithes* cannot be removed until the produce has been harvested and measured (t.Maas.1.1a). The first definition of when tithes *must* be removed is therefore the time when produce is collected in containers and 'smoothed over.'[12] This tractate appears to give various definitions of the time when tithing must take place: first, the time when produce is gathered to a place of safety (i.e., the home or a secured courtyard—cf. m.Maas.1.5); then, the time when it has reached the market (cf. m.Maas.1.5); and then, the time when it is used to prepare a meal (cf. m.Maas.4.2).

This apparent diversity of answers to the question '*When* must you tithe?' represents a diversity of viewpoints. From the viewpoint of the farmer, tithing cannot take place until the produce has been collected in a secure place and measured, because it is only then that he knows how much produce he has and how much would be one-tenth. From the viewpoint of a merchant or a farmer who takes goods to market, he does not have to tithe them until he stops to prepare his own meal from them at a lodging house at the end of the day. From the viewpoint of the consumer, the goods do not have to be tithed until they are prepared as a meal, because until that

---

[12] Cf. m.Pea.1.6, etc. and esp. m.Pea.4.7 which is quoted in t.Maas.1.7.

point it is undecided whether the goods will be used as animal feed, as seed for planting, or as oil for lamps, none of which require tithing.

We hear nothing about how the *first tithe* was distributed. Torah said that it should go to a Levite who then gave a tenth to a priest (Num.18.26-28), and Mishnah assumes that this procedure was followed (e.g., m.Ter.2.2; m.MS.5.9, 10). Outside rabbinic literature, however, there are hints that most tithes were given to the priests.[13] This may indicate that the *first tithe* was actually given to priests and not to Levites because there were far more priests than Levites after the Exile (as Safrai suggests[14]). Another explanation, which fits well with evidence from the Mishnah, is that the *first tithe* was rarely separated so that the bulk of tithes consisted of *elevation offerings* which went to the priests—so in pactice, virtually all tithes went to the priests. The tractate *Demay* assumes that pious Jews separated the *elevation offering* of the *first tithe* from all food which they bought from the market, just in case the *first tithe* had not been separated. The *first tithe could* be separated at various stages, by the farmer, by the merchant or by the householder, and so each one could justifiably leave the task (and the loss) to someone else. Only the *elevation offering* was actually dangerous to eat, so the householder could separate just one-hundredth and thereafter treat the food as edible. Therefore, for most produce, the Levite's *first tithe* was never separated, but the taboo about avoiding *elevation offering* and other priestly portions was so strong that this was separated even in cases of doubt.

Until the food is tithed, it cannot be eaten except as a *snack*. *Snacking* is an extension of the concept of the ox eating the grain while treading it (Deut.25.4, cf. m.Maas.2.7). This was extended to humans who worked on the farm, who are subject to some of the same laws as an ox in Mishnah (cf. on m.Maas.2.4). It was assumed that the ox did not tithe his food before he ate it, snf so, as long as there was no intention to prepare a meal from the food, small portions can be consumed as a *snack* without tithing. This concept was already recognized before 70 CE (m.Maas.2.4; 4.2) though it developed considerably after 70 CE. A householder who bought produce at the market was allowed to continue *snacking* on it until they used it to prepare a meal.

This tractate assumes that food bought at the market has had the *elevation offering* separated, but the *first* and *second tithes* have not been removed. Although Associates and other strictly observant Jews were willing to pay higher prices for food which they knew to be fully tithed, they bought this food only from fellow Associates whom they could trust (cf. m.Dem.2.2a). This produce would cost up to 20 percent more

---

[13] Immediately after the Exile it was assumed that *firstfruits* were given to the priests and tithes to the Levites who then passed on the *elevation offering* from those tithes to the priests (Neh.10.35-38), but Judith and Jubilees assumes that both *firstfruits* and tithes were given to the priests (Jdt.11.13; Jub.13.25-28) while others assume that 'tithes' went to the priests (Philo.*Virt*.95; Jos.*Life*.80; Heb.7.5).

[14] *CRINT* 1.II.585.

than untithed food, and so few non-Associates would buy it. Therefore merchants did not tithe food but they left it to each consumer to do their own tithing. If the consumer was strict they would tithe it properly (i.e., remove two lots of 10 percent), but many would simply regard it as *doubtful* and remove only the 1 percent which represented the *minor elevation offering* (see the Introduction to tractate *Demay*).

Before 70 CE, it is likely that merchants did not separate *elevation offerings* until they reached the market, where *elevation offerings* were handed to the Temple Treasurer or his representative who distributed them to the priests (cf. m.Pea.1.6; 2.8). After 70 CE the *elevation offerings* could be given to any local priest, and so if it was separated at the farm, there was less to transport. This resulted in a long time gap between the start of tithing (the *elevation offerings*) and the end of tithing (the *first* and *second tithes*). R. Eliezer, who represented the older opinions, did not think that *snacks* should be allowed after tithing had started, but he was overruled (m.Maas.2.4). He was also stricter than the majority on tithing the seeds of herbs (m.Maas.4.5b), which indicates that herbs were already tithed before 70 CE, but the debate on the details of tithing herbs occurred mainly just after 70 CE.

Tractate *Maaser Sheni*: Second Tithe

Definitions and Outline

Torah has complex rules on tithing and there appears to be a contradiction between Deuteronomy and the other books. Leviticus speaks about one-tenth which is given to the Lord (Lev.27.30-32) and Numbers explains that this offering belongs to the Levites (Num.18.24-32), but Deuteronomy says that one-tenth has to be put aside for eating in Jerusalem and that every third year there was a tithe for the Levites and the poor (Deut.12.17-19; 14.23-29; 26.12-15). The rabbis understood these texts as describing two separate tithes: the *first tithe* (*maaser rishon*, מַעֲשֵׂר רִאשׁוֹן) which was for the Levites and the *second tithe* (*maaser sheni*, מַעֲשֵׂר שֵׁנִי) which was for eating in Jerusalem except every third year when it became the *poor tithe* (*maaser ani*, מַעֲשֵׂר עָנִי). The passage in Leviticus 27 is traditionally interpreted as referring to *second tithe* because it speaks about redeeming the tithed produce, which was necessary only for *second tithe*.

If you lived too far from Jerusalem (Deut.14.24), you could redeem your *second tithe* produce at the cost of its *full value* plus an *added fifth* (*homesh*, חֹמֶשׁ) (Lev.27.31). The produce was exchanged for *second tithe silver* (כֶּסֶף מַעֲשֵׂר עָנִי, *maaser ani keseph*, as specified in Deut.14.25). The normal coin used for this was a silver *sela* (סֶלַע) which was worth two normal *shekels* or one 'sacred *shekel*' (the value of a theoretical coin derived from the Old Testament). Those actual coins were set aside for carrying to Jerusalem (Deut.14.25: "bind up the money in your hand") though if these coins were accidentally used wrongly, their *valuation* (דָּמִים, *damim*) could be replaced.

At the end of the third year there was a ceremony of *removal* (*biur*, בִּיעוּר) when you declared before the Lord that you had paid your *poor tithe* (Deut.26.12-15) and this later became a declaration that all *consecrated* produce had been distributed or destroyed.

The fruit of the *fourth-year plant* (*neta rebai*, נֶטַע רְבָעִי) was also brought to Jerusalem and consumed there (Lev.19.23-25). This similarity with the *second tithe* is probably the reason why it is dealt with in this tractate.

m.MS.1.1–2.4: *Second tithe* produce

Second tithe produce which you bring to Jerusalem or purchase there must be eaten there; you cannot trade with it or purchase non-food items, though any container you purchase with it can be taken home.

m.MS.2.5–3.4: *Second tithe silver*

Second tithe silver should consist of silver coins and you should keep the original coins if possible. You can spend it on a friend's produce or on produce at home away from Jerusalem, but that produce must then be eaten in Jerusalem, in *purity*.

m.MS.3.5-13: Problems re *second tithe* produce

Second tithe produce should not be taken out of Jerusalem once it is there, but how do you define "in" Jerusalem? And what about produce which became contaminated so that it cannot be eaten as *second tithe*?

m.MS.4.1-12: Problems re *second tithe silver*

All the *second tithe silver* must be spent on produce in Jerusalem, but how do you decide the price? If you find some coins, can you assume they are not *second tithe silver*?

m.MS.5.1-5: *Fourth-year fruit*

Fourth-year fruit can be redeemed like *second tithe*, but do the other *second tithe* laws of *added fifth* and *removal* also apply to *fourth-year fruit*?

m.MS.5.6-15: *Removal* of *consecrated* produce

Destruction of *second tithes* at the time of *removal* can be avoided by redeeming them or by not tithing them until later. The ancient declaration at the Removal ceremony (from Deut.26.13-15) is expounded line by line.

m.MS.1.1-7: Purchasing and selling *second tithe* produce

Summary of Mishnah: You do not carry out commercial transactions with *second tithe* produce or other *consecrated* goods, though you can offer them as a gift (1.1). Farmers cannot use a tithed animal for commercial transactions, though a priest can use *firstborn* animals in this way (1.2). You may not redeem *second tithe* produce with dubious coinage (1.2). Food bought with *second tithe silver* is *consecrated*, though the container is not—this includes a sealed bottle, animal hide, or grape skins from the winepress (1.3) but does not include hides of animals which cannot be eaten, or open containers (1.4). You cannot spend *second tithe silver* on things which cannot be eaten as a meal or cannot be taken to Jerusalem before it perishes. If it was an accident, it can be returned, but if it was deliberate, it must be taken to Jerusalem immediately, or (after its destruction) left to rot (1.5-6). If you purchase non-food items with *second tithe silver* you must purchase the same *valuation* of food as *second tithe* (1.7).

The following traditions have elements (marked in bold) for which there is evidence of an origin before 70 CE:

m.MS.1.3-4: Purchasing second tithe produce which has containers

He who purchases a farm animal [with *second tithe silver*]	הלוקח בהמה
for sacrifices of *peace offerings*	לזבחי שלמים,
or [he who purchases] a wild animal for eating meat:	או חיה לבשר תאוה,
The hide becomes *deconsecrated*,	יצא העור לחולין,
even if the [value of the] hide	אף על פי שהעור
is greater than the meat.	מרובה על הבשר.
Jugs of wine [which are] sealed	כדי יין סתומות,
from a place where [they are] normally sold	מקום שדרכן למכר
sealed [so the jug is inseparable from the wine]:	סתומות,
The jug becomes *deconsecrated*.	יצא קנקן לחולין.
Nuts and almonds:	האגוזים והשקדים,
Their shells become *deconsecrated*.	יצאו קלפיהם לחולין.
Lees wine while it is not [yet] fermented:	התמד עד שלא החמיץ,
It may not be bought with [*second*] *tithe silver*,	אינו נלקח בכסף מעשר.
but when it is fermented,	ומשהחמיץ,
it may be bought with [*second*] *tithe silver*.	נלקח בכסף מעשר.
4) He who purchases a wild animal [with *second tithe silver*]	הלוקח חיה
for sacrifices of *peace offerings*	לזבחי שלמים,
[or he who purchases] a farm animal for eating meat:	בהמה לבשר תאוה,
The hide does not become *deconsecrated*.	לא יצא העור לחולין.
Jugs of wine [which are] open or sealed	כדי יין פתוחות או סתומות,
from a place where [they are] normally sold	מקום שדרכן למכר
open [so the jug is not inseparable from the wine]:	פתוחות,
The jug does not become *deconsecrated*.	לא יצא קנקן לחולין.
Baskets of olives and baskets of grapes	סלי זיתים וסלי ענבים
[which are sold] with the container:	עם הכלי,
The *valuation* of the container does not	לא יצאו דמי הכלי
become *deconsecrated*.	לחולין.

Comments: The *second tithe silver* had to be spent on food in Jerusalem, and when you spent it, the money became *deconsecrated* because the *second tithe* status passed to the food which you purchased. If the food included a container (such as the hide of an animal or a closed jug) this container was *deconsecrated* so that it was not subject to *second tithe* restrictions. If the purchase could not be eaten as *second tithe* then one had to sell it again and purchase something which could. This meant that the hide of an unsuitable animal was still '*consecrated*' because it was part of the *valuation* which had to be sold to buy *second tithe* food.

Most people would have spent their *second tithe* money while they were in Jerusalem for a festival. The food had to be eaten in *purity*, and so this was a good opportunity to sacrifice a *peace offering* which was eaten in *purity* by the offerer and his household. This ruling assumes that if you were going to eat an animal which *could* be offered as a *peace offering*, you should do so. You could also purchase any other type of meat or food, and normally you would purchase more luxurious food than you usually ate, because Torah commanded that you should "rejoice" and that you should eat "whatever you desire" (Deut.12.18; 14.26). However, you could also purchase the cheapest food, like lees wine which was made by pouring water through lees (the material sieved out during wine making—cf. comments on t.Ter.7.11; 10.12).

Any non-food which was inseparably part of the food could also be counted as purchased with the *second tithe*. Therefore a hide or shells or sealed jug could be taken home from Jerusalem even if it had been bought with *second tithe silver*. But if it was an open jug or an open basket, it was not inseparable from the food. Wine was sometimes sold in amphorae which were closed at the vineyard (a 'sealed jug') or it was sold from a barrel and poured into a container when it was purchased (an 'open jug'). When it was filled from the barrel, the jug was not an inseparable part of the wine, so even if it was sealed after being filled, it could not be counted as a purchase with *second tithe silver*. In this type of situation the jug was often regarded as a loan (see m.MS.3.13 below).

If you bought something which could not be eaten in *purity*, such as meat which had been improperly made into a *peace offering* or meat which *could* have been a *peace offering* which was not offered in the Temple, this was not a valid purchase with *second tithe silver*, and so neither the hide or shells or jug count as valid *second tithe* purchases, even if these are not for eating.

Dating (2): The purchase of produce for consumption in Jerusalem stopped after 70 CE (see on t.MS.3.13-14 below) though the reason for this is not clear, because the Temple was not necessary for doing this. Latter rabbis had various ways to explain this, mainly by showing that *second tithe* should be eaten in a similar way to *firstborn*.[1] The rulings here at m.MS.1.3-4 give the best clue for explaining the change, because they assume that any domestic animal purchased with *second tithe* money would be offered as a *peace offering*—which is also seen as normal practice in the school debate in m.Hag.1.3.

This suggests that the *second tithe* was normally consumed at a festival and that the meat (which was the most expensive and therefore the most important part of the

---

[1] These arguments are collected at Sif.Deut.106 where they are attributed to R. Ishmael [T3].

festival) would normally be offered as a *peace offering*. Therefore, after 70 CE, it would have seemed very strange to come to Jerusalem and consume *second tithe* when there was no festival atmosphere and when it was impossible to make a *peace offering*. It would, in any case, be difficult to "rejoice" (Deut.12.18; 14.26) while the Temple was not standing. Pious Jews therefore redeemed all their *second tithe* produce and saved the money in the hope of spending it in Jerusalem when it was rebuilt.[2]

It is likely that the first part of these two mishnahs formed a single ruling and that the rest was added at a later date as a derivation based on the principle that they established. Although these later rulings also concern purchasing produce with *second tithe silver*, they may nevertheless date from after 70 CE because issues like this were still debated as theoretical matters by later generations, especially in the generation T4 (mid second century) (cf. m.MS.3.2, 5, 10-12; 4.10).

m.MS.1.5-6: Spending *second tithe* improperly

He who purchases [with *second tithe silver*]	הלוקח
water or salt	מים, ומלח,
or produce which is attached to the soil,	ופרות המחוברים לקרקע,
or produce which is not able	או פרות שאינן יכולין
to reach Jerusalem [for eating, before spoiling]:	להגיע לירושלים,
He has not acquired [goods with the status of *second*] tithe.	לא קנה מעשר.
He who purchases produce accidentally	הלוקח פרות, שוגג,
[using *second tithe silver* outside Jerusalem]:	
Its *valuation* must be returned to its place.	יחזרו דמים למקומן.
[He who does it] deliberately, he must bring it up	מזיד, יעלו
and he must eat it in the Place [i.e., Jerusalem].	ויאכלו במקום.
And if there is no Holy [Place], it must rot.	ואם אין מקדש, ירקבו.
6) He who purchases a farm animal accidentally	הלוקח בהמה, שוגג,
[using *second tithe silver* outside Jerusalem]:	
The payment must be returned to its place.	יחזרו דמיה למקומן.
[He who does it] deliberately, let him bring it up	מזיד, תעלה
and let him eat [it] in the Place [i.e., Jerusalem].	ותאכל במקום.
And if there is no Holy [Place],	ואם אין מקדש,
it should be buried, together with its hide.	תקבר על ידי עורה.

Comments: What should you do if you use *second tithe silver* on an ordinary purchase? If it is not food, or if it cannot be taken to Jerusalem before it spoils, or it was an accidental purchase, the money should be replaced. But if you knew it was *second tithe silver* then you *must* take it to Jerusalem and eat it there, or let it rot.

---

[2] In later traditions there are occasional references to collections of *second tithe* money—e.g., b.Pes.7a; b.San.30a.

Dating (8): The core of this subject reflects the pre-70 practice of bringing produce to Jerusalem, and the addition of 'if the Holy [Place] does not exist' suggests that an earlier ruling has had to be changed in order to accommodate new circumstances. This type of circumstance became more important after 70 CE when households were starting to accumulate *second tithe silver* which could not be spent.

Before 70 CE it would have been unnecessary to add the ruling about purchasing meat because it was obvious that the ruling about produce would also apply to meat. But after 70 CE, when the different ending was added ('let it be buried, with its hide' instead of 'let it rot'), the separate ruling was important. If this ruling did not exist, the law of the produce could have opened a potential loophole for spending the otherwise unspendable *second tithe silver*, because someone could purchase an animal, remove the valuable hide, and let the meat rot. It is therefore likely that this ruling was added later to prevent this practice.

m.MS.1.7: What you cannot purchase with *second tithe silver*

One should not purchase	אֵין לוֹקְחִין
men servants or maid servants	עֲבָדִים וּשְׁפָחוֹת
or land or *impure* animal	וְקַרְקָעוֹת וּבְהֵמָה טְמֵאָה
from the *valuation of second tithe*.	מִדְּמֵי מַעֲשֵׂר שֵׁנִי.
And if he purchases [these with *second tithe silver*]	וְאִם לָקַח,
he should eat the equivalent [value as *second tithe*].	יֹאכַל כְּנֶגְדָּן.
One should not bring	אֵין מְבִיאִין
the sacrificial birds of *men suffering discharge*	קִנֵּי זָבִים,
or the sacrificial birds of *women suffering discharge*	וְקִנֵּי זָבוֹת,
or the sacrificial birds of *women in confinement*	וְקִנֵּי יוֹלְדוֹת,
or *sin offerings* or *guilt offerings*	חַטָּאוֹת, וַאֲשָׁמוֹת,
from the *valuation of second tithe*.	מִדְּמֵי מַעֲשֵׂר שֵׁנִי.
And if he brought [any of these with *second tithe silver*]	וְאִם הֵבִיא,
he must eat the equivalent [value as *second tithe*].	יֹאכַל כְּנֶגְדָּם.
This is the general principle:	זֶה הַכְּלָל,
Everything except which is	כֹּל שֶׁהוּא חוּץ
for eating or for drinking or for anointing	לַאֲכִילָה וְלִשְׁתִיָּה וְלִסִיכָה
[which is purchased] from the *valuation* of *second tithe*	מִדְּמֵי מַעֲשֵׂר שֵׁנִי,
he must eat the equivalent [value as *second tithe*].	יֹאכַל כְּנֶגְדּוֹ.

Comments: You can only buy food items with *second tithe silver,* and if you bought other things you had to purchase the equivalent value of food and eat it as *second tithe*. The difference between this mishnah and the preceding ones (m.MS.1.5-6) is probably that they concern invalid purchases outside Jerusalem while this one assumes an invalid purchase inside Jerusalem, because the previous mishnahs said one should replace the money but this mishnah says one should eat the equivalent value.

Dating (8): There would be no need for creating this type of ruling after 70 CE, and the reference to both spending *second tithe silver* and paying for sacrifices are very specifically pre-70.

The general principle at the end is almost certainly later, especially with the addition of the word "anointing" which is not present in the preceding passage. It is possible that *second tithe* oil was used for anointing even after 70 CE, because it was discussed by Simeon b. Yohai [T4] (m.MS.2.2-3), though it is likely that this was merely a theoretical debate about what used to be done.

m.MS.2.1-4: Using *second tithe* produce

Summary of Mishnah: If *second tithe* produce is accidentally mixed with spices, its value increases in proportion with the spices (2.1). *Second tithe silver* must purchase only produce which can be eaten, though you can anoint yourself with the eating oil (just like priests can use *elevation offering* oil and fenugreek as non-foods—2.2-3). Can vetches become *deconsecrated* when they become *impure* (like *elevation offerings* can) (2.4)?

The digression at m.MS.2.3 includes a school debate concerning *elevation offerings* of fenugreek and vetches. This tradition is dealt with at the end of the chapter on *Terumot*. There is no evidence that any of this section originated before 70 CE.

m.MS.2.5-10: Mixing *consecrated* and *deconsecrated* coins

Summary of Mishnah: If *consecrated* coins become mixed with *deconsecrated*, you can pick up any coins to the same *valuation* and treat them as the *consecrated* coins (2.5). If they are silver coins, you *deconsecrate* the silver coins with copper coins and then chose the best silver coins (2.6). Can you exchange them for gold coins (2.7)? Can you ever exchange *second tithe silver* for other silver coins (2.8-9)? If you say 'this *second tithe silver consecrates* part of the meal,' then *impure* people who eat with you can be assumed to eat the *deconsecrated* part (2.10).

The following traditions have elements (marked in bold) for which there is evidence of an origin before 70 CE:

t.MS.2.4 (Z 2.6): Accidental mixing of *consecrated* coins with others

Deconsecrated coins and *dedication* coins	מעות חולין ומעות הקדש
which became scattered [and mixed]:	שנתפזרו,
What he gathered is gathered as *dedication* [coins].	משלקט לקט להקדש.
One [and the same rule applies to]	אחד

coins [scattered and mixed] with coins,	מָעוֹת בְּמָעוֹת,
[pieces of] of produce with [pieces of] produce	פֵּירוֹת בְּפֵירוֹת,
and pomegranates with pomegranates,	וְרִמּוֹנִין בְּרִמּוֹנִין,
or any thing which intermingles.	וְכָל דָּבָר שֶׁדַּרְכּוֹ לִיבָּלֵל.
But a thing which does not intermingle:	אֲבָל דָּבָר שֶׁאֵין דַּרְכּוֹ לִיבָּלֵל,
That which he gathered is gathered for both	מַה שֶּׁלָּקַט לָקַט לִשְׁנֵיהֶם,
[categories and separated accordingly]	
and that which remains [if an excess is gathered]	וּמַה שֶּׁהוֹתִיר
remains for both [to be shared proportionately].	הוֹתִיר לִשְׁנֵיהֶם.

Mishnaic parallel: m.MS.2.5

Comments: If two baskets of money or produce both spilled and you could not decide what should go into which basket, you erred on the side of the *consecrated* goods. This prevented you from accidentally spending a *dedicated* coin or eating *dedicated* produce. The rule is in this tractate because it applied equally to *second tithe* coins and produce as well as to to *first tithe* or *elevation offerings* which were probably collected and taken to Jerusalem or to a local Temple representative before 70 CE (see Comments at m.Ter.5.1).

Dating (8): These rulings reflect pre-70 practices because after 70 CE *dedications* were very rarely made (because they were for the upkeep of the Temple) and produce of other kinds was not stored, waiting for transportation to Jerusalem, as it was before 70 CE. After 70 CE the *elevation offerings* and *first tithe* were given to local priests and Levites, respectively, and the *second tithe* was converted into coins.

The text in m.MS.2.5 is almost identical, except that it speaks about *second tithe* coins instead of *dedication* coins and pieces of produce. This version reflects a post-70 context when *second tithe silver* was of preeminent concern because it started to accumulate in peoples' houses while they awaited the rebuilding of the Temple.

In t.MS.2.5-9 there is more discussion about *dedicated* coins, but some of this is by later rabbis from generations T3 (Ben Azzai) and then T5 (Eleazar b. Simeon and Judah haNasi). They use the principles delineated in this older tradition to discuss the problems associated with *second tithe silver*.

m.MS.2.7-9: Exchanging *second tithe silver* for other coins

The School of Shammai says:	בֵּית שַׁמַּאי אוֹמְרִים,
One may not make [silver] *selas*	לֹא יַעֲשֶׂה אָדָם אֶת סִלְעָיו
[of second tithe into] gold *dinars*.	דִּינְרֵי זָהָב.
But the School of Hillel permits [it].	וּבֵית הִלֵּל מַתִּירִין.
R. Akiba [T3] said:	אָמַר רַבִּי עֲקִיבָה,
I made, for Rn. Gamaliel [II, T2]	אֲנִי עָשִׂיתִי לְרַבָּן גַּמְלִיאֵל
and for R. Joshua [(b. Hananiah, T2),	וּלְרַבִּי יְהוֹשֻׁעַ
[silver] *selas* into gold *dinars*.	אֶת כַּסְפָּן דִּינְרֵי זָהָב.

8) He who changes a [silver] *sela*	הפורט סלע
from coins of *second tithe*:	ממעות מעשר שני,
The School of Shammai says:	בית שמאי אומרים,
The whole *sela* [must be changed for copper] coins.	כל הסלע מעות.
But the School of Hillel says: [You may change it for]	ובית הלל אומרים,
a *shekel* of silver and a *shekel* of [copper] coins.	שקל כסף ושקל מעות.
R. Meir [T4] says:	רבי מאיר אומר,
One should not *deconsecrate* [*second tithe*] silver	אין מחללין כסף
or [*second tithe*] produce with [other coins of] silver.	ופרות על הכסף,
But the Sages permit [it].	וחכמים מתירים.
9) He who changes a [silver] *sela*	הפורט סלע
which is *second tithe* in Jerusalem:	של מעשר שני בירושלים,
The School of Shammai says:	בית שמאי אומרים,
The whole *sela* [must be changed for copper] coins.	כל הסלע מעות.
But the School of Hillel says: [You may change it for]	ובית הלל אומרים,
a *shekel* of silver and a *shekel* of [copper] coins.	שקל כסף ושקל מעות.
The disputants before the Sages say:	הדנין לפני חכמים אומרים,
[The *sela* may be changed] for three silver *dinars*	בשלשה דינרין כסף
and [one] *dinar* of [copper] coins.	ודינר מעות.
R. Akiba [T3] says:	רבי עקיבה אומר,
[The *sela* may be changed] for three silver *dinars*	שלשה דינרין כסף,
and a fourth [*dinar* of copper] coins.	ורביעית מעות.
R. Tarfon [T3] says:	רבי טרפון אומר,
The "four" [are] *aspers* of silver	ארבעה אספרי כסף.
[which is four-fifths of a *sela* and the one-fifth is of copper].	
Shammai [1st C BCE] says:	שמאי אומר,
He must deposit [the *sela*] in a shop	יניחנה בחנות
and he must eat the equivalent [value as *second tithe*].	ויאכל כנגדה.

Mishnaic parallel: m.MS.1.9-10

Comments: Once *second tithe* produce has been redeemed with coins, those actual coins gain the status of *second tithe* and you should not exchange them for other coins if you can avoid it. The Torah specified "silver" (Deut.14.25) which was interpreted as a silver *sela* (cf. the T5 discussion at b.Bekh.50b) which was worth two silver *shekels* or four silver *dinars* or five silver *aspers* or a multitude of copper coins.

A large denomination coin such as a *sela* was difficult to spend, and so you had to break it up, and a large number of *selas* were difficult to carry, and so you might want to convert it to gold. The Shammaites did not allow anyone to convert *selas* into any gold or silver coins, but the reason is not given. The most likely reason is that they did not want anyone to interpret "silver" in Torah as any other coin than a *sela,* and so they did not allow anyone to change the coins into any other form.

The number of copper coins which were exchanged for one *sela* were too unwieldy to carry easily, and so the Hellenites allowed half of the *sela* to be converted into silver, and later rabbis allowed more and more of the *sela* to be converted into silver (Akiba allowed three quarters and Tarfon allowed four *added fifths*).

Shammai himself did not like changing the *sela* at all and said that one should give the whole coin to a shopkeeper who kept an account of what was bought until that *sela* was spent.

Dating (1): There is no reason to doubt that the school dispute about changing the *selas* into smaller coins dates from before 70 CE, though it is possible that the similar dispute about changing them into larger denomination gold coins may be a later creation based on the other one. After 70 CE, when *second tithe* money was accumulating because it could not be spent, people would be increasingly wanting to change their coins for larger less bulky denominations. However, this might also be an issue before 70 CE for farmers who had large quantities of coins to carry to Jerusalem.

The tradition about Shammai is a stricter version of the Shammaite teaching, and so it fits in with the progression of the history and there was no reason for anyone to make it up at a later date. It also employs unusual vocabulary which is untypical for the Mishnah, except for the phrase at the end of this saying which was probably later imported from m.MS.1.7 in order to help fit this tradition into the rest of the tractate.

The two versions of the school dispute about changing *selas* into smaller denominations are identical except for the words "coins of" and "in Jerusalem." It is difficult to know whether the word "Jerusalem" was added later in order to remind later generations why one might want to have smaller denomination coins (i.e., in order to spend them in Jerusalem) or whether the word "Jerusalem" was later removed because no one took them to Jerusalem any more. The two versions are also both preserved in m.Ed.1.9-10 along with the later discussions which are also found here.

The later discussions were probably mainly for academic interest because there would be little need to change the coins into smaller denominations when no one could spend them. The progress of the dispute appears to be as follows:

> T2 or earlier: A debate before the Sages which said something like: If a *sela* can be changed for one silver coin (a *shekel*) and some copper ones, then it can also be changed for "three silver *dinars* and a *dinar* [of copper] coins."
>
> T3: Akiba transmitted this traditions with one extra word: "three silver *dinars* and a fourth [*dinar* of copper] coins."
>
> T3: Tarfon interpreted this tradition as "three silver *dinars* or four coins," and concluded that the four coins were *aspers*.

This progression gives us an insight into the progressive abbreviation of traditions which sometimes results in reinterpretation.

m.MS.3.1-4: Spending *second tithe silver*

Summary of Mishnah: *Second tithe* can be shared as a gift but not divided equally like a debt (3.1). Do not spend *second tithe silver* on *elevation offerings*. What about vice versa (3.2)? In Jerusalem you can *deconsecrate second tithe silver* with a friend's produce (which must then be eaten in *purity*) (3.3) or with food which you own outside Jerusalem (which must then be brought to Jerusalem) (3.4), or you can *deconsecrate second tithe silver* with produce in Jerusalem (3.4).

There is no evidence that any traditions in this section predate 70 CE. Although the subject of *deconsecrating second tithe* money with food was only of theoretical interest after 70 CE, we know that this topic was still debated (e.g., by R. Simeon b. Yohai, T4, in this section at m.MS.3.2), and so it is unsafe to conclude that any of this predates 70 CE without any further confirmation.

m.MS.3.5-8: *Second tithe* inside and outside Jerusalem

Summary of Mishnah: You may take *second tithe silver* out of Jerusalem without consuming it, but not *second tithe* produce (3.5) unless it was *doubtful second tithe* (3.6). *Second tithe* from produce which was in Jerusalem before it was tithed cannot be redeemed but must be returned and eaten there, unless perhaps it was not fully processed before it left Jerusalem (3.6). Fruit on a tree outside Jerusalem is 'inside' if its branch overhangs the city wall, and perhaps similarly for vats and presses which straddle the wall (3.7). However, with Temple buildings which extend beyond the sanctified area it depends on where their entrance opens (3.8).

The tradition in m.MS.3.8 concerning Temple chambers which are partly inside and outside sanctified space is probably pre-70 and is discussed at m.Mid.1.6.

The following traditions have elements (marked in bold) for which there is evidence of an origin before 70 CE:

m.MS.3.5: *Second tithe* produce may not leave Jerusalem

[*Second tithe*] coins	מעות
may enter Jerusalem and may leave,	נכנסות לירושלים ויוצאות,
while [*second tithe*] produce	ופרות
may enter but may not leave.	נכנסין ואינן יוצאין.
Rabban Simeon b. Gamaliel [II, T4] says:	רבן שמעון בן גמליאל אומר,
Produce, too, may enter and may leave.	**אף** הפרות נכנסין ויוצאין.

Comments: Once *second tithe* produce has been brought to Jerusalem it must be consumed or redeemed. It cannot be taken home again and then brought again to Jerusalem because it was likely to spoil in the meantime.

This rule was particularly difficult for merchants who sold food which still contained the *first* and *second tithes*, because they could not take unsold produce out of Jerusalem for selling in another town or for bringing bring back to the Jerusalem market on another day. Simeon's ruling was probably on their behalf, though the Jerusalem Talmud says that he was thinking of those who bake bread outside the city and bring it back to eat it.

Dating (2): The next mishnah contains a school dispute where both sides assume this ruling is already in force.

Before 70 CE there were probably fewer merchants who sold untithed goods because they did their tithing of *elevation offerings* when they reached the city, and so they were likely to do all their tithing at the same time (cf. Conclusions to the chapter on *Maaserot*). After 70 CE, when anyone could give *elevation offerings* to local priests, they could pretend that they had already removed the other tithes. The whole subject of *doubtfully tithed food* suggests that many merchants were suspected of not tithing the *first* and *second tithes*, though they were always assumed to tithe the *major elevation offering* properly (cf. Conclusions to the chapter on *Demay*).

Rn. Simeon appears to assume that some merchants have not removed the *second tithe* and that this has become normal practice. So, he wants to provide a way whereby they can freely move their goods. The Jerusalem Talmud may not wish to believe that Rn. Simeon would 'wink' at their lax tithing in this way.

m.MS.3.6: *Second tithe* after produce came from Jerusalem

[*Untithed*] produce whose processing is completed	פרות שנגמרה מלאכתן
and was removed from within Jerusalem:	ועברו בתוך ירושלים,
The *second tithe* of it must be returned	יחזור מעשר שני שלהן
and must be eaten in Jerusalem.	ויאכל בירושלים.
And [produce] whose processing is not completed	ושלא נגמרה מלאכתן
[and was removed from within Jerusalem],	
such as grapes [on their way to] the vat	סלי ענבים לגת
or such as figs [on their way to] the drying shed:	וסלי האנים למוקצה,
The School of Shammai says:	בית שמאי אומרים,
The *second tithe* of it must be returned	יחזור מעשר שני שלהם
and must be eaten in Jerusalem.	ויאכל בירושלים.
But the School of Hillel says:	ובית הלל אומרים,
It must be redeemed and eaten in any place.	יפדה ויאכל בכל מקום.
R. Simeon b. Judah [T6] says	רבי שמעון בן יהודה אומר
in the name of R. Jose [b. Halafta, T4]:	משום רבי יוסי,
The School of Shammai and the School of Hillel	לא נחלקו בית שמאי ובית הלל

were not divided	
about produce	עַל פֵּרוֹת
whose processing is not completed,	שֶׁלֹּא נִגְמְרָה מְלַאכְתָּן,
that the *second tithe* of it must be redeemed	שֶׁיִּפְדֶּה מַעֲשֵׂר שֵׁנִי שֶׁלָּהֶם
and it must be eaten in any place.	וְיֵאָכֵל בְּכָל מָקוֹם.
But about what were they divided?	וְעַל מַה נֶחְלְקוּ,
About produce whose processing is completed,	עַל פֵּרוֹת שֶׁנִּגְמְרָה מְלַאכְתָּן,
[about] which the School of Shammai says:	שֶׁבֵּית שַׁמַּאי אוֹמְרִים,
The *second tithe* of it must be returned	יַחֲזוֹר מַעֲשֵׂר שֵׁנִי שֶׁלָּהֶם
and he must eat [it] in Jerusalem.	וְיֵאָכֵל בִּירוּשָׁלַיִם.
But the School of Hillel says:	וּבֵית הִלֵּל אוֹמְרִים,
It must be redeemed and eaten in any place.	יִפָּדֶה וְיֵאָכֵל בְּכָל מָקוֹם.
And [*second tithe* put aside from] *doubtfully tithed food*	וְהַדְּמַאי,
enters and leaves [Jerusalem] and [then] is redeemed.	נִכְנָס וְיוֹצֵא וְנִפְדֶּה.

Comments: Produce became liable to *first* and *second tithe* when the processing was complete (cf. re t.Maas.1.1a), and so both schools agreed that it should not be taken out of the city after this. If it *was* taken out, then the *second tithe* must be brought back and cannot be redeemed, because it should never have left the city. However, if the produce was not fully processed when it was taken out of the city it was not yet liable to *second tithe*, and so the Hillelites allowed you to redeem its *second tithe*.

R. Jose [T4] thought that both schools agreed that *second tithe* from unprocessed food could be redeemed and that Hillelites also allowed you to redeem *second tithe* from processed food. He may have said this in order to support the merchants who sold untithed food, like Rn. Simeon did according to the previous mishnah.

Dating (1): There is no reason to doubt that these school disputes date from before 70 CE. It is likely that R. Simeon's version is incorrect because it stands in line with a revision of the previous mishnah which also originated in the generation T4.

The examples ('grapes to the vat' and 'olives to the drying shed') were perhaps added later because this dispute probably originated at the same time as the dispute in the next mishnah which concerned an olive press.

m.MS.3.7: Trees and rooms which are partly inside and outside Jerusalem

A tree which stands inside [the city of Jerusalem]	אִילָן שֶׁהוּא עוֹמֵד בִּפְנִים
and [one branch] stretches outside,	וְנוֹטֶה לַחוּץ,
or [one which] stands outside [the city]	אוֹ עוֹמֵד בַּחוּץ
and [one branch] stretches inside:	וְנוֹטֶה לִפְנִים,
[The bit] next to the wall and inside [from there]	מִכְּנֶגֶד הַחוֹמָה וְלִפְנִים,
is [counted as] inside.	כְּלִפְנִים.
[That which is] next to the wall and outside [from there]	מִכְּנֶגֶד הַחוֹמָה וְלַחוּץ,
is [counted as] outside.	כְּלַחוּץ.
Olive presses whose entrances [are] inside	בָּתֵּי הַבַּדִּים שֶׁפִּתְחֵיהֶן לִפְנִים

and [whose] internal [rooms] are outside [the city wall],	וחללן לחוץ,
or whose entrances are outside	או שפתחיהן לחוץ
and [whose] internal [rooms] are inside [the city wall]:	וחללן לפנים.
The School of Shammai says:	בית שמאי אומרים,
All [are treated] as inside [the city wall].	הכל כלפנים.
But the School of Hillel says:	ובית הלל אומרים,
[That which is] adjacent to the wall	מכנגד החומה
and towards the inside is [counted as] inside.	ולפנים, כלפנים.
[That which is] adjacent to the wall	מכנגד החומה
and towards the outside is [counted as] outside.	ולחוץ, כלחוץ.

Comments: If a tree was inside Jerusalem you cannot carry its fruit outside until it has been tithed, because you cannot carry *second tithe* produce out of Jerusalem. But if a branch extends over the city wall, this restriction only applies to fruit which actually grows within the wall. This ruling is supported by a school dispute about an olive press which was built into the city wall, which the Shammaites said was 'inside' while the Hillelites said that the part which extended beyond the wall was 'outside.'

This dispute presumably originated from an actual case brought by the owner of such an olive press, for whom this decision was very important. If the press was 'inside' the city then the *second tithe* would have to be removed from any oil which was taken out of the city because the oil had been inside the city when it became fully processed. This would mean that he would have to charge the higher price for pretithed oil, but not everyone was willing to pay this price. Most people bought oil for a multitude of uses (cooking, anointing, fuel for lamps, etc.) but they needed to tithe it only if it was used for food, and so they would buy non-tithed oil and tithe it themselves when necessary.

Hillel's solution was useful because he could make sure that the final stages of processing the oil took place in the part of the press which was outside the city, so that the oil did not become liable to compulsory *second tithe*. In the discussion of Dating (below) we will conclude that Hillel actually replied that "the one whose entrance opens inside, is inside, and the one whose entrance opens outside is outside." This would mean that the owner of this type of press should make sure that he only had one entrance (outside the city), and then the whole press was considered to be 'outside.'

Dating (1): There is no reason to doubt that the schools did debate this issue, but there has been some corruption to the record of the Hillelite response, as seen by the confusion of different reports in the Mishnah and Tosefta (t.MS.2.12 cf. t.Arak.5.15).

Mishnah has:

> An olive press whose entrance is inside but whose enclosure is outside
> or whose entrance is outside but whose enclosure is inside:
> Shammaites: All [should be treated] as inside.

Hillelites: The area adjacent the wall and toward the inside is inside.
and the area adjacent the wall and toward the outside is outside.

Tosefta has a version which is attributed to Akiba:

Shammaites: Regarding the *second tithe* it is inside
and regarding eating *lesser holy things* it is outside.
Hillelites The area adjacent the wall and toward the inside is inside.
and the area adjacent the wall and toward the outside is outside.

Tosefta also has a 'First' version:

Shammaites: Regarding *second tithe* it is inside
and regarding eating *consecrated* things it is outside
Hillelites Lo, they are like [Temple] chambers:
The one whose entrance opens inside is inside,
and the one whose entrance opens outside is outside.

All of the various versions of the school dispute have problems associated with them. Both of the versions in Tosefta are too unbalanced to be correct because normally the school disputes were recorded with as much symmetry as possible, in order to make them easier to memorise, but the pairs of opinions in Tosefta do not even relate to each other. If we assume that the Shammaite ruling in Mishnah is the original (because none of the Hillelite responses balance the other Shammaite rulings), and that the question (which is the same in Mishnah and Tosefta) has been preserved correctly, there are two possible 'original' versions of the Hillelite ruling, the first from Tosefta and the second from Mishnah.

An olive press whose entrance is inside but whose enclosure is outside
or whose entrance is outside but whose enclosure is inside:
Shammaites: All [i.e., both] [should be treated] as inside.
Hillelites The one whose entrance opens inside, is inside
and the one whose entrance opens outside is outside.

Or:

Shammaites: All [i.e., the whole area] [should be treated] as inside.
Hillelites: The area adjacent the wall and toward the inside is inside.
and the area adjacent the wall and toward the outside is outside.

The original case presumably involved an olive press which extended inside the wall but had an entrance outside, because if its only entrance was into the city there would be no dispute about the fact that the fully processed oil was taken into the city before it was taken out. Either of the Hillelite solutions would help in this situation, but the second one would be relevant only if the press was partly inside and partly outside the city, and we would expect this detail to be present in the question. Therefore the first version (which is found only in Tosefta) was probably the original. The second version may have been inspired by a different interpretation of the Shammaite "All" or by the preceding mishnah about overhanging trees or by the mishnah about Temple spaces which follows.

Both Mishnah and Tosefta are followed by a mishnah about Temple spaces (m.MS.3.8 // t.MS.2.13-15):

> Chambers built in the holy space and open to unsanctified space:
> Their enclosure is unsanctified but their roof is holy.
> Chambers built in unsanctified space and open to the holy space:
> Their enclosure is holy but their roof is unsanctified.
> Chambers built in partly unsanctified and in holy space and open to both:
> For both enclosures and roof:
> that which is adjacent to the holy and toward the holy is holy, and
> that which is adjacent to the unsanctified and toward the unsanctified is unsanctified.

This tradition is dealt with in greater detail in the chapter on *Middot*, but it should be noted here that the tradition in m.Mid.1.6 partly contradicts m.MS.3.8 and that a later authority in T2 or T3 attempted to harmonize them. The room described in m.Mid.1.6 had a single entrance to the holy space and according to the tradition in m.MS.3.8 the whole of this room should be holy, but according to m.Mid.1.6 there were flagstones down the center of the room to mark the holy half from the unsanctified half. This contradiction was harmonized in m.Mid.1.7 by saying that the chamber described in m.Mid.1.6 actually had another entrance which opened to the unsanctified space, so that this agreed with m.MS.3.8 which says that a room which opened to both areas should be divided. This harmonization is commented on by R. Judah [T4] who answers the question, 'Why was the second door not mentioned before?' by saying, 'It was only a *small* door.' This suggests that the anonymous explanation preceded R. Judah by one or two generations.

The recognition that there was a contradiction suggests that both the traditions in m.Mid.1.6 and in m.MS.3.8 were already too well established to alter by the time that the harmonization was suggested, so they both originate from before 70 CE.

It was concluded above that an earlier version of the Hillelite ruling in the school dispute in m.MS.3.7 was preserved in t.MS.2.12. The later version in m.MS.3.7 (which divided an enclosure which only had one entrance) appears to be based on m.Mid.1.6 without the harmonization which came later. If this is true, the second version was already in circulation before 70 CE.

There is no way of knowing if the ruling about the tree branches dates before 70 CE.

m.MS.3.9-13: *Second tithe* produce which became *impure*

Summary of Mishnah: If *second tithe* produce in Jerusalem became *impure* must it still be eaten in Jerusalem after you have redeemed it (3.9)? And does this apply when it was purchased with *second tithe silver*, or should you destroy it (3.10)? If you do destroy it, you also destroy the valuable container with it (3.11), unless the vendor stated that the container was 'on loan' before he closed it (3.12). When a wine jug is corked it must be treated as single item of food (3.12), and so if the vendor does not want to sell the jug, is it sufficient just to uncork it (3.13)?

The following traditions have elements (marked in bold) for which there is evidence of an origin before 70 CE:

m.MS.3.9: *Second tithe* produce of Jerusalem which became *impure*

Second tithe [produce] which entered	מעשר שני שנכנס
Jerusalem and became *impure*:	לירושלים ונטמא,
Whether it became *impure* from a *source of impurity*, [or]	בין שנטמא באב הטומאה
whether it became *impure* from *transmitted impurity*,	בין שנטמא בולד הטומאה,
whether [it became *impure* while] inside [Jerusalem],	בין בפנים
[or] whether [it became *impure* while] outside [Jerusalem]:	בין בחוץ,
The School of Shammai says:	בית שמאי אומרים,
It must be redeemed and must be eaten,	יפדה ויאכל
all [of it], inside [the city]	הכל בפנים,
except that which became *impure*	חוץ משנטמא
from a *source of impurity* [while] outside [the city].	באב הטומאה בחוץ.
But the School of Hillel says:	ובית הלל אומרים,
It must all be redeemed and must be eaten	הכל יפדה ויאכל
outside [the city]	בחוץ,
except that which became *impure*	חוץ משנטמא
from *transmitted impurity* [while] inside [the city].	בולד הטומאה בפנים.

Comments: *Second tithe* had to be eaten in *purity*, and so if it became *impure* it had to be redeemed, but it still retained some *second tithe* status. So, could you take it out of the city? The Shammaites almost never let you take it out because they said that even *second tithe* which was *on its way to* the city retains its status, unless it was seriously contaminated on its way. The Hillelites almost always let you take it out because they said only *second tithe* which *actually entered* the city and only that which was lightly contaminated retained *second tithe* status.

The different emphases of the schools is conveyed by a subtle movement of the word "all" from the verb "eaten" in the Shammaite saying to the verb "redeemed" in the Hillelite version. The Shammaites emphasized that anything which had been brought to the city with the status of *second tithe* should be *eaten* inside Jerusalem—

though they drew the line at bringing into the city produce which had been contaminated with a *source of impurity*. The Hillelites emphasized that any *second tithe* which had become contaminated should be *redeemed*, and that after it was redeemed you could eat it anywhere—though they drew the line at removing from the city *second tithe* which had only minor contamination.

Dating (1): There is no reason to doubt that this school dispute dates from before 70 CE. The subject is debated again by Eliezer [T2] and later rabbis in t.MS.2.16.

t.MS.2.16c (Z 2.18c): Where to eat redeemed *impure second tithes*

The School of Shammai says:	שבית שמיי אומרים
It is redeemed in the Place [i.e., Jerusalem]	נפדה במקום
and so it must be eaten in the Place.	ויאכל במקום
But the School of Hillel says:	ובית הלל אומרים
It is redeemed in the Place	נפדה במקום
and so it must be eaten in any place.	ויאכל בכל המקומות.

Comments: This concerns *second tithe* which had been brought to Jerusalem but became contaminated, and it makes plain what was hidden in the subtle movement of the word "all" in the school dispute of m.MS.3.9. The Shammaites said that *second tithe* could not be taken out of Jerusalem even after it was contaminated and redeemed, but the Hillelites said that if it was redeemed you could eat it anywhere.

Dating (1): It is possible that this school dispute was a later version which was invented as an easier way to remember the subtle teaching which was embedded in the school dispute of m.MS.3.9. It is not recorded anywhere in Mishnah and the tradition in Tosefta was transmitted by Simeon b. Eleazar of the generation T5 (late second century). The language could have been derived from other traditions such as m.MS.1.5-6 or m.MS.3.6.

However, the Shammaites have the upper hand in this record of the dispute, because their saying has a natural logic to it and a memorable simplicity. The Hillelite reply is clever, but it does not overcome the simple logic of the Shammaites. It is unlikely that anyone would invent a saying in support of the Shammaite opinion after 70 CE when the Shammaites had lost all influence and had virtually disappeared.

m.MS.3.13a: How a vendor can sell wine but not the corked jug

[How can a wine merchant sell wine as *second tithe* and not *consecrate* the jug?]:

The School of Shammai says:	בית שמאי אומרים,
[By] unsealing [the jug] and pouring [the wine]	מפתח ומערה
into the vat [and back into the jug].	לגת.
But the School of Hillel says:	ובית הלל אומרים,
[By] unsealing [the jug], but it is not necessary	מפתח ואינו צריך

to pour [the wine into the vat and back again].	לַעֲרוֹת.
In what situations do they say [this]?	בַּמֶּה דְבָרִים אֲמוּרִים,
In the place where it is normal	בְּמָקוֹם שֶׁדַּרְכָּן
to sell sealed [jugs, this rule applies],	לִמְכֹּר סְתוּמוֹת.
but in the place where it is normal	אֲבָל בְּמָקוֹם שֶׁדַּרְכָּן
to sell open [jugs]	לִמְכֹּר פְּתוּחוֹת,
the jug has not become *deconsecrated*.	לֹא יָצָא קַנְקַן לְחֻלִּין.

Comments: Many wine merchants sold open wine cheaply in the expectation that the container would be returned to them. However, if you bought a sealed container with *second tithe* money, the money also purchased the container, and you were able to take this home with you. Many people wanted to do this so that they could spend their *second tithe* money on something which they could take home. How could a wine merchant ensure that the container was not sold with the wine if he was selling corked amphorae? It appears that the Hillelites allowed him simply to uncork the amphora at the time of the sale, but the Shammaites said that the amphora had to be filled at the time of the sale.

Dating (1): There is no reason to doubt that this school dispute dates from before 70 CE. It is also likely that some of the previous mishnah predates this, because it is necessary to read this in order to infer the question which this dispute was answering. However it is also possible that the school dispute was added onto a later debate and that the opening question which was attached to this dispute was removed as unnecessary in the combined tradition.

m.MS.4.1-7: The cost of redeeming *second tithe* produce

Summary of Mishnah: *Second tithe* produce is accounted with the *valuation* it has when it is eaten in Jerusalem or when it is redeemed (4.1), even if you do not have the cash with you (4.6). The value is the lowest price at that time and place (4.2), though a higher bidder gets preference (4.3). If you redeem your own produce, you pay its *full value* plus an *added fifth* (4.3), but not if an adult member of the family redeems your produce (4.4) or if you give it away and then redeem it (4.5). Do you have to declare that your purchase is a redemption (4.7)?

There is no evidence that any traditions in this section of Mishnah predate 70 CE but a couple of school traditions are preserved in the Tosefta at this point.

t.MS.3.13-14 (Z 3.13): *Second tithe* produce after the Temple's destruction

One should not redeem *second tithe*	אֵין פּוֹדִין מַעֲשֵׂר שֵׁנִי
in Jerusalem at this time [i.e., after the destruction].	בִּירוּשָׁלַיִם בַּזְּמַן הַזֶּה,
And one should not set aside *second tithe*	וְאֵין מַפְרִישִׁין מַעֲשֵׂר שֵׁנִי

in Jerusalem at this time.	בִּירוּשָׁלַיִם בַּזְּמַן הַזֶּה,
And one should not *deconsecrate second tithe* [money]	וְאֵין מְחַלְּלִין מַעֲשֵׂר שֵׁינִי
in Jerusalem at this time.	בִּירוּשָׁלַיִם בַּזְּמַן הַזֶּה,
And one should not sell [produce] as *second tithe*	וְאֵין מוֹכְרִין מַעֲשֵׂר שֵׁינִי
in Jerusalem at this time.	בִּירוּשָׁלַיִם בַּזְּמַן הַזֶּה,
And one should not take out *second tithe*	וְאֵין מוֹצִיאִין מַעֲשֵׂר שֵׁינִי
from Jerusalem at this time.	בִּירוּשָׁלַיִם בַּזְּמַן הַזֶּה,
And if it was taken out [of Jerusalem]	וְאִם הוֹצִיא
lo, one must let it rot.	הֲרֵי אֵלּוּ יֵרָקֵבוּ.
14) Those *deconsecrating* coins with produce	מְחַלְּלִין מָעוֹת עַל פֵּירוֹת
in Jerusalem at this time:	בִּירוּשָׁלַיִם בַּזְּמַן הַזֶּה,
The School of Shammai says:	בֵּית שַׁמַּיִ אוֹמְרִים
This and that [i.e., both coins and produce]	זֶה וָזֶה
[have the status of] *second tithe*.	מַעֲשֵׂר שֵׁינִי,
But the School of Hillel says:	וּבֵית הִלֵּל אוֹמְרִים
The coins remain the same*	הַמָּעוֹת כְּמוֹת שֶׁהוּא,
and the produce remains the same.	וְהַפֵּירוֹת כְּמוֹת שֶׁהָיוּ.

*Z omits שהוא 'the same' from this one line

Comments: After 70 CE when they stopped taking *second tithe* produce or coins to Jerusalem, they redeemed all *second tithe* produce and put the coins aside in hope that they could spend them one day when the Temple was rebuilt. Theoretically it was still possible to eat *second tithe* produce in Jerusalem in a state of *purity*, because the Temple was not necessary for this, but it did not seem right to rejoice in Jerusalem, and it soon became established practice to save up *second tithe* money in hope of a rebuilt Temple (cf. on m.MS.1.3-4).

It is difficult to know if this was a ruling (i.e., "One should not redeem *second tithe* in Jerusalem at this time") or a statement of normal behavior (i.e., "They do not . . ."). In Mishnah, the impersonal plural usually carried a jussive force, especially with a negative, and so it is best to translate "One should not. . . ." This might suggest that some people wanted to continue going to Jerusalem to spend their *second tithe,* and they had to be told to wait, in hope of a rebuilt Temple.

Dating (1): This school dispute is very unusual in that, as it occurs here, it appears to come from a post-70 context, ruling about a situation after the destruction of the Temple. It is likely that the opening question has been changed or (more likely) that it has been made more specific so that a ruling which was made before 70 CE has been reapplied to the post-70 context.

Probably this dispute originally concerned "those *deconsecrating* coins with produce invalidly," i.e., those who bought *impure* produce or bought produce outside Jerusalem. It may have been related to the group of rulings in m.MS.1.3-6 which all concern invalid purchases, because it would fit seamlessly onto the end of this collection where the introductions to the rulings would no longer need to repeat that the purchase was invalid:

> He who purchases produce accidentally
> [using *second tithe silver* outside Jerusalem]:
> Its valuation should be returned to its place.
> [He who does it] deliberately, he should bring it up
> and he should eat it in the Place [i.e., Jerusalem].
> And if there is no Holy [Place], it should rot.

The presence of "let it rot" at the end of this and here in t.MS.3.13 just before the school dispute helps to confirm that this dispute may originally have been attached to the end of this collection.

This Hillelite ruling was useful after 70 CE to solve the problem of *second tithe* coins which were accidentally spent in Jerusalem after the destruction. The authority for this new ruling (that no one can purchase or eat *second tithe* produce in Jerusalem) could thereby be based on the authority of the schools.

Therefore the school dispute is likely to be genuine, though the question introducing it has been slightly changed and the rulings to which it is attached are post-70. The rulings by the two schools are usually balanced to make them easier to remember. It is likely that the Hillelite ruling was expanded in order to make it clearer, and this may explain the slight differences in textual traditions. Therefore the original School dispute was probably something like:

> Those *deconsecrating* [*second tithe*] coins with produce [in an invalid way]:
> Shammaites: This and that [i.e., both coins and produce] [have status of] *second tithe*.
> Hillelites This and that [i.e., both coins and produce] remain the same.

It is impossible to determine when these rulings about *second tithe* after the destruction originated, but the principle that *second tithes* should not be eaten after 70 CE appear to have been universally accepted by the time the Mishnah was edited at the beginning of the third century, because the Mishnah simply assumes it.

t.MS.3.15 (Z 3.14): Eating doubtful *second tithe* without setting it aside

The School of Hillel says:	בית הלל אומרים
One may set aside the *first tithe*	מפריש אדם מעשר ראשון
which is [from food whose tithing is] *doubtful*[*1]	של דמיי
and *elevate* [the *elevation offering* from] it	ותורמו
and [then] eat it;	ואוכלו,
and **it is not necessary to set aside *second* [tithe].**	ואין צריך להפריש שני.
The School of Shammai says:	בית שמיי אומרים
It is necessary to set aside *second* [tithe]	צריך להפריש שיני,
for I say: [i.e., they would argue that:][*2]	שאני אומר

[If] the *second* [tithe] is separate [already]	הורם השני
[then] the *first* [tithe] is separate [already]	הורם הראשון,
[but if] the *first* [tithe] is separate [already]	הורם הראשון
the *second* [tithe] is not [necessarily] separate [already].	לא הורם השני.
And the *halakhah* is according to the words of	והלכה כדברי
the School of Shammai.	בית שמיי.

*1 Z has what became the more conventional spelling דמאי.
*2 Z omits this line. L reads שיני which is probably an error.

Comments: *Doubtfully tithed food* was assumed to have the *major elevation offering* separated, so that one only had to designate the *first tithe* and *second tithe* and separate the *minor elevation offering* from the *first tithe*. In practice you did not actually discard the *first tithe* and *second tithe* but merely designated where they were in order to remove the *minor elevation offering* from the *first tithe* (see m.Dem.4.3). This ruling suggests that some Hillelites did not bother to designate the *second tithe* because it served no practical purpose.

After 70 CE the designation of the *second tithe did* have a practical purpose because all *second tithes* were redeemed. Before 70 CE, when *second tithe* could be put aside for consumption in Jerusalem, they could ignore the small quantities in a normal meal because it was impractical to carry them. A scrupulous person might destroy these portions by crumbling them or throwing them on the fire (cf. m.Hal.4.8), but most people simply let them mix with the rest of the meal. But after 70 CE, when all *second tithes* were redeemed, they could no longer resort to this convenience, and so they had to put aside money for every small portion of *second tithe* (cf. the formula for tithing *doubtfully tithed food* at m.Dem.7.1).

Dating (1): There is no reason to doubt that this was a genuine school dispute. Even though the Shammaite position is best suited to the situation after 70 CE, there is no reason to believe that it was not followed by them before 70 CE. If later authorities had wanted to *invent* a school dispute in order to bolster a new ruling, they would let the Hillelites represent their own position, rather than assign the 'correct' ruling to the Shammaites who normally represent the rejected ruling. We know from the school dispute in m.MS.4.8b that some *second tithes* from *doubtfully tithed food* were already redeemed before 70 CE, which tends to confirm that a significant number of people followed the Shammaite ruling even before 70 CE.

This debate was taken further in generation T2 (soon after 70 CE) when Eliezer said that the *second tithe* did not need to be delineated in the years when it was a *poor tithe* (see m.Dem.4.3). Eliezer appeared to be making a last effort to preserve some part of the Hillelite ruling. He presumably argued that although the *second tithe* had a high status because it was *consecrated*, the *poor tithe* did not have such a high status. In both cases, here and at m.Dem.4.3, the majority voted that designating the *second tithe* was necessary.

It is unusual for the majority after 70 CE to follow the Shammaite ruling, but it was done in this case because this ruling fitted better with the changed circumstances after the destruction of the Temple, when all *second tithes* were redeemed for money. They could no longer argue that designation of *second tithe* had no practical value.

The wording of the school dispute appears to have been altered, because the normal form is for the question to be stated before the Schools give their opinion. The original may have been:

> If someone sets aside the *first tithe*:
> Hillelites: It is not necessary to set aside the *second*.
> Shammaites: It is necessary to set aside the *second*.

The question may have been expanded and moved to become part of the Hillelite words when the dispute became part of the tractate *Maaser Sheni*. If the dispute had been inserted into the tractate *Demay* there would have been no need to add the extra explanation. Perhaps it was originally transmitted together with other traditions about *doubtfully tithed food*.

m.MS.4.8-12: Spending and storing *second tithe* silver

Summary of Mishnah: You spend *second tithe silver* according to the value it has when you spend it, until there is no more than one-tenth (or one-eleventh?) of an *issar* left (4.8). If you find coins which might be *second tithe*, you may assume they are not, unless you were expecting to find similar coins (4.12) or unless they are in a container marked 'tithe' (4.9)—and if it says 'offering' or an abbreviation for *consecrated* goods, its contents must be assumed to be *consecrated* (4.10-11).

The following traditions have elements (marked in bold) for which there is evidence of an origin before 70 CE:

m.MS.4.8b: How little must be left for *second tithe silver* to be counted as 'spent'

He who puts aside an *issar* as *second tithe*	הַמַּנִּיחַ אָסָר שֶׁל מַעֲשֵׂר שֵׁנִי,
eats [food in Jerusalem] according to its [value]	אוֹכֵל עָלָיו
[until no more than] an eleventh of an *issar* [remains]	אֶחָד עָשָׂר בְּאָסָר
[if it is from *doubtfully tithed food*, but if it is from a *certainly untithed* food,]	
[until no more than] one-hundredth of an *issar* [remains].	וְאֶחָד מִמֵּאָה בְּאָסָר.
The School of Shammai says:	בֵּית שַׁמַּאי אוֹמְרִים,
In every [case, eat until no more than a] tenth [remains]	הַכֹּל עֲשָׂרָה.
But the School of Hillel says:	וּבֵית הִלֵּל אוֹמְרִים,
For *certainly untithed* food [until] an eleventh [remains]	בְּוַדַּאי אֶחָד עָשָׂר,
and for *doubtfully tithed* food [until] a tenth [remains].	וּבִדְמַאי עֲשָׂרָה.

Comments: When was the *second tithe* money fully spent? The Shammaites said one had to spend it until there was no more than one-tenth of an *issar* left—i.e., a little less than the smallest coin, the *perutah* which was worth an eighth of an *issar* (cf. m.Qid.1.1). The Hillelites made a distinction between money which came from proper *second tithe* and that which came from *doubtfully tithed food* (see t.MS.3.15 above). They said that for *doubtfully tithed food* a tenth is alright, but for proper *second tithe* it must be less than a tenth (i.e., an eleventh). Later authorities changed these to an eleventh and a hundredth respectively.

The reason for these quantities are unlikely to have anything to do with the value of the coins, because there is no coin worth one-tenth of an *issar*. It is most probably related to the concept of *neutralizing consecrated* food by dilution with one hundred parts (cf. m.Ter.4.7–5.9), but the reasons for these precise quantities is not certain.

Dating (1): There is no reason to doubt that this school dispute dates from before 70 CE, especially as it ties in the school dispute in t.MS.3.15.

The reasoning for these different rulings is now obscure, but at a guess I would say that originally the *issar* itself represented the smallest amount which could remain because it is worth one-hundredth of a *sela*, which is the coin which was used for *second tithe* money (cf. m.MS.2.7-9). Also the *issar* was the smallest useful coin for buying food—the *perutah* is used in Mishnah only to indicate 'the smallest possible value' and has little practical value, while the *issar* is often mentioned with regard to purchasing small quantities of food.

The Shammaites were able to spend down to a smaller quantity than an *issar* because they often followed the practice of Shammai who gave all his *second tithe* money to a shopkeeper and procured food from him until it was spent. Therefore the Shammaites were able to follow the rule that it must be spent down to the impractically small value of one-hundredth of an *issar*. The Hillelites did not want to be outdone and said that one-tenth was alright for *second tithes* of *doubtfully tithed food* (which only the Shammaites used—cf. t.MS.3.15 above) but *they* spent down below one-tenth to one-eleventh. Later authorities went further still and took it to extremes (one-hundredth of an *issar*), which was impossible to measure by any coinage, but they were able to do this because they never, in practice, actually spent any *second tithe* money. This reconstructed history of the rulings is of course speculative.

m.MS.5.1-5: *Fourth-year* produce of vineyards

Summary of Mishnah: During Sabbath Years, *fourth-year vineyards* are marked with clods of earth, and younger vineyards are marked with clay to warn people—and graves are marked with lime [not just in Sabbath Years] (5.1). *Fourth-year vineyard* produce was redeemed only if it grew more than a day's journey from Jerusalem, until it became too abundant (5.2). Do the laws of *added fifth*, *removal* and harvest *leftovers* apply to *fourth-year vineyard* produce (5.3)? It is redeemed at the highest price from three potential purchasers including the cost of harvesting (5.4). In the Sabbath Year you redeem your own produce at its value plus harvesting costs and an *added fifth*, unless you declare it *ownerless* (5.5).

The school debate at 5.3 about the *added fifth* and *removal* with regard to *fourth-year fruits* is a duplicate of m.Pea.7.6 where it is discussed.

The following traditions have elements (marked in bold) for which there is evidence of an origin before 70 CE:

m.MS.5.2: What *fourth-year* produce can be redeemed?

[Produce from] a *fourth [year] vineyard*	כרם רבעי
was brought up to Jerusalem [if it is within]	היה עולה לירושלים
one day's [journey] in any direction.	מהלך יום אחד לכל צד.
And what are the limits?	ואיזו היא תחומה,
Ayeleth to the south	**אילת מן הדרום**
and Akrabah to the north,	ועקרבה מן הצפון,
Lod to the west	לוד מן המערב
and the Jordan to the east.	והירדן מן המזרח.
But when the produce increased	ומשרבו הפרות,
they *decreed* **that it is to be redeemed**	התקינו שיהא נפדה
[even if it grows] close to the wall.	סמוך לחומה.
And there was a condition on this ruling:	ותנאי היה בדבר,
That at the time when they wish	שאימתי שירצו,
the ruling will reverse to remain as it was.	יחזור הדבר לכמות שהיה.
R. Jose [b. Halfta, T4] says:	רבי יוסי אומר,
From when the Temple was destroyed	משחרב בית המקדש,
this condition was made,	היה התנאי הזה.
and [the wording of] the condition was:	ותנאי היה,
At the time when they [re]build the Temple	אימתי שיבנה בית המקדש,
the ruling will reverse to remain as it was.	יחזור הדבר לכמות שהיה.

Comments: *Fourth-year fruit* had to be to be consumed in Jerusalem, but if the vineyard was more than a day's journey away one could redeem the produce and bring the money instead. At some point there were too many vineyards near Jerusalem, and so they suspended this ruling—perhaps too many vines were planted the same year after a period of warfare or drought—but later rabbis ruled that the original ruling should be reestablished when the Temple is rebuilt.

A whole year's harvest of a vineyard could represent a large amount of produce which was much more than the owner or his family and friends could consume.

Tosefta says that "he divides it among his neighbors, his family and his friends, and he decorates the public road with it" (t.MS.5.14), though this is part of a debate in generation T4 (mid second century).

Dating (2): This ruling only makes sense in the time of the Temple, and it is unlikely that it was made up later because its destruction necessitated a special suspension of the ruling which was not strictly applicable. The original suspension applied when there was a surplus of produce and ended when the surplus ended, but this suspension was converted into a wait until the Temple was rebuilt.

It is not clear when this suspension was reapplied after the destruction, but R. Jose does not claim to be the originator of it—he reported that this condition was in place since the time that the Temple was destroyed. This may not be strictly so, but for him to believe it (or get away with stating it) this condition must have been already established as tradition for more than two generations, because otherwise someone might say: "This ruling was first stated by my teacher." Therefore this revised condition is likely to date back to generation T2 (soon after 70 CE), which means that the original condition, which must come from at least one generation earlier, dates back to before 70 CE. This conclusion is assumed in the Tosefta where an anonymous source says, "When the Temple was destroyed, the first court said nothing about it, but the later court prescribed that: it should be redeemed [even if it grows] close to the wall" (t.MS.5.15). Tosefta assumes that this later court's ruling was in force at the time of Eliezer (see below).

The limits of the one day journey may have been added later, but they are given credence by a story about R. Eliezer in t.MS.5.15-16. According to this story, he had a vineyard "east of Lod" and he wanted to escape the cost of redeeming the produce by keeping it until after the time of *removal* and then destroying it, but his disciples pointed out the ruling that it should be redeemed. It is possible that this story is a late invention (like many biographical stories), especially as the butt of the story is Eliezer who was later regarded as a heretic. On the other hand, this ruling shows Eliezer disagreeing with the Shammaites who said that the law of *removal* did not apply to *fourth-year fruit* (m.MS.5.3 // m.Pea.7.6, dealt with in *Peah*) and that one had to redeem produce at the time of *removal* (m.MS.5.7). Later stories tend to regard Eliezer as a Shammaite (cf. b.Shab.130b; b.Nid.7b) whereas in fact he sometimes disagreed with the Shammaites (cf. m.Dem.4.3 re the *second tithe* at t.MS.3.15).

t.MS.5.18 (Z 5.11b): Can you prune *fourth-year fruit*?

[A *fourth-year vineyard*:]

The School of Shammai says:	בית שמיי אומרים
One may not prune it [i.e., a *fourth-year vineyard*]	אין גוממין אותו,
But the School of Hillel says:	ובית הלל אומרים
One may prune it.	גוממין אותו

Comments: The Shammaites allowed the poor to help themselves to harvest *leftovers* (see m.Pea.7.6), and so this ruling probably relates to vines which still have fruit on them after the harvest time. It is similar to the principle which the Shammaites had in m.Shebi.4.10 where they say that branches bearing Sabbath Year fruit cannot be cut down, whereas the Hillelites restricted this prohibition only to the time when the fruit was optimally ripe.

Dating (1): There is no reason to doubt that this was a genuine school dispute. The opening question is missing, and the context in Tosefta suggests that it should share the same question as the previous two school disputes which precede a short distance above in t.MS.5.17 // m.MS.5.3 // m.Pea.7.6 and t.MS.5.14 // m.MS.5.2, i.e., "a *fourth-year vineyard.*" As suggested in the Comments above, this ruling makes more sense if the question also involved the continued presence of fruit, so that it might have been something like: "a *fourth-year vineyard* with harvest *leftovers.*" However this is the first of three school disputes which share the same distinctive formula "they do not ... it [אותו]," and the other two appear to have the same introductory question. So the most likely original form of this school dispute is:

> A *fourth-year vineyard*:
> Shammaites: They do not prune it.
> Hillelites: They do prune it.

t.MS.5.19 (Z 5.11c): Do you redeem grapes or wine?

The School of Shammai says:	בית שמיי אומרים
One may not redeem it [i.e., a *fourth-year vineyard*]	אין פודין אותו
[as] grapes, but [they do redeem] wine.	ענבים אלא יין,
But the School of Hillel says:	ובית הלל אומרים
[One may redeem it as both] wine and grapes.	יין וענבים,
But they all agree	אבל הכל מודין
that one may not redeem [*fourth-year fruit*]	שאין פודין
[which is] attached to the ground.	במחובר לקרקע

Comments: The Shammaites only redeemed the produce of *fourth-year vineyards* after it had been fully processed, while Hillelites allowed it to be redeemed while it was still unprocessed.

This ruling would make more sense if it was reversed, because Hillelites said that the whole of *fourth-year vineyard* harvests should go to the vat while Shammaites allowed the poor to redeem the harvest *leftovers* (m.MS.5.3 // m.Pea.7.6, dealt with in *Peah*). Also the Hillelites treated *fourth-year fruit* with the same rules as *second tithe* (which was liable to tithing and redemption only after the last stage of processing), whereas the Shammaites regarded it as subject to different rules than *second tithe* (see m.Pea.7.6).

Before 70 CE, when the *fourth-year fruit* was taken to Jerusalem, the easier policy would be to process it as wine, so that there was bulk to carry to Jerusalem and it would be more enjoyable to consume. After 70 CE, when all *fourth-year fruit* had to be redeemed, the cheaper policy would be to redeem it at the lower value of the grapes.

Dating (1): There is no reason to doubt that this represents a genuine school dispute though there may be some indications that the wording has been changed. The opening question is missing, but it is likely to be the same as that of the previous school disputes (see Dating re t.MS.5.18). The wording of the Shammaites starts off as a direct parallel with the previous school dispute from Tosefta (t.MS.5.18), and so it is possible that the Hillelite wording was also parallel. Also, as is pointed out in the Comments, it is possible that the rulings have become reversed. Therefore the original version may have been:

> A *fourth-year vineyard*:
> Shammaites: They do redeem it.
> Hillelites: They do not redeem it.

At some point someone has reversed the rulings (perhaps influenced by the previous and following rulings which are very similar) and then added to the Shammaite ruling 'grapes, but [they do redeem] wine,' perhaps in order to explain the fact that they allow the poor to redeem it at m.MS.5.3 // m.Pea.7.6. The Hillelite "they do not redeem it" was impossible after 70 CE, and so this was dropped off and replaced with "wine and grapes" to correspond with the new Shammaite ruling. All this is very conjectural, but it does help to explain the strange construction, "they do not redeem it, grapes but wine," which would have been much simpler as "they do not redeem grapes but wine."

t.MS.5.20 (Z 5.11d): Do you allow a *fourth year* to coincide with Sabbath Year?

The School of Shammai says:	בית שמיי אומרים
One may not plant it [i.e., a vineyard]	אין נוטעין אותו
during the *fourth [year]*	ברביעית,
because the *fourth [year fruit]* will happen to turn*	שהרביעי שלו חל
to fall on the Seventh [Year].	להיות בשביעית,
But the School of Hillel permits.	ובית הלל מתירין.

*Z has שהרביעית.

Comments: In the Sabbath Year anyone could help themselves to any crop, but if it was *fourth-year fruit* they had to eat it in Jerusalem. According to an undateable tradition in m.MS.5.1 they especially marked such vines so that no one would accidentally eat the fruit incorrectly.

Farmers might deliberately grow a vine during the *fourth year* of the cycle so that the *fourth year* coincided with the Sabbath Year, because this would release them from the financial burden of redeeming the crop. This probably explains why there is a ruling on this issue and no equivalent ruling which warns against planting in the fifth or sixth years which would result in one of the first three years when produce was uneatable coinciding with the Sabbath Year. Therefore the ruling was introduced in order to prevent farmers from exploiting the Law for financial gain rather than to protect the public from eating forbidden fruit during the Sabbath Year.

Dating (1): There is no reason to doubt that this is a genuine school dispute though this ruling became much more important after 70 CE when no one could take the *fourth-year fruit* to Jerusalem and everyone had to redeem it.

This uses the same distinct formula as the previous three school disputes, though details have been added to explain the ruling. We cannot know when those details were added, and given the similarities with the other related rulings it is likely that the original form of this one was:

> A *fourth-year vineyard*:
> Shammaites: They do not plant it in the *fourth [year]*.
> Hillelites: They do plant it in the *fourth [year]*.

t.MS.5.22 (Z 5.12b): If you accidentally dedicate some *second tithe* produce

He who *dedicates* [to the Temple] *second tithe*:*	הַמַּקְדִּישׁ מַעֲשֵׂר שֵׁנִי,
Behold, he redeems this with the intention	הֲרֵי זֶה פּוֹדֶה עַל מְנָת
to give to the *dedication* as its own	לִיתֵּן לְהַקְדִּישׁ אֶת שֶׁלּוֹ
and to the *second tithe* as its own.	וּלְמַעֲשֵׂר שֵׁנִי אֶת שֶׁלּוֹ.

---

*Z adds שֶׁלּוֹ, 'its own.'

Comments: If you *dedicate* some produce to the Temple and then discover that it was actually *second tithe*, you can redeem it so that the produce remains a *dedication* and the money becomes the *second tithe*.

Dating (9): This would have no relevance after 70 CE both because there were no *dedications* (i.e., gifts for Temple upkeep) and because all *second tithe* would be redeemed as a matter of course. However, this tradition has no corroborating evidence of an early origin.

m.MS.5.6-15: *Removal* of *consecrated* produce

Summary of Mishnah: The day of *removal* is the day before the first *holyday* of *Pesach* (Passover) in the *fourth* and Sabbath years, when all tithes must have been given away or destroyed (5.6). After the destruction of the Temple, is *second tithe* produce redeemed or destroyed (5.7)? Tithes which have not yet been put aside are exempt (5.8), and tithes which are elsewhere can be given away by oral declaration (5.9). The ancient ceremony of removal was followed by a confession based on Deuteronomy 26.13-15 that the proper produce has been given to the Levites, priests, and the poor (5.10); that the *first tithe* was separated before the *second* and separated from each type of produce with thanks using the Name (5.11); and that it was dealt with in *purity* (5.12) so that God will bless them and their harvest (5.13). This confession was recited by any Jew who owned land in Israel (5.14) until it was abolished by John Hyrcanus, who also abolished the Psalm of Awakening, stunning sacrificial animals, and loud work during *ordinary festival days*; and in his day even the *impious* tithed properly (5.15).

The following traditions have elements (marked in bold) for which there is evidence of an origin before 70 CE:

m.MS.5.6: The time and process of *removal*

On the eve of the first *holyday**	ערב יום טוב הראשון
of *Pesach* of the *fourth [year]*	של פסח של רביעית
and of the Seventh [Year in the seven-year cycle]	ושל שביעית,
was the [time of] *removal*. How [was it done]?	היה בעור. כיצד,
One should give the *elevation offerings*	נותנין תרומה
and *elevation offerings* of the [*first*] *tithe*	ותרומת מעשר
to [those entitled to be] its owners [i.e., priests],	לבעלים,
and the *first tithe* to its owners [i.e., Levites],	ומעשר ראשון לבעליו,
and the *poor tithe* to its owners [i.e., the poor],	ומעשר עני לבעליו.
but *second tithe* and *firstfruits*	ומעשר שני והבכורים
were *removed* [i.e., destroyed]	מתבערים
in all places.	בכל מקום.
R. Simeon [b. Yohai, T4] says:	רבי שמעון אומר,
Firstfruits are given to the priests	הבכורים נתנין לכהנים
like *elevation offerings*.	כתרומה.
That which is cooked:	התבשיל,
The School of Shammai says:	בית שמאי אומרים,
It is necessary to *remove* [it].	צריך לבער.
But the School of Hillel says:	ובית הלל אומרים,
Behold, it is like that which is *removed* [already].	הרי הוא כמבוער.

* A few MS read האחרון, 'last' instead of הראשון, 'first.'

Comments: Any *consecrated* food which could still be given away on that day had to be given to those to whom it was due, except for *second tithe* and *firstfruits* which had to be eaten in Jerusalem. A possible explanation of the phrase "in all places" is given below.

The tradition about the confession of Removal at m.MS.5.10 suggests that *second tithes* could still be eaten during this *Pesach* (Passover) because the confession does not take place until the end of the festival.

Cooking the food was the same as *removing* or destroying it because it had to be eaten immediately.

Dating (1): The process of *removal* was almost certainly practiced before 70 CE as witnessed by the debate in m.MS.5.9 by scholars of T2 (soon after 70 CE) who assumed this was an established practice. There are also other traditions concerning the time of *removal* which appear to date from before 70 CE (dealt with below), though each of these have difficulties concerning dating. The best witness to the process of *removal* is this tradition, and there is no reason to doubt its genuineness.

The description of *removal* looks like something which would have been composed by later generations to describe what *used* to be done, especially the second half starting "How?" which looks like an added commentary. The detail at the end of this second half, that *second tithe* and *firstfruits* were destroyed "in all places," would mean different things before and after 70 CE. If it was composed before 70 CE it would mean "even near Jerusalem," indicating that even if you were within a day's journey of Jerusalem you should destroy it just in case you don't arrive in time. If it was composed after 70 CE it would mean "even in Jerusalem" because you could no longer consume the produce there.

The date "eve of the first *holyday* of *Pesach*" coincides with the removal of leaven (cf. m.Pes.1.3) so it was a good time for the day of *removal*. But it seems likely that the original date for the *removal* was the last *holyday* of *Pesach* (as suggested in m.MS.5.10), which meant that people would have time to eat their *second tithes* during the festival, as was normal (see m.MS.1.3-4). This agrees with the minority reading of the Palestinian Mishnah and a few MSS.[3] Therefore it is likely that this whole tradition other than the school dispute is late, though there is no reason to believe that the details are inaccurate except for the date.

m.MS.5.7: Redeeming or destroying produce subject to *removal*

One who had [*second tithe*] produce	מִי שֶׁהָיוּ לוֹ פֵרוֹת
at this time [i.e., after the destruction of the Temple]	בַּזְּמַן הַזֶּה
and the time of *removal* arrived:	וְהִגִּיעָה שְׁעַת הַבִּעוּר,
The School of Shammai says:	בֵּית שַׁמַּאי אוֹמְרִים,
It is necessary to *deconsecrate* it with silver.	צָרִיךְ לְחַלְּלָן עַל הַכֶּסֶף.
But the School of Hillel says:	וּבֵית הִלֵּל אוֹמְרִים,
It is the same whether it is silver	אֶחָד שֶׁהֵן כֶּסֶף
or whether it is produce.	וְאֶחָד שֶׁהֵן פֵרוֹת.

---

[3] See footnote 57 in Neusner's translation of y.MS.5.3.

Comments: One way to avoid paying redemption money for *second tithe* was to keep it until the time of *removal* and then destroy it, but the Shammaites did not allow this. This issue became much more important after 70 CE when all *second tithe* had to be redeemed and no one could spend the *second tithe* money. As the later rabbis said: "Even if one were to *deconsecrate* the produce [with money], what good would it do?" (y.MS.5.7 V).

Dating (1): The question at the beginning clearly dates from after 70 CE, but this does not mean that the school dispute was not genuine. Although the issue became much more important after 70 CE, it was also important before 70 CE for those who lived a long way from Jerusalem or who had too much *second tithe* produce to consume. A story of Eliezer [T2] at t.MS.5.15-16 says he kept the *fourth-year vineyard* produce until the day of *removal* to escape paying the redemption, and so he appears to be following this Hillelite ruling, though it is possible that this story was a later invention—see the discussion at Dating at m.MS.5.2.

It is therefore likely that this was a genuine school dispute but the opening question was changed to reflect the new circumstances.

m.MS.5.10-13: The ancient confession of Removal

On the afternoon of the last *holyday*	במנחה ביום טוב האחרון
[of *Pesach*] **they used to confess.**	היו מתודין.
How was the confession? [from Deut.26.13-15:]	כיצד היה הודוי,
"I have *removed consecrated* things from [my] house"	בערתי הקודש מן הבית
—this is *second tithe* and *fourth-year plant*.	זה מעשר שני ונטע רבעי.
"I have given it to the Levite"	נתתיו ללוי,
—this is the Levite's tithe [i.e., *first tithe*].	זה מעשר לוי.
"And I have also given it"	וגם נתתיו,
—this is *elevation offering*	זו תרומה
and *elevation offering* of the [*first*] *tithe*	ותרומת מעשר.
"to the foreigner, to the orphan and to the widow"	לגר ליתום ולאלמנה,
—this is *poor tithe*, *gleanings*	זה מעשר עני, הלקט
and *forgotten* and *corner* [produce left for the poor],	והשכחה והפאה,
even though [nonperformance of] these do not	אף על פי שאינן
prevent the confession.	מעכבין את הודוי.
"From [my] house"	מן הבית,
—this is *dough offering*.	זו חלה.
11) "According to all the commands	ככל מצותך
which you commanded me"	אשר צויתני,
—thus, if he first [put aside] *second tithe*	הא אם הקדים מעשר שני
before [he put aside] the *first* [*tithe*]	לראשון,
he is not able to confess.	אינו יכול להתודות.
"I did not transgress your commands"	לא עברתי ממצותיך,

—I did not set aside from [one] kind   לא הפרשתי ממין

for that [other different] kind;   על שאינו מינו,

and not from picked [produce] for unpicked,   ולא מן התלוש על המחובר,

and not from unpicked [produce] for picked,   ולא מן המחובר על התלוש,

and not from new for old [i.e., last year's],   ולא מן החדש על הישן,

and not from old for new [i.e., this year's],   ולא מן הישן על החדש.

"and I have not forgotten"   ולא שכחתי,

—I did not forget to bless you   לא שכחתי מלברכך

or to commemorate your Name over it.   ומלהזכיר שמך עליו.

12) "I did not eat from it during my mourning."[4]   לא אכלתי באוני ממנו,

—thus if he ate it during mourning   הא אם אכלו באנינה

he is not able to Confess.   אינו יכול להתודות.

"and I did not *remove* [any] from it in *impurity*"   ולא בערתי ממנו בטמא,

—thus if he set aside [any] in *impurity*   הא אם הפרישו בטומאה

he is not able to confess.   אינו יכול להתודות.

"And I did not give [any] from it to the dead"   ולא נתתי ממנו למת,

—I did not purchase from it[s value] a coffin   לא לקחתי ממנו ארון

or shrouds for the dead,   ותכריכים למת,

and I did not give it to other mourners.   ולא נתתיו לאוננים אחרים.

"I have listened to the voice of the Lord my God"   שמעתי בקול ה׳ אלהי,

—I have brought it to the Chosen House.   הבאתיו לבית הבחירה.

"I have done all which you commanded me"   עשיתי ככל אשר צויתני,

—I rejoiced and made [others] rejoice with it.   שמחתי ושמחתי בו.

13) "Look down from your Holy Dwelling   השקיפה ממעון קדשך

from the heavens"   מן השמים,

—we did what you prescribed for us, [therefore]   עשינו מה שגזרת עלינו,

also you do what you promised us.   אף אתה עשה מה שהבטחתנו,

"Look down from your Holy Dwelling   השקיפה ממעון קדשך

from the heavens   מן השמים

and bless your people Israel"   וברך את עמך את ישראל,

—with sons and daughters   בבנים ובבנות.

"and the soil which you have given to us"   ואת האדמה אשר נתתה לנו,

—with dew and rain and offspring of cattle.   בטל ומטר ובולדות בהמה.

"as you swore to our Fathers: כאשר נשבעת לאבותינו

'a land flowing with milk and honey.'"   ארץ זבת חלב ודבש,

—so as to give flavor to the produce.   כדי שתתן טעם בפרות.

Comments: This tradition assumes that the passage in Deuteronomy 26.13-15 was literally spoken as a confession by each householder at the Temple at the ceremony of Removal—a practice which finished at the end of the second century BCE according

---

[4] The translation "mourning" is not strictly correct, because *aninah*, אֲנִינָה, refers only to the time between death and burial.

to m.MS.5.15. The passage which they quoted for the Confession is interpreted here phrase by phrase.

The original context suggests that this confession concerned mainly the *poor tithe* ("When you have ended tithing all the tithes of your increase in the third year, the year of tithing, and have given it to the Levite, the stranger, the orphan and the widow," Deut.26.12), but it is interpreted here as though it concerns many types of *consecrated* produce: *elevation offerings, first tithe, second tithe, fourth-year fruit, poor tithe,* harvest *leftovers,* and *dough offering.* In order to include all of these, a couple of phrases have to be interpreted twice. Therefore "I have *removed consecrated* things from [my] house" is related to *second tithe* and *fourth-year fruit* (perhaps because they are taken from the house to Jerusalem), and then "from [my] house" is also related to *dough offering* (perhaps because *dough offering* is always in the house, whereas others can be kept in a barn). Similarly "I have given them to the Levite" is related to the *first tithe* (because this tithe went to the Levites[5]), and "and I have also given them" is related to *elevation offerings.*

The main point of these interpretations is to suggest that this confession related not only to the *poor tithe* (as the context suggests) but also to all the other tithes on produce. The time of *removal* was important to pious Jews as a way of disposing of tithes which had built up and which could not be dealt with properly. Produce which was too expensive to redeem (e.g., the *fourth-year fruit* of a vineyard owner), or which had become too stale to give to Levites or priests, or perhaps even to the poor, could be disposed of by destroying it at the time of *removal*. This was more important before 70 CE when food was stored for taking to Jerusalem and could go stale, but it was also important after 70 CE.

The next lines are interpreted as a list of conditions which, if met, result in a fulfilment of the blessings in the last lines. These blessings are interpreted as a promise which is virtually demanded: "We did what you decreed for us; you also do what you promised us." This promise was probably inferred from the verses shortly after this confession: "You have today caused the Lord to promise to become your God, . . . and the Lord has today caused you to promise to become his people" (Deut.26.17-18).[6] This type of prayer was very unusual—Exod.R.16.1 says that this was the *only* occasion when the Jews approached God with a 'prayer of force.'

Dating (9): The whole passage is written as if such things "used to" happen (היו, which is normally used to indicate the past, e.g., in m.Ber.9.5; m.Pea.2.4; 4.5, 7-8; t.Ter.1.1), though the opening sentence may originate from an earlier tradition because it uses a different form of the word "confession" than the rest of this tradition

---

[5] In Num.18.24 this tithe goes to the Levites, but in Deuteronomy the Levites benefited from the *second* or *poor tithe*, cf. Deut.12.18; 14.27.

[6] "Cause to promise" is the hiphil of כרת.

(מתודין instead of הודיין, hithpael instead of hiphil, both from יָדָה) and because it has a date which contradicts the normal date for the time of *removal* in m.MS.5.6. It would be simple to resolve this contradiction by saying that *removal* took place before the first *holyday* (as in m.MS.5.6) and the confession took place on the last *holyday* (as stated here), but later rabbis did not choose this easy solution.[7] It seems more likely that the contradiction is due to a change in the date for *removal*, as discussed above (see Dating of m.MS.5.6), and that the date here was the original one.

It is difficult to know when the text of the confession and interpretations of each phrase were added. Some of the exegesis fits better into a post-70 context because the second use of "And I have also given them" was probably justified by the particle "also" (גַם), which was a particle of extension in post-70 exegesis—i.e., it indicated that another ruling was hidden within a ruling.[8] The other phrase which was used twice ("from [my] house") did not need this type of justification because although this had been cited as part of a previous phrase which had already been interpreted, it was not a necessary part of that phrase—the only necessary part was "I have *removed consecrated* things."

On the other hand there are also early features which might indicate a date before 70 CE, especially the unusual prayer of demand. Heinemann[9] points out that this type of forceful prayer is only found elsewhere in the Lord's Prayer ('forgive as we have forgiven') and the prayer of Honi the Circler which is criticized by Simeon b. Shetah (although this may have been a later criticism which was put in his mouth; similar criticisms are frequent, including the early one at m.Ber.5.3—see the Comment there). Another possible indication of a pre-70 date is the interpretation of "I have listened to the voice of the LORD my God" as "I have brought it to the Chosen House" because this appears to assume that the Temple was still standing even though there was nothing in the text to demand a mention of the Temple.

The lengthy explanation of "a kind for a [different] kind" as "not picked for unpicked . . . and not new for old . . ." may be an explanation which was added later, because the wording is exactly the same as at m.Ter.1.5. Another possible later addition is the text and interpretation which is a prayer of demand, "'Look down from your Holy Dwelling from the heavens'—we did what you decreed for us; [therefore] also you do what you promised us," because this is followed by a strange

---

[7] The Jerusalem Talmud (y.MS.5.5.I) noted this contradiction but tried to solve it by pointing out that R. Simeon [T4] exempted *firstfruits* from the *removal* (m.Bik.2.2), with the implication that later rabbis also exempted *second tithe*. However there is no evidence for this, and R. Simeon was exempting *firstfruits* for a different reason (because they were offered at a later festival).

[8] See my *Techniques,* pp. 19-20.

[9] *Prayer,* pp. 200-201.

repetition of "Look down from your Holy Dwelling from the heavens," which is not interpreted separately when it is repeated.

Therefore an early feature (the prayer of demand) is likely to be one of the latest elements in this tradition, which may indicate that the whole tradition is early. However, the dating of this prayer of demand is very uncertain.

m.MS.5.15: The Removal confession finished after Johanan

Johanan the High Priest [John Hyrcanus BCE 2]	יוחנן כהן גדול
removed the Confession of Tithing.	העביר הודיות המעשר.
Also he annulled the Awakeners	אף הוא בטל את המעוררים,
and the Stunners.	ואת הנוקפים.
And until his day	ועד ימיו היה
a hammer struck in Jerusalem.	פטיש מכה בירושלים.
And in his day it was not necessary for someone	ובימיו אין אדם צריך
to inquire about doubtfully tithed food.	לשאול על הדמאי.

Mishnaic parallel: m.Sot.9.10

Comments: This largely obscure list of changes which took place during the office of John Hyrcanus I (about 135–105 BCE) is explained in the Talmuds (y.MS.5.5.XI-XVII; b.Sot.48a), though the explanations are largely undateable and may have late origins. The "Awakeners" were Levites who used to sing Psalm 44.24 loudly in the mornings: "Awake, why do you sleep O Lord?" The "Stunners" were those who hit a sacrificial victim on the head to make them more compliant when their throat was cut—this was replaced by using a nose ring and a head restraint. The "hammer struck in Jerusalem" referred to noisy work which was not allowed during *ordinary festival days* during his period of office. The inquiries about *doubtfully tithed food* were unnecessary because there were officials who checked that tithes had been separated from food which was sold in the market.

Dating (11): The obscure terms used here probably indicate an early origin for all of these items, though the collection here has signs of being a compilation because the items are linked by "Also he ... And until his day ... And in his day...." The last item about *doubtfully tithed food* is the least obscure and the most likely to be a later invention—it says, in effect, "in the golden days of the past, everyone tithed properly"—though, in fairness, the later rabbis said that this referred to the officials who Johanan put in place when he discovered that people were *not* tithing properly (y.MS.5.5.XIV-XV; b.Yom.9a).

It is impossible to date any of this tradition with any confidence, though there is no conceivable reason why this tradition should be invented at a later date.

Related early traditions from other tractates

t.San.2.6: Letters from Rn. Gamaliel

It happened: Concerning Rn. Gamaliel [I, T1]	מעשה ברבן גמליאל
and the Elders who used to stand [i.e., in session]	וזקנים שהיו עומדין
upon the arch of the steps of the Temple Mount.	על גב מעלות בהר הבית
And Johanan the scribe went before them,	ויוחנן סופר הלך לפניהם
and they said, Write: To our brothers,	ואמרו כתוב לאחנא
people of Upper Galilee	בני גלילא עילאה
and people of Lower Galilee:	ובני גלילא תתאי
May your peace increase.	שלמכון יסגא
We inform you	מהודעין אנחנא לכון
that the time of *removal* is approaching	דמטא זמן בעורא
to bring out tithes	לאפוקיא מעשריא
from vats of olives.	ממעטניא זיתיא
And [write]: To our brothers,	ולאחנא
people of Upper South	בני דרומא עילאה
and people of Lower South:	ובני דרומא תתאה
May your peace increase.	שלמכון יסגא
We inform you	מהודעין אנחנא לכון
that the time [of *removal*] approaches	דימטן זמן
to bring out tithes	לאפוקי מעשריא
from sheaves of grain.	מעומרי שובילא
And [write]: To our brothers,	ולאחנא
people of Exile of Babylon	בני גלותא דבבל
and people of Exile of Media	ובני גלותא דמדי
and to the rest of all [other]	ושאר כל
people of the Exile of Israel:	בני גלותא דישראל
May your peace increase.	שלמכון יסגא
We inform you	מהודעין אנחנא לכון
that young pigeons are [still] weak	דגוזליא רכיכין
and the lambs are [still] tender	ואמריא דעדקין
so the appointing of Abib is not approaching,*	וזימניה דאביבא לא מטא
and it seems best in my sight	ושפר באנפאי
and in the sight of my associates	ובאנפי חבראי
that we add to this year	ואוספנא על שתא דא
[an extra] thirty days.	תלתין יומין.

*This line is missing from the version in b.San.11b.

Comments: Gamaliel the Elder is seen here dictating letters to Jewish communities in the provinces and the Diaspora on matters of the calendar. The Jewish lunar calendars had an average length of 28.5 days, and so they often had to add an extra month before Nisan (also known as Abib, 'spring') in order to keep in line with the solar calendar. They met on the Temple steps at the southern main entrace, which largely survived the destruction and have now been excavated.

The purpose of this tradition is to show the influence of Gamaliel and the Elders and to suggest that the forerunners of the Rabbis really did rule over the whole of Judaism. However, there are hints in this tradition that their role and influence was rather less grand. They met on the steps of the Temple in the open sun and among the crowds coming and going through the three public gates into the Temple. Why did they not meet instead in the grand porticoes inside the Temple where there was shade and ample room for large meetings, or in the Chamber of Hewn Stone where the Sanhedrin met for court cases (cf. m.Pea.2.6)? This venue suggests that they were an unimportant group who were unable to obtain permission to use a more suitable place. The meeting only appears to include Pharisees because there is no hint of anyone except the Elders and no hint of any dissension or a divided opinion.

It is likely that Gamaliel was the head of the Pharisee party at the time, or at least their spokesman, but there is no indication that he was presiding over the Sanhedrin. We have no indication that the Pharisees were ever out of step with the calendar of the Temple, and so either the Sanhedrin followed the decisions of a Pharisee subgroup on this matter, or perhaps Gamaliel is passing on the decisions of the whole Sanhedrin as though the Pharisees alone had made them. It may be significant that they do not tell the people of Galilee and the South that the month of Abib is starting but only that the time of *removal* is coming, which may suggest that the Sanhedrin had already sent out letters concerning the start of the month but only the Pharisees were concerned to remind people about the time of *removal*. The *removal* of tithes from peoples' homes may have been a conscious replacement for the Temple ceremony which ended in the second century BCE.

> The rabbis in the Babylonian Talmud were amazed that Gamaliel, one of the greatest rabbis of his time, should be seen in such lowly circumstances. Some suggested that this incident may have occurred during the period when Gamaliel was deposed from being *Nasi* (b.San.11b)—even though it was Gamaliel II who was deposed, not Gamaliel I (see b.Ber.27b-28a).

Dating (1): There is no reason to doubt that these letters are genuine, and the details about the lowly circumstances in which they were written suggests that it has not been made up, though they have of course been abbreviated and stylized. The line about the month of Abib may have been added as an explanation because it is missing from the versions in the Talmuds. The fact that Gamaliel is not called "the Elder" here is an additional indication that this is an old tradition which was fixed at a time where there was no need to distinguish him from Gamaliel II [T2].

New Testament: This is the same Gamaliel who spoke up in the Sanhedrin suggesting that the new Christian sect should not be persecuted (Acts 5.34) and who

Paul claims was his teacher (Acts 22.3). His status in this tradition suggests that his role in Acts 5.34 may have been as a spokesman for the Pharisees within the Sanhedrin. Although it is possible that he was a personal teacher of Paul, it is also possible that Paul merely attended his lectures.

Summary and Conclusions

Only the first and last chapters of this tractate appear to have originated at an early date because although chapters 2–4 contain early traditions, these are largely woven into later discussions where they are presented as proofs or foundations for later practices.

The concerns about *second tithe* before and after 70 CE were very different. Before 70 CE the main concerns were how to purchase and consume *second tithe* produce in Jerusalem, but after 70 CE the main concerns were how to redeem *second tithe* produce and how to avoid redeeming large amounts of produce by keeping it until the time of *removal*.

Before 70 CE there is every indication that *second tithes* were put aside or redeemed by a large proportion of the population, and that this became their food and spending money during *ordinary festival days* (m.MS.1.3-4). They often had too much money or produce, and so they tried to find ways to buy other commodities with this money (m.MS.1.5-7) and found ways to buy pelts and jars by purchasing whole animals (including their hides) and sealed containers of food or drink (m.MS.1.3-5; 3.11-13). The Shammaites were very strict about *second tithe* produce never leaving Jerusalem (m.MS.3.5-9), even if it had been redeemed (t.MS.2.16c), and about keeping *second tithe* money in silver coinage (m.MS.2.7-9). They also insisted that the whole of *fourth-year fruit* had to be redeemed and did not allow the farmer to escape this by pruning (t.MS.5.18) or by making this *fourth year* coincide with the Sabbath Year rest when he was not responsible for the crop (t.MS.5.20), or by waiting for the time of *removal* (m.MS.5.2—as Eliezer wanted in t.MS.5.15-16).

When the Temple was destroyed it might still be theoretically possible to come and eat *second tithes* and *fourth-year fruit* in Jerusalem in *purity*, but it was no longer possible to 'rejoice' in Jerusalem (as Deut.12.18; 14.26 demanded) or to buy *peace offerings* during festivals (which was a normal purchase with *second tithe* money—cf. m.MS.1.3-4). We do not know when the decision was made to stop spending *second tithe* in Jerusalem, but probably there was no need for any formal decision. The closest we have to a formal ruling was when an older temporary suspension about bringing *fourth-year fruit* was adapted soon after 70 CE to become a suspension during the absence of the Temple (m.MS.5.2).

Debates in Mishnah and Tosefta about *second tithe* and *fourth-year fruit* are almost absent for generations T2 and T3 (from just after 70 CE until after Bar

Kokhba's revolt),[10] as if they were waiting for normality to assert itself after the Temple was rebuilt. When it was obvious that they would not have a Temple for a very long time, the generation T4 started discussing *second tithes* in order to make new rules for a new age. They also discussed the spending of *second tithe* money though their purely theoretical interest is sometimes seen in the impractical conclusions they come to (e.g. m.MS.4.8b).

The school disputes were employed by these later generations to provide guidelines about redeeming *second tithe* produce and storing the *second tithe* money. The stricter Shammaite rulings were largely rejected in favor of the more practical Hillelite ones, except where Shammaite rulings better fitted the post-70 situation (e.g., t.MS.3.15 about designating *doubtful second tithe* which the Hillelites ignored).

The tradition about Gamaliel sending out letters concerning the time of *removal* (t.San.2.6) is meant to show that everyone listened to the forerunners of the Rabbis, but actually suggests that the non-Pharisees were not concerned about *removal*. The time of *removal* was important to Jews who were not able to bring their produce to Jerusalem and could not afford to redeem it. It became more important after 70 CE because this was one way to avoid redeeming *second tithe*, because it could be destroyed instead. The date for this *removal* was the first *holyday* of *Pesach* (Passover) every third year, so that *consecrated* goods were cleared out at the same time as the leaven. However, there are indications that originally it was on the last *holyday* of *Pesach*, so that the *second tithes* could still be consumed during this festival. The confession of Removal in Deuteronomy 26.13-15 was remembered as a ceremony in the Temple which ended in the second century BCE, though it is difficult to know if any details about this ceremony are accurate. The Pharisaic ruling about a *removal* which was carried out in peoples' homes may have been a replacement for this ceremony.

---

[10] Possible exceptions are the comment by Tarfon [T3] in m.MS.2.4 concerning the consumption of vetches (though this did not originally concern *second tithe*) and the opinion of Ishmael b. Elisha [T3] that the sharecropper who lives nearer Jerusalem should keep the *second tithe* of a crop.

Tractate *Ḥallah*: Dough Offering

Definitions and Outline

Torah said that an *elevation offering* should be given to the Lord from the bread of the new Land (Num.15.18-21). This offering was called "the *elevation offering* of the threshing floor" (v. 20) which might suggest that grain should be given, but it was also called "the first of the kneading trough" (עֲרִיסָה, *arisah*, 'dough' or 'trough'— meaning uncertain) (vv. 20, 21), and so the offering was made from dough (עִיסָה, *isah*). The offering was to be made in the form of a "cake" (חַלָּה, *ḥallah*), from which this tractate is named. The gift should be given "to the Lord" and it was called an *'elevation offering'* (v.20), and so the offering was given to the priests to be eaten by them in purity, like other *elevation offerings* (see tractate *Terumot*), and it could *taint* and be *neutralized* like *elevation offerings* (this is dealt with in tractate *Orlah*).

Torah did not define what 'bread' was, or how much should be given, and it did not say at what stage the dough became liable to this tithe, and so all this had to be decided, as recorded in this tractate. Their definition for 'bread' in this tractate became also the definition for fulfilling the laws concerning bread for *Pesach* (Passover) and *community markers* (*érubim*).

Although this law appeared to apply only to produce of the Land, *dough offering* was also separated outside the Land though this was burned or eaten by a priest in lesser states of *purity*. This offering continued to be given to priests after 70 CE.

m.Hal.1.1–2.2: Bread which is liable to *dough offering*

Dough offerings are liable from any bread made from cereals, and this definition applies to other laws concerning bread. The *dough offering* is treated like *elevation offering* in most respects.

m.Hal.2.3-8: How to separate a *dough offering*

You should separate one-twenty-fourth from any lump of dough which is larger than 1 *qab* plus an *added fifth*, and you should be in a state of *purity*.

m.Hal.3.1-6: When to separate a *dough offering*

The *dough offering* should be removed when the dough is fully processed (i.e., rolled out), if it belongs to an Israelite at that time.

m.Hal.3.7–4.6: A *dough offering* **from** *mixtures* **or different batches**

Small lumps of dough which are smaller than 1 *qab* can combine and become liable if they are similar to each other, and one batch can be tithed on behalf of another if it is similar.

m.Hal.4.7-11: A *dough offering* **from outside the Land**

Dough from outside the Land is separated but not sent to Jerusalem. Various other things were taken to Jerusalem priests, but they refused various offerings, especially from outside the Land.

m.Hal.1.1-3: Species which are liable to *dough offering*

Summary of Mishnah: *Dough offerings* are due from five species: wheat, barley, spelt, oats, and rye. *Dough offerings* are due even when they are mixed with a lesser amount of other species. These species cannot be harvested before the waving of the *first sheaf* (1.1). At *Pesach* (Passover) you must eat at least one olive's bulk of unleavened bread from these species or a mixture, but if you eat the same with leaven, you suffer extirpation. If you vow to avoid bread, your vow refers to these species (1.2). Most produce which is exempt from tithes is nevertheless subject to *dough offering* (1.3).

The following traditions have elements (marked in bold) for which there is evidence of an origin before 70 CE:

m.Hal.1.3: Food which is liable to dough offering but not to tithes

These are liable to a *dough offering*	אלו חייבין בחלה
but exempt from tithes:	ופטורים מן המעשרות,
The *gleanings*, or the *forgotten* [produce during harvest]	הלקט, והשכחה,
or the *corners* [of the field during harvest]	והפאה,
and [produce which has been declared] *ownerless*	וההפקר,
and *first tithe*	ומעשר ראשון
from which the *elevation offering* has been removed	שנטלה תרומתו,
and *second tithe*	ומעשר שני
and a *dedication* which was redeemed	והקדש שנפדו,
and the remainder of the *first sheaf*	ומותר העומר,
and produce	ותבואה
which has not reached one-third [of its growth].	שלא הביאה של יש.
R. Eliezer [b. Hyrcanus, T2] says:	רבי אליעזר אומר,
Grain which has not [yet] grown one-third	תבואה שלא הביאה של יש,
is exempt from a *dough offering*.	פטורה מן החלה.

Comments: *Dough offerings* were due from almost all sources of grain, even those which were not subject to other tithing, i.e., the harvest *leftovers* for the poor (*gleanings, forgotten, corners,* and *ownerless*—see tractate *Peah*). Any tithes which did not belong to the priests or the Temple were tithed again by their owners (i.e., Levites tithed *dough offerings* from the *first tithe*, and the owners of *second tithe* or redeemed *dedications* tithed them), and even the redeemed remains of the *first sheaf* (see m.Men.10.4) were tithed again.

In other words, any bread which did not already belong to the priests had a priest's portion inside it, the *dough offering*, which needed to be removed before it was permitted safe to eat. The only exception was bread which was made from a crop which had not yet experienced one-third of its expected growth. This may be because the plant was considered too immature to produce 'seed' (as in Deut.14.22, "You shall tithe all the growth of your seed"[1]) or because the dough produced by immature seed was not good enough for such holy purposes (cf. the discussion at t.Ter.2.14).

Dating (2): The last element of this list is datable by the fact that Eliezer [T2, just after 70 CE] disputed it, and it was probably imported from t.Ter.2.14 where exactly the same words are used about *elevation offerings* in general.[2]

If this last addition is removed, the whole list is based on the principle that the *dough offering* is due from everything which does not already belong to the priests. On the assumption that new items tended to be added to the end of a list (cf. m.Dem.1.1a; 1.3), this makes it likely that the whole list dates from before 70 CE. Although this is not certain, some parts of the list do have early features. The reference to a *dedication* helps to suggest that this list originated before 70 CE though it is equally likely that this was merely part of the phrase "*second tithe* and *dedication* which is redeemed" which occurs as a standard phrase in Mishnah (see "Dating anonymous sayings" in the Introductions). The ruling about the remainder of the *first sheaf* must date to at least T2 (soon after 70 CE) because it is disputed by Akiba [T3] (m.Men.10.4).

m.Hal.1.4-8: Dough which is exempt from the *dough offering*

Summary of Mishnah: Leavened food made from other species or made from less than 1.25 *qab* of the five species, or made from a mixture of *consecrated* and unconsecrated grain is subject to tithes but not to *dough offering* (1.4). Dough

---

[1] R. Zeira said that it came from this text but emphasized 'seed' and argued that plants less than one-third grown cannot be said to have produced 'seed' because the seed is too immature to sprout (y.Hal.1.3 VI).
[2] As suggested in y.Hal.1.3 VI, though later rabbis had other explanations.

prepared like sponge cake from beginning to end is exempt from *dough offering*, but if it was prepared at the beginning or end like bread, it is liable to *dough offering*; and even bread crumbs are liable (1.5). One school includes one type of dumplings while another includes a different type. Loaves with a Nazirite offering are exempt if they were made for personal use (1.6). Dough less than the prescribed minimum which is given to a baker for baking your own bread is exempt, but if he used his own dough, it is liable (1.7). Dough is liable for a *dough offering* if it is good enough for a shepherd to eat, which means that it is also suitable for making a *community marker*, for blessing at meals, and for eating at festivals (1.8).

The following traditions have elements (marked in bold) for which there is evidence of an origin before 70 CE:

m.Hal.1.6: Are pancakes/wafers or dumplings/cakes liable?

Pancake:	הַמְעִיסָה,
The School of Shammai exempts	בית שמאי פוטרין,
and the School of Hillel obligates.	ובית הלל מחייבין.
Dumpling:	הַחֲלִיטָה,
The School of Shammai obligates	בית שמאי מחייבין,
and the School of Hillel exempts.	ובית הלל פוטרין.
Cakes of a *thank offering*	חלות תודה
and wafers of a Nazirite [offering]	ורקיקי נזיר
[if they are] made for himself [they] are exempt,	עשאן לעצמו, פטור.
[but if they are made] to sell in the market,	למכור בשוק,
[they are] liable.	חייב.

Mishnaic parallel: m.Ed.5.2

Comments: R. Jose b. Halafta [T4] explained in t.Hal.1.1-2 that a 'pancake' (מְעִיסָה, *meisah*) is flour paste to which hot water is added, while a 'dumpling' (חֲלִיטָה, *halitah*) is flour which is added to hot water, but it is difficult to know how these translate into modern language. The translation here is based on R. Jose's explanation and on the link with the *thank offerings* which consisted of 'wafers' and 'cakes' (Lev.7.12; Num.6.15 for the Nazirite's *thank offering*). These traditions are probably introduced here because the 'cakes' (חַלָּה, pl. חַלּ֖ת, *hallot*) were assumed to be related to the similar-sounding 'dumplings' (*halitah*), and the 'wafers' and 'pancakes' were related because they were both flat (though this is very uncertain).

The reason for the Shammaite exemption for a 'pancake' is presumably that this food is nothing like a 'cake' (the *hallah* after which this tractate was named). The reason for the Hillelite exemption is less easy to understand, but it may be related to the ruling which followed. It is possible that the Hillelites countered the Shammaite exemption of pancakes by pointing, the 'wafers' of the *thank offering* and Nazirite's offering, which were certainly liable to *dough offering* because they accompanied the 'cake' (חַלָּה, *hallah*—the same word which means *dough offerings*). The Shammaites may have replied that these cakes and wafers were not liable to a *dough offering* because they were already owned by the Temple, as opposed to those which were on sale in the market.

Dating (1): There is no reason to doubt that this school debate originated before 70 CE.

The ruling about the cakes and wafers in the market may have been added at a later time as a way to explain or reverse the strange Hillelite exemption for dumplings, because after 70 CE, when *thank offerings* ceased, people were continuing to sell similar cakes and wafers in the market.

However it is also possible that this ruling was the Shammaite reply to the Hillelite argument about pancakes (as described above) because when this rule was attributed to Eliezer b. Hyrcanus [T2, just after 70 CE], Eleazar b. Azariah [T2] replied that this was an old traditional ruling ("it was spoken at Mt. Horeb"— t.Hal.1.6).

Tosefta has another related ruling:

> The Sages say: The same for both [pancakes and dumplings]; that which is made in a stewpot or in a boiling pot is exempt and that which is made in an oven is liable. (t.Hal.1.2)

It it likely that the Mishnah ruling about the market and Tosefta tradition about boiling were both added with the same purpose—to explain or reverse the strange Hillelite exemption with regard to dumplings. The Mishnah saying probably originated before 70 CE (perhaps from Shammaites), but there is no evidence that Tosefta's tradition about boiling originated before 70 CE.

In practice they both come to the same conclusion, because boiled dumplings or pancakes would not be suitable for selling in the market. Therefore it is likely that these later rulings were influenced by the principle that 'bread' is anything which is baked, not boiled. This principle is also seen behind rule of Akiba [T3, mid second century] that it becomes liable for *dough offering* 'when the crust forms' (m.Hal.3.6).

m.Hal.1.9–2.2: The holiness of *dough offering*

Summary of Mishnah: *Dough offerings* are like *elevation offerings* in that nonpriests may not eat them (punishment for deliberate offense is death, and for accidental offense it is payment of *full value* plus the *added fifth*), they are *neutralized* when they are diluted with 100 parts, priests must eat them in *purity*, one cannot separate from one batch for another unless they are touching, and one cannot designate the whole batch as *elevation offering* or *dough offering* (1.9). Dough made in Israel from foreign produce is liable, but what about dough made abroad from produce of the Land (2.1)? Produce brought here by ship is liable only once the ship has grounded. Dough kneaded with fruit juice is liable but the *dough offering* can be eaten with *impure* hands (2.2).

The following traditions have elements (marked in bold) for which there is evidence of an origin before 70 CE:

m.Hal.2.1: *Dough offerings* from produce outside the Land

Produce from outside the Land	פרות חוצה לארץ
which is brought into the Land:	שנכנסו לארץ,
[It is] liable to a *dough offering*.	חייבים בחלה.
[Produce which is] exported from here to there:	יצאו מכאן לשם,
R. Eliezer [b. Hyrcanus, T2] obligates [it]	רבי אליעזר מחייב,
but R. Akiba [T3] exempts [it from a *dough offering*].	ורבי עקיבה פוטר.

Comments: Torah links the *dough offering* to the Land (Num.15.18-19), but what about produce which is imported or exported? The principle appears to be that it becomes liable when it is made into dough, and so grain imports are liable but exports are not.

Dating (2): The ruling about imports probably predates the debate about exports which appears to have been tagged onto the end. The debate about exports dates from T2/T3 (at the beginning of the second century), so that the ruling about imports is probably pre-70, though this is not certain.

In later generations, *dough offering* became liable outside the Land (cf. y.Orl.3.7.II), where it was burned instead of being given to a priest (cf. m.Hal.4.8), though some Jews outside the Land separated *dough offerings* even without any ruling to require them (see m.Hal.4.9).

m.Hal.2.3-8: How to separate the *dough offering*

Summary of Mishnah: You must separate the *dough offering* in *purity* (so a man must not be naked though a woman can be because she can cover her nakedness while sitting), but if you cannot, then process the dough in 1 *qab* batches or designate it as '*impure dough offering*' (2.3). Two portions of 1 *qab* each which touch each other become liable—but what if they were made up of crumbs from the oven (2.4)? Flour cannot be separated as a *dough offering* until it is made into dough, and if you *have* separated *dough offering* from it (and it is over 1 *qab*), it is still liable to a *dough offering*, and so it cannot be eaten by either priest or nonpriest (2.5).

A minimum of 1.25 *qab* of flour is liable for a *dough offering*, though if the coarse flour is removed temporally, making it less than 1.25 *qab*, and then returned, the mixture is not liable (2.6). A baker separates one-forty-eighth for a *dough offering* but a private individual separates one-twenty-fourth, even if he is baking for a large number of people. For *impure* dough you separate only one-forty-eighth unless you deliberately made it *impure* (2.7). You cannot separate a *dough offering* from *pure* dough on behalf of *impure* dough, though Eliezer allows it if you connect the two lumps by a tiny third one which is too small to spread the *impurity* (2.8).

The following traditions have elements (marked in bold) for which there is evidence of an origin before 70 CE:

m.Hal.2.4: Portions of 1 *qab* can combine to become liable

He who makes his dough in [portions of 1] *qab*	העושה עסתו קבים
and they touched each other:	ונגעו זה בזה,
They are exempt from *dough offering*	פטורים מן החלה
—unless they become attached.	עד שישוכו.
R. Eliezer [b. Hyrcanus, T2] says:	רבי אל יעזר אומר,
Also he who removes [pieces from the oven]	אף הרודה
and puts them in a basket [so they touch each other],	ונותן לסל,
the basket combines them	הסל מצרפן
into [a portion large enough to be liable to] *dough offering*.	לחלה.

Comments: Dough less than one *qab* in size is too small to be liable but small portions can combine and become liable. See m.Ed.1.2 in Related Traditions (below) for a discussion of this quantity.

The ruling by Eliezer appears, in the context, to say that lumps of dough which are collected in a single vessel should be assumed to combine even if they haven't become attached. However, the traditional interpretation is that he is talking about scrapings from an oven. Although dough becomes liable when it was rolled out (m.Hal.3.1), it was offered as a 'cake,' and so it was more convenient for a baker to separate it *after* baking, which meant that the scrapings inside the oven had to be tithed as well.

Dating (2): The ruling of Eliezer [T2, just after 70 CE] assumes that dough which touches can combine, which means that this first ruling predates 70 CE. The words "unless they become attached" were probably added later as a transition to explain Eliezer's ruling, because although the concept of 'attaching' occurs in a school debate (m.TY.1.1), it was probably added later (see the discussion in Related Traditions below).

At a later time, portions of dough were considered to be combined even if they accidentally touched each other (cf. 4.1). When this became accepted, the ruling of Eliezer became self-evident, so it was assumed that he was talking about something else—hence the interpretation about scrapings from an oven.

New Testament: It is possible that the fragments of bread which were put in baskets after the feeding of the thousands (Mt.14.19; Mk.6.41; 8.6; Lk.9.16) would become liable to *dough offering*. If they considered the bread to be *doubtfully tithed* they would presumably break off a *dough offering* as well as the *elevation offering* of the *first tithe* (though the earliest reference to *dough offering* which is *doubtful* in m.Hal.4.6 cannot be shown to originate before 70 CE). According to the ruling of Eliezer, these small portions would combine when they were collected in a basket.

m.Hal.2.5: A *dough offering* separated from flour is not valid

He who sets aside his *dough offering* [from] flour:	הַמַּפְרִישׁ חַלָּתוֹ קֶמַח,
It is not a *dough offering*,	אֵינָהּ חַלָּה,
and [even if] it is stolen [and comes] into the hand of a priest,	וְגָזַל בְּיַד כֹּהֵן,
that dough itself [made from the flour which was tithed]	הָעִסָּה עַצְמָהּ,
is [still] liable to *dough offering*.	חַיֶּבֶת בְּחַלָּה,
And the flour [which was separated as a *dough offering*],	וְהַקֶּמַח,
if it has [the minimum] measure [i.e., a qab],	אִם יֵשׁ בּוֹ כַּשִּׁעוּר,
It is [also] liable to *dough offering*.	חַיֶּבֶת בְּחַלָּה,
And it is prohibited to nonpriests	וַאֲסוּרָה לְזָרִים,
—the words of R. Joshua [(b. Hananiah, T2].	דִּבְרֵי רַבִּי יְהוֹשֻׁעַ.
They [the Sages] said to him: It happened that:	אָמְרוּ לוֹ, מַעֲשֶׂה
A nonpriest Elder grabbed [this type of portion and ate it].	וְקִפְּשָׁהּ זָקֵן זָר.
He said to them:	אָמַר לָהֶם,
He has both corrupted himself [by a sinful act]	אַף הוּא קִלְקֵל לְעַצְמוֹ
and *decreed* it for others [because an Elder sets a precedent].	וְתִקֵּן לַאֲחֵרִים.

Comments: *Dough offerings* cannot be separated before the flour is made into dough (and rolled out, according to the definition in m.Hal.3.1), and if it is separated prematurely, the separated flour and the remaining batch are both still liable to *dough offering*, even if the separated portion gets into the hands of a priest.

Joshua pointed out that the separated portion is actually prohibited to a priest, because it has not been tithed properly, but others replied that an unnamed Elder had set a precedent in this case. It is difficult to know if this nonpriest was 'elderly' or 'an Elder,' but the reply by Joshua assumes the latter.

Dating (2): Joshua [T2, just after 70 CE] is commenting on an established ruling so that this predates 70 CE. Other Rabbis replied with a story which presumably came from a previous generation, so this too must be pre-70.

m.Hal.3.1-6: When to separate a *dough offering*

Summary of Mishnah: You **can** *snack* on dough until it is fully processed—i.e., until wheat dough is rolled out or until barley dough is in a lump (or when a crust forms, according to Akiba, 3.6), though you **should** separate the *dough offering* as soon as water is mixed with all the flour, except for the last 1.25 *qab* [which is not liable—cf. 2.6] (3.1). If it becomes unfit for *dough offering* (due to mixture with *consecrated* flour or due to the woman's *impurity*) before it is rolled out, it is not liable for *dough offering*, but if it becomes unfit afterward, it is liable (3.2).

If you both *dedicated* it and redeemed it before or after it was rolled out, it is still liable to a *dough offering*, but if you *dedicated* it before and redeemed it after it was rolled out, it is exempt from a *dough offering* [because it belonged to the Temple when it became liable] (3.3)—and the same applies to other *dedicated* produce when it becomes liable to tithes (3.4). If you roll out dough which belongs to a gentile it is not liable for a *dough offering*, but if he gives it to you so you own it when you roll it out, it is liable (3.5). Dough owned by a convert is liable if he rolls it out after he converts (3.6).

The following traditions have elements (marked in bold) for which there is evidence of an origin before 70 CE:

m.Hal.3.3: *Dedicating dough to the Temple and redeeming it*

[If] she *dedicated* her dough [to the Temple]	הקדישה עסתה
before she rolled out [the dough]	עד שלא גלגלה,
and [then] redeemed it: [It is] liable [to a *dough offering*].	ופדאתה, חייבת.
[If] she *dedicated* her dough having rolled it out	משגלגלה,
and [then] redeemed it: [It is] liable [to a *dough offering*].	ופדאתה, חייבת.
[If] she *dedicated* it [to the Temple]	הקדישתה
before she rolled out [the dough]	עד שלא גלגלה,
and the [Temple] Treasurer rolled it out	וגלגלה הגזבר,
and after that she redeemed it, [it is] exempt.	ואחר כך פדאתה, פטורה,
For at the time it became liable [to a *dough offering*]	שבשעת חובתה
it was exempt [since it belonged to the Temple].	היתה פטורה.

Comments: The Temple did not have to pay itself tithes, and so if the dough belonged to the Temple at the time that the *dough offering* became due, there were no tithes to pay, even if it was subsequently redeemed.

Dough is a strange thing to *dedicate* to the Temple, and probably they expected you to redeem this type of *dedication*. We can imagine a woman who was praying as she worked and impulsively *dedicated* her dough to the Temple while she was kneading it. Having done so, she would redeem her *dedication* (at its *full value* plus the *added fifth*) and give the money to the local Temple Treasurer (they were found at various collection points, cf. Comments at m.Pea.4.7-8).

The reference to a Temple Treasurer who "rolled it out" is probably theoretical. Even if a woman was foolish enough to take the actual dough to the Treasurer, although he would feel obliged to receive it, he would probably leave it to rot because it was not worth dealing with.

Dating (9): The reference to a Temple Treasurer makes it possible that this was a pre-70 tradition, though it is equally possible that this is a purely theoretical discussion based on the more likely scenario in m.Pea.4.8 where a field is *dedicated*.

m.Hal.3.4: *Dedicating* and redeeming crops during harvest

This is identical to m.Pea.4.8 where it is discussed.

m.Hal.3.7–4.6: *Dough offerings* from *mixtures* or different batches

Summary of Mishnah: Bread made from a wheat and rice flour mixture is counted as 'bread' if it tastes of cereals (3.7). If a small piece of untithed dough is added as leaven to tithed dough, and there is no other untithed dough to tithe in its place, the mixture must be tithed again (3.8); and similarly for untithed harvest produce which becomes mixed with a collection of Peah [which would not otherwise need tithing] (3.9); and similarly if untithed leaven is added to rice dough [which would not otherwise be liable to *dough offering*], but only if the resultant dough tastes of cereals (3.10).

Two portions of 1 *qab* each become liable to *dough offering* if they touch [because they form a single lump of greater than 1.25 *qab*], unless they belong to different women or they are different species (4.1), though wheat can combine with spelt, and barley can combine with anything except wheat (4.2). Two lumps can combine if they both touch a third lump which is already tithed, though not if the third lump is not liable to tithes (4.3). What if one lump is from the old harvest and one is from the new (4.4)? What if you tithe a 1-*qab* lump? Akiba says it is valid *dough offering* (4.4), and so he says if you tithe two such lumps which are then combined, it does not need retithing (4.5). *Dough offering* must be removed even from dough which is going to be used later, or which is not going to be used at all except for tithing on behalf of *doubtfully tithed* dough (4.6).

There is no evidence that any of this section originated before 70 CE.

m.Hal.4.7-11: Dough offerings from outside the Land

Summary of Mishnah: Israelites in Syria (which in some respects was part of the Land) who sharecrop with gentiles: should they separate *dough offering* twice [once for their gentile partner] (4.7)? The second portion [for the gentile] is burned and the first can be eaten by a priest even if he is not entirely *pure* (4.8).

A list of things which can be given to a priest (4.9): *dough offering* from outside the Land which has been refused by priests, as also *firstfruits* brought before *Shabuot* (Pentecost) (4.10) or *firstborn* from outside the land. A family who came for the Second Passover was even turned away (4.11).

Although the list in m.Hal.4.9 includes some offerings which ceased with the destruction of the Temple, there is no evidence that this list originated before 70 CE. The list is much enlarged in t.Hal.2.7-10.

The following traditions have elements (marked in bold) for which there is evidence of an origin before 70 CE:

m.Hal.4.7: The *dough offering* and tithes from Syria

Israelites who [farm at] fixed shares	ישראל שהיו אריסין
for gentiles in Syria:	לנכרים בסוריא,
R. Eliezer [b. Hyrcanus, T2] [said]:	רבי אליעזר
Their produce is liable	מחייב פרותיהם
to tithes and to Sabbath Year [regulations].	במעשרות ובשביעית,
but Rn. Gamaliel [I T1] exempted [it].	ורבן גמליאל פוטר.
Rn. Gamaliel says:	רבן גמליאל אומר,
Two [portions of] *dough offering* [for those] in Syria,	שתי חלות בסוריא.
but R. Eliezer [b. Hyrcanus, T2] says:	ורבי אליעזר אומר,
One *dough offering*.	חלה אחת.
[In the past] they accepted the lenient [ruling]	**אחזו קולו**
of Rn. Gamaliel [for the first matter]	של רבן גמליאל
and the lenient [ruling] of R. Eliezer [in the second].	וקולו של רבי אליעזר.
[Then] they reverted to follow the rulings of	חזרו לנהוג כדברי
Rn. Gamaliel in both matters.	רבן גמליאל בשתי דרכים.

Comments: An Israelite who owned a crop in Syria was liable for tithes (m.Maas.5.5) and Sabbath Year restrictions (m.Shebi.6.2), but he could get round it if a gentile did the preparation of the ground during the Sabbath Year and the actual harvesting. The Israelite could do his portion of the work by processing the harvest and selling it. Eliezer tried to plug this loophole by saying that the shared work meant they were both doing the work, and so the whole harvest was liable to tithes and Sabbath Year restrictions, but Gamaliel I had already declared that it was not.

Gamaliel's logic is explained by the second ruling, in which he says that the Israelite must set aside two portions of *dough offering*, one for himself and one for his gentile partner. The next mishnah explains that the gentile's portion must be burned, while the Israelite's portion can be eaten by a priest. Eliezer countered that only one portion of *dough offering* is put aside. In other words, Gamaliel regarded the harvest as two separate halves, each of which required a *dough offering* but neither of which required tithes—the gentile's half was not tithed because it belonged to a gentile, and the Israelite's half was not tithed because he did not harvest it himself. But Eliezer said it was all one crop, and so one portion of *dough offering* was given, presumably on behalf of the whole crop.

Dating (1): This was probably not a debate, because although Rn. Gamaliel [I T2] could have lived long enough to meet R. Eliezer b. Hyrcanus [T2], it is unlikely that they would have been regarded as equal enough to be recorded in the same debate. From this tradition alone one would assume that Eliezer is debating with Gamaliel II [T2], but Tosefta records a tradition which suggests that this is Gamaliel I:

> R. Eleazar b. R. Zadok [T2] says: Rn. Gamaliel used to [declare an Israelite in Syria] liable to only one *dough offering*. (t.Hal.2.5)

This tradition must refer to Gamaliel I, not II, because Eleazar is passing on his saying as it if comes from a previous generation. This tradition contradicts Mishnah, and so it is unlikely that someone invented it at a later date (because it would carry very little weight).

The version in Tosefta may be reflected in the comment that "they accepted the . . . lenient ruling of Eliezer," i.e., "one *dough offering*." This later comment by an editor (who remembered that there was an authoritative ruling about one *dough offering*) actually represents a misunderstanding of Eliezer, because Eliezer presumably meant 'one *dough offering* from the whole of the produce' whereas if it was a 'lenient ruling' he must have meant 'a *dough offering* just from the half belonging to the Israelite.'

The above is a possible explanation of this confusion, but it is impossible to be certain. However, the very existence of this confusion suggests that both contradictory traditions were well established at an early stage so that neither of them could be changed sufficiently to produce a proper harmony.

There is another tradition concerning Eleazar b. R. Zadok and Gamaliel earlier in t.Hal.2.5, but this is very likely to be a later invention, because it attempts to exonerate Gamaliel from the charge that he helped Israelites to circumvent the Sabbath Year restrictions in Syria. It says that although Gamaliel ruled that Israelites sharecropping with gentiles were exempt from Sabbath Year restrictions, he actually told Israelites that they should not sharecrop with gentiles during the Sabbath Year. But no tradition is presented to show that Gamaliel actually said this.

m.Hal.4.10-11: Bringing offerings to Jerusalem

Nittai, a gentleman of Tekoa, brought	נתאי איש תקוע הביא
dough offerings from Bethar	חלות מביתר,
and they [the priests] did not accept them from him.	ולא קבלו ממנו.

The people of Alexandria brought	אנשי אלכסנדריא הביאו
their *dough offerings* from Alexandria	חלותיהן מאלכסנדריא,
and they did not accept them from them.	ולא קבלו מהם.
The men of Mt. Tzeboim brought	אנשי הר צבועים הביאו
their *firstfruits* before the Assembly [Pentecost]	בכוריהם קודם עצרת,
and they did not accept them from them.	ולא קבלו מהם,
—because of what is written in the Torah [Exod.23.16]:	מפני הכתוב שבתורה
"And [at] the Festival of Harvest [Pentecost],	וחג הקציר
the *firstfruits* of your labor	בכורי מעשיך
which you sowed in the field."	אשר תזרע בשדה.
11) Ben Antigonus brought up	בן אנטינוס העלה
the *firstborn* from Babylon	בכורות מבבל,
and they did not accept them from him.	ולא קבלו ממנו.
Joseph the Priest brought	יוסף הכהן הביא
firstfruits of wine and oil	בכורי יין ושמן,
and they did not accept them from him.	ולא קבלו ממנו.
Also he brought up	אף הוא העלה
his sons and the sons [i.e., men] of his household	בניו ובני ביתו,
to observe the Minor *Pesach* in Jerusalem,	לעשות פסח קטן בירושלים,
and they turned him back	והחזירוהו,
so that it should not [become]	שלא יקבע
a fixed obligatory ruling.	הדבר חובה.
Ariston brought his *firstfruits*	אריסטון הביא בכוריו
from Apamia and they did accept them from him,	מאפמיא וקבלו ממנו,
because they said: A land buyer in Syria	מפני שאמרו, הקונה בסוריא,
[is] like a land buyer in a district of Jerusalem.	כקונה בפרור שבירושלים.

Comments: *Dough offerings* and *firstfruit* could be eaten only by a priest. They had to originate from the Land (cf. m.Hal.2.1), and so the Alexandrians and Babylonians were refused even though these were centers of Jewish observance. Offerings also had to be brought at the right time, and so *firstfruits* had to wait until *Shabuot* (Pentecost) (cf. m.Bik.1.3, 6).

Why was Nittai refused?—he was a Jew from within the Land (Tekoa was near Bethlehem) who brought *dough offering* from Bethar which was the town where Bar Kokhba made his last stand, about 10 km west of Bethlehem.[3] Neither Tosefta nor Jerusalem Talmud give an explanation, and so presumably it was obvious. Perhaps this man came from the other Tekoa in Northern Galilee[4] which was probably regarded as the southern border of Syria because it was roughly in line with Chezib

---

[3] This is largely confirmed by some inscriptions found in ruins northwest of the Arab village of Battir—see the article "Bethar" in *Encyclopaedia Judaica*.
[4] See Richard J. A. Talbert, *Barrington Atlas of the Greek and Roman World*, 1 (Princeton: Princeton University Press, 2000), map 69 B4.

on the coast (i.e., Ecdippa, which defined the border in m.Hal.4.8). This ruling would then provide the basis of a principle that non-Israelites cannot bring *dough offering* to the Temple even if it is otherwise valid. Or perhaps Bethar, from where he brought the *firstfruits*, was a different Bethar outside Israel.

The last two in the list are also mysteries, but a later editor has added explanations for them. Why was the offering by a priest rejected?—the explanation implies that it would have set a precedent, because priests normally kept the tithes from their own produce (cf. m.Dem.6.3).[5] The editor points that he almost set another precedent when he brought all his sons and other males of his household (which probably implies his household slaves)[6] to the Second Passover, presumably because they missed the first due to *impurity* (Num.7.3-11). He was refused because, as an elder in the community, this would set a precedent (cf. m.Hal.2.5). Therefore if he, as a priest of high standing, decided to bring his priestly tithes to the Temple, every priest would feel they had to follow this precedent. The man from Apamia whose gift was accepted is explained by a saying that parts of Syrian land which are in Jewish ownership are treated like the Land (cf. similar compromises re Syria at m.Shebi.6.2; m.Maas.5.5; m.Hal.4.7).

The discussion of *dough offering* alongside *firstfruits* in this tradition may suggest that a representative collection of *dough offerings* from each community was taken to the Temple along with *firstfruits*. *Dough offerings* appear to be brought by a representative or a delegation from the community ("The people of Alexandria brought their *dough offerings* from Alexandria"), which agrees with m.Bik.3.3 which describes the procession of delegations from each community when they brought their *firstfruits*. These delegations were met at the gates of Jerusalem by Temple authorities who greeted them: "Brothers, men of such-and-such a place, Welcome!" This meeting would be a suitable time either to welcome or refuse them, rather than causing trouble by rejecting their offering in the Temple.

Dating (8): The reference to Temple activities suggests that this originated before 70 CE, though this is very uncertain. However the tradition does not appear to have been created with any ulterior purpose, such as criticism or praise of the priests or of any historical character, and so it is unlikely that it was made up. The fact that *dough offerings* are seen as taken to Jerusalem (when they were given to local priests after 70 CE) and the fact that the details are difficult to understand increase the likelihood that this was an old tradition.

---

[5] An anonymous voice in Jerusalem Talmud has another explanation based on a quote from m.Ter.11.3: "They may not bring *firstfruits* in the form of liquids," so that he may not bring oil and wine but should instead have brought olives and grapes. However this quote stops too soon because the next words are "except for that which is produced from olives or grapes."
[6] This has been altered to emphasize that women did not come — see the parallel discussed at t.Pes.8.10.

When the various explanations are removed we have a list of six similar instances of people whom 'they' accepted or did not accept in Jerusalem. It is likely that this was the original core to which the explanations were added by later rabbis. We are not told who was accepting or refusing these offerings, and so this tradition was probably compiled at a time when this was obvious and uncontentious—i.e., when it was accepted that the priests were in charge of the Temple and there was no need to claim that the Pharisees advised them (cf. m.Yom.1.3; t.Yom.1.8).

New Testament: This tradition shows that at least some Jews in the Diaspora were separating *dough offering* even though this was not required of them before 70 CE (cf. m.Hal.2.1), and that some of them would have liked to bring them to Jerusalem. Paul refers to these dough offerings as 'holy' in Romans 11.16:

If the firstfruits (ἀπαρχή) is holy, so is the [rest of the lump of] dough (φύραμα).

Paul is almost certainly alluding to the Septuagint "firstfruits of dough" (ἀπαρχὴν φυράματος, Num.15.20, 21), which is in the context of *firstfruits*, and not the MT reference to "bread of firstfruits" (Lev.23.20, which is ἄρτων τοῦ πρωτο—γεννήματος in the LXX Lev.23.19), which is in the context of *waving the first sheaf* after Passover. Philo uses the same terminology when he says, "God commands those who are making bread, to take of all the fat and of all the dough (φυράματος), a loaf as firstfruits (ἀπαρχὴν) for the use of the priests" (Philo.*Spec*.I.27, 132). The Greek ἀπαρχὴν translates the Hebrew "First of" (רֵאשִׁית, *reshit*) as it does in the context of several other offerings.[7] We should probably translate both the Greek and Hebrew terms as *"first offering"* because they are sometimes used synonymous with *"firstfruit"* (Deut.18.4a; 26.10; 2Chr.31.5), and sometimes used alongside *"firstfruit"* (בִּכּוּרִים, *bikkurim*—e.g., Exod.23.19) though it also sometimes refers to other offerings such as *firstborn, first sheaf,* and *dough offering* (e.g., Lev.23.10; Num.15.20; Deut.18.4). The Greek term is almost always used in a cultic context both in biblical and nonbiblical Greek.

The use of *"first offering"* (ἀπαρχὴν) to refer to *dough offering* in Romans 11.16 is therefore perfectly correct, though the MT equivalent (רֵאשִׁית, *reshit*) never occurs with this meaning in Mishnah. It is possible that Jews in the Diaspora preferred to speak of *dough offering* in this way because this is one of the few cultic acts which they could share in, if only in a restricted way. It is therefore significant that when Paul and James spoke about converts as *'first offerings'* (usually misleadingly

---

[7] The context is *dough* in Neh.10.37; *firstfruit* in Exod.23.19; Deut.18.4a; 26.10; 2Chr.31.5; *firstborn* in Deut.18.4b; the *first sheaf* in Lev.23.10 and nonspecific first offering in Exod.34.26; Lev.2.12; Ezek.20.40. The only exceptions are Ezek.48.14 where the LXX uses πρωτογένημα, 'firstfruit,' and Jer.2.3 where Israel is the "first of the Lord's produce" and the LXX uses the simple ἀρχή ('first' with no cultic undertones).

translated as '*firstfruits*'),[8] they did not refer to the passage in Jeremiah where Israel is called 'the first of the Lord's harvest' (Jer.2.3, LXX ἀρχὴ γενημάτων) but instead used the word ἀπαρχήν, which alludes to the *first offerings* in Torah.

It is also possible that *dough offerings* were taken to Jerusalem in the form of *firstfruits* before 70 CE—see m.Bik.3.3.

Related early traditions from other tractates

m.Ed.1.2: A *dough offering* from one *qab* or two?

Shammai [T0] says: [Dough which is made]	שמאי אומר,
from a *qab* [of flour is liable] to *dough offering*.	מקב לחלה.
But Hillel says: [Dough which is made]	והלל אומר,
from [two] *qabs* [is liable to *dough offering*]	מקביים.
And the Sages say:	וחכמים אומרים,
[It is not according to the ruling of this [one]	לא כדברי זה
nor the ruling of that [one].	ולא כדברי זה,
But: [Dough made from] a *qab* and a half [of flour]	אלא קב ומחצה
is liable to *dough offering*.	חייבים בחלה.
And [after] measurements increased they said:	ומשהגדילו המדות אמרו,
[Dough made with] five fourths [of a *qab*] is liable.	חמשת רבעים חייבין.
R. Jose [b. Halafta, T4] says: [If it is made from exactly]	רבי יוסי אומר,
five, it is exempt, [but if it is made from]	חמשה פטורין.
five and more, it is liable.	חמשה ועוד, חייבין.

Comments: Hillel and Shammai themselves left very few rulings (traditionally, only three, cf. b.Shab.14b based on m.Ed.1.1-3), and this one seems minor but it would have had a huge influence on daily life in almost every household. Hillel's ruling made it possible for most women to totally avoid the need to separate *dough offering* because a *qab* was about 2.5 liters, and it is unlikely that someone would want to knead more than 5 liters of dough at a time. The Sages made a compromise which later changed when official measurements changed. Even with their changes, it was still likely that most women could avoid separating *dough offerings* so long as they kept individual lumps of dough separate.

The logic behind these quantities is probably the principle that *consecrated* food can be *neutralized* by breaking it up into small portions so that no more than an egg volume is eaten at once (see m.Ter.5.1-3—which specifically mentions 'dough'; cf. m.Hal.2.8; m.Orl.2.4-5). There are twenty-four egg volumes in a *qab*, and the normal *dough offering* for a householder is one-twenty-fourth; so the *dough offering* from a

---

[8] Re converts in Rom.16.5; 1Cor.16.15; Jas.1.18; Rev.14.4; cf. re Christ in 1Cor.15.20, 23 and re the Spirit in Rom.8.23.

qab would be small enough to be regarded as *neutralized*. The ruling of Hillel probably assumed that a householder could make a *dough offering* of one-forty-eighth, like bakers did (cf. m.Hal.2.7).

Dating (1): There is no reason to doubt that these are genuine traditions of Hillel and Shammai. The fact that the later Sages reject both rulings means that this was not invented in order to give authority to a new ruling.

m.TY.1.1a: Combining lumps of dough or a *dough offering*

He who gathers [lumps of] *dough offering*	המכנס חלות
[intending] to reckon them separately	על מנת להפריש,
but they clustered together:	ונשכו,
The School of Shammai says:	בית שמאי אומרים,
They are joined,	חבור
with [regard to passing on] *impurity for a day.*	בטבול יום.
But the School of Hillel says:	ובית הלל אומרים,
They are not joined.	אינו חבור.

Comments: The Hillelites did not count lumps of *dough offering* as a single lump if they accidentally adhered. This means that if one lump was *impure*, it would not pass its *impurity* to the other lumps.

Dating (1): There is no reason to doubt that this was a genuine school dispute, but the heading and the line about *impurity for a day* may not be part of the original debate. The voluminous discussions about combining lumps are all later than 70 CE, except for the debate in m.Hal.2.4 which rejects the concept of combination, though a later editor has changed this by the addition of "unless they become attached."

The original debate probably concerned lumps of dough from which the *dough offering* had not been separated. Hillel wanted to minimize the necessity of householders to separate *dough offerings* (as in m.Ed.1.2), and this was in line with that purpose. Later generations followed the Shammaite ruling that one could join small lumps of dough to make one which was liable for *dough offering*, but the natural inclination of the later rabbis was to follow Hillelite rulings. They therefore assumed that this dispute did not concern untithed lumps of dough, but lumps of *dough offering* which might *taint* each other.

Summary and Conclusions

Very little in this tractate can be traced back to before 70 CE, which may indicate that this was a minor issue. It was assumed that dough was only liable if it was significantly larger than 1 *qab* (m.Hal.2.4; though there was some dispute about the exact size, m.Ed.1.2) and if it was made within the Land (m.Hal.2.1; 4.7, 10), and that at least some was taken to Jerusalem (m.Hal.4.10; cf. m.Betz.1.6) or given to the local Temple representatives (m.Hal.3.3). The insistence that the separation must take place after the flour has been made into dough (m.Hal.2.5; 3.3) meant that this was mainly the task of women, though in practice this was easy to avoid by making batches of dough of less than 1 *qab* (about 2 liters).

Before 70 CE there was some debate about what types of flour-based foods were liable, as seen in the school dispute about pancakes and dumplings (or whatever they were—see m.Hal.1.6), but soon after 70 CE there was a general consensus that *dough offering* applied only to baked bread, not boiled food (t.Hal.1.2) or sponge cake (m.Hal.1.5). The proportion of dough which was offered was probably not settled before 70 CE (cf. m.Ed.1.2; m.Hal.2.7).

Soon after 70 CE there was also a great deal of debate about batches and mixtures which combined (the second half of m.Hal.2.4 and then the long section m.Hal.3.7–4.6 of which nothing can be shown to originate before 70 CE). There was also much debate about whether *dough offering* was liable outside the Land, and later rabbis decided that it *was* liable but it must be burned and not given to a priest (on the basis of m.Hal.4.8).

There is no discussion in these early sources about removing the *dough offering* from *doubtfully tithed* bread (the earliest reference to this occurs at m.Hal.4.6), and so it was crucial that the *dough offering* should be removed. The men were at the mercy of their wives or bakers before 70 CE, though shortly after this a pious man could remove a small portion off every loaf and burn it if he suspected that the *dough offering* had not been given. This former state of affairs explains why the *dough offering* was treated so seriously that women who neglected it were thought to die in childbirth (m.Shab.2.6) or could be divorced without their *ketubbah* (m.Ket.7.6).

Tractate *Orlah*: Forefruit of Young Trees

Definitions and Outline

Torah taught that newly planted trees could not be harvested for three years and that the next year's fruit was *consecrated* (Lev.19.23-25). The first three years' fruit, the *forefruit* (*orlah*, עָרְלָה, lit. 'foreskin'), was left on the plant, and the fruit of the *fourth-year plant* (*neta rebai*, נֶטַע רְבָעִי) was brought to Jerusalem and consumed there (dealt with at m.Pea.7.6; m.MS.5.1-5).

The rabbis had to define what Torah meant by 'planting,' 'food,' and 'fruit' in Leviticus 19.23. They decided that 'planting' did not include replanting in the same spot if a tree blew down, that 'food' included that which was processed using non-food products of the tree, and that 'fruit' included non-food products of the fruit. They also had to decide how these products might *taint* others, and decided that *forefruit tainted* twice as much as *elevation offerings* (i.e., in a proportion of one two-hundredth instead of one one-hundredth). This led them to compare and contrast *forefruit* with other contaminating products, especially with *mixtures in a vineyard* (which are dealt with mainly at m.Kil.4-7). They discussed not only *tainting* by a measure (i.e., one one-hundredth or one two-hundredth) but also *tainting* by its effect such as leavening or flavoring.

m.Orl.1.1-5: Which trees are subject to *forefruit*?

Any tree which is newly planted is subject to *forefruit* for three years.

m.Orl.1.6-9: Forbidden produce of *forefruit* trees

Any food from the trees and anything made from its fruit is forbidden.

m.Orl.2.1-3: *Tainting* by a measure of *forefruit* (and others)

Forefruit, like *mixtures in a vineyard, taints* in any concentration higher than one part in 200 of *deconsecrated* food.

m.Orl.2.4-17: *Tainting* by the effect of *forefruit* (and others)

Forefruit taints in any quantity if it flavors or leavens the whole.

m.Orl.3.1-9: *Tainting* by tiny portions of *forefruit* (and others), outside the Land

Some *forefruit* can *taint* in the tiniest quantity, even outside the Land.

m.Orl.1.1-5: Which trees are subject to *forefruit*?

Summary of Mishnah: A tree is liable only if it is planted for food (1.1), though the food does not have to be for personal consumption (1.2). Replanting is not 'planting', if it was uprooted with enough soil to support it (1.3), or if it was replanted where the bulk of its root still remained (1.4), but it is replanting if an uprooted tree puts out shoots which become roots (1.5).

There is no evidence that any of this section originated before 70 CE.

m.Orl.1.6-9: Forbidden produce of *forefruit* trees

Summary of Mishnah: *Forefruit* or *mixtures in a vineyard* is *neutralized* by 200 parts (1.6). Non-food products are exempt from the law of *forefruit, fourth year,* and Nazirite vow (unless perhaps they are used for processing other food), but are liable to the law of Asherah idolatry [Exod.34.13; Deut.7.5; 12.3; 16.21-22] (1.7). Non-food portions of the fruit are prohibited under all these laws except *fourth-year fruit* (1.8). You cannot plant the fruit of *forefruit*, but you can graft shoots of *forefruit* (1.9).

The following traditions have elements (marked in bold) for which there is evidence of an origin before 70 CE:

m.Orl.1.7: Non-food and non-fruit portions of *forefruit* plants

The leaves and shoots	הֶעָלִים וְהַלּוּלָבִים
and sap and blossoms	וּמֵי גְפָנִים וְסַמָּדַר,
are permitted in [laws of] ***forefruit***	מוּתָּרִים בְּעָרְלָה
and in [the laws of] *fourth [year]* and Nazirite [vow],	וּבְרְבָעִי וּבְנָזִיר,
but they are prohibited in [the law of] Asherah.	וַאֲסוּרִים בָּאֲשֵׁרָה.
R. Jose [b. Halfta, T4] says:	רַבִּי יוֹסֵי אוֹמֵר,
The blossom is prohibited	הַסַּמָּדַר אָסוּר,
because it becomes fruit.	מִפְּנֵי שֶׁהוּא פְרִי.
R. Eliezer [b. Hyrcanus, T2] says:	רַבִּי אֱלִיעֶזֶר אוֹמֵר,
The curdling [of milk] with resin of *forefruit*:	הַמַּעֲמִיד בִּשְׂרַף הָעָרְלָה,
[The cheese is] prohibited.	אָסוּר.
Said R. Joshua [b. Hananiah, T2]:	אָמַר רַבִּי יְהוֹשֻׁעַ,
I heard explicitly	שָׁמַעְתִּי בְּפֵרוּשׁ,
that the curdling with resin of leaves	שֶׁהַמַּעֲמִיד בִּשְׂרַף הֶעָלִים,
or with resin of roots: [The milk is] permitted;	וּבִשְׂרַף הָעִקָּרִים, מוּתָּר.
[but curdling with] resin of unripe fruit [is] prohibited	בִּשְׂרַף הַפַּגִּים, אָסוּר,
because they are [the same] as fruit.	מִפְּנֵי שֶׁהֵם פְּרִי.

Comments: 'Fruits' and 'food' from *forefruit* plants are prohibited in Torah, but what about using non-food products of the plant for processing other food? Eliezer says that this is prohibited, but Joshua says it is prohibited only if the product comes from the fruit.

It is difficult to know whether 'resin' (שְׂרָף, *seraph*) is the same as 'sap' (מֵי גְפָנִים, *mé gephanim*, 'water of the vine') or whether one is a subset of the other. I have assumed here that 'sap' is the moisture in the stem, while 'resin' is a generic term for moisture elsewhere such as in the leaf, roots, and fruit. Therefore Eliezer is not contradicting or refining the reference to 'sap' in the opening ruling, but he is introducing a new item to the list, viz., 'resin.'

These exceptions can also apply to the prohibition of *fourth-year fruit* and the prohibition of grape products for Nazirites, but not to the prohibition of products of trees which have been used in the context of Asherah worship.

Dating (2): Eliezer and Joshua are both from T2 (soon after 70 CE) and both assumed that the preceding ruling was already established, so it must originate before 70 CE.

m.Orl.2.1-3: Tainting by a measure of *forefruit* (and others)

Summary of Mishnah: *Doubtful elevation offerings, dough offerings,* and *firstfruits* or combinations of these are *neutralized* by 100 parts, and you give the priest a replacement portion, though *forefruits* and *mixtures in a vineyard* or combinations of these are *neutralized* by 200 parts and you do not replace the portion (2.1). One portion of *elevation offering* and half a portion of *forefruit* can *neutralize* each other if they fall into 99 portions of *deconsecrated* produce (2.2). One portion of *forefruits* or *mixtures in a vineyard* can *neutralize* another if one was *neutralized* by 200 portions and then the other fell in later (2.3).

The following traditions have elements (marked in bold) for which there is evidence of an origin before 70 CE:

m.Orl.2.1: Combining of similar sources of tainting

Elevation offering	התרומה
and *elevation offering* of the [*first*] *tithe*	ותרומת מעשר
which [is from] *doubtfully tithed food*	של דמאי,
[and] *dough offerings* and *firstfruits*	החלה והבכורים,
are *neutralized* by a hundred and one [parts]	עולים באחד ומאה,
and one can combine together	ומצטרפין זה עם זה,
[to make a higher concentration,]	
and it is necessary to *elevate* [a replacement offering].	וצריך להרים.

Forefruit **and** *mixtures of the vineyard*	הערלה וכלאי הכרם,
are *neutralized* **by [two] hundred and one [parts]**	עולים באחד ומאתים,
and one can combine together	ומצטרפין זה עם זה,
[to make a higher concentration,]	
and it is not necessary to *elevate* [a replacement offering].	ואינו צריך להרים.
R. Simeon [b. Yohai, T4] says:	רבי שמעון אומר,
They [do] not combine [to make a higher concentration].	אינן מצטרפין.
R. Eliezer [b. Hyrcanus, T2] says:	רבי אליעזר אומר,
They do combine	מצטרפין
when [they still] give [a detectable] flavor	בנותן טעם,
but [otherwise the combined produce is] not prohibited.	אבל לא לאסור.

Comments: This summarizes the law of *tainting* by *consecrated* produce and divides this type of produce into two groups: that which is *neutralized* by a dilution in 100 parts (*elevation offerings, doubtful elevation offerings, dough offerings,* and *firstfruits*) and in 200 parts (*forefruit* and *mixtures in a vineyard*). The reason for the higher dilution of the latter is to discourage farmers from picking more in order to *neutralize* some prohibited fruit (according to m.Orl.1.6[1]). Another difference between the two groups is that you do not have to provide a replacement offering of *forefruit* or *mixtures of a vineyard* (cf. m.Ter.5.2).

What if two separate portions of *consecrated* produce fell in, which were less than one one-hundredth of the whole but when added together they brought the concentration above the one one-hundredth (or one two-hundredth) mark? The anonymous majority view is that they can add together but Simeon disagrees and Eliezer only agrees if they spread a flavor throughout the *tainted* produce (cf. Comments at m.Orl.2.4 below).

Dating (5): Eliezer's disagreement with this anonymous opinion suggests that the principle of combining sources of *tainting* was already in place in his day (just after 70 CE). The generalized ruling by Joshua b. Hananiah [T2, just after 70 CE] appears to be based on the different rates of *neutralization*, so these too were already in place before 70 CE. These two references to principles which occur in this ruling suggest that at least these principles originate before 70 CE.

The ruling itself as recorded here may not originate before 70 CE because the first list, of things which *taint* with a one-hundredth, does not include *dedications* (which were no longer made after 70 CE) or *second tithes* (which were always redeemed after 70 CE and they were not likely to fall into any containers before they were declared to be redeemed). However, this is not necessarily an indication that the ruling is late (see the note of caution about a similar situation at m.Orl.2.4-5), and it is likely that the original ruling simply said "*elevation offering*" and that this was extended into a list

---

[1] m.Orl.1.6: ". . . so that he does not purposely [pick more produce to neutralize it]."

after 70 CE. Similarly, the second list, of things which *taint* with a two-hundredth, may have originally simply said *"forefruits"* and *"mixtures of a vineyard"* may have been added later, though it may equally have listed both in the first place. This is confirmed to some extent by the way m.Orl.2.4 appears to refer to this ruling using a list which consists of *"elevation offerings* or *forefruits* or *mixtures of a vineyard."*

It is also possible that the reference to Eliezer is inaccurate and that this was originally a debate between R. Eleazar [b. Shammua, T4] and Simeon b. Yohai (who often debated together), because Eleazar and Eliezer are often confused for each other in rabbinic texts (the only difference is the *yod* in Eliezer's name). The reason for changing Eleazar to Eliezer would be that Eleazar is nowhere else interested in the topic of *elevation offerings* or this type of *tainting*, whereas Eliezer is. However, their two opinions are presented in isolation and not as a debate with each other, because although they both interact with the preceding ruling they do not interact with each other, and so there is no substantial reason to doubt that this is Eliezer.

Therefore, although only the main principles of this ruling can be shown to originate before 70 CE, it is likely that the core of the wording was part of a pre-70 ruling.

m.Orl.2.4-17: *Tainting* by the effect of *forefruit* (and others)

Summary of Mishnah: *Tainting* can be by any amount which leavens or flavors the whole—but is there a minimum quantity as there is with *impurity* (2.4-5)? This ruling can have both strict and lenient applications (2.6-7). Leaven can *taint* even if other leaven already leavened most or all of the lump (2.8-9). Can spices, which would not flavor the whole by themselves, combine to *taint* (2.10)? And who may eat them (2.15)? Can lumps of leaven, which would not leaven the whole by themselves, combine to *taint* (2.11-12)? And who may eat them (2.14)? If you wiped *impure* and *pure* oil into leather, does *tainting* depend on the first or the last wiping (2.13)? If different portions of sacrifices *taint* a dish, who may eat it (2.16-17)?

The following traditions have elements (marked in bold) for which there is evidence of an origin before 70 CE:

The traditions at m.Orl.2.16-17 which concern various types of sacrificial meat may possibly date back to Temple times, but it is equally possible that this was based on a theoretical discussion in the days of R. Simeon b. Yohai [T4] who comments on similar matters at m.MS.3.2, or that it was inspired by the discussion at m.Meil.4.3-4 about combining some of these same categories of meat (which, as seen below at m.Meil.4.3, probably postdates 70 CE). Therefore m.Orl.2.16-17 is not included here.

m.Orl.2.4-5: *Tainting* by leavening or flavoring

Whatever [*consecrated* food] leavens or spices	כל המחמץ והמתבל
or *taints* [by a fixed concentration]	והמדמע
[whether] by *elevation offering* or by *forefruits*	בתרומה ובערלה
or by *mixtures of a vineyard*:	ובכלאי הכרם,
[The *tainted* food is] prohibited.	אסור.
And the School of Shammai says:	ובית שמאי אומרים,
[This amount of *tainting*] also makes [it] *impure*.	אף מטמא.
But the School of Hillel says:	ובית הלל אומרים,
[This amount] will never make [it] *impure*	לעולם אינו מטמא,
unless there is [at least] an egg-sized [amount] in it.	עד שיהא בו כביצה.
5) Dosethai of Kefar Yithmah [T1]	דוסתאי איש כפר יתמה,
who was a disciple of the School of Shammai	היה מתלמידי בית שמאי,
said: I heard from Shammai the Elder [1st C BCE]	ואמר, שמעתי משמאי הזקן
who said: [It] can only make [it] *impure*	שאמר, לעולם אינו מטמא
if there is [at least] an egg-sized [amount] in it.	עד שיהא בו כביצה.

Comments: If some *elevation offering* or other *consecrated* produce falls into *deconsecrated* produce, it is *tainted* and becomes *consecrated*, though if it forms a concentration of less than one one-hundredth (or one two-hundredth in some cases—cf. m.Orl.1.6; 2.1-3), the *tainting* is *neutralized* (see tractate *Terumot*). This ruling points out that sources of *tainting* which spread throughout the whole, like leaven or spices which spread their flavor, can *taint* at a lower concentration than one one-hundredth. The schools said that *impurity* can also be passed on in the same way, so that the merest amount of *impure* leaven or spices can *taint* anything into which it falls. The Hillelites agreed, but they said that the source of *tainting* must be at least an egg-sized quantity, and one Shammaite said that Shammai himself had also said this.

This was a very important debate for the average householder because a tiny portion of *impure* leaven could fall into a tub of flour and *taint* several months' food supply, or a crumb of leaven could fall from the hand of an *impure* person and *taint* a whole batch of dough. The restriction by the Hillelites made it into a much more practical ruling for the householder.

Dating (1): There is no reason to doubt that this is a genuine school dispute, and there would be little point in inventing the tradition that Shammai himself agreed with the Hillelite position, except perhaps before 70 CE while the Shammaites were in the ascendancy.

This school dispute is assumed in m.Toh.1.5 which is concerned with *impurity* passed on by an egg-sized quantity, and so this might have been the original context of this dispute. This suggests that the ruling about *tainting* by leavening and flavoring predates 70 CE, which is confirmed by the fact that Eliezer b. Hyrcanus [T2, just after 70 CE] assumed that flavor can *taint* even when the concentration is less than one-hundredth (m.Orl.2.1; see m.Orl.2.11), and by the early ruling about *tainting* from the flavor of fenugreek (m.Ter.10.5).

The list of *elevation offerings*, *forefruits* and *mixtures of a vineyard* may have been added later because the list omits other types of *consecrated* produce which were not sources of contamination after 70 CE—i.e., *second tithes* and *dedications* (cf. a similar omission in m.Orl.2.1). However, the list also omits *dough offerings* (which are also *elevation offerings*—cf. Num.15.20) which would have been a very obvious member of this list (especially in the context of leavening), and so the shortened list may merely be representative and we should not read too much into what is missing.

The text of 2.4a became the starting point for further exposition in m.Orl.2.6-10 which periodically refers back to these words.

New Testament: Leaven in the NT is regarded in both a positive and a negative light—leavening illustrates the spread of the Kingdom (Mt.13.33 // Lk.13.21) but also the spread of hypocrisy (Mt.16.6 // Mk.8.15 // Lk.12.1), boasting (1Cor.5.6), and bad doctrine (Gal.5.9). This spreading negative influence cannot be related to the clear-out of leaven at *Pesach* (Passover) because this practice does not imply the concept of spreading. It is much more likely that this NT imagery reflects the concerns of this tradition about the spread of *tainting* by *consecrated* or *impure* leaven. The fact that the schools were debating this subject, and the fact that this debate was so important for the average householder (see Comments above), made it an ideal illustration for Jesus and Paul to use. However, any reference to leaven also carries an allusion to the Feast of Unleavened Bread (i.e., Passover), and so Paul links "Christ our Passover" with the lack of leaven (1Cor.5.6).

m.Orl.2.11-12: Combining leavening sources of *tainting*

Leaven which is *deconsecrated*	שְׂאוֹר שֶׁל חוּלִין
and [leaven] which is *elevation offering*	וְשֶׁל תְּרוּמָה
which [both] fell into the middle of dough;	שֶׁנָּפְלוּ לְתוֹךְ עִסָּה,
[if] there is not [enough] in this [piece of *deconsecrated* leaven] to leaven [the whole]	לֹא בָזֶה כְדִי לְחַמֵּץ
and there is not [enough] in this [piece of *elevation offering* leaven] to leaven [the whole]	וְלֹא בָזֶה כְדִי לְחַמֵּץ,
but [when] they are combined, they leaven it:	וְנִצְטָרְפוּ וְחִמְּצוּ,
R. Eliezer [b. Hyrcanus, T2] says:	רַבִּי אֱלִיעֶזֶר אוֹמֵר,
I follow [the status] of the last [leaven].	אַחַר הָאַחֲרוֹן אֲנִי בָא.
But the Sages say:	וַחֲכָמִים אוֹמְרִים,
Whether the prohibited leaven [fell in]	בֵּין שֶׁנָּפַל אִסוּר
at the start or at the end,	בַּתְּחִלָּה בֵּין בַּסוֹף,
[it] can only [make it] prohibited	לְעוֹלָם אֵינוּ אוֹסֵר
if there is [enough] to leaven [the whole].	עַד שֶׁיְּהֵא בוֹ כְדִי לְחַמֵּץ.
12) Joezer of the Birah [T1]	יוֹעֶזֶר אִישׁ הַבִּירָה

was a disciple of the School of Shammai	הָיָה מִתַּלְמִידֵי בֵית שַׁמַּאי,
and he said: I inquired of	וְאָמַר שָׁאַלְתִּי אֶת
Rn. Gamaliel the Elder [I, T1] who was standing	רַבָּן גַּמְלִיאֵל הַזָּקֵן עוֹמֵד
at the East Gate, and he said:	בְּשַׁעַר הַמִּזְרָח, וְאָמַר,
[It] can only [make it] prohibited	לְעוֹלָם אֵינוּ אוֹסֵר,
if there is [enough] to leaven [the whole].	עַד שֶׁיְּהֵא בוֹ כְּדֵי לְחַמֵּץ.

Comments: If two lumps of leaven fell into some dough, neither of which was large enough to leaven the whole of it, and only one of them was *consecrated*, was the dough *tainted*? The Sages said no, because the *consecrated* lump has to be big enough to leaven all of it by itself (even if some of it is actually leavened by the other lump). Their reply is very similar to the Hillelite ruling in m.Orl.2.4,[2] and a Shammaite said that he remembered Gamaliel saying the same thing.

Eliezer says that it depends on which lump fell in last—if the *consecrated* lump fell in first and was not able to leaven it all, then the dough did not become *tainted*, but if it fell in last so that it was able to complete the leavening of the dough, then the whole dough must be regarded as *tainted*. This was even stricter than the Shammaite ruling of m.Orl.2.4, because it made it possible for the tiniest amount of *consecrated* leaven to *taint* a very large batch of dough which was almost all leavened. The Sages limited this *tainting* to lumps which were actually large enough to *taint* the whole batch by themselves.

The detail about Gamaliel standing at the East Gate may indicate that this was one of the gates where courts were held (cf. m.San.11.2), or it may be significant as a holy spot, in sight of the Holy of Holies (cf. m.Ber.9.5).

Dating (1): The transmission of a tradition about Gamaliel by a Shammaite is unusual, but this makes its veracity more likely. In the debate between the majority and Eliezer [T2, just after 70 CE], both sides assume that the *consecrated* lump does not actually have to leaven the whole but only has to leaven part of it, and so this principle must predate 70 CE. The question at the start of this tradition encapsulates this principle very well, and the tradition which is attributed to Gamaliel forms a suitable answer to it, and so it is likely that this is the original core of the tradition. The explanations ("[if] there is not [enough] in this [piece . . .]") were probably added later.

New Testament: The comment in Acts 5.35 that Gamaliel was "honored by all the people" coheres with this tradition that the Shammaites respected him.

---

[2] The Sages say: "[it] can only [make it] prohibited if there is [enough] to leaven [the whole] in it," which is only two words different from the Hillelite ruling in m.Orl.2.4: "it can only make [it] *impure* if there is an egg-sized [contaminant] in it," and both use the same unusual construction.

m.Orl.2.13: *Tainting* leather goods with impure oil

[Leather] goods which one greased with *impure* oil	כלים שסכן בשמן טמא,
and he returned and greased with *pure* oil	וחזר וסכן בשמן טהור,
or which one greased with *pure* oil	או שסכן בשמן טהור,
and he returned and later greased with *impure* oil:	וחזר וסכן בשמן טמא,
R. Eliezer [b. Hyrcanus, T2] says	רבי אליעזר אומר,
I follow [the status] of the first [oil].	אחר הראשון אני בא.
But the Sages say:	וחכמים אומרים,
[We follow the status] of the last [oil].	אחר האחרון.

Comments: If you grease a leather sandal or bag with oil, it is liable to exude a little of that oil, so that using *impure* oil can make the whole object *impure*. A householder or a servant could therefore unknowingly cause extremely expensive damage. The majority of the Sages said that you could undo the mistake by regreasing with *pure* oil, but Eliezer disagreed.

The word translated "[leather] goods" (כְּלִי, *keli*) more often means 'a vessel,' which can be earthenware, leather, or glass, etc., but it can also be used for tools and anything made by a craftsman (cf. m.Pea.6.2), especially for leather goods (cf. m.Dem.1.3). The debate by later rabbis in the Jerusalem Talmud (y.Orl.2.7) assumes that it refers to leather bottles or bowls which are lubricated on the outside until the oil exudes through to the inside, so that *impure* oil would *taint* its contents when it is filled, but it could equally refer to any leather goods.

Dating (5): Both the Sages and Eliezer (just after 70 CE) assume that *impurity* could spread by this means, which suggests that this type of *tainting* was already recognized before 70 CE. Eliezer's reply is clearly related to his reply in m.Orl.2.11, which is probably why this ruling is placed here.

New Testament: The Pharisees who looked aghast at the prostitute who anointed Jesus' feet (Lk.7.36-39) were probably thinking about this issue among all the other issues of *impurity* which this event provoked. The oil which she used would have been made *impure* by her (unless she was keeping the purity laws, which might be considered unlikely), and although Jesus could bathe himself and be *pure* at sunset, his sandals could have been ruined if he replaced them without washing his feet, unless he followed the Sages' advice and greased them later with *pure* oil. There is, of course, no indication that Jesus regarded this issue as important.

m.Orl.3.1-9: Tainting by the tiniest portion of forefruit (and others), even outside the Land

Summary of Mishnah: A thread which is dyed with fruit of *forefruit*, or a garment which contains it, must be burned—but can it be *neutralized* (3.1-2)? Similarly you

must burn sacks with a hair of a *firstborn* or a Nazirite or other *holy things* (3.3).
Food cooked with fuel of *forefruit* rind must be burned if it is not *neutralized* (3.4-5).
Fenugreek grown as a *mixture of a vineyard* must be burned—but it can be
neutralized (3.6), unlike six or seven other food items (though Meir says more) (3.7-
8). Produce which might perhaps be *forefruit* or *mixtures in a vineyard* may not be
eaten in the Land but they may be purchased and eaten outside the Land. *Forefruit*
applies outside the Land (according to traditional *halakhah*), as do *mixtures* with
vines (according to the Scribes) (3.9).

Although m.Orl.3.3 refers to Nazirites and *firstborn* (both of which ended at 70 CE)
there is nothing to show that this discussion originated before 70 CE. The following
traditions have elements (marked in bold) for which there is evidence of an origin
before 70 CE:

m.Orl.3.9: *Forefruit* inside and outside the Land

Uncertain [fruit which might be] *forefruit*:	ספק ערלה,
In the Land of Israel it is prohibited [as if it is *forefruit*]	בארץ ישראל אסור,
but in Syria it is permitted.	ובסוריא מותר,
And outside the Land	ובחוצה לארץ
one may go down and buy [it from a *non-Jew*],	יורד ולוקח,
but only [if] one does not see him gather it	ובלבד שלא יראנו לוקט.
[from a plant which is subject to *forefruit*].	
A vineyard which is planted [as a *mixture* **with] vegetables,**	כרם נטוע ירק,
and vegetables are sold outside it:	וירק נמכר חוצה לו,
In the Land of Israel it is prohibited	בארץ ישראל אסור,
but in Syria it is permitted.	ובסוריא מותר,
And outside the Land one may go down	ובחוצה לארץ יורד
and gather but only [if] one does not	ולוקט, ובלבד שלא
gather it in [one's own] hand.	ילקוט ביד.
The *new produce* is prohibited [before waving the *first sheaf*],	החדש, אסור
according to [written] Torah,	מן התורה
in all places [even outside the Land];	בכל מקום.
and *forefruit* [is prohibited in all places]	
[by] *halakhah* [Oral Torah];	והערלה, הלכה.
and *mixtures* [are prohibited in all places];	והכלאים,
by the rulings of the Scribes.	מדברי סופרים.

t.Orl.1.8: No *forefruit* outside the Land

R. Eleazar b. R. Jose [the Galilean, T4]	רבי אליעזר בן רבי יוסי
said in the name of	אומר משום
R. Jose son of the Damascene [T3]	רבי יוסי בן דורמסקית
who said in the name of	שאמר משם

R. Johanan b. Nuri [T3]	רבי יוחנן בן נורי
who said in the name of	שאמר משם
R. Eliezer the Great [b. Hyrcanus, T2]:	רבי אליעזר הגדול
There is no *forefruits* outside the Land.	אין ערלה בחוצה לארץ.

Comments: If you are uncertain whether some produce is from *forefruit* plants or *mixtures in a vineyard*, you have to err on the side of caution within Israel, but not outside Israel, unless you actually see them gathered or gather them yourself from a prohibited plant.

Laws which apply outside Israel include the prohibition of eating *new produce* (which may not be eaten before waving the *first sheaf*, cf. m.Hal.1.1), *forefruit,* and *mixtures*—the first is in Torah, the second in *halakhah,* and the last in the rulings of the Scribes. Later rabbis debated in the Jerusalem Talmud about what is meant by "*halakhah*"—it is either a voluntarily adopted law or a law passed down orally from Mt. Sinai (y.Orl.3.7.III). The "Scribes" are generally regarded as the teachers who preceded the Tannaim (the authorities cited in the Mishnah), and their rulings are regarded as additional to the Written Torah and in some respects more important (cf. m.San.11.3; m.Par.11.4-6).

Dating (2): According to Tosefta, Eleazar b. Hyrcanus [T2, just after 70 CE] disagreed with the majority who applied the law of *forefruits* outside the Land. It is possible that he represented the status quo (as he often did) so that these laws were extended outside the Land only after 70 CE. However, according to m.Qid.1.9 (see below), Eliezer appears to accept a ruling which says that *forefruits do* apply outside Israel. It is likely that t.Orl.1.8 represents the status quo just before 70 CE, which was wrongly attributed to Eliezer. The long chain of scholars in t.Orl.1.8 indicates that this is a tradition which was not recorded in Eliezer's name until long after his time.

New produce, forefruit, and *mixtures* (which are listed at the end of m.Orl.3.9) were applied outside Israel even though Torah appears to apply them only within the Land. The later rabbis in Jerusalem Talmud debated why *dough offering* was not added to this list because by their time *dough offering* was also obligatory outside Israel. Although some in the Diaspora already set aside *dough offering* before 70 CE (cf. m.Hal.4.10), it is unlikely that it was obligatory until after 70 CE (see m.Hal.2.1). The silence about *dough offering* at the end of m.Orl.3.9 suggests that this list dates from after 70 CE, but it cannot date from before 70 CE because it already includes *new produce* which was added by Eliezer (cf. m.Qid.1.9 below), and so it probably comes from about 70 CE.

This change in the law concerning *forefruit* helps to explain the apparent contradictions in the rulings in m.Orl.3.9, which appear to make a threefold distinction between Israel, Syria, and outside Israel, even though the rules about parts of Syria are the same as for outside Israel. It is likely that the first parts of these rulings originated in the days when the laws of *forefruit* only applied in Israel, and they were applied in a lesser way in Syria (which was considered as an adjunct to Israel—cf.m.Hal.4.10-11 and Comments there). Later generations applied the rules about Syria to other lands 'outside Israel' and added the examples.

Related early traditions from other tractates

m.Qid.1.9: Commandments which are dependent on the Land

All commands which depend on the Land	כל מצוה שהיא תלויה בארץ,
are not carried out except in the Land,	אינה אלא בארץ.
and those which do not depend on the Land	ושאינה תלויה בארץ,
are carried out both in the Land	נוהגת בין בארץ
and outside the Land,	בין בחוצה לארץ,
except for *forefruits* and *mixtures*.	חוץ מן הערלה והכלאים.
R. Eliezer [b. Hyrcanus, T2] says:	רבי אליעזר אומר,
New produce is also [an exception].	אף מן החדש.

Comments: Commands where Torah referred to the Land, such as tithing of harvests, *leftovers* for the poor, and the Sabbath Year rest for the land, were obligatory only within Israel. The exceptions to this were *mixtures* and *forefruits*, but Eliezer added another exception—the restriction on eating any of the *new produce* until after the ceremonial waving of the *first sheaf*. This restriction continued after 70 CE in spite of the fact that the accompanying sacrifice was impossible, and Johanan b. Zakkai [T1, just before 70 CE and just after] made a ruling about how it should be celebrated "far from Jerusalem" (i.e., in the provinces of Israel—m.Men.10.5). It is possible that Eliezer interpreted this to mean that it applied outside Israel.

Dating (2): The addition by Eliezer [T2, just after 70 CE] does not have the form of a debate—he is appending his ruling to a received tradition, which suggests that this tradition originated before 70 CE.

There is some doubt that Eliezer would have added his ruling to this tradition which extends the laws of *forefruits* and *mixtures* outside the Land, because t.Orl.1.8 records that Eliezer did not agree about extending the law of *forefruits* outside Israel. However, it is likely that this tradition was mistaken (as discussed above at m.Orl.3.9), especially as m.Qid.1.9 reflects the pre-70 situation in every other respect—agricultural tithing was not extended outside Israel (m.Dem.1.3), nor Sabbath Year regulations (m.Yad.4.3, discussed at the end of *Peah*), and the undateable tradition in m.Orl.3.9 said that *mixtures* was enacted outside Israel by authority of the Scribes, and so the Tannaim after 70 CE already regarded it as an established law.

m.Meil.4.3: Combining similar impure sources of *tainting*

All [forms of] *invalid offerings*	כל הפגולין
combine together [to *taint*].	מצטרפין זה עם זה.
[And] all [forms of] *leftover offering*	כל הנותרין
combine together [to *taint*].	מצטרפין זה עם זה.
[And] all [forms of] *carrion*	כל הנבלות
combine together [to *taint*].	מצטרפות זו עם זו.
[And] all [forms of] *creeping things*	כל השרצים
combine together [to *taint*].	מצטרפין זה עם זה.
The blood of a *creeping thing*	דם השרץ
and its flesh combine [to *taint*].	ובשרו מצטרפין.
The general rule stated by R. Joshua [b. Hananiah, T2]:	כלל אמר רבי יהושע
All whose *impurity* and measure are alike	כל שטומאתו ושעורו שוין,
combine together [to *taint*].	מצטרפין זה עם זה.
[If they are alike in] *impurity* but not measure,	טומאתו ולא שעורו,
[or] measure but not *impurity*,	שעורו ולא טומאתו,
[or] neither *impurity* nor measure,	לא טומאתו ולא שעורו,
they do not combine together [to *taint*].	אין מצטרפין זה עם זה.

Comments: If two pieces of meat which a priest may not eat fell into a pot, and neither of them were large enough on their own to *taint* the food, could they combine to *taint* it? Joshua said they could, but only if they were similar with regard to their '*impurity* and measure'—which is traditionally regarded as meaning 'the length of time it remains *impure*,' and 'the minimum measure which conveys *impurity*.'

Dating (5): None of this tradition can be shown to originate from before 70 CE, but the fact that Joshua is making a general rule suggests that there were already previous disparate rules which he was attempting to bring together. This means that the principle of combining sources of *tainting* already existed.

This ruling is related to the dispute in m.Orl.2.16-17 regarding the combination of *invalid offerings* and *leftover offerings* which together flavored a pot. It is also likely that it is related to the principle that sources of *tainting* can only combine if they are *neutralized* by the same measure (m.Orl.2.1).

This general rule is not altogether suitable for adjudicating in this situation, because all four types of contamination had the same consequences with regard to *impurity* (a punishment of 40 stripes—see m.Makk.3.2) and three of them (*invalid offerings, leftover offerings,* and *carrion*) conveyed *impurity* by the same minimum measure (an olive's bulk, and for *creeping things* it was a lentil's bulk—see m.Toh.3.4). It is therefore likely that this general rule was constructed in a different context. The most likely original context is m.Orl.2.1 with regard to the general rules about combining sources of *tainting*. In this context the reference to 'measures' makes much more sense because it would measure the amount needed to *neutralize*, and the reference to *impurity* would make sense because it was related to the school dispute concerning the amount needed to spread *impurity* (m.Orl.2.4).

Therefore it is likely that Joshua's generalization was originally a comment on the rulings in m.Orl.2.1&4, and that it was later applied to the context where we find it here.

Summary and Conclusions

Very little discussion of *forefruits* is found in the early strata of this tractate, except where it provides insights into other matters such as *tainting* by *elevation offering*. The reason for this is probably that the laws of *forefruit* concern mainly a fruit farmer and do not impinge much on the average householder. All that a householder needed to remember was that a new fruit tree or vine should not be harvested for three years, and that they should treat the *fourth year fruit* like *second tithe*. However, if a fruit farmer ignored his crop for four years, this could spell financial ruin, because he still needed to pay rent on the land and hire laborers to tend the plants.[3]

The farmers increasingly looked for new ways to gain income from their *forefruit* trees, such as selling the sap for curdling milk (m.Orl.1.7), or making dye and fuel from the fruit (m.Orl.3.1-5), but anything which involved using the 'fruit' or 'food' was prohibited (m.Orl.1.7) because of the use of these two words in Leviticus 19.23. They presumably also wanted to use the land between the fruit trees or vines for another crop, especially during the first four years when they were not too concerned to tend the plants regularly because there was little point in maximizing their crop. They could probably get away with planting crops among trees of an orchard (tractate *Kilayim* makes almost no mention of this, and tractate *Shebiit* assumes that orchards were ploughed not necessarily just for the sake of the trees—cf. m.Shebi.1.2), but they could certainly not plant crops among vines (called *mixtures in a vineyard*) because this *sanctified* (i.e., made inedible) both the vines and the crops (m.Kil.4.1–5.8).

The principle that *consecrated* food could be *neutralized* by *deconsecrated* food could have provided a loophole for large producers. If, for example, they had two young *forefruit* plants which each produced half the crop of a full-grown plant, this could be *neutralized* by the harvest from another 100 plants. So, the *neutralizing* was increased to one part in 200 to make this loophole less tempting (as suggested by m.Orl.1.6). The principle that sources of *tainting* can combine (m.Orl.2.1) was

---

[3] It is possible that they could avoid some of the regulations by grafting onto existing stumps instead of replacing their older stock, though grafting was regarded as new growth with regard to the Seventh Year (m.Shebi.2.6), and so it is likely that this applied also to *forefruit*, though there are no early traditions which state this.

probably introduced at the same time as an added barrier to those who tried to deliberately circumvent this law. The idea that there were Jews who looked for such loopholes is, of source, purely speculative.

The concern about combining sources of *tainting* spread to the subjects of *elevation offerings* and other *consecrated* food (m.Orl.2.1) which was similar to *forefruit* because they could be *neutralized* by a specific measure. It also spread to the subject of *tainting* by *impure* food (m.Orl.2.4-5) which was very similar to *forefruit*, as far as a householder was concerned, because if either fell into a store of food, the whole store had to be destroyed (unless it was large enough to *neutralize* it).

The problem of *tainting* was more serious when the source of *tainting* was able to affect the food it fell into by leavening it or flavoring it. In these cases it could not necessarily be *neutralized* by 100 parts or even by 200 parts, because it *tainted* any amount which it could leaven or flavor by itself (m.Orl.2.4), or in combination with other contamination (m.Orl.2.11-12; m.Meil.4.3). *Tainting* was even capable of permanently ruining leather goods (m.Orl.2.13) and clothing (m.Orl.3.1-2—though this is probably post-70).

Before 70 CE it is unlikely that the laws of *forefruit* were applied outside the Land, and they were applied slightly less strictly in Syria, but after 70 CE the regulations for Syria were applied everywhere outside the Land (m.Orl.3.9; m.Qid.1.9).

It is difficult to know how widely these regulations were applied by householders and especially by farmers. The suggestion that the introduction of the two-hundredth measure and the principles of combining sources of *tainting* (neither of which have any basis in Scripture) were probably inspired by farmers who tried to circumvent these regulations implies that these regulations were recognized and grudgingly followed even by those who did not 'delight in the Law.'

Tractate *Bikkurim*: Firstfruits

Definitions and Outline

Torah said that Israelites should bring *firstfruits* (בִּכּוּרִים, *bikkurim*) of their land to the Temple (Exod.23.19) and they should offer it to a priest in a basket and with a profession of thanks for bringing them into the Land (Deut.26.1-10). The actual offering is not defined, but the rabbis decided that it included only the seven species named in Deuteronomy 8.8 (though other species could accompany them as a supplement), and the profession of thanks was a recitation of Deuteronomy 26.3b, 5b-10a.

No quantities were specified in Torah, and the rabbis did not prescribe any. There also is considerable freedom about when *firstfruits* should be designated, set apart, and offered, so long as it is between the festivals of *Shabuot* and *Sukkot* (i.e., Pentecost and Tabernacles), though some sections of Judaism regarded the end of *Shabuot* as a fixed date for a Day of Firstfruits (cf. Jub.6.21f; 16.13f; 22.1). There is much more discussion about the celebrations on the journey, the decorations of the basket, and the recitation before the priest. It was regarded as a joyful occasion with relatively few regulations.

The Torah said "of your land" (Exod.23.19; Deut.26.2) which was "the land which the Lord your God is giving you as an inheritance" (Deut.26.1), and so the rabbis were concerned that the *firstfruits* should come from Israel and from land which the offerer owned himself. The recitation also includes "which the Lord swore to our Fathers to give us" (Deut.26.3), and so the rabbis had to define who was an Israelite (who could say "our Fathers") and who was worthy enough (to whom God could be said to "give").

Firstfruits could no longer be offered after 70 CE because their reception by a priest was accompanied by a sacrificial offering and waving before the altar (m.Bik.2.4), and because the *firstfruits* had to be brought to the Temple (Deut.26.2, 4; cf. m.Bik.1.8-9). However, it is clear in m.Sheq.8.8 that some individuals continued to set aside *firstfruits* and considered them to be holy because R. Simeon b. Yohai [T4, mid second century] stood out against this and said that these *firstfruits* could be eaten like any other food (m.Sheq.8.8; m.Bik.2.2).

Various comparisons are made between *firstfruits*, tithes, and *elevation offerings*, and these lead into other unrelated comparisons concerning plants, blood, the mysterious creatures called 'koy' (which are neither wild nor domesticated) and hermaphrodites (who have both male and female characteristics).

m.Bik.1.1-11: Who can bring *firstfruits* and who can recite?

If you own suitable crops you can bring them at a suitable time, and if you are a free male Israelite who owns the land you can also recite the profession of thanks.

m.Bik.2.1-5: Comparing *firstfruits* with tithes and *elevation offerings*

In some ways *firstfruit* is similar to *elevation offering* and *second tithe*, and in other ways it is different from them.

m.Bik.2.6-11: Other comparisons

Comparisons of citron trees with vegetables, human blood with animal blood, and koy as a wild animal with koy as a domesticated animal.

m.Bik.3.1-7: Bringing *firstfruits* to the Temple

Separating *firstfruits* before or after harvest, traveling to Jerusalem, and offering them with the recitation.

m.Bik.3.8-12: Offerings accompanying the *firstfruits*

Firstfruits belong to the priests and can be brought in an expensive basket, with decorations, and supplementary offerings.

m.Bik.4.1-5: Comparison of hermaphrodites with men and women

This is a later supplement to the tractate, expanding t.Bik.2.3. It is missing from many editions, and the text varies in others.

m.Bik.1.1-11: Who can bring *firstfruits* and who can recite?

Summary of Mishnah: Some can bring *firstfruits* and recite the blessing (from Deut.26.3-10), while others can bring *firstfruits* but cannot recite, and others cannot even bring *firstfruits* (1.1). You cannot bring *firstfruits* if the plants are not completely grown on your own land because it says "of your land" (Deut.26.2) (1.1-2, contra Judah in 1.11). You can bring only the seven species for which the Land is famous [i.e., wheat, barley, grapes, figs, pomegranates, oil (i.e., olives), and honey (i.e., dates)], and you must not bring them before *Shabuot* (Pentecost) or after *Sukkot* (Tabernacles) (1.3, 10). You cannot recite (or marry a priest, 1.5) if your mother was not an Israelite because you cannot say "which the Lord swore to our fathers" (Deut.26.3) (1.4). You cannot recite if you are an executor, agent, slave, woman, of doubtful sex, or androgynous because you cannot say "which you O Lord have given me" (Deut.26.10) (1.5). What if you did not own the land during the whole time the plant was growing (1.6-7)? Or what if you do not own all of the land (1.11)? If your *firstfruits* become lost or spoiled, you bring replacements but do not recite, though if you got as far as the Temple Court before you spoilt them you don't offer them or replace them (1.8) because you have fulfilled the words "to the house of the Lord" (1.9).

The tradition at m.Bik.1.5 concerns Eliezer b. Jacob who could be either one of two individuals, from T2 or T4 (soon after 70 CE or mid second century). This Eliezer is almost certainly Eliezer b. Jacob II [T4] who elsewhere debates this same subject with Judah b. Illai [T4] (y.Bik.1.5.I) and with R. Jose b. Halfta [T4] (m.Qid.4.7). So, this tradition is likely to be post-70.

The following traditions have elements (marked in bold) for which there is evidence of an origin before 70 CE:

m.Bik.1.3: Bring the seven species before Shabuot (Pentecost)

One should only bring *firstfruits*	אֵין מְבִיאִין בִּכּוּרִים
from [produce of] the seven species [listed in Deut.8.8].	חוּץ מִשִּׁבְעַת הַמִּינִים.
[Though] not from the dates of the hilltops	לֹא מִתְּמָרִים שֶׁבֶּהָרִים,
and not from the fruit of the valleys	וְלֹא מִפֵּרוֹת שֶׁבָּעֲמָקִים,
and not from olives for [making] oil	וְלֹא מִזֵּיתֵי שֶׁמֶן
(for these are not from the choicest [quality]).	שֶׁאֵינָם מִן הַמּוּבְחָר.
One should not bring *firstfruits*	אֵין מְבִיאִין בִּכּוּרִים
before the Assembly [Day of Pentecost].	קוֹדֶם לָעֲצֶרֶת.
The men of Mt. Tzeboim brought	אַנְשֵׁי הַר צְבוֹעִים הֵבִיאוּ
their *firstfruits* before the Assembly	בִּכּוּרֵיהֶם קוֹדֶם לָעֲצֶרֶת,
and they [the priests] did not receive them from them	וְלֹא קִבְּלוּ מֵהֶם.
—because of what is written in the Torah [Exod.23.16]:	מִפְּנֵי הַכָּתוּב שֶׁבַּתּוֹרָה
"And [at] the Festival of Harvest, the *firstfruits* of	וְחַג הַקָּצִיר בִּכּוּרֵי
your labor [which] you sowed in the field."	מַעֲשֶׂיךָ אֲשֶׁר תִּזְרַע בַּשָּׂדֶה.

Comments: Torah did not define what one should bring or when, though the rabbis found hints about this in Deuteronomy 8.8 (which lists the wonderful produce which Israel could look forward to in the new Land) and Exodus 23.16 (which calls *Shabuot*, the first harvest festival, "the *firstfruits* of your labor"). It was obvious that they could not bring all the seven species at *Shabuot*, because they were not all ripe, and so they assumed that this was the earliest date for bringing them.

The tradition about the men of Mt. Tzeboim and its proof text is cited from m.Hul.4.10, where it is discussed. The Assembly of *Shabuot* (the Day of Pentecost) is discussed below at m.Bik.1.6.

The seven species listed at Deuteronomy 8.8 are wheat, barley, vines, figs, pomegranates, olive oil, and honey from dates.[1] The exceptions given in Mishnah are comments on this list, in order to ensure that only the best produce is brought. Dates must not be too dry (as they might be if they were grown on the exposed hilltops where they get too much sun and there is less moist☐ure in the soil) but on the other hand they must not suffer from too little sun (as they might in a steep valley). The olives must not come from a crop which would normally be used only for oil and not for eating, because this indicates that it is an inferior crop, even though Torah merely stipulates "olive oil" (Deut.8.8).

Tosefta adds two additional caveats with the same purpose of insuring that only the best is offered:

> Rn. Simeon b. Gamaliel [T2] says: They do not bring *firstfruits* of dates, apart from those dates which [grow] in Jericho. And they recite only over the *kotebet* [best quality dates].
> R. Eliezer [T2] says: Pomegranates of the valley. (t.Bik.1.5)

Tosefta says that Simeon allowed only the best dates (the *kotebet* dates from Jericho) and that Eliezer made an exception to the exception about valleys because the best pomegranates were grown in valleys.

Dating (5): The list of exceptions in Mishnah looks like something which has grown gradually. First someone pointed out that the dates which grow on exposed hilltops are not among the best, then someone balanced this by excluding any crops which grow in dark valleys, then someone added olives which are used for oil, and finally someone added the explanation for this. The further exceptions in Tosefta are both refinements on the rules in Mishnah: Simeon restricted the dates even further by allowing only dates which were grown in Jericho, and Eliezer adds an exception to Mishnah's exception about produce grown in valleys. The comment about *kotebet* dates may have been added later, either as a further refinement or as an explanation.

The fact that Eliezer comments on the rule in Mishnah about valleys means that this rule was already established by his time (just after 70 CE) so it predates 70 CE. If Eliezer and Simeon added their comments at the same time, then this is Rn. Simeon b. Gamaliel I [T1], though it may possibly be Rn. Simeon b. Gamaliel II [T4].

m.Bik.1.6b: Bringing *firstfruits* after *Shabuot* (Pentecost)

From the Assembly [Day of Pentecost]	מֵעֲצֶרֶת
and until the Feast [*Sukkot*, Tabernacles]:	וְעַד הֶחָג,

---

[1] The same word for 'honey' is used for both date honey and comb honey, but dates fit in with the rest of the list much better than honeycombs. Jerusalem Talmud concludes that it must refer to dates because honeycomb is not liable to tithes (y.Bik.1.3.I).

He may bring [*firstfruits*] and may recite [Deut.26.5b-10a].   מביא וקורא.
From the Feast [Sukkot, Tabernacles]   מן החג
and until *Ḥanukkah* [the Festival of Lights]:   ועד חנוכה,
He may bring but may not recite.   מביא ואינו קורא.
R. Judah b. Bathyra [T2] says: רבי יהודה בן בתירה אומר,
He may bring and recite.   מביא וקורא.

Comments: *Firstfruits* should be brought between the festival of *Shabuot* (Pentecost) and the festival of *Sukkot* (Tabernacles), and someone who brings it late cannot take part in the ceremony of reciting. The reason for the starting date is that Torah calls the festival of *Shabuot* "the Day of Firstfruits" (Num.28.26), and m.Bik.1.3 gives Exodus 23.16 as a further prooftext.

This tradition gives two finishing dates for bringing *firstfruits*—the anonymous majority allow them to be brought until *Sukkot*, but Judah b. Bathyra allows them to be brought until the Festival of *Ḥanukkah* (Lights). The reason for an endpoint at *Sukkot* may be that this too had an "Assembly," so they projected the "Assembly" in Numbers 28.26 from one to the other. The term 'Assembly' (עֲצֶרֶת, *atzeret*) is used in Torah for the eighth day of *Sukkot* (Lev.23.36; Num.29.35) and for the seventh day of *Pesach* (Passover) (Deut.16.8) and for the day of *Shabuot* (Pentecost) (Num.28.26). In Mishnah it always refers to the day of *Shabuot*,[2] while the festival of *Sukkot* was often referred to simply as "the Feast" (חג, *ḥag*), as here.

Dating (2): The second half of m.Bik.1.6 is complete in itself and is not related to the first half except by the repeated phrases "he brings and recites" and "he brings but does not recite," which are also found throughout this section in m.Bik.1.4-7. The comment by Judah b. Bathyra could be either his contribution to a debate taking place during his time, or his dissension from a ruling which was already accepted by his time. The latter is probably the case, because otherwise we would expect the contrary opinion to be attached to the name of the rabbi who disputed with him, and perhaps a rejoinder to show why Judah b. Bathyra was wrong.

One might think that this dispute should be located alongside m.Bik.1.3b which discusses whether one can bring *firstfruits* before *Shabuot*. It is probably recorded here instead because it is part of a collection of traditions about those who "bring and do not recite," while 1.3 is in the section concerning those who neither bring nor recite (see Conclusions below).

---

[2] It is also used this way by Akiba (T3, m.Sheq.3.1 // m.Bek.9.5), Johanan b. Nuri (T3, m.Ed.2.10) and Simeon b. Yohai (T4, m.Shebi.2.1). Later rabbis used "Assembly" also to refer to the last day of *Sukkot*, which came to be known as *Shemini Atzeret*, and marked the last day of the one-year reading cycle for Torah—cf. b.Meg.31a, though this describes the situation outside Israel where *Shemini Atzeret* is a two-day festival and the Torah reading cycle ends on the second day. The one-year cycle replaced the three-year cycle probably at about the time that this new festival was introduced.

m.Bik.1.8: *Firstfruits* which are lost or spilled in the Temple Court

[If] he put aside his *firstfruits*,	הִפְרִישׁ בְּכּוּרָיו,
and they became plundered, squashed,	נִבְזְזוּ, נִמְקוּ,
stolen, destroyed or *impure*:	נִגְנְבוּ, אָבְדוּ, אוֹ שֶׁנִּטְמְאוּ,
He brings other [produce] instead	מֵבִיא אֲחֵרִים תַּחְתֵּיהֶם
but he does not recite.	וְאֵינוֹ קוֹרֵא.
And the substitutes [for the lost *firstfruit*]	וְהַשְּׁנִיִּים
are not liable	אֵינָם חַיָּבִים
to the *added fifth* [unless they are eaten accidentally].	עֲלֵיהֶם חֹמֶשׁ.
[If] they become *impure* [by spilling] in the [Temple] Court,	נִטְמְאוּ בָעֲזָרָה,
he scatters [them] and he does not recite.	נוֹפֵץ וְאֵינוֹ קוֹרֵא.

Comments: If the fruit which was designated as *firstfruits* cannot be used, then it can be replaced, unless it has already been brought as far as the Temple Court. The next mishnah explains that if you have brought it that far, you have already carried out the command to "bring it into the House of the Lord" (Exod.23.19).

The list of possible ways in which the *firstfruits* may be lost is very different from the ways in which other tractates discuss *consecrated* produce. They normally assume that accidents such as *tainting* or accidental consumption will spoil the goods, whereas this tradition implies that they can also be spoiled by various acts of theft or physical damage. This either indicates a great deal of lawlessness, where thieves and vandals break into food stores, or (more likely) is talking about incidents before the fruit is harvested. According to m.Bik.3.1, *firstfruits* are designated by the farmer when he sees the first plants which are fruiting, and he marks them out by tying a reed around them. During the following weeks, while waiting for those fruit to ripen, any number of accidents or incidents of casual theft by passers-by could occur. It must have been a common experience for the farmer to return just before harvest and find that the plants which he had designated as *firstfruits* contained no fruit or spoiled fruit.

Dating (8): The tradition in m.Bik.1.9 which explains the ruling by means of a prooftext is almost certainly added later. The reference to the Temple Court indicates an interest in pre-70 practice but does not by itself indicate a pre-70 origin, because the exegesis which follows may have been the origin of this detail. However, if the text of Exodus 23.19 had been the inspiration for the ruling about the Temple Court, one would have expected that it would speak instead about the "House of the Lord" (as in Exod.23.19) or the equivalent, which is the "Temple Mount" (as in m.Bik.1.9).

This series of rulings deals with very practical issues in a way which appears to reflect real life, unlike the comparisons with *elevation offerings* and *second tithes* (m.Bik.2.1-5) which are concerned with the usual matters of *consecrated* or *impure* sources of *tainting*—matters which were important, but less common. The accidental spoiling of *firstfruits* in the Temple Court was also the type of accident which actually happened. Thousands of people, all carrying their own baskets, jostling to reach the altar at one end of the Temple Court, must often have spilled their fruit. This suggests that these rulings arose out of actual problems during the period before 70 CE when *firstfruits* were brought to the Temple. It is possible that the ruling about no *added fifth* for substitutions was added later.

The concept of not reciting over substitutions may have been the inspiration for the later development of the whole of the section concerning whether or not to recite (m.Bik.1.4-9).

m.Bik.2.1-5:   Comparing *firstfruits* with tithes and *elevation offerings*

Summary of Mishnah: *Elevation offering*s and *firstfruits* (unlike tithes) result in extirpation for nonpriests who eat deliberately or payment plus the *added fifth* if it is accidental; they are *neutralized* by 100 parts; and priests eat them in *purity* (2.1). *Second tithe*s and *firstfruits* (unlike *elevation offerings*) are brought to Jerusalem, recited over, forbidden to *mourners*, subject to *removal*, and cannot be *neutralized* in Jerusalem (2.2). *Elevation offering*s and tithes (unlike *firstfruits*) must be separated from produce before eating any, have a prescribed quantity, and can be offered from all species, even when there is no Temple (2.3). *Firstfruits* (unlike *elevation offerings* or tithes) can be designated before harvest, in any quantity, replaced if not offered, and require a [Peace] offering, singing by Levites, waving by the priest, and an overnight stay in Jerusalem [Deut.16.7] (2.4). *Elevation offering*s of the [*first*] *tithe* like *firstfruits* can be replaced *pure* produce for *impure* produce and produce from one location for produce from elsewhere, but unlike *firstfruits* they render produce uneatable before they are separated, and they have a prescribed quantity (2.5).

There is no evidence that any of this section originated before 70 CE.

m.Bik.2.6-11: Other comparisons

Summary of Mishnah: Citron trees are like other trees re *forefruits*, *fourth-year fruit* and Sabbath Year produce; but they are like vegetables re tithing (2.6). Blood of humans is like blood of domesticated animals in that it defiles seeds; but it is like the blood of reptiles in that drinking it is not punished by extirpation (2.7). A koy is like both a farm animal and a wild animal (2.8). Like a wild animal you must cover its blood and you must not slaughter it on a festival (though if you do, you do not cover its blood); its fat conveys *impurity* (though its own *impurity* is uncertain) and you cannot redeem a *firstborn* ass with it (2.9). Like a farm animal you must not eat its fat (though if you do, you do not suffer extirpation), you cannot buy it with *second tithe* money, and you must give the priests the shoulder, cheeks, and stomach (2.10). It is like neither category in that it cannot be yoked with either, and if you mention it either in a will or a vow, you cannot be said to have a koy in mind. It is like both in that you cannot eat it without ritual slaughter, or if it was partly eaten by *carrion,* or if the rest of it is still alive (2.11).

The following traditions have elements (marked in bold) for which there is evidence of an origin before 70 CE:

m.Bik.2.9-10: A *koy* is both like a farm animal and like a wild animal

How is [a *koy*] like a wild animal?	כיצד שוה לחיה,
Its blood is required to be covered	דמו טעון כסוי
like blood of a wild animal [Lev.17.13].	כדם חיה,
And one should not slaughter it on a *holyday*,	ואין שוחטין אותו ביום טוב,
and if one [does] slaughter it [on a *holyday*],	ואם שחטו,
one does not cover the blood [m.Betz.1.2 // m.Ed.4.2].	אין מכסין את דמו,
And **its fat makes [one]** *impure*	וחלבו מטמא
with *carrion* impurity, like a wild animal [Lev.7.24]	בטומאת נבלה כחיה,
but its *impurity* is in doubt	וטומאתו בספק,
and **one should not redeem with it**	ואין פודין בו
the *firstborn* **of an ass** [Exod.13.13; m.Bek.1.5].	פטר חמור.
10) How is [a *koy*] like a farm animal?	כיצד שוה לבהמה,
Its fat is prohibited like the fat of farm animals;	חלבו אסור כחלב בהמה,
but one is not liable to extirpation for [eating] it;	ואין חייבין עליו כרת,
and it is not bought with [*second*] *tithe silver*	ואינו נלקח בכסף מעשר
to eat in Jerusalem;	לאכול בירושלים,
and **one is liable [to give the priests]**	וחייב
the shoulder and cheeks and stomach [Deut.18.3].	בזרוע ולחיים וקבה.
R. Eliezer [b. Hyrcanus, T2] exempts,	רבי אליעזר פוטר,
for [the priest] who [wishes to] takes [his due from]	שהמוציא
from his associate,	מחברו
upon him [rests the burden of] proof	עליו
[to show that a *koy* is a farm animal].	הראיה.

Comments: A *koy* (כוֹי, *koy*) was probably a type of wild sheep or goat, because they discussed the possibility that it might be used to redeem the *firstborn* of an ass, which should be redeemed by a lamb (Exod.13.13).[3] It was in some ways a wild

---

[3] Jastrow says it is a type of bearded deer or antelope, probably based on b.Hul.79b // y.Bik.2.6.I which say it is the offspring of a male goat and a hind. Judith Wegner (in *Chattel or Person* [Oxford: Oxford University Press, 1988], p. 7, n. 13) suggests that this is similar to the classical Greek concept of a 'goat stag' (*tragelaphos*), "a fantastic animal represented on Eastern carpets and the like" (Henry George Liddell, Robert Scott, and Sir Henry Stuart Jones

animal and in other ways a farm animal, so some rules about wild animals applied to it and some rules about domestic farm animals applied to it.

This digression is one of the discussions which were inspired by the compare-and-contrast section in m.Bik.2.1-5.

Dating (5): The compilation of this section is probably late, but it is based on some elements which originated before 70 CE. Some elements depend on early traditions, such as the school dispute about whether or not to cover blood of slaughter on a *holyday* (m.Betz.1.2 // m.Ed.4.2) but this does not mean that the related conclusions about the *koy* should be dated early. However, some elements were commented on by Eliezer, which suggests that the debate about the *koy* dates back to before 70 CE.

Eliezer comments on the decision that a *koy* cannot be used to redeem the *firstborn* of an ass (m.Bek.1.5), on the rule that a *koy* is liable for the shoulder, cheeks, and stomach (m.Bik.2.10), and on eating the fat of a *koy* (b.Ker.17b). In Tosefta Eliezer answers the question which is raised by m.Bik.2.9, concerning what someone should do if they accidentally ate the fat of a *koy*.[4] There are other Eliezer traditions relating to the *koy*,[5] but it is now impossible to know if some of the ones which are recorded only in Talmud did actually originate with him, or whether later traditions became associated with Eliezer because he had already made other rulings in this area. Nevertheless it is relatively certain that the discussions concerning the *koy* started before 70 CE, and it is likely that the contributions which are attributed to Eliezer in Mishnah and Tosefta are accurate.

m.Bik.3.1-7: Bringing *firstfruits* to the Temple

Summary of Mishnah: When the first fruits start to ripen you mark them as *firstfruits* by tying a reed round them (3.1). The members of the Standing (the *Maamad,* one of the twenty-four divisions which manned the Temple) spend the night in the open [to avoid *corpse impurity*] before going up to the Temple (3.2). People bring figs and grapes (or dried fruit if they come from afar) in a celebratory procession, and the leaders of the priests and craftsmen come out of Jerusalem to meet them (3.3). On the Temple Mount you must carry it yourself, and the Levites greet you singing Psalm 30 (3.4). Any pigeons accompanying the *firstfruits* are also offered (3.5), then you recite Deuteronomy 26.3-5a, and then the priest waves your

---

et al., *A Greek-English Lexicon*, 9th ed. [Oxford: Clarendon, 1996], p. 1809), which is a standard paradigm for a hybrid and logically nonsensical category (cf. Plato *Republic* 6:488A).
[4] In t.Bik.1.5 Eliezer says that they should bring a *suspected guilt offering* (אָשָׁם תָּלוּי, *asham taluy*), which is based on Lev.5.17-19.
[5] E.g., b.Ned.15b 'if he sanctifies all his animals'; b.Hul.79b re yoking with young animals; b.Hul.132a.

basket while the Levites recite Deuteronomy 26.5b-10 [with you] before leaving the basket at the altar (3.6). At first they only help you recite if you cannot read, but this discouraged non-readers from coming (3.7).

Although the traditions in this section cannot be dated with any certainty, it is likely that they are based on a core of ancient material, and because of the importance of this ceremony, an attempt will be made here to extract the earlier material. Indications of pre-70 origins in these traditions include the presence of details which later rabbis found confusing and incidental details which later rabbis would have regarded as insignificant.

m.Bik.3.2: A division of priests gathers before going to Jerusalem

How should one bring in the *firstfruits*?	כיצד מעלין את הבכורים,
[From] all the towns which are in [the] Standing	כל העירות שבמעמד
[which is about to start its period of service]	
gather [priest, Levites, and lay people who will serve in the Temple]	מתכנסות ,
into the [main] town of that Standing	לעיר של מעמד
and they sleep the town square.	ולנין ברחובה של עיר,
And they did not use to enter into houses	ולא היו נכנסין לבתים.
[to avoid unforeseen *corpse impurity*].	
And early [the next morning]	ולמשכים
the appointed [leader] used to say:*	היה הממונה אומר,
"Arise and let us go up to Zion	קומו ונעלה ציון
to the House of the Lord our God" [Jer.31.5(6)]	אל בית ה_אלהינו.

---

*Some editions have הממנה, perhaps from מנה, 'to count.' Presumably it is the name for the leader of a Standing.

Comments: This describes the start of the process of bringing *firstfruits* from the point of view of a Standing (*Maamad*, מַעֲמָד)—one of the twenty-four divisions into which the priesthood was divided. According to m.Taan.4.2, a Standing consists of priests, Levites and Israelites (i.e., Jews who are neither priests nor Levites). All of these assembled in the main town of their division when their period of service was about to start. The priests in each division were called a Watch (מִשְׁמָר, *Mishmar*, 'guard'), and so the term 'Standing' (*Maamad*) is often used to refer only to the lay Israelites. Their name may come from the fact that they were 'standing' there in order to represent other Israelites during communal sacrifices. This is apparently the explanation in m.Taan.4.2 which says: "How can a person's offering be made, while he is not standing by its side?" However, this explanation may simply be based on their curious name. Another possible origin of the name is a verbal link with the Eighteen Benedictions which was also known as the *Amidah* (the 'Standing' prayer). They read portions of Genesis 1 during their week of duty (m.Taan.4.3) and perhaps also prayed.

Their period of duty consisted of two weeks a year, plus each of the three major festivals when all the divisions were on duty. The context of this passage in Mishnah suggests that the occasion envisaged here is the preparation for serving at the festival of *Shabuot* (Pentecost), when most communities would bring their *firstfruits*, and when every Standing was on duty.

The quotation from Jeremiah 38.6 deviates from the MT by adding "House of." This addition may be due to a conflation with Isaiah 2.3 or Jerermiah 31.5[6], or it may be the result of using a different text tradition which was similar to that used by LXX A which reads 'Mountain of.' This type of amendment is an attempt to remove the anthropomorphic idea that they are going to visit God, as if he lives in the Temple. The significance of this verse lies in the words which precede the quotation: "There shall be a day when the watchmen (נֹצְרִים, *notzerim*) on Mount Ephraim call out: 'Arise. . . .'" This forms a link in with the theme of a Watch, though a different Hebrew word is used. The LXX changes "the watchmen" to "those who plead" (ἀπολογουμένων)[7] which would have been very significant for the members of the Standing if their role included prayer.

Dating (8): There is nothing here which can be dated before 70 CE with any certainty, but there are some hints that this is early material. The fact that this tradition is written from the viewpoint of the Standing rather than the Watch is striking because there are so few references to the Standing, and if a later author had tried to envisage the scene he would be much more likely to concentrate on the priestly Watch.

The quotation from Jeremiah 31.5(6) with the additional word ('House of') may indicate that this was a form of the Hebrew text at the time when this tradition originated, which would suggest an early date. Or it may be a quotation from a variant text which was related to the variant in LXX A (see above), especially if this tradition originated in the circles of the Standing who would have liked the LXX reading "those who plead." Hebrew manuscripts of the vorlage of the LXX were still extant in the first century,[8] but later texts conformed much more closely to the form which was preserved in the MT.

The detail that they slept in an open area of the town during the night before going up to Jerusalem is strange, but it is presumably related to the fact that they had to remain pure before their period of duty (cf. m.Taan.2.7). The detail about not entering houses may be a later gloss to explain that they were avoiding even the remote possibility that someone in a house might die during the night, so that they would

---

[6] Suggested to me by Stefan Reif.
[7] This is also used for pleading with God in Jer.12.1.
[8] Two texts at Qumran, 4Q Jer b, d clearly follow the LXX of Jeremiah where the verse order is different from the MT.

suffer *corpse impurity* by being under the same roof. This explanation did not convince some later rabbis who said that they could have stayed in the local synagogue, though even this might not be safe because one of their own number might possibly die (cf. y.Bik.3.2.I). The fact that explanations and discussions were necessary suggests that this was a detail which was not obvious to later generations, which helps to confirm that this was an old tradition.

New Testament: Luke's gospel opens with Zechariah in Jerusalem serving with the rest of his division, and then returning after the end of their period of service (Lk.1.23).

m.Bik.3.3: Procession to Jerusalem with *firstfruits*

Those [traveling from] nearby bring	הקרובים מביאים
figs and grapes	התאנים והענבים,
and those [traveling from] afar bring	והרחוקים מביאים
dried figs and raisins.	גרוגרות וצמוקים.
And an ox went before them,	והשור הולך לפניהם,
its horns overlaid with gold	וקרניו מצופות זהב,
and a crown of olive [leaves] on its head.	ועטרה של זית בראשו.
A flute played before them	החליל מכה לפניהם,
until their arrival near to Jerusalem.	עד שמגיעים קרוב לירושלים.
[When] they arrived near to Jerusalem,	הגיעו קרוב לירושלים,
they sent [a message] before them	שלחו לפניהם,
and they crowned their *firstfruits* [with decorations].	ועטרו את בכוריהם.
The Rulers, Deputies [of the Priests,]	הפחות, הסגנים
and Treasurers came out to address them.	והגזברים יוצאים לקראתם.
According to the honor of those gathered,	לפי כבוד הנכנסים
those [of appropriate ranks] used to come out.	היו יוצאים.
And all the craftsmen of Jerusalem	וכל בעלי אומניות שבירושלים
stood before them and greeted them	עומדים לפניהם ושואלין בשלומם,
[lit., 'asked after their welfare']:	
Brothers, men of such-and-such a place,	אחינו אנשי המקום פלוני,
Welcome! [lit., You have come to peace.]	באתם לשלום.

Comments: *Firstfruits* consisted of dried produce if fresh produce was in danger of spoiling during the journey. The gifts were brought with a great deal of ceremony, and the flute may indicate that there was also singing and perhaps dancing by the men. Each community came in its own procession, led by the ox decorated with a crown of olive leaves and gilded horns.[9] This ox was later slaughtered as their *peace offering*[10] which they would eat at a feast together in the city.

When they reached the edge of Jerusalem they stopped to add final decorations to their baskets of *firstfruits*. Various undateable regulations about these decorations (m.Bik.3.8-12) say that they can consist of any produce which is not among the seven species (see m.Bik.1.3) and that these decorations and the baskets themselves (which could be made of gold or silver) became the personal property of the priests.[11] They also sent out a messenger to announce their arrival.

The Temple dignitaries came out to greet them, though the size and importance of the community procession determined who actually came out. The dignitaries and the local people greeted each procession by name ('brothers, men of Bethlehem,' or whatever) and welcomed them into the city. The "craftsmen" in this tradition (*baelé omaniyot*, בעלי אומניות, 'masters of trades') were probably the market traders (in the marketplace or in the city gate), whom the procession passed as they entered into the city. The way that this tradition is written seems to suggest that the official greeting came from these traders, but perhaps the dignitaries announced the greeting and similar or shorter greetings were repeated by everyone else.

The Torah law of *firstfruits* applied only to the Land,[12] and this is unquestioned by later rabbis—even though they applied the laws of *forefruits*, *mixtures*, and *new produce* outside the Land (see m.Qid.1.9 dealt with in the chapter on *Kilayim*). However, the fact that some people had to bring dried produce (because fresh produce would have spoiled during their journey) may suggest that they came from outside Israel. A tradition in m.Hal.4.10-11 shows that communities outside Israel did attempt to bring their *firstfruits,* and although the priests accepted offerings from Syria (which was regarded as quasi Israel), they did not accept offerings from locations such as Alexandria. This produce was probably only a representative

---

[9] Sacrificial offerings were decorated with crowns of olive leaves in the Graeco-Roman world (cf. refs in TDNT II:722 n.13). Saul Lieberman traces this to a Greek influence—see *Hellenism in Jewish Palestine: Studies in the Literary Transmission, Beliefs and Manners of Palestine in the I century B. C. E.-IV Century C. E*. Texts and Studies of the Jewish Theological Seminary of America, v. 18 (New York: Jewish Theological Seminary of America, 1950), p. 144. Moshe Weinfeld finds a Hittite parallel—see "Traces of Hittite Cult in Shiloah, Bethel and in Jerusalem" in Bernd Janowski, *Religionsgeschichtliche Beziehungen zwischen Kleinasien, Nordsyrien und dem Alten Testament*, Orbis biblicus et orientalis 129 (Freiburg/Schweiz; Göttingen: Universitätsverlag; Vandenhoeck & Ruprecht, 1993), pp. 455-72, esp. p. 468.

[10] We are not told this, but it is a reasonable supposition by later rabbis in y.Bik.3.3.II.

[11] Later rabbis in early fourth century said that priests did not keep the more expensive baskets—b.BQ.92a.

[12] Deut.26.1-2: "When you have come in to the Land which the Lord your God is giving to you as an inheritance, and you have possessed it and lived in it, you shall take of the first of all the fruits of the ground which you shall bring in out of your land which the Lord your God is giving to you and put it in a basket. . . ."

offering, because they also brought financial contributions based on their *firstfruits* (see Philo *Legat* 156).

Dating (9): This account contains some colorful and irrelevant details which one would expect from an original eyewitness account but not from a later third-party summary of the event. There is nothing of theological significance or any comment which shows that this ceremony fulfills Scripture in any way, which one might expect in an account which was constructed by later generations. The reason for bringing an ox is not stated, and although the Jerusalem Talmud suggests a very reasonable conclusion that this was a *peace offering*, the fact that they felt they had to explain this detail rather than change it helps to imply that this account was not constructed by later generations.

New Testament: The colorful and public ceremony of bringing in *firstfruits* makes this otherwise minor offering a spectacular event, and so it is not surprising to find several references to *firstfruits* in the New Testament (Rom:8.23; 11.16; 16.5; 1Cor.15.20, 23; Jas.1.18; Rev.14.4). All but two of these use *firstfruits* as a metaphor for converts, which is perhaps due to the fact that most *firstfruits* were offered at or around the Festival of *Shabuot* (Pentecost) which, for the church, represented its first harvest of converts.

The greetings by Temple officials for each procession as it arrived in Jerusalem (cf. m.Hal.4.10-11 and Comments above) may explain why the account of the church's first Pentecost included a list of all the nationalities which were present. Although the priests did not accept *firstfruits* from outside Israel, they presumably still greeted each group if they arrived while they were on duty to greet visitors from Israel.

This group of officials is probably similar to those listed in Acts 14.1 ("priests and captain of the Temple and Sadducees") who came to stop the apostles preaching in the Temple.

m.Bik.3.4-5: Carrying *firstfruits* through Jerusalem to the Temple

A flute played before them	החליל מכה לפניהם
until their arrival at the Temple Mount.	עד שמגיעין להר הבית.
[When] they arrived at the Temple Mount	הגיעו להר הבית,
even Agrippa the King carried	אפילו אגריפס המלך נוטל
the basket upon his shoulder and went in [with it]	הסל על כתפו ונכנס,
until he reached the [Temple] Court.	עד שמגיע לעזרה.
He reached the [Temple] Court	הגיע לעזרה
and the Levites sang the hymn [Ps.30.1]:	ודברו הלוים בשיר,
"I will exalt you Lord for you raised me up	ארוממך יהוה כי דליתני
and did not let my enemies rejoice over me."	ולא שמחת אויבי לי.
5) The pigeons	הגוזלות

which were on top of the baskets:	שֶׁעַל גַּבֵּי הַסַּלִּים,
They were [offered as] *burnt offerings*.	הָיוּ עוֹלוֹת,
And those [pigeons] which [were] in their hands	וּמַה שֶּׁבְּיָדָם,
were given to the priest [as a gift].	נוֹתְנִים לַכֹּהֲנִים.

Comments: The procession continued through Jerusalem with flute playing (and perhaps singing and dancing) until they reached the entrance to the Temple Mount. At this point each offerer, however important they were, would pick up their own basket and carry it to the Temple Court where the Levites would greet them with a Psalm.

Why would there be pigeons on top of the baskets and why should they be given as sacrifices rather than those which they brought in their hands? Later rabbis thought that this should be the other way around, because if the pigeons on the baskets were additional offerings ('decorations'), they would have belonged to the priests (m.Bik.3.10) and would not be sacrificed, while birds in their hands were being brought like normal *burnt offerings* (y.Bik.3.4.I-II). Perhaps there were live birds on the top which were feeding on the offerings while people waited in the queue, and these were deemed to be *consecrated* as a result?

Dating (8): Although this clearly describes pre-70 activities, there is nothing to confirm that this tradition originated before 70 CE. However, the presence of confusing details (such as the pigeons) and theologically irrelevant details (such as the flutes) helps to suggest that this was not invented at a later date.

The repeat of "a flute plays before them" (in the middle of m.Bik.3.3 and the start of 3.4) may indicate that the second occurrence is either the start of an expansion based on this phrase, or an insertion which takes this phrase as its cue. However, it is more likely that the repeated phrase is part of the structure of the passage which divides the journey into three sections: approach to Jerusalem, approach to the Temple, and approach to the altar in the Temple Court.

There is clearly something wrong with the "and . . ." after the phrase "he reaches the [Temple] Court." Perhaps this phrase was added in order to agree with the similar symmetry in the two preceding similar phrases:

3.3: . . . until their arrival near to Jerusalem. [When] they arrive near to Jerusalem . . .
3.4: . . . until their arrival near to Jerusalem. [When] they arrive near to Jerusalem . . .
3.4: . . . until he reaches the [Temple] Court. [When] he reaches the [Temple] Court . . .

If the phrase "[When] he reaches the [Temple] Court" is removed, the phrase "and the Levites sang" fits into the passage smoothly. It is unlikely that this is a later invention because there are many Psalms which celebrate God's harvest (which one might expect a later rabbi to choose), and no reason is given for choosing Psalm 30 which concerns death and possibly resurrection.

The reference to Agrippa does not necessarily indicate a historical event and could mean "even *if someone as great as* Agrippa. . . ." However, this does not mean that the comment did not originate early, and it may have been part of a series of traditions about Agrippa (see m.Bik.3.6).

New Testament: The picture of Christ as the "firstfruit (ἀπαρχή) of the dead" (1Cor.15.20-23) may indicate that the Day of Firstfruits was associated with the concept of resurrection or new life. This may have been prompted by the Levites' singing of Psalm 30 (or perhaps their choice of this Psalm was prompted by this association), or by the use of the word "firstfruits" with regard to the loaves made from the *first sheaf* (Lev.23.17, 20). Modern Messianic Jews continue this tradition by celebrating the Day of Firstfruits during *Pesach* (Passover) (based on Deut.16.8—see m.Bik.1.6b), when they celebrate the resurrection.

m.Bik.3.6: Offering the *firstfruits* and reciting

While the basket is on his shoulder	עודהו הסל על כתפו,
he recites from "I declare this day	קורא מהגדתי היום
to the Lord your God" [Deut.26.3]	לה׳ אלהיך
until [he] finishes the whole passage.	עד שגומר כל הפרשה.
R. Judah [b. Illai, T4] says: [He recites]	רבי יהודה אומר
until "A wandering Aramean was my father" [Deut.26.5].	עד ארמי אובד אבי.
[When] he reached	הגיע
"A wandering Aramean was my father"	לארמי אובד אבי,
he lowers the basket from off his shoulder	מוריד הסל מעל כתפו
and holds it by its edges, and the priest	ואוחזו בשפתותיו, וכהן
puts his hand under it and waves it	מניח ידו תחתיו ומניפו,
and [the offerer] recites	וקורא
from "A wandering Aramean was my father"	מארמי אובד אבי
until he finishes the whole passage.	עד שהוא גומר כל הפרשה,
And he puts it [the basket] by the side of the altar,	ומניחו בצד המזבח,
and he bows and leaves.	והשתחוה ויצא.

Comments: Having carried the basket to the Temple Court he keeps it aloft while reciting Deuteronomy 26.3b, 5b-10a, then he puts it down by the altar and leaves. The interjection by R. Judah is inspired by the text of Deuteronomy which divides the first verse of recitation (v. 3b) from the rest (vv. 5b-10a) with the instructions that "the priest shall take the basket out of your hand and place it before the altar of the Lord your God" (v. 4). However, the end of the passage says that the offerer "should place it [the basket] before the Lord your God and bow before the Lord your God," so why did they give it to the priest in v. 4? Judah solves this problem by having the priest wave the basket during the recitation.

Dating (8): The tradition by R. Judah was either interjected into an older tradition which originally included the concluding line "And he puts it by the side of the altar and he bows and leaves," or the tradition of Judah has been added onto the end of a tradition which ended with "until he finishes the whole passage." The latter is more likely because it is very unusual to insert later comments into the middle of an established tradition, and because the closing remark (about putting the basket by the altar and bowing) comes from an exegesis of Scripture (Deut.24.10). As suggested in the Comments above, the fact that the priest waved the offering was probably also based on exegesis of the text rather than on memories of what actually happened.

The ruling concerning the waving of the *firstfruits* is referred to at m.Men.5.6 and y.Bik.2.3.II as a tradition of Eliezer b. Jacob. There were two individuals called Eliezer b. Jacob (I, T2 and II, T4), and the earlier one was well known for his reminiscences about the Temple (e.g., m.Arak.2.6; m.Tam.5.2; m.Mid.1.2, 9; 2.5-6; 5.4). However, the fact that Judah b. Illai is from the generation T4, and that Eliezer b. Jacob [T4] has another debate with Judah b. Illai in this tractate (m.Bik.1.5; cf. y.Bik.1.5.I), suggests that the Eliezer who ruled on waving is the later individual.

There are a significant number of links between this passage (m.Bik.3.4-6) and m.Sot.7.8 (dealt with at the end of *Shebiit*) which may suggest that they both originated from the same collection or that they were related in some other way. Both traditions mention the role of Agrippa in a ceremony in the Temple Court (m.Sot.7.8 concerns the ceremony at the end of the Sabbath Year), and both involve recitations from Deuteronomy. Both traditions also include exactly the same the phrase—"he recites from . . . until he finishes the whole passage"—which is distinctive because both passages use a verbal participle for "recite" without adding a subject. Although this type of abbreviation is not uncommon in Mishnah, it is significant that when R. Judah copied this phrase in his addition, he *did* include a personal particle as a subject:

Agrippa tradition in m.Bik.3.6; m.Sot.7.8:

    "until [he] finishes the whole passage"   עד שגומר כל הפרשה

R. Judah in m.Bik.3.6:

    "until he finishes the whole passage"   עד שהוא גומר כל הפרשה

m.Bik.3.7: Help with reciting for *firstfruits*

At first everyone who was able to recite	בראשונה כל מי שיודע לקרות,
would recite [the Scripture by themselves],	קורא.
and [for] all who were not able to recite	וכל מי שאינו יודע לקרות,
they [the priests would lead] him in the recitation.	מקרין אותו.
[When they saw] they held back from bringing [*firstfruits*]	נמנעו מלהביא,
and they *decreed* that they [the priests] recite	התקינו שיהו מקרין
[both] with one who knows [how to recite]	את מי שיודע
and with one who does not know [how to recite].	ואת מי שאינו יודע.

Comments: Those who could not remember (or read?) the words of the recitation were assisted by the priest who would recite with them. But many people were ashamed that their neighbors who offered alongside them might recognize their ignorance, so they avoided bringing these offerings. When the priests realized this they decided to recite alongside every offerer so that no one would feel embarrassed.

The verb 'to recite' (קָרֵי, *qeré*) is used of 'reciting' Scripture or 'reading' in general, and so it could imply that some people were unable to read and were ashamed of this fact. However, this word is often used in contexts where it would be impractical to read (such as 'reciting' the Shema before sunrise and at night—cf. m.Ber.1.1-2). Also, if they were so ashamed of their illiteracy, they could have overcome this by the simple expedient of learning the passage. It is more likely that everyone was expected to memorize it and that some were embarrassed when, in the excitement of the hour, they forgot some words and had to be prompted. Memorizing it would have been especially difficult for the uneducated because it had to be said in Hebrew (according to m.Sot.7.2) unlike most other recitations by the laity (m.Sot.7.1).

Dating (9): It is unlikely that this kind of tradition would be made up because later rabbis would want to suggest that the former generations of the glorious Temple times were *well* educated. However, the reporting of this detail is clearly late, and it is possible that this is an attempt to explain why the priest normally recited with the offerer even though Scripture said that the offerer should recite on his own ("you shall come to the priest . . . and say to him . . ." Deut.26.3). Therefore this tradition is a reliable witness only to the fact that priests used to help the offerers, but it is not certain that offerers could originally recite on their own if they wished.

m.Bik.3.8-12: Offerings accompanying the *firstfruits*

Summary of Mishnah: The rich bring their *firstfruits* in silver and gold baskets while the poor bring willow baskets (3.8). You may decorate the baskets with other gifts of fruit (3.9). If these gifts come from the seven species (cf. 1.3), they must also be eaten in *purity* and are not liable re *doubtful* tithing (3.10-11). The *firstfruits* belong to the priests as personal property (3.12).

There is no evidence that any of this section originated before 70 CE.

m.Bik.4.1-5:   Comparison of hermaphrodites with men and women

Summary of Mishnah: A hermaphrodite is somewhat like a man and somewhat like a woman (4.1). He is like a man with regard to some matters (such as seminal discharge, not being alone with a woman, marriage, haircut) (4.2), but he is like a woman with regard to others (such as menstruation, not being alone with a man, inheritance, priestly purity, and court testimony) (4.3). Like all men and women he may not be assaulted or cursed and he may inherit (4.4), but unlike normal men and women he cannot be guilty of extirpation for *impurity* [seminal or menstrual discharge] in the Temple and he cannot be sold as a slave (4.5).

There is no evidence that any of this section originated before 70 CE.

Summary and Conclusions

Torah said little about how to celebrate *firstfruits* and the rabbis did not create a highly structured law as they might have done. They could have defined when to designate fruit as *firstfruits*, or how and when to pick the fruit, and they could have defined the quantities of fruit, perhaps different for different fruits, or the dates when they should be presented. The only regulations which are presented are relatively general—the species which can be presented (the seven species of Deut.8.8, cf. m.Bik.1.3, though others could be added, m.Bik.3.9-10[13]) and a very wide range of time (between the festivals of *Shabuot* and *Sukkot*, i.e., Pentecost and Tabernacles, m.Bik.1.6).

The only aspects which are dealt with in any detail are the source of the *firstfruits* (must be grown on one's own land within Israel, m.Bik.1.1-2) and your own worthiness (it cannot be offered by a gentile or disreputable persons, m.Bik.1.4-5), though there is no evidence that these rulings predate 70 CE. Beyond that, there are considerable descriptions of the actual ceremonies (m.Bik.3.2-7), which were later elaborated on the basis of Scripture exegesis (the offering is waved, see m.Bik.3.6; and the offerer originally recited on his own, see m.Bik.3.7).

The rabbis are relatively uninterested in the many possible accidents which might happen, such as *tainting* with other *consecrated* products, or the accidental consumption of *firstfruits*. They are content to say that *firstfruits* which cannot be offered should be replaced (m.Bik.1.8). The only accident which they deal with in

---

[13] This is a later tradition, but the fact that the *firstfruits* are "decorated" (m.Bik.3.3) implied that other species were employed.

any detail is the possibility that the fruit may be spilled within the Temple Court (m.Bik.1.8).

Later rabbis were interested in comparisons between *firstfruits* and other *consecrated* produce, especially *elevation offerings* and *second tithes*, and the presence of this section of compare-and-contrast (m.Bik.2.1-5) 'attracted' other traditions which compared one thing with another. There are a few small groups of comparisons concerning citron trees and blood, but the largest group of comparisons concern the *koy*, which is either a wild animal or a domesticated farm animal. Although the whole of this section is late, some of the traditions which discuss the *koy* originated before 70 CE (m.Bik.2.9-10). A later group of comparisons concerning hermaphrodites was added to the end of this tractate.

Most of the early traditions in this tractate have been inserted into a structure which appears to be late. The start of this tractate (m.Bik.1.1–2.4) is very highly structured, and although this structure is partly determined by the subject matter, it is significantly more structured than most parts of Mishnah. The first mishnah lists three situations:

(i) those who bring and recite
(ii) those who bring but do not recite
(iii) those who do not bring [and do not recite]

These three are then dealt with in reverse order:

(iii) Those who cannot bring (for various reasons)—m.Bik.1.2-3
(ii) Those who cannot recite (for various reasons)—m.Bik.1.4-9
(i) Those who bring and recite—m.Bik.1.10-11

The comparisons with other types of offerings in m.Bik.2.1-4 are similarly highly structured:

(2.1) Features of *elevation offerings* and *firstfruits* which are not shared by tithes
(2.2) Features of tithes and *firstfruits* which are not shared by *elevation offerings*
(2.3) Features of *elevation offerings* and tithes which are not shared by *firstfruits*
(2.4) Features of *firstfruits* which are not shared by *elevation offerings* or tithes

Both sets of material appear to have been edited at a later stage to highlight the structure. This is more obvious in the second set where clarification has been inserted between each set of comparisons. In the following, the primary structure is in bold.

2.1 *Elevation offerings* and *firstfruits*: <a series of shared features>
Lo, these [restrictions apply] to *elevation offerings* and to *firstfruits* but not to tithes.
2.2 Some [apply] to tithes and to *firstfruits* which do not to *elevation offerings*.
For tithes and *firstfruits*: <a series of shared features>
Lo, these [apply] to tithes and to *firstfruits* but not to *elevation offerings*.
2.3 Some [apply] to *elevation offerings* and to tithes which do not [apply] to *firstfruits*.

For *elevation offerings* and tithes: <a series of shared features>
Lo, these [apply] to *elevation offerings* and to tithes but not to *firstfruits*.
2.4 And some [apply] to *firstfruits* but not to *elevation offerings* or tithes.
For *firstfruits*: <a series of shared features>

Unusually for Mishnah and other *halakhic* literature, this structure involves a lot of redundant repetition, and so it is likely that the secondary structure was added later by an editor who wished to emphasize the structure without removing any words from the original. The fact that this editor has not added the introductory formula to the first section or the final closing formula to the final section means that he was more concerned to emphasize the divisions than to give each section a standard wording. It also implies that this body of material did not include m.Bik.2.5 which has a completely different structure though it deals with a similar topic.[14]

Therefore there are fragments of early material in this tractate inserted into a later structure. These early traditions portray the Day of Firstfruits as an enjoyable and relatively unregulated festival. There was a continued interest in *firstfruits* after 70 CE as a form of tithing, but little interest in the Temple ceremony. The comparisons of *firstfruits* with other types of *consecrated* produce became associated with other traditions about comparing categories, such as the discussion of hermaphroditism.

---

[14] "*Elevation offerings* of the [*first*] *tithe* is like *firstfruits* in two ways and [like] *elevation offerings* in two ways: . . ."

Mishnaic Hebrew Glossary

Grammatical differences with biblical Hebrew

Mishnaic Hebrew is similar to biblical Hebrew, though the grammar is simpler and the vocabulary is more extensive. Some aspects of Aramaic grammar and vocabulary appear in Mishnaic Hebrew, though they remained as thoroughly separate languages. Small portions of Aramaic occur in Mishnah, usually when quoting older sources.[1] In the Talmuds, which are written in Aramaic, Mishnaic Hebrew occurs in the *beraytot*, though in the Babylonian Talmud it begins to conform again to biblical Hebrew, especially in fictitious *beraytot*.

The verbal system is easier to grasp because, generally speaking, the perfect = past, imperfect = future, and participle = present. The verb *to be* is used with participles to construct tenses like continuous future or subjunctive (future יִהְיֶה with participle—'he will be doing' or 'he would do'), continuous past (past הָיָה with participle, 'used to do') and imperative (imperative הֱוֵה with participle—'be doing').

The imperfect is also commonly used as an optative in prayer ('may you do') or a strong jussive ('must do'), and the negative is formed with לֹא instead of אַל. The impersonal participle ('one does') often has the force of a custom ('one normally does') or a jussive especially as a negative ('one may not do') or as a plural ("they do," which is best translated as "one should do"). When the passive participle is impersonal it is often like the Latin gerundive ('it is to be done' or 'it should be done').

Feminine and sometimes plural endings are dropped in favor of masculine singular, and verbal agreement is often neglected. The Hebrew plural ־ים often becomes like the Aramaic ־ין (especially for impersonal participles), and the Aramaic definite article (א as a suffix) occurs frequently. The *construct* is often indicated by the word שֶׁל, and sentence word order is generally *subject-verb-object*.

The vocabulary contains many new words imported from Latin and Greek, as well as many new constructs from Hebrew roots. New nouns have been formed by prefixing מ or ה or sometimes ת, and new verbs have been formed by prefixing a שׁ. In some texts, vowels are expressed by inserting a ו or י, and these can be doubled to indicate when they should be read as a consonant.

---

[1]m.Taan.2.8; m.Meg.4.9; m.Yeb.15.3; m.Ket.4.7-12; m.Git.9.3; m.BM.9.3; m.BB.10.2; m.Ed.8.4; m.Ab.1.13; 2.6; 4.5; 5.22f.

Various new prefixes occur as well as those in biblical Hebrew:

ב   means 'in, on, with, by' and also 'son of'

ד   acts like a relative pronoun, like שׁ (see below)

ה   is a definite article or marks the causative hiphil, etc. (as in biblical Hebrew) but is also used as an interrogative at the start of a question, or converts a verb to noun

ו   means 'and, or, but' though it is not used for vav-conversive.

י   indicates imperfect (as in biblical Hebrew) which is future in Mishnaic Hebrew

כ   means 'like, according to, as' (as in biblical Hebrew)

ל   forms a verbal infinitive and means 'to, for' (as in biblical Hebrew)

מ   means 'from, some of' and transforms a verb into a noun or a participle (as in biblical Hebrew)

נ   indicates a perfect niphal (reflexive, as in biblical Hebrew) .

שׁ   is an abbreviation of אֲשֶׁר, 'which, who'

Transliteration

Transliteration is simplified in these volumes, as in most Jewish works. Soft-sounding letters are indicated by a following *h*, i.e., כ is *kh*, פ is *ph*, but no distinction is made between ת and תּ or ד and דּ. The soft ב after vowels is a single *b*, and the hard ב after vowels is a double *bb* and a single *b* at other times. Both ת and ט are transliterated as *t* and both שׂ and ס are transliterated as *s*, but צ is indicated by *tz*. Silent א or ע are not transliterated, and vowels are indicated simply by their nearest equivalent simple letter, though יְ is transliterated as *é*.

When pronouncing the transliterated text, a single 'b' which follows a vowel is pronounced 'v' (a soft ב), and any double vowel should be pronounced as two vowels—e.g., *Maamad* and *Amoraim* are pronounced *Ma-amad* and *Amora-im*. The harsh *h* (ח) is indicated by *ḥ* at the start of a word and *ch* in the middle of a word, which is pronounced as in 'loch.'

Glossary of technical vocabulary

ab ha-tumah	אַב הַטּוּמְאָה	*source of impurity* ('father of impurity') — transmitted by *discharge*, *menstruation*, childbirth, leprosy, semen, corpses, etc.
aggadah	אַגָּדָה	nonlegal teaching ('narrative')
am ha-aretz (pl. *ammé ha-aretz*)	עַם הָאָרֶץ עַמֵּי הָאָרֶץ	*impious* (in Mishnah) or *ignorant* (in Talmud) ('people of the land')—those who do not follow all the rules re tithing and *impurity*
Amidah	עֲמִידָה	another name for the Eighteen Benedictions ('standing,' i.e., the Standing Prayer)
Amora (pl. *Amoraim*)	אֲמוֹרָא אֲמוֹרָאִים	teachers from early third century CE, after R. Judah ha-Nasi until the Talmuds were finished at the end of fourth and fifth century CE
aninah	אֲנִינָה	*mourning* between the time of death and burial
aray	עֲרָאִי	*snack* ('incidental [meal]')—a small amount of food which can be eaten from untithed food because it is still being harvested and stored
asham	אָשָׁם	*guilt offering*
asham taluy	אָשָׁם תָּלוּי	*doubtful guilt offering* for a suspected sin
asham va-day	אָשָׁם וַדָּאִי	*undoubted guilt offering* for an undoubted sin
atzeret	עֲצֶרֶת	the Assembly [Day of Pentecost]. In Torah it is used for the last day of *Sukkot* (Tabernacles, Lev.23.36; Num.29.35), the last day of *Pesach* (Deut.16.8) and for *Shabuot* (Pentecost, Num.28.26). In Mishnah and other rabbinic texts it is normally the Day of Pentecost—cf. m.Bek.9.5
baraytah (pl. *beraytot*)	בְּרִיתָה בְּרִיתוֹת	('outside')—a *tannaitic* tradition found outside only in Talmuds or Midrashim
bekhor (pl. *bekhorot*)	בְּכוֹר בְּכוֹרוֹת	*firstborn* son or animal; tractate *Bekhorot*
berakhah (pl. *berakhot*)	בְּרָכָה בְּרָכוֹת	*benediction* or blessing—a prayer starting with "Blessed . . ."; tractate *Berakhot*
bét din	בֵּית דִּין	Courthouse ('house of judgment')

Bét ha-Midrash	בֵּית הַמִּדְרָשׁ	School of Midrash ('House of Interpretation'), i.e., the rabbinic Schoolhouse.
Bét ha-Miqdash (or *Miqdash*)	בֵּית הַמִּקְדָּשׁ	the Sanctuary ('House of Holiness'), i.e., the Temple in Jerusalem
bikkurah (pl. *bikkurim*)	בִּכּוּרָה בִּכּוּרִים	*firstfruits*—an offering from the first productive plants; tractate *Bikkurim*
biur	בִּיעוּר	*removal* of Sabbath Year food at the time of the new harvest; or: annual ceremony of Removal in the Temple or: *removal* of undistributed tithes at *Pesach* of the fourth and seventh years
demay	דְּמַאי	*doubtful* or *doubtfully tithed* food—which might not have the *minor elevation offering* removed; tractate *Demay*
dama	דֶּמַע	*taint* ('mix')—accidental mixing of *elevation offering* with *deconsecrated*, so it has to be sold cheaply to a priest
damim	דָּמִים	valuation, e.g., of *second tithe* or compensation
dinar	דִּינָר	a silver coin equivalent to a *zuz*
éphah	אֵיפָה	a measure of dry volume equivalent to 432 eggs
Eretz Yisrael	אֶרֶץ יִשְׂרָאֵל	the Land of Israel
érub (pl. *érubin*)	עֵירוּב עֵירוּבִין	*community marker* ('conjunction')—a deposit of food, placed away from the home, to extend the Sabbath day limit for walking or carrying; tractate *Érubin*
Gaon (pl. *Geonim*)	גָּאוֹן גָּאוֹנִים	a rabbinic leader of the Babylonian Academies from late sixth to mid eleventh century CE
Gemara	גְּמָרָא	('thorough learning')—the discussions of the *Amoraim* which form a commentary on Mishnah in the Talmuds
goy (pl. *goyim*)	גּוֹי גּוֹיִם	*non-Jew*. Often replaced by censors with עוֹבְדֵי כּוֹכָבִים, *obedé kokhabim*, 'worshippers of stars'
Habdalah	הַבְדָּלָה	('separation')—a prayer at the end of Sabbath which celebrates differences between the holy and profane, Sabbath and weekday, etc.

haber (pl. haberim)	חָבֵר חֲבֵרִים	Associate—someone who can be trusted re tithing and *impurity*
hadash	חָדָשׁ	*new produce* ('new, fresh')—produce which can be eaten after waving the *first sheaf*
Hag (pl. haggim)	חַג חַגִּים	the Feast (i.e., Tabernacles) ('feast')—either the whole of *Sukkot* or its *holydays*; plural (and sometimes singular) refers to any festival
hagigah	חֲגִיגָה	*festival offering*—a *peace offering* when one visits Jerusalem at a festival, esp. at *Pesach*; tractate *Hagigah*
Hakhamim	חֲכָמִים	Sages—a collective title for *rabbinic* teachers
halakhah (pl. halakhot)	הֲלָכָה הֲלָכוֹת	('law')—a ruling, or a collection of rulings or legal teaching; or: a paragraph of the Mishnah in Jeremiah Talmud
hallah	חַלָּה	*dough offering* ('bun')—a portion of bread for the priests; tractate *Hallah*
Hanukkah	חֲנוּכָּה	festival of *Hanukkah* (Lights) ('dedication')
ha-qodesh	הַקֹּדֶשׁ	the *consecrated* thing—see *qodesh* (not to be confused with *heqdesh*); or: Temple or God
hasid (pl. hasidim)	חָסִיד חֲסִידִים	a Pietist ('charitable')—a holy man or ascetic. The name was use for different groups at different times
hatat	חַטָּאת	*sin offering* for inadvertent sins
hephqer	הֶפְקֵר	*ownerless property* ('free')
heqdesh	הֶקְדֵּשׁ	*dedication*—to the Temple as an offering or for its upkeep
heresh	חֵרֵשׁ	*deaf-mute* ('choked')—a deaf person (assumed also to be mute), who is not legally responsible
hiqdish (Hifil) hoqdash (Hofal)	הִקְדִּישׁ הֻקְדַּשׁ	*sanctify*—separate something for use in the Temple
Hol ha-Moed	חֹל הַמּוֹעֵד	*ordinary festival day* ('unconsecrated [day] of a festival') in the middle of *Pesach* and *Sukkot* (which start and end with a *holyday*) when *labor* restrictions are relaxed; tractate *Moed Qatan*

ḥomesh	חֹמֶשׁ	added fifth ('fifth')—added to a *full value* for redeeming *consecrated* goods or restoring *misappropriated* goods
ḥullin	חוּלִּין נללה	deconsecrated ('profane')—all tithes, including the *minor elevation offering,* have been removed; or: animals which are not suitable for the Temple; tractate *Hullin*
ḥullin metuqqanim	חוּלִּין מְתֻקָּנִים	corrected deconsecrated ('profane adjusted')—*doubtfully tithed* food which has all the tithes removed to make it into *deconsecrated* food
karet	כָּרֵת	extirpation ('cut off')—execution or excommunication, or heavenly judgment through premature or childless death
keseph	כֶּסֶף	second tithe silver ('silver')—e.g., *second tithe* should be paid from silver coins if possible (Deut.14.25)
ketubbah (pl. *ketubbot*)	כְּתוּבָּה כְּתוּבּוֹת	marriage settlement ('writ')—the document or the payment of money owed to a wife at divorce or widowhood; tractate *Ketubbot*
Ketubim	כְּתוּבִים	The Writings—Psalms–Chronicles, including Wisdom books
kilayim	כִּלְאַיִם	mixtures or mixture (the plural is always used)—plants, animals, and cloth of different kinds which are forbidden together; tractate *Kilayim*
kohen (pl. *kohanim*)	כֹּהֵן כֹּהֲנִים	priest
leqet	לֶקֶט	gleanings—crop which is fallen, gleaned by the poor after harvest
levi	לֵוִי	a Levite
log (pl. *luggin*)	לֹג לוּגִּין	a measure of liquid, equal to six eggs
Maamad	מַעֲמָד	the Standing ('standing')—one of the twenty-four divisions of priest, Levites, and supporting lay people; or: the lay people of the division
maasar (pl. *maaserot*)	מַעֲשֵׂר מַעְשְׂרוֹת	tithe—a tenth of all produce; plural tithes is *first tithe* and *second tithe* (or *poor tithe*), and sometimes also *elevation offering*
maaser ani	מַעֲשֵׂר עָנִי	poor tithe—the *second tithe* in the third and sixth year of the seven-year cycle

maaser rishon	מַעֲשֵׂר רִאשׁוֹן	first tithe—one-tenth for the Levites; tractate Maaserot
maaser sheni	מַעֲשֵׂר שֵׁנִי	second tithe—one-tenth removed every first, second, fourth, fifth year, to be consumed in Jerusalem; tractate Maaser Sheni
malqosh	מַלְקוֹשׁ	late rain which falls in spring
mamzer (f. mamzeret)	מַמְזֵר מַמְזֶרֶת	an illegitimate, i.e., someone born from a forbidden relationship
maneh	מָנֶה	weight of about 1 pound; or: 'a hundred', esp. 100 zuz
Mar or Rab	מָר רַב	title for a Babylonian Amora
massekhet (pl. massekhtot)	מַסֶּכֶת מַסֶּכְתּוֹת	tractate of Mishnah, Tosefta, or Talmud
meén	מֵעֵין	abstract—abbreviated version of the Eighteen Benedictions
meilah	מְעִילָה	misappropriation ('fraud')—using consecrated property; tractate Meilah
metuqqan	מְתֻקָּן	corrected—short for hullin metuqqanim (q.v.)
mezuzah	מְזוּזָה	('doorpost')—a case containing small scrolls of Deut.6.4-9; 11.13-21, attached to doorposts
midrash	מִדְרָשׁ	a commentary on Scripture, halakhic and aggadic
minchah (pl. menachot)	מִנְחָה מְנָחוֹת	Afternoon Prayers ('offering'); or: meal offering; tractate Menachot
Miqra	מִקְרָא	Scripture ('read'), i.e., written Scripture (all three sections)
Mishmar	מִשְׁמָר	Watch ('guard')—one of the twenty-four priestly divisions
mishnah (pl. mishnayot)	מִשְׁנָה מִשְׁנָיוֹת	a paragraph from the Mishnah
mitzvah (pl. mitzvot)	מִצְוָה מִצְווֹת	commandment—scriptural or rabbinic

moed	מוֹעֵד	*festival* ('appointed time'); or: abbreviation of *Ḥol ha-Moed, ordinary festival days* Order Moed
nakhri	נָכְרִי	gentile ('stranger'); often replaced by censors with עוֹבְדֵי כּוֹכָבִים, *obedé kokhabim,* 'worshippers of stars.' Genizah texts often read גּוֹיִם, *goyim,* which is normally the original version
Nasi	נָשִׂיא	President—he and the Head of the Court made up the ruling Pair
neta rebai	נֶטַע רְבָעִי	*fourth-year plant*—fruit on four-year-old plants which was eaten in Jerusalem like *second tithe*
nazir	נָזִיר	Nazirite ('abstainer'); tractate *Nazir*
neeman	נֶאֱמָן	a Trusted one—who can be trusted re tithing
nebelah	נְבֵלָה	*carrion* ('decayed')—animal corpses
Nebiim	נְבִיאִים	The Prophets—Joshua–Malachi
niddah	נִדָּה	*menstruant* ('isolation'); tractate *Niddah*
notar	נוֹתָר	*leftover offering* ('left over') which remained beyond the legal time for eating and must be burned
ohel (pl. *oholot*)	אוֹהֶל אֲהָלוֹת	*overhang* ('tent'), esp. a roof over a corpse; tractate *Oholot*
olelot	עוֹלֵלוֹת	*defective bunches* ('bunches')—grapes which are left for the poor at harvest
olah	עָלָה	*neutralize* ('raise')—restore food which has been *tainted* with *consecrated* food
olah (pl. *olot*)	עוֹלָה עוֹלוֹת	*burnt offering* ('ascending')
omer	עוֹמֶר	the *first sheaf* ('sheaf') which is waved on sixteenth Nisan, after which the new harvest can be eaten
orlah	עָרְלָה	*forefruit* ('foreskin')—the fruit of trees in the first three years; tractate *Orlah*

peah	פֵּאָה	*corner crop* ('corner')—left for the poor at harvest; or: a designated sum of one-sixtieth of the total crop or: a generic term for all the types of *harvest leftovers*; tractate *Peah*
pereq (pl. *Peraqim*)	פֶּרֶק פְּרָקִים	a chapter
peret	פֶּרֶט	*separated grapes* ('separate')—fallen off bunches; they are left for the poor
pérot rebai	פֵּירוֹת רְבָעִי	*fourth-year fruit*—fruit on four-year-old plants which was eaten in Jerusalem like *second tithe*
Perushim	פְּרוּשִׁים	*separatists*—related to Pharisees
perutah	פְּרוּטָה	the smallest possible amount of money
Pesach (pl. *Pesachim*)	פֶּסַח פְּסָחִים	*Passover* festival. The plural includes the Second Passover for those who could not attend the first; tractate *Pesachim*
piggul	פִּגּוּל	*invalid offering* ('abomination')
poseq (pl. *poseqim*)	פּוֹסֵק פּוֹסְקִים	*halakhic* authority
prozbul	פְּרוֹזְבּוּל	from πρὸς βουλῆ, via a Court—a debt paid via the Court to escape the Sabbath Year *release* of debts
Purim	פּוּרִים	Festival of *Purim* ('lots')
qab (pl. *qabbin*)	קַב קַבִּין	a measure of dry grain, about 2.5 pints, or area of land which can be sown with this amount
qadosh (piel *qiddesh*)	קָדֵשׁ קָדוֹשׁ קִדֵּשׁ	*sanctified* ('holy'); piel 'to make holy, *sanctify*'; or: *betroth*
qal va-ḥomer	קַל וָחוֹמֶר	*minor and major* ('light and heavy')—an exegetical argument *a minus ad majorem*, i.e., "if this is so, then surely this also is so"
qatan	קָטָן	a *minor* ('small')—one who is not legally responsible
qen (pl. *qinnim*)	קֵן קִנִּים	nest, esp. re sacrificial birds; tractate *Qinnim*

qeren	קֶרֶן	*full value* of recompense, with the *added fifth*; or: *horn damage*—damage caused by an animal's horn; or: other intentional damage done by an animal
qiddush (pl. *qiddushin*)	קִדּוּשׁ קִדּוּשִׁין	the *Qiddush*—a prayer re God's holiness; or: *betrothal*—the setting apart of a girl for marriage; tractate *Qiddushin*
qinyan	קִנְיָן	purchase or transfer of property ownership
qodesh	קוֹדֶשׁ	*consecrated* ('holy')—whatever is given to priests and requires an *added fifth* as in Lev.22.14
qodashim	קוֹדֶשׁ	*holy things*, esp. sacrifices which are eaten in a state of purity; offerings in general (cf. m.Hag.3.1) Order *Qodashim*
Rab or Mar	רַב מַר	title for a Babylonian *Amora*
Rabban	רַבָּן	('our teacher')—title for the President of the Sanhedrin
Rabbi	רַבִּי	('my teacher')—title for ordained teachers after 70 CE; or: an informal title before 70 CE
rebai	רְבָעִי	*fourth year [fruit]* ('fourth')—short for *neta rebai* (q.v.)
rebii letumah	רְבִיעִי לְטוּמְאָה	*fourth grade impurity* ('fourth to impurity'); transmitted from a *third grade impurity*
rebiit	רְבִיעִית	a measure, a quarter *log*
Rishon (pl. *Rishonim*)	רִאשׁוֹן רִאשׁוֹנִים	a rabbinic leader in the period after the *Geonim*, before the publication of the *Shulchan Arukh*, about 1000–1500 CE
Rosh ha-Shanah	רֹאשׁ הַשָּׁנָה	*Rosh ha-Shanah* (New Year) festival; tractate *Rosh ha-Shanah*
Sanhedrin	סַנְהֶדְרִין	the highest Jewish court in the Hall of Hewn Stone in the Jerusalem Temple courts and later in Yavneh; tractate *Sanhedrin*
seder (pl. *sedarim*)	סֵדֶר סְדָרִים	an *order* esp. of Mishnah
sela (pl. *selaim*)	סֶלַע סְלָעִים	a silver shekel, worth 4 *zuz*

shaatnez	שַׁעַטְנֵז	a mixture of wool and linen, prohibited for making a garment
Shabbat	שַׁבָּת	Sabbath, seventh day of the week; tractate *Shabbat*
shabua	שָׁבוּעַ	week;
Shabuot	שָׁבוּעוֹת	plural 'weeks' is usually the *Shabuot* (Pentecost)
shebiit	שְׁבִיעִית	Sabbath Year when the land rests; tractate *Shebiit*
shebut	שְׁבוּת	a rest, esp. from work on Sabbaths and *holydays*
shelamim	שְׁלָמִים	*peace offering*
Shema	שְׁמַע	hear, esp. the *Shema*—readings and prayers at morning and evening
shemittah	שְׁמִטָּה	*release*, esp. Year of Release—the end of the seven-year cycle
Shemoneh Esreh	שְׁמוֹנֶה עֶשְׂרֵה	Eighteen Benedictions ('eighteen')
sheqel	שֶׁקֶל	*shekel*, a silver coin, worth 4 *zuz*; tractate *Sheqalim* re the half shekel Temple tax
sheretz (pl. *sheratzim*)	שֶׁרֶץ שְׁרָצִים	*creeping thing*—species whose corpse transmits *impurity*
shikhbat zara	שִׁכְבַת זָרַע	semen
shikhechah	שִׁכְחָה	*forgotten*—crop which is accidentally unharvested or uncollected, so it belongs to the poor
shoteh	שׁוֹטֶה	*imbecile*, i.e., mad or foolish; one who is not legally responsible
Shulchan Arukh	שֻׁלְחָן עָרוּךְ	an authoritative sixteenth-century summary of *halakhic* decisions, by Joseph Caro
sopherim	סוֹפְרִים	Scribes or Men of the Great Assembly—leaders from Ezra until approximately the third century BCE; or: scribes—the profession
sukkah (pl. *Sukkot*)	סוּכָּה סֻכּוֹת	*booth*; plural *Sukkot* (Tabernacles); tractate *Sukkah*
tahor	טָהוֹר	*pure* for ritual use

tallit	טַלִּ ית	cloak, esp. a prayer shawl
talmid	תַּלְמִיד	disciple ('learner')
tamid	תָּמִיד	*daily offering* ('continuous'), burnt offerings in the Temple; tractate *Tamid*
Tanna (pl. *Tannaim*)	תַּנָּא תַּנָּאִים	rabbinic teacher from the first–second century CE until Mishnah was finished at the end of the second century CE
Tanna qamma	תַּנָּא קַמָּא	the anonymous speaker of the first opinion stated in a mishnah
taqqanah (pl. *taqqanot*)	תַּקָּנָה תַּקָּנוֹת	*decree*—a rabbinic rule for which there is no biblical prescription
tebel	טֶבֶל	*untithed* ('liable')—liable to *tithes*
tebilah	טְבִילָה	*immersion* ('dipping')—for purification; tractate *Tebul Yom*
tebul yom (f. *tebulat yom*)	טְבוּל יוֹם טְבוּלַת יוֹם	*impurity for a day* ('immersed of the day')—partial impurity after immersion, which lasts until evening
teme met	טְמֵא מֵת	*corpse impurity* ('impurity of death'), equivalent to *originating source of impurity*, transmits *source of impurity*
temurah	תְּמוּרָה	*redemption* ('substitution')—exchanging a sacrifice for another or for money; tractate *Temurah*
tephach (pl. *tephachim*)	טֶפַח טְפָחִים	*palm*—a measure of four finger-breadths of a closed hand
Tefillah	תְּפִלָּה	the Prayer ('prayer')—the Eighteen Benedictions
tefillin	תְּפִלִּין	*tefillin* or *phylacteries* ('prayers'), worn during prayer times on head and hand, containing Scripture passages; or: the Scripture portions they contain
teréphah	טְרֵיפָה	*stricken*—an animal torn by beasts or fatally ill, which cannot be sacrificed or eaten
terumah (pl. *terumot*)	תְּרוּמָה תְּרוּמוֹת	*elevation offering* ('elevation'), which can be eaten only by priests and their families in a state of *purity*; tractate *Terumot*
terumah gedolah	תְּרוּמָה גְּדוֹלָה	*major elevation offering*—about one-fiftieth separated from every crop by the farmer

terumah qetannah	תְּרוּמָה קְטַנָּה	minor elevation offering—the elevation offering of a first tithe, i.e., one-hundredth of every food item
todah	תּוֹדָה	thank offering
toharah (pl. toharot)	טָהֳרָה טָהֳרוֹת	purity, esp. re food, sacrifices, people, intentions, and vessels; free of tummah; Order and tractate Toharot
Torah	תּוֹרָה	the five Books of Moses, the basis of Jewish law
tummah (pl. tumaot)	טֻמְאָה טוּמְאוֹת	impurity, esp. levitical impurity, due to human fluids, food, disease, and death
tzaraat	צָרַעַת	plague—esp. leprosy
tzarah	צָרָה	rival wife—when a man has two wives
Tzedukim	צְדוּקִים	Sadducees
vadday	וַדַּאי	certainly untithed food ('certain')—which has no tithes removed, not even the major elevation offering
velad ha-tumah	וְלַד הַטּוּמְאָה	transmitted impurity ('child of impurity'), a generic term which includes first grade impurity, second grade impurity, etc.
yabam (pl. yebamin)	יָבָם יְבָמִין	levirate husband—a man who is obligated to marry his brother's childless widow
yad (pl. yadayim)	יָד יָדַיִם	hand; tractate Yadayim
yebamah (pl. yebamot)	יְבָמָה	levirate wife—a childless widow who becomes the responsibility of her husband's brother; tractate Yebamot
yibbum	יִבּוּם	levirate marriage—i.e., between a childless widow and her dead husband's brother
yoledet	יוֹלֶדֶת	woman in confinement ('bearer')—a woman during or after childbirth
Yom ha- Kippurim	יוֹם הַכִּפּוּרִים	Day of Atonement; tractate Yoma
yom tob (pl. Yamim Tobim)	יוֹם טוֹב יָמִים טוֹבִים	holyday—i.e., the first day and last day of a festival, when labor is forbidden, similar to a Sabbath; tractate Bétzah is Yom Tob in Tosefta

yoreh	יוֹרֶה	early rain, which falls after *Sukkot*
zab (f. *zabah*) (pl. *zabim*)	זָב זָבָה זָבִים	discharge, esp. a *man suffering discharge* or a *woman suffering discharge*, e.g., gonorrhoea; tractate *Zabim*
zaqen (pl. *zeqenim*)	זָקֵן זְקֵנִים	elder, esp. Elder, member of the Sanhedrin, or *Beth Din*, or a distinguished leader
zar (pl. *zarim*)	זָר זָרִים	*layman* ('stranger'), i.e., nonpriest
zebach (pl. *zebachim*)	זֶבַח זְבָחִים	*Sacrifice*, esp. re *peace offerings*; tractate *Zebachim*
Zeqenim ha-Rishonim	זְקֵנִים הָרִאשׁוֹנִים	Former Elders—collective title for pre-*tannaitic* teachers
zeraim	זְרָעִים	Seeds, esp. for sowing *Order Zeraim*
zimmun	זִימּוּן	the Grace after Meal—('invitation'), i.e., the invitation by the leader to say the Grace after meals
Zugot	זוּגוֹת	the Pairs—leaders listed in *Abot*, from Jose b. Joezer second century BCE to Hillel and Shammai in the first century BCE
zuz	זוּז	a silver coin equivalent to a silver *dinar*

Index of Named Individuals and Places

Index of Subjects

Index of References to Ancient Literature